A New
Reference Grammar of
Modern Spanish

Second Edition

John Butt

Carmen Benjamin

NTC Publishing Group
Lincolnwood, Illinois USA

This edition first published in 1995 by NTC Publishing Group, 4255 West Touchy Avenue,
Lincolnwood (Chicago), Illinois 60646–1975, USA
Second impression 1996

© 1994, 1988 John Butt and Carmen Benjamin

Originally published by Edward Arnold, a member of the Hodder Headline Group.

Library of Congress Cataloging-in-Publication Data
Butt, John 1943-
    A new reference grammar of modern Spanish/John Butt, Carmen Benjamin—2nd ed.
        p. cm.
    Includes bibliographical references (p. 499) and index.

ISBN 0-8442-7088-1
1. Spanish language—Grammar.
I. Benjamin, Carmen.   II. Title.
PC4112.B88   1994
468.2'421—dc20

Manufactured in Great Britain.

*A New Reference Grammar of
Modern Spanish*

Contents

Preface to the first edition (abridged and revised)   vii
Preface to the second edition   xi
Conventions, spelling and abbreviations   xiii

 1   Gender of nouns   1
 2   Plural of nouns   17
 3   Articles   30
 4   Adjectives   51
 5   Comparison of adjectives and adverbs   73
 6   Demonstrative adjectives and pronouns   83
 7   Neuter article and pronouns   89
 8   Possessive adjectives and pronouns   94
 9   Miscellaneous adjectives and pronouns   101
10   Numerals   114
11   Personal pronouns   123
12   *Le/les* and *lo/la/los/las*   143
13   Forms of verbs   156
14   Use of indicative (non-continuous) verb forms   207
15   Continuous forms of the verb   230
16   The subjunctive   237
17   The imperative   273
18   The infinitive   281
19   Participles   292
20   The gerund   298
21   Modal auxiliary verbs   307
22   Personal *a*   312
23   Negation   319
24   Interrogation and exclamation   329
25   Conditional sentences   335
26   Pronominal verbs   341
27   Verbs of becoming   358
28   Passive and impersonal sentences   362
29   *Ser* and *estar*   375
30   Existential sentences('there is/are', etc.)   382
31   Adverbs   385
32   Expressions of time   401
33   Conjunctions   410

34   Prepositions   419
35   Relative clauses and pronouns   448
36   Nominalizers and cleft sentences   458
37   Word order   464
38   Diminutive, augmentative and pejorative suffixes   476
39   Spelling, accent rules, punctuation and word division   483
Bibliography and sources   499
Index of English words   503
Index of Spanish words and grammatical points   506

Preface to the first edition (abridged and revised)

This reference grammar offers intermediate and advanced students a reasonably comprehensive guide to the morphology and syntax of educated speech and plain prose in Spain and Latin America at the end of the twentieth century.

Spanish is the main, usually the sole official language of twenty-one countries,[1] and it is set fair to overtake English by the year 2000 in numbers of native speakers.[2] This vast geographical and political diversity ensures that Spanish is a good deal less unified than French, German or even English, the latter more or less internationally standardized according to either American or British norms.

Until the 1960s, the criteria of internationally correct Spanish were dictated by the *Real Academia Española*, but the prestige of this institution has now sunk so low that its most solemn decrees are hardly taken seriously – witness the fate of the spelling reforms listed in the *Nuevas normas de prosodia y ortografía*, which were supposed to come into force in all Spanish-speaking countries in 1959 and, nearly forty years later, are still selectively ignored by publishers and literate persons everywhere. The fact is that in Spanish 'correctness' is nowadays decided, as it is in all living languages, by the consensus of native speakers; but consensus about linguistic usage is obviously difficult to achieve between more than twenty independent, widely scattered and sometimes mutually hostile countries.

Peninsular Spanish is itself in flux. Since the end of Franco's dictatorship in 1975 the language of the old Establishment has steadily yielded to a standard based on the speech of the new middle classes of Madrid, but this evolution has been resisted by purists and there are constant disputes about what constitutes correct Spanish.

---

[1] Argentina, Bolivia, Chile, Colombia, Costa Rica, Cuba, The Dominican Republic, Ecuador, Equatorial Guinea (on the African Atlantic coast between Gabon and Cameroun), Guatemala, Honduras, Mexico, Nicaragua, Panama, Paraguay, Peru, Puerto Rico, El Salvador, Spain, Uruguay and Venezuela.

[2] English will continue to have more speakers for whom it is a *second* language. Chinese (Putonghua) has more native speakers than either, but it is geographically more restricted.

But it is above all the variety, vigour and constantly rising prestige of Latin-American Spanish that makes the task of lexicographers and grammarians difficult. The day is (or should be) long past when one could claim that the only variety of Spanish worth serious study and imitation is the standard language of Spain, which is based on the Castilian dialect of the North and Centre, a variety nowadays spoken by less than eight per cent of the Spanish-speaking world. But now that European Castilian has lost its standing as a pan-Hispanic model, no new model has replaced it and there is no longer any one national Spanish-speaking linguistic or cultural centre to which the other countries and regions defer. This absence of universally acknowledged pan-Hispanic linguistic norms will no doubt persist for the foreseeable future.

This is not to say that Spanish is no longer one language: anyone who knows one variety well can travel the Spanish-speaking world with no more problems of communication than would afflict Britons, Americans and Australians travelling in the various English-speaking countries – and probably less. But *at the level of detail*, i.e. at the level at which textbooks like this one must work, there are regional and national variations of vocabulary and, to a much lesser extent, syntax, that can be very disconcerting when it comes to laying down the law about what is 'correct' or recommended usage. These differences do not only separate European and 'Latin-American' Spanish. Strictly speaking, the latter does not exist: Mexican, Cuban, Colombian, Peruvian, Argentine and all the other national varieties differ from one another, above all in colloquial vocabulary, and the distance between, for example, Mexican and Argentine is probably as great as between Argentine and European Spanish.

This problem of diversity need not worry the beginner who is struggling with basic grammar and vocabulary, but it grows more acute as one advances beyond the intermediate level. It disheartens a foreign student to find that *Collins Spanish-English English-Spanish* dictionary gives twelve different national Latin-American meanings for the word *chiva* including 'goat', 'sheep', 'goatee', 'bus', 'car', 'blanket', 'naughty girl', 'immoral woman' and 'knapsack' (although any one Spanish-speaker will usually know only a few of these possible meanings). The dimensions of the problem become clearer when one reads headlines in a popular Peruvian daily like *Choros chupan tres palos a Cristal* ('Thieves steal three million *soles* from Crystal Brewery') or *Lorchos datean que los afilaron tres años* ('Peruvians claim they were trained for three years'), language that baffles Argentines and Mexicans as much as Spaniards. This problem of variety must frequently perplex the fair-minded grammarian who can no more denounce as 'incorrect' a typical Latin-American sentence such as *Es con ella que quiero hablar* ('It's her that I want to talk to', Spaniards insist on *Es con ella **con la** que quiero hablar*), than assert that *dentro de* is the 'correct' Spanish for 'inside' when a writer as famous as Borges uses the form *adentro de* - unacceptable to Spaniards.

Many textbooks of Spanish sidestep this problem of diversity by ignoring or understating the variety of Latin-American usage or by confining their discussion to a colourless pan-Hispanic *lingua franca* of the sort found in *Selecciones del Reader's Digest*, a language stripped of all the colloquialisms and regionalisms that give everyday Spanish its immense vigour and charm.

We reject both of these solutions and have adopted the working method of illustrating as many important points as possible with Latin-American examples which, except where stated, seem to us also to be good European Spanish and therefore indicative of what one assumes is international Spanish usage. We hope that this method will give readers a sense of authentic Spanish and also do justice to the status of Latin-American language.

Despite this, it is certain that some of our everyday Peninsular examples will amuse or puzzle readers from the Americas. We apologize for this, and we hope that the spirit of this grammar is as pan-Hispanic as it can be in the face of the ultimately irreconcilable claims of all the subtly different national and regional varieties of the language.

We often quote familiar dialogue from plays and novels as well as extracts from a range of texts, including the press and popular material like cookery books, leisure and hobby magazines and occasionally spontaneous utterances by native speakers. The fact that some of these sources are not usually considered to be linguistically prestigious does not mean that all their language is necessarily corrupt: all our examples are good Spanish except where stated. The alternative would have been to quote only elegant literary texts by famous authors or the editorials of one or two up-market newspapers, and this would have given a false picture of the language.

As far as possible we indicate whether the language described is formal, colloquial, familiar or popular. Foreign students will constantly hear colloquial and popular forms, but pending real fluency in the language they should use them – especially popular forms – with caution. In any language some things that pass unnoticed in relaxed native speech sound shocking when spoken with a foreign accent.

With rare exceptions, examples of written language are taken from texts published since the 1960s, many of them from the 1980s and 1990s. Severe problems of space have obliged us to omit historical considerations. The grammar also concentrates on syntactic and morphological questions: lexical issues such as word formation (except diminutive and other affective suffixes) are barely discussed, mainly because of acute lack of space, but also because teaching foreigners how to coin new words encourages badly-formed vocabulary.

The approach and terminology of the grammar are conservative and points are often clarified by example rather than by theoretical argument, which is kept to a minimum. The fact that we use traditional terms like 'subject', 'object', 'indirect object', 'demonstratives', etc. does not mean that we are completely ignorant of the unscientific nature of such labels. But to speak of 'nominals', 'disjuncts', 'deictics' and so on would frighten off the type of reader we have in mind. Words and constructions are discussed under those headings by which readers unfamiliar with modern linguistic terms will most easily recognize them.

We assume that readers have a native knowledge of English, and explanations have been drastically shortened by reference to English wherever the languages seem to coincide. Since interference from French and occasionally Italian and Portuguese is a perennial problem for teachers of Spanish, sporadic mention of these languages is made in order to emphasize some peculiarity of Spanish.

Acknowledgments

Like everyone in the field, we are indebted to the labours of Andrés Bello, María Moliner, Ramsey and Spaulding, Manuel Seco and other eminent grammarians and lexicographers. Of the works mentioned in the bibliography, we have drawn heavily on E. García (1975) and C.E. Kany (Chicago, 1945, reprinted and translated into Spanish). Three other works often provided information, explanations and insights: R. Quirk et al. (1972), A. Judge and F.G. Healey (1983), and the first edition of A.E. Hammer (1971), perusal of which originally inspired the present work.

A very large number of Spanish speakers from many countries have helped us and we cannot name them all. Our sincere thanks go to every one: without them we could not have finished. We are, however, heavily indebted to Antonia Moreira and María Álvarez for their thoughtful opinions on Peninsular usage; to Sheila Hague for her valuable criticisms of the proofs; to Lynn Ingamells of Queen Mary College, London who generously read and commented on the first draft; to Steve Jones and to his Colombian wife Candy, whose protests often reminded us that Peninsular Spanish is but one variety among many, and to Professor Alan Paterson of St Andrew's University whose kind words of encouragement raised morale at critical moments more, perhaps, than he realized.

Despite all this invaluable assistance we are acutely aware that a book of this nature must contain mistakes, omissions and inaccuracies for which we alone assume responsibility.

John Butt
Carmen Benjamin

King's College, London

Preface to the second edition

We have rewritten several chapters and made numerous additions and clari-
fications in most of the others. A number of new chapters are included, on
the Imperative, Expressions of time, Existential sentences (i.e. ways of saying
'there is'/'there are'), and on Modal Auxiliaries like *haber, deber, poder*, etc.
Verbs meaning 'to become' are now discussed in a separate chapter, as is
the vexed question of the difference between the pronouns *le* and *lo*.

English translations are shown more systematically than in the first edition,
except in a few obvious cases and in some long lists of verbs. A number
of footnotes have been added with items of interest or information about
the language that are often missing from dictionaries. The appendix on
pronunciation has been deleted: it contained nothing that cannot be found
in countless beginners' course-books.

We have included more Mexican examples, since this, the most populous
Spanish-speaking country, was under-represented in the first edition. In this
regard John Butt thanks Professor David Hook for arranging, and King's
College, London for granting assistance towards a journey to Mexico in
Autumn 1992. In connection with the Latin-American examples, we should
point out that a remark like 'in Spain the word used is . . .' does not exclude
the possibility that what we know is good European usage is also current in
some or all of the American republics: it is clearly impossible to check every
fact country by country.

The term 'Spanish America(n)', which irritates some Latin Americans, has
been replaced by 'Latin America(n)'. It should be obvious that we are talking
about Latin-American Spanish and not the continent's other Latin-based
languages.

In response to several complaints, the Argentine author Ernesto Sábato has
been given back his accent, despite the fact that many publishers print his
name Sabato, Italian-style.

The success of this book in the USA raised problems of trans-Atlantic
variety in English that were more troublesome than we foresaw: a number of
American readers questioned our British spelling, punctuation and idiom. In
this new edition we have made an effort to avoid (insofar as Britons can) what
seems to be exclusively British usage, and we include American equivalents
of British words that we think may cause confusion across the Atlantic.

We again owe heartfelt thanks to numerous readers, colleagues, friends
and students who helped us with their remarks and criticisms, especially
to Professors Steven L. Hartman and Leo Hickey, to Carmen Gleadow and

María Brown. We are again much indebted to Antonia Moreira for her unfailing interest and numerous invaluable comments.

Once more we declare that we alone are responsible for any omissions or errors.

London, 1994

Conventions, spelling and abbreviations

El mujer: a preceding asterisk marks a form that is not Spanish. It is occasionally also used for forms that may be heard but are very aberrant.

?*Se puso detrás mío*, ?*Se los dije*: a preceding uninverted question mark shows that a form is doubtful or disputed and not accepted by all speakers.

'Colloquial' describes forms that are accepted in spontaneous educated speech but are usually avoided in formal speech or writing, e.g. *Si tuviera dinero me compraba un piso* 'If I had some money I'd buy a flat/apartment' for *me compraría un piso*.

'Familiar' describes forms that are commonly heard in spontaneous speech, e.g. ?*el chico que fui con él* 'the boy I went with' (i.e. *el chico con el que fui*), but should be avoided or used with great caution by foreign learners.

'Popular' describes commonly-heard forms that may be stigmatized as uneducated, for example ?*Habían muchos* for *Había muchos* 'There were lots of them'.

Forms separated by / are alternatives, either alternatives that have different meanings but use the same construction, e.g. *yo sé/él sabe* 'I know'/'(s)he knows', or alternative ways of saying the same thing, e.g. *antes de que/antes que* 'before'.

Words in round brackets may be optionally deleted with no or only slight effect on meaning or style, e.g. *con tal (de) que* 'provided that'.

The European equivalents of distinctly Latin-American forms are noted, e.g. *el plomero* (Spain *el fontanero*) 'plumber', but Latin-American equivalents of European forms are not systematically shown. It would be beyond the scope of this, and probably of any book, to list every national or regional Latin-American equivalent of words used in Spain.

Except where stated otherwise, all examples represent usage worthy of imitation by foreigners. The Latin-American quotations are also good European Spanish unless stated otherwise. Latin-American texts published outside their author's home country may have been 'normalized' by editors, particularly in the case of the numerous famous Latin-American novels published in Spain.

Words that represent the speech of fictional characters are marked 'dialogue' to show that they reflect spoken usage and to avoid their language being attributed to their author.

The spelling of Spanish words follows the original text or, in the case of unattributed examples, the Academy's rules laid down in the *Nuevas normas de prosodia y ortografía* of 1959, although we follow general usage where this is clearly at odds with the Academy's prescriptions. In the cases of the word *sólo/solo* 'only'/'alone' and of the demonstrative pronouns *este/éste, ese/ése, aquel/aquél*, modern written usage usually flouts the Academy's rules and we show both forms.

The spellings *México, mexicano* are used throughout for *Méjico, mejicano* on the grounds that Mexicans prefer them, as does the prestigious Spanish daily *El País*.

The English used throughout is British, although we try to indicate US usage where confusion may arise (e.g. 'lecturer'/(US) 'professor', etc.). British habits will be particularly obvious in the punctuation (particularly our habit of writing punctuation outside inverted commas), in certain spellings, in the writing of dates,[1] and most of all in the translations of colloquial Spanish, where our colloquial British will sometimes puzzle or amuse North Americans.

Grammar books constantly make even the simplest language ambiguous by quoting it out of context. This problem is severe in a language like Spanish which regularly omits subject pronouns and does not systematically mark sex, number or person in its object pronouns. Thus *Se lo daba* can mean 'I gave it to her/him/them/you', 'He/she gave it to him/her/them/you', 'You (*usted*) gave it to him/her/them/you', '(S)he gave it to himself/herself', and so on. One cannot show all of the possibilities each time, but the temptation to translate such sentences always using masculine English pronouns is misleading and possibly shows sexual bias. For this reason we often use English feminine forms in the translations, if only to recall that a native Spanish-speaker does not automatically form a mental picture of a man on hearing the verb *tosió* '(S)he/you/it coughed', and to remind readers that, out of context, there is no special reason for translating *Habla ruso* as 'He speaks Russian' rather than 'She speaks Russian' or 'You speak Russian'.

The following abbreviations are used:

Esbozo	Real Academia de la Lengua, *Esbozo de una nueva gramática de la lengua española* (Madrid 1973)
lit.	'literally', 'literal translation'
Nuevas normas	*Nuevas normas de prosodia y ortografía. Nuevo texto definitivo* (Madrid 1959)
Lat. Am.	Latin America(n)

---

[1] E.g. 10 July 1998 = North American 7-10-1998, European 10-7-1998.

1

Gender of nouns

1.1 General

All nouns in Spanish are either masculine or feminine in gender, except for one or two nouns of undecided gender. There are no Spanish nouns of neuter gender, but there are some neuter pronouns: see Chapter 7.

Discussion of the gender of Spanish nouns is clarified by dividing nouns into two groups:

(a) nouns that refer to human beings or to domesticated animals, and also a few well-known wild animals. These are discussed in 1.2.

(b) nouns that refer to inanimate things or to plants, or to the animals not included in 1.2. These are discussed in 1.3 and 1.4.

1.2 Nouns referring to human beings and domesticated animals (and a few wild animals)

Nouns referring to male human beings or to male domesticated animals and to the male of a few well-known wild animals such as wolves, lions, tigers, elephants, bears and foxes, are almost always masculine, and those referring to females are feminine.

This remark is not as obvious as it seems: the gender of such nouns is more biological in Spanish than in French where *le professeur* or *le docteur* can be a woman and *la recrue* 'recruit' can be a man, or in Italian where a policeman may be *la guardia* (forms like *la recluta*, *la centinela* used to be applied to men in Golden-Age Spanish, but one now says *el recluta* for a male recruit, *la recluta* for a female). However, a few Spanish nouns of fixed gender, e.g. *la víctima*, *la celebridad*, *el ligue* may refer to both males and females: see 1.2.11 for a selection.

1.2.1 Special forms for male and female

Some nouns have special forms for the male and female which must be learnt separately. The following list is not exhaustive:

el abad	la abadesa	abbot/abbess
el actor	la actriz	actor/actress
el barón	la baronesa	baron/baroness
el caballo	la yegua	stallion/mare
el carnero	la oveja**	ram/ewe
el conde	la condesa	count/countess
el duque	la duquesa	duke/duchess

el emperador	la emperatriz	emperor/empress
el gallo	la gallina**	cockerel/hen
el héroe	la heroína	hero/heroine (or heroin)
el jabalí	la jabalina	wild boar/wild sow
el marido	la mujer	husband/wife (or woman)
el padre	la madre	father/mother
el príncipe	la princesa	prince/princess
el rey	la reina	king/queen
el sacerdote	la sacerdotisa	priest/priestess
el toro	la vaca	bull/cow
el yerno	la nuera	son-in-law/daughter-in law
	(*la yerna* is heard	
	in parts of Lat. Am.)	
el varón [1]	la hembra	male/female
(el macho)		
el zar	la zarina	Tsar/Tsarina

Note

** A feminine form which is also used for the species in general. Normally the masculine is the generic form: *los caballos* = 'horses' as well as 'stallions'.

1.2.2 Feminine of nouns ending in -o

The great majority of nouns referring to human beings or to the animals included in this group make their feminine in -*a*:

el abuelo	la abuela	grandfather/grandmother	el novio	la novia	boyfriend/girlfriend
el amigo	la amiga	friend	el oso	la osa	bear/she-bear
el candidato	la candidata	candidate	el perro	la perra	dog/bitch
el ganso	la gansa	gander/goose	el tío	la tía	uncle/aunt
el gato	la gata	cat	el zorro	la zorra	fox/vixen
el hermano	la hermana	brother/sister	etc.		

But some words denoting professions or activities are invariable in form, and the sex of the person referred to is shown by an article or adjective:

el/la modelo	model; *modelos francesas* 'female French models'	el/la soprano	soprano
el/la piloto	pilot/racing driver	el/la testigo	witness (*la testiga* is popular Spanish)
el/la reo	accused (in court)		
el/la soldado	soldier; *una soldado israelí* 'an Israeli woman soldier'		

Others, like *el médico/la médica*, 'doctor' are controversial. See 1.2.7 for a discussion.

1.2.3 Feminine of nouns ending in -or, -ón, -ín, -és

Nouns referring to members of this group and ending in -*or*, -*ón*, *ín* and -*és* make their feminine in -*a*:

el asesor	la asesora	adviser/consultant	el anfitrión	la anfitriona	host/hostess
			el bailarín	la bailarina	dancer

---

[1] *El varón* = human male; *el macho* = male of other animals.

el burgués	la burguesa	bourgeois/	el león	la leona	lion/lioness
		bourgeoise	el profesor	la profesora	teacher
el campeón	la campeona	champion	el programador	la programadora	programmer
el doctor	la doctora	doctor	etc.		

Notes
(i) Adjectives (which in Spanish can almost always double as nouns) ending in *-és* make their feminine in *-a*: *el francés/la francesa* 'Frenchman'/'Frenchwoman'. The only important exception is *cortés/descortés* 'courteous'/'discourteous' (masc. and fem. singular; the plural is *(des)corteses)*. Adjectives are discussed in detail in Chapter 4.
(ii) *El/la peatón* 'pedestrian' seems to be the only invariable noun in *-ón*: *La peatón recibió graves heridas* (*La Voz de Galicia*, Spain, confirmed by native informants) 'The woman pedestrian received severe injuries'.

1.2.4 Nouns ending in -*a*
These are invariable:

el/la artista	artist	el/la espía	spy
el/la astronauta	astronaut	el/la guía	guide (*la guía* also
el/la atleta	athlete		'guide book')
el/la camarada	comrade	el/la nómada	nomad
el/la colega	colleague/workmate	etc.	

Occasional uneducated masculine forms in *-isto* are heard. *El modisto* 'fashion designer' is well-established in everyday Peninsular usage: *Todo las separa, los lazos de sangre, el destino, e incluso los modistos* (*El Mundo*, Madrid) 'Everything stands between them, blood ties, fate and even fashion designers'. Manuel Seco and *El País* recommend *el/la modista*.

1.2.5 Feminine of nouns ending in -*nte*
The majority are invariable:

el/la adolescente	adolescent	el/la creyente	believer
el/la agente	police officer/agent	el/la descendiente	descendant
el/la amante	lover	el/la representante	representative
el/la cantante	singer	etc.	

But a few feminine forms in *-nta* are in standard use (at least in Spain; they may be unacceptable in parts of Latin America):

el acompañante/la acompañanta	companion/escort
el asistente/la asistenta	valet/daily help
el comediante/la comedianta	'actor'/'actress'[2]
el dependiente/la dependienta	shop assistant/(US) sales clerk
el gigante/la giganta	giant
el infante/la infanta	royal prince/princess
el pariente/la parienta	relative
el principiante/la principianta	beginner
el sirviente/la sirvienta	servant

---

[2] These words tend to be derogatory in Peninsular usage, particularly the feminine: *¡Qué comediante/a eres!* 'What an act you put on!' Polite forms are *actor cómico/actriz cómica* 'comic actor'.

In general, the tendency to form the feminine in *-nta* may spread, although forms like **la estudianta* for *la estudiante* 'female student' are considered substandard. There are a few popular nouns/adjectives that form a feminine in *-nta*: *el golfante/la golfanta* 'lout'/'good-for-nothing', *el atorrante/la atorranta* (Lat. Am.) 'tramp'/(US) 'bum'/'slacker'.

Note
The following also occur, the invariable form being more formal: *el/la asistente social* 'social worker' (also *la asistenta social*), *el/la cliente*, 'customer' (familiarly *la clienta*), *el/la presidente*, 'president' (also *la presidenta*, which Seco recommends).

1.2.6 Feminine of nouns ending in -e or a consonant
Apart from those already mentioned, these are mostly invariable:

el/la alférez	subaltern	*el/la rehén*	hostage
el/la enlace	union representative/	*el/la mártir*	martyr
	(British) shop steward	*el/la médium*	(spiritualist) medium
el/la intérprete	interpreter	*el/la tigre (la tigresa*	tiger
el/la líder	(political) leader	is heard)	
el/la joven	young man/woman	etc.	

But *el huésped/la huéspeda* 'guest' (also *la huésped*), *el monje/la monja* 'monk'/'nun', *el sastre/la sastra* 'tailor'. For *la jefa* see 1.2.7.

1.2.7 Feminine of nouns referring to professions
Like other Latin-based languages, Spanish is afflicted with the relatively new problem of what title to use for professional women. Until quite recently feminine forms of professional or educational titles had pejorative or comic overtones or denoted the wife of the male, cf. *el bachiller* (someone who has passed the equivalent of the baccalaureat or pre-university examination), *la bachillera* 'blue stocking' (i.e. a woman sneered at for being too intellectual), *el sargento/la sargenta* 'sergeant'/'battle-axe' (i.e. a fierce woman), *el general/la generala* 'general'/'the general's wife'.

In parts of the Spanish-speaking world, especially in Spain, a lingering stigma still attaches to the feminine form of words referring to professionals, so formal language tends to show respect by using the masculine form with a feminine article, e.g. *el/la abogado* 'lawyer/'legal counsel' (*la abogada*, originally 'intercessionary saint', is however now widespread for a woman lawyer).

Further examples (the comments reflect usage in Spain; the feminine forms may be more acceptable in Latin America):

el/la catedrático 'professor'.[3] *La catedrática* is gaining ground, but is often avoided when addressing the woman concerned;

el juez/la jueza 'judge'. In Spain, *la juez* is used in formal language; *El País* insists on it. *La jueza* may still mean 'the judge's wife' in rural usage;

el/la médico 'doctor'. *La médica* is spreading and is considered normal in

---

[3] *El catedrático* = 'professor' in the European sense, i.e. someone who occupies a university chair or *cátedra* and is usually, but not always, chairperson of the department. US 'professor' = *profesor universitario*.

much of Latin America, cf. *una médica blanca sudafricana* (*Granma*, Cuba) 'a white South-African female doctor', but it is thought disrespectful by many speakers of European Spanish. *Doctora* is, however, normal as a form of address;

el/la miembro 'member' (of clubs). *El socio* is said of men and *la socio* sometimes of women, but *la socia* is avoided, in Spain if not elsewhere, because it may be slang for prostitute;

el/la ministro 'minister' is common, but *la ministra* is increasingly acceptable. Both *la primer ministro* and *la primera ministra* are used for a woman prime minister. The former is more common, although *El País* and Manuel Seco both recommend *la primera ministra*.

In much of Latin America *la jefa* is an accepted feminine of *el/la jefe* 'boss', but it may sound disrespectful in Spain.

Other nouns in *-o* may be regular: *el arquitecto/la arquitecta* 'architect', *el biólogo/la bióloga* 'biologist', *el filósofo/la filósofa* 'philosopher', *el letrado/la letrada* 'counsel'/'legal representative', *el político/la política* 'politician', *el sociólogo/la socióloga* 'sociologist', etc. Nevertheless, forms like *la arquitecto, la filósofo, la letrado* may be preferred in Spain and are common in respectful language.

Very often the feminine form is only used when the woman referred to is not present: *¿Qué tal te llevas con la nueva jefa?* 'How are you getting on with your new woman boss?', but *Me han dicho que usted es la jefe del departamento* 'They tell me that you are the head of the department'.

1.2.8 Nouns referring to mixed groups of males and females
With rare exceptions (some noted at 1.2.1), the masculine plural denotes either a group of males, or of males and females:

los ingleses	English men/the English	*los profesores*	men teachers/teachers in general
los niños	little boys/children	*los reyes*	kings/the kings and queens
los padres	fathers/parents	etc.	
los perros	male dogs/dogs in general		

Since masculine plural nouns indicate either males or mixed groups and feminine nouns refer only to females, use of the masculine noun is obligatory in sentences like *No tengo más amigos que mujeres* 'The only friends I have are women' or *Todos los profesores son mujeres* 'All the teachers are women'. *No tengo más amigas que mujeres* would have the absurd meaning 'The only female friends I have are women'.

Care must also be taken with words like *uno, otro*. If a woman from Madrid says *Todos los madrileños me caen gordos* 'All the people from Madrid get on my nerves' one could reply *¡Pero tú eres uno de ellos!* 'But you're one of them!'[4], but not *. . .una de ellos*, since *madrileños* includes both males and females.

Compare

Ana es una de las profesoras	Ana is one of the women teachers

---

[4] Though *Pero ¡tú eres madrileña también!* 'But you're from Madrid too!' avoids the problem.

and

Ana es uno de los profesores   Ana is one of the teachers (who include males)

However, this principle is not applied consistently. In sentences like the following, use of the feminine noun does not necessarily exclude males:

María es la mejor profesora del instituto	Maria's the best teacher in the school (may or may not include males)
Emilia Pardo Bazán es la mejor intérprete de la vida rural de toda la literatura española del siglo XIX	Emilia Pardo Bazán is the best interpreter of rural life in the whole of 19th-century Spanish literature

For this reason, ambiguity must be removed in sentences like *Emilia Pardo Bazán es la mayor novelista **femenina** española del siglo pasado* 'Emilia Pardo Bazán is the greatest Spanish woman novelist of the last century'.

In some cases usage seems uncertain. A woman might say either *Unos están a favor y otros en contra. Yo soy de **las** que están a favor* or . . . *de **los** que están a favor* 'Some are for, others are against. I'm one of those who are for it'.

1.2.9 Gender of inanimate nouns when applied to humans
Feminine nouns applied to male humans may acquire masculine gender:

la cámara	camera	*el cámara*	camera man
la piel	skin	*el piel roja*	redskin
la primera clase	first class	*un primera clase*	someone first-class
la superventa	top sale	*el superventa*	top seller (male)
la trompeta	trumpet	*el trompeta*	trumpet-player
etc.			

The reverse case is better avoided: *la que toca la trompeta* 'the woman playing the trumpet', not *la trompeta*, which is the instrument.

1.2.10 Gender of names applied across sex boundaries
A female name applied to a male acquires masculine gender: *Tú eres **un** Margaret Thatcher* 'You're a Margaret Thatcher' (said to a man of his right-wing political ideas). But men's names usually remain masculine: *María, tú eres **un** Hitler con faldas* 'Maria, you're a female Hitler' (lit. 'Hitler in skirts').

1.2.11 Nouns of invariable gender applied to either sex
The following are some common words which, although applied to human beings, do not change their gender. One says *El bebé está enfermo* 'The baby is ill', whatever its sex[5]:

el ángel	angel	*el genio*	genius
el bebé	baby	*el ligue*	'date'/casual boy or
la celebridad	celebrity		girlfriend
el desastre	'disaster'	*la persona*	person
el esperpento	'fright'/weird-looking person	*el personaje*	character (in novels, etc.)
		la víctima	victim
la estrella	star (TV, etc.)		

---

[5] *Bebé* is considered to be a Gallicism in Spain and *niño/niña* are more common in everyday speech.

and a few other words, most involving sexual innuendo or comparisons with objects, cf. *el pendón* 'trollop' (lit. 'pennant'), *el marimacho* 'tom-boy', etc.

Note
The titles *Alteza* 'Highness', *Excelencia*, *Ilustrísima* 'Grace', (title of bishops) and *Majestad* 'Majesty' are feminine, but the person addressed keeps his/her gender: *Su Majestad estará cansado* (to king), 'Your Majesty must be tired'.

1.3 Nouns referring to animals not included under 1.2.1–1.2.11

Nouns that refer to animals not included in the preceding sections – i.e. to most wild animals – are treated as though they referred to inanimates, i.e. the noun is of fixed, arbitrary gender:

la araña	spider	*el panda*	panda
la ardilla	squirrel	*el puma*	puma
la ballena	whale	*la rana*	frog
el canguro[6]	kangaroo	*el sapo*	toad
el castor	beaver	*el tejón*	badger
la marsopa	porpoise	*el tiburón*	shark
la nutria	otter	etc.	

If sex must be distinguished, the male is denoted by adding *macho* 'male' and the female by adding *hembra* 'female': *la ardilla macho* 'male squirrel', *el cangrejo hembra* 'female crab', etc.

Agreement of adjectives in good Spanish is with the noun, not with the animal: *La rana macho está muerta* 'the male frog is dead', *El ratón hembra es blanco* 'the female mouse is white'.

Neither *macho* nor *hembra* agrees in gender or number: *las cebras macho* 'male zebras', *los gavilanes hembra* 'female sparrowhawks'.

Note
There is a tendency in familiar language and popular journalism to give such nouns biological gender: *el/la gorila* 'he-gorilla' and 'she-gorilla' (properly invariably *el gorila*), *el/la jirafa* 'giraffe' (*la jirafa* is properly invariably feminine).

1.4 Gender of nouns referring to inanimates

The gender of nouns referring to inanimates (and to plants) must be learned for each noun. The gender of these nouns is arbitrary and cannot be predicted from the meaning of the word. It also has no sexual implications and occasionally varies from place to place or century to century (e.g. Golden Age *la puente*, modern *el puente* 'bridge').

There are few infallible rules, and only those are quoted which in our view do not encourage false generalizations.

---

[6] *La canguro* is used in Spain to mean 'child-minder'.

The other Romance languages are uncertain guides to the gender of Spanish nouns, as the following list shows:

Spanish	French	Portuguese (o = masc. a = fem.)	Italian
el análisis	l'analyse (fem.)	a análise	l'analisi (fem.)
la duda	le doute	a dúvida	il dubbio
la estratagema	le stratagème	o estratagema	lo stratagemma (masc.)
el fin	la fin	o fim	la fine
la flor	la fleur	a flor	il fiore
la sal	le sel	o sal	il sale

There are many disagreements of this kind.

1.4.1 Masculine by meaning

Many nouns acquire the gender of an underlying or implied noun (metonymic gender). The following are typical:

(a) Rivers (*el río*): *el Amazonas* 'the Amazon', *el Jarama, el Manzanares, el Plata* 'the River Plate', *el Sena* 'the Seine' (French *la Seine*), *el Támesis* 'the Thames', *el Volga.*

Locally some rivers may be feminine, but outsiders rarely know this and the masculine is always correct.

(b) Mountains, oceans, seas and lakes (*el monte, el océano, el mar, el lago*): *el Etna, el Everest, el Himalaya* (singular), *el Pacífico, el Caribe* 'Caribbean', *el Windermere.*

(c) The names of cars, boats and aircraft (*el coche, el barco, el avión*): *un Fiesta, un Mercedes, un haiga* (colloquial Peninsular Spanish 'flashy car'), *el Queen Elisabeth, el Marie Celeste, un DC10, un Mig 21.*

Also *el caza* 'fighter aircraft'. Light aircraft are usually feminine because of the underlying noun *la avioneta: una Cessna.*

(d) Months and days of the week (*los meses y los días de la semana*): *enero/abril pasado, el lunes, el viernes.*

(e) Wines (*el vino*): *el Borgoña* 'Burgundy', *el champaña/el champán* 'champagne', *el Chianti, un Rioja.*

(f) Pictures (*el cuadro*) by named artists: *un Constable, un Leonardo, un Rembrandt, un Riley.*

(g) Sports teams (*el equipo*): *el Barça* 'Barcelona soccer club' (pronounced [bársa]), *el Betis* 'Seville soccer club', *el España, el Bilbao,* etc.

(h) All infinitives and all words referred to for grammatical or typographical purposes: *el fumar* 'smoking', *el escupir* 'spitting'.

Quita el "de" y pon un "del" (printer talking)	Take out the 'of' and put an 'of the'
El "cama" no se lee	You can't read the word 'bed'
No viene la señal, el "siga" que él esperaba (E. Poniatowska, Mexico)	The signal doesn't come, the 'go on' that he was expecting

(i) Any adverb, interjection or other genderless word used as a noun: *un algo* 'a "something"', *un no sé qué,* 'a *je ne sais quoi*' (i.e. 'indefinable quality'), *Ella está siempre con un "ay"* 'She's always sighing'/'always got troubles'.

(j) Numbers (*el número*): *un seis, un 5, la Generación del 98* 'the Generation of 98', *el dos por ciento* 'two per cent'.

(k) Musical notes: *el fa, el la* (underlying noun unclear).

(l) Colours (*el color*): *el azul* 'blue', *el rosa* 'pink', *el ocre* 'ochre', *Con lentitud se amplía el naranja del horizonte* 'The orange of the horizon spreads gradually wider' (A. Gala, Spain).

(m) Certain trees (*el árbol*) whose fruit is feminine, e.g.

Tree	Fruit	
el almendro	*la almendra*	almond
el avellano	*la avellana*	hazel
el banano	*la banana*	banana (Lat. Am.)
el castaño	*la castaña*	chestnut
el cerezo	*la cereza*	cherry
el ciruelo	*la ciruela*	plum
el granado	*la granada*	pomegranate
el guayabo	*la guayaba*	guava
el guindo	*la guinda*	morello cherry
el mandarino	*la mandarina*	tangerine
el manzano	*la manzana*	apple
el naranjo	*la naranja*	orange
el nogal	*la nuez*	walnut (or simply 'nut')
el papayo	*la papaya*	papaya
el peral	*la pera*	pear

But some fruits are masculine: *el limón* 'lemon', *el aguacate* 'avocado' (called *la palta* in southern Latin America), *el melón* 'melon', *el albaricoque* 'apricot', *el plátano* 'banana', (Spain), *la higuera* 'fig tree', but *el higo* 'fig'.

1.4.2 Masculine by form

(a) Nouns ending in *-o*: *el eco* 'echo', *el tiro* 'shot'.

Exceptions:

la dinamo	dynamo (also *la dínamo*)
la foto	photo
la Gestapo	the Gestapo
la libido	libido
la magneto	magneto (masc. in Lat. Am.)
la mano	hand (diminutive *la manita* (Spain), *la manito* (Lat. Am.))
la moto	motorbike
la nao	ship (archaic)
la polio	polio
la porno	porn(ography) (i.e. *la pornografía*)

La radio 'radio' is feminine in Spain and in the Southern Cone, but in Mexico and Central America and sporadically in northern parts of South America it is masculine: *el radio*. In some places *el radio* is 'radio set' and *la radio* is 'radio station'. *El radio* also everywhere means 'radius', 'radium' and 'radiogram'.

(b) Words ending in *-aje, -or, -án, -ambre* or a stressed vowel:

el equipaje	luggage	*el amor*	love
el paisaje	landscape	*el calor*	heat

el color	colour	*Canadá*	(masc.) Canada
el valor	value	*el champú*	shampoo
el mazapán	marzipan	*el sofá*	sofa/couch
el refrán	proverb	*el rubí*	ruby
el calambre	spasm/twinge	etc.	
el enjambre	swarm		

But: *la labor* 'labour', *la flor*, 'flower'. *El hambre* 'hunger' is also feminine: see 3.1.2 for explanation of the masculine article.

The forms *la calor* and *la color* for *el calor* 'heat' and *el color* 'colour' are heard in dialect and rural speech in Spain and in parts of Latin America. *La televisor* for *el televisor* 'television set' and one or two other unusual genders are also found in local Latin-American dialects.

1.4.3 Common masculine nouns ending in -*a*

Many errors are caused by the assumption that nouns ending in -*a* are feminine. Many nouns ending in -*ma*, and several other nouns ending in -*a* are masculine:

el anagrama	anagram
el anatema	anathema
el aroma	aroma
el cisma	schism
el clima	climate
el coma	coma (*la coma* = 'comma')
el crisma	holy oil (but *Te rompo la crisma* 'I'll knock your block off')
el crucigrama	crossword puzzle
el diagrama	diagram
el dilema	dilemma
el diploma	diploma
el dogma	dogma
el drama	drama
el eczema/eccema	eczema
el emblema	emblem
el enigma	enigma
el esquema	scheme
el estigma	stigma
el fantasma	ghost
el fonema	phoneme
el holograma	hologram
el lema	slogan/watchword
el magma	magma
el miasma	miasma
el panorama	panorama
el pijama	pyjamas/(US) 'pajamas' (*la pijama* or *la piyama* in Lat. Am.)
el plasma	plasma
el poema	poem
el prisma	prism
el problema	problem
el programa	program(me)
el radiograma	radiogram
el reúma	rheumatism (less commonly *el reuma*)

el síntoma	symptom
el sistema	system
el telegrama	telegram
el tema	theme/topic/subject
el trauma	trauma

and most other scientific or technical words ending in *-ma*. These words are masculine because the Greek words they are derived from are neuter. However, *la estratagema* 'stratagem', *el asma* 'asthma' (see 3.1.2 for explanation of the masculine article) and *la flema* 'phlegm' are feminine in Spanish even though the Greek originals are neuter.

For a list of feminine words in *-ma* see 1.4.6.

Notes
(i) A few of these words are feminine in popular speech, dialects and pre-nineteenth-century texts, especially *problema, clima, miasma* and *fantasma,* cf. *pobre fantasma soñadora* in Lorca's *El maleficio de la mariposa.*
(ii) Also masculine are: *el aleluya* 'halleluya' (*la aleluya* is 'doggerel'/'jingle'), *el alerta* 'alert' (*el alerta rojo* 'red alert'; *la alerta* is spreading), *el caza* 'fighter plane', *el cometa* 'comet' (*la cometa* = 'kite', the toy), *el día* 'day', *el extra* 'extra', *el guardarropa* 'wardrobe' (all such compounds are masculine), *el insecticida* 'insecticide' (and all chemicals ending in *-icida*), *el mañana* 'the morrow'/'tomorrow' (*la mañana* = 'morning'), *el mapa* 'map', *el mediodía* 'noon', *el nirvana, el planeta* 'planet', *el telesilla* 'ski-lift', *el tranvía* 'tram', *el vodka, el yoga.*

1.4.4 Feminine by meaning
The following are feminine, usually because of an underlying noun:
(a) Companies (*la compañía, la firma*): *la Westinghouse, la ICI, la Seat, la Hertz, la Volkswagen, la Ford.*
(b) Letters of the alphabet (*la letra*): *una b, una c, una h, la omega. El delta* 'river delta' is masculine.
(c) Islands (*la isla*): *las Azores, las Baleares, las Antillas* 'West Indies', *las Canarias,* etc.
(d) Roads (*la carretera* 'road' or *la autopista* 'motorway'/US 'freeway'): *la N11, la M4.*

1.4.5 Feminine by form
Nouns ending in *-eza, -ción, -sión, -dad, -tad, -tud, -umbre, -ie, -nza, -cia, -sis, -itis*:

la pereza	laziness	*la superficie*	surface
la acción	action	*la esperanza*	hope
la versión	version	*la presencia*	presence
la verdad	truth	*la crisis*	crisis
la libertad	freedom	*la tesis*	thesis
la virtud	virtue	*la diagnosis*	diagnosis
la muchedumbre	crowd/multitude	*la bronquitis*	bronchitis
la servidumbre	servitude	etc.	
la serie	series		

But the following are masculine:

el análisis	analysis	*el éxtasis*	ecstasy
el apocalipsis	apocalypse	*el paréntesis*	parenthesis/bracket
el énfasis	emphasis/pomposity of style		

1.4.6 Common feminine nouns ending in -*ma*

The majority of nouns ending in -*ma* are masculine (see 1.4.3), but many are feminine. The following are common examples (asterisked forms require the masculine article for reasons explained at 3.1.2, despite the fact that they are feminine nouns):

la alarma	alarm	*la forma*	shape
el alma*	soul	*la gama*	selection/range
la amalgama	amalgam	*la goma*	rubber
el arma*	weapon	*la lágrima*	tear (i.e. teardrop)
el asma*	asthma	*la lima*	(wood, nail)
la broma	joke		file/lime (fruit)
la calma	calm	*la llama*	flame/llama
la cama	bed	*la loma*	hillock
la cima	summit	*la máxima*	maxim
la crema	cream	*la merma*	decrease
la Cuaresma	Lent	*la norma*	norm
la chusma	rabble	*la palma*	palm
la diadema	diadem/tiara	*la paloma*	dove
la doma	breaking-in/taming	*la pantomima*	pantomime
	(= *la domadura*)	*la prima*	female cousin/
la dracma	drachma		bonus/prize
la enzima	enzyme	*la quema*	burning
la escama	scale (fish)	*la rama*	branch
la esgrima	fencing (with swords)	*la rima*	rhyme
la/el esperma	sperm	*la sima*	chasm/abyss
la estima	esteem	*la suma*	sum
la estratagema	stratagem	*la toma*	taking
la firma	firm/signature	*la yema*	egg yolk/fingertip
la flema	phlegm		

1.4.7 Gender of countries, provinces, regions

Countries, provinces or regions ending in unstressed -*a* are feminine:

la España/Francia/Argentina de hoy	Spain/France/Argentina today
la conservadora Gran Bretaña	conservative Britain

The rest are masculine: (*el*) *Perú*, (*el*) *Paraguay*, (*el*) *Canadá*; *Aragón*, *Devon*, *Tennessee*.

Some place names include the definite article and may exceptionally be feminine, cf. *las Hurdes* (near Salamanca, Spain). For use of the article with countries and place names, see 3.2.17.

Note
Such constructions as *todo Colombia lo sabe* 'all Colombia knows it' are nevertheless normal and correct, especially with the adjectives *todo*, *medio*, *mismo*, etc., probably because the underlying noun is felt to be *pueblo* 'people'. Cf. *Todo Piura está muerta* 'The whole of Piura is dead' (M. Vargas Llosa, Peru, dialogue).

1.4.8 Gender of cities, towns and villages

Cities ending in unstressed -*a* are usually feminine, the rest are masculine:

la Barcelona de ayer	the Barcelona of yesterday
la Roma de Horacio	Horace's Rome

el Londres de Dickens	Dickens's London
el Moscú turístico	the tourist's Moscow

But there are exceptions like *Nueva York*, **la** *antigua Cartago*, and spontaneous language often makes cities feminine because of the influence of the underlying noun *la ciudad* 'city':

Bogotá, antes de ser remodelada . . .	Bogota, before it was refashioned . . .
(Colombian press, in *Variedades*, 20)	

Villages are usually masculine even when they end in *-a*, because of underlying *el pueblo* 'village'.

For the construction *Todo Barcelona habla de ello* see the note to 1.4.7.

1.4.9 Gender of compound nouns

Compound nouns consisting of a verb plus a noun (frequent) are masculine:

el cazamariposas	butterfly net	*el paraguas*	umbrella
el cuentarrevoluciones	tachometer/	*el sacacorchos*	corkscrew
	rev-counter	*el saltamontes*	grasshopper
el lanzallamas	flamethrower	etc.	

The gender of other compound nouns should be learned separately.

1.4.10 Gender of foreign words

Words that refer to human beings will be feminine or masculine according to the gender of the person referred to: *los yuppies*, *el recordman* 'record-holder' (probably borrowed from French), but *la nanny*.

Foreign words referring to inanimates may be feminine if they closely resemble a familiar feminine Spanish word in form or meaning or, sometimes, because they are feminine in the original language:

la beautiful people	the rich set in Madrid (because of *la gente*?)
la chance	chance (Lat. Am. only, sometimes masc.)
la élite	élite (best pronounced as in French)
la Guinness	because of *la cerveza* 'beer'
la hi-fi	because of *la alta fidelidad*
la Kneset	the Knesset (Israeli parliament, because of *las Cortes*?)
la Motorola	portable phone
la NASA	because of *la agencia*
la opus	in music (cf. *la obra*), but *El Opus* = Opus Dei
la pizza	
la roulotte	caravan
la sauna	(masc. in Argentina)
la suite	suite (all senses)

But if the word is un-Spanish in spelling or ending, or is not clearly associated with a feminine Spanish word, it will be masculine. The great majority of foreign-looking words are therefore masculine, even though some of them are feminine in their original language:

el affaire	affair (love or political; fem. in French)
el after-shave	

el Big Bang	also *la Gran Explosión*
el best-seller	
los boxes	pits (in motor racing, more correctly *el taller; el box* is also sometimes used for 'casing', e.g. of an electrical component)
el boom	financial boom
el/la cassette (or *el/la casete*)	(*el cassette* is the player, *la cassette* the tape)
el chalet	(British) detached house, i.e. a house built on its own land
el chándal	track-suit
el Christmas	Christmas card
el déficit	economic deficit
el diskette	floppy disk; also *el disquete*
el dumping	commercial dumping
el echarpe	(light) scarf (fem. in French; pronounced as a Spanish word)
el eslogan/los eslóganes	advertising slogan/catch-phrase
el entrecot	entrecote steak (fem. in French)
el fax	
el footing	jogging (from French)
el gel de baño	bath gel
el hardware	(colloquially *el hard*; the Academy prefers *el soporte físico*)
el jazz	
el karaoke	
el joystick	joystick/(US) yoke (of an aeroplane)
el long play	L-P (record)
el marketing	
el modem	
el performance	performance (of a machine)
el poster	
el pub	(in Spain, a fashionable bar with music)
el quark	cf. *el neutrón, el protón* and *el electrón*, but *las partículas subatómicas*
el ranking	
el reprise	pick-up (i.e. acceleration of a car)
el scroll	e.g. *hacer un scroll de pantalla* 'to scroll the screen' (in computing)
el slip	men's underpants/(US) 'shorts'
el slogan	(publicity) slogan
el software	(colloquially *el soft*; the Academy prefers *el soporte lógico*)
el (e)spray	aerosol
el standing	e.g. *un piso alto standing* 'desirable flat/apartment'

The formation of the plural of foreign words is discussed at 2.1.5.

There is wide variation between the various Hispanic countries as to the source and number of recent loanwords, so no universally valid list can be drawn up.

1.4.11 Gender of abbreviations

This is determined by the gender of the main noun:

la ONU	UN
la OTAN	NATO
la CEE	EEC
las FF.AA. (*Fuerzas Armadas*)	Armed Forces
la UVI (*Unidad de Vigilancia Intensiva*)	Intensive Care Unit
el FBI	

el BOE	*Boletín Oficial del Estado* (where Spanish laws are published)
la CIA	
la EGB	*Educación General Básica*, the basic course in Spanish schools
el OVNI (objeto volante no identificado)	UFO

If the gender of the underlying noun is unknown the abbreviation is masculine unless there is a good reason otherwise: *el IRA* 'the IRA (Irish Republican Army; *la ira* = 'anger'), but *la RAF, la USAF* (because of *las fuerzas aéreas* 'air force'), etc.

1.4.12 Gender acquired from underlying noun (metonymic gender)

Many of the examples in previous sections illustrate cases of a noun acquiring the gender of another that has been deleted. This accounts for many apparent gender anomalies, cf. *el Psicosis = el Bar Psicosis*, (*la (p)sicosis* = 'psychosis'), *el Avenida = el Cine Avenida*, (*la avenida* = 'avenue'), *una EBRO = una camioneta EBRO* 'an EBRO light truck', *la Modelo = la Cárcel Modelo* 'Model Jail', *Radio Nacional de España, la número uno* (RNE, 11-1-92, *la emisora* 'broadcasting station' omitted) 'National Radio of Spain, the number one (station)', *la (número) setenta y tres = la habitación número setenta y tres* 'room seventy-three'.

1.4.13 Doubtful genders

There are a few words of doubtful gender. The following list gives the more common gender in the modern language in Spain (and usually elsewhere). Where both genders are in use, the more usual comes first:

el azúcar	sugar; it is usually masculine, though curiously a following adjective may correctly be feminine, e.g. *el azúcar moreno/a* 'brown sugar'
el calor	heat (*la calor* is rustic)
el color	colour (*la color* is rustic)
la dote	dowry/gifts (in plural – *tiene dotes* 'he's gifted')
la/el duermevela	snooze/nap/light sleep
los herpes	herpes
el hojaldre	puff pastry
el/la interrogante	question
el lente	lens (but *las lentillas* 'contact lenses')
el/la linde	boundary
la/el pelambre	thick hair/mop of hair
la/el pringue	fat/grease/sticky dirt (*esto está pringoso* 'this is sticky')
la sartén	frying pan (masc. in Bilbao and locally in Spain, and in many parts of Lat. Am.; fem. in Mexico)
el/la testuz	forehead (of animals)
la tilde	the sign over an ñ
el/la tizne	soot/black smear or stain
la/el tortícolis	stiff neck
el trípode	tripod

Pre-twentieth century texts may contain now obsolete genders, e.g. *la puente* 'bridge', *la fin* 'end', *la análisis* 'analysis', etc.

1.4.14 Gender of *mar*, 'sea'

Masculine, except in poetry, the speech of sailors and fishermen, in nautical terms (*la pleamar/la bajamar* 'high/low tide', *la mar llana* 'dead calm') and whenever the word is used as a colloquial intensifier: *la mar de tonto* 'absolutely stupid', *la mar de gente* '"loads"' of people'.

1.4.15 Some Latin-American genders

Some words are given different genders in provincial Spain and/or some parts of Latin America. Examples current in educated usage and writing in some (but not all) Latin-American countries are:

el bombillo	(Sp. *la bombilla*)	light bulb
el llamado	(*la llamada*)	call
el vuelto	(*la vuelta*)	change (money)
el protesto	(*la protesta*)	protest

There are surely many other examples, locally more or less accepted in educated speech.

1.4.16 Words with two genders

A number of common words have meanings differentiated solely by their gender. Well-known examples are:

	Masculine	Feminine
cometa	comet	kite (toy)
coma	coma	comma
consonante	rhyming word	consonant
cólera	cholera	wrath/anger
corte	cut	the Court/'Madrid'
capital	capital (money)	capital (city)
cura	priest	cure
delta	river delta	delta (Greek letter)
doblez	fold/crease	duplicity
editorial	editorial	publishing house
escucha	radio monitor/listening device/phone 'bug'	listening/monitoring
frente	front (military)	forehead
guardia	policeman	guard
génesis	Genesis (Bible)	genesis (= birth)
mañana	tomorrow/morrow	morning
margen	margin	riverbank
moral	mulberry tree	morals/morale
orden	order (opposite of disorder)	order (=command or religious order)
ordenanza	messenger/orderly	decree/ordinance
parte	official bulletin	part
pendiente	earring	slope
pez	fish	pitch (i.e. 'tar')
policía	policeman	police force
radio	radius/radium/spoke	radio
terminal	terminal (computers, electrical)	terminus
vocal	member of a board	vowel

Notes
(i) *Arte* 'art' is usually masculine in the singular, but feminine in the plural: *el arte español* 'Spanish art', *las bellas artes* 'fine arts'. But note set phrase *el arte poética* 'Ars Poetica'/'treatise on poetry'.
   But Manuel Seco (1992) 51, notes that a phrase like *esta nueva arte* 'this new art-form' is not incorrect, and that *los artes de pesca* 'fishing gear' (of a trawler) is standard usage.
(ii) *Radio* in the meaning of 'radio' is masculine from Colombia northwards, feminine elsewhere.

2

Plural of nouns

2.1 Formation of the plural of nouns

2.1.1 Summary of rules

The vast majority of Spanish nouns form their plural in one of the following three ways:

Method	Main type of noun	Example of plural
Add -s	Ending in an unstressed vowel Many foreign words ending in a consonant	*las casas* *los chalets* *los shows*
Add -es	Spanish (not foreign) nouns ending in a consonant other than -s Nouns ending in a stressed vowel + -s Many nouns ending in a stressed vowel	*las flores* *los ingleses* *los iraníes*
No change	Nouns already ending with an **unstressed** vowel + -s Families (people or things)	*las crisis* *los virus* *los Blanco* *los Ford*

Exceptions to these rules are discussed in the following sections.

2.1.2 Plural in -s

(a) Nouns ending in an unstressed vowel:

la cama	*las camas*	table
la serie	*las series*	series
el quinqui	*los quinquis*	'tinkers', itinerant peddlers (US 'pedlars')[1]
el huevo	*los huevos*	egg
la tribu	*las tribus*	tribe
el ecu	*los ecus*	Ecu (European Currency Unit)

---

[1] *Los quinquis* (Spain only) live much like the gypsies but keep apart from them. For many people the word is a synonym for 'gangster'.

(b) Nouns ending in stressed *-e*, including words of one syllable ending in *-e*:

el café	*los cafés*	coffee/café
el pie	*los pies*	foot/feet
el té	*los tés*	tea (the accent distinguishes this from the pronoun *te*)

(c) Nouns of more than one syllable ending in *-ó* (rare):

el dominó	*los dominós*	domino(es)
el buró	*los burós*	(roll-top) desk

(d) Many foreign words ending in a consonant, e.g. *el club/los clubs* (or *los clubes*). See 2.1.5.

2.1.3 Plural in -es

(a) Native (or nativized) nouns ending in a consonant other than *-s*:

el avión	*los aviones*	aeroplane
el color	*los colores*	colour
el cuásar	*los cuásares*	quasar
el/la chófer	*los/las chóferes*	driver
(*el chofer/los choferes* in many American republics)		
la verdad	*las verdades*	truth
el rey	*los reyes*	king
el suéter	*los suéteres*	sweater[2]
la vez	*las veces*	time (as in 'three times')

(b) Nouns ending in a stressed vowel plus *-s*, and all words of one syllable not ending in *-e*:

el anís	*los anises*	anis (an alcoholic drink)
el autobús	*los autobuses*	bus
el francés	*los franceses*	Frenchman
el dios	*los dioses*	god
el mes	*los meses*	month
el país	*los países*	country
la tos	*las toses*	cough
	los síes y los noes	the 'yesses' and 'noes', usually *sís y nos* in speech

Exception: *el mentís/los mentís* 'denial' (literary styles).

(c) Nouns ending in *-í*, *-ú* or *-á*:
The following plural forms are considered correct in formal or written language. For the use of the written accent in these words, see notes (iii) and (iv):

el bisturí	*los bisturíes*	scalpel
el maniquí	*los maniquíes*	tailor's dummy (*la maniquí* = female model)
el rubí	*los rubíes*	ruby
No intento siquiera poner el punto sobre las íes (A. Gala, Spain)		I'm not even trying to dot the Is

---

[2] This is the Academy's recommended form, but *los suéters* is commonly heard.

el zulú	*los zulúes*	Zulu
el tabú	*los tabúes*	taboo
el ombú	*los ombúes*[3]	ombu tree (Lat. Am.)
el bajá	*los bajaes*[3]	pasha
el jacarandá	*los jacarandaes*	jacaranda tree

Exceptions:

papá/papás	father/dad	*el menú/los menús*	menu
mamá/mamás	mother/mum/mom	*el tisú/los tisús*	(paper) tissues
sofá/sofás (illiterate **sofases*)	sofa/couch		

However, words of this kind usually simply add *-s* in spontaneous speech: *los iranís* 'Iranians' (properly *los iraníes*), *los jabalís* (properly *jabalíes*) 'wild boars', *los jacarandás, los rubís, los tabús, los zahorís* 'clairvoyants'/'water diviners'. A literary plural form of a truly popular word, e.g. *la gachí/las gachís* 'woman' (Spanish slang) would sound ridiculous.

The Latin-American words *el ají* 'chili'/'chili sauce', and *el maní* 'peanut' (Spain *el cacahuete*) often form the plurals *los ajises, los manises* in speech.

Notes

(i) If *-es* is added to a final *z*, the *z* becomes *c*: *la paz/las paces* 'peace', *la voz/las voces* 'voice'.

For words ending in *-g* (rare) or *-c* see 2.1.5.

(ii) If, when *-es* is added, the stress naturally falls on the last syllable but one, any accent written in the singular disappears:

el alacrán	*los alacranes*	scorpion
el irlandés	*los irlandeses*	Irishman
la nación	*las naciones*	nation
el/la rehén	*los/las rehenes*	hostage
etc.		

This does not apply to words that end in *-í* or *-ú*: *el pakistaní/los pakistaníes* (or *el paquistaní/los paquistaníes*) 'Pakistani', *el tabú/los tabúes* 'taboo'. These are discussed above at 2.1.3c and in note (iv) below.

(iii) Words ending in *-en* (but not *-én*!) require an accent in the plural to preserve the position of the stress. Since they are frequently misspelled, the following commonly-seen forms should be noted:

el carmen	*los cármenes*	villa with a garden (esp. in Andalusia)
el crimen	*los crímenes*	crime
el germen	*los gérmenes*	germ
la imagen	*las imágenes*	image
el lumen	*los lúmenes*	lumen (in physics)
el/la margen	*los/las márgenes*	margin (masc.)/river-bank (fem.)
el origen	*los orígenes*	origin
la virgen	*las vírgenes*	virgin

This also affects the nativized word *el mitin/los mítines* 'political meeting'.[4]

For the irregular plurals of *el régimen* and *el espécimen* see 2.1.8a.

(iv) When an accent written on *í* or *ú* shows that these vowels are pronounced

---

[3] The combination *ae* never forms a diphthong so it does not require an accent.

[4] A non-political meeting, e.g. of a department, family, shareholders, etc., is *la reunión*.

separately and do not form a diphthong, the accent is retained in the plural after the addition of -*es*:

el baúl	los baúles	trunk/chest
el laúd	los laúdes	lute
el país	los países	country
la raíz	las raíces	root

2.1.4 No change in the plural

(a) Words ending in an unstressed vowel plus *s*:

el/los análisis	analysis
el/los atlas	atlas
el/los campus	campus
la/las crisis	crisis
el/los lunes	Monday (similarly all weekdays)
el/los mecenas	patron of the arts
el/los paréntesis	bracket
la/las tesis	thesis
el/los virus	virus

In words of one syllable like *la tos* 'cough', the vowel is always stressed, so the plural ends in -*es*: *las toses*.

(b) Words ending in -*x*, e.g. *el/los dúplex* (US) 'duplex apartment'/(British) 'maisonette', *el/los fénix* 'phoenix', *el/los fax* 'fax': *No bajamos de tres o cuatro fax por día* (interview in *Cambio16*, Spain) 'We don't send less than three or four faxes a day'.

(c) Latin words ending in -*t* (at least in careful language):

los altos déficit presupuestarios (El País)　　high budgetary deficits

Likewise *los superávit* 'budgetary surpluses', *los accésit* 'second prizes', *el/los quórum*. But in everyday usage words in -*um* usually form their plural in -*ums*: *el memorándum/los memorándums, el referéndum/los referéndums, el ultimátum/los ultimátums, el currículum vitae/los currículums vitae*.

El País prefers the plurals *memorandos, referendos, ultimatos* and *currículos*, though common usage says -*ums*. The corresponding singular forms, *el memorando, el referendo, el ultimato* are Academy recommendations that the public has not accepted. *El currículo* 'curriculum' has recently spread in Peninsular colloquial language (and possibly also elsewhere).

In spontaneous speech all Latin words may be treated like other foreign words (see 2.1.5). Spanish speakers do not try to impress by using Latin plurals, cf. our (incorrect) 'referenda' for 'referendums'.

(d) Words ending in a consonant plus -*s*: *los bíceps, los fórceps*.

2.1.5 Plural of foreign words ending in a consonant

The universal tendency is to treat them all as English words and add -*s*, whatever language they come from. This produces words that end in two consonants, which goes against the spirit of the Spanish language and irritates grammarians. As a result, some foreign words have recommended written plurals in -*es* and everyday spoken plurals in -*s*, e.g. *los cócteles/los cóctels* 'cocktail', *los córneres/los córners* 'corner' (in soccer), *los fraques/los fracs* 'dress-coat'/'tails'.[5]

As a rule, if a word ends in *b, c, f, g, k, m, p, t, v,* or *w,* or in any two or more consonants, it is almost certainly a foreign word and will make its plural in *-s* unless it ends with a *s, sh* or *ch* sound, cf. *el kibutz* 'kibbutz', *el flash, el lunch, el sketch,* in which case it will probably be invariable in spontaneous speech. Well-informed speakers may use foreign plurals like *los flashes, los kibutzim, los sketches.* Examples:

el álbum	*los álbums*	(written form *los álbumes*)
el barman	*los barmans*	barman (the most usual colloquial plural in Spain, although *los barmen* is heard)
el boicot	*los boicots*	boycott
el complot	*los complots*	(political) plot
el coñac	*los coñacs*	cognac
el chalet	*los chalets*	detached house
el esnob	*los esnobs*	'snob'/'trendy'[6]
el hit	*los hits*	hit parade
el hobby	*los hobbys*	hobby/hobbies
el iceberg	*los icebergs*	iceberg
el kart	*los karts*	go-kart
el penalty[7]	*los penaltys*	(in soccer)
el quark	*los quarks*	quark (in physics)
el tic	*los tics*	tic
etc.		

Notes

(i) *El sandwich* (different from a *bocadillo,* which is a filled bread roll), makes the plural *los sandwiches* in educated usage, but *los sandwich* is frequently heard. It is pronounced [sángwich]. The Academy's word for 'sandwich', *el emparedado,* has never found favour.

(ii) Some modern loanwords are treated as Spanish words. This happens most readily when the word ends in *-l, -n* or *-r:*

el bar	*los bares*	bar
el dólar	*los dólares*	dollar
el electrón	*los electrones*	electron
el escáner	*los escáneres*	scanner (also *el scanner/los scanners*)
	los espaguetis	spaghetti (also *los espagueti*)
el gol	*los goles*	goal (in sport)
el hotel	*los hoteles*	hotel
el neutrón	*los neutrones*	neutron
el quasar	*los quasares*	quasar (preferably *el cuásar/los cuásares*)
etc.		

(iii) Academy plurals like *el gong/los gongues* 'gong', *el zizgzag/los zigzagues* 'zigzag', etc. are not used; *-s* alone is added. However *el film(e)/los filmes* is not uncommon and is recommended by *El País* (the everyday word is *la película*), and *el club/los clubes*

---

[5] Grammarians often recommend Hispanized forms of foreign words, e.g. *güisqui* for *whisky, yip* for *jeep, yaz* for *jazz, yóquey* or *yoqui* for *jockey,* etc. Since use of such forms suggests ignorance of foreign languages, it is unlikely that many of them will be adopted.

[6] In Spain *esnob* can also be applied to objects, in which case it means 'trendy' or 'flashy': *un coche esnob* = 'a flashy car'.

[7] Pronounced [elpenálti].

'club' is normal in Latin America for the common Peninsular *los clubs* (*El País* prefers *los clubes*).

(iv) Some writers and editors occasionally treat foreign words ending in a consonant like Latin words (see 2.1.4c), so forms like *los hit*, *los láser* are sometimes seen; *El País* recommends *los láser*. Zero plural forms are often given to foreign words in spontaneous everyday speech.

2.1.6 Proper names

If a proper name refers to a collective entity such as a family, it has no plural form: *los Franco, los Mallol, los Pérez; en casa de los Riba* (E. Poniatowska, Mexico) 'in the Ribas' house'.

A group of individuals who merely happen to have the same name will be pluralized according to the usual rules, although names in -z are almost always invariable:

Este pueblo está lleno de Morenos, Blancos y Péreces/Pérez	This village is full of Morenos, Blancos and Perezes
no todos los Juan Pérez del mundo (J. Donoso, Chile)	not all the Juan Perezes in the world
los Góngoras del siglo dieciocho	the Gongoras of the eighteenth century

Notes

(i) The same principle also applies to objects that form families: *los Ford* 'Ford cars', *los Chevrolet, los Simca*.

(ii) Royal houses are considered to be successive individuals: *los Borbones* 'the Bourbons', *los Habsburgos*.

2.1.7 Compound nouns

(a) Those (the most common) consisting of a verb plus a plural noun do not change in the plural:

el/los abrelatas	tin-opener
el elevalunas	automatic window opener (in a car)
el/los lanzamisiles	missile-launcher
el/los limpiabotas	shoe-shine
el/los portaaviones	aircraft carrier

(b) There is a growing class of compounds consisting of two juxtaposed nouns. Normally only the first noun is pluralized. The following forms have been noted from various written sources:

el año luz	*los años luz*	light year
el arco iris	*los arcos iris*	rainbow
la cárcel modelo	*las cárceles modelo*	model prison
el coche cama	*los coches cama*	sleeping car
el hombre rana	*los hombres rana*[8]	frogman
la hora punta	*las horas punta*	rush hour (lit. 'point hour')
el experimento piloto	*los experimentos piloto*	pilot experiment
el niño prodigio	*los niños prodigio*	child prodigy
el perro policía	*los perros policía*	police dog
el sistema antimisil	*los sistemas antimisil*	antimissile system

---

[8] Manuel Seco (1992), 223, says the plural should be *los hombres-ranas*, but neither the hyphen nor the double plural reflects general usage.

But always:

el país miembro	*los países miembros*	member country
la tierra virgen	*las tierras vírgenes*	virgin land

Pluralization of the second noun robs it of its adjectival force: *los hombres ranas* sounds like 'men who are frogs', cf.

las ediciones pirata	pirate editions	*los editores piratas*	pirate publishers
los niños modelo	model children	*los niños modelos*	child models

(c) Other compound nouns are treated as single words with regular plurals:

altavoz	*los altavoces*	loudspeaker (Lat. Am. *el altoparlante*)
bocacalle	*las bocacalles*	side street
correveidile	*los correveidiles*	tell-tale
sordomudo	*los sordomudos*	deaf-mute
hidalgo	*los hidalgos*	nobleman (the old plural was *hijosdalgo*)

2.1.8 Irregular plurals

There are only two or three irregular plural nouns.

(a) Three common nouns shift their stress in the plural:

el carácter	*los caracteres*	character (*los carácteres is not Spanish!)
el espécimen	*los especímenes*	specimen
el régimen	*los regímenes*	régime

(b) *El lord* (British) 'lord' has the plural *los lores*: *la Cámara de los Lores* 'The House of Lords'.

The scholarly word *el hipérbaton* 'hyperbaton' usually forms the plural *los hipérbatos*.

2.2   Syntax and semantics of plural nouns

2.2.1   Mass nouns and count nouns in Spanish and English

A count noun refers to countable items, 'egg'/'two eggs'. Mass or uncountable nouns denote non-countable items, 'justice', 'bread', but not *'two justices', *'two breads'.

In both English and Spanish, mass or uncountable nouns can often be pluralized to mean different varieties of the thing in question: 'her fear'/'her fears', 'my love'/'my loves', 'I love French wine'/'I love French wines'.

This device is far more frequent in Spanish than in English, and idiomatic translation of the resulting plural noun may require thought, e.g.:

Si aparece por tu casa, lo echas sin contemplaciones (J. Marsé, Spain, dialogue)	If he turns up at your house, throw him out on the spot/without second thoughts
Para nosotros existen dos urgencias (interview in *Cambio16*, Spain)	For us there are two urgent issues (lit. 'urgencies')

A number of Spanish nouns can be pluralized in this way whereas their English translation cannot.[9] Examples:

la amistad	friendship	*las amistades*	friends
la atención	attention	*las atenciones*	acts of kindness

---

[9] Some of these examples are from Iannucci (1952) and Stockwell *et al.* (1965).

la bondad	goodness	*las bondades*	good acts
la carne	meat	*las carnes*	fleshy parts
la crueldad	cruelty	*las crueldades*	cruel acts
la gente	people	*las gentes*	peoples
la información	information	*las informaciones*	news items
el negocio	business	*los negocios*	business affairs
el pan	bread	*los panes*	loaves of bread
el progreso	progress	*los progresos*	advances
la tostada	toast	*las tostadas*	slices of toast
la tristeza	sadness	*las tristezas*	sorrows
el trueno	thunder	*los truenos*	thunderclaps
etc.			

2.2.2 Nouns denoting symmetrical objects
As in English, these nouns are usually invariably plural:

los auriculares	earphones
las gafas	glasses (Lat. Am. *los anteojos*)
los gemelos	binoculars/cuff-links/twins
las tijeras	scissors

But usage is uncertain in some cases, with a colloquial tendency towards the singular. The more usual form (in Spain) comes first:

los alicates/el alicate	pliers/pincer
las bragas/la braga	knickers/panties
los calzoncillos/un calzoncillo	underpants/(US, shorts
la nariz/las narices	nose (the plural is colloquial)
las pinzas/la pinza	peg/pincers/tweezers/dart (in sewing)
el pantalón/los pantalones	trousers/(US, pants (both Spanish forms equally common[10])
las tenazas/la tenaza	tongs/pliers

Note
las escaleras/la escalera 'stairs' (plural more common), but singular if it means 'a ladder'.

2.2.3 Nouns always plural in Spanish
As happens in English, some nouns or phrases are normally found only in the plural. The following list is by no means exhaustive:

las afueras	outskirts
los alrededores	surroundings
los altos (Lat. Am.)	upstairs flat/apartment
los bajos (Lat. Am.)	downstairs flat/apartment
los bienes	goods, provisions
buenos días	good morning
buenas noches	good night (greeting or goodbye)
buenas tardes	good afternoon
las cosquillas	tickling
los enseres	goods and chattels/ household goods
las exequias	funeral rites
las ganas	urge/desire
las nupcias (archaic)	wedding rites

---

[10] But always *En casa es ella la que lleva los pantalones* 'She's the one who wears the trousers round the house' (i.e. 'she's the boss').

las tinieblas	darkness
los ultramarinos	groceries
las vacaciones	holiday/vacation
etc.	

2.2.4 Singular for objects of which a person has only one

The English sentence 'they cut their knees' is ambiguous: one knee or both? Spanish normally clarifies the issue by using the singular if only one each is implied or if only one thing is possessed:

Les cortaron la cabeza	They cut off their heads
Se quitaron el sombrero	They took off their hats
Todos tenían novia	All had girlfriends (one each)
tres israelíes con pasaporte alemán	three Israelis with German passports
(*Cambio16*, Spain)	
La cara de Antonio no refleja el mismo	Antonio's face doesn't reflect the same
entusiasmo. Ni **la** *de sus cuñados*	enthusiasm. Nor do (lit. 'nor does that
tampoco (Carmen Rico-Godoy, Spain)	of') those of his brothers-in-law

This rule is sometimes ignored in Latin-American speech: *Nos hemos mojado las cabezas* (Bolivia, quoted Kany, 26) 'We've wet our heads', *Lo hacían para que no les viéramos las caras* (L. Spota, dialogue, Mexico) 'They were doing it so we wouldn't see their faces'.

2.2.5 Singular for plural

Singular nouns may sometimes be used to represent large numbers after words like *mucho, tanto*, etc., often, but not exclusively, with an ironic tone:

En verano viene mucho inglés . . .	In summer you get a lot of English . . .
con tanto anglófilo como anda por ahí . . .	with all those Anglophiles about . . .
Se emocionó de ver tanto libro junto	He was moved to see so many books
(L. Sepúlveda, Chile)	together

This construction is colloquial and tends to sound mocking.

2.3 Number agreement rules

This section covers various aspects of number agreement, mainly with nouns. For further remarks on the agreement of adjectives see 4.7. For the agreement of possessive adjectives, see 8.3.2. For agreement with *cuyo* see 35.7. For tense agreement see 16.16.

2.3.1 Number agreement with collective nouns

(a) Adjectives that modify a collective noun (one that refers to a group of persons or things) are singular and the verb is in the singular when it immediately follows the collective noun: *La mayoría musulmana* **ha** *reaccionado* . . . 'The Muslim majority have/has reacted . . .', *La policía británica* **busca** *a dos individuos* 'The British police are looking for two individuals'. As the translations show, such nouns may be treated as plurals in English – especially in spoken British English, cf.

El gobierno considera . . .	The government consider(s)
La gente dice . . .	People say . . .
La tripulación está a su disposición	The crew is/are at your disposal

(b) If the collective noun is linked to a plural noun (usually by *de*), the safest option is to make the adjective or verb plural: *un grupo de vecinos airados* 'a group of angry neighbours', *una mayoría de españoles creen que...* 'a majority of Spaniards think that...'. The singular is, in fact, quite common in such constructions, but use of the plural will prevent beginners uttering nonsense like **un grupo de mujeres embarazado* 'a pregnant group of women' for *un grupo de mujeres embarazadas* 'a group of pregnant women'.

Examples:

Un mínimo de 13 presos habían sido asistidos de heridas (El País, Spain)	A minimum of 13 prisoners had been treated for injuries
La mayoría duermen, hechos ovillos (M. Vargas Llosa, Peru; *duerme* would sound wrong here because of the adjacent plural participle *hechos*)	The majority are curled up asleep

As mentioned above, singular agreement is very common when the meaning allows it:

Un sinnúmero de personas observaba el famoso Big Ben (El Comercio, Peru)	A vast crowd of people was/were watching the famous Big Ben
*La masa de los creyentes no **era** menos compleja que sus creencias* (O. Paz, Mexico)	The mass of believers were no less complex than their beliefs
*El resto de mis bienes **es** ya vuestro* (A. Gala, Spain)	The rest of my goods are yours now

Notes

(i) The question of agreement with collective nouns in constructions like *una mayoría de personas* is controversial. Seco (1992), 110, advocates the plural, but the style book of *El País* recommends the singular wherever possible.

Native speakers will sometimes hesitate over agreement with collective nouns: *una pareja amiga que se llama/llaman Mario y Ana* 'a couple who are friends of ours and are called Mario and Ana'.

(ii) When the collective noun is separated from the verb by intervening words, plural agreement is normal: *Una muchedumbre entró en el Palacio Real, pero al encontrarse con las tropas, huyeron* 'A crowd entered the Royal Palace, but on encountering the troops, they fled'.

(iii) For constructions like *Esa gente **son** unos desgraciados, El comité **son** unos mentirosos*, see 2.3.3.

2.3.2 Plural noun after *tipo de*, etc.

After *tipo de* and similar phrases, count nouns are often made plural:

Ya que ese tipo de rostros es frecuente en los países sudamericanos (E. Sábato, Argentina)	Since that type of face is frequent in South American countries
¿Por qué hacen los hombres este tipo de cosas? (C. Rico-Godoy, Spain)	Why do men do this kind of thing?

2.3.3 *Esto son lentejas, todo son problemas*, etc.

When *ser* (and occasionally a few other verbs like *volverse*) has a singular subject and a plural noun for its predicate, the verb agrees in number with the predicate, a construction which is unfamiliar to English speakers and difficult to analyse according to the traditional rules of grammar.

This most commonly occurs after neuter pronouns like *todo* 'everything. . .', *esto* 'this. . .', etc.

A similar phenomenon is found in French and German, which say 'it are lies': *ce **sont** des mensonges, es **sind** Lügen*:

*Esa gente **son** unos ladrones*	Those people are thieves
*Esto **son** lentejas y eso **son** guisantes*	This is lentils and that's peas
*Todo **son** problemas*	It's all problems
*El escrito **eran** sus 'condiciones' para que las Fuerzas Armadas aceptaran el sistema establecido (Cambio16, Spain)*	The document was his 'conditions' for the Armed Forces accepting the established system
*Su morada más común **son** las ruinas . . . .* (J.L. Borges, Argentina)	Their most usual dwelling-place is (in) ruins
*Al perro flaco todo se le **vuelven** pulgas*	Everything turns to fleas for a skinny dog (i.e. one misfortune follows another)

However, the following example suggests that this rule is not rigidly applied everywhere:

*En la terrible escasez que vive el país, lo único que no falta **es** cigarrillos* (M. Vargas Llosa, Peru, for *son cigarrillos*)	Amidst the terrible shortages the country is living through, the only thing that isn't lacking is cigarettes

Note
For this rule to be applied, the predicate must literally refer to a series of different things. In the following example the statement does not refer to something that is literally plural:

*María **es** en realidad muchas personas diferentes*	Maria is really a lot of different people (i.e. she has lots of different personalities)

María son muchas personas diferentes would mean that there are a lot of people who are assumed to be Maria.

2.3.4 Agreement with nouns linked by y, o and phrases meaning 'as well as'

(a) Nouns linked by *y* require plural agreement unless they are felt to form a single concept. Compare

Su padre y su madre estaban preocupados and	His father and his mother were worried
un atolondrado ir y venir	a mad coming and going

Further examples:

Su modestia y dulzura me encantaba (or *encantaban*)	Her modesty and gentleness charmed me
. . . el derrumbe del socialismo y la desaparición de la URSS causó el mayor daño en el orden económico (speech by Fidel Castro in *Cuba Internacional*; *causaron* equally possible)	. . . the collapse of socialism and the disappearance of the Soviet Union caused the greatest damage in the economic sphere

Note
As in any language, a speaker may start an utterance with a single noun and then

add further nouns as an afterthought. In this case the rules of agreement will not be applied:

Por supuesto que podemos pensar que en el juicio de Lope pesaba la rivalidad, el resentimiento, y la cercanía (E. Sábato, *Argentina, interview; pesaban* equally possible)	Obviously we can suppose that rivalry, resentment and closeness to the events played their part in Lope's assessment[11]

(b) With *o* agreement is optional, but the singular stresses the idea of 'one or the other' more than the plural:

Viene(n) Mario o Antonia	Mario or Antonia is/are coming

Singular agreement is usual when the nouns represent a single idea:

la depresión o tristeza que afecta(n) . . .	the depression or sadness that affect(s) . . .

(c) Agreement after phrases that mean 'as well as', 'likewise', etc. seems to be optional, although the plural is more common:

Tanto Mario como María pensaba(n) que . . .	both Mario and Maria thought that . . .

---

[11] The 17th-century playwright Lope de Vega allegedly said that *Don Quixote* was the worst book he had ever read.

3

Articles

Use of the definite article *el/la/los/las* is discussed in sections 3.2. The indefinite article *un/una/unos/unas* is discussed in section 3.3. *Unos/unas* is discussed at 3.4.

For the use of the definite article to replace a possessive adjective, e.g. *Se ha roto **el** brazo* 'He's broken his arm', *Me dejé **la** cartera en casa* 'I left my wallet at home', see 8.3.4. For the definite article in superlatives see 5.3. For the 'neuter article' *lo* see 7.2.

3.1 Forms of the definite article

3.1.1 Masculine and feminine definite articles

	Masculine	Feminine
Singular	*el*	*la*
Plural	*los*	*las*

La is always written in full in modern Spanish. Compare Spanish *la artista* 'woman artist' with Italian *l'artista*. The *-a* is not elided in pronunciation before words beginning with a vowel other than *a*: *la emisora* 'radio station' is pronounced [laemisóra], not [lemisóra].

3.1.2 Use of *el* and *un* before certain feminine nouns

El and *un* are always used immediately before singular feminine nouns beginning with stressed *a-* or *ha-*, despite the fact that all the adjectives and pronouns that modify these nouns must be in the feminine form. This feature of Spanish has no counterpart in other Romance languages.

This important rule must not be broken, although it is not always observed in pre-nineteenth-century texts and in some dialects. The following are some common examples:

el/un abra	mountain pass (Lat. Am., *el puerto*)
el África contemporánea	contemporary Africa
el agua	water
el/un águila	eagle
el/un alba	dawn (poetic)
el/un alma humana	the human soul

el/un alza	rise/increase
el/un ancla	anchor
el/un área	area
el/un arma	weapon
el/un arpa	harp
el Asia de hoy	Asia today
el asma	asthma
el/un aula	lecture room
el/un haba	bean
el/un habla	language/speech form
el/un hacha	axe/(US) ax
el/un hada	fairy
el/un hambre	hunger
el hampa madrileña	the Madrid criminal underworld
el/un haya	beech

Compare the following words which do not begin with a stressed *a*:

la/una amnistía	amnesty
la/una apertura	opening
la/una armonía	harmony
la/una hamaca	hammock

Exceptions:

la a, la hache	'a', 'h' (letters of the alphabet)
la Ángela, la Ana	and other women's names (see 3.2.2 for the rare use of the article with personal names)
La Haya	the Hague
la/una haz	surface/face (archaic; also *el haz* although fem.; *el haz,* masc. = bundle/sheaf)
la árabe	Arab woman
la ácrata	anarchist woman

Notes
(i) The plural is always with *las/unas*: *las águilas* 'eagles', *las hachas* 'axes'. The feminine article must be used if any word intervenes between the article and the noun: *una peligrosa arma* 'a dangerous weapon', *la misma área* 'the same area'.
(ii) The rule applies only to nouns, not to adjectives: *la/una ardua lucha* 'the/an arduous struggle', . . . *una amplia estancia con libros y cuadros* (F. Umbral, Spain) 'a wide room with books and paintings', *la/una ancha puerta* 'wide door', *Suele asumir la forma de una alta mujer silenciosa* (J.L. Borges, Argentina) 'She usually takes the form of a tall silent woman'.
(iii) This rule should apply to those rare feminine compound nouns whose first element would have begun with a stressed *a* had it stood alone: *el aguamarina* 'aquamarine', *un avemaría* 'an Ave Maria'.
(iv) It is a bad error to treat such words as masculine in the singular. One must say *un aula oscura* 'a dark lecture hall', not **un aula oscuro*, *la última alza* 'the latest rise', not **el último alza*, etc.
   However, mistakes like ?*Habrá que encontrar otro aula* 'We'll have to find another lecture-room' (for *otra aula*) or *el habla popular hispanoamericano* 'popular Spanish-American speech' (seen in a Spanish grammar book!) are extremely common, and constructions like ?*Tengo un hambre bárbaro* 'I'm starving hungry' or ?*Tengo mucho hambre* 'I'm very hungry' pass unnoticed in relaxed Latin-American speech, although they are not allowed in formal language.
(v) The forms *algún* 'some', *ningún* 'no' are normal in spontaneous speech before such nouns, but *alguna*, *ninguna* are the recommended written forms.
   Este 'this', *ese* and *aquel* 'that' are also common in spontaneous speech before such

nouns, but the feminine forms should be used in writing: *esta área* 'this area', *esta agua* 'that water'.

(vi) The usual explanation of the use of *el* before feminine nouns beginning with stressed *a-* is that the ancient form of the feminine article, *ela*, was abbreviated to *el* before such nouns: *ela arma>el arma*. But this does not explain why the masculine form is not used before adjectives beginning with stressed *a-*, e.g. *la ancha puerta*, never **el ancha puerta*.

3.1.3 *Del* and *al*

De plus *el* is shortened to *del* 'of the'. *A* plus *el* is shortened to *al* 'to the'. *De él* 'of him' and *a él* 'to him' are not abbreviated in modern Spanish.

The abbreviated forms are not used (at least in writing) if the article is part of a proper name:

la primera página de El Comercio	page one of *El Comercio*
Viajaron a El Cairo	They journeyed to Cairo
el autor de El intruso	the author of *The Intruder*

3.2 Uses and omission of the definite article

3.2.1 General remarks on the use of the definite article

Article usage is especially difficult to define, and usage of the definite article notoriously so: why *does* one say *en la práctica* 'in practice' but *en teoría* 'in theory'?

Article usage also varies in detail from region to region in the Spanish-speaking world, so the following remarks must be supplemented by careful study of good writing and educated speech.

Perhaps the most striking difference between Spanish and English is the use of the definite article with generic nouns, i.e. nouns which refer to a concept or object in general: *la naturaleza* 'nature', *la democracia* 'democracy', *el espacio* 'space' (in general) or 'the space', *las vacas* 'cows' (in general) or 'the cows'. But this rule is by no means hard and fast.

Careful study of the following pages should make it clear to students of French that although use of the Spanish definite article resembles French usage, the definite article in Spanish is in fact less used than its modern French counterpart, and is apparently less used than fifty years ago.

3.2.2 The French and Spanish definite articles

The following summary of the main differences may be useful.

French	Spanish
Usual with unqualified names of countries, provinces, continents: *L'Espagne est un beau pays, L'Amérique,* etc.	Not used (with occasional exceptions – see 3.2.17): *España es un hermoso país, América,* etc.
Often used when addressing people: *Salut les gars!, Oui, monsieur le Président*	Not used: *¡Hola muchachos!, Sí, señor Presidente*

Used without preposition with numerous time words: *le soir* 'in the evening', *le matin* 'in the morning', *le lendemain* 'the next day'	Preposition often required: *por la tarde, por la mañana, al día siguiente,* but *el año pasado,* 'last year', etc.
Not used in time expressions of the type *il est huit heures*	Used: *son **las** ocho*
Used with generic nouns: *Le vin est mauvais pour la foie* 'Wine's bad for the liver', *l'amour est aveugle* 'love is blind'	Very similar, but not identical (see 3.2.6 - 3.2.10): *El vino es malo para el hígado, **El** amor es ciego*
Used instead of possessives with parts of the body, clothing, mental faculties: *Il ferme **les** yeux, Il a perdu **la** mémoire,* etc.	Same, but more extensive: *Cierra **los** ojos, Ha perdido **la** memoria;* also *Te he aparcado **el** coche* 'I've parked your car', etc. See 8.3.4
Double article in superlatives when adjective follows noun: *le livre **le** plus intéressant*	Only one article, *el libro más interesante.* See 5.3
Used with superlative adverbs: *C'est lui qui chante **le** mieux*	Not used: *Él es quien mejor canta.* See 5.4.
De used before partitive nouns (i.e. to express 'some'): *Il boit de l'eau, Il y avait de la neige*	No article or preposition in partitive constructions: *Bebe agua, Había nieve* (except occasionally before demonstratives; see 3.2.8 note ii)

3.2.3 A useful generalization about the Spanish definite article
With two important exceptions, if the definite article is used in English it is also used in Spanish:

*la caída **del** gobierno*	**the** fall of **the** government
*Es difícil definir **el** uso **del** artículo definido*	It is difficult to define **the** use of **the** definite article

Exceptions:
(a) Ordinal numbers with kings, popes, etc.: *Fernando séptimo* 'Ferdinand **the** Seventh', *Carlos quinto* 'Charles **the** Fifth'.
(b) A number of set phrases in Spanish take no article whereas their English equivalent usually does. They must be learned separately:

a corto/largo plazo	in **the** short/long run	*en nombre de*	in the name of
cuesta abajo	down (the) hill	*hacia oriente*	towards the east
cuesta arriba	up (the) hill	*(hacia el este)*	
a gusto de	to the liking of	*a título de*	in the capacity of
en alta mar	on the high seas	*a voluntad de*	at the discretion of
en camino	on the way	*de plantilla*	on the payroll/staff
en dicho mes	in the said month	etc.	
en manos de	at/in the hands of		

This applies only to set adverbial phrases: compare *en **las** manos de Julia* 'in Julia's hands'. Note also *a fuerza de* 'by dint of', and *a **la** fuerza/por fuerza* 'by force'.

Note
The converse is not true: the Spanish definite article is constantly used where English

uses none, e.g. *El feminismo ha mejorado la condición de **las** mujeres* 'Feminism has improved the condition of women'.

3.2.4 Definite article with more than one noun

If two or more nouns appear together, each has its own article if they are individually particularized or are felt to indicate different things (see 3.2.7 for further remarks on lists of nouns).

In this respect Spanish differs sharply from English, which allows omission of the second article, possessive or demonstrative in phrases like 'the sun and moon', 'a dog and cat', 'my brother and sister', 'those men and women'. Spanish says *el sol y **la** luna*, ***un** perro y **un** gato*, ***mi** hermano y **mi** hermana*, ***esos** hombres y **esas** mujeres*. *?Un gato y perro* sounds like a cross between a cat and a dog:

el padre y la madre	the father and mother
entre el hotel y la playa	between the hotel and (the) beach
el agua y la leche	the water and (the) milk
Por el contrario, ello ayuda a mantener el país	On the contrary, it helps to keep the
en el subdesarrollo, es decir la pobreza,	country in a state of underdevelopment –
la desigualdad y la dependencia (M. Vargas	i.e. poverty, inequality and dependence
Llosa, Peru)	

But if the nouns are felt to form a single complex idea or are felt to be aspects of the same thing (often the case when they are joined by *o* 'or'), all but the first article may be omitted, especially in writing:

***el** misterio o enigma del origen* . . . (O. Paz, Mexico)	the mystery or enigma of the origin . . .
El procedimiento y consecuencias son semejantes (M. Vargas Llosa, Peru)	The procedure and consequences are similar
*Si una universidad debe pagar el precio de la enseñanza gratuita renunciando a contar con **los** laboratorios, equipos, bibliotecas, aulas, sistemas audiovisuales indispensables para cumplir con su trabajo [...] aquella solución es una falsa solución* (M. Vargas Llosa, Peru)	If a university has to pay the price of free education by giving up the laboratories, equipment, libraries, lecture rooms, audiovisual systems indispensable for it to do its work, that solution is a false solution

Notes

(i) Nouns may constitute similar things in one context and not in another. One says *Voy a comprarme **un** libro y **una** revista* 'I'm going to buy a book and a magazine' (two different things), but '*Los libros y (las) revistas están en el estante de arriba* 'The books and magazines are on the top shelf' (books and magazines both seen as members of the set 'publications').

(ii) If the first noun in a list is feminine and the second masculine, good style requires that the article should appear before both. One could say *las aulas y **los** equipos* 'lecture rooms and equipment' or *los equipos y aulas* but preferably not *las aulas y equipos*.

This rule is sometimes broken, cf *Las liebres, **las** perdices y faisanes, los cacé esta mañana* (M. Vargas Llosa, Peru, dialogue) 'I shot the hares, partridges and pheasants this morning' (*el faisán* = 'pheasant').

(iii) In pairs of animate nouns of different sex both require the article: *el toro y **la** vaca* 'the bull and (the) cow', never **el toro y vaca*.

(iv) In doubtful cases retention of the articles is safer: *Tráeme **los** tenedores y **las** cucharas* 'Bring me the forks and spoons'.

3.2.5 Omission of articles in proverbs

Articles, definite and indefinite, are often omitted in proverbs and in statements that are meant to sound proverbial:

Gato escaldado del agua fría huye	A scalded cat runs from cold water
Afectaremos a muchos turistas extranjeros, señor Presidente, y turista que se enoja, no regresa (Luis Spota, Mexico, dialogue)	We'll affect a lot of foreign tourists, Mr President, and **an** angry tourist doesn't come back
Virtudes y defectos van unidos	Virtues and defects go together

3.2.6 Definite article with generic nouns

With the exceptions noted at 3.2.10, the definite article is required before generic nouns, i.e. nouns that refer to something in general. These are typically:

(a) Abstract nouns:

la informalidad	informality/unreliability
la democracia	democracy
el catolicismo español	Spanish catholicism

(b) Substances in general:

El salvado es bueno para la digestión	Bran is good for the digestion
El acero inoxidable es carísimo	Stainless steel is extremely expensive
La sangre no tiene precio	Blood has no price

Colour nouns are members of this class of noun and require the article: *el azul* 'blue', *el negro* 'black', *El amarillo es un color que no me gusta* 'Yellow is a colour I don't like'.

(c) Countable nouns which refer to all the members of their class:

Los belgas beben mucha cerveza	(The) Belgians (in general) drink a lot of beer
Reivindicaban los derechos de la mujer moderna	They were campaigning for the rights of (the) modern woman/of modern women
El tigre es un animal peligroso	The tiger is a dangerous animal

Notes
(i) These rules are especially binding when the noun is the subject of a verb. The article cannot be omitted in the following sentences (but see 3.2.7 for the omission of the article from lists of two or more generic nouns): *No me gusta la manzanilla* 'I don't like camomile', (lit. 'camomile doesn't please me'), *El azúcar es malo para los dientes* 'sugar is bad for the teeth'.

But when the generic noun is the object of a verb or is preceded by a preposition, the definite article may be omitted in certain circumstances. See 3.2.10 for examples.

See 3.4.2 for sentences like *Expertos americanos dicen . . .* 'American experts say . . .' in which the noun may in fact be partitive, i.e. it does not really apply to every member of the class it denotes.

(ii) Sentences like *Me gusta el vino, Me gustan las cerezas* are therefore ambiguous out of context: 'I like the wine/the cherries' or 'I like wine/cherries'. In practice context or intonation makes the meaning clear, or a demonstrative – *este vino* 'this wine', *estas cerezas* 'these cherries' – can be used for the first meaning.

3.2.7 Omission of the article in lists

When two or more generic nouns follow one another, all the articles may be omitted, especially in literary style.

One must say *Esto podrá interesar a los jóvenes* 'This may interest the young' (i.e. 'young people'), but in both languages one could omit the bracketed items in *Esto podrá interesar a (los) jóvenes y (a los) viejos* 'This may interest (the) young and (the) old'.

This is presumably done to avoid the tedium of too many definite articles:

Los ingredientes con que se amasa el ser humano: amor, terror, fracaso, destino, libertad, fe, esperanza, risa, y llanto (Última Hora, Bolivia)	The ingredients that go to make up the human being: love, terror, failure, fate, freedom, faith, hope, laughter and tears
Ingleses y alemanes, en cuyos idiomas no existe la ñ, encuentran cierta dificultad en pronunciarla (instead of *Los ingleses y los alemanes*)	Englishmen and Germans, in whose languages *ñ* does not exist, find it somewhat difficult to pronounce
. . . esas apariencias que Historia y Tradición te exigen respetar (L. Spota, Mexico, dialogue)	Those appearances that History and Tradition require you to respect

Note
The nouns must be generic for omission to be possible. One can only say *el padre y la madre de Antonio* 'Antonio's father and mother', both nouns being specific in reference.

3.2.8 Omission of the article before partitive nouns
The article is omitted before nouns that refer not to the whole but only to part of something ('partitive' nouns):
(a) Before partitive mass (uncountable) nouns, i.e. nouns that refer only to a part of the whole:

Quiero cerveza	I want (some) beer
Eso necesita valor	That needs courage
No hay agua	There isn't any water/there's no water

The difference between generic and non-generic mass nouns is, however, not always obvious - as in the sentence *Como carne* 'I eat meat', where 'meat' is apparently generic. See 3.2.10 for further comments on the subject.
(b) Before partitive count nouns, i.e. countable nouns that in English could normally be preceded by 'some':

No se te olvide traer clavos	Don't forget to bring (some) nails
Incluso nos dieron flores	They even gave us (some) flowers
Llevan armas	They're carrying weapons

Notes
(i) Unqualified partitive nouns rarely appear in front of the verb of which they are the subject: *Caían bombas por todas partes* (not **Bombas caían por todas partes*) 'Bombs were falling everywhere'.
However, partitive nouns modified by some expression like *como ése/ese* 'like that one' may appear in front of the verb of which they are the subject: *Cosas como ésas/esas sólo/solo te pasan a ti* (example from M. Moliner) 'Things like that only happen to you', *Hombres como él no se encuentran a menudo* 'One doesn't often find men like him'.
For *Expertos americanos dicen que . . .* 'American experts say that . . .' see 3.4.2.
(ii) French and Italian regularly uses *de* or *di* before partitive nouns: *Il a des roses rouges*/*Ha delle rose rosse* = *Tiene rosas rojas* '(S)he's got some red roses'. *De* is not used in this way in Spanish, but it may occasionally appear before a demonstrative adjective to make it clear that 'some of' rather than 'all of' is meant. Compare *Tráenos de ese vino tan bueno que nos serviste ayer* 'Bring us **some of** that really good wine you served us yesterday', and *Tráenos ese vino tan bueno que nos serviste ayer* 'Bring us that really good wine you served us yesterday'.

3.2.9 Definite article required before nouns restricted by a qualifier

As in English, a noun that does not require the definite article when it stands alone usually requires it when it is qualified by a following word or phrase. Compare *Está hecho de oro* 'It's made of gold', and *Está hecho del oro que trajeron de las Indias* 'It's made from the gold they brought from the Indies'. Cf also *Admiramos al Cervantes humanista* 'We admire the humanist (in) Cervantes', *recuerdos de la España medieval* 'memories/souvenirs of Medieval Spain'.

This rule must be understood to override any of the rules of article omission that follow. However, a qualifier does not always make a noun specific: the resulting noun phrase may still be generic in its own right. This is especially true when the qualifier is an adjective:

Está hecho de oro macizo	It's made of solid gold
Estamos hablando de religión antigua	We're talking about ancient religion
No hablo con traidores de su patria	I don't talk to traitors to their own country

3.2.10 Apparent exceptions to the rules outlined in 3.2.6

The general rule given at 3.2.6 – that generic nouns take the definite article – has exceptions.

In the sentence *Yo como carne* 'I eat meat', *carne* seems to be generic: it refers to all meat and should apparently require the definite article. Such exceptions usually arise because the noun does not really refer to the whole of its class but only to a part, although this may not always be obvious. This is especially true of nouns which (a) follow prepositions or (b) are the object of certain kinds of verb.

(a) Omission after prepositions

Nouns following prepositions very often really only denote a part or an aspect of the thing they refer to. If this is the case, they take no definite article:

Le gusta salir con ingleses	She/He likes going out with English people (one or a few at a time, not the whole species at once)
El Ministerio de Justicia	The Ministry of Justice (local, not universal justice)
Sólo una minoría cuenta con electricidad	Only a minority have electricity (only quantities of electricitry, not electricity in general)
Dio una conferencia sobre poesía árabe	He gave a lecture on Arabic poetry (aspects of it, not the whole thing)
Me suena a mentira	It sounds like a lie

(b) After certain verbs, e.g. of consuming, desiring, producing, nouns which at first sight seem generic may on examination be seen to be partitive:

Los lagartos comen moscas	Lizards eat flies (one or two at a time, not the whole species at once)
Escribo novelas de ciencia ficción	I write science-fiction novels
Claro que uso jabón	Of course I use soap
Queremos paz	We want peace

But if the verb really affects the whole of its object in general – usually the case with verbs of human emotion like 'love', 'hate', 'admire', 'criticize', 'censure', 'reject', etc. – then the article is required:

*Odio **las** novelas de ciencia ficción*	I hate science-fiction novels
*Adoro **el** helado de vainilla*	I love vanilla ice cream
*Hay que combatir **el** terrorismo*	Terrorism must be fought

(c) Omission in adverbial phrases

The article is omitted in many adverbial phrases consisting of a preposition plus a noun:

la confusión por antonomasia	confusion personified/par excellence
a cántaros	in pitcherfuls
en balde	pointlessly/in vain
a quemarropa	point-blank
por avión	by plane
en tren/coche	by train/car
Estamos aquí de observadores	We're here as observers
De niña yo sólo hablaba catalán	As a little girl I only spoke Catalan

See Chapter 34 for detailed examples of prepositional usage.

Note
Omission or retention of the article with abstract and mass nouns after a preposition often depends on the point of view of the speaker. One can say either *Publicó tres artículos sobre poesía* 'He published three articles on poetry' or . . . *sobre la poesía* 'on Poetry'. The latter implies the universal concept 'Poetry'; the former implies 'aspects of poetry'. The difference is slight, and the strong modern tendency is to omit the article.

3.2.11 The definite article after *de*
When two nouns are joined by *de* to form what is effectively a compound noun, the article is omitted before the second noun. Compare *la rueda **del** coche* 'the wheel of/from the car', and *una rueda **de** coche* 'a car wheel':

la carne de la vaca	the meat of the cow
la carne de vaca	beef
los sombreros de las mujeres	the women's hats
los sombreros de mujer	women's hats
el dolor de muelas	toothache
un crimen de pasión	a crime of passion
lecciones de contabilidad	lessons in accountancy

Such combinations are often denoted in English by compound nouns: *la noche de la fiesta* 'the night of the party', *la noche de fiesta* 'party night'.

3.2.12 Use of the definite article after *haber* ('there is'/'there are')
Use of the articles with *haber/hay* meaning 'there is'/'there are' is discussed separately at 30.2.1 note (iii), but it is worth repeating here that Spanish does not normally allow the definite article to appear after *haber*: *Hay agua* 'There's water', *Hubo una tormenta* 'There was a storm', but *Ahí **está** el cartero* 'There's the postman'.

3.2.13 Omission of the definite articles in book, film and other titles
At the beginning of titles of works of literature or art the definite article is

often suppressed before nouns that are not felt to be unique entities:

Política y estado bajo el régimen de Franco	*Politics and the State under the Franco Régime*
Casa de campo, de José Donoso	*The Country House*, by J. Donoso
Selección de poemas	*Selected Poems*

But with unique entities or proper names the article is retained:

La casa verde, de M. Vargas Llosa	*The Green House*, by . . .
La Iglesia en España ayer y mañana	*The Church in Spain yesterday and tomorrow*

For the use of capital letters in book titles, see 39.3.2d.

3.2.14 Omission in headlines

In Spain the grammar of headline language is fairly normal and article omission follows the general rules. In Latin America a type of headline jargon has emerged which follows English in omitting articles:

Ingleses toman Islas Georgias luego de combate de 2 horas (*La Prensa*, Peru)	British take Georgias after two-hour battle
Causa de deslizamiento verán expertos (idem)	Experts to investigate cause of landslide
Afirma divorcios producen temblor (*Última Hora*, Dominican Republic, quoted in *Variedades* 20)	'Divorces cause Earthquakes' Claim

For the word order of these Latin-American headlines see 37.5.1, note (iii).

3.2.15 The definite article with names of unique entities

As in English, the definite article is used with nouns which refer to things of which there is only one.

Unlike English, Spanish also uses the definite article with mountains, volcanoes, Heaven and Hell: *El Taj Mahal, el Atlántico, el Infierno* 'Hell', *el Cielo/el Paraíso* 'Heaven'/'Paradise', *el Diablo* 'the Devil', *la Virgen* 'the Virgin', *el Everest, el Mont Blanc.*

As in English, it is not used with personal names as opposed to epithets or titles: *Dios* 'God', *Cristo* 'Christ' (very rarely *el Cristo*), *Jesucristo* 'Jesus Christ', *Satanás* 'Satan'.

For the article before ordinary personal names see 3.2.21.

3.2.16 Definite article with names of languages

Usage is capricious and departures from the following rules may occur:

(a) No article after *en*, or, usually, after *saber, aprender, hablar*:

en español, en inglés	in Spanish, in English
Sé quechua	I know Quechua
Aprendo alemán, habla griego	I'm learning German, he speaks Greek

(b) Optional article after *entender* 'understand', *escribir* 'write', *estudiar* 'study':

Entiendo (el) inglés	I understand English
Escribe (el) italiano	He writes Italian

(c) After *de* meaning 'from' and after other prepositions, the article is used:

traducir del español al francés	to translate from Spanish to French
una palabra del griego	a word from Greek
Comparado con el ruso, el español parece poco complicado	Compared with Russian, Spanish seems uncomplicated

(d) After *de* meaning 'of', the article is used only if the whole language is meant: *curso de español* 'Spanish course' (really 'aspects of Spanish'), *dificultades del español* 'difficulties of Spanish' (in general), *las sutilezas del japonés* 'the subtleties of Japanese';

(e) After *traducir* 'translate', *dominar* 'master', *chapurrear* 'speak badly', *destrozar* 'murder' and other verbs and prepositions not discussed above, the article is used: *Domina perfectamente el portugués* 'He's a complete master of Portuguese', *Chapurrea el inglés* 'He speaks broken English';

(f) If the language is the subject of a verb it requires the article:

El francés es difícil	French is difficult
El español es una lengua hermosa	Spanish is a beautiful language

(g) If the language is qualified by a following word or phrase, the article is required:

el español de Colombia	the Spanish of Colombia
el inglés que se habla en Tennessee	the English spoken in Tennessee

3.2.17 Definite article with names of countries

This is a difficult problem since spoken usage varies and is out of line with the most modern written styles. *El País* (*Libro de estilo* 8.28) orders its journalists to write all countries without the article except *la India, el Reino Unido* 'the United Kingdom' and *los Países Bajos* 'the Low Countries'; one even sees *en Reino Unido* in advertisements.[1]

The rules of everyday spoken language seem to be:

(a) Obligatory: *la India, El Salvador, El Reino Unido* 'the United Kingdom';

(b) Usual: *el Camerún* 'Cameroon', *el Congo, el Líbano* 'Lebanon', *la China, el Oriente Medio* 'The Middle East', *el Senegal, el Sudán, la Somalia, el Yemen*;

(c) Optional: *(la) Arabia Saudita, (la) Argentina* (article always used in Argentina itself), *(el) Brasil, (el) Canadá, (el) Ecuador, (las) Filipinas* 'The Philippines', *(el) Irak, (el) Irán, (el) Japón, (el) Nepal, (el) Pakistán, (el) Paraguay, (el) Perú, (el) Tibet, (el) Uruguay, (el) Vietnam*.

The article is frequently heard with these nouns in everyday speech, probably more so in Latin America than in Spain.

Other countries do not take the article: *tres años en Australia/Egipto/Noruega/Europa Oriental/África del Sur* 'three years in Australia/Egypt/Norway/Eastern Europe/South Africa'.

Notes
(i) 'The United States' is either *los Estados Unidos* (plural agreement) or *Estados Unidos* (singular agreement and no article). The latter is common in Latin-American usage and is the only form allowed in *El País* (Spain).

Gran Bretaña 'Great Britain' does not take the article, but *el Reino Unido* 'the United Kingdom' does.
(ii) In older texts, particularly in solemn diplomatic language, names of countries occasionally appear with the article: *la Francia, la Inglaterra*, etc.

---

[1] In this respect we must differ from Batchelor and Pountain (1992), 297, who say that 'use of the article is more typical of the written registers'. The reverse is true.

(iii) All place names require the article when they are qualified or restricted by a following adjective, phrase or clause, unless the qualifier is part of an official name:

la España contemporánea	contemporary Spain
la Suecia que yo conocía	the Sweden I knew

but

en Australia Occidental	in Western Australia
en Irlanda del Norte	in Northern Ireland

3.2.18 Definite article with provinces, regions, cities and towns

Some place names include the article as an inseparable feature: *Los Ángeles, El Cairo*[2], *La Coruña, El Escorial, La Habana* 'Havana', *El Havre, La Haya* 'the Hague', *la Mancha, La Meca* 'Mecca', *La Paz, la Plata, la Rioja*, etc.

Otherwise the article is not used – unless 3.2.9 applies, as in *el Buenos Aires de hoy* 'Buenos Aires today', *la Roma de Cicerón* 'Cicero's Rome', etc.

3.2.19 Definite article before names of streets, roads, squares, etc.

The definite article is used before roads, squares, avenues, lanes, alleys and similar places:

*Vive en **la** plaza/**la** calle de la Independencia*	He lives in Independence square/street
*la panadería de **la** avenida Fleming*	the baker's in Fleming Avenue

3.2.20 Definite articles with days of the week

The definite article appears with days of the week, but it does not appear when the day is the predicate of *ser* 'to be', or after *de* when it means 'from'. The article is also not used in dates:

Llegan el martes	They're arriving on Tuesday
cerrado los viernes	closed on Friday(s)
Odio los lunes	I hate Mondays
El miércoles es cuando habrá menos	Wednesday's the day there'll be least
a partir del domingo	after Sunday

but

*Hoy **es** lunes*	Today is Monday
*Trabajo **de** lunes a jueves*	I work from Monday to Thursday
miércoles 23 de marzo de 1943	Wednesday 23 March 1943

When *de* means 'of' the article is used:

Ocurrió en la noche del viernes	It happened on Friday night

3.2.21 Definite article with personal names

The definite article occasionally appears before the surname of very famous women: *la Loren, la Garbo, la Callas, la Pardo Bazán.*

It is not used in this way before the names of men, except occasionally in law courts to refer to the accused.

---

[2] The article is usually written with a capital letter only in the case of cities (Seco 1992, 162). This is the practice of *El País*.

Use of the article before first names, e.g. *la María, la Josefa, el Mario*, is considered substandard or regional or typical of court-room language or police reports, unless the name is qualified, as in *la simpática Inés* 'the kindly Inés'.

The definite article usually appears before nicknames: *El Che nunca fue derrotado* '"Che" (Guevara) was never defeated' (*Cuba Internacional*, Cuba)[3], *Detuvieron a Ramón Pérez "el Duque"* 'They arrested Ramón Pérez, (alias) "the Duke"' (in Spain virtually all notorious criminals are identified by nicknames).

In some places, e.g. Chile and Catalonia, use of the article before first names is quite common even in educated speech, but it is generally best avoided by foreign learners since it may sound condescending. Students of Portuguese should remember to omit the article in Spanish: *o António quer um café* = *Antonio quiere un café*.

3.2.22 Definite article with sports teams
The masculine article is used before sports teams: *el Granada* 'Granada FC', *el Manchester United, el Argentina*.

3.2.23 Definite article before nouns of family relationship
Abuelo/abuela takes the article: *Entré a dar un beso a la abuela* 'I went in to give grandmother a kiss', *El abuelo comía en silencio* 'Grandfather was eating in silence'.

Tío/tía 'uncle/aunt' also take the article: *Di un beso a la tía* 'I gave auntie a kiss'. But if the person is named the article is omitted – at least in educated language: *Le di un beso a tía Julia* 'I kissed aunt Julia'. (This rule may not be observed everywhere, but children in Madrid are – or were until recently – rebuked for saying *a la tía Julia*.)

In rural areas *tío/tía* may be used before the first names of local worthies: *el tío José/la tía Paca* 'old José'/'old Paca'.[4]

With *papá/mamá* use of the article may also sound uneducated to some speakers if the noun stands alone: *Dale un beso a papá* 'Give daddy a kiss'.

3.2.24 Definite article with personal titles
The definite article is used before the title of a person being talked about: *el señor Moreira, el profesor Smith, el general Rodríguez, el presidente Belaúnde, el doctor Fleming, el padre Blanco* 'Father Blanco'. It is not used if the person is directly addressed: *Pase usted, señor Sender/señor Presidente/padre Blanco* 'Come in Mr Sender/Mr President/ Father Blanco'.

The definite article is not, however, used before *don, doña, fray, san, santa, sor*, or before foreign titles like *míster, monsieur, Herr*: *don Miguel, fray Bentos, santa Teresa, sor Juana, míster Smith*, etc.

---

[3] But a few lines above in the same article *Che nunca fue derrotado*, no doubt because the revolutionary hero's nickname 'Che' is sometimes felt to be a proper name.

[4] *El tío, la tía* are nowadays very frequent in Spain as a rather vulgar word roughly meaning 'guy' (French *type*): *No conozco al tío ese* 'I don't know that guy'/(British) 'bloke'. Latin-Americans and well-spoken Spaniards use the more refined *el tipo*.

Notes

(i) *Don/doña* are used before the first names of older persons of respected social status and on envelopes (less now than formerly): *señor don Miguel Ramírez, doña Josefa, don Miguel*.

(ii) For the military forms of address *mi general* 'General', *mi coronel* 'Colonel' see 8.3.3.

3.2.25 Definite article in apposition

The definite article is omitted in apposition:

Madrid, capital de España	Madrid, the capital of Spain
Simón Bolívar, libertador de América	Simón Bolívar, the liberator of Latin America

But it is retained:

(a) if the following phrase is used to remove a possible confusion of identity: *Miró, **el** autor* 'Miró, the author' (not the painter); *Córdoba, **la** ciudad argentina* 'Cordoba, the Argentine city' (not the one in Spain).

(b) if the following phrase is a comparative or superlative: *Cervantes, **el** mayor novelista español* 'Cervantes, the greatest Spanish novelist', *Joaquín, el **más** listo de los dos* 'Joaquín, the cleverer of the two'.

(c) if the phrase is qualified by a following word or phrase:

*Javier Marcos, **el** arquitecto que diseñó las dos fuentes*	Javier Marcos, the architect who designed the two fountains

3.2.26 Definite article with numbered nouns

Unlike English, nouns identified by a number take the article:

*Vivo en **el** piso 38*	I live in apartment 38
*una disposición **del** artículo 277 de la Constitución*	a provision in Art. 277 of the Constitution
*unas fotos **del** 93*	some photos from the year 1993
el diez por ciento	ten per cent

The article is also used in expressions like *Murió a **los** ochenta años* 'He died at the age of eighty', but not when translating '*n* years old': *Tiene ochenta años* 'He's eighty'.

3.2.27 Definite article in phrases denoting place

The following require the definite article in Spanish:

*a/en/de **la** cama*	to/in/from bed
a/en/de la iglesia	to/in/from church
al/en el/del cielo/infierno	to/in/from Heaven/Hell
al/en el/del hospital	to/in/from hospital
en la cárcel/en el colegio/en el trabajo	in prison/at school/at work
en el escenario	on stage
en la televisión	on television
en el espacio	in space
en el mar	at sea, on/in the sea
debajo de la tierra (but *bajo tierra*)	underground

en todas partes	everywhere
(cf. *en todos los sitios*	everywhere)
a/en/de casa (often *a/en/de la casa* in Lat. Am.)	at/in/from home
en clase	in class

Some speakers differentiate *estar en la cama* 'to be in bed' and *estar en cama* 'to be ill/sick in bed', but the distinction is not universal.

3.2.28 Definite article after the verb *jugar*
The verb *jugar* requires the article: *jugar a la pelota* 'to play ball/with a ball', *jugar al ajedrez* 'to play chess', *jugar a las cartas* 'to play cards', *jugar al escondite* 'to play hide and seek'.

3.2.29 Definite article with personal pronouns
The definite article is required after first and second-person plural pronouns in phrases like the following: *ustedes **los** uruguayos* 'you Uruguayans', *nosotros **los** pobres* 'we poor people', *vosotras **las** españolas* 'you Spanish women . . .' It is also used when the pronoun is deleted:

Las *mujeres de los mineros siempre estamos en vilo pensando en los hombres* (A. López Salinas, Spain, dialogue)	We miners' wives are always on tenterhooks thinking about the men
Los *ingleses siempre ocultáis vuestras emociones*	You English always hide your emotions

3.2.30 Colloquial use of *la de*
In familiar language, *la de* may mean 'lots of':

Con la de números de abogado que vienen en la guía . . .	With all the dozens of lawyers' numbers there are in the directory . . .
. . . la de veces que han dicho eso	. . . the number of times they've said that!
. . . la de lágrimas que solté (L. Sepúlveda, Chile, dialogue)	the amount of tears I shed . . .

3.3 The indefinite article

3.3.1 Forms of the indefinite article

	Masculine	Feminine
Singular	*un*	*una*
Plural	*unos*	*unas*

For the use of *un* before feminine nouns beginning with a stressed *a*, e.g. *un arma, un alma*, see 3.1.2.

3.3.2 General remarks on the use of the indefinite article
In general terms, use of the indefinite article in Spanish corresponds to the use of 'a'/'an' in English, but there are two important differences:

(a) it is omitted before singular count nouns in certain contexts described at
3.3.6–12: *Tengo coche* 'I've got a car', *Mario es ingeniero* 'Mario's an engineer', *Lo
abrió sin llave* 'He opened it without a key', *Es mentira* 'It's a lie'
(b) It can appear in the plural: **unos** *pantalones* 'a pair of trousers', *Han
organizado* **unas** *manifestaciones* 'They've organized demonstrations', *Son* **unos**
genios incomprendidos 'They're misunderstood geniuses'.
For *uno/una* as an impersonal pronoun see 28.7.1.

3.3.3 The indefinite article in Spanish and French
Use of the indefinite article corresponds quite closely in these two Romance
languages, but Spanish almost never uses partitive *de*, cf *Tengo vino* and *J'ai
du vin* 'I've got some wine' (see 3.2.8 note (ii) for discussion) and French has
no plural form of *un/une*, cf. Spanish **unos** *guantes* 'some gloves', French **des**
gants. Unlike French, Spanish regularly omits the article in sentences of the
type *Tiene secretaria* 'He's got a secretary', cf *Il a* **une** *secrétaire*. See 3.3.8.

3.3.4 Indefinite article before more than one noun
When more than one noun occurs in a sequence, the indefinite article is
required before each noun. English tends to omit the article in such cases:

Entraron **un** *hombre y* **una** *mujer*	A man and (a) woman entered
Compré una máquina de escribir y una	I bought a typewriter and (a) wastepaper
papelera para mi despacho	basket for my office

However, omission is necessary when the nouns refer to the same thing or
to different aspects of the same thing:

una actriz y cantante	an actress and singer (same woman)
un cuchillo y abrelatas	a combined knife and tin-opener
Este libro está escrito con una maestría y	This novel is written with unusual skill
delicadeza insólitas	and delicacy

3.3.5 Omission before singular nouns: general
Un/una is quite often omitted before singular count nouns in circumstances
that are difficult to explain.
This happens whenever the generic or universal features of the noun are
being stressed. Compare *Pepe tiene secretaria* 'Pepe's got a secretary' (like most
bosses) and *Pepe tiene* **una** *secretaria que habla chino* 'Pepe's got a Chinese-
speaking secretary' (unlike most bosses).
The following sections 3.3.6–13 illustrate the main cases in which *un/una*
are omitted. For the omission of *un/una* in proverbs, see 3.2.5.

3.3.6 Omission before nouns denoting professions, occupations, social
status, sex
(This is a very common case of the phenomenon described in 3.3.7.)
Un/una are regularly omitted before nouns which describe profession,
occupation, social status, sex, etc. In this case the noun can be thought of
as a sort of adjective that simply allocates the noun to a general type:

Soy piloto/son buzos	I'm a pilot/they're divers
Mi mujer es enfermera	My wife's a nurse
Es soltero/es casada (compare *está casada*	He's a bachelor/she's a married woman
'she's married'; see 29.4.1a for further	
details)	

Se hizo detective	He became a detective
. . . y aunque Alejandra era mujer . . .	. . . and although Alejandra was a
(E. Sábato, Argentina)	woman . . .
Veo que es usted mujer de buen gusto	I see you're a woman of good taste

But nouns denoting personal qualities rather than membership of a profession or other group require the article: compare *Es negrero* 'He is a slave-trader' and *Es **un** negrero* 'He's a "slave driver"' (i.e. makes you work too hard), *Eres un genio* 'You're a genius', *Es un ladrón* 'He's a thief' (i.e. not professionally).

Notes
(i) The article is retained if it means 'one of . . .': — *¿Quién es ese que ha saludado? — Es un profesor* '"Who was that who said hello?" "He's one of the teachers"'.
(ii) If a noun of the type discussed above is qualified, it usually becomes particularized (non-generic) and therefore requires the article. Compare *es actor* 'He's an actor' and *Es un actor que nunca encuentra trabajo* 'He's an actor who never finds work'.
But the resulting noun phrase may still be a recognized profession or a generic type, so no article will be used: *Soy profesor de español.* See 3.3.9 for discussion.

3.3.7 Omission of the indefinite article with *ser* and nouns not included in 3.3.6

Omission of the indefinite article after *ser* is frequent (a) in certain common phrases, (b) in literary style. A rare English counterpart is the optional omission of 'a' with 'part': 'This is (a) part of our heritage' *Esto es (una) parte de nuestro patrimonio.*

Omission is more common in negative sentences and apparently more frequent in Peninsular Spanish than in Latin-American.
(a) In the following phrases omission seems to be optional:

Es (una) coincidencia	It's a coincidence
Es (una) cuestión de dinero	It's a question of money
Es (una) víctima de las circunstancias	He/she's a victim of circumstances

No clear rule can be formulated since the article is retained in other common phrases of a similar type:

Es una lata (colloquial)	It's a nuisance
Es una pena	It's a pity
Es un problema	It's a problem
Ha sido un éxito	It was a success

Omission may occur after the negative verb even though it is not usual after the positive verb:

No es molestia/problema	It's no bother/problem
No es exageración	It's no exaggeration
No es desventaja	It's not a disadvantage

(b) In other cases, omission often, but not always, produces a literary effect:

Es mar de veras (M. Vargas Llosa, Peruvian dialogue)	It's (a) real sea
La codorniz es ave tiernísima (M. Delibes)	The quail is an extremely tender bird (to eat)
¡Váyanse! ¿Qué vienen a ver? ¡Esta es cuestión que a ustedes no les importa! (J. Ibargüengoitia, Mexico, dialogue)	Go away! What have you come here to look at? This is an affair that has nothing to do with you!

Es privilegio peculiar de ciertos linajes de pura sangre celta (J. L. Borges, Argentina)	It is a special privilege of certain thoroughbred Celtic families

In all the above examples the article could be used.

Notes
(i) If the following noun is not generic but merely implies the possession of certain qualities, *un/una* is used: *El hombre es **un** lobo para el hombre* 'Man is a wolf to man' (but not a member of the wolf species), *Esos muchachos son **unas** niñas* 'Those boys are (behaving like) little girls'.
(ii) In literary styles, omission of *un/una* is normal in definitions when the subject comes first: *Novela es toda obra de ficción que . . .* 'A novel is any work of fiction that . . .'.
(iii) Omission of the indefinite article before a qualified noun tends to produce an archaic or heavily literary effect, as in *Entra una señora con sombrero verde con plumas de avestruz* 'A lady with a green hat with ostrich feathers enters', where *un sombrero verde* would nowadays be much more normal.
   Similarly, where Unamuno wrote *Era un viejecillo [. . .] con levitón de largos bolsillos* 'He was a little old man . . . with a large frock-coat with deep pockets', a modern writer might prefer *un levitón*. Purists occasionally complain about this increasing use of the indefinite article, which they attribute to English or French influence.
(iv) For constructions like *Expertos americanos dicen que . . .* 'American experts say that . . .' see 3.4.2.

3.3.8 Omission of *un/una* after other verbs
Spanish omits *un/una* after a number of verbs such as *tener* 'have', *sacar* 'take'/'draw out' (with cinema tickets, etc. = 'buy'/'book'), *buscar* 'look for', *llevar* 'wear', when their object is a certain type of noun.
   These nouns refer to things of which one would normally have or be carrying only one at a time: umbrella, pen, spoon, nanny, valet, cook, hat, etc. Sometimes the noun denotes some object or person – wife, garden, video recorder, telephone, freezer, lover – which in some way defines the social status of the speaker:

¿Tenías idea de lo que serías capaz de hacer?	Did you have any idea of what you'd be able to do?
Ya he sacado entrada	I've already got a ticket
Vamos a buscarle novia	Let's look for a girlfriend for him
Siempre lleva anillo	He always wears a ring
Hubo quien se ofendió y sacó pistola (M. Vargas Llosa, Peru)	There was one person who took offence/(US) 'offense' and pulled a gun
Barcelona tiene puerto y parque y tranvía y metro y autobús y cine (L. Goytisolo, Spain)	Barcelona has a port, park, tramway, metro, buses and cinema(s)
Voy a pedir hora (*una hora* = one hour or a specific time)	I'm going to ask for an appointment

The indefinite article reappears if the particular identity of the object is relevant:

*Llevaba **una** falda blanca*	She was wearing a white skirt
Tenía [. . .] una carita de chico pecoso . . . (F. Umbral, Spain)	She had a cute face like a freckled boy's

   Use of *un/una* with unqualified nouns may therefore hint at some suppressed comment: *Tiene una mujer . . .* 'He's got a wife . . . (and she is . . .)', *Tiene un coche . . .* 'You should see his car. . .'. This may sound insinuating.

Note
If it would be normal to have more than one of the things denoted, or if the idea of
'one' is relevant, the article must be used: *¿Tienes **un** hermano?* Do you have a brother?
– not **¿Tienes hermano?*:

¿Tienes un dólar?	Have you got a dollar?
¿Has comprado una novela?	Have you bought a novel?
Tiene un novio en Burgos y otro en Huelva	She's got one boyfriend in Burgos and another in Huelva

3.3.9 Retention of indefinite article before qualified nouns
As soon as nouns are qualified (restricted) by a clause, phrase or adjective
they become specific and the article is obligatory: *Tengo padre* 'I've got a
father', *Tengo **un** padre que es inaguantable* 'I've got an unbearable father'. But
if the resulting noun phrase is still generic the article may still be omitted:
Tú eres hombre respetable 'You're a respectable man', *Es pastor protestante* 'He's
a protestant vicar'.

Note
This rule also applies in the plural: *Es un conservador arrepentido/Son unos conservadores
arrepentidos* 'He's a repentant conservative'/'They're repentant conservatives':

*Es **un** ejemplo/Son **unos** ejemplos que hemos encontrado en tu novela*	It's an example/They're examples we found in your novel
*El tipo había estudiado su carrera en Inglaterra y en seguida me llené de **unos** celos juveniles hacia él* (F. Umbral, Spain)	The fellow/guy had studied for his degree in England, and I was immediately filled with juvenile jealousy towards him

3.3.10 Omission of indefinite article in apposition
The indefinite article is normally omitted in appositive phrases in written
language:

El Español de hoy, lengua en ebullición	*Spanish today, a Language in Ferment* (book title)
a orillas del Huisne, arroyo de apariencia tranquila . . (J. L. Borges, Argentina)	On the banks of the Huisne, a seemingly tranquil stream . . .

But in informal language, or if the noun in apposition is qualified by an
adjective or clause, the article may optionally be retained:

*. . . el Coronel Gaddafi de Libia, **un** ardiente admirador del ayatollah Jomeini . . .* (Cambio16, Spain)	. . . Colonel Gaddafi of Libya, a fervent admirer of Ayatollah Khomeini . . .

3.3.11 Indefinite article to distinguish nouns from adjectives
Many Spanish nouns are indistinguishable in form from adjectives: use of
un/una indicates that the noun is meant:

Juan es cobarde	John is cowardly
Juan es un cobarde	John is a coward
Papá es (un) fascista	Father is a fascist
Soy (un) extranjero	I'm foreign/a foreigner

Papá es fascista implies 'he's a committed Fascist', whereas *Papá es **un** fascista*
suggests 'he acts like a fascist'. The indefinite article is also used in the plural
so as to retain the distinction: *Son desgraciados* 'They're unhappy', *Son **unos**
desgraciados* 'They're wretches'.

3.3.12 Omission after *como*, *a modo/manera de*, *por*, *sin*, *con*

(a) The indefinite article is omitted after *a manera de*, *a modo de* and after *como* when it means 'in the capacity of' or 'by way of':

a manera de prólogo	by way of a prologue
a modo de bastón	as/like a walking stick
como ejemplo	as an example
Utilicé mi zapato como martillo	I used my shoe as a hammer
Vino como ayudante	He came as an assistant

(b) It is omitted after *por* when it means 'instead of', 'in place of' or 'for' in phrases like: *Por respuesta le dio un beso* 'She gave him a kiss as a reply', *Por toda comida me dieron un plato de arroz* 'For a meal they gave me a plate of rice' (i.e. 'all I got for a meal was . . .').

(c) It is usually omitted after *sin* 'without':

No lo vas a poder cortar sin cuchillo/No vas a poder cortarlo sin cuchillo	You won't be able to cut it without a knife
Ha venido sin camisa	He's come without a shirt on
un gato sin cola	a cat without a tail

But if the idea of 'one' is stressed, the article is required:

sin una peseta	without a (single) peseta
sin un amigo a quien contar sus problemas	without a friend to tell his problems to

(d) It is omitted after *con* when it means 'wearing', 'equipped with' and in many other adverbial phrases:

Siempre va con abrigo	He always wears an overcoat
una casa con jardín	a house with a garden
La Esfinge [. . .] es un león echado en la tierra y con cabeza de hombre (J. L. Borges, Argentina)	The Sphinx is a lion stretched out on the ground, with a man's head
Lo escribí con lápiz	I wrote it with a pencil
con ganas/violencia	enthusiastically/violently
etc.	

3.3.13 Omission in exclamations, after *qué*, and before *tal*, *medio*, *cierto*, *otro*

The following constructions differ from English:

¡Extraña coincidencia!	What a strange coincidence!
¡Qué cantidad!/ruido!/pena!	What a quantity/noise/pity!
¿Cómo ha podido hacer tal/semejante cosa? (colloquially *una cosa así*; *un tal* = 'a certain')	How could he have done such a thing?
media pinta/medio kilo	half a pint/kilo
cierta mujer/otra cerveza	a certain woman/another beer

See 9.7 for *cierto* and 9.13 for *otro*.

3.4 *Unos/unas*

Spanish is unusual in that the indefinite article can be used in the plural with a variety of meanings.

For a comparison of *algunos* and *unos*, which may both sometimes mean 'some', see 9.4.2.

3.4.1 Uses of *unos/unas*

(The pronoun *uno* is discussed at 9.3 note (iv) and 28.7.1.)

The Spanish indefinite article appears in the plural with various meanings :

(a) before numbers, 'approximately':

unos trescientos mil pesos	about 300,000 pesos
Se calculó que el terremoto duró unos 25 segundos	It was calculated that the earthquake lasted some twenty-five seconds

(b) before plural nouns, 'some':

Le dieron unas monedas	They gave him some coins
Tomamos unas cervezas	We had some beers
Todavía tenía unos restos de fe	He still had some vestiges of faith

When used thus it may merely moderate the force of a following noun. It can therefore add a modest note and may sometimes be the equivalent of the colloquial disclaimer 'just a couple of':

El gobierno ha organizado unas elecciones (*Cambio16*, Spain)	The government has organized elections

(Omission of *unas* would imply something grander, e.g. general elections.)

Sonreí . . . pero fue peor: unos dientes amarillos aparecieron (C. Rico-Godoy, Spain)	I smiled, but it was worse: a set of yellow teeth appeared (or 'some yellow teeth appeared')
Mira estas fotos – son unas vistas tomadas en Guadalajara	Look at these photos – they're a couple of shots taken in Guadalajara

But sometimes use of *unos* makes little difference:

El pacifismo debería traducirse en unos comportamientos políticos que no tuviesen ninguna indulgencia con los violentos (*La Vanguardia*, *unos* deletable)	Pacifism ought to be translated into (a set of) patterns of political behaviour which show no indulgence towards the violent

(c) Before nouns that only appear in the plural, to show that only one is meant. If the noun denotes a symmetrical object like trousers, binoculars, scissors, *unos/unas* means 'a pair of':

Me he caído por unas escaleras	I've fallen/I fell down some/a flight of stairs
Voy a tomarme unas vacaciones	I'm going to have a holiday/vacation
Llevaba unos pantalones a rayas	He was wearing striped trousers
Se había puesto unas gafas que no intelectualizaban su rostro (F. Umbral, Spain)	She had put on a pair of glasses which did not give her face an intellectual air
He comprado unas cortinas	I've bought a pair of curtains

(d) Use of *unos/unas* may show that the plural noun which follows is not being used generically:

Son niñas	They're little girls
Son unas niñas	They're (acting like) little girls
Son payasos	They're (circus) clowns
Son unos payasos	They're (acting like) clowns

(e) *Unos/unas* may be needed to show that the following noun is a noun and not an adjective or noun used as an adjective. See 3.3.11 for examples.

3.4.2 Omission of *unos/unas*

There is a growing tendency in written Spanish, especially in journalism, to avoid the use of *unos* (and of *algunos*) in sentences of the kind:

Expertos americanos afirman que . . .	American experts claim that . . .

It is not clear whether *los, algunos* or *unos* has been omitted here. The omission is no doubt a journalistic ruse designed to gloss over the fact that only one or two experts were actually consulted. Spoken Spanish requires *los* if the meaning is 'all American experts', *algunos* if the meaning is 'some', and *unos* if 'a few' is intended.

In other cases omission produces a literary effect:

Eléctricas letras verdes intermitentes anunciaron la salida del vuelo (M. Vázquez Montalbán, Spain)	Flashing green electric lights announced the departure of the flight

where **unas** *letras verdes eléctricas e intermitentes* . . . would have been more normal.

4

Adjectives

4.1 General

(a) Spanish adjectives agree with nouns and pronouns in number and, if possible, gender. This means that nearly all adjectives have at least two forms, e.g. *natural/naturales*, and in many cases four different forms: *bueno/buena/buenos/buenas*. However, a small group of rather unusual adjectives, e.g. *macho, violeta*, are invariable in form. They are discussed at 4.2.3.

(b) One problem facing the student of Spanish is the position of an adjective with respect to the noun it modifies, the difference between *un problema difícil* and *un difícil problema* 'a difficult problem' or *una nube lejana* and *una lejana nube* 'a distant cloud' being virtually untranslatable in English. This problem is discussed in section 4.11.

(c) It is necessary to distinguish 'descriptive' and 'attributive'[1] adjectives. Descriptive adjectives can be thought of as replacing a simple relative clause: *un libro aburrido* 'a boring book' is the same as *un libro que es aburrido* 'a book that is boring'. Attributive adjectives usually replace a noun + *de*: *la presión sanguínea* 'blood pressure' = *la presión de la sangre*, *un programa televisivo* = *un programa de televisión*. Unlike descriptive adjectives, attributive adjectives always follow the noun. They are discussed in detail at 4.12.

(d) As in other Romance languages, adjectives in Spanish become nouns if an article, demonstrative, numeral or other qualifier is added: *viejo/el viejo* 'old'/'the old man' or 'the old one', *enfermo/estos enfermos* 'ill'/'these ill/sick people', *reptil/tres reptiles* 'reptilian'/'three reptiles', etc. In this respect the difference between adjectives and nouns in Spanish is not very clear, especially in view of the fact that nouns can occasionally be used like adjectives, as in *Ella es más mujer que Ana* 'She's more (of a) woman than Ana' (or 'more feminine'). Such adjectival use of nouns is discussed at 4.10.

However, although adjectives can serve as nouns, adjectives are nevertheless formed in unpredictable ways from nouns: *automóvil* > *automovilístico*, *legislación* > *legislativo*, *montaña* > *montañoso*, *leche* > *lácteo* 'milk', etc. Only a few nouns, e.g. *miembro, virgen*, function as adjectives without a change of form, cf. *los países miembros* 'member countries', *las tierras vírgenes* 'virgin territories', etc.

---

[1] This is the term used in *Collins Spanish-English/English-Spanish Dictionary*. Judge and Healey (1983) use the term 'relational'.

(e) Some adjectives can be used with object pronouns and the verb *ser*: *Me es importante* 'It's important to me', *Nos es imprescindible* 'He's indispensable to us', *Estas materias primas le son muy necesarias* 'These raw materials are very necessary for him/you'; but most cannot. See 11.9 for discussion.

(f) Adjectival participles ending in *-ante*, *-iente* are discussed under participles at 19.4.

(g) The gerund in *-ndo* is a verbal form in Spanish and must not therefore be used as an adjective: *una muñeca que anda* 'a walking doll', not *una muñeca andando* 'a doll **walking**'. For two exceptions to this rule, see 4.4; for a general discussion of the gerund see Chapter 20.

(h) A few adjectives may also function as adverbs, e.g. *Los teléfonos están* ***fatal*** 'The phones are in a dreadful state'. See 31.3.3. for discussion.

4.2 Morphology of adjectives

Spanish adjectives are of three types:

> **Type 1** show agreement in number and gender with the noun.
>
> **Type 2** show agreement for number but not for gender.
>
> **Type 3** are invariable in form (few, and mostly colours).

4.2.1 Type 1 adjectives (marked for number and gender)

These include adjectives whose masculine singular ends in:

-o,	with the rare exceptions noted at 4.2.3
-án	
-és	except *cortés* 'courteous' and *descortés* 'discourteous', which are type 2
-ín	usually a diminutive suffix (but see note iii)
-ón	usually an augmentative suffix (but see note iii)
-or	with the dozen or so exceptions listed in note (i)
-ote	
-ete	

and adjectives of place of origin or nationality not ending in *-a*, *-í*, *-e*, *-al* or *-ar*, e.g. *español/española*, but not *celta*, *iraní*, *provenzal*, *balear*, which are type 2. (*Español* and *andaluz* are in fact the only two common type 1 adjectives ending in a consonant other than *-n*.)

The feminine of type 1 adjectives is formed thus:

(1) if the masculine singular ends in a vowel, change the vowel to *-a*: *colombiano* > *colombiana*[2] 'Colombian';

(2) if the masculine singular ends in a consonant, add *-a*: *pillín* > *pillina* 'mischievous'. By the normal rules of spelling (explained at 39.2.1), an accent on the final vowel of the masculine is dropped.

---

[2] Adjectives in Spanish are almost always written with a lower-case letter. See 39.3.1 for occasional exceptions.

The plural of type 1 adjectives is formed thus:

(1) add *-s* to a vowel: *colombiano* > *colombianos, colombiana* > *colombianas*;

(2) add *-es* to a consonant to form the masculine, *pillín* > *pillines*, and *-as* to form the feminine *pillina* > *pillinas*. By the normal rules of spelling, a final *-z* is changed to *c* before *e*. Examples:

	Singular	Plural	
Masc.	*bueno*	*buenos*	good
Fem.	*buena*	*buenas*	
	musulmán	*musulmanes*	Muslim
	musulmana	*musulmanas*	
	aragonés	*aragoneses*	Aragonese
	aragonesa	*aragonesas*	
	saltarín	*saltarines*	restless, fidgety
	saltarina	*saltarinas*	
	mandón	*mandones*	bossy
	mandona	*mandonas*	
	hablador	*habladores*	talkative
	habladora	*habladoras*	
	regordete	*regordetes*	plump
	regordeta	*regordetas*	
	español	*españoles*	Spanish
	española	*españolas*	
	andaluz	*andaluces*	Andalusian
	andaluza	*andaluzas*	

Notes
(i) Adjectives in *-or* that have a comparative meaning are all type 2, i.e. they have no separate feminine form. These are: *anterior* 'previous', *exterior* 'outer', *inferior* 'lower'/'inferior', *interior* 'inner'/'interior', *mayor* 'greater'/'older', *mejor* 'better', *menor* 'minor'/'smaller/younger', *peor* 'worse', *posterior* 'later'/'subsequent', *superior** 'upper'/'superior', *ulterior* 'later'/'further'.
*Exception: *la madre superiora* 'mother superior'.
(ii) *Cortés,* 'courteous' and *descortés* 'discourteous' are type 2 adjectives. *Montés* 'wild' (i.e. not domesticated) is also usually type 2: *el gato montés* 'wild/untamed cat', *la cabra montés* 'wild goat', *las hierbas monteses* 'mountain herbs'.
(iii) One or two adjectives ending in *-ín* or *-ón* are type 2: *marrón* 'brown'[3], *afín* 'related'/'similar': *una camisa marrón*, 'a brown shirt', *ideas afines* 'related ideas'.

4.2.2 Type 2 adjectives (no separate feminine form)
No difference between masculine and feminine. This class includes (with the exceptions noted above):

(a) all adjectives whose masculine singular ends in a consonant other than *-n* or *-és*;
(b) adjectives ending in *-a, -e, -ú, -í*.

The plural is formed:

---

[3]There is no single word for 'brown' in Peninsular Spanish. *Marrón* is chiefly used for artificial things like shoes. *Castaño* is used for hair and eyes: *pelo castaño, ojos castaños*. 'Brown skin' is *piel morena*. 'Brown earth' is *tierra parda* or *tierra rojiza*. *Café* (no agreement) is used for 'brown' in many parts of Latin America.

(1)   if the adjective ends in a consonant or *-í* or *-ú*, by adding *-es*. *-z* is written *c* before *e*;

(2)   in all other cases, by adding *-s*.

Examples:

Singular	Plural	
azteca	*aztecas*	Aztec
suicida	*suicidas*	suicidal
grande	*grandes*	big/great
farsante	*farsantes*	fraud/'pseudo'
iraní	*iraníes*	Iranian
hindú	*hindúes*	Hindu/Indian (see 4.8.1 note iii)
cortés	*corteses*	courteous
gris	*grises*	grey
feliz	*felices*	happy

Notes

(i) Adjectives ending in *-í* often make their plural in *-ís* in spontaneous speech, e.g. *los iranís* 'Iranians', although *los iraníes* is the standard written form. Some words, e.g. *maorí/maoríes* or *maorís* 'Maori' are uncertain, but at the present stage of the language, *-íes* is still generally felt to be the correct written plural ending of adjectives ending in *-í*.

(ii) If a diminutive or augmentative suffix is added to one of these adjectives, it then becomes type 1: *mayorcito/mayorcita* 'grown-up', *grandote/grandota* 'extremely large'.

(iii) *Dominante* forms a popular feminine *dominanta* 'bossy'/'domineering'. A few other popular or slang forms in *-nta* occur, e.g. *atorrante/atorranta* (Lat. Am.) 'lazy'/'loafer', but in general adjectives ending in *-nte* are not marked for gender, whereas some nouns ending in *-nte* are. See 1.2.5 and 19.4 for further discussion.

4.2.3 Type 3 adjectives (marked for neither number nor gender)

Members of this group, which also includes a number of colour adjectives discussed 4.2.4, are invariable in form, presumably because they are felt to be nouns rather than adjectives. (See also 2.1.7b for discussion of compound nouns like *perro policía* 'police dog', *hombre rana* 'frogman'):

Singular	Plural	
una rata macho	*unas ratas macho*	male rat(s)
la camisa beige (*El País* uses the spelling *beis*)	*las camisas beige*	beige shirt(s)

Other common members of this class are:

alerta*	alert	*estamos alerta*	we're alert
clave*	key	*el punto clave/los puntos clave*	the key issue(s)
encinta	(literary) pregnant	*tres mujeres encinta*	three pregnant women (Manuel Seco recommends the plural *encintas*)
extra*		*pagos extra*	extra payments
hembra	female	*los ratones hembra*	female mice
esnob	snobbish/trendy		
modelo		*las granjas modelo*	model farms
monstruo	monster	*una casa monstruo*	a monster/giant house
sport		*los coches sport*	sports cars
tabú*	taboo		
ultra*	extreme right-wing		

Notes

(i) This group is unstable, and the words asterisked often agree in the plural: *los problemas claves, los pagos extras, los temas tabúes, Nuestra obligación es vivir constantemente alertas* (M. Vargas Llosa, Peru) 'Our obligation is to live constantly alert . . .'.

(ii) Although they look like nouns, *maestro, virgen* and *perro* agree like normal adjectives: *llaves maestras* 'master keys', *tierras vírgenes* 'virgin territories', *¡Qué vida más perra!* 'What a rotten life!'

(iii) *Varón* 'male' (of humans) is type 2: *niños varones* 'male children'.

(iv) Pluralization of the adjectival word restores its full function as a noun. Compare *niños modelo* 'model children' and *niños modelos* 'child models'. See 2.1.7b for discussion.

(v) A similar phenomenon is found in French with a few adjectives, cf. *des chemises marron* 'brown shirts'.

4.2.4 Invariable adjectives of colour

The more usual adjectives denoting colours – *negro, rojo, azul* – are ordinary type 1 or type 2 adjectives. However, any suitable noun, preceded by *color, de color* or *color de*, can describe a colour: *ojos color (de) humo* 'smoke-coloured eyes', *color barquillo* 'wafer-coloured'. The phrase with *color* is sometimes dropped and the noun is then used like a type 3 adjective, i.e. it does not agree in number and gender: *tres botones naranja/rosa/beige/malva/violeta/esmeralda* 'three orange/pink/beige/mauve/violet/emerald buttons', *corbatas salmón* 'salmon ties', *cintas fresa* 'strawberry-colour ribbons'. Other nouns so used are:

añil	indigo	*granate*	garnet/dark red
azafrán	saffron	*lila*	lilac
azur	azure	*oro*	gold (*dorado* = golden)
café	coffee-coloured/brown	*paja*	straw-coloured
carmesí	crimson	*sepia*	sepia
cereza	cherry	*turquesa*	turquoise
chocolate	chocolate brown	etc.	
escarlata	scarlet		
grana	dark red (*Se puso como la grana* 'He turned deep red')		

Notes

(i) Colloquially, and in the work of some writers, especially Latin-American, *naranja, rosa, malva, violeta* and a few others may be pluralized: *flores malvas* 'mauve flowers', *Los jacarandaes se pusieron violetas* (E. Sábato, Argentina) 'The jacarandas turned violet', *las uñas violetas* 'violet finger-nails' (C. Barral, Spain), . . . *los ojos violetas eran de Mary* (C. Fuentes, Mexico) 'the violet eyes were Mary's'. But this seems to be avoided in careful language: . . . *sus ojos violeta parpadean* (J. Marsé, Spain) 'her violet eyes are blinking', . . . *rayos ultravioleta* (El País, Spain) 'ultraviolet rays', *pliegos de papel llegados de Europa, azules, malva, rosa, verdes* (F. Umbral, Spain) 'folds of paper from Europe, blue, mauve, pink, green'.

Carmesí 'crimson' is always pluralized like a regular type 2 adjective (*carmesíes*) by the Spanish writer Antonio Gala in his best-selling novel *El manuscrito carmesí* (1991). It is also pluralized in the novels of the Mexican, Luis Spota.

(ii) It is unusual to find such adjectives before a noun, except in poetry: *Como sonreía la rosa mañana* (Antonio Machado, Spain, written before 1910) 'As pink dawn was smiling'.

(iii) *Color* or *de color* is, in practice, usually inserted before such words in everyday language: *una bicicleta color naranja* 'an orange bicycle', *zapatos (de) color mostaza* 'mustard-colour shoes'.

4.3 Compound colour adjectives

All compound colour adjectives of the type 'dark blue', 'light green', 'signal red' are invariable in form:

hojas verde oscuro	dark green leaves
calcetines rojo claro	pale/light red socks
una masa gris castaño	a grey-brown mass
[Mis ojos] son azul	My eyes are pale blue,
pálido como los de las	like the wet-nurses'
nodrizas (E. Poniatowska,	
Mexico)	

In this respect Spanish resembles French: *des yeux bleu clair*.

Notes
(i) Well-established compound adjectives of this kind may be used on their own, but new or unusual formations may require the formula *de color* . . ., e.g. *una mancha de color* rojo apagado 'a dull red stain/patch', not ?*una mancha rojo apagado*.
(ii) There are special words for some common mixed colours: *verdirrojo* 'red-green', *verdiblanco* 'greenish white', *verdinegro* 'very dark green', *blanquiazul* 'bluish white', *blanquinegro* 'black and white', *blanquirrojo* 'red and white'. These agree like normal adjectives: *verdinegros/verdinegras*, etc.

4.4 *Hirviendo* and *ardiendo*

Gerunds cannot be used as adjectives in Spanish: one cannot say **un objeto volando* for 'a flying object' (un *objeto volante* or un *objeto que vuela/volaba*, etc.). See 20.3 for a more detailed discussion.

There are two exceptions, *hirviendo* 'boiling' and *ardiendo* 'burning' which, despite having the form of gerunds, can be used as adjective:

Tráeme agua hirviendo	Bring me some boiling water
Tienes la frente ardiendo	Your forehead is burning
Yo más bien soy un carbón ardiendo	I feel more like a burning coal
(i.e. sexually excited; dialogue in	
M. Vargas Llosa, Peru)	

Chorreando 'dripping wet' may be another exception in *Llevo la ropa chorreando* 'my clothes are dripping wet'.

Hirviendo and *ardiendo* are invariable in form, take no suffixes and cannot appear before a noun.

4.5 Adjectives formed from two words

Some compound adjectives are made into single words and behave like any adjective: *muchachas pelirrojas* 'red-haired girls' (from *pelo* 'hair' and *rojo* 'red'), *cuernos puntiagudos* 'sharp-pointed horns' (from *punta* 'point' and *agudo* 'sharp').

In compound adjectives joined by a hyphen, only the second word agrees with the noun:

movimientos político-militares	political-military movements
teorías histórico-críticas	historical-critical theories

Such examples excepted, use of a hyphen to join words is very rare in Spanish; cf. *contrarrevolucionario* 'counter-revolutionary', *latinoamericano* 'Latin-American'. See 39.4.6 for details about the use of the hyphen.

4.6 Short forms of some adjectives

A number of common adjectives lose their final syllable in certain circumstances.

(a) The singular of *grande* is shortened to *gran* before any noun: *un **gran** momento* 'a great moment', *una **gran** comida* 'a great meal'. The *-de* is occasionally retained in literary styles for purposes of emphasis or before words beginning with a vowel: *este grande héroe nacional* 'this great national hero'.

Grande is not shortened if *más* or *menos* precede: *el más grande pintor del mundo* 'the greatest painter in the world' (*el mayor pintor* is better).

(b) The following lose their final vowel when placed before a singular **masculine** noun or combination of adjective and masculine noun:

alguno	**algún** *remoto día*	some remote day
bueno	*un **buen** cocinero*	a good cook
malo	*un **mal** ingeniero*	a bad engineer
ninguno	*en **ningún** momento*	at no moment
postrero	*tu **postrer** día*	your last day (archaic)
primero	*mi **primer** gran amor*	my first great love
tercero	*el **tercer** candidato*	the third candidate

Notes
(i) The full form must be used if any conjunction or adverb separates the adjective from the noun or noun phrase: *esta **grande** pero costosa victoria* 'this great but costly victory', *un **bueno** aunque agrio vino* 'a good though sour wine'.
(ii) Popular speech, especially Latin-American, sometimes uses short forms of adjectives before feminine nouns as well. This usage is also occasionally seen in several good Spanish writers of the first half of the twentieth century, but it is nowadays avoided: *la primera mujer* 'the first woman', not **la primer mujer*, *buena parte de* 'a good part of', not **buen parte de*.
(iii) *Algún* and *ningún* are found in spontaneous speech before feminine nouns beginning with a stressed *a-* or *ha-*, but the full feminine forms should be used in writing. See 3.1.2, 9.4 and 23.5.5 for details.
(iv) For *cualquiera* see 9.8.
(v) *Santo* 'saint' is shortened to *San* before the names of all male saints except those beginning with *Do-* or *To-*: *san Juan, san Blas, santo Tomás, Santo Domingo*. It is not shortened when it means 'holy': *el santo Padre* 'the Holy Father', *todo el santo día* 'the whole day through', *el Santo Oficio* 'the Holy Office' (i.e. the Inquisition).
(vi) For the short forms of *tanto* and *cuánto* (*tan* and *cuán*) see 9.16 and 24.6.

4.7 Agreement of adjectives[4]

Some questions of number agreement of adjectives are also discussed under 2.3, particularly agreement with collectives nouns (2.3.1).

For the agreement of adjectives with titles like *Alteza* 'Highness', *Excelencia* 'Excellency' see 1.2.4.

---

[4] Some of the examples and arguments in this section are inspired by Judge and Healey (1983) 11.2.

4.7.1 Agreement of adjectives that follow the noun

(a) One or more masculine nouns require a masculine adjective: *un elefante asiático* 'an Asian elephant', *platos combinados* 'meals on a plate' (e.g. hamburger, vegetables, potatoes all served together, foreign-style), *cien mil pesos mexicanos*, '100,000 Mexican pesos', *Mi padre es inglés* 'My father is English'.

One or more feminine nouns require a feminine adjective: *la Grecia antigua* 'ancient Greece', *mil pesetas españolas* '1000 Spanish pesetas', *Mi madre es inglesa* 'My mother is English'.

Two or more nouns of different gender require a masculine plural adjective:

profesores y profesoras ingleses	English men and women teachers
puentes y casas decrépitos	derelict bridges and houses

(b) If several adjectives follow a plural noun and each adjective refers to only one individual item, the adjective will be singular: *los presidentes venezolano y peruano* 'the Peruvian president and the Venezuelan president'. *Los presidentes venezolanos y peruanos* means 'the presidents of Venezuela and the presidents of Peru'.

Notes

(i) Seco (1992), 112, notes the possibility of singular agreement with two or more nouns denoting a single complex idea: *talento y habilidad extremada* 'extreme talent and skill' or *talento y habilidad extremados*. In the former case the adjective agrees in gender with the last noun in the series, but plural agreement is much more usual in everyday language.

(ii) A plural adjective is occasionally given the gender of the last noun in the list even though it qualifies all the nouns: *los arbustos y las flores marchitas* 'withered bushes and flowers' – although the most obvious reading is 'bushes and withered flowers'. *Los arbustos y las flores marchitos* makes the adjective refer unambiguously to both nouns and is the normal construction.

Spanish is more tolerant than French of a masculine adjective following a feminine noun. French rejects constructions like **des hommes et des femmes gros* = *hombres y mujeres gordos* 'fat men and women'.

(iii) Adjectives may sometimes function as adverbs, in which case they are invariably masculine singular in form: *María habla muy claro* 'Maria speaks very clearly'. See 31.3.3 for further discussion.

4.7.2 Agreement with nouns joined by o or ni

(a) With the conjunction *o* agreement is optional. Plural agreement emphasizes the fact that the *o* is not exclusive (i.e. either one or the other or possibly both) and it indicates that the adjective refers to both nouns:

Buscaban una tienda o un restaurante abiertos (*abiertos* unambiguously refers to both)	They were looking for an open shop or (an open) restaurant
Buscaban la mujer o el hombre capaces de asumir el cargo (for the absence of personal *a* see 22.2)	They were looking for the woman or man capable of taking on the job

Singular agreement emphasizes exclusivity:

Puede *venir Mario o su hermano, pero no los dos*	Mario or his brother can come, but not both

(b) With *ni* 'nor' the plural is usual:

*Ni Mario ni Juan **eran** tontos*	Neither Mario nor Juan were stupid

4.7.3 Agreement with collective nouns
An adjective that modifies a collective noun is singular:

La organización de profesores se dio por *vencida*	The teachers' association gave up/admitted defeat

However, if words that refer to the people belonging to the collective noun intervene between the collective noun and the adjective or verb, the latter are usually in the plural. Compare *Sólo/Solo una minoría **es** culta* 'Only a minority are educated' and *Sólo/Solo una minoría de los empleados **son cultos*** 'Only a minority of the employees are educated'.

For further details on agreement with collective nouns, including *minoría, parte, resto, mitad* and similar words, see 2.3.1.

4.7.4 Agreement of pre-posed adjectives
When an adjective precedes two or more nouns and modifies them all, it usually agrees only with the first noun. This avoids the awkward combination of a plural adjective with a singular noun:

con exagerada cortesía y deferencia *Henrique Ureña . . . con **su habitual*** *sabiduría y tolerancia* (E. Sábato, Argentina, interview)	with exaggerated courtesy and deference Henrique Ureña, with his usual wisdom and tolerance
*. . . **esta creciente** generalización y* *abstracción de la ciencia* (ibid.)	this growing generalization and abstraction of science

The plural may, however, be used to avoid severe ambiguities: *sus amados hijo y nieto* 'his beloved son and grandson' (different people, both beloved).

Note
French does not allow this construction. Compare *. . . una profunda inspiración y reflexión* and *une inspiration et une réflexion profondes* 'deep inspiration and reflection'.[5]

4.7.5 'Neuter' agreement
An adjective that refers to no noun in particular is masculine singular in form:

Es absurdo hacerlo sin ayuda	It's absurd to do it without help
Fantástico . . . la cantidad de dinero que *gasta en tabaco*	Fantastic . . . the amount of money he spends on tobacco
La miseria no tiene nada de sano y *placentero* (M. Vargas Llosa, Peru)	Extreme poverty has nothing healthy or agreeable about it

Notes
(i) Neuter agreement is sometimes found even where a noun is present: *Tampoco es bueno demasiada natación* (L. Goytisolo, Spain, dialogue) 'Too much swimming isn't good either'. Here the adjective does not modify the noun *natación* but the idea *demasiada natación*. *Buena* would also be correct.
(ii) For adjectives with the article *lo* (*lo bueno, lo grande,* etc.), see 7.2.

---

[5] P. Gerboin and C. Leroy (1991), 33.

4.8 Formation of adjectives of place

4.8.1 Adjectives from countries and regions
These are formed unpredictably. The following are noteworthy (for the use of the definite article with the names of countries, see 3.2.17):

Alemania	*alemán*	
América	*americano*	(often 'Latin-American'. See note i)
Argelia	*argelino*	Algeria, Algerian
(la) Argentina	*argentino*	
Austria	*austriaco*	
Bélgica	*belga*	
Bolivia	*boliviano*	
(el) Brasil	*brasileño*	
(el) Canadá	*canadiense*	
Canarias	*canario*	
Castilla	*castellano*	Castile/Castilian. (See note ii)
Cataluña	*catalán*	
Chile	*chileno*	
(la) China	*chino*	
Colombia	*colombiano*	
Costa Rica	*costarriqueño, costarricense*	
Dinamarca	*danés*	Danish
Ecuador	*ecuatoriano*	
Egipto	*egipcio* (not *egipciano*)	
Escocia	*escocés*	Scottish
Estados Unidos	*estadounidense*	(rare in speech. See note (i))
Europa	*europeo*	
Francia	*francés*	
Gales	*galés*	Wales/Welsh
Galicia	*gallego*	
Gibraltar	*gibraltareño*	
Grecia	*griego*	
Guatemala	*guatemalteco*	
Holanda	*holandés*	
Honduras	*hondureño*	
Hungría	*húngaro*	
Inglaterra	*inglés*	(often used for 'British')
Irlanda	*irlandés*	
(el) Japón	*japonés*	
la India	*indio*	(see note iii for *hindú*)
Marruecos	*marroquí*	Moroccan
Méjico/México	*mejicano/mexicano*	(see note iv)
Nicaragua	*nicaragüense*	
Panamá	*panameño*	
(el) Paraguay	*paraguayo*	
(el) Perú	*peruano*	
Polonia	*polaco*	Polish
Portugal	*portugués*	
Puerto Rico	*puertorriqueño/ portorriqueño*	(the former is used on the island and is spreading)
El Salvador	*salvadoreño*	
Rusia	*ruso*	
Suecia	*sueco*	Swedish
Suiza	*suizo*	
(el) Uruguay	*uruguayo*	

Vascongadas	*vasco*
(País Vasco)	
Venezuela	*venezolano*

Notes

(i) The adjective from *América Latina* or *Latinoamérica* is *latinoamericano*. Spanish-speaking Latin-Americans dislike terms like *hispanoamericano* or 'Spanish-American' for the same reason that US citizens would not like to be called 'British Americans'. However, *Latinoamérica* includes countries where other Latin-based languages are spoken – e.g. Brazil, Haiti, Martinique, French Guyana – so 'Latin-American' is linguistically misleading.

In Latin America *norteamericano* is taken to mean our 'American' and is more common than *estadounidense*, which is rarely used in spoken Spanish. *Americano* is assumed to mean *latinoamericano*, although in Spain it means the same as our 'American'.

The adjective from *América del sur* or *Sudamérica* 'South America' – which does not include Central America, Mexico or the Caribbean – is **sud***americano*. The form *suramericano* is rejected by the style-book of *El País* and is generally considered incorrect in Spain, but it and similar forms, e.g. *Suráfrica*, *suroeste* 'South-West', *sureste* 'South-East' are common in Latin America. Standard Peninsular usage prefers *sud-* in all of these, though *sur-* is increasingly common.

For agreement with *Estados Unidos*, see 3.2.17.

(ii) *Castellano* is the Castilian language, i.e. the language described in this book, strictly speaking the dialect of Castile, which came to be the dominant literary language of Spain. *El castellano* now means the same as *el español*, 'the Spanish language'. However *el español* has political overtones for autonomists, and now that Spain has several official languages, Catalans, Basques and Galicians sometimes object to *el castellano* being called *el español*. The same objection is also heard from some Latin-Americans.

(iii) In Latin America the word *indio* is always assumed to mean 'Amerindian', so *hindú* is normally used there – but not in Spain – for Asian Indian, despite the fact that it properly means the Hindu religion: *los empleados* **hindús** *del raj británico*[6] (C. Fuentes, dialogue, Mexico), 'the Indian employees under the British Raj'.

In Spain, *indiano* used to denote a 'colonial' who had made a fortune in Latin America and returned home.

(iv) Mexicans always spell the words *México/mexicano*, even though they are pronounced *Méjico*, *mejicano*. The spelling with *x* honours the memory of the Mexica or Aztecs, as their neighbours called them. *El País* (Spain) always prints *México*, *mexicano*, but Manuel Seco objects on the grounds that it encourages Spanish news-readers to pronounce them [méksiko], [meksikáno].

A few other Mexican place names are similarly affected, e.g. Oaxaca, Xalapa (or Jalapa). See 39.1.3 for further remarks on the pronunciation of *x*.

(v) *Árabe* means 'Arab' or 'Arabic'.

4.8.2 Adjectives from towns

There is no general rule for deriving adjectives from the names of towns, and some places pride themselves on obscure forms, e.g. *Huelva – onubense*.

Some of the more common are:

Álava	*alavés*	
Alcalá	*complutense*	(used of the ancient university of Alcalá, now in Madrid)
Ávila	*abulense*	
Badajoz	*pacense*	

---

[6] *Hindús*, colloquial for *hindúes*. See 2.1.3c.

Barcelona	barcelonés	
Bilbao	bilbaíno	
Bogotá	bogotano	
Buenos Aires	porteño	
Burgos	burgalés	
Cádiz	gaditano	
Caracas	caraqueño	
Córdoba	cordobés	
La Coruña	coruñés	
Florencia	florentino	
Granada	granadino	
La Habana	habanero	
Lima	limeño	
Londres	londinense	(note spelling)
Lugo	lucense	
Madrid	madrileño	
Málaga	malagueño	
Moscú	moscovita	
Murcia	murciano	
Nápoles	napolitano	
Nueva York	neoyorquino	
Oviedo	ovetense	
Pamplona	pamplonés/pamplonica	
París	parisiense	(*El País* censures the use of *parisién* and *parisino*)
La Paz	paceño/pacense	
Quito	quiteño	
Río de Janeiro	carioca	(after a local Indian tribe)
Roma	romano	
Salamanca	salmantino/salamanqués	
San Sebastián	donostiarra	(a Basque word)
Santander	santanderino	
Santiago	santiaguino (Chile)	
	santiagués (Spain)	
Sevilla	sevillano	
Toledo	toledano	
Valencia	valenciano	
Valladolid	vallisoletano	
Zaragoza	zaragozano	

4.9 Intensive forms of the adjective

4.9.1 The suffix -*ísimo*: meaning and formation

The suffix -*ísimo* can be added to many adjectives. It intensifies the original meaning – *Ana es riquísima* 'Ana is extremely rich' (from *rico)* – and should be used sparingly. It cannot be added to all adjectives, and there are irregularities.

This suffix is sometimes misnamed a 'superlative' suffix, but it cannot be used in comparisons and is best thought of simply as an intensifier.

-*ísimo* is added after removing any final vowel: *grande/grandísimo, guapa/guapísima.*

(a) Adjectives ending -*co/-ca* and -*go/-ga* require spelling changes to keep the hard sound of the *c* or *g*: *rico/riquísimo* 'rich', *vago/vaguísimo* 'vague'/'lazy'.

(b) Adjectives ending in -z change the z to c: *feliz/felicísimo* 'happy', *feroz/ferocísimo* 'ferocious'.
(c) For adjectives ending in two vowels, see 4.9.2.
(d) Adjectives ending in *-ble* change this ending to *-bil*: *amable/amabilísimo* 'friendly', *posible/posibilísimo. Endeble/endeblísimo* 'feeble' is a rare exception.

4.9.2 Adjectives which do not take *-ísimo*
The following adjectives do not take the suffix *-ísimo*:
(a) Those ending in *-í, -uo, -io,* or *-eo* if not stressed on the *e*: e.g. *baladí* 'trivial', *arduo* 'arduous', *espontáneo* 'spontaneous', *rubio* 'blond', *tardío* 'late'.
   Exceptions: *agrio/agrísimo* 'sour', *amplio/amplísimo* 'wide'/'extensive', *frío/friísimo* 'cold', *limpio/limpísimo* 'clean', *ordinario/ordinarísimo* 'ordinary'/ 'vulgar', *pío/piísimo* 'pious', *sucio/sucísimo* 'dirty', *vacío/vaciísimo* 'empty'.
(b) Words stressed on the antepenultimate syllable (*esdrújulas*) ending in *-ico, -fero, -geno, -voro*: *político* 'political', *mamífero* 'mammal(ian)', *homogéneo* 'homogeneous', *carnívoro* 'carnivorous'.
(c) Augmentatives, diminutives and comparatives: *preguntón* 'inquisitive', *bonito* 'pretty', *grandote* 'enormous', *menor* 'smaller'/'younger'.

Note
Mayorcísimo 'very old' is often heard, e.g. *Es mayorcísimo* 'He's very old'.

(d) Compound adjectives, e.g. *patizambo* 'knock-kneed', *ojituerto* 'one-eyed'.
(e) Many adjectives of more than three syllables ending in *-ble*: *inexplicable, incontestable* 'unquestionable', *desmontable* 'collapsible'. There are exceptions, though some are uncommon: *agradable/agradabilísimo* 'agreeable', *apacible/apacibilísimo*, 'mild', *miserable/miserabilísimo* 'wretched', *venerable/venerabilísimo* 'venerable'.
(f) Those whose meaning cannot be further intensified: *fantástico, ideal, infinito, inmortal* 'immortal', *total*, etc.
   Exceptions: *mismo/mismísimo* 'very' (*la mismísima persona* 'the very same person'), *singular/singularísimo*.
(g) Time and number adjectives: *anual* 'annual', *diario* 'daily', *nocturno* 'nighttime', *semanal* 'weekly', *quinto* 'fifth', *último* 'last', *vigésimo* 'twentieth', etc.
   Exception: *primer/primerísimo* 'first'/'very first of all'.
(h) *Hirviendo* 'boiling' and *ardiendo* 'burning'.
(i) Technical and scientific adjectives and most adjectives ending in *-ista*, e.g. *decimal, termonuclear* 'thermo-nuclear', *transformacional* 'transformational', *comunista* 'Communist', *nacionalista* 'nationalist', etc.

4.9.3 Irregular intensive forms
(a) The following are best learnt as separate words:

antiquísimo	(from *antiguo*)	ancient
cursilísimo	(from *cursi*)	affected/pseudo-refined
ínfimo	(from *inferior*)	inferior/least/lowest (literary)
jovencísimo	(from *joven*)	young
máximo	(from *mayor*)	supreme/greatest
mínimo	(from *menor*)	slightest/least
óptimo	(from *mejor*)	superb (literary)
pésimo	(from *peor*)	bad/dreadful
supremo	(from *superior*)	superior/supreme

(b) The following forms are occasionally found in older texts and or in flowery written styles:

		Literary form	Current form
amigo	friendly/keen	*amicísimo*	*amiguísimo*
áspero	harsh	*aspérrimo*	*asperísimo*
benévolo	charitable/benevolent	*benevolentísimo*	not used
célebre	famous	*celebérrimo*	not used
cruel	cruel	*crudelísimo*	*cruelísimo*
difícil	difficult	*dificílimo*	*dificilísimo*
fácil	easy	*facílimo*	*facilísimo*
fiel	faithful	*fidelísimo*	*fidelísimo*
frío	cold	*frigidísimo*	*friísimo*
íntegro	whole/entire	*integérrimo*	*integrísimo*
libre	free	*libérrimo*	*librísimo* (familiar)
magnífice	magnificent	*magnificentísimo*	not used
mísero	wretched (archaic)	*misérrimo*	not used?
munífice	munificent	*munificentísimo*	not used
pobre	poor	*paupérrimo*	*pobrísimo*
sabio	wise	*sapientísimo*	not used
sagrado	sacred	*sacratísimo*	not used

(c) The old rule whereby the diphthongs *ue* and *ie* are simplified to *o* or *e* when -*ísimo* is added, is nowadays usually ignored although *novísimo* 'very recent' must be distinguished from *nuevísimo* 'very new':

bueno	*buenísimo*	(*bonísimo*)	good
cierto	*ciertísimo*	(*certísimo*)	certain
fuerte	*fuertísimo*	(*fortísimo*)	strong
reciente	*recientísimo*	(*recentísimo*)	recent
tierno	*tiernísimo*	(*ternísimo*)	tender

Some words never suffered modification: *viejo/viejísimo* 'old', *cuerdo/cuerdísimo* 'sane', etc.

4.10 Use of nouns as adjectives

Nouns may occasionally be used adjectivally, although this construction is not particularly common in written language:

*Tienes que ser más **persona decente***	You've got to be more of a decent person
*Este libro es menos **novela** que el otro*	This book is less of a novel than the other
*Es más **bailarina** que actriz*	She's more (of) a dancer than an actress
*Su reacción es puro **teatro***	His reaction is pure theatre

Such nouns do not agree in number or gender with the word they modify, and when they are modified by words like *más, menos, tan* they are not accompanied by a definite or indefinite article.

4.11 Position of adjectives in relation to nouns

4.11.1 General

For the position of *alguno, ninguno, cualquiera, mismo*, see 9.4.1a, 23.5.5, 9.8a and 9.11 respectively. For the position of ordinal numerals see 10.12.3.

It is hardly true to say that the adjective 'normally' follows the noun in Spanish. Adjective position is much more flexible than in English and a good deal more flexible than in French, but the underlying rules are difficult to formulate. Many factors of convention, sound and above all style and meaning combine to determine whether, for example, one says *un lejano ruido* or *un ruido lejano* 'a distant noise'. Moreover there seem to be as yet unresearched differences between Peninsular and American-Spanish, the latter apparently allowing some pre-posed constructions unacceptable in Spain. The basic rule seems to be:

(a) Restrictive adjectives follow the noun.

(b) Non-restrictive adjectives may precede or follow the noun. Some always precede the noun.

Restrictive adjectives narrow the scope of the noun that precedes them: *vino espumoso* 'sparkling wine' denotes a restricted type of wine; *Odio las novelas históricas* 'I hate historical novels' refers only to those novels which are historical.

Non-restrictive adjectives typically refer to the whole of the entity denoted by the noun: *las aburridas conferencias del decano* 'the dean's boring lectures', *la poco apetitosa cocina británica* 'unappetizing British cooking' are both generalizations that attribute a quality to every member or aspect of the class of things denoted by the noun.

Unfortunately, the distinction between restrictive and non-restrictive adjectives is not always clear, and the decision about where to put the adjective often relies on a feel for the language rare among non-natives.

As a useful, though not absolutely fool-proof guide to whether an adjective is restrictive, native speakers of English may apply the following test:

If an English adjective sounds correct when spoken with a heavy stress (or, more accurately, with falling intonation) – 'I don't like **sour** apples, but I do like **sweet** apples' – then it is almost certainly restrictive, and its Spanish equivalent will follow the noun: *No me gustan las manzanas **agrias**, pero sí me gustan las manzanas **dulces***.

If an English adjective sounds wrong when stressed, it is probably non-restrictive and its Spanish counterpart may well precede the noun. Thus if one stresses 'beautiful' in 'the beautiful sun of Spain', the phrase suggests that there is another Spanish sun that is not beautiful; the absurdity of this strongly suggests that the Spanish adjective precedes the noun: *el hermoso sol de España*.

4.11.2 Examples of restrictive (post-posed) adjectives

The following adjectives are restrictive and therefore always follow the noun:
(a) Those that create a new type or sub-set of the thing described by the noun:

el pan integral	wholemeal bread
el papel secante	blotting paper
los cazas computerizados	computerized fighter aircraft
la tracción delantera	front-wheel drive

All the other examples in this section are in fact instances of this type of adjective, which can be thought of as a transformed clause: *la poesía romántica*

= *aquella poesía que es romántica, las manzanas verdes* = *aquellas manzanas que están verdes.*

(b) Those used for purposes of contrast, whether explicit or implied:

Tráigame una espumadera limpia, no una sucia	Bring me a clean ladle, not a dirty one
Tengo un boli verde y otro azul	I have a green ball-point pen and a blue one
Adoro los ojos azules	I adore blue eyes

(c) Scientific or technical adjectives used to define or specify a noun (as is almost always the case):

la gramática transformativa	transformational grammar
la crítica estructuralista	structuralist criticism
el laboratorio lingüístico	language laboratory

Only the most far-fetched styles would use such adjectives poetically or as epithets, though some, e.g. *unilateral, microscópico, (p)sicoanalítico, materialista*, might conceivably be used as value judgements (see 4.11.4a).

(d) Attributive adjectives. These express the origin, substance, contents or purpose of a noun. Their use is discussed at 4.12.

la nave espacial	space ship
el túnel ferroviario	railway tunnel
la guerra nuclear	nuclear war
el material bélico (= *material de guerra*)	war matériel

(e) Adjectives of nationality, which are almost always restrictive:

el clima argentino	the Argentine climate
la paella valenciana	paella Valencia-style
los monumentos mayas	the Mayan monuments

Note
Adjectives of nationality may occasionally be used as epithets (because they express allegedly typical qualities. See 4.11.4 for a discussion of epithets): *Mi española impulsividad me hace escribir estas líneas* (reader's letter in *Cambio16*, Spain) 'My Spanish impulsiveness makes me write these lines', *su británica reserva* 'her/his British reserve'.

(f) With *tener* + *el/la/los/las* followed by a noun denoting a part of the body:

Tiene las manos largas	She has long hands
Tiene el pelo rizado	He's got curly hair

4.11.3 Pre-posed (non-restrictive) adjectives indicating impression, reaction, subjective evaluation

The most common reason for putting an adjective before the noun is to emphasize its emotional or subjective content, e.g. *una **tremenda** tragedia* 'a tremendous tragedy', *un **gran** poeta* 'a great poet', *el **inquietante** problema del efecto invernadero* 'the worrying problem of the greenhouse effect'. These adjectives are non-restrictive because the speaker wishes to eliminate from the utterance any reference to another tragedy, poet or problem; no comparison or contrast with other nouns is suggested.

Such adjectives may describe the speaker's impression, assessment or evaluation of a thing, or its appearance. They can include a vast range of adjectives indicating shape, distance, size, colour, texture, passage of time, praise, blame or subjective appraisal of any kind.

Since the use of such pre-posed adjectives conveys an emotional message, the decision whether to put such adjectives in front of a noun often depends on stylistic and other subjective factors. Literary, solemn or poetic styles, journalism and advertising particularly favour pre-posed adjectives:

las magníficas ruinas de Machu Picchu	the magnificent ruins at Macchu Picchu
un profesor de historia del arte, dueño de una amplísima cultura (S. Pitol, Mexico, dialogue)	a lecturer (US 'professor') in Art History, a highly-educated man
¡Sensacional oferta de verano!	Sensational Summer Offer!

Sometimes the difference between post-posed and pre-posed adjectives can be significant, as in *el poético lenguaje de Lorca* 'the poetic language of Lorca' (aesthetic judgement) and *el lenguaje poético de Lorca* 'the language of Lorca's poetry' (factual), or *las decimonónicas actitudes del ministro* 'the nineteenth-century attitudes of the minister' (value judgement) and *la novela decimonónica* 'the nineteenth-century novel' (factual).

But very often the difference is merely stylistic, a pre-posed adjective being more literary, poetic or dramatic, a post-posed one more matter-of-fact. The following examples will help to train the ear; in every case the adjective could have followed the noun or noun-phrase:

el casi olvidado nombre de James MacPherson (J.L. Borges, Argentina)	the almost forgotten name of James MacPherson
Además, en el mar hay barcos anclados en permanente contacto con los aviones nocturnos (G. García Márquez, Colombia, dialogue)	Moreover, there are boats anchored at sea in permanent contact with the night aircraft
la ciudad donde, en el anterior siglo, se habían casado Bécquer y Casta Esteban	the city where, in the previous century, Bécquer and Casta Esteban had married
La revolución significó para mí una justa redistribución de la riqueza (M. Vargas Llosa, Perú)	The revolution meant for me a just redistribution of wealth
una guirnalda de blancas flores (L. Goytisolo, Spain)	a wreath of white flowers
La pera es de fácil digestión (cookery book, Spain)	Pears are easily digested
el creciente costo de la tierra urbana	the rising cost of land within the cities

Notes
(i) Adjective position is arbitrarily fixed in many set phrases: *Alto Egipto* 'Upper Egypt', *el Sumo Pontífice* 'the Pope', *Baja California* 'Lower California' (cf. *América Central, los Estados Unidos, la China Popular*, 'People's China', etc.), *altos hornos* 'blast furnaces', *en alta mar* 'on the high seas', *Dios Todopoderoso* 'Almighty God', *sentido común* 'common sense', *gramática parda* 'smartness'/'cunning', etc.
(ii) If an adjective is qualified by an adverb it usually follows the noun in ordinary styles: *esta noticia altamente reveladora* 'this highly revealing news item', *una chica frígidamente agresiva*, 'a frigidly aggressive girl', *con tres amigos igualmente roñosos* 'with three equally mean friends'. Compare: *Anuncian una útil linterna* (not *linterna útil*) 'They are advertising a useful torch' and *Anuncian una linterna muy útil* 'They are advertising a **very** useful torch'.

With *más* and *menos* either position is possible: *el más popular presentador de la TV italiana* (*Cambio16*, Spain) 'the most popular presenter on Italian TV', or *el presentador más popular de la TV*.

Constructions like *la altamente reveladora noticia* 'the highly revealing news item', *la siempre inquieta juventud* 'ever-restless youth', *las ya de por sí interesantes confesiones del autor* 'the in themselves interesting confessions of the author', are however, found in literary style and can be explained in terms of contrast between restrictive and non-restrictive adjectives.

(iii) Nouns with two or more adjectives: the restrictive adjective follows, the non-restrictive (i.e. least important) normally precedes: *los blancos ejércitos angélicos* 'the white armies of the angels, *una elegante camisa blanca* 'an elegant white shirt', *una siniestra cruz gamada* 'a sinister swastika', *una enorme cúpula blanca* 'an enormous white dome'.

4.11.4 Other uses of pre-posed non-restrictive adjectives

The following types of non-restrictive adjectives are also pre-posed:

(a) Epithets, i.e. adjectives used to describe qualities typically associated with the noun. These are infrequent in everyday or scientific or technical language, except in set phrases. They are very common in literary, poetic or other types of emotive or affective language:

mi distinguido colega	my distinguished colleague
el peligroso tigre asiático	the dangerous Asian tiger
un valiente torero	a brave bull-fighter
los volubles dioses romanos	the fickle Roman gods

Epithets describe predictable or typical qualities: one can say *un enorme elefante* 'an enormous elephant' but only *un elefante cojo* 'a lame elephant' since lameness is not typical of elephants, *mi leal amigo* 'my loyal friend' but only *mi amigo vegetariano* 'my vegetarian friend', *un difícil problema* or *un problema difícil* 'a difficult problem', but only *un problema (p)sicológico*, since problems are not typically psychological.

(b) Adjectives that unambiguously refer to every one of the items denoted by a plural noun: *Tuvo que parar en boxes para cambiar sus deterioradas ruedas* (*El País*) 'He had to stop in the pits to change his worn tyres' (*ruedas deterioradas* might imply that only some of his tyres were worn):

muchas gracias por las magníficas rosas	many thanks for the magnificent roses
(*rosas magníficas* allows the possibility that some of the roses were not magnificent)	
las simpáticas peticiones de nuestros oyentes	our listeners' kind requests

For this reason, adjectives applied to unique entities are likely to be pre-posed, unless they apply only to an aspect or part of the thing:

Desde nuestro campamento se veía el imponente Everest	one could see imposing mount Everest from our camp
El izquierdista Frente Farabundo Martí	the left-wing Farabundo Martí Front

but

Existe un Unamuno político y comprometido, y otro contemplativo	There is a political, committed Unamuno, and another contemplative one
También visitamos la ciudad moderna	We also visited the modern (part of the) city

(c) Intensifiers, hyperboles and swearwords – which are extreme examples of adjectives used emotively and often stripped of all real meaning. If they are post-posed, they often recover their literal meaning:

mi negra suerte	my rotten luck
¡esta maldita máquina de escribir!	this damned typewriter!
Valiente soldado eres tú	A great soldier you are (I don't think . . .)
tu dichosa familia	your blessed family
estas condenadas hormigas	these damned ants

4.11.5 Position of adjectives with compound nouns

Choice of position here depends on whether the noun phrase is felt to be a compound word (i.e. a new idea) or merely a loose conjunction of words. Thus *las flores de España* 'the flowers of Spain' is not a compound, so one says *las flores silvestres de España* 'the wild flowers of Spain' not **las flores de España silvestres*. But *una casa de muñecas* 'a dolls' house' is a compound and is therefore inseparable: *una casa de muñecas barata* 'a cheap dolls' house', not **una casa barata de muñecas*. Only long familiarity with the language will provide a certain guide to what is or is not a compound noun.

Some noun phrases are uncertain: one can say *una bicicleta amarilla de hombre* or *una bicicleta de hombre amarilla* 'a yellow man's bicycle' (the Spanish is unambiguous!). Further examples:

un cochecito de niño verde	a green pram/baby carriage
un médico de cabecera simpático	a nice family doctor

4.11.6 Position of *bueno, malo, grande, pequeño*

The general rule applies: when they are clearly restrictive, they follow the noun. When used restrictively, they usually indicate objective qualities. When they precede the noun they usually express a subjective evaluation (which is usually the case, but see note (iv) for the special case of *pequeño*).

(a) Objective qualities:

Tengo un abrigo bueno para los fines de semana, y uno regular para los laborables	I've got a good coat for weekends, and a so-so one for weekdays
Deme un melón bueno (objective, i.e. one that's not bad)	Give me a good melon
Oscar Wilde dijo que no hay libros buenos o malos sino libros bien o mal escritos (J.L. Borges, Argentina, contrast)	Oscar Wilde said there are no good or bad books, only well or badly written books
Trae la llave grande	Bring the big key/spanner
Era un hombre grande	He was a big man
mi hermana mayor/menor	my elder/younger sister

(b) Subjective qualities:

un buen carpintero	a good carpenter
un buen vino tinto	a good red wine
un gran éxito	a great success
un gran ruido/poeta/embustero	a great noise/poet/liar
los grandes narcotraficantes	the major drug dealers
un pequeño problema (see note iv)	a slight problem
No hubo mayores problemas	There were no major problems
el mayor poeta mexicano	the greatest Mexican poet
ni la menor impresión de insinceridad	not even the slightest impression of insincerity

Notes
(i) With *hombre* and *mujer*, *bueno* tends to mean 'good' after the noun and 'harmless' before: *un buen hombre* means 'a harmless/simple man'. *Malo* is weaker before the noun. *Mala mujer* may be a euphemism for prostitute.

(ii) There are many set expressions: *Lo hizo de buena gana* 'He did it willingly', *oro de buena ley* 'pure gold', *En buen lío te has metido* 'You're in a fine mess', *A mí siempre me pone buena cara* 'He always makes an effort to be nice to me', *¡Qué mala pata!* 'What bad luck!', etc.
(iii) *Grande* is pre-posed when it means 'great', but it may mean 'big' in either position.
(iv) *Un pequeño problema* is normal since 'problem' is an abstract noun. However, *?una pequeña casa* is not usual for 'a little house', which is *una casita*. For discussion of this phenomenon see 38.2.

4.11.7 Position of *nuevo* and *viejo*
The usual explanation is that these are pre-posed when they mean 'another' and 'previous'/'long-standing' respectively, but in practice it is doubtful whether the distinction is always clear-cut: *Tenemos un nuevo presidente/un presidente nuevo* 'We've got a new president', *nuevos progresos técnicos* 'new (i.e. more) technological developments', *un viejo amigo* 'an old friend' (i.e. long-standing, not necessarily old in years).

Nuevo is usually post-posed when it means 'brand-new', as is *viejo* when it means 'not new': *un coche nuevo* 'a brand-new car', *un coche viejo* 'an old car'. *Viejo* may be pre-posed when it means 'not young': *un viejo americano* 'an old American'. This distinction is overridden for purposes of contrast: *Prefiero el coche nuevo al viejo* 'I prefer our new (i.e. 'latest') car to the old (i.e. 'previous') one'.

4.11.8 Adjectives whose meaning varies according to position
The following are some common examples of changes of meaning determined by adjective position, but in many cases the distinction is not rigid and a good dictionary should be consulted for further information:

	After noun	Before noun
alto	tall	high/top (*un alto funcionario* top civil servant/government official)
antiguo	ancient	former or ancient
cierto	certain	certain (= sure)
(en ciertos trenes	on certain trains)	
medio	average	half
pobre	poor (= not rich)	miserable/wretched
puro	pure/clean	sheer
raro	strange/rare	rare
rico	rich	delicious
simple	simple-minded	simple (= mere)
triste	sad	wretched
valiente	courageous	great (ironic)
varios	assorted/various	several

For *mismo* see 9.11, *propio* 9.14, *solo/sólo* 9.15.

4.11.9 Adjectives that occur only in front of the noun
The following phrases contain adjectives that normally occur only in front of a noun:

Lo haré en **ambos** casos	I'll do it in both cases
las **llamadas** democracias	the so-called 'democracies'
la **mera** mención del asunto	the mere mention of the topic
Llevaba **mucho** dinero	He was carrying a lot of money
Busquemos **otro** médico	Let's look for another doctor

*Me dejó en **pleno** centro*	He left me right in the town centre
*el **presunto** culpable*	the allegedly guilty person
***poca** paciencia*	little patience
*el **pretendido** autor*	the alleged/supposed author
*un **sedicente** budista*	a self-styled Buddhist
*Trajeron **sendos** paquetes* (literary)	They brought a parcel each
*ante **tamaña** tontería*	in the face of such a great act of stupidity
*No puedo comer **tanta** cantidad*	I can't eat such a quantity

4.12 Attributive adjectives

Spanish readily forms attributive adjectives from nouns, cf. *mañana-**matinal*** (*la televisión matinal* 'breakfast TV'), *impuesto-**impositivo*** (*política impositiva* 'taxation policy'). These adjectives usually replace *de* plus a noun in compound nouns of the type *la vida de familia = la vida familiar* 'family life'.

Many new attributive adjectives have been coined in recent decades, perhaps because the result has a pleasing brevity or a satisfying technical ring. Many of them are rejected as jargon or journalese by careful speakers, and many have not found their way into dictionaries or speech.

There is no fixed rule for forming such adjectives from nouns, and Latin-American coinages may differ from Peninsular inventions. In a few cases, e.g. *viento > **eólico*** 'wind' (*la energía eólica* 'wind energy'), the adjective is derived from a completely different root. The following are taken from various printed sources, mostly journalistic:

de + noun	Attributive adjective	
problemas de presupuesto	*problemas prepuestarios* (Lat. Am. *presupuestales*)	budget problems
estancia en la cárcel	*estancia carcelaria*	prison term
carestía de petróleo	*carestía petrolera*	high oil prices
programa de televisión	*programa televisivo*	television programme
medios de masas	*medios masivos*	mass media
política de energía	*política energética*	energy policy
programa de informaciones	*programa informativo*	information programme
proceso de autonomía	*proceso autonómico*	process of development towards autonomy
industria de automóviles	*industria automovilística*	car industry
crisis de la banca	*crisis bancaria*	bank crisis
esfuerzo de defensa	*esfuerzo defensivo*	defence/(US) defense effort
defectos del oído	*defectos auditivos*	hearing defects
industria de hoteles	*industria hotelera*	hotel industry
sindicato de pilotos	*sindicato piloteril*	pilots' union
etc.		

Note

In both languages an adjective may be descriptive or attributive according to context: compare 'theatrical equipment' (attributive) and 'theatrical behaviour' (descriptive). Such pairs seem to be more common in Spanish and this may confuse English-speakers, who tend to misinterpret a phrase like *calidad constructiva* as meaning 'constructive quality' when it in fact means 'quality of construction'. Further examples: *lenguaje shakespeariano* 'Shakespearean language'/'the language of Shakespeare', *una cantidad masiva* 'a massive quantity', *los medios masivos* 'the mass media', *literatura fantástica* 'fantastic literature'/'literature of fantasy', *política defensiva* 'defence (US 'defense') policy', *actitud defensiva* 'defensive attitude', *poesía amorosa* 'love poetry', *una sonrisa amorosa* 'a loving smile'.

4.13 Translating the English prefix 'un-'

The Spanish prefix *in-* is much less common than the English 'un-' and English speakers should resist the temptation to invent imaginary words like **ineconómico* from 'uneconomical' *(poco económico)*. The two languages often coincide:

inimaginable	unimaginable	*intocable*	untouchable
insobornable	unbribable	*irreal*	unreal
		etc.	

but often a solution with *poco*, *no* or *sin* must be found:

poco profesional	unprofessional	*no usado*	unused
poco caritativo	uncharitable	*no autorizado/*	unauthorized
poco atractivo	unattractive	*sin autorizar*	
poco apetitoso	unappetizing	*sin principios*	unprincipled
poco amistoso	unfriendly	*sin probar*	untried
poco favorable	unfavourable	*sin comprender*	uncomprehending
poco práctico	impractical	*sin convencer*	unconvinced
	(not **impráctico)*	etc.	
poco inteligente	unintelligent		

The above list shows that *poco*, like the French *peu*, negates an adjective: *poco deseable* means 'undesirable', not 'a little desirable'. A preceding indefinite article restores the meaning 'little': *un poco cansado* 'a little tired'/'rather tired'.

5

Comparison of adjectives and adverbs

Comparison in Spanish is not particularly complex, but English-speaking students are often hindered by interference from French, which encourages misuse of the article in the superlative and failure to use *tanto como* 'as . . . as' in comparisons of equality (cf. French *aussi . . . que*). Foreigners also tend to overlook the difference between *más de* and *más que* and often fail to use *del que* or *de lo que* before clauses, verb phrases or neuter adjectives.

5.1 Regular comparison

With the exception of the six adjectives and adverbs listed at 5.2, all adjectives and adverbs form the comparative with *más . . . que* 'more . . . than' or *menos . . . que* 'less . . . than':

Los limones son más agrios que las cerezas	Lemons are more bitter than cherries
Tú andas más despacio que yo	You walk slower/more slowly than me
Tiene un traje menos/más formal	He's got a less/more formal suit

Notes

(i) For the difference between *más/menos que* and *más/menos de* see 5.5.

(ii) Before clauses, verb phrases and 'neuter' adjectives and participles, *más/menos de lo que* or the appropriate gender and number of *más/menos del que* are required. See 5.6 for discussion.

(iii) The comparative of adverbs and, in some circumstances, of adjectives, is not distinguishable by form from the superlative. See 5.3.2 for discussion.

(iv) *Más* and *menos* need not be repeated: *Él es más inteligente y emprendedor que su hermano* 'He's more intelligent and enterprising than his brother', *Es menos cómodo y limpio* 'It's less comfortable and clean'.

5.2 Irregular comparative forms

There are six adjectives and adverbs that have irregular comparative forms which are not marked for gender:

bueno/bien	good/well	*mejor*	better
malo/mal	bad/badly	*peor*	worse
pequeño	small	*menor* (or *más pequeño*)	smaller
grande	big	*mayor* (or *más grande*)	bigger/greater
poco	little	*menos*	less
mucho	much	*más*	more

When they are used as adjectives, the plural of these words is regularly formed by adding *-es*: *mejores, mayores,* etc. When they are used as adverbs they are invariable, as are *menos* and *más*. Examples:

Estas manzanas son mejores que las de la semana pasada	These apples are better than last week's
El mundo es peor que yo (E. Mendoza, Spain)	The world is worse than me/than I
Sus hermanas hablan mejor que ella (adverb)	Her sisters speak better than she does
Aquí estamos mejor (adverb)	It's better for us here/We're better off here

Notes

(i) The uses of *mayor* and *menor* are discussed at 5.8 and 5.9.

(ii) *Más bueno, más malo* are used of moral qualities though *mejor/peor* are more usual: *Pedro es mejor/más bueno que Ricardo* 'Pedro is better (i.e. a better person) than Ricardo', *A mí no me gusta pegar a los niños . . . pero es que éste es el más malo de todos* (E. Arenas, Spain, dialogue) 'I don't like hitting children, but this one's the worst of all', *Es más bueno que el pan* (set phrase) 'He has a heart of gold' (lit. 'He is more good than bread').

(iii) Use of *más* or *menos*, e.g. **más mejor*, with these comparative forms is substandard and comparable to English forms like **'more better', *'less worse'*.

5.3 Superlative of adjectives

See 5.4 for the superlative of adverbs. See 16.14.4 for the use of the subjunctive after superlative expressions.

5.3.1 Superlative formed with *el más/menos*

In statements of the type 'the nearest station', 'the smallest tree', the superlative of adjectives is formed with *el/la/los/las más* 'the most' or *el/la/los/las menos* 'the least'. In certain cases, listed at 5.3.2, the definite article is not used.

el más complicado problema/el problema más complicado	the most complicated problem
Chesterton, el escritor más popular de su tiempo, es una de las figuras más simpáticas de la literatura (J.L. Borges, Argentina)	Chesterton, the most popular writer of his time, is one of the most likable figures in literature
lo mejor/peor que te puede suceder . . .	the best/worst thing that can happen to you . . .

Notes

(i) Students of French must avoid repeating the article: *l'exemple le plus intéressant* = *el ejemplo más interesante* or *el más interesante ejemplo*. **El ejemplo el más interesante* is not Spanish.

(ii) Translation of sentences like 'the best restaurant in Argentina' usually require *de* not *en*: i.e. *el mejor restaurante de (la) Argentina*. See 34.7.1 for discussion.

5.3.2 Superlative of adjectives formed without the definite article

The definite article is not used in superlative constructions in the following cases:

(a) When the subject refers to a course of action rather than to a thing or person:

Sería más fácil dejar su carta sin contestar	It would be easiest (or 'easier') to leave his letter unanswered

This can be differentiated from the comparative by using *lo*: *Lo más fácil sería dejar su carta sin contestar.*

(b) When a possessive adjective precedes *más* or *menos*:

mi más leal amigo/mi amigo más leal	my most loyal friend

. . . *pero mi capa más profunda se entristeció* (E. Sábato, Argentina)	but the deepest layer in me (lit. 'my deepest layer') was saddened

Compare the French *mon ami le plus loyal*.

(c) After *estar, resultar, parecer, ponerse* (and other verbs of becoming) and *quedar(se)*:

Ella es la que está más alterada	She's the one who's most upset
Este caballo está más cansado	This horse is the most tired
Aurora parece menos española	Aurora looks least/less Spanish
María se pone más nerviosa cuando mencionan esas cosas	Maria gets most nervous when they mention those things
Queda mejor así	It's best/better like that

Such sentences could also be understood as comparatives. The issue could be clarified by recasting the sentence using *ser*: *Ella es **la** más alterada, Este caballo es **el** más cansado, Aurora es **la que** parece menos española, Este/Éste es **el que** queda mejor.*

(d) In relative clauses and after nominalizers, i.e. after *el/la/los/las que, quien, aquel que*, etc. meaning 'the one(s) who/which':

el curso que es menos interesante es . . .	the course that's least interesting is . . .
la que es más abordable	the girl/woman who's most approachable
El patrón fue uno de los que más peces capturó durante los 40 minutos que se dedicaron a la pesca (*Granma*, Cuba)	The skipper was one of those who caught most fish during the forty minutes dedicated to fishing

(e) When the superlative does not involve comparison with another noun (this includes cases in which something is compared with itself):

El idealismo siempre es más fácil cuando uno es joven	Idealism is always easiest (or 'easier') when one's young
Es en su poemas largos donde es menos convincente	It is in his long poems that he is least (or 'less') convincing
Los domingos es cuando la lluvia es más deprimente	It's on Sundays that the rain is most depressing
Aquí es donde el Rin es más romántico (the Rhine compared with itself)	The Rhine is at its most romantic here

Compare the following where true comparison with another noun is involved:

*El amor sin celos es **el** más noble* (compared with other loves)	Love without jealousy is the noblest
*Las pizzas con anchoas son **las** mejores*	Pizzas with anchovies are (the) best

5.4 Superlative of adverbs

The definite article cannot be used to form the superlative of an adverb, with the result that the superlative is not always clearly distinguishable from the comparative. Students of French must remember not to use the article: compare *C'est Richard qui danse le mieux* and *Ricardo es el que mejor baila*.

Examples:

De las tres niñas la que canta mejor es Ana	Of the three girls, the one who sings best is Ana

Él trabaja menos/más rápido	He works least/fastest (or 'less'/'faster')
Cuando más llueve es en verano	It's in summer that it rains most (or 'more')
Pero el caso de U . . . es el que más conmoción ha causado en los medios periodísticos (*El País; mayor* possible)	But the case of U. . . is the one which has caused most stir in journalistic circles

In the unlikely event of real ambiguity, one of the following constructions can be used for the superlative:

Él habla mejor que todos	He speaks better than everyone
Él habla mejor que ninguno	He speaks better than any of them
Él es quien habla mejor de todos	He is the one who speaks best of all of them

Note
The difference between *el que más me gusta* and *el que me gusta más* 'the one I like more/most' is one of emphasis, the former being stronger and therefore more likely to carry a superlative meaning.

5.5 *Más/menos que* or *más/menos de*?

The difference is crucial: *más de* is used before numbers or quantities:

Mi abuelo tiene más de cien años	My grandfather is more than 100 years old
Son más de las tres y media	It's past 3.30
Estaba seguro de que no aguantarías quieta durante más de 6 meses (A. Mastretta, Mexico, dialogue)	I was sure you wouldn't stay still for more than six months

Compare the following examples in which the expression following *más* or *menos* is not a quantity:

Este restaurante es más caro que antes	This restaurant is dearer than before
Cansa más el viaje que el empleo	The travelling is more tiring than the job

Notes
(i) Care must be taken not to confuse this construction with *no . . . más que . . .* meaning 'only': *No he traído más que mil* (= *Sólo/solo he traído mil*) 'I've **only** brought 1,000', *No he traído más de mil* 'I haven't brought **more than** 1,000', *No hay más que cuatro gatos* 'There isn't a soul around'/'The place is completely dead' (lit. 'There are only four cats here'), *No hay más gasolina que la que necesitamos* 'There's only enough petrol/(US) 'gas' as we'll need', *No he traído más que lo que usted ha pedido* 'I've only brought what you asked for'.
(ii) In the following examples *que* must be used, even though a number follows: *Tiene más fuerzas que tres hombres juntos* 'He's stronger than three men together', *Habla más que siete* 'He/She never stops talking' (lit. 'He talks more than seven people').
The reason is that there is no comparison with an actual number. Spanish thus removes an ambiguity that affects English: *Comiste más que tres* 'You ate more than three people **(eat)**', *Comiste (a) más de tres* 'You ate more than three people' (cannibalism).

5.6 Comparison of quantity with clauses, verb phrases and neuter adjectives/participles

In the preceding section it was noted that 'more/less than' must be translated *más/menos de* before numerals or other quantities.

However, if the quantity is represented by a clause, verb phrase or adjective/participle, as in the English sentences 'He is more intelligent **than you think**', 'It's less difficult **than expected**', a problem arises since *más/menos de* can only appear before nouns or noun phrases: **Es más inteligente de crees* is clearly not Spanish.

In such cases the appropriate form of *del que* must be used to convert the verb phrase into a noun phrase: *Es más inteligente de lo que crees*.

(a) If a comparison of quantity is made with a clause containing a noun or pronoun, *del que* must be used and must agree in number and gender:

*Has traído menos aceite **del que** necesitábamos*	You've brought less oil than we needed
*Han venido más **de las que** se matricularon para el curso*	More girls/women have come than registered for the course
*Tiene más años **de los que** dice*	He's older than he says

(b) If the comparison is made with a verb phrase, a participle or an adjective, *de lo que* must be used:

*El viento me vuelve mucho más loca **de lo que** mi marido y ex maridos dicen que estoy* (Carmen Rico-Godoy, Spain)	The wind drives me much crazier than my husbands and ex-husbands say I am
*Lo hicieron menos bien **de lo que** esperábamos*	They did it less well than we hoped
*No se haga el estúpido más **de lo que** es* (M. Vargas Llosa, Peru, dialogue; Spain *no se haga más estúpido de lo que es*)	Don't try to be more stupid than you are
*más impresionante **de lo** esperado* (= *de lo que se esperaba*)	more impressive than was hoped
*. . . o si la noche era cálida y menos húmeda **de lo** habitual* (E. Mendoza, Spain)	. . . or if the night was warm and less humid than usual

Notes

(i) This construction often seems awkward to English speakers, but it is necessary in Spanish because *más/menos de* can only precede nouns and because *más que* before a verb or adjective usually means 'rather than': *Gasta más que gana* 'He spends more (i.e. 'rather') than he earns'.

(ii) Constructions on the lines of **Eres más inteligente que pareces* have been attested in good writers in the past, and a few informants thought they might occur in spontaneous speech. Most informants condemned them as badly formed.

(iii) Use of *del que/de lo que* is apparently not always obligatory in Latin America: *Había hecho más **que lo** posible para que Ángela Vicario se muriera en vida* (G. García Márquez, Colombia; Spain *más **de lo** posible*), 'She had done more than was possible so that Angela Vicario would have no life at all' (lit. 'die while alive').

(iv) Comparison between two non-neuter adjectives requires *que*: *más azul que verde* 'more blue than red', *más muertos que vivos* 'more dead than alive'.

(v) French is free of the problems raised by *del/de lo que*, but unlike Spanish it uses a redundant negative in comparisons with a clause: *Il en sait plus qu'il n'avoue* = *Él sabe más **de lo que** admite* 'He knows more than he admits'.

(vi) 'Than ever . . .' is translated *que nunca* (not **que jamás*): *¡Estás más joven que nunca!* 'You're younger than ever!'. This use of *nunca* and of other negative words used with a positive meaning, is discussed at 23.4.

5.7 Más as a colloquial intensifier

Más is often used as an intensifier in familiar speech, without any comparative meaning:

Es que eres más tonto . . .	Heavens you're stupid . . .
Está más borracho . . .	Is he *drunk*!

5.8 Uses of mayor

Más is used before plural nouns, e.g. *Tengo más amigos que tú* 'I've got more friends than you', and before quantities: *Tiene más dinero que yo* 'He's got more money than me'.

Mayor, which means both 'greater' and 'bigger', is used as follows:
(a) In the same way as *más grande* 'bigger' in comparisons involving physical objects, although it is not normally used of small things like pins, insects, etc:

Esta aula es más grande/mayor que la otra	This lecture room is bigger than the other
Mallorca es la más grande/la mayor de las Baleares	Majorca is the biggest of the Balearic Islands

One can never say **lo mayor*: *Lo más grande lo ponemos abajo* 'Let's put the biggest things underneath'.
(b) To translate 'older' or 'oldest' when applied to people:

Mi hermano es mayor que el tuyo	My brother is older than yours
mi hermano mayor	my elder brother
Tienes dieciséis años pero pareces mayor	You're sixteen but you look older
. . . es ya mayor que su hermana mayor . . .	. . . she's already older than her elder
en realidad mayor de lo que fue nunca Teresa	sister . . . actually older than Teresa ever
(J. Marías, *Spain*, dialogue)	was

Mayor is also a euphemism for *viejo*: *una señora mayor* 'an elderly lady'.
(c) *Mayor* is used to mean 'greater' or 'greatest': *su mayor éxito* 'his greatest success', *el mayor criminal del mundo* 'the greatest criminal in the world', *el mayor peligro* 'the greatest danger', *su mayor preocupación/alegría* 'his/her greatest worry/joy'.
(d) Before nouns denoting size, intensity, frequency, power or quantity, *mayor* or *más* can be used, with *mayor* considered more elegant: *mayor/más anchura* 'greater width', *mayor/más intensidad* 'greater intensity', *mayor/más fuerza* 'greater strength', *mayor/más potencia* 'more power', *mayor/más frecuencia* 'greater frequency', *mayor/más peso* 'more weight'. Further examples:

Más acentuado será el sabor del ajo, cuanta mayor cantidad lleve	The greater the quantity it contains, the more pronounced the garlic flavour will be
El rojo produce mayor efecto de sensualidad	The red produces a greater effect of sensuality
Deseo recibir mayor información	I would like to receive more information
Tiene mayor contenido vitamínico	It has a greater vitamin content

In all these examples *más* is possible, though less elegant.
(e) Before *número* or words and phrases indicating number, *mayor* is obligatory: *en mayor número de casos* 'in a greater number of cases', *mayor índice de mortalidad infantil* 'a higher rate of infantile mortality', *mayor incidencia de accidentes de tráfico* 'a higher rate of traffic accidents'.
(f) Set phrases: *mayor de edad* 'of age', *hacerse mayor* 'to get old', *ganado mayor* 'cattle' (horses, cows, mules only), *calle mayor* 'high street', etc.

(g) *Más grande* can be used as a superlative: *el más grande/mayor pensador moderno* 'the greatest modern thinker', but not in pejorative statements: *el mayor granuja del país* 'the biggest rogue in the country'.

5.9 Uses of *menor*

Menos is used before plural nouns – *Tengo menos amigos que tú* 'I've got less friends than you' – and before quantities: *Tiene menos dinero que yo* 'He's got less money than me'.

Menor differs from *mayor* in that it cannot refer to dimensions: *Esta habitación es más pequeña que ésa/esa* not **menor que ésa/esa, Ella es más pequeña de tamaño/más baja* 'She's smaller in size'. It can be used for dimensions only where English would allow 'less': *El área es menor de lo que parece* 'The area is less/smaller than it looks'.

Note also *mi hermano menor/pequeño* 'my younger brother', but *Mi hermano es más joven/pequeño que yo* 'My brother is younger than me'. Also *el más pequeño de la familia*.

*Lo menor is also impossible: *lo más pequeño* 'what's smallest'/'the smallest things'.

Menor is used in the same contexts as *mayor* in (b), (c), (d) and (e) in the previous section.

Examples:

Diego es tres años menor que Martita y cuatro que Sergio (C. Rico-Godoy, Spain)	Diego is three years younger than Martita and four younger than Sergio
Virginia era unos meses menor que yo (A. Mastretta, Mexico, dialogue)	Virginia was a few months younger than me
Usted no tendrá la menor dificultad (or *mínima* or *más pequeña*)	You won't have the slightest difficulty
El riesgo de un enfrentamiento es cada vez menor	The risk of a confrontation is declining

Common set phrases: *menor de edad* 'under age', *apto para menores* 'suitable for minors/young people'.

5.10 *Mucho más, mucho menos, poco más, etc.*

Before *más, menos, mayor* and *menor* when these qualify a noun, *mucho* and *poco* are used as adjectives and must agree in number and gender with the noun that follows – a fact that English-speakers are prone to forget:

Tienen muchos más hijos que tú	They have many more children than you
El proyecto era de mucha más envergadura que el anterior	The plan was much wider in scope than the previous one
Cincuenta personas eran muchas menos que en ocasiones anteriores	Fifty people was much less than on previous occasions
mucha menor cantidad	a much smaller quantity

Elsewhere, before adjectives and adverbs, *mucho* and *poco* are used as adverbs and are invariable in form:

La diferencia era mucho mayor/menor	The difference was much greater/less
Los alijos de hashish eran mucho más grandes de lo que se esperaba (*El País*)	The hauls of hashish were much greater than expected

Los problemas son mucho menos complejos de lo que se temía	The problems are much less complex than feared

5.11 'The more . . . the more . . .'/'the less . . . the less . . .'

Cuanto más . . . más . . . , cuanto menos . . . menos . . . are the standard formulas:

Cuanto más pensaba más me afligía . . . (J. Cortázar, Argentina, dialogue)	The more I thought, the more upset I got
Cuanto menos lo pienses de antemano, menos te va a doler	The less you think about it beforehand, the less it'll hurt
Cuanto mayor sea la distancia de una galaxia a la Tierra, más deprisa se aleja (ABC, Spain)	The greater the distance between a galaxy and the Earth, the faster it recedes
Cuantos más, mejor	the more the better

Colloquial speech may replace *cuanto* by *mientras* in this construction; this sounds popular or substandard in Spain but it is considered normal by educated Latin-Americans. Use of *contra* or *entre* for *cuanto* in this construction is typical of everyday speech in many parts of Latin America, but it is usually avoided in formal writing:

. . . mientras más pienses en ella, más tuya la harás (C. Fuentes, Mexico, dialogue)	The more you think of her, the more you will make her yours
. . . la cabeza gacha, entre menos me vea, mejor . . . (E. Poniatowska, Mexico, dialogue)	. . . with my head bowed, the less he sees of me the better . . .

See 24.6 note (i) for the use of the accent with *cuanto*.

Note
'All the more . . .', 'not so much . . . but that . . .' may be translated by *tanto . . . cuanto*: *No es tanto que entre dos personas . . . no haya secretos porque así lo deciden . . . cuanto que no es posible dejar de contar . . .* (J. Marías, Spain) 'It's not so much that there are no secrets between two people because they decide it should be this way, but that it's not possible to avoid telling . . .'.

5.12 'More and more . . .', 'less and less . . .'

Cada vez más/menos are the standard translations:

Está cada vez más delgado	He's getting thinner and thinner
Hace cada vez menos calor	The weather's getting less and less hot

5.13 Superlative time expressions

A neuter construction may be required:

Cenamos lo más tarde a las ocho	We have dinner/supper at eight o'clock at the latest
Lo antes/más temprano que puedo salir de casa es a la una	The earliest I can leave the house is at one

5.14 Miscellaneous translations of English comparatives and superlatives

Todos le interesaban, el párroco no el que menos	All the men interested her, not least the parish priest

Ninguno trabaja mucho, y tú menos que todos	None of them works much, and you least of all
lo menos que podrías hacer	the least you could do
De los dos, este libro es el que más se lee	Of the two, this book is read more/the most
Dale cuanto dinero puedas/Dale todo el dinero que puedas	Give him as much money as you can
la mejor solución posible	the best possible solution
el segundo mejor/peor	the second best/worst
Tan duquesa es como mi padre	She's as much a duchess as I am (ironic. Lit. 'She's as much a duchess as my father is')

5.15 Comparisons of equality

5.15.1 *Tan como, tanto como*

The formula is *tan . . . como* or *tanto . . . como* 'as . . . as', not *tanto . . . que* which can only mean 'so much that': *Se rió tanto que por poco revienta* 'He laughed so much he nearly burst'. *Tan* is used before adjectives, adverbs and nouns; *tanto* is used before *como* itself or when nothing follows:

Estos/Éstos no parecen tan grandes como los anteriores	These don't seem as big as the previous ones
Usted lo sabe tan bien como yo (M. Vargas Llosa, Peru, dialogue)	You know as well as I do
Contestó tan inteligentemente como quien más	She answered as intelligently as the best of them
No eres tan hombre como él	You're not as much of a man as him
No hablo tanto como tú	I don't talk as much as you

Other non-comparative uses of *tan* and *tanto* are discussed at 9.16.

5.15.2 *Igual que, lo mismo que, tal como*

These are used to express equality. *Igual que* is used after verbs, not *igual a* (for which see 5.15.3):

Escribe igual que/lo mismo que tú (not *igual como, *lo mismo como*)	She writes the same way as you
Me trató igual que siempre (G. García Márquez, Colombia)	She treated me the same as always
Lo hice tal como me lo dijiste	I did it just/exactly as you told me to

Notes
(i) Comparison of equality with verb phrases can also be expressed by the formula *del mismo modo que/de la misma manera que/de igual modo que/de igual manera que*: *Argüía de la misma manera que muchos filósofos de la época* 'He argued in the same way as many philosophers of the day'.
(ii) *Diferente, distinto*: *Es diferente del que tú tienes* 'It's different from the one that you've got', *Esta silla es diferente de la otra* 'This chair is different from the other one', *Es diferente/distinto a ti* 'He's different to you'.[2]

For Latin-American colloquial constructions like *Piensa distinto* 'He thinks differently' (for *Piensa de manera distinta*), see the note to 31.3.3.
See 9.11 for further discussion of *mismo*.

---

[2] Speakers of North-American English may prefer 'different than' in these sentences.

5.15.3 *Igual or igualmente?*

Igualmente means 'equally', but *igual* (as well as being an adjective meaning 'equal') is an invariable adverb in its own right meaning 'the same'.

otros problemas igualmente difíciles	other equally difficult problems

but:

una bata que le caía igual que hecha a medida (L. Goytisolo, Spain)	a housecoat that fitted her exactly as if it had been made to measure
¿Por qué todos lo hacen igual? (C. Rico-Godoy, Spain)	Why do all men do the same?
En eso ustedes son igual a las mujeres (M. Puig, Argentina, dialogue) (also *igual que. . .*)	You're the same as women in that respect
Es igual que tú (also *igual a ti*)	She's the same as you
Tú eres igualmente delgado/Tú eres igual de delgado	You're equally slim
Lo hace igual de bien que tú	She does it as well as you do

Note

In Spain, *igual* very often functions colloquially as an adverb meaning 'maybe' (i.e. meaning *quizá*, *tal vez* or a *lo mejor*, discussed at 16.3.2): *Yo no sé lo que me espera hoy. Igual llego tarde* (Carmen Rico-Godoy, Spain, dialogue) 'I don't know what's in store for me today. Maybe I'll get back late'.

This is familiar style, rejected by some as 'common' and probably confined to Spain. Latin-Americans may interpret *igual* as meaning 'anyway', e.g. *Igual nos vemos mañana* 'We're seeing one another tomorrow anyway'.

6

Demonstrative adjectives and pronouns

Spanish demonstrative adjectives and demonstrative pronouns are identical in form: *este* means 'this' or 'this one' (masc.), *esas* and *aquellas* mean 'those' or 'those ones' (fem.). The ambiguities that very rarely arise from this can be removed by spelling the pronouns with an accent; see 6.3 for discussion.

Spanish differs from French, German and English in having two words for 'that', depending on the distance in time or space between the speaker and the object referred to.[1]

6.1 Forms of demonstrative adjectives and pronouns

	this	that (near)	that (far)
masc.	este	ese	aquel
fem.	esta	esa	aquella

	these	those (near)	those (far)
masc.	estos	esos	aquellos
fem.	estas	esas	aquellas

The demonstratives have neuter forms, *esto*, *eso* and *aquello*, which are discussed separately in Chapter 7.

Notes
(i) See 6.3 for when to write these with an accent.
(ii) The masculine singular forms do not end in *-o*!
(iii) *Esta*, *esa* and *aquella* should be used before feminine nouns beginning with stressed *a-* or *ha-*: *esta agua* 'this water', *esa aula* 'that lecture hall', *aquella haya* 'that beech tree over there'. But forms like *este arma* 'this weapon', *este área* 'this area' are very common in spontaneous speech and sometimes appear in informal written styles.

---

[1] The first edition of this grammar explained *este*, *ese* and *aquel* in terms of the pronoun system: *este* 'this near me', *ese* 'that near you', *aquel* 'that near him/her'. It now seems to us more accurate to say that the difference between *ese* and *aquel* simply reflects distance from the speaker.

(iv) In Latin America *este*, and in Spain *esto*, are used and abused like the English 'er
. . .' to fill pauses while the speaker is thinking.
(v) When two or more nouns are involved, the demonstratives are repeated unless the
nouns refer to the same thing: *este hombre y esta mujer* 'this man and (this) woman' but
este poeta y filósofo 'this poet and philosopher' (same man).

6.2 Position of demonstrative adjectives

Normally before the noun: *esta miel* 'this honey', *ese árbol* 'that tree', *aquellas
regiones* 'those regions'.

   In spoken language they may appear after the noun, in which case they
strongly imply that the thing referred to has been mentioned before or is very
familiar. In many cases this implies irritation, exasperation or an ironic tone
and the construction should be used with caution. Compare *esa mujer* 'that
woman' (neutral tone) and *la mujer esa* 'that woman . . .' (sarcastic or weary
tone).

   However, a demonstrative adjective placed after the noun may simply
indicate another reference to a well-known topic, as in *Fue él quien se casó
con la gallega esa* 'He was the one who married that Galician girl (whom we
were talking about, whom we both know)'.

Examples:

Pero con la agencia esa que ha montado, se está forrando el riñón (A. Buero Vallejo, Spain, dialogue)	But with that agency he's set up, he's simply raking it in
En seguida dejé de tener importancia para la gente aquella (F. Umbral, Spain, dialogue)	I immediately ceased to have any importance for those people

   The definite article is obligatory if a demonstrative adjective follows the
noun. The demonstrative in this case remains an adjective even though it
follows the noun, so it is not written with an accent.

6.3 When does one write *este, ese, aquel* with an accent?

The present confused situation can be summarized thus:
(a) According to the Academy the accent is virtually never necessary on
these words, so the best advice to learners is when in doubt leave it out.
Omission of the accent looks much less illiterate than incorrect use of it.
(b) The neuter pronouns, *esto, eso* and *aquello* are **never** written with an
accent.

   The old rules of spelling required that the demonstrative pronouns should
always be distinguished from the adjectives by adding an accent, but even
in carefully edited texts printed before 1959, many inconsistencies appear.
The Academy's *Nuevas normas* of 1959 now state that the accent is required
only to remove ambiguities of the sort found in *esta protesta* 'this protest'
and *ésta protesta* 'this woman is protesting' or *ese español* 'that Spaniard' and
ése español 'that Spanish **one**'. Since such ambiguities almost never appear
in written Spanish (because context makes the meaning clear), the accent
can in practice be omitted. Both the Academy and Seco (1992), 189, now
consider sentences like *esta es mía* 'this one's mine', *un libro como ese* 'a book
like that one' to be correct.

Nevertheless, most publishing houses, newspaper editors, the more cautious grammarians and ordinary citizens everywhere still write – or try to write – the accent on the demonstrative pronouns even when there is no ambiguity: *El País* orders its journalists to ignore the Academy and always write the accent on the pronouns. The foreign student must therefore choose between following the Academy and thereby offending the eye of educated Spanish-speakers, or trying systematically to distinguish demonstrative adjectives from pronouns, which is not always easy.

In this book we show both possibilities, e.g. *un libro como ese/ése* 'a book like that one', although we omit the accent in a few cases where we cannot decide whether the demonstrative is an adjective or a pronoun.

There is one important inconsistency in printed usage. It has always been the practice in modern times, even before 1959 and among the most conservative writers, to omit the accent from demonstrative pronouns that are the antecedent of a relative clause or act as nominalizers (*aquel que, este de*, etc.); the reason for this is not entirely clear. As a result we write *Esta novela es mejor que **aquella** en que* . . . 'This novel is better than that in which . . .', ***este/ese** que* . . . 'this/that one that . . .', ***aquel** de ayer* . . . 'the one from yesterday . . .', etc.

Point **(b)** above can hardly be over-stressed: the neuter pronouns *esto, eso* and *aquello* (discussed in Chapter 7) are **never** written with an accent.

Examples of demonstrative pronouns:

Dame otro cuchillo – este/éste no corta	Give me another knife – this one doesn't cut
Antonio salía cada vez más de casa, circunstancia esta/ésta que a su madre no le pasaba inadvertida (Note position of dem. pronoun in apposition)	Antonio left the house more and more, this being a circumstance which did not pass unnoticed by his mother
*. . . su proximidad o lejanía respecto de la persona que habla o de **aquella** a quien se habla* (Academy Grammar, 1928 edition, 39; accent omitted from **aquella** followed by rel. pronoun)	. . . one's closeness or distance in relation to the person speaking or to whom one is speaking

Note
Use of demonstratives to refer to someone present is humorous or insulting: *Pregúntaselo a éste* 'Ask this one here' (e.g. pointing to her husband), *¡Éstos/Estos fuera!* 'Get this lot out!'

6.4 Use of *este, ese* and *aquel*

6.4.1. General
(a) *Este* refers to things near to or associated with the speaker and is equivalent to 'this': *este libro* 'this book', *estos arbustos* 'these bushes', *esta catástrofe* 'this catastrophe (that has just happened)'.
(b) As far as physical distance is concerned, *ese* means 'that': *ese libro* 'that book', *esos árboles* 'those trees'. It can refer to objects at any distance from the speaker and can therefore replace *aquel* provided no contrast is made with something even further away.

As far as time is concerned, *ese* refers to something in the past: *esa catástrofe* 'that catastrophe (that we were talking about before)', *en esas circunstancias* 'in those circumstances (we referred to earlier)'.

Examples:

este/éste de aquí	this one here
ese/ése de ahí	that one just there
aquel/aquél de allí[2]	that one over there
no ese/ése sino aquel/aquél	not that one, but that one over there
Prefiero ese que tú tienes	I prefer that one (masc.) that you've got
¿Quién se acuerda ya de aquellas tardes sin televisión?	Who can still remember those evenings without television?

6.4.2 *Aquel* or *ese*?

Aquel may be yielding ground to *ese* in some dialects: some grammarians complain about a tendency to use *ese* where *aquel* is more elegant. But the distinction is a real one for the immense majority of speakers on both continents, and must be respected by the foreign student in those contexts in which a distinction is obligatory.

(a) As far as spatial distance is concerned, *aquel* is only necessary when we need to differentiate between 'there' and 'further over there':

—*¿Quién plantó ese árbol?*	'Who planted that tree?'
—*¿Ese/Ése?*	'That one?'
—*No, **aquel** de detrás*	'No, the one behind'
*no esa torre sino **aquélla/aquella***	not that tower but the one further away

(b) It is **optionally** used to indicate something at some distance from the speaker:

Tráeme aquella/esa taza (que está allí)	Bring me that cup (from over there)
¿Ves aquella/esa montaña?	Can you see that mountain?

(c) As far as time is concerned, *aquel* indicates the distant past. Once an event in the past has been mentioned, *ese* can be used in subsequent references to it:

Recuerdo que aquel día hubo tormenta y que en aquella/esa ocasión yo había salido sin paraguas	I remember that that day there was a storm and on that occasion I'd gone out without an umbrella
¿Te acuerdas del 39? Pues en aquella/esa época yo vivía en Bilbao (Esa is possible here because the year is specified)	Do you remember '39? Well, at that time I was living in Bilbao
Debe de haber andado ya por los sesenta años cuando se embarcó con aquel horror de mujer (S. Pitol, Mexico, dialogue; she is no longer in his life.	He must have been getting on for sixty when he fell in with (lit. 'set sail with') that frightful woman

In some phrases *aquel* is obligatory:

¡Qué noche aquélla/aquella!	What a night that was!
¡Qué tiempos aquéllos/aquellos!	What times they were!

---

[2] *Ahí* '(just) there' suggests a middle distance between *aquí* 'here' and *allí* '(over) there'. See 31.6.1 for details.

Further examples of *ese* and *aquel*:

Era como uno de esos payasos de circo que dan miedo a los niños (*Aquellos* would only be possible here if such circus clowns no longer existed)	He was like one of those circus clowns who frighten the children
¿Te acuerdas de aquel escritorio que el abuelo quemó cuando tenías cinco años? (*Aquel* appropriate for something no longer in existence)	Do you remember that desk that grandfather burnt when you were five?
. . . la luna ya como de invierno, con su halo violeta de medusa y aquellas estrellas como un hielo hecho añicos (L. Goytisolo, Spain) (*Aquellas* appropriate for a childhood memory)	. . . the moon like a winter moon now, with its violet halo like a jellyfish's, and those stars like shattered ice

Notes
(i) In writing, *aquel que* (no written accent) replaces *el que* if the latter is followed by a relative pronoun. See 6.5c and 35.13 for examples.
(ii) *Aquel* should not be used in conjunction with a historic present because of the absurdity of simultaneously stressing the remoteness and the immediacy of an action; i.e. not **en aquel año Cervantes escribe el Quijote* 'in that year Cervantes wrote *Don Quixote*' but either *en **este** año Cervantes **escribe** Don Quijote*, or *en **aquel** año Cervantes **escribió** el Quijote*.

6.4.3 'The former, the latter'
Since *aquél/aquel* denotes something remote and *éste/este* something close, they conveniently translate 'former' and 'latter':

*La Universidad de México . . . no favorece ni los estudios ni la amistad. La ausencia de disciplina y normas de selección impide **aquéllos**; la plétora indiscriminada de una población de doscientos mil estudiantes dificulta **ésta*** (C. Fuentes, Mexico, dialogue)	Mexico University encourages neither study nor friendship. The lack of discipline and admission qualifications prevents the former; the undifferentiated mass of a student population of 200,000 hinders the latter

6.5 Translation problems involving demonstratives

(a) 'The . . . which/who', 'those . . . who', etc.
El que or *quien* are the usual equivalents; *aquel que* (usually written without an accent) is used in formal language: *Que se ponga de pie la que ha dicho eso* 'Stand up the girl who said that', etc. See Chapter 36 (Nominalizers) for discussion.
(b) 'Those of them', 'those of you', etc. *Aquellos de* is frowned on, except perhaps before *ustedes* or *vosotros*:

los que vivimos en Gibraltar	those of us who live in Gibraltar
los nicaragüenses que sabemos la verdad	those of us Nicaraguans who know the truth
aquellos de (entre) ustedes que afirman eso	those of you who claim that
los que no hayan firmado el formulario	those (of them/you) who haven't signed the form

Note
*Los de ellos or **aquellos de ellos* in this context is not Spanish.

(c) 'The one in which', 'those where', etc.

Aquel, customarily written without an accent in this construction, is a literary replacement for *el que* when a preposition governs a relative pronoun, i.e. one writes *La habitacion era más cómoda que **aquella** en que había dormido antes* 'The room was more comfortable than the one he had slept in before'. The spoken language usually prefers to repeat the noun: *La habitación era más cómoda que la habitación en la que/donde había dormido antes*; **la en que* is not possible. See 35.13 for details.

(d) 'That's why . . .', 'that's where', 'that's who', 'that was when', etc.

Translation of these phrases may involve the problem of 'cleft' sentences, e.g.:

*Fue por eso **por lo que** pagó demasiado*	That was why he paid too much
(Lat. Am. *Fue por eso que pagó demasiado*)	
*Fue con ésa/esa **con la que** se casó*	It was that girl whom he married

See 36.2 for a detailed discussion of 'cleft' sentences.

7

Neuter article and pronouns

7.1 Neuter gender: general

Nouns in Classical Latin could have one of three genders, masculine, feminine or neuter. Most neuter nouns came to be confused with masculine nouns in Vulgar Latin, and nowadays all traces of the neuter have vanished from the Spanish noun system.

However a few neuter pronouns and an article have survived in Spanish and remain as important features of the modern language. These forms are the 'neuter article' *lo*, the neuter third-person pronoun *ello* and its object form *lo*, the neuter relative pronouns *lo que* and *lo cual*, the neuter nominalizers *lo que* and *lo de*, and the neuter demonstrative pronouns *esto*, *eso* and *aquello*.

Neuter pronouns are necessary in Spanish to refer to concepts or ideas that have no gender. Masculine and feminine articles and pronouns can refer only to nouns or pronouns, present or implied, and nouns can be only masculine or feminine. Examples should make this clear:

No quiero hablar de aquel/aquél/aquella/	I don't want to talk about **that one** (i.e.
aquélla[1]	some masc./fem. noun)
No quiero hablar de aquello	I don't want to talk about **that**
No me gusta ese/ése/esa/ésa[1]	I don't like **that one** (French *celui-là/celle-là*)
No me gusta eso	I don't like **that** (*cela*)
los nuevos/las nuevas	the new ones (masc./fem.)
lo nuevo	what is new

For *lo que*, *lo cual* as relative pronouns (meaning 'which . . .'), see 35.6.

For *lo que* and *lo de* as nominalizers (i.e. 'the thing that/of . . .'), see 36.1.3 and 36.1.5. For the humorous *la que . . .* for *lo que . . .* see 36.1.4 note (iii).

For the colloquial *la de* meaning 'lots of' see 3.2.30.

For *lo* as a masculine direct object pronoun = 'him/it', see Chapter 12.

For the neuter pronouns *todo* 'everything', *algo* 'something', *mucho* 'a lot', and *poco* 'a little', see Chapter 9.

7.2 The 'neuter article' *lo*

7.2.1 *Lo* with masculine singular adjectives or with adverbs

A masculine singular adjective, or an adverb preceded by *lo*, becomes a sort of abstract noun. An adjective then often becomes a rough equivalent of an

---

[1] For the optional use of the accent on these pronouns, see 6.3.

English adjective + 'thing', but in many cases translation requires ingenuity:
(a) with adjectives:

Lo importante es que diga la verdad	The important thing is that he should tell the truth
Lo bueno sería que tú volvieras a perder el dinero	What would be great (ironic) is if you lost the money again
Lo bueno de tu casa es que tiene mucha luz	The good thing about your house is that it's full of light
Lo malo es que no quiere	The trouble is that she doesn't want to
¿Estoy en lo correcto?	Am I on the right lines?
Papá se ha enterado de lo nuestro	Father has found out about us
A la impresión de enorme antigüedad se agregaron otras: la de lo interminable, la de lo atroz, la de lo completamente insensato (J.L. Borges, Argentina)	To the impression of enormous antiquity were added others: the impression of endlessness, of horror, of utter irrationality
a pesar de lo antes dicho	despite what was said earlier
Lo verdaderamente increíble es que yo te haya encontrado (S. Puértolas, Spain)	The really incredible thing is the fact that I've found you
lo nunca visto en Estados Unidos	what has never been seen before in the USA

Note
In sentences with *ser* the verb apparently agrees with the predicate: *Lo mejor de la película **son** los actores* 'The best thing in the film is (lit. 'are') the actors'. This topic of the unexpected agreement of *ser* (and a few other verbs) with its predicate is discussed more fully at 2.3.3.

(b) with adverbs or adverbial phrases:

Hazlo lo más rápidamente que puedas	Do it as quickly as you can
Cuélgalo lo más arriba/atrás que puedas	Hang it as far up/back as you can
Lo antes que puedo salir de casa es a las seis	The earliest I can leave home is at six
Baja lo de allí arriba	Take down everything from up there

Notes
(i) Other Romance languages lack this device: *le plus tragique* can mean both 'the most tragic thing' and 'the most tragic one'; the Italian *il bello e il brutto* can mean 'beauty and ugliness' or 'the beautiful one and the ugly one'.
(ii) For the choice between the indicative and the subjunctive in constructions with *lo* + adjective + *es que*, e.g. *lo curioso es que . . .*, see 16.6.3.
(iii) *Lo* is occasionally found with a noun used adjectivally, although this construction is uncommon: *Ya te salió lo mujer* (A. Mastretta, Mexico, dialogue) 'Here goes the woman in you' (lit. 'the woman in you came out'), *Ya sabes lo torbellino que es* 'You know what a whirlwind he is'.
(iv) When *bastante* and *suficiente* occur in phrases of the kind 'clever enough to . . .', 'he did it well enough to . . .', they are preceded by *lo* and followed by *para*. The *lo* survives even if *para* and what follows are deleted: *El cuello de su gabardina estaba lo bastante abierto para permitirme contemplar el collar de perlas* (J. Marías, Spain) 'The collar of her raincoat was open enough to let me see her pearl necklace', *No la conozco lo suficiente para invitarla/No la conozco lo suficiente* 'I don't know her well enough to invite her'/'I don't know her well enough'.
(v) Colours may be turned into rather vague abstract nouns by using *lo*: *lo verde* 'greenness', *lo azul del cielo* 'the blueness of the sky'. However, when followed by *de*, colours are not usually vague abstractions but masculine nouns, and are translatable by the usual English names of specific colours: *El verde de sus ojos me fascina* 'The green of his/her eyes fascinates me', *el amarillo del poniente* 'the yellow of the sunset'.

7.2.2 *Lo* plus adjectives or adverbs translating 'how', etc.

Lo with an adjective or adverb often translates the English 'how' or some similar word + an adjective or adverb.

It commonly occurs after verbs of perception ('see', 'realize', 'understand', 'know') and liking or disliking. When used thus the adjective must agree with the noun:

(a) with adjectives and nouns used adjectivally:

No me había dado cuenta de lo guapa que era	I hadn't realized how attractive she was
Me irritan por lo tontos que son	I find them irritating because of their silliness
¿No te has fijado en lo delgada que se ha quedado? (A. Buero Vallejo, Spain, dialogue)	Haven't you noticed how thin she's become?
Tal vez no haya salido todo lo buena que yo creía (M. Puig, Argentina, dialogue)	Perhaps she hasn't turned out to be as good as I thought
Pues sí, Diego, ya sabes lo desastre que soy (C. Martin-Godoy, Spain; noun used as adjective)	Well yes, Diego, you know what a disaster I am

(b) with adverbs and adverbial phrases:

Yo llegué confiando en lo bien que lo iba a pasar	I arrived sure of what a good time I was going to have
Haga que hablen de usted por lo bien que habla inglés (Newspaper advertisement, Spain)	Get them talking about you because you speak English so well
Hay que ver lo tarde que es	I can't believe how late it is (lit. 'you have to see how late it is')

Notes

(i) A common colloquial construction is *con lo* + adjective. Translation varies with context: *Pobre Ana, con lo enferma que está . . .* 'Poor Anna, and her being so ill', *Parece mentira que no te guste, con lo rico que está* 'It seems impossible that you don't like it. It's so delicious', etc.

(ii) *De* + *lo* + comparative adjective is also found in familiar speech as an intensifying phrase: *Viene de lo más arregladita* 'She's coming all dressed up', *Tomaban su cerveza de lo más tranquilos* (M. Vargas Llosa, Peru, dialogue) 'They were drinking their beer really quietly'.

(iii) In expressions of cause *por* or *de* can be used before *lo* + adjective: *No pudo pasar por lo gordo que estaba/No pudo pasar de (lo) gordo que estaba* 'He couldn't get through because he was so fat'.

7.3 *Ello*

This is a neuter third-person pronoun. It is invariable in form and can be used to translate 'it' when this pronoun does not refer to any specific noun. Compare *En cuanto al régimen militar, prefiero no hablar de él* 'As for the military regime, I prefer not to talk about it' (masc. singular) and *Todo fue tremendamente violento, y prefiero no hablar de ello* 'It was all tremendously embarrassing, and I prefer not to talk about it' (neuter).

Ello can be used as a subject pronoun or it can be combined with a preposition, but it cannot be used as a direct object pronoun: *lo* is its direct object form.

When it is the subject of a verb, it normally requires translation by 'this'.

This use as a subject is rather literary; *esto* comes more readily in speech:

No te preocupes por ello, que no se me olvida²	Don't worry about that – I haven't forgotten about it
Por ello ya no se fía de nadie	Because of that she doesn't trust anybody any more
Habitó un siglo en la Ciudad de los Inmortales. Cuando la derribaron, aconsejó la fundación de otra. Ello no debe sorprendernos . . . (J.L. Borges, Argentina)	He dwelt for a century in the City of the Immortals. When they demolished it, he recommended the foundation of another. This (fact) should not surprise us . . .

7.4 *Lo* as a neuter pronoun

Lo is the direct object pronoun corresponding to *ello*.

For *lo* 'him'/'it' (referring to masculine nouns) see Chapter 12.

¿Lo hacemos o no?	Shall we do it or not?
¿No sabíais que estaba prohibido? No, no lo sabíamos	Didn't you know it was forbidden? No, we didn't know (it)
Ya nadie la llamaba Clarita, como lo habían hecho siempre sus difuntos padres y marido (M. Puig, Argentina, dialogue)	By now nobody called her Clarita, as her deceased parents and husband had done

Notes

(i) *Lo* is used to echo or resume the predicate of *ser* and *estar* and the object of *haber* 'there is/are': —*Parece buena la tierra desde aquí.* —*Lo es* '"The land looks good from here." "It is", (lit. 'it is it'), —*Usted no es don Antonio.* —*¿Y si lo fuera?* '"You're not don Antonio." "And (what) if I were?"', *La luna está muerta y lo ha estado siempre* 'The Moon is dead and always has been', *¿Tolera estar solo, o tolera la necesidad que tenga su cónyuge de estarlo?* (quiz on marriage in *ABC*, Spain), 'Can you stand being alone, or can you stand your partner's need to be (alone)?'.

This resumptive *lo* is often omitted from Latin-American speech and sometimes in Latin-American writing.

See 30.2.2 for the resumptive pronoun with *haber* 'there is/are'.

(ii) *Lo* is used in many colloquial phrases to indicate something implied but not specified: *El ministro lo tiene difícil* (*Cambio16*, Spain.) 'The minister is in a difficult situation', *En eso las mujeres lo tenemos mejor* (C. Rico-Godoy, Spain) 'In that respect we women are better off', *Se lo están poniendo mal* 'They're making things difficult for him/her'.

(iii) *Lo* is sometimes used redundantly before *todo* to make the latter more specific in meaning: compare *Miguel lo sabe todo* 'Miguel knows it all/all about it', and *Miguel sabe todo* 'Miguel knows everything'.

(iv) For Latin-American *?se los dije* 'I said it to them', see 11.13.2.

7.5 Neuter demonstrative pronouns

These take the invariable forms *esto*, *eso* and *aquello*. Since they cannot be confused with demonstrative adjectives, they *never* take the written accent – a fact that learners and native speakers constantly forget.

They refer to no noun in particular (cf. French. *ceci*, *cela*).

The difference between *esto* 'this', *eso* 'that' and *aquello* 'that', (distant) reflects the difference between *este*, *ese*, and *aquel*, discussed at 6.4:

¿Quién ha hecho esto?	Who did this?

---

² See 33.4.4b for this use of *que*.

Quisiera llamar a cobro revertido. De eso nada

I'd like to make a transfer charge/collect call. No way/Out of the question

. . . había comprendido cómo todo aquello jamás tuvo nada que ver con el humor ni con el buen humor (A. Bryce Echenique, Peru)

. . . I had understood how all that never had anything to do with humour or good temper

Prefiero no pensar en todo aquello/eso

I'd rather not think about all that

¿Qué hay de aquello/eso de los billetes falsos?

What's happening about that business of the forged notes?

¿Cómo podía yo pensar que aquello que parecía tan mentira era verdadero? (J. Cortázar, Argentina, dialogue)

How could I think that that thing which seemed such a lie was true?

Notes

(i) *Aquello* often corresponds to 'the saying that', though *eso* may also be used: *En realidad todo se reduce a aquello de que ojos que no ven* ˙. . . (J. Cortázar, Argentina. dialogue) 'Really it all boils down to "what the eye doesn't see . . ."'

(ii) The choice between a neuter or non-neuter demonstrative may cause problems: compare *Esto es un soneto* 'This is a sonnet' and *Éste/Este es un soneto – los demás sólo tienen trece versos* 'This (*poema*) is a sonnet – the rest have only thirteen lines'.

If the speaker has in mind a specific noun, the masculine or feminine pronoun must be used as appropriate unless the speaker is referring to a type of thing. For example, pointing to a coat in a shop window one could say *Eso es lo que quiero* 'That's the (type of) thing I want' or *Ese/Ése es el que quiero* 'That's the **one** I want'. Compare the following: *No tengo ni talento, ni fuerza. Esa/Ésa es la verdad* (E. Sábato, Argentina, dialogue; *eso* also possible because it refers to the whole of the statement) 'I have neither talent nor strength. That's the truth', *Esa/Ésa es otra de las invenciones de ustedes* (M. Vargas Llosa, Peru, dialogue) 'That's another of your inventions', *¿Qué es esto?* 'What's this?', *¿Quién es éste/este?* 'Who's this (man or boy)?', *Este/Éste es el problema* 'This is the problem', *Esto es un problema* 'This is **a** problem', *Esto no es una limosna sino un derecho* 'This isn't charity (lit. 'alms') but a right', *Si a esto se puede llamar marido, que venga Dios y lo vea* (neuter pronoun appropriate, given the tone of the remark) 'If you can call this (thing) a husband, then I'm a Dutchman' (lit. 'then let God come and see it').

When the subject of the verb is a noun, the pronoun agrees with it: *La verdad es ésta/esta*, 'The truth is this', *Los problemas son éstos/estos* 'The problems are these'.

8

Possessive adjectives and pronouns

8.1 General

Spanish possessives have two forms. The short forms, *mi*, *tu*, *su*, etc. are the normal, unstressed possessive adjectives and appear in front of a noun or noun phrase. These correspond to the English 'my', 'your', 'his', 'her': *mi libro* 'my book', *su casa* 'her/his/your house'.

The full forms, *mío*, *tuyo*, *suyo*, etc. roughly correspond to the English 'mine', 'yours', 'hers', etc. and can only follow the noun or stand alone: *un amigo mío* 'a friend of mine', *De los dos prefiero el tuyo* 'Of the two I prefer yours', etc.

Number and gender agreement is determined by the number and gender of the noun possessed. All forms agree in number, but only those whose masculine singular ends in *-o* agree in gender.

Points to watch are:

(a) Replacement of the possessive adjectives by the definite article when the identity of the possessor is obvious: *Me he roto **el** brazo* 'I've broken my arm', *Dame **la** mano* 'Give me your hand' (see 8.3.4). This occurs much more frequently than in French;

(b) The difference between *es mío* and *es el mío* (see 8.4.2).

8.2 Forms of the possessives

8.2.1 Short forms of possessives

Personal pronoun	Singular	Plural	
yo	*mi*	*mis*	my
tú (and vos)	*tu*	*tus*	your (familiar)
él/ella	*su*	*sus*	his/her
usted	*su*	*sus*	your (polite)
ellos/ellas	*su*	*sus*	their
ustedes	*su*	*sus*	your (polite)

Only *nuestro* and *vuestro* are marked for gender:

nosotros/nosotras	masc.	*nuestro*	*nuestros*	our
	fem	*nuestra*	*nuestras*	
vosotros/vosotras	masc.	*vuestro*	*vuestros*	your
	fem.	*vuestra*	*vuestras*	(familiar)

Vuestro is not used in Latin America and is replaced by *su*. See 8.6 for discussion of Latin-American usage.

8.2.2 Long forms of possessives
All are marked for number and gender:

Personal pronoun	Masculine	Feminine	
yo	mío/míos	mía/mías	mine
tú/vos	tuyo/tuyos	tuya/tuyas	yours
él/ella	suyo/suyos	suya/suyas	his/hers
usted	suyo/suyos	suya/suyas	yours
nosotros/nosotras	nuestro/nuestros	nuestra/nuestras	ours
vosotros/vosotras	vuestro/vuestros	vuestra/vuestras	yours
ellos/ellas	suyo/suyos	suya/suyas	theirs
ustedes	suyo/suyos	suya/suyas	yours

Note
Vuestro is not used in Latin America and is replaced by *suyo*. See 8.6 for discussion of Latin-American usage.

8.3 Use of the short form of possessives

8.3.I Basic uses
This is straightforward provided the rules of agreement are mastered: the possessive agrees in number with the thing possessed and *nuestro* and *vuestro* agree in gender as well:

mi padre/mis padres	my father/my parents
mi madre/mis flores	my mother/my flowers
¿Dónde está tu coche?	Where's your car?
¿Dónde están tus zapatos?	Where are your shoes?
Me fío de su amigo	I trust his/her/your friend
Me fío de sus amigos	I trust his/her/your friends
nuestro dinero/nuestra dignidad	our money/our dignity
vuestra casa/vuestras casas	your house/your houses
Si ustedes quieren dejar sus cosas aquí . . .	If you want to leave your/his/her/their things here . . .
Si ellos no quieren dejarnos su cortacésped . . .	If they don't want to lend us their lawnmower . . .

8.3.2 Possessives with more than one noun
If a possessive refers to more than one noun, Spanish differs from English in that the possessives are deleted only if the following nouns are felt to refer to the same or aspects of the same thing.

One says **mi** *padre y* **mi** *madre* 'my father and mother' (different people) but **mi** *amigo y colega* 'my friend and colleague' (same person), **su** *paciencia y valor* 'his patience and courage' (aspects of a single virtue), **nuestros** *cuentos y novelas* 'our short stories and novels' (aspects of a single œuvre).

8.3.3 Possessives in military usage
In military circles, possessives are used to address officers: *Sí, mi general* 'Yes, General', *No, mi coronel* 'No, Colonel'.

8.3.4 Definite article instead of possessives

Spanish uses possessive adjectives much more sparingly than English and French, and frequently replaces them by the definite article.

A sentence like *Sacó **su** pañuelo de **su** bolso* 'He took his handkerchief out of his pocket', although grammatically correct, sounds unnatural: *Sacó el pañuelo **del** bolso* (if the pocket is someone else's) or *Se sacó el pañuelo **del** bolso* (from his own pocket) are much more idiomatic. The Academy's *Esbozo...*, 3.10.9a., remarks that sentences like *Pase sus vacaciones en la playa de X*, 'Spend your holidays/vacation on the beach at X' for *Pase las vacaciones . . .* have a foreign ring to them.

Possessive adjectives are replaced by the definite article:

(a) If context makes it clear that the thing possessed belongs to the speaker or to the person who is the focus of the sentence. Compare *He dejado **el** coche en **el** garaje* 'I've left my/the car in my/the garage' and *He dejado tu coche en mi/el garaje* 'I've left **your** car in **my** garage'.

Use of the definite article is normal with parts of the body, clothing and other intimate possessions, especially articles of which one normally has only one, e.g. wrist-watch, purse, wallet/notebook, pen, pencil, glasses, etc.

Examples:

*Metí . . . en una bolsa de playa el bronceador, las toallas, la radio portátil, el libro que estoy leyendo, dos camisetas, **el** monedero . . .* (C. Rico-Godoy, Spain)[1]	I put the sun-tan lotion, the towels, the portable radio, the book I'm reading, two T-shirts, *my* purse . . . in a beach-bag
Junté las manos y bajé la cabeza (C. Fuentes, Mexico, dialogue)	I joined my hands and bowed my head
Cierre la boca	Shut your mouth
Perdió la vida	She lost her life
Siempre la recuerdo con las uñas pintadas de azul	I always remember her with her nails painted blue
Tengo los ojos azules	My eyes are blue/I've got blue eyes

(b) When the thing possessed belongs to the person indicated by an indirect object pronoun. Compare *He dejado tu coche en el garaje* 'I've left your car in my/the garage' and *Te he dejado **el** coche en el garaje* 'I've left your car in the garage (for you)'. **Te he dejado tu coche . . .* is incorrect.

Ricardo se aflojó la corbata	Richard loosened his (own) tie
Bébete el café	Drink your coffee
Arréglate el pelo	Tidy your hair
Les robaron el coche	They stole their/your car
Vio que ella se ponía las manos sobre la cara como si le dolieran las sienes (J.L. Borges, Argentina)	He saw her putting her hands over her face as though she had a pain in her temples

However, when the thing possessed is emphasized or particularized by context, by an adjective or by other words, or whenever ambiguity must be avoided, the possessive adjective usually reappears:

---

[1] This shows how Spanish is often content to let the meaning of a noun clarify the identity of the possessor. *El monedero* is here certainly 'my purse' since the writer is a woman, but, as far as one can tell from the context, the other items preceded by the definite article belong jointly to her and her husband.

*Que el Pelícano se abre el pecho y alimenta con **su propia** sangre a los hijos es la versión común de la fábula* (J.L. Borges, Argentina: **la propia sangre* is not possible)	That the pelican tears open its breast and feeds its children with its own blood is the common version of the fable
*Vi **sus** ojos grandes, fatigados, sonrientes y como lacrimosos* (F. Umbral, Spain)	I saw her eyes, big, tired, smiling and seemingly tearful
*Acerqué **mi** cabeza a la suya* (C. Fuentes, Mexico, dialogue; contrast)	I moved my head close to his
*X deja **sus** manos suaves y perfumadas* (or *le deja las manos . . .*)	X leaves your hands soft and perfumed
*Toco **tus** labios . . .* (popular song)	I touch your lips . . .

Notes

(i) Use of the definite article plays down the importance of the thing possessed. *Te toco los labios* sounds accidental or matter-of-fact. A mother says *Dame la mano, que vamos a cruzar la calle* 'Hold my hand, we're going to cross the road', an old-fashioned lover might say *Dame tu mano y te haré feliz* 'Give me your hand (i.e. 'in marriage') and I will make you happy'.

For the same reason, one does not, in polite speech, use the definite article when the thing possessed is a human being: *¡Cuánto echo de menos a mis hijas!* 'I miss my daughters so much!' *Siempre voy de vacaciones con mi mujer/mi novia* (?*con la mujer/la novia* is either humorous or popular, cf. British 'with the wife') 'I always go on holiday/vacation with my wife/girlfriend'.

(ii) As mentioned above, the possessive adjective must be used when the object possessed is the subject of a verb, unless an indirect object pronoun identifies the possessor: *Su cabeza se destacaba contra el cielo* 'His head stood out against the sky', *Sus ojos parecían cansados* 'Her eyes seemed tired', but *Se le cae el pelo* 'His hair's falling out', *Le dolían las piernas* 'Her/his legs hurt'.

(iii) In Latin America possessive adjectives are often used in combination with *le/les*: *Les pintamos su casa* (street sign, Oaxaca, Mexico) 'We'll paint your house for you', *Me duele mi cabeza* (popular colloquial Mexican) 'My head aches', standard Spanish *Me duele la cabeza*.

8.4 Long or pronominal forms of the possessives

8.4.1 Use of the long or pronominal forms of the possessive

(a) To translate English '. . . of mine/yours/his/ours', etc.:

un amigo mío	a friend of mine
un poema muy malo mío (interview in *Granma*, Cuba; Spain *un poema mío muy malo*)	a very bad poem of mine
un pariente vuestro	a relation of yours
Antonio ha vuelto a hacer una de las suyas	Antonio's up to his usual tricks again (lit. 'a trick of his')
una actitud muy suya	a very typical attitude of his/hers/ yours/theirs
algo mío	something of mine
nada nuestro	nothing of ours

(b) As a literary, rather stilted variation of the usual possessive:

en mi novela/en la novela mía	in my novel/in this novel of mine
nuestro pan/el pan nuestro de cada día	our daily bread

(c) In Spain, in formulas of address:

Bueno, hijo mío/hija mía, me voy   Well, dear, I'm off

(Lit. 'my son'/'my daughter', a term of
endearment used between friends)
Latin-American Spanish says mi hijo, mi
hija, etc.

(d) To translate the pronouns 'mine', 'yours' (see the following section for the
use of the definite article in this construction):

Este garabato es tuyo   This scrawl is yours
Este/Éste es el vuestro, ¿verdad?   This one is yours, isn't it?

Note
The long forms are used in a number of set phrases: *de nuestra parte/de parte nuestra*
'for our part', *a pesar mío/suyo* 'despite me/him', *a costa mía* 'at my cost', *en torno suyo*
'around him/her/them/you', *a propuesta suya* 'at his suggestion', *muy señor mío* 'Dear Sir'
(in letters).

8.4.2 Definite article with the long forms
The definite article is obligatory in the following cases:
(a) After prepositions. Compare *¿De quién es el coche? Mío* 'Whose car is it?
Mine' and *¿En qué coche vamos? En el mío* 'Which car are we going in? In
mine'.

Further examples:

No hablo del tuyo sino del nuestro   I'm not talking about yours but ours
A tu primo sí le/lo conozco, pero no al suyo   I know your cousin, but not his/hers

(b) When the pronoun is the subject or object of a verb (even though the verb
may be deleted):

Coge el mío   Take mine
Tu padre te deja salir, el mío no   Your father lets you go out, mine doesn't
Los dos vídeos son buenos, pero el nuestro es   The two videos are good but ours is
mejor   better
Qué vida tan triste la suya   What a sad life his/hers/yours/theirs is

(c) After *ser* 'to be', omission of the article stresses actual possession. Thus
one would say *Esta casa es mía* 'This house is mine' (it is my property or I live
in it), but in an office where there are several telephones one would say *Ese
teléfono que suena es **el** tuyo* 'That phone that's ringing is yours' (i.e. the one you
use, not your property):

Compare

Este libro es mío   This book belongs to me
La culpa es tuya   It's your fault
la casa de Jeremiah Saint-Amour, que desde   Jeremiah Saint-Amour's house, which
ahora era suya (G. García Márquez,   from now on was hers . . .
Colombia)
and
*¿Ves estas tres camas? Esta/ésta es **la** mía,*   Do you see these three beds? This is
*esa/ésa es **la** tuya y aquella/aquélla es la de*   mine, that's yours and that one's Rafael's
Rafael (implies use, not possession)

8.4.3 The neuter article with *lo mío, lo suyo*, etc.

The neuter form of the possessive has various meanings:

Mi marido sabe lo nuestro	My husband knows about us
Ahora estás en lo tuyo	Now you're in your element
Lo vuestro es alucinante	What happened to you is mind-boggling

See Chapter 7 for more details about neuter forms.

8.5 Replacement of possessive by *de* + pronoun

In some cases a possessive can optionally be replaced by *de* + a pronoun.
This happens:
(a) When it is necessary to clarify the meaning of *su/suyo*, which can have six translations: 'his', 'her', 'its', 'your' (*usted*), 'their', 'your' (*ustedes*).

Context nearly always makes the meaning clear, but ownership may be stressed or ambiguities removed by using *de él/ella, de usted, de ellos/ellas, de ustedes*: *los paraguas de ustedes* 'your (plural) umbrellas', *la camisa de él* 'his shirt'.

In Spain, *su* is assumed out of context to be third-person, so that *de usted/ustedes* may need to be added to emphasize the meaning 'your'. (For Latin-American usage, see 8.6)

The possibility of ambiguity is illustrated by the question 'Is this handkerchief yours or hers?', which one would probably say *¿Este pañuelo es de usted o de ella?* whereas *¿Este pañuelo es suyo?* 'Is this handkerchief yours?' is clear if no one else is present. Examples: *Conozco a la madre de él* 'I know *his* mother', *¿Este sombrero es de ella?* 'Is this hat hers?'
(b) When *de* means 'from' or 'about' and not 'of':

*Hace tiempo que no tengo noticias vuestras/**de** vosotros*	It's been some time since I've had news about you

8.6 Possessives: Latin-American usage

Latin-American usage differs from European in a number of ways:
(a) Possessives in areas of *voseo*

Tu/tuyo are the forms corresponding to *vos* in *voseo* areas of Latin America: cf. *Vos tenés tu birome* (Argentina, *la birome* is feminine) 'You've got your ballpoint pen'; Spain *Tú tienes tu bolígrafo*.
(b) Possessives corresponding to *usted/ustedes* and to third-person pronouns

Vuestro is not used in Latin America, except in liturgical and other ceremonial language; it is replaced by *ustedes*.[2] *Su/sus* is therefore the only second-person possessive form and is used for both formal and informal address.
(c) In Latin America *su/suyo* is assumed, out of context, to mean *de usted/de ustedes* 'of you'. Third-person possession may be represented in everyday

---

[2] *Vuestro* is, however, found as a polite plural possessive in Argentine business correspondance: . . . *dada la recomposición de relaciones entre la Argentina y vuestro país* '. . . given the re-establishment of relations between Argentina and your country' (from a business letter sent to England).

speech by the following construction: *de él* 'his/its' (masc.), *de ella* 'her/its' (fem.), *de ellos* 'their' (masc.), *de ellas* 'their' (fem.): *¿Quieres que vayamos al cuarto de él a ver si está?* (Costa Rican dialogue, quoted Kany, 69) 'Do you want to go to his room to see if he's there?'.

(d) *De nosotros* for *nuestro* is also common in Latin-American speech: *La casa de nosotros está en la esquina* (Colombian informant, standard Spanish *nuestra casa*) 'Our house is on the corner', *—¿A quién se lo entregó? —Al jefe de nosotros* (*Vindicación de Cuba*, Cuba) '"Who did you hand it over to?" "To our boss"', (standard Spanish *nuestro jefe).*

8.7 Possessives after prepositions and adverbs

A common construction in colloquial Latin-American Spanish, also found in popular speech in Spain, is the use of possessive pronoun forms after prepositions followed by *de*, and after some adverbs: *?detrás mío = detrás de mí* 'behind me', and even, in sub-standard speech, *?Entró antes mío* 'He went in before me', for *Entró antes que yo*.

This usage is so deep-rooted in Argentina that it is found in the best writers, but it is considered colloquial in other Latin-American countries and incorrect in Spain and Mexico:

Adentro mío yo soy igual que todos los reaccionarios (M. Puig, Argentina, dialogue; Spain *dentro de mí* or *por dentro*)	Inside (me) I'm the same as all the reactionaries
Quiero estar cerca tuyo (ibid., Spain *cerca de ti*)	I want to be near you
No lo consiguió por lo intimidado que estaba en mi delante (M. Vargas Llosa, Peru, dialogue; Spain *delante de mí*)	He was so intimidated in my presence that he didn't manage it

and also (the bracketed forms are used in standard Spanish):

?alrededor mío	*(a mi alrededor[3]/alrededor de mí)*	around me
?encima mía	*(encima de mí)*	above/over me
?enfrente suyo	*(enfrente de él/ella/usted/ustedes/ellos/ellas)*	opposite him/her/you/them
?en su delante	*(delante de él/ella,* etc.)	in front of him, etc.
?aparte suyo	*(aparte de él/ella,* etc.)	apart from him/her, etc.
?fuera suyo	*(fuera de él/ella,* etc.)	apart from him/her, etc.

Foreign students should avoid this construction. However, *en torno nuestro* (literary) 'around us' is considered correct.

Note

Both *contra mí/ti* and *en contra mía/tuya*, 'against me/you', etc. are correct, but there is a tendency to make the possessive precede in Latin America and this usage seems to be spreading to Spain:

Está en mi contra (Peanuts, Argentina)	He/she/it is against me
El hecho de que el teléfono se hubiera puesto en mi contra . . . (S. Puértolas, Spain)	The fact that the phone had turned against me

---

[3] *A mi alrededor* is the usual form in Spain.

9

Miscellaneous adjectives and pronouns

Many of the words discussed in this chapter are of problematic classification and have multiple uses as adjectives, pronouns or adverbs. For easy reference they are, where possible, discussed under a single heading.

9.1 *Ajeno*: adjective, marked for number and gender

A rather literary word meaning 'someone else's': *el dolor ajeno* (*el dolor de otros*) 'other people's sorrow', *en casa ajena* (*en casa de otro*) 'in another person's house', *Se preocupa demasiado por lo ajeno* 'He concerns himself too much with other people's business'.

It is not used in this meaning after *ser*:

Esta agenda es de otro   This is someone else's diary

Note
Ajeno often translates 'a stranger to', 'remote from': *Éstos/Estos son problemas ajenos a mi responsabilidad* 'These are problems outside my responsibility', . . . *una mujer adulta pero atractiva que tomaba el sol tumbada y ajena, aparentemente, a todo* (C. Rico-Godoy, Spain) '. . . an adult but attractive woman who was lying there sun-bathing and apparently oblivious to everything'.

9.2 *Algo*: invariable pronoun/adverb

The usual equivalent of 'something' or, in questions or after *poco* and a few other words that form 'pseudo-negative' sentences (discussed at 23.4), 'anything' (French *quelquechose*):

Aquí hay algo que no me suena	There's something here that doesn't sound right to me
¿Ves algo?	Can you see anything?
Serán pocos los que hayan traído algo	There probably won't be many who have brought anything

Adverbially it means 'rather', 'somewhat', though *un poco, un tanto* or *más bien* are equally common in speech:

Es algo complicado explicarlo	It's rather complicated to explain
Te has apartado algo del asunto	You've rather wandered off the subject

Notes
(i) *Algo así, algo así como* are translations of 'something like . . .': *Pesa algo así como siete kilos* 'It weighs around 7 kilos', *Se llama Nicanora, o algo así* 'She's called Nicanora, or something like that'.

(ii) In negative sentences *nada* translates 'anything': *No sabe nada* 'He doesn't know anything', *Yo no sé dónde está nada en esta casa* 'I don't know where anything is in this house'.

(iii) The English question-opener 'Do you know something . . .?' must be translated *¿Sabes una cosa?*. *¿Sabes algo?* means 'Do you know anything?'.

9.3 *Alguien*: invariable pronoun

'Someone'/'somebody'. It also translates 'anyone'/'anybody' in questions (see 23.4.) It is not marked for gender.

Ha venido alguien a cobrar el recibo de la luz	Someone's come to take the money for the electricity bill
¿Conoces a alguien que pueda darme un presupuesto para reparar el coche?	Do you know anyone who could give me an estimate for mending my car?

Notes

(i) **Alguien de los estudiantes*, **alguien de ellos* are rejected by grammarians in favour of *alguno de los estudiantes*, *alguno de (entre) ellos*, although *alguien de entre ustedes* is accepted by some authorities: *Si alguien de entre ustedes/alguno de ustedes lo sabe, que lo diga* 'If someone among you/any of you knows, say so'.

Occasionally *alguien de* is necessary since, unlike *alguno*, it does not indicate gender: *Yo creo que alude a alguien de esta casa* 'I think he's alluding to someone in this house'.

(ii) María Moliner notes that *?darle una cosa a alguien que él no desea* offends the ear since *alguien* is too vague for a specifically masculine pronoun: *darle una cosa a alguien que no lo desea* 'to give something to someone who doesn't want it'.

(iii) 'Give it to someone else' is *Dáselo a algún otro/alguna otra/alguna otra persona*. **Alguien otro* is not Spanish.

(iv) *Uno* is sometimes colloquially used for 'someone' when gender is an important part of the message (for other uses of *uno* as a pronoun see 28.7.1): *Se ha peleado con uno en la calle* 'He's had a fight with some man in the street', *Se casó con una de Valencia* 'He married some girl from Valencia'.

9.4 *Algún*, *alguno*, *algunos*; *alguna*, *algunas*: adjective/pronoun marked for number and gender

9.4.1 General uses of *alguno*

The appropriate form of *alguno* may be used either as an adjective or (except for the short form *algún*) as a pronoun.

(a) As an adjective:

The usual translation is 'some', (French *quelque*). It is shortened to *algún* before a singular masculine noun or noun phrase: *algún día* 'some day', *algún remoto rincón de Extremadura* 'some remote corner of Extremadura', but *alguna región* 'some region'.

Algún is also common in spoken Spanish immediately before feminine nouns beginning with a stressed *a-* or *ha-*: *algún alma perdida* 'some lost soul', *algún arma defensiva* 'some defensive weapon'; but *alguna* should be used in writing.

In the singular, *alguno* and *uno* are often interchangeable, but *alguno* often means 'one or maybe more' and is roughly equivalent to 'one or another', 'some or other'. (For the difference between *unos* and *algunos*, see 9.4.2):

Tienes que prometerme que si algún/un día te cansas me lo dirás en seguida	You must promise me that if some day you get tired, you'll tell me straight away
Sólo se veía por las desiertas playas algún turista extranjero	All one could see along the deserted beaches was the occasional foreign tourist
—¿Tiene usted algún manual de programación?	'Do you have any programming manuals?'
—Sí, alguno hay	'Yes, there may be one.'

Note

In formal style, *alguno* may follow a noun, in which case it is an emphatic equivalent of *ninguno*, 'none', 'no . . . at all': *No cultivaba forma alguna de contacto con el pueblo* (J. Marsé, Spain) 'He cultivated absolutely no kind of contact with the common people', *En modo alguno entraba en mis propósitos ingresar en el ejército* 'In no way at all was it part of my plans to join the army', . . . *o mejor una lista de palabras que no tuviera orden alguno* (G. Cabrera Infante, Cuba, dialogue) '. . . or better a list of words with no order at all'.

(b) *Alguno* as a pronoun:

Se lo habrá llevado alguna de las vendedoras	One of the salesgirls must have taken it away
—¿Has recibido cartas de tu familia?	'Have you had any letters from your family?'
—Bueno, alguna, sí	'Well, one or two, yes'

In the plural, 'some' or 'a few' are the usual translations: *Con algunos de tercero vas a tener que hacer ejercicios de verbos irregulares* 'You're going to have to do irregular verb exercises with some of the third year'.

Notes

(i) When the singular of *alguno* is combined with a second-person pronoun, the verb agrees optionally with the pronoun or with the third person, although the latter is more usual: *si alguno de vosotros lo sabéis/lo sabe* 'if any of you know(s) it'.

In the plural, agreement is always with the pronoun: *algunas de vosotras lo sabéis* 'some of you women know'. This is also true of the first-person plural: *Algunas de nosotras generalmente caminamos despacito* (*La Jornada*, Mexico) 'Some of us women generally walk slowly'.

(ii) 'Some' (and 'any') has no visible equivalent in Spanish when it precedes a partitive noun, i.e. a noun that denotes only part of what it refers to, as in 'Give me some water' *Dame agua*, 'You haven't bought any pins' *No has comprado alfileres*.

In some cases *un poco* or *ninguno* may be appropriate translations of 'some'. 'Any' in the sense of 'it doesn't matter which' is *cualquiera* (see 9.8): *¿Tiene usted pan integral?* 'Have you got any wholemeal bread?', *¿Chuletas de ternera? No tenemos* 'Veal chops? We haven't got any', *No tenemos ninguno/ninguna* 'We haven't got a single one' (masc.).

(iii) When *alguno* is the object, direct or indirect, and is placed before the verb for purposes of focus, agreement is governed by the number of an accompanying noun or pronoun: *A alguno de vosotros os quisiera ver yo en un lío como éste/este* 'I'd like to see one of you in a mess like this', *A alguno de ellos les quiere dar el premio* 'It's one of them that he wants to give the prize to'.

9.4.2 *Unos* and *algunos* contrasted

English speakers often have difficulty in differentiating these two plural words.

Unos has various meanings discussed at 3.4.

(a) *Algunos . . . otros* and *unos . . . otros*

The two words are interchangeable when accompanied by *otros/otras*:

Algunos/Unos vinieron, otros no	Some came, others didn't
Algunos/Unos días estoy de mal humor, otros no	Some days I'm in a bad mood, others I'm not

(b) Only *algunos* is possible in the phrase *algunos de*: *salí a cenar con algunos de los alumnos* 'I went out to dinner with some of the students'. *Algunos* is also used when no contrast is intended: *Algunos mexicanos hablan tres idiomas* 'Some Mexicans speak three languages', *Algunos días estoy de mal humor* 'Some days I'm in a bad mood'.

(c) *Unos* 'some' and *unos cuantos* 'a few' can both be used when no specific reference to quantity is intended: *Tráeme unas (cuantas) patatas* 'Bring me a few/some/a couple of potatoes', *Esta tarde vinieron unos (cuantos) amigos* 'Some/a few friends came this afternoon', *He traído unas (cuantas) cerezas* 'I've brought some/a few cherries'. However, sentences like *Salí anoche con unos amigos de Barcelona* 'I went out last night with some friends from Barcelona' and *. . . con unos cuantos amigos de Barcelona* '. . . with *a few* friends from Barcelona' may mean slightly different things, as they do in English.

(d) *Algunos/unos cuantos* are interchangeable in the meaning of 'a few' when they do not appear before a noun: *—¿Tienes monedas de cinco pesetas? —Algunas/unas cuantas* '"Have you got any 5-pesetas coins?" "A few."'.

9.5 *Ambos*: adjective marked for number and gender

'Both', though it is rather literary and *los/las dos* usually replaces it in speech.

en ambos/los dos casos	in both cases
¿Cuál de los dos es correcto? Ambos/Los dos	Which of the two is correct? Both

9.6 *Cada*: invariable

'Each', 'every'. *Cada* always precedes the noun:

Cada loco con su tema	'Each to his own' (lit. 'every madman with his obsession')
un libro por cada tres alumnos	one book for every three students
No puedes estar molestando a la gente cada dos por tres	You can't keep bothering people every two minutes

Notes

(i) *Cada vez más/menos* usually translate 'more and more' and 'less and less': *Es cada vez más complicado* 'It gets more and more complicated', *Era cada vez menos generosa* 'She was less and less generous'.

(ii) In familiar speech, *cada* roughly means 'all sorts of . . .': *Dice cada tontería* 'The nonsense he talks . . .', *Hay cada ladrón por ahí* 'There are all sorts of thieves around there', *¡Me hace usted cada pregunta!* (S. Pitol, Mexico, dialogue) 'The questions you ask me!'.

(iii) 'Each one', 'each person': *Que cada uno* (or *cada cual/cada quien*) *haga la lectura que le parezca conveniente* 'Let each person read it as it suits him/her'.

(iv) *?Me baño cada día* or *?voy cada mañana* for *. . . todos los días, . . . todas las mañanas* are said to be spreading, but are rejected by careful speakers.

9.7 *Cierto*: adjective, marked for number and gender

'Certain' i.e. 'specific'. Used thus it precedes the noun:

en ciertos casos	in certain cases
cierto alemán	a certain German
en cierta novela suya	in a certain novel of his

Determinado is a more formal synonym: *En determinados trenes existe un servicio de camareros* 'On certain trains waiter service is provided'.

Notes
(i) *Un cierto/una cierta* for 'a certain' are sometimes condemned as Gallicisms or Anglicisms, but are very common in all styles. *Un cierto* is found before partitive nouns – *Yo era consciente de (una) cierta tendencia suya a exagerar* 'I was aware of a certain tendency of his to exaggerate' – and as a colloquial alternative to *un tal*: *Se casó con un cierto Dionisio de México* 'She married a certain Dionisio from Mexico'.
(ii) Placed after the noun *cierto* means 'fixed'/'accurate': *Hemos tenido noticias ciertas de otro enfrentamiento en la frontera* 'We have received accurate reports of another frontier clash'.

9.8 *Cualquier, cualquiera, cualesquiera*: adjective/pronoun, marked for number

As an adjective 'any'; as a pronoun 'anybody'/'any one' (French *n'importe quel*).
(a) As an adjective:
   Before any noun or noun phrase, the *a* of *cualquiera* (but not usually of *cualesquiera*), is dropped: *en cualquier momento* 'at any moment', *cualquier mujer* 'any woman', *en cualquier triste pueblo andino* 'in any wretched village of the Andes'.
   However, the plural adjective *cualesquiera* is nowadays normally expressed by the singular since the meaning is almost the same: *cualquier mujer que no simpatice con el feminismo* . . . 'any woman who doesn't/any women who don't sympathize with feminism . . .'.
   Cualquier(a) normally precedes the noun. The idea of random choice is strengthened if it is put after the noun, cf. English 'any at all'. When used thus of people the effect is often pejorative, as is the English 'any old':

Vamos a pasear por una calle cualquiera	Let's just walk down any street
Su esposa no es una mujer cualquiera	His wife isn't just any woman (i.e. she is rather special)

Note
Cualquiera before a feminine noun is an occasional and doubtful colloquial variant, cf. *?de cualquiera manera* (dialogue in C. Fuentes, Mexico), *?y más malvados que cualquiera otra tribu* (M. Vargas Llosa, Peru, dialogue) 'and more wicked than any other tribe'. It is, however, attested in Ortega y Gasset, Valera and a few other pre-mid 20th-century stylists.

(b) As a pronoun:
   The final *-a* is always retained. The plural *cualesquiera* is hardly used in speech and is disappearing even in writing:

Puede usted elegir cualquiera de estos tres modelos	You can choose any one of these three models

Cualquiera diría que eres un millonario	Anybody would think you're a millionaire
Eso lo sabe cualquiera	Anyone knows that
Se les garantiza plaza escolar a sus hijos cualquiera que sean sus estudios (El País – singular for plural)	Their children are guaranteed schoolplaces, whatever their studies (i.e. whatever they have studied)
Cualesquiera que sean las dificultades, cualesquiera que sean los desafíos en el camino de la construcción del comunismo . . . (Fidel Castro, speech)	Whatever the difficulties, whatever the challenges along the path to the building of Communism . . .

9.9 *Demasiado*: adjective marked for number and gender, or invariable adverb

As an adjective 'too many'/'too much'; as an adverb 'too', 'too well'.
(a) Used as an adjective, it must agree in number and gender:

No (le) conviene al trigo que caiga demasiada lluvia	It isn't good for the wheat for too much rain to fall
Esto ha sucedido en demasiados casos	This has happened in too many cases
Llévate un poco de carne – has traído demasiada	Take away a bit of meat – you've brought too much
Has traído demasiados pocos tornillos (*demasiado* is treated as an adjective before *poco*)	You've brought too few screws

Nowadays *demasiado* is always placed before the noun.
(b) As an adverb (invariable in form):

Tú hablas demasiado	You talk too much
A ése/ese me lo conozco demasiado	I know him only too well

9.10 *Medio*

In standard Peninsular usage this word functions as an adverb (invariable in form) or as an adjective (inflected for number and gender), both meaning 'half':

Están medio borrachos	They're half drunk
La recogieron medio muerta	They picked her up half dead
media pinta/media luna	half a pint/half moon
media hora	half an hour

In Latin America is often used to mean 'rather', 'pretty' as in *Es medio linda* 'She's rather attractive'/'pretty good-looking', *Son medio tontos* 'They're pretty stupid'.

In Galicia and throughout Latin America there is a widespread colloquial tendency to make the adverb agree in gender: *Ella es media loca* 'She's half crazy', for *medio loca*, *Es media chiquita la casa* (Spain *Es bastante pequeña*) 'The house is pretty small', *Llegó media desilusionada* (popular Mexican, quoted Kany, 55) 'She arrived pretty disillusioned'.

9.11 *Mismo* (and Latin-American variants): adjective, marked for gender and number

(a) 'The same'

When it means 'the same' it is always placed before any noun or noun phrase that it qualifies:

Lleváis la misma blusa	You're wearing the same blouse
Estos dos casos son el mismo	These two cases are the same (i.e. identical)
Estos dos son los mismos	These two are the same (i.e. as before)
—¿Es usted don Francisco? —El mismo	'Are you Don Francisco?' 'I am indeed' (lit. 'the same')

Notes

(i) *Lo mismo* may mean *la misma cosa*, or it may be adverbial. *Lo mismo* is heard in familiar European Spanish with the meaning 'perhaps': *Como me vuelvan a decir lo mismo/la misma cosa . . .* 'If they say the same thing to me again . . .', *No nos divertimos lo mismo que si hubieras estado tú* 'We didn't have such a good time as we would have if you'd been there', *Lo mismo te da una propina* 'Maybe he'll give you a tip'.

*Lo mismo como is substandard for *lo mismo que*.

(ii) The following should be noted: *Esa casa es lo mismo que (igual que) aquélla/aquella* 'That house is the same as that other one' (i.e. the same is true of it), *Esa casa es la misma que compró Agustín* 'That house is the same one that Agustín bought'.

(b) Placed either before or after a noun, but always after a pronoun, *mismo* means 'selfsame'/'very'/'right':

Vivo en Madrid mismo/en el mismo Madrid	I live in Madrid itself
Aparca el helicóptero en su mismo jardín/su jardín mismo	He parks the helicopter right in his garden

If there is danger of ambiguity, *mismo* must be placed after the noun if it means 'very', 'selfsame': *el mismo Papa* 'the Pope himself' or 'the same Pope', *el Papa mismo* = only 'the Pope himself'.

Propio (see 9.14b) means the same as *mismo* in this sense, but it is not used with pronouns.

(c) Placed after a pronoun it adds emphasis e.g. *yo mismo* 'I myself', *ella misma* 'she . . . herself':

—¿Quién construyó el chalet?[1] —Yo mismo/misma	'Who built the house?' 'I did myself'

(d) Placed after an adverb or adverbial phrase, *mismo* is itself an adverb and is therefore invariable:

por eso mismo	for that very reason
ahora mismo/ya mismo	right now/right away
aquí mismo	right here

But if the adverbial phrase contains a noun not accompanied by the definite article, *mismo* may or may not agree with it (Seco (1992), 262, recommends agreement):

esta noche mismo/misma	this very night
Vino esta mañana mismo/misma	It came this very morning

---

[1] *El chalet* (Spain) 'detached house.'

En España mismo/misma no se pudo evitar la In Spain itself it was impossible to
llegada del bikini prevent the arrival of the bikini

However, if the definite article is present, *mismo* is an adjective and must agree in number and gender: *Lo descubrieron en la chimenea misma* 'They found it in the chimney itself'.

Notes
(i) *Mismísimo* is a colloquial emphatic form of *mismo* in sense **(b)**: *El mismísimo presidente le/lo felicitó* 'The President himself congratulated him'.
(ii) Mexican and Central-American spontaneous speech often uses *mero* in contexts under **(b)**: *en la mera (misma) esquina* 'right on the corner', *Lo hizo él mero (él mismo)* 'He did it himself', *ya mero (ahora mismo)* 'right now'.
   In various parts of Latin America, from Chile to Mexico, *puro* may be used in the same way: *en la pura cabeza (en la misma cabeza)* 'right on the head', etc. (from Kany, 57ff).[2]
(iii) *Mismamente* (= *igual*) is rustic or jocular.

9.12 *Mucho* and *poco*: adjectives, marked for number and gender, or invariable adverbs

(a) Adjectival uses:

Mis hijos no me hacen mucho caso My children don't pay much attention to me
En el patio hay muchos limoneros There are a lot of lemon trees in the patio
Pon poca pimienta Don't put much pepper on/in it
Somos muchos/pocos There are a lot/not many of us
Lo poco gusta, lo mucho cansa Brevity is the soul of wit (lit. 'little pleases, much tires')

Note
In the following sentences *mucho* and *poco* do not agree with the preceding noun, but refer to the general idea underlying the sentence: *¿Trescientos mil dólares? Es mucho* '300,000 dollars? It's a lot', *¿Mil cajas de ciruelas? Es poco* '1000 boxes of plums? That's not much'. Compare *Mil cajas para cien días son pocas* '1000 boxes for 100 days isn't/aren't a lot' and *Setenta libros por estante son muchos* '70 books to a shelf is/are a lot'.

(b) Adverbial uses:

Estoy añorando mucho mi patria I'm missing my home country a lot
Sale poco últimamente He hasn't been out much lately
Por mucho que te quejes . . . However much you complain . . .
Por poco que lo quieras However little you want it . . .
No sabes lo poco que me gusta ese hombre You don't know how little I like that man

Notes
(i) Before *más, menos, mayor* and *menor*, when these are followed by a noun (present or implied), *mucho* or *poco* are adjectives and must agree in number and gender – a fact that English-speakers are prone to forget: *Tienen muchos más hijos que tú/tienen muchos más que tú* 'They have many more children than you/They have many more than you', *No en balde han transcurrido 27 años, hay mucha más experiencia, mucha más*

---

[2] *Puro* may be used adverbially in some Latin-American countries, cf. *a puro Villa* (announcement by a bus-driver in Tabasco, Mexico) '(I'm going) only to Villahermosa', Spain *sólo/solo a . . . .* Also *Había puras mujeres* (colloquial Chilean, informant) 'There were only women there' (Spain *No había más que mujeres*).

madurez (Fidel Castro, Cuba) 'Twenty-seven years have not passed in vain, there is much more experience, much more maturity'.

But before adjectives and adverbs, *mucho* and *poco* are adverbs and invariable in form: *Los problemas eran mucho mayores* 'The problems were much greater'.

For further examples see 5.10.

(ii) *Muy* 'very' can be thought of as a shortened form of *mucho*, used before adjectives and adverbs. The full form therefore reappears when it is used alone: —*¿Es laborioso?* —*Mucho*. '"Is he hard-working?" "Very"'.

(iii) *Poco* negates an adjective: *poco frecuente* = *no frecuente*: *Estoy poco acostumbrado al trabajo manual* 'I'm not used to manual labour', *El argumento es poco convincente* 'The argument is unconvincing', *Es poco más honrado de lo que tú dices* 'He is no more honest than you say'.

Compare *Es **un** poco más honrado de lo que tú dices* 'He's a bit more honest than you say'.

(iv) 'Very much' = *muchísimo*. *Muy mucho* is archaic or jocular.

(v) *Un poco de* is invariable, but phrases like ?*una poca de sal* 'a bit of salt' are heard in very popular or jocular speech.

9.13 *Otro*: adjective/pronoun, marked for number and gender

Adjectivally 'other'/'another'; pronominally 'another one'/'others':

Otra persona no te creería	Another person wouldn't believe you
Ponle otro sello (Lat. Am. *estampilla*)	Put another stamp on it
por otra parte . . .	on the other hand . . .
En circunstancias otras que aquellas en que . . .	In circumstances other than those in which . . .
El que lo hizo fue otro	The one who did it was someone else
Hay quienes ven la vida lógica y ordenada, otros la sabemos absurda y confusa (G. Cabrera Infante, Cuba, dialogue)	There are some who see life as logical and ordered, others of us know it s absurd and confused

Notes

(i) **Un otro* 'another' (French *un autre*, Catalan *un altre*) is not Spanish: *Dame otro* – 'Give me another'.

(ii) The possessives *mi, tu, su, nuestro, vuestro* precede *otro*, but other adjectives follow it, although *mucho* may appear in either position: *tu otro pantalón* 'your other trousers', *Sé que estoy manipulada como otra mucha gente* (interview in *Cambio16*, also *mucha otra* . . .) 'I know I'm being manipulated like a lot of other people', . . . *cosa que sólo celebraron Carmen Serdán y otras cuatro maestras* (A. Mastretta, Mexico, dialogue) 'something that only Carmen Serdán and four other women teachers greeted enthusiastically', *en otros pocos casos* (cf. *en pocos otros casos* 'in not many other cases'), 'in a few other cases', *otras dos Coca Colas* 'two more Coca Colas'.

(iii) *Los/las demás* may be a synonym of *los otros/las otras* if the latter means 'the rest'/'the remaining': *el resto de los/los otros/los demás países europeos* 'the other European countries'.

9.14 *Propio*: adjective, marked for number and gender

(a) Usually it means 'own', as in:

mi propio taxi	my own taxi
tus propias convicciones	your own convictions
Tiene chófer propio	He has his own driver
Es suyo propio	It's his own
Intentar comprender su realidad es comprender mejor la tuya propia (Queen Sofía of Spain, quoted in *El País*)	Trying to understand their [i.e. artists'] reality is to understand better your own

(b) 'Selfsame', 'very', etc. (same as *mismo* at 9.11b.):

Las tachaduras son del propio autor	The crossing out is by the author himself
Nos dio audiencia el propio obispo	The Bishop himself granted us an audience

(c) 'Appropriate', 'right', 'peculiar', 'characteristic':

Ese lenguaje no es propio de un diplomático	That language is not suitable for a diplomat
Es propio de ella llegar tres horas tarde	It's just like her to arrive three hours late

9.15 *Solo*: adjective, marked for number and gender; *sólo*: invariable adverb

The adjective means 'alone', the adverb means 'only'. The adverb used always to be distinguished by the written accent, but the Academy's *Nuevas normas* of 1959 decree that an accent is now necessary only to avoid ambiguity, so one may legitimately now write *solo tres* or *sólo tres* for 'only three'. Nearly thirty years later most editors still follow the old rules and there is much inconsistency.

Ambiguity is only possible with the masculine singular adjective, e.g. *un hombre solo/un hombre sólo* 'a man alone/only one man' *solo en casa/sólo en casa* 'alone in the house/only at home'. *Solamente* is an unambiguous equivalent of *sólo*.

(a) Adjectival uses:

No renunciaré, aunque todos ustedes dimitan y yo me quede solo	I won't give up, even if all of you resign and I am left alone
Usted sola no podrá hacerlo	You (fem.) won't be able to manage it alone
El solo anuncio de su llegada ha despertado una avalancha de protestas	The mere announcement of his arrival has aroused an avalanche of protests
dos cafés solos	two black coffees
(cf. *dos cafés sólo*	only two coffees)

(b) Adverbial examples:

Millones de personas disfrutan de la luz eléctrica con sólo/solo accionar un simple conmutador	Millions of people enjoy electric light merely at the press of a switch
Sólo/Solo así se solucionarán estos problemas	Only in this way will these problems be solved

Notes
(i) A negative + *más . . . que* is a common way of translating 'only' (cf. French *ne . . . que . . .*): *No hizo más que reírse* 'All he did was laugh', *No piensa más que en sí misma* 'She only thinks of herself'.

Más que must not be confused with *más de*. The latter is used with numerical values and means 'more than'. See 5.5 for discussion.

(ii) *A solas* strictly means 'alone' (i.e. unaccompanied), and is occasionally required for the sake of clarity, e.g. *Lo solucionó a solas* 'He solved it alone (no one else present)', *Lo solucionó solo* 'He solved it alone' (without help).

A solas cannot be used of inanimate things. In sentences like *Estuvo a solas con sus pensamientos* 'He was alone with his thoughts', it is an elegant, rather poetic alternative to *solo*.

(iii) Translating 'the only . . .', 'the only one . . .', 'his only', etc. *Único* is required if no noun follows: *Él es el único que sabe conducir* 'He's the only one who can drive',

Lo único es que no sé nadar 'The only thing is I can't swim', *Es hijo único* 'He's an only child'.

But *el único/solo ser por quien deseo vivir* 'the only person I want to live for', *Son el único/solo sustento del gobierno* 'They're the government's only support'.

9.16 *Tanto*: adjective, marked for number and gender; or invariable adverb

For the use of *tanto* and *tan* in comparisons see 5.15.1.

These words basically mean 'so much', 'so many' (French *tant de*):

(a) As an adjective it must agree in number and gender:

Se me fue el santo al cielo de tanto hablar (adverbially, *de hablar tanto*)	I clean forgot from so much talking (lit. 'my Saint went up to Heaven with so much talking')
Te he advertido tantas veces	I've warned you so many times
No creí que se atrevería a tanto	I didn't think he would be that daring
Cobran un tanto por ciento de comisión	They take a certain percent as commission

(b) As an adverb it is invariable in form:

—*Hay más de tres kilos.* —*¡No tanto!*	There are more than three kilos. Not that much!
Corrió tanto que no podía hablar	He ran so much that he couldn't speak
Tanto era así que . . . (see note (ii) for *?tan era así...*).	So much was it so, that . . .
Tanto mejor/tanto peor para ellos	All the better/so much the worse for them
La rana es tanto un plato favorito de los franceses como buena presa para las serpientes	The frog is both a favourite dish of the French and a good prey for snakes

Notes

(i) Before adjectives or adverbs, *tan* is required: *Usted ha sido tan acogedor* 'You've been so welcoming', *Se levanta tan de mañana que nadie le/lo ve salir* 'He gets up so early in the morning that no one sees him leave', *Lo hizo tan de pronto* 'He did it so suddenly', *tan a propósito* 'so much on purpose'/'so relevantly', *tan inteligentemente* 'so intelligently'.

Mejor, peor, mayor and *menor* are exceptions: *tanto mejor/peor para usted* 'so much the better/worse for you', *El peligro era tanto mayor debido a la radiactividad* 'The danger was so much greater due to radioactivity'.

(ii) *?Tan es así*, *?tan se conocían*, for *tanto es así* or *tanto se conocían*, are considered substandard in Spain but are found in Latin-American speech and writing.

(iii) *Tanto* plus a singular noun is a colloquial expression for 'lots of', 'so many': *Hay tanto ricacho por aquí* 'There are loads of stinking rich people round here'.

(v) *Tanto . . . que* for 'as much as' is not Spanish: *No viaja tanto como tú* 'He doesn't travel as much as you'. For further details on *tanto* in comparisons see 5.15.1.

9.17 *Todo*: adjective/pronoun, marked for number and gender

'All', 'every', 'the whole of', 'any':

(a) When it is not followed by *un* or *el* it usually means 'every' or 'any':

todo producto alimenticio que contenga colorantes artificiales . . .	any food product containing artificial colouring . . .
todo español sabe que . . .	every Spaniard knows that . . .
en todo caso	in any case

In all these cases *cualquier* could replace *todo*.

(b) With the definite article, possessives or demonstratives, or before proper names it usually translates 'the whole of'/'all':

toda la noche	all night
todos los griegos	all (the) Greeks
todos los cinco	all five of them
Todo aquel febrero no paró de llover	All that February it didn't stop raining
Todo Barcelona habla de ello (See 1.4.7, note, for the gender of *todo* in this example)	All Barcelona's talking about it

(c) With definite article and periods of time, 'every':

El fontanero (Lat. Am. *plomero*) *viene todos los meses*	The plumber comes every/once a month
todos los viernes/años	every Friday/year

Notes

(i) *Cada* must be used if the actions are new ones rather than repetitions, or when the period of time is preceded by a number: *Cada día sale con una chica nueva* 'Every day he goes out with a new girl,' *Cada diez minutos sale con alguna nueva burrada* 'Every ten minutes he comes out with some new nonsense', *tres gotas cada cuatro horas* 'three drops every four hours'.

(ii) Moliner, II, 1330, notes that *al* . . . is more elegant than *todos los* . . . when describing rate or quantity per period of time: *Se fuma cuatro paquetes al día* 'He smokes four packets a day', *Lee un par de novelas a la semana* 'He reads a couple of novels a week', etc.

(iii) *Cuanto* may be used to translate 'absolutely every': *No es cosa de obligar a leer cuanto libro se ha escrito* (E. Sábato, Argentina, interview) 'It's not a question of obliging people to read every book that was ever written'.

Cuanto is not used thus in phrases like *todos los días* 'every day'. *Cuanto* or *todo cuanto* may also translate 'absolutely everything': *Heredó de él una tremenda bronca a (todo) cuanto sonara a autoridad* (L. Sepúlveda, Chile)[3] 'He inherited from him a tremendous rage against everything that sounded like authority'.

(d) Pronominally, the singular means 'everything', the plural 'everyone'/'everybody'/'all of them': *Se enfada por todo* 'He gets cross about everything', *Es todo propaganda* 'It's all propaganda'.

—*¿Dónde están las fresas?*	'Where are the strawberries?'
—*Me las he comido todas*	'I've eaten them all'

Note

After a neuter *todo* – as after all singular nouns and pronouns – Spanish makes the verb *ser* (and one or two others) agree with a following plural noun: *Todo son mentiras* 'It's all lies', *Con nuestro nuevo plan de ahorros, todo son ventajas* 'With our new savings plan it's all advantages'. See 2.3.3 for further discussion.

(e) Agreement of *todo* should be noted in the following examples:

Su cara era toda pecas	Her face was all freckles
El cielo era todo nubes	The sky was all clouds
Esa niña es toda ojos (from Moliner, II, 1930)	That girl's all eyes

---

[3] *Bronca* means 'row'/'dispute' outside the Southern Cone.

But the adverbial *todo* is not uncommon in this construction: *Estas chuletas son todo hueso* 'These chops are all bone', *Tu amiga es todo sonrisas esta mañana* 'Your friend's all smiles this morning'.

(f) Relative clauses involving *todo*

The following sentences, many inspired by Hammer (1971), 189, illustrate some translation problems:

todos los que dicen eso	all who say that
todo el que diga eso/todo aquel que diga eso (latter is literary)	anyone who says that
Todo lo que escribe es bueno	Everything he writes is good
Cuanto/todo cuanto escribe es bueno (literary)	Everything he writes is good
Este poeta, cuyas palabras todas quedarán grabadas en nuestro corazón . . .	This poet, whose every word will remain engraved on our hearts . . .
El césped, por toda cuya superficie crecían malas hierbas . . .	The lawn, over whose entire surface weeds were growing . . .
Esta ciudad, de la que conozco todas las iglesias . . .	This city, all of whose churches I know . . .
Estas novelas, todas las cuales he leído . . .	These novels, all of which I have read . . .
Estos niños, los padres de todos los cuales yo conozco . . .	These children, all of whose parents I know . . .
Estas páginas, escritas todas ellas en japonés . . .	These pages, all of which are written in Japanese . . .
El palacio, del que no hay habitación que yo no haya visitado . . .	The palace, all of whose rooms I have visited . . .

Notes

(i) *Todo* occasionally follows the noun in flowery styles: *El cielo todo estaba sembrado de estrellas* 'The whole sky was strewn with stars', *El mundo todo le parecía un jardín encantado* 'The whole world seemed to him an enchanted garden'.

(ii) *Todo el mundo* (singular agreement) is a set phrase meaning 'everybody'.

(iii) *Todo* followed by the indefinite article usually translates 'a whole . . .': *Se comió toda una tarta de melocotones* 'He ate a whole peach tart', *Hubo toda una serie de malentendidos* 'There was a whole series of misunderstandings'.

9.18 *Varios*: adjective, marked for number and gender

(a) 'Several', in which case it normally – but not invariably – precedes the noun:

en varias partes del país	in several parts of the country
Mis motivos son varios	My motives are several

(b) 'Various', 'varied' (usually follows the noun):

flores de colores varios	flowers of various colours
La fauna de esta zona es muy varia/variada	The fauna of this zone is very varied

Note

Translating 'various': *en **diversas** ocasiones* 'on various occasions', *en **diferentes** puntos de los Andes* 'in various places in the Andes'.

10

Numerals

Spanish numerals are neither complex nor plagued with exceptions, although this regularity makes the three unexpected forms *quinientos* 500 (**not** **cinco cientos*), *setecientos* 700 (**not** **sietecientos*), and *novecientos* 900 (**not** **nuevecientos*) much easier to forget. Also easily forgotten is the rule that 16-19 and 21-29 are written as one word, whereas the other numbers joined by *y* are not.

10.1 Cardinal numbers

Spanish cardinal numerals are invariable in form, with the important exceptions of *uno* 'one' and *cientos* 'hundreds', which agree in gender with the noun counted.

The ordinal numbers above *décimo* 'tenth' are usually avoided in informal language and are replaced by the corresponding cardinal numbers. See 10.12.2.

0 *cero*	11 *once*	22 *veintidós*	40 *cuarenta*
1 *uno/una*	12 *doce*	23 *veintitrés*	50 *cincuenta*
2 *dos*	13 *trece*	24 *veinticuatro*	60 *sesenta*
3 *tres*	14 *catorce*	25 *veinticinco*	70 *setenta*
4 *cuatro*	15 *quince*	26 *veintiséis*	80 *ochenta*
5 *cinco*	16 *dieciséis*	27 *veintisiete*	90 *noventa*
6 *seis*	17 *diecisiete*	28 *veintiocho*	100 *cien/ciento*
7 *siete*	18 *dieciocho*	29 *veintinueve*	101 *ciento uno/una*
8 *ocho*	19 *diecinueve*	30 *treinta*	102 *ciento dos*
9 *nueve*	20 *veinte*	31 *treinta y uno/una*	
10 *diez*	21 *veintiuno/a*	32 *treinta y dos*	

185	*ciento ochenta y cinco*
200	*docientos/doscientas*
205	*doscientos cinco/doscientas cinco*
300	*trescientos/trescientas*
357	*trescientos cincuenta y siete/trescientas cincuenta y siete*
400	*cuatrocientos/cuatrocientas*
500	***quinientos/quinientas***
600	*seiscientos/seiscientas*
700	*setecientos/setecientas*
800	*ochocientos/ochocientas*
900	*novecientos/novecientas*
1000	*mil*
1006	*mil seis* (but see note (iv) for *mil y uno/una* 1001)
1107	*mil ciento siete*
1998	*mil novecientos/as noventa y ocho*
2022	*dos mil veintidós*

5000	*cinco mil*
10.000	*diez mil*
500.014	*quinientos/as mil catorce*
936.257	*novecientos/as treinta y seis mil doscientos/as cincuenta y siete*
1.000.000	*un millón*
100.000.000	*cien millones*
$1.000.000	*un millón de dólares*
7.678.456	*ptas: siete millones seiscientas setenta y ocho mil cuatrocientas cincuenta y seis pesetas*
1.000.000.000.000	*un billón*[1]

Notes

(i) 16-19 and 21-29 are rather arbitrarily written as one word, as are 200, 300, 400, 500, 600, 700, 800, 900. Forms like *diez y seis* for *dieciséis* are old-fashioned.

(ii) *Uno* is not used before *ciento* and *mil* except in rare cases of ambiguity: *Hay ciento veinte coches* 'There are 120 cars', *más de mil colegios equipados con televisores en color* 'more than one thousand schools equipped with colour television', but –

*trescientos/as **un** mil ochenta y cuatro*	*301.084*
trescientos/as mil ochenta y cuatro	*300.084*

(iii) A comma separates decimals: *3,05* = our 3.05, and a point is used to separate thousands: *19.000 dólares* = *$19,000*; but Mexico follows our conventions and Cuba writes 10 000 for ten thousand. Typists often write years with a point, e.g. *1.998*, but the best authorities condemn this.

(iv) Seco (1992), 369, notes that *mil y uno* 'a thousand and one' comes from the famous stories *Las mil y una noches* 'A Thousand and One Nights' and is correct only in the vague sense of 'a lot', cf. *Es sólo un ejemplo de los mil y un casos de todos los días* (*El País*, quoted Gerboin and Leroy (1991), 91) 'It's only one example among the thousand and one cases of every day'.

However, the form . . . *y uno* is commonly used in speech after thousands: *mil y una pesetas* '1001 pesetas', *tres mil y un dólares* '3001 dollars'. Theoretically correct forms like *mil una pesetas* are confined to formal writing.

(v) Certain forms ending in *-ón* are used pejoratively to refer to people of a specific age: *un cuarentón* 'a forty-year old man', *un cincuentón* 'a fifty-year old', *una sesentona* 'a sixty-year old woman'.

10.2 Gender of numbers

Numbers, unlike letters of the alphabet, are masculine:

Yo puse un siete, no un nueve	I put a 7, not a 9
un cinco de bastos	a five of clubs
Tú eres el cinco	You're number five

This is also true of *cientos* and *miles* when they are used as nouns (i.e. when they are followed by *de*):

los miles de víctimas	the thousands of victims
los escasos cientos de personas que asistían	the few hundred persons present

Note

In informal styles *miles de* is quite often made to agree with a following feminine noun: *La acumulación de los plaguicidas es un continuo peligro de envenenamiento para **las** miles de aves* (*La Vanguardia*, Spain) 'The accumulation of pesticides represents (lit.

---

[1] *Un billón* is a million million – as everywhere except in the English-speaking world.

'is') a continual threat of poisoning for the thousands of birds'. *Los miles de aves* is recommended.

10.3 Agreement of *uno* and the hundreds

Uno and *cientos* (but not *ciento/cien*) must agree in gender with the noun counted – a rule constantly overlooked by foreign students:

un peso/una peseta	one peso/one peseta
veintiuna pesetas	twenty-one pesetas
quinientos dólares	five hundred dollars
setecientas libras	seven hundred pounds
en la página quinientas catorce	on page 514
Yo duermo en la cuatrocientas (*habitación* omitted)	I'm sleeping in (room) 400

Note

Tens plus a thousand (21,000, 31,000, 41,000, etc.) are problematic. Logically one should say *veintiuna mil pesetas/mujeres* '21,000 pesetas/women' since the nouns are feminine and *mil* is in this case an adjective, not a masculine noun. However, forms like *veintiún mil pesetas*, *treinta y un mil mujeres* '31,000 women', etc., are in fact in general use and most speakers will not accept *veintiuna/treinta y una mil*.

With hundreds the expected gender agreement must be used: *doscientas mil pesetas* '200,000 ptas', never **doscientos mil pesetas*.

10.4 Millions

Millón is a masculine noun and is connected by *de* to a following noun or noun phrase:

. . . *una inversión global de más de 6.000 millones de pesetas, de los que mil millones se invertirán el próximo año* (*El País*)	. . . an overall investment of more than 6,000 million ptas of which 1,000 million will be invested next year

Un millón is a collective noun and a following adjective or verb must agree accordingly: *El millón y medio restante fue invertido* . . . 'The remaining million and a half were/was invested . . .'. See 2.3.1 for details.

10.5 *Un* or *uno*?

Uno loses its final vowel before a masculine noun or noun phrase, as does *una* before nouns beginning with stressed *a-* or *ha-*. *Veintiuno* is shortened to *veintiún* in the same contexts:

un tigre, dos tigres, tres tigres	one tiger, two tigers, three tigers (a tongue-twister)
veintiún mil hombres	21,000 men
veintiún mil mujeres (see note to 10.3)	21,000 women
un águila, veintiún armas, treinta y un hachas	one eagle, 21 weapons, 31 axes

In the following examples the final vowel is retained since the numeral does not precede a noun:

No hay más que veintiuno	There are only twenty-one
párrafo ciento uno	paragraph 101
Inglaterra, país tradicional de los fantasmas, ve uno nuevo por sus calles (*Cambio16*, Spain)	England, the traditional land of ghosts, is witnessing a new one in its streets

10.6 *Cien* or *ciento*?

Ciento is shortened to *cien* before another numeral which it multiplies, or before a noun or noun phrase:

cien mil bolívares	100,000 bolivares
cien millones	100 million
cien buenas razones	100 good reasons
but	
ciento once	one hundred and eleven
en la página ciento dieciocho	on page one hundred and eighteen

The old rule (still respected by some purists and by some older speakers in Spain) was that *ciento* should be used when the number stands alone:

— ¿Cuántos son? — Ciento	'How many are there?' 'A hundred'
Vendimos más de ciento	We sold over a hundred

But this rule is completely obsolete in Latin America and virtually extinct in Spain:

Yo vivo en el cien	I live in number 100
Pues faltan cien o sobran cincuenta	Well, there are either a hundred missing
(A. Mastretta, Mexico, dialogue)	or fifty too many

However, *ciento* is used in percentages: see 10.7.

10.7 Expression of percentages

Ciento is used with all numbers, although the phrase *cien por cien* 'one hundred per cent' is also found for *ciento por ciento*.

Forms like *cincuenta por cien*, *diez por cien* are heard colloquially in Latin America (and occasionally in Spain), but . . . *por ciento* is used in writing on both continents:

El PCE sólo obtuvo el 8 y pico por ciento de los votos (El País)	The Spanish Communist Party only obtained slightly more than 8 per cent of the votes
. . . el costo de la construcción creció el 0,7 por ciento (La Nación, Argentina)	building costs rose 0.7 per cent
. . . la seguridad, cien por cien, de que los vertidos son inocuos (El País)	. . . the hundred per cent certainty that the material to be dumped is harmless

10.8 Collective numerals

There is a series of collective numerals, cf. our 'score', sometimes used to express approximate quantities:

un par de veces	a couple of times
una decena	ten
una docena	a dozen (used less in Spanish)
una veintena	a score/about twenty
la cuarentena	about forty/quarantine
una cincuentena	about fifty
un centenar	about a hundred
un millar	about a thousand

Notes

(i) *Cuatro* is used colloquially in Spain, Mexico and no doubt elsewhere to mean 'a couple'/'a handful': *No hay más que cuatro gatos* 'There's not a soul about' (lit. '. . . only four cats about'), *No son más que cuatro desgraciados los que ponen las pegatinas fascistas* 'It's only a handful of wretches who put up fascist stickers'.

(ii) *Centenar* and *millar* are used for expressing rate: *mil dólares el centenar/millar* '1000 dollars the hundred/the thousand' (or, more colloquially, . . . *cada cien/por cada cien, cada mil*).

(iii) Like all collective nouns, collective numerals are often treated as singular: *Una veintena de casas se ordenaba formando una calle frente al río* (L. Sepúlveda, Chile) 'A score of houses were laid out to form a street in front of the river'. See 2.3.1 for further remarks on agreement with collective nouns.

10.9 Mathematical expressions

Dos y tres son cinco	Two plus three equals five
Dos por tres son seis	Two times three equals six
Ocho dividido por dos son cuatro	Eight divided by two equals four
(sometimes *ocho entre dos* . . .)	
Once menos nueve son dos	Eleven minus nine equals two
Tres es la raíz cuadrada de nueve	Three is the square root of nine
Nueve es el cuadrado de tres	Nine is three squared
Forma un cuadrado de diez metros	It's 10 metres square
dos metros cuadrados	Two square metres

The division sign is a colon, e.g. $3:6 = 0,5$ (*tres dividido por seis son cero coma cinco*) '$3/6 = 0.5$'.

10.10 Fractions

1/2 *una mitad*	1/5 *un quinto*
1/3 *un tercio*	3/7 *tres séptimos*
2/3 *dos tercios*	7/10 *siete décimos*
1/4 *un cuarto*	

For fractions based on larger numbers, the masculine or the feminine of the ordinal form may be used (the feminine form agrees with the word *parte* 'part', deleted):

un centésimo/una centésima	a hundredth
un milésimo/una milésima	a thousandth
un millonésimo/una millonésima	a millionth
A partir de la primera cienmilésima de	After the first one hundred thousandth of
segundo, el Universo empieza a cobrar un	a second the Universe begins to take on
aspecto conocido (*ABC*, Spain)	a familiar appearance

Forms ending in *-avo* are also found in technical and mathematical language: *cuatro quinceavos* 'four fifteenths', *tres cincuentavos* 'three fiftieths'. These forms should not be used as ordinal numbers. See 10.12.2 for discussion.

La tercera parte 'a third', *la quinta parte* 'a fifth', *la décima parte* 'a tenth', etc. are normally used in non-mathematical contexts: *la tercera parte de los accidentes de tráfico* 'a third of traffic accidents'.

10.11 Articles with numbers

Certain common numerical expressions, especially percentages, usually appear with the article. This is particularly true when the numerical value is preceded by a preposition:

Vivo en el cinco	I live in number 5
La inflación ha subido en un tres por ciento	Inflation has risen by 3 per cent
El porcentaje de éxito llega al 70 por ciento	The success rate reaches 70%

But *Ha costado entre tres mil y cinco mil ptas* 'It cost between 3,000 and 5,000 ptas'.

10.12 Ordinal numbers

10.12.1 Ordinals 'first' to 'tenth'

Ordinals agree in number and gender: *el quinto libro/la quinta casa* 'the fifth book'/'the fifth house'. Ordinals 1st–10th are in everyday use, but the cardinals encroach even on them in phrases like *el siglo nueve/noveno* 'the ninth century', *Alfonso diez/décimo* 'Alfonso the tenth', the ordinal being considered more correct:

primer(o)	first	*sexto*	sixth
segundo	second	*séptimo/sétimo*	seventh
tercer(o)	third	*octavo*	eighth
cuarto	fourth	*noveno*	ninth
quinto	fifth	*décimo*	tenth

Examples:

el tercer hombre	the third man
Carlos III (tercero)	Charles III
Fernando VII (séptimo)	Ferdinand VII
la tercera vez	the third time
el siglo décimo/diez	the tenth century

Notes
(i) *Primero* and *tercero* lose their final vowel before a masculine singular noun or noun phrase: *el primer récord mundial* 'the first world record', *el tercer gran éxito* 'the third great success'.
(ii) *Séptimo* is often pronounced *sétimo* and the Academy approves of this as an alternative spelling. Most Spanish-speakers do not.
(iii) *Nono* is used for *noveno* when referring to Popes: *Pío nono* 'Pope Pius IX'.

See 32.9 for how to say and write dates.

10.12.2 Ordinal numbers above 'tenth'

The use of special ordinal forms for these numbers is declining, and they are now mainly used only in official or formal language.

Forms in the rightmost column are used for fractions in technical language: *tres doceavos* 'three-twelfths'. They are used as ordinals in Latin America: *la doceava parte de un sexenio* (Carlos Fuentes, Mexico, dialogue) 'one twelfth of six years'. This usage is found occasionally in Spain but it is condemned by connoisseurs of good usage, including Manuel Seco and the *Libro de estilo* of *El País*, despite the fact that the phrase *doceava edición* 'twelfth edition' is seen, arbitrarily, in well-printed books.

undécimo	eleventh	*onceavo*
duodécimo	twelfth	*doceavo*
decimotercero	thirteenth	*treceavo*
(decimotercer		
before sing. masc. nouns)		
decimocuarto	fourteenth	*catorceavo*
decimoquinto	fifteenth	*quinceavo*
decimosexto	sixteenth	*dieciseisavo*
decimoséptimo	seventeenth	*diecisieteavo*
decimoctavo	eighteenth	*dieciochavo*
decimonoveno/decimonono	nineteenth	*diecinueveavo*
vigésimo	twentieth	*veinteavo*
vigésimo/a primero/a	twenty-first	
primero/a		
(vigésimo primer before sing. masc. nouns)		
vigésimo/a quinto/a etc.	twenty-fifth	*veinticincavo*
trigésimo	thirtieth	*treintavo*
trigésimo/a sexto/a	thirty-sixth	
cuadragésimo	fortieth	*cuarentavo*
quincuagésimo	fiftieth	*cincuentavo*
sexagésimo	sixtieth	*sesentavo*
septuagésimo	seventieth	*setentavo*
octogésimo	eightieth	*ochentavo*
nonagésimo	ninetieth	*noventavo*
centésimo (in common use)	hundredth	*centavo*
ducentésimo	two hundredth	
tricentésimo	three hundredth	
cuadringentésimo	four hundredth	
quingentésimo	five hundredth	
sexcentésimo	six hundredth	
septingentésimo	seven hundredth	
octingentésimo	eight hundredth	
noningentésimo	nine hundredth	
milésimo (in common use)	thousandth	
dosmilésimo	two thousandth	
cuatrocientosmilésimo	four hundred thousandth	
millonésimo	millionth	

Notes

(i) In informal styles, written and spoken, ordinal forms over 'tenth' are either avoided, e.g. *Mañana cumple treinta años* 'Tomorrow's his thirtieth birthday', —*¿En qué capítulo viene? —En el trece* ' "What chapter's it in?" "Thirteen" ', or the ordinary ordinal number is used, e.g. *el veinticinco aniversario* 'the twenty-fifth anniversary', *la trescientas cincuenta reunión del comité* 'the 350th meeting of the committee', *El tren de alta velocidad español está a punto de contabilizar su pasajero medio millón* (*El País*) 'The Spanish High Speed Train is about to get (lit. 'to enter into its accounts') its 500,000th passenger'.

(ii) *Decimoprimero, *decimosegundo, for *undécimo*, *duodécimo*, are common mistakes in spoken Spanish.

(iii) Forms like *décimo tercero*, *décimo cuarto*, in which both words agree in number and gender, are nowadays old-fashioned. Forms like *vigesimoquinto/a*, *vigesimoséptimo/a*, etc. are also increasingly common for 21st to 29th.

10.12.3 Position of ordinals

Like most adjectives, they may follow or precede a noun, occasionally with changes of meaning. They usually precede, but used emphatically or contrastively, or with titles, they follow the noun:

en el tercer capítulo/en el capítulo tercero (latter order unusual)	in the third chapter
los tres párrafos primeros	the first three paragraphs (i.e. paras 1, 2 and 3)
los tres primeros párrafos	the three first paragraphs (i.e. para 1 of 3 different chapters)
Isabel segunda (Isabel II)	Elizabeth the Second
por la enésima vez	for the umpteenth time

10.13 Distribution

Di cien mil pesos a cada uno	I gave 100,000 pesos to each of them
Traían sendos ramilletes de flores (literary style, informally *cada uno traía un ramillete*)	Each bore a bouquet of flowers/Each one was carrying a bouquet
cada cinco meses	every five months

10.14 'Single', 'twofold', 'double', 'treble', etc.

un billete de ida	a single ticket
una habitación individual	a single room
todos y cada uno de los problemas	every single problem
con una sola excepción/con una excepción única	with a single exception
ni uno solo	not a single one
Mi sueldo es el doble del suyo	My salary is double his
el doble acristalamiento	double glazing
una cama de matrimonio	double bed
Duplicaron la suma	They doubled the sum
Esta cantidad es el triple de ésa/esa	This quantity is triple that

10.15 Dimensions and other numerical expressions

Este cuarto mide 2,5 (dos coma cinco) por 3,75 (tres coma setenta y cinco metros)	This room measures 2.5 metres by 3.75
El área es de tres metros cuadrados	The area is 3 square metres
Forma un cuadrado de dos metros	It's two metres square
mil centímetros cúbicos	1000 cc
El cable tiene cien metros de largo/de longitud	The cable's 100m long
Tiene cinco metros de hondo/ancho	It's five metres deep/wide
un motor de ocho caballos	an 8 horsepower engine
un motor de dos tiempos	a two-stroke engine
un ángulo de treinta grados	a 30-degree angle
Forma un ángulo recto	It makes a right-angle
Debe haber cinco bajo cero	It must be five degrees below zero
números pares/impares/primos	even/odd/prime numbers
dos nueveavos dividido por tres sieteavos (see 12.2 for discussion of *-avo*)	two ninths divided by three sevenths
diez elevado al cubo/sexto/noveno	ten to the third/sixth/ninth

10.16 Numerals: rules for writing

There is no universal agreement about the rules for writing numbers. The following recommendations reflect Martínez de Sousa (1977), 294-5, checked against the *Libro de estilo* of *El País*.

Figures are used:

(a) for all numbers over nine;

(b) for all numbers, when some of them are over nine: *3 ministros, 45 senadores y 100 diputados* 'three ministers, 45 senators and 100 members of Congress' (example from *Libro de estilo de El País*). Approximate numbers are, however, spelled out. See (b) below;

(c) in timetables: *salida a las 20:30* 'departure at 20.30', *llegada a las 09.15* 'arrival at 09.15';

(d) for dates: *el 23 de marzo de 1995* (occasionally seen written 1.995, although use of the point is not recommended in dates). See 32.9 for discussion of the format of dates. Numbers are used for years (*1998, 2005*) but not for decades: *los años noventa* 'the nineties';

(e) for exact figures, including addresses: *2,38 kilómetros* '2.38 kilometres', *58 por ciento* '58 per cent', *419 páginas* '419 pages', *63 grados bajo cero* '63 degrees below zero', *223 habitantes* '223 inhabitants', *Avenida de la Libertad 7, 2° izquierdo* '7 Liberty Avenue, left-hand flat/apartment on second floor'.

Words are used:

(a) for time elapsed: *veinticinco años* 'twenty-five years', *han pasado quince segundos* 'fifteen seconds have gone by';

(b) for approximate figures: *Hubo más de quinientos heridos* 'There were more than five hundred injured';

(c) for numbers that are quoted as spoken by someone: *Me dijo que quería comprar quince* 'He told me wanted to buy fifteen';

(d) for telling the time (in literary works): *Llegó a las diez y media/cuatro cuarenta y cinco* 'He arrived at 10.30/4.45'.

Note
It is considered bad written style to begin a sentence with a number except in headlines and abbreviated messages. *El País* expressly forbids its journalists to open with *Diez personas resultaron heridas . . .*; this should be recast as *Un total de diez personas resultaron heridas* (*Libro de estilo*, 10.10).

10.17 Telephone numbers

The *Libro de estilo* of *El País* recommends that phone numbers should be expressed by pairs: 54-06-72 *cincuenta y cuatro cero seis setenta y dos*.

If the number of figures is uneven, the first group should be in the hundreds: *542-67-22 = quinientos cuarenta y dos sesenta y siete veintidós. Cinco cuarenta y dos sesenta y siete veintidós* is also possible.

Codes and extensions are sometimes written in brackets: (033) 527-76-89 (19) = our 033-527 7689 (ext. 19). As the examples show, phone numbers are optionally written with hyphens separating the figures that are spoken as single numbers.

11

Personal pronouns

Index to chapter:

Forms of personal pronouns	11.1
Use of subject pronouns	11.2
Formal and informal modes of address	11.3
nosotros	11.4
Forms of pronouns after prepositions	11.5
The pronoun *sí*	11.5.3
Pronouns and agreement	11.6
First and second-person object pronouns	
(*me, te, nos, os*)	11.7
Pronouns with verbs of motion	11.8
Pronouns with *ser* and *resultar*	11.9
'Resumptive' *lo* with *ser* and *estar*	11.10
Object pronouns used to show personal	
involvement	11.11
Order of object pronouns	11.12
Replacement of *le* by *se*	11.13
Position of object pronouns in sentences	11.14
Quiero verlo or *lo quiero ver*?	11.14.4
Emphasis of object pronouns	11.15
'Redundant' object pronouns	11.16

The use of the third-person object pronouns *le* and *lo* is discussed separately in Chapter 12.

For possessive adjectives and pronouns, see Chapter 8.

11.1 Classification and forms

'Subject' pronouns may be optionally used to emphasize the subject of a verb: *yo hablo*, 'I'm talking', *él duerme* 'he's sleeping'.

'Object' pronouns (other than third-person) may be used *either* for the direct object *or* for the indirect object of the verb, *Te quiero* 'I love you', *Te hablo* 'I'm talking to you', *Nos vio* 'He saw us', *Nos dio* 'He gave (to) us'.

As a result of this dual function there is no need to distinguish between 'direct' and 'indirect' object pronouns in Spanish except in the case of the third person, where the difference between the 'direct' object forms (*lo/la/los/las*) and the 'indirect' forms (*le/les*) only partly coincides with the traditional distinction between direct and indirect objects. This latter problem is discussed separately in Chapter 12.

Spanish has an incomplete set of prepositional personal pronouns (*mí, ti, sí*) which must be used after prepositions. The ordinary subject pronouns are used for the other persons; see 11.5.

Se is traditionally called a 'reflexive' third-person object pronoun, but it is usually not reflexive and it sometimes apparently functions as a subject. It is discussed at length in Chapters 26 and 28.

TABLE I *Spanish personal pronouns*

This table contains all the personal pronoun forms currently in use.

PERSON	EMPHATIC SUBJECT	OBJECT	PREPOSITIONAL	
SINGULAR				
I	yo	me	mí	I
2	tú	te	ti	you (familiar)
	vos	te	vos	you (familiar)[1]
	usted	lo/la/le	usted	you (polite)
3	él	lo/la/le	él	he, it
	ella	la/le	ella	she, it
	ello[2]	lo/le	ello	it (neuter)
	se		sí	'reflexive'
PLURAL				
I	nosotros	nos	nosotros	we (masc.)
	nosotras	nos	nosotras	we (fem.)
2	vosotros	os	vosotros	you (familiar masc. Spain)
	vosotras	os	vosotras	you (familiar fem. Spain)
	ustedes	los/las/les	ustedes	you (polite, also familiar in Lat. Am.)
3	ellos	los/les	ellos	they (masc.)
	ellas	las/les	ellas	they (fem.)
	se[3]		sí	'reflexive'

11.2 Use of subject pronouns

11.2.1 Emphasis

The ordinary subject pronoun is expressed by the verb ending: *hablo* 'I speak', *habló* 'he/she/you spoke', *vendimos* 'we sold', *salieron* 'they/you went out', etc. The forms *yo/tú/él/ella/ustedes/ellos/ellas* are therefore usually only required for emphasis.

It is a bad error, very common among English speakers, to use Spanish subject pronouns when no emphasis is intended. To do so draws confusing attention to the subject of the verb, as in an English sentence pronounced with unnecessary stress on the pronoun, e.g. '*I* got up at eight, *I* showered, *I* had coffee, *I* went to work . . .'.

The subject pronouns are used:

(a) When the pronoun stands alone;

---

[1] In parts of Latin America only; acceptability dependent on country and style.
[2] Discussed at 7.3.
[3] Discussed in Chapters 26 and 28.

—¿*Quién ha venido?*	'Who's come?'
—*Ellos*	'They have'
—¿*Quién lo ha hecho?*	'Who did it?'
—*Nosotros*	'We did'
—¿*Quién es?*	'Who is it?'
—*Yo*	'Me'

(b) In contrast;

Tú eres listo, pero ella es genial	You're clever but she's a genius
Yo no, pero ustedes sí	I don't (or 'not me'), but you do (or 'you')

(c) *usted/ustedes* 'you' are used more frequently, either to avoid ambiguity or to stress the polite tone of an utterance;

¿*Adónde van ustedes?*	Where are you going?
Si (usted) quiere, iré con usted	If you like, I'll go with you

(d) Third-person pronouns may sometimes be required for clarity since a sentence like *Viene mañana* is ambiguous out of context: **Ella** *viene mañana* 'She's coming tomorrow', **Usted** *viene mañana* 'You're coming tomorrow', **Él** *habla inglés* 'He speaks English', etc.

Other subject pronouns may occasionally be used to clarify ambiguous verb endings: *Yo tenía/Él tenía* 'I had'/'he had', *que yo fuese/que él fuese* 'that I should go/be'/'that he should go/be'.

However, in both cases context usually makes the meaning clear.

11.2.2 Subject pronouns for inanimate nouns

Although *él/ella/ellos/ellas* may translate 'it' or 'them' when applied to inanimate things, in practice they are usually taken to stand for human beings when they are used as the subject of a verb.

For this reason one does not pronominalize *El viento sopla* 'The wind's blowing' as **Él sopla*, which is understood as 'He's blowing'; *sopla* = 'it's blowing'. But subject pronouns are sometimes used in Latin America to replace an inanimate subject where Peninsular speakers would use either no pronoun at all or an appropriate form of *éste* 'this'/'the latter':

La "oposición" ha desaparecido de la radio, de la televisión y de la prensa diaria en el Perú. **Ella** *subsiste, mínima, hostigada, desde las columnas de todos los periódicos* (M. Vargas Llosa, Peru)	The 'opposition' has vanished from radio, television and daily press in Peru. It continues to operate, minimal, harassed, from the columns of all the newspapers
. . . si algún "interés" tengo que defender como autor, **él** *está mucho más cerca de los países socialistas que de los capitalistas* (M. Vargas Llosa, Peru)	if I have any 'interest' to defend as an author, it is much closer to the socialist countries than the capitalist

11.3 Formal and informal modes of address

11.3.1 *Voseo*

Vos replaces *tú* (see next section) in many parts of Latin America, but it may be too intimate for casual use by foreigners. It is everywhere stylistically informal, and is replaced by *tú* in prayers and other solemn language: God, Jesus and the Virgin are usually addressed as *tú*, not as *vos*.

It is used in the spoken language of all social circles in Argentina, and in most social circles in Uruguay, Paraguay and most of Central America. It is also used in the extreme south of Mexico. In Colombia, Chile, Ecuador and Venezuela it is often heard, is possibly spreading, but may be considered 'lower-class' or provincial, although usage and attitudes vary between countries and regions.

It is not usual in Bolivia, Peru, Panama, Cuba, Mexico and Puerto Rico, but there are local pockets of *voseo* in some of these countries. Even where *voseo* is current in speech, *tú* is often written, even in intimate letters.

The possessive adjective for *vos* is *tu/tus*, the object pronoun is *te*, and the prepositional form is *vos*: *¿Te das cuenta de que estoy hablando de **vos** y de **tu** amiga?* 'Do you realize I'm talking about you and your friend?'.

The verb forms used with *vos* fluctuate according to region and are best learnt locally. For details on the verb forms used with Argentine *voseo* see 13.1. and 16.2.8

Note
Voseo descends from the Golden Age use of *vos* as a polite second-person singular pronoun. *Vos* was still current in early nineteenth-century Spain to judge from Larra's *Artículos de costumbres* of the 1830s, and it survives in Spain in ritual language in official documents and in pseudo-archaic style - e.g. in Buero Vallejo's play *Las meninas* (in this case it is comparable to the use of 'thou' in modern English). In Spain this archaic singular pronoun *vos* takes the normal verb endings for *vosotros*, and the possessive adjective/pronoun is *vuestro/a/os/as*.

11.3.2 *Tú (vos)* or *usted*?
The basic rule - at least as far as Spain is concerned - is that *tú* is used for anyone with whom one is on first-name terms.[4] *Tú* (or, where it is used, *vos*) is therefore used between friends, family members, when speaking to children or to animals, generally between strangers under the age of about thirty, and in prayers.

It therefore follows that, in Spain, *tú* is used much more readily than the French *tu* or German *Du*; its use is much more common in Spain than fifty years ago. However *tú/vos* should not be used to persons in authority or to older strangers or elderly persons unless they invite its use.

Use of *tú* where *usted* is expected may express contempt or threat: criminals call their victims *tú*, not *usted*.

Note
Generalization about the use of *tú* and *usted* is hazardous. In most of Latin America *tú/vos* is not used so readily[5] and one finds dialects (e.g. Antioquía, Colombia) where all three pronouns, *usted*, *tú* and *vos*, may be used in the course of a single conversation, depending on the degree of intimacy reached at any moment.[6]

---

[4] An exception occurs when addressing respected subordinates: *María, no se le olvide limpiar el horno* 'Maria, don't forget to clean the oven'.
[5] It is very noticeable that in the Spanish department of King's College, London, which contains both Spanish and Latin-American students, the former readily address the teachers as *tú* whereas the latter often find it embarrassing to do so.
[6] Batchelor and Pountain (1992) 284 report that in Chile husbands and wives may affectionately call one another *usted*.

11.3.3 *Vosotros/as* or *ustedes*?

Vosotros (*vosotras* to two or more females) is the plural of *tú* and is used in Spain for two or more persons with whom the speaker is on first-name terms.

It is used in all styles in standard European Spanish, but in Latin America it is replaced by *ustedes* in all but archaic styles, a phenomenon also found in popular speech in Southern Spain and the Canary Islands. A mother in Latin America addresses her child as *tú* or, in some places, as *vos*, and her children as *ustedes*. Even animals are called *ustedes* in Latin America.

Note
Vosotros, in the shape of its possessive *vuestro*, is however found in business correspondence in Argentina and perhaps elsewhere in Latin America. See footnote to 8.6b for an example.

11.3.4 Use of *usted, ustedes*

These are polite forms roughly equivalent to French *vous*, German *Sie* – but French and German usage is a poor guide, so see 11.3.2 and 11.3.3 for details of the relationship between *tú/vos* and *usted/ustedes*.

They require third-person verb forms: *Usted habla* 'You speak', *Ustedes hablan* 'You (plural) speak'. In writing, *usted/ustedes* may optionally be abbreviated to *V./Vs.*, *Vd./Vds.*, or *Ud./Uds.*

Object forms of *usted/ustedes* are discussed under third-person pronouns (11.7.3).

Notes
(i) As subject pronouns *usted/ustedes* need only appear once at the beginning of a text or utterance and then occasionally thereafter to recall the politeness of tone. Whereas total omission of *usted/ustedes* may sound too informal, constant repetition may sound obsequious.
(ii) Agreement when one subject is *tú* and the other *usted* or *ustedes*, or one *vosotros* and the other *usted/ustedes*, is as for *ustedes*: *Tú y usted, quédense aquí* 'You and you stay here'.

11.4 *Nosotros/as, nos*

Females referring to themselves and other females use *nosotras*.

The first-person plural is constantly used in books and articles when the author is modestly referring to her/himself. It is less pompous than the English 'royal We': *En este trabajo hemos procurado enfocar el problema de la inflación desde* . . . 'In this work I ('we') have tried to approach the problem of inflation from . . .'.

Nos for *nosotros* is obsolete, but is used by popes, bishops and monarchs in official documents or ritual utterances.

Note
The following construction is peculiar to Latin America, especially Argentina: *Fuimos con mi hermano* . . . (Spain *Fui con mi hermano/Mi hermano y yo fuimos*) 'I went with my brother' (lit. 'We went with my brother'), *Y así nos fuimos a la Patagonia, con Matilde* (E. Sábato, Argentina, interview; Spain *Fui con Matilde/Matilde y yo fuimos*), 'So Matilde and I went to Patagonia'.

11.5 Forms of pronouns after prepositions

11.5.1 Use after prepositions
Only *yo, tú* and *se* have separate prepositional forms: *mí, ti* and *sí* (the latter is discussed at 11.5.3). In the other cases the normal subject forms, *él, ella, ello, nosotros, vosotros, usteded/ustedes, ellos/ellas,* are used after prepositions.

No sabe nada de mí	He knows nothing about me
No tengo nada contra ti	I've nothing against you
Creo en vos (Argentina, etc.)	I believe in you
no delante de usted	not in front of you
Me refiero a él/ella	I'm referring to him/her
Confiamos en ustedes	We trust in you
Corrió tras ellos	He ran after them
aparte de ellas	except for them (fem.)

However, seven prepositions or preposition-like words require the ordinary form of all the subject pronouns (but not of the pronoun *se* – see 11.5.3 note (i)). These are:

entre	between/among
excepto	except
hasta	when it means 'even' rather than 'as far as'
incluso	including/even
menos	except
salvo	except/save
según	according to
Todos lo hicieron menos/excepto/salvo tú	They all did it except/save you
Que se quede entre tú y yo	Let's keep it between you and me
Hasta tú puedes hacer eso . . .	Even you can do that . . .
según tú y él	according to you and him

Notes
(i) Note also the set phrases *de tú a tú* 'on equal terms', *hablar de tú* (i.e. *tutear*) 'to address someone as *tú*'. Also *Dije entre mí* 'I said to myself'.
(ii) For constructions like *?detrás tuyo* for *detrás de ti* 'behind you', or *?delante mío* for *delante de mí* 'in front of me' (frequent in colloquial Latin-American Spanish, substandard or popular in Spain), see 8.7.

11.5.2 *Conmigo, contigo*
These special forms replace *con + yo, con + tú*: *¿Vienes conmigo?* 'Are you coming with me?', *No quiero discutir contigo* 'I don't want to argue with you'.

In areas of *voseo, contigo* is rarely heard: *No quiero discutir con vos* 'I don't want to argue with you'.

11.5.3 *Sí, consigo*
These are special prepositional forms of the pronoun *se*.

Sí is used after prepositions other than *con*; the accent distinguishes it from *si* meaning 'if'.

Consigo replaces *con + se* and means 'with him/herself'. *Sí* is often combined with *mismo* when it is used reflexively:

Están muy contentos de sí mismos	They're very pleased with themselves
No se refiere a sí misma	She's not referring to herself
Este fenómeno ya es muy interesante de por sí	this phenomenon is in itself very interesting

Un brillante que para sí lo quisieran muchos (advertisement)	A diamond many would like for themselves
Volvió en sí	(S)he came round (regained consciousness)
No puede dar más de sí	He's doing the best he can
Está disgustada consigo misma	She's cross with herself

Notes

(i) *Se* is unique in being the only pronoun requiring a prepositional form after *entre*: *entre tú y yo*, but *entre sí* 'among themselves'. *Entre sí* may also mean 'to himself': *Dijo entre sí* 'He said to himself'/'He murmured under his breath'.

(ii) *Sí* is not always really 'reflexive' as the following example shows: *El acento sirve para que se distingan los ingleses entre sí* 'Accent enables Englishmen to distinguish themselves from one another'.

(iii) There is a curious colloquial tendency to reject other persons of *volver en sí* 'to regain consciousness' and *dar de sí* 'to give of oneself'. One hears *recobré el conocimiento* (correct) or even *?volví en sí*, but the expected *volví en mí* is often avoided, even by educated speakers: *Volví en sí ya estando en la clínica* (interview, *El Nacional*, Mexico) 'I came round when I was (lit. 'already being') in the clinic', —*Perdona, ¿no te importa ponerte de pie para que te veamos? —Estoy de pie, es que no doy más de sí* (E. Arenas, dialogue, Spain) '"Excuse me, would you mind standing up so we can see you?" "I *am* standing up. This is all there is of me"'.

(iv) There is a good deal of disagreement about *sí* in the modern language. When *sí* refers to a specific person, the modern tendency is to prefer a non-reflexive prepositional pronoun. In answer to a questionnaire, the great majority of informants (professional people and students, Spanish) rejected *sí* in the following sentences:

*Hablan francés entre **ellos** (?entre sí)*	They speak French among themselves
*Yo sé que usted toca para **usted** misma* (?para sí misma)	I know you play (music) for yourself
*Lo mantuvo contra **ella** con uno de sus brazos* (E. Sábato, Argentina)	She held him against herself with one arm
*Tenía las manos apoyadas en la barra, delante de **él** (?ante sí)*	His hands were resting on the bar, in front of him(self)
*Cerró la puerta tras **él** (?tras sí)*	He shut the door after him(self)
*Usted tiene ante **usted** a un hombre que . . .* (interview, *El Nacional*, Mexico)	You have before you a man who . . .
*El policía los vio venir hacia **él** (?hacia sí)*	The policeman saw them coming towards him(self)
Guárdeselo para usted	Keep it for yourself

11.6 Pronouns and agreement

Verbs sometimes agree with personal pronouns in ways unfamiliar to English speakers:

Soy yo/somos nosotros/fuisteis vosotros/fueron ellos	it's me/it's us/it was you/it was them[7] (lit. 'I am me', 'we are we','you were you', 'they were they')
*El feo de la foto **eres** tú*	The ugly one in the photo is you
*—¿Quién ha dicho eso? —**He** sido yo* (Lat. Am. *–¿Quién dijo eso? —Fui yo*)	'Who said that?' 'It was me'

---

[7] Or, as some English-speakers insist, 'it is I', 'it is we', 'it was they', etc.

L

When answering the phone one says *soy Ana* 'it's Ana (here)' (lit. 'I'm Ana'), *soy Antonio* 'it's Antonio speaking'. *Es Ana* 'it's Ana' is only possible when said by someone else about Ana.

11.7 Object pronouns

The term 'object pronouns' is used in this book to refer to the forms *me/te/lo/la/le/nos/os/los/las/les* and *se* – although the latter apparently sometimes functions as a grammatical subject, as in *se vive* 'one lives', *Se está mejor aquí* 'One's better off here'. See 28.6 for further discussion of this construction.

Traditional grammars often divide these pronouns into two lists, 'accusative' or 'direct object' pronouns, and 'dative' or 'indirect object' pronouns, but only the third-person set has two forms (*le/les* as opposed to *lo/la/los/las*), and the difference between them only partly coincides with the traditional distinction between 'direct' and 'indirect' objects.

The difference between *le* and *lo* is discussed separately in Chapter 12. For 'pronominal' verbs (sometimes inaccurately called 'reflexive' verbs), see Chapter 26.

11.7.1 Forms of first and second-person object pronouns

	singular	**plural**
First person	*me*	*nos*
Second person	*te*	*os* (see note (iii))

Notes
(i) *Usted/ustedes* take third-person object pronouns.
(ii) *Te* is the object form of *tú* or *vos* (where *vos* is used): *Vos sabés que te vi ayer* (Argentina) 'You know I saw you yesterday', *Vos te arrepentirás* (Argentina) 'You'll be sorry'.
(iii) *Os* corresponds to *vosotros* and is therefore not heard in Latin America, where *ustedes* is used for both polite and familiar address; see 11.3.3 for discussion.

11.7.2 Use of first and second-person object pronouns
The main problem raised for the English-speaking learner by these (and by the third-person) object pronouns is the variety of translations possible for each form.

Basically Spanish object pronouns merely indicate the person 'affected' by a verb phrase. They do not indicate *how* the object is affected; this must be worked out from the meaning of the verb, from context or by common sense. English makes the meaning much more explicit, so *me* can, for example, be translated into English in at least thirteen ways in the following sentences:

Me han visto	They've seen **me**
Me dejó una finca	He left an estate **to me**
Me ha aparcado el coche	He's parked the car **for me**
Entró en mi tienda y me compró una agenda	He came into my shop/(US) 'store' and bought a diary **off/from me**
Me sacaron tres balas	They took three bullets **out of me**
Me han quitado a mis hijos	They've taken my children **from me**
Me tiene envidia	He's envious **of me**
Me tiró una bola de nieve	He threw a snowball **at me**
Me encontraron mil pesetas	They found 1000 ptas **on me**

Me echaron una manta	They threw a blanket **over me**
Voy a comprarme un helado	I'm going to buy **myself** an ice cream
Siempre me pone pegas	He always finds fault **with me**
Me rompió el brazo	He broke **my** arm

It is not clear whether the terms 'direct object' and 'indirect object' are helpful descriptions of these various uses. 'Indirect object' may encourage students to limit their use of object pronouns to dative constructions and to neglect such sentences as *Me quitó el libro* 'He took the book **off** me'.

Lists A and B (at 12.3 and 12.4) show numerous examples of sentences in which *me/te/os/nos* could be substituted for *le/les* or *lo/la/los* where the meaning is appropriate.

A special case arises when the object pronoun and the subject pronoun (usually indicated by the verb ending) refer to the same person or thing, e.g. ***Me** lavo* 'I'm washing (myself)', ***Te** equivocaste* 'You were mistaken', *Miguel **se** va* 'Miguel's leaving', ***Nos** caímos* 'We fell over'. We call such verbs 'pronominal verbs' and discuss them in Chapter 26.

11.7.3 Use of third-person object pronouns
The distinction between *le/les* and *lo/las/los/las* is discussed in Chapter 12.

These overworked pronouns also have a second-person meaning since they are used for *usted/ustedes* 'you':

Doctora Smith, le aseguro que la llamé ayer	Dr Smith (fem.), I assure you I rang you/her yesterday
Le vi ayer (Spain only; see 12.5.1, 2)	I saw you/him yesterday
Lo vi ayer (Lat. Am. and, optionally, Spain)	I saw it/him/you yesterday
Los vi ayer	I saw you/them yesterday

11.8 Pronouns with verbs of motion

Object pronouns cannot replace the preposition *a* plus a noun if mere physical arrival or approach is involved: *Voy a la reunión* > *voy allí* (not **le voy*) 'I'm going to the meeting' > 'I'm going to it', *Acude a ella* 'He goes to her':

Cuando tiene problemas siempre va a ella	When he has problems he always goes to her
Me dirijo a ustedes	I'm turning to you/addressing you/writing to you
todo el occidente que vino a nosotros (M. Vargas Llosa, Peru)	the whole of the west (i.e. western world) which came to us
Suele recurrir a él	(S)he usually turns to him

However, object pronouns are often used colloquially with the following verbs, particularly if the verb is third-person:

Se me acercó/Se acercó a mí	He approached me
Él se le acercó por la espalda (J. Marsé, Spain)	He approached her from behind
Ella se le reunió al doblar la esquina (L. Goytisolo, Spain)	She caught up with him as she turned the corner
No sólo los sollozos de los niños y de los nativos se alzaron entonces, sino que se les unieron los de los sirvientes (José Donoso, Chile)	Not only did sobbing from the children and natives break out then, but the servants' (sobs) were added to it

Notes

(i) This construction is rare in the first and second persons: *Se le opuso* 'He opposed him', but *Te opusiste a él* 'You opposed him' rather than ?*Te le opusiste.*

Forms with first and second persons may occur in Latin America, especially in Mexico,[8] where sentences like *Me le acerqué* (i.e. *Me acerqué a él*) 'I approached him', *Te ruego que te nos incorpores* (for . . . *que te incorpores a nosotros*) 'I'm asking you to join us' are common. A Mexican informant claimed that ?*Me le arrodillé a la Virgen* 'I kneeled before/to the Virgin' is heard in his country, but the sentence was rejected by Spaniards and Argentines in favour of *Me arrodillé delante de la Virgen.*

(ii) *Se le puso delante, Se me puso delante* 'He stood in front of him', 'He stood in front of me' occur colloquially for *Se puso delante de él/Se puso delante de mí*, and are more emotional in tone.

(iii) The example from José Donoso is an exception to the rule that object pronouns are not used with such verbs when the sentence refers to a non-human entity: the normal construction would be *Se acercó al puente* 'He approached the bridge' > *Se acercó a él* 'He approached it', not **Se le acercó.*

(iv) Object pronouns are used to denote a person affected by *llegar* and *venirse* (if their subject is inanimate) and by *venir con*: *El armario se le vino encima* 'The cupboard/(US) "closet" collapsed on him/her/you', *Siempre me viene con pejigueras* 'He's always coming to me with irritating details', *cuando me llegó la noticia de su triunfo* 'when news of his triumph reached me'.

(v) In *Le viene a decir que* . . . He's coming to tell him that . . .' the *le* belongs to the *decir*: *Viene a decirle que* . . .

In *Le viene bien* 'It suits him' and *¿Qué tal te va?* 'How are things going'/'How're you doing?', advantage, not motion, is involved.

11.9 Pronouns with *ser* and *resultar*

(a) With adjectives:

The choice is between *Me es necesario* and *Es necesario para mí*. The former is possible with *ser* only if the adjective expresses a meaning included in List A, 12.3. *Resultar* allows the construction with a wider range of adjectives, and may be thought of as the 'involving' counterpart of *ser*:

Les es/resulta necesario	It's necessary for them
Me es/resulta importante	It's important to me
Nos era imprescindible contactar a sus padres	It was absolutely necessary for us to contact her parents
Le era más fácil soportar los dolores ajenos que los propios (G. García Márquez, Colombia)	It was easier for him to put up with other people's suffering than his own

but

La casa era demasiado blanca para mí/me resultaba demasiado blanca (not **me era demasiado blanca*)	The house was too white for me
Era muy feo para ella	**It** was very ugly for her
Le resultaba muy feo	**He** seemed very ugly to her

The following list will give an idea of the kind of adjective that can take object pronouns with *ser*:

---

[8] J. Lope Blanch (1991), 20.

agradable/desagradable	agreeable/disagreeable
conocido/desconocido	known/unknown
conveniente/inconveniente	suitable/unsuitable
fácil/difícil	easy/difficult
grato/ingrato	pleasing/displeasing
indiferente	indifferent
leal	loyal
molesto	bothersome
necesario/innecesario	necessary/unnecessary
permitido/prohibido	allowed/prohibited
posible/imposible	possible/impossible
simpático/antipático	nice/nasty (persons)
sincero, franco	sincere, frank
suficiente/insuficiente	sufficient/insufficient
urgent	urgent
útil/inútil	useful/useless

Notes
(i) Many of these adjectives could also be constructed with *para* or *con*: *Es conveniente para ellos/Les es conveniente* 'It's suitable for/to them', *Voy a ser franco con usted/Le voy a ser franco* 'I'll be frank with you'. The object pronouns convey a higher level of personal involvement.
(ii) *Grande, pequeño* take *le/les* if they mean 'too big', 'too small': *Ese puesto le está grande* 'That job's too big for him'. Otherwise *resultar* or *ser para* must be used: *Es grande para él* 'It's big to/for him', etc.
(iii) The nuance conveyed by *resultar* is often virtually untranslatable. Compare *Es feo* = 'It/He's ugly' and *Resulta feo* 'The effect is ugly'/'He/It is ugly as a result'.

(b) *Ser* plus personal pronouns with nouns:
This occurs only with a few nouns, most derived from or close in meaning to the adjectives listed above.

Si le es molestia, dígamelo	If it's a nuisance for you, tell me
Me/Le era un gran placer/Era un gran placer para mí/él	It was a great pleasure for/to me/him,
Nos es de interés	It's of interest to us

Notes
(i) Spanish does not allow a pronominal construction in translations of sentences like 'I was always a good mother to him' *Siempre fui una buena madre para él* (not *siempre le fui . . .*).
(ii) *Resultar* has limited use with nouns: *Mi temporada aquí me está resultando un verdadero viaje de estudios* (J.L. Borges, Argentina, letter style) 'My stay here is turning out to be a real study trip for me', *Si le resulta un problema* 'If it turns out to be a problem to you'.

11.10 'Resumptive' *lo* with *ser*, *estar* and *parecer*

The predicate of *ser*, *estar* and *parecer* is echoed or resumed by *lo*: —*Parece buena la tierra desde aquí.* —*Lo es* '"The land looks good from here." "It is"'. This construction is discussed at 7.4, note (i).

11.11 Object pronouns used to denote personal involvement

Object pronouns may be included in a verb phrase to show that a person is intensely affected. Compare the indignant Frenchman's *Regardez-moi ça!* 'Just look at that for me!', 'Just look at that, will you!'.

Usually the effect cannot be translated into standard English, although popular English sometimes uses 'on me', 'on you', etc. in order to include the person affected. Compare *Se **me** han ido de casa* 'They've left home "on me"', *Se **le** ha averiado el coche* 'His car's broken down "on him"'. In Spanish this device is more typical of familiar speech or when there is a strong emotional involvement on the speaker's part, e.g. when parents are speaking about their child:

*Mi marido se **me** está quedando delgadísimo*	My husband's getting terribly thin
***Me** le has estropeado tres camisas*	You've spoilt three of his shirts for me
*Pues, yo eché a una porque **me** fumaba y ahora tengo otra que, además de fumar, **me** bebe* (E. Arenas, Spain, dialogue, very colloquial)	Well, I fired one [maid] because she smoked ('on me') and now I've got another who not only smokes but drinks ('on me')
Péiname al niño	Do the child's hair for me
Sírvamele un café a la señorita (Argentina, quoted García (1975); Spain *sírvale un café* . . .)	Serve a coffee to the young lady for me
Cuídamele (or *Cuídamelo*) *bien*	Look after him well for me

This device of including mention of an interested party is more favoured in parts of Latin America than in Spain. *Me le pintaste la mesa* 'You painted the table for him for me' is apparently acceptable for some Latin American speakers. Peninsular Spanish tends to avoid clusters of two object pronouns when neither is a direct object.

11.12 Order of object pronouns

The invariable order of object pronouns when two or more appear together is:

se	*te/os*	*me/nos*	*le/lo/la/les/los/las*

i.e. *se*, if it occurs, comes first, second person precedes first, and third-person pronouns come last:

María te lo dijo	Maria told it to you
Me lo habré dejado en casa	I must have left it at home
Te lo llevé al tinte (or *a la tintorería*)	I took it to the cleaner's for you
No querían comunicárnoslo	They didn't want to tell it to us
¿Por qué no se lo prueba?	Why don't you try it on?
Se te ha caído la tinta	You've dropped the ink
Se le ha muerto un hijo	A son of his/hers has died
Nos los vamos a comprar	We're going to buy them for ourselves
Se nos ha vuelto listísimo	He's turned into a genius 'on us'
Yo me le fui encima, pero ella chilló (J. Cortázar, Argentina; Spain *Yo me le eché encima* . . .)	I lunged at her, but she screamed

Notes
(i) Reversal of the correct order, e.g. ?*Me se ha caído* for *Se me ha caído* 'I've dropped it' (lit. 'It's fallen down "on me"'), ?*¿Me se oye?* for *¿Se me oye?* 'Can anyone hear me?'/'Is anyone listening?', is a classic mistake of uneducated speech.
(ii) The order shown is invariable for all persons, unlike in French. Compare *Me lo da* and *Il **me le** donne* 'He gives it to me' (same order) and *Se lo da* and *Il **le lui** donne* 'He gives it to him'.

11.13 Replacement of *le* by *se*

11.13.1 *Se* for *le* when the latter is followed by a pronoun beginning with *l*

If *le* or *les* are immediately followed by an object pronoun beginning with *l*, i.e. by *lo*, *la*, *los* or *las*, the *le* or *les* must be replaced by *se*: *le doy* 'I give to him/her/you' + *lo* 'it' > *se lo doy* 'I give it to him/her/you' – **never** **le lo doy*:

Quiero dárselo	I want to give it to him
Se lo dije a ella	I told her
Se lo dije a ellos	I told them (masc.)
*¿Quiere usted que **se** lo envuelva?*	Do you want me to wrap it for you?

Note
This phenomenon, unique to Spanish among the Romance languages, is traditionally explained by the alleged ugliness of too many *l*'s. Whether this is the reason or not, it is useful to remember that in Spanish two object pronouns beginning with *l* can **never** stand side-by-side.

11.13.2 Latin-American *se los* for *se lo*

The combination *se lo* is very ambiguous. For example, *se lo dije* may mean 'I told it to him, her, you (*usted*)', 'them' (*ellos* or *ellas*) or 'you' (*ustedes*)'. *A él/ella/usted/ellos/ellas/ustedes* may be added if context does not make the issue clear: *Se lo dije a ustedes* 'I told **you**', etc.

There is a universal but grammatically illogical tendency in spontaneous Latin-American speech, very common even in educated language, to show that *se* stands for *les* by pluralizing the *direct* object pronoun, i.e. ?*Se **los** dije*, for *Se lo dije* 'I told it to **them**':

*. . . a un policía le había gustado más bien poco la gracia y se **los** había dicho* (J. Cortázar, Argentina, dialogue, for *se lo había dicho*)	one policeman didn't really like the joke and told them so
Se los dije, hijos, ganó 'Tierra y Libertad' (A. Mastretta, Mexico, dialogue; Spain *se lo dije* or, in this case, *os lo dije*)	I told you all/(US) 'you guys', 'Land and Liberty' won

This construction is very deep-rooted in spontaneous Latin-American speech but it is vehemently rejected by Spaniards. It is not accepted in formal written styles in Latin America.

11.14 Position of object pronouns

The position of object pronouns in relation to a verb depends on the form of the verb.

11.14.1 Pronouns with verbs in finite tenses

Pronouns come immediately before the verb in the order given at 11.12. In compound tenses the pronouns are placed before the auxiliary verb:

Se los entregamos	We gave them (masc.) to him/her/it/them/you
Te los enviaré luego	I'll send you them (masc.) later
Os las guardaré (Spain)	I'll keep them (fem.) for you
La he visto	I've seen her/it/you
Se me ha roto el cinturón	My belt's broken

Notes

(i) No word may come between the object pronoun and a verb, and they are pronounced as though they formed part of the verb, e.g. *te lo dijo* 'he said it to you' is pronounced *telodíjo*.

(ii) In pre-twentieth century literary style, object pronouns were often joined to verbs in finite tenses: *Contestóles así* 'He answered them thus' = *Les contestó así*, *Encontrábase exiliado* 'He found himself exiled' = *Se encontraba exiliado*, *Ocurriósele* 'It occurred to him/her' = *Se le ocurrió*.

Rules for this construction are omitted here since it is now extinct for practical purposes, except in a few set phrases, e.g. *habráse visto . . .* 'well, did you ever . . .', *diríase* (literary) 'one might say', *dícese* (literary) 'it is said', etc.[9] The construction is still occasionally found in burlesque or very flowery styles, and also in headlines in some Latin-American countries: *Entrevístanse Gorbachov y Fidel en Moscú* (*Granma*, Cuba) 'Gorbachev and Fidel hold talks in Moscow'.

11.14.2 Position with imperatives
See 17.4.

11.14.3 Position with infinitives

(a) If the infinitive is used as a noun or follows an adjective or a participle plus a preposition, pronouns are suffixed to it in the usual order:

Sería una locura decírselo	It would be madness to tell it to him
mejor enviárselo ahora	best send it to him/her/them now
Rechazaron el proyecto por considerarlo demasiado caro	They rejected the project on the grounds that it was too expensive
Estamos hartos de oírtelo	We're fed up with hearing it from you

As the examples show, when more than one pronoun is attached to the infinitive a written accent is needed to show that the position of the stress has not changed.

(b) If the infinitive depends on a previous verb, there are two possibilities:

  (i) Join the pronouns to the infinitive as in the previous examples.

Quiero hacerlo	I want to do it
Pudieron salvarla	They managed to save her
Propusieron alquilárnoslos	They suggested renting them to us
Acabo de dártelo	I've just given it to you

This is the safest, and in the view of some excessively strict purists, the only 'correct' option.[10]

  (ii) Place the pronouns before the finite verb: *lo quiero hacer*, etc. See the following section for discussion.

11.14.4 *Quiero verlo* or *lo quiero ver*?
Suffixed object pronouns are very often shifted leftwards when the infinitive depends on a preceding verb: *Quiero verlo* > *Lo quiero ver* 'I want to see it', etc. This construction, which has a long history, is possible with a large

---

[9] *Dícese* survives in various forms in spoken Latin-American Spanish, e.g. *dizque*. See 28.4.

[10] Francisco Marsá (1986), 6.1.2, says that *no se debe decir* is 'incorrect' for *no debe decirse*, although he admits that violations of this 'rule' – even by him – are very common. Cervantes's *Don Quijote*, which is the purists' Bible, contains many instances of shifted pronouns.

number of common verbs, but it is subject to controversy and apparently arbitrary constraints.

When shifting is possible, the two constructions seem to occur in Spain with about equal frequency in ordinary speech – although the shifted forms predominate in relaxed styles. To judge by the dialogue of modern novels, Latin-American speech strongly prefers the shifted forms. The suffixed forms are everywhere preferred in formal written styles.

The following are everyday examples current on both continents:

querer
Te la quiero enviar/Quiero enviártela — I want to send it (fem.) to you
poder
No puedo atenderle/No le puedo atender en este momento — I can't attend to you/her/him at this moment
deber
Deberías explicárnoslo/Nos lo deberías explicar — You ought to explain it to us
tener que
Tiene que devolvértelo/Te lo tiene que devolver — He has to give it back to you
acabar de
Pero si acabo de verlo/lo acabo de ver — But I've just seen him! (contradicting *si*)
llegar a
Incluso llegué a caerme/me llegué a caer por unas escaleras — I even managed to fall down a flight of stairs
haber de
He de consultarlo/Lo he de consultar con la almohada — I'd better sleep on it (lit. 'consult my pillow')
dejar de
No dejes de llamarla/No la dejes de llamar — Don't forget to phone her
ir a
Me temía que Roberto fuera a contárselo/se lo fuera a contar a mamá — I was worried that Roberto would go and tell it to mother
volver a
Como vuelvas a decírmelo/Como me lo vuelvas a decir, me voy — If you say it to me again, I'm going
hacer
Me hizo abrirlo/Me lo hizo abrir — He made me open it

The list at 18.2.3 indicates those common verbs which allow this shifting of suffixed pronouns, although some verbs, e.g. *fingir*, are controversial.

Pronouns cannot be shifted in this way if:

(a) The earlier verb is a 'pronominal' verb (see Chapter 26 for a discussion of pronominal verbs).

Volverse 'to turn round' is a pronominal verb in its own right (discussed at 26.6.2 and 27.2), so one says *Se volvió a mirarla* 'He turned to look at her' but not *Se la volvió a mirar*. The latter is only possible if we take the *se* to stand for *le* and the verb to be *volver* and not *volverse*, as in *El médico volvió a mirarle la lengua* 'The doctor looked at his tongue again' > *Se la volvió a mirar* 'He looked at it again'.

Compare the following examples in which *ver* and *dejar* are **not** pronominal verbs and therefore allow pronoun shifting:

Nos ha visto hacerlo/Nos lo ha visto hacer — He saw us do it
Os dejaron llamarla/Os la dejaron llamar — They let you ring her

Other common pronominal verbs that do not allow pronoun shifting are: *ponerse a* 'to begin', *echarse a* 'to begin' (the non-pronominal verb of the same meaning, *echar a*, also does not allow pronoun shifting), *meterse a* 'to begin'. The asterisked forms in the following examples are not correct Spanish:

Se puso a hacerlo (not **Se lo puso a hacer*)	He started to do it
(Se) lo echó a perder (not **(Se) echó a perderlo*)	(roughly) He lost it/'Off he goes and loses it'
Se metió a venderlos (not **Se los metió a vender*)	He started to sell them

(b) If any other word intervenes between the verb phrase and the following infinitive: *Trató varias veces de hacerlo* 'He tried several times to do it' but not **Lo trató varias veces de hacer*; *Quisiera no hacerlo* 'I'd prefer not to do it' but not **Lo quisiera no hacer*; *Quiero mucho verla*, not **La quiero mucho ver* for *Quiero mucho verla* 'I really want to see her', etc.

An exception is made of a few common verb phrases that include a preposition, usually *a* or *de* or the conjunction *que*: *Lo trató **de** hacer* 'He tried to do it', *Le tengo **que** hablar* 'I've got to talk to her', *Lo empezó **a** hacer* 'He began to do it'.

The rule is also sometimes broken in familiar speech, cf. *No le tengo **nada** que envidiar*, familiar for *No tengo nada que envidiarle* 'I've got nothing to envy him/her/you for':

El que no se tiene que andar metiendo eres tú (A. Mastretta, Mexico, dialogue)	The one who shouldn't go round getting involved is you

(c) If the main verb is a positive imperative: *Procura hacerlo* 'Try to do it', *Ven a verme* 'Come and see me'. Forms like *Venme a ver* are popular or familiar. But negative imperatives can be shifted in informal styles: *No intentes hacerlo* or *No lo intentes hacer* 'Don't try to do it', *No vengas a verme/No me vengas a ver* 'Don't come and see me'.

Notes
(i) In *Voy a verla* 'I'm going to see her' either motion or futurity is meant. Usually *La voy a ver* can only be interpreted as a future form of the verb: 'I'll see her', although familiar speech may allow shifting with both meanings: *Ellos me fueron a comprar el billete* (Interview in *Triunfo*, Spain) 'They went and bought my ticket for me'.
(ii) If more than one infinitive is involved in a construction that allows pronoun shifting, several solutions are possible, the first being safest for foreigners:

No quiero volver a decírtelo	I don't want to tell you it again
No quiero volvértelo a decir	" "
No te lo quiero volver a decir	" "
Puedes empezar a hacerlo	You can start to do it
Puedes empezarlo a hacer	" "
Lo puedes empezar a hacer	" "
Debes tratar de hacerlo	You must try to do it
Debes tratarlo de hacer	" "
Lo debes tratar de hacer	" "

However, if two pronouns are joined as suffixes they must stay together if they are shifted. In other words, starting from *Tienes que vérselo hacer* which, for Peninsular speakers at least, is the correct way of saying 'You have to see him doing it', the only permitted colloquial shift is *Se lo tienes que ver hacer*. However, we found that

Latin-American informants rejected *Se lo tienes que ver hacer* in favour of *Le tienes que ver hacerlo*.

(iii) It is difficult to explain why some verbal phrases allow pronoun shifting whereas others do not. The difference between a phrase like *tratar de* 'to try to', which allows pronoun shifting, and *tardar en* 'to be late in'/'to take time over . . .', which does not, is presumably that the preposition *de* has become so intimately fused with *tratar* that the two words are processed by the speaker as a single word. Only long familiarity with the language can resolve this problem of when pronoun shifting is possible.

11.14.5 Position of pronouns with the gerund

(a) In combination with *estar* (continuous verb forms) and a few other auxiliary verbs like *andar, ir, venir*, the pronouns may be either attached or shifted:

Te lo estoy contando/Estoy contándotelo	I'm telling you it
Nos estuvieron esperando/Estuvieron esperándonos	They waited for us
Os lo estoy diciendo/Estoy diciéndooslo	I'm saying it to you (*vosotros*)
Se me quedó mirando/Se quedó mirándome (the *se* belongs to *quedarse*)	He remained gazing at me

The second construction is slightly more formal and is probably safer for foreign students.

(b) In other cases the pronouns are always attached to the gerund: *Disfruta mirándolo* 'He enjoys himself looking at it', *Se divierte quemándolos* 'He amuses himself by burning them', *Contesta insultándolos* 'He replies by insulting them'.

Notes
(i) *Seguir* allows both constructions, but some native speakers did not accept pronoun shifting with *continuar*: *Se seguían viendo/Seguían viéndose* 'They went on seeing one another', *Me sigue dando la lata/Sigue dándome la lata* 'He's still pestering me', but *Continuaban viéndose, Continúa dándome la lata*.

(ii) In case **(a)**, if the auxiliary verb is an infinitive preceded by one of the verbs that allow pronoun shifting (see 11.14.4), several solutions are possible: *Debe estar recordándolo/Debe estarlo recordando/Lo debe estar recordando* 'He must be remembering it/him', *Tenía que quedarse mirándola/Tenía que quedársela mirando/Se la tenía que quedar mirando* 'He had to remain looking at her'.

11.14.6 Position with past participles

Pronouns come before the auxiliary verb:

Se ha equivocado	She's made a mistake
Se lo ha traído de China	He's brought it from China
Te lo hemos mandado ya	We've already sent it to you

Notes
(i) In phrases in which pronoun shifting is possible (discussed at 11.14.4), there are two options:

Se lo hemos tenido que vender/Hemos tenido que vendérselo	We had to sell it to him
La he vuelto a ver/He vuelto a verla	I've seen her again
No he podido abrirlo/No lo he podido abrir	I couldn't open it
Ha debido hablarle/Le ha debido hablar	He must have spoken to him

(ii) Literary language used to join personal pronouns to past participles when the auxiliary verb was deleted, but this is now only seen in flowery writing in some Latin-American Republics, e.g. *un accidente ocurrídole en el corral de yeguas* 'an accident that happened to him in the yard where the mares are kept' (Uruguay, cited Kany, 156), usually *que le había ocurrido*.

11.15 Emphasis of object pronouns

(a) Object pronouns may be emphasized by adding *a* and the prepositional form of the pronoun:

*La vi **a ella**, pero no **a él***	I saw **her** but not **him**
*Te lo darán **a ti**, pero no **a él***	They'll give it to **you**, but not to **him**
*¡**A mí** me lo dices!*	You're telling **me**!?

(b) Reflexive phrases may be emphasized by the appropriate number and gender of *mismo* added to a prepositional pronoun. Reciprocal sentences can be emphasized by the appropriate form of *el uno* and *el otro*:

Se lavaron	They washed (themselves)/They were washed
*Se lavaron **a sí mismos***	They washed **themselves**
Es difícil vivir con quien no se estima a sí mismo (*ABC*, Spain)	It's difficult to live with someone who does not value himself ('herself' is no doubt also intended)
Se quieren el uno al otro	They love one another
Se quieren la una a la otra (two females)	They love one another
Se envidian los unos a los otros	They envy one another (more than two involved)

Note

If both males and females are involved in a reciprocal sentence, the logical form might be thought to be *el uno a la otra*, but both pronouns are masculine: *Antonio y María se quieren **el uno al otro*** 'Antonio and Maria love one another'.

11.16 Redundant object pronouns

Spanish makes constant use of pronouns even when the thing they refer to is named by a noun: cf. ***Le** di un anillo a María* 'I gave Maria a ring' (lit. 'I gave to her to Maria a ring'), *Los demás **los** tienes que dejar aquí* 'The rest you'll have to leave here' (lit. 'the rest you'll have to leave them here'). Some of these redundant pronouns are virtually obligatory, others are more typical of informal styles.

11.16.1 Redundancy when object precedes verb

If, for purposes of emphasis or focus, the direct or indirect object of a verb precedes the verb, a redundant pronoun is usually obligatory. Compare *Compré esta casa hace cinco años* and *Esta casa **la** compré hace cinco años* 'I bought this house five years ago'. Examples:

*Lo que dice en público jamás **lo** consentiría ninguno de los dirigentes de la pequeña pantalla* (*Cambio16*, Spain)	What he says in public would never be tolerated by the people in charge of the 'small screen' (TV)
*A alguno de vosotros **os** quisiera ver yo en un buen fregado* (D. Sueiro, familiar Spanish dialogue)	I'd like to see one of you in a real mess
*Eso no me **lo** negarás*	You won't deny me that
*Al profesor Berlin no **le** parece tan importante*	It does not seem so important to

que Maquiavelo propusiera esa disyuntiva (M. Vargas Llosa, Peru)	Professor Berlin that Machiavelli suggested this dilemma

Notes
(i) The pronoun is omitted after *eso* in such phrases as *Eso creo yo* 'That's what I think', *Eso digo yo* 'That's what I think' (but compare *Eso lo digo yo* 'That's what I **say**'). Omission in other cases is very rare, but not unknown.
(ii) For a discussion of the effect of putting the object before the verb see 28.2.3.
(iii) The redundant pronoun is not used when the object noun is not preceded by an article or demonstrative adjective: *Mucha prisa ha debido tener* 'He *must* have been in a hurry', *Muchas cosas quiero contarte* 'I want to tell you a lot of things', *Aviones tenemos aquí que han costado más de cincuenta millones* 'We've got planes here that cost more than 50 million . . .'.

11.16.2 Redundant pronouns and 'indirect objects'
A redundant pronoun is normally inserted to show that a noun is 'involved', by the verb in one of the ways listed in List A at 12.3 (i.e. 'receiving', 'losing', 'advantage', 'involvement', etc.):

Esta solución le pareció a doña Matilde la más acertada (J.M. Guelbenzu, Spain)	This solution seemed to be the best one to Doña Matilde
Bueno, si no le dicen a uno cómo hay que hacerlo . . .	Well, if they don't tell one how to do it . . .
A vos te la tienen jurada (M. Puig, Argentina, dialogue)	They've got it in for you
Le puso un nuevo conmutador a la radio	He put a new knob on the radio
Tráigale un jugo[11] de naranja a la niña (A. Mastretta, Mexico, dialogue)	Bring the little girl an orange juice

Note
Omission of the redundant pronoun depersonalizes the indirect object and would be appropriate in formal writing, official documents or business letters when a distant tone is required: *Comunique los detalles al señor Presidente* 'Inform the President of the details', *Esto no corresponde a Odradek* (J.L. Borges: Odradek is a non-human creature) 'This is not a trait of Odradek's', *Es necesario dar cera a este tipo de suelo todas las semanas* (instruction leaflet, Spain) 'This type of floor must be waxed every week'.
   In most cases the redundant pronoun is used, more so than fifty years ago and always with proper names: *Dáselo a Mario* 'Give it to Mario', *Se lo robaron a Julia* 'They stole it from Juliet' (*robar a . . .* 'to steal from . . .').

11.16.3 *Le* for redundant *les*
There is a strong tendency in spontaneous language everywhere to use the singular *le* in this construction for the plural *les*, especially (but not exclusively) when the pronoun refers to something inanimate:

Cualquiera le da vuelta a las razones por las que te viniste conmigo (J.M. Guelbenzu, Spain, dialogue)	Anyone might ponder on the reasons why you came to me
no darle importancia a los detalles	not to ascribe importance to details
¿Quieres devolverle la isla de Manhattan a los Algonquins? (C. Fuentes, Mexico, dialogue)	Do you want to give Manhattan Island back to the Algonquins?
Y ese pequeño elemento ya justificaría que yo le pusiera la firma a sus papeles (M. Puig, Argentina, dialogue)	And that little detail would be enough to justify my signing your papers

[11] In Spain *el zumo* is used for the juice of fruits and vegetables, *el jugo* for meat juices.

Le viene natural a los niños (educated Spaniard, overheard)	It comes naturally to children
Bayardo San Román le puso término a tantas conjeturas (G. García Márquez, Colombia)	Bayardo San Román put an end to so many conjectures

This tendency is so deep-rooted, even in educated speech, that sentences like *Él les* (for *le*) *da mucha importancia a las apariencias* 'He ascribes a lot of importance to appearances' sound frankly odd to many speakers. But it is technically 'wrong', and should be avoided in formal writing, e.g. in this case by omitting the redundant pronoun altogether.

11.16.4 Redundant direct object pronouns

As was said at 11.16.1, a redundant pronoun is usually obligatory when an object precedes the verb.

When the direct object *follows* the verb, use of a redundant object pronoun is common with *todo* and is required when it is necessary to reinforce an object pronoun, e.g. *La vi a ella pero no a él* 'I saw *her* but not *him*' (not *vi a ella*).

In other cases use of a redundant pronoun with *direct objects* is avoided in Spain. However, it is very common in Latin America in spontaneous speech, and in Argentina it appears even in literary styles, especially with proper names:

Ahora me lo tienes que contar todo (normal with *todo*)	Now you have to tell me everything
Morgan . . . también lo mandó llamar a Abdulmalik (J.L. Borges, Argentina dialogue; Spain. . .mandó llamar a Abdulmalik)*	Morgan also had Abdulmalik sent for
Le quiere mucho a ese hijo (Spain, familiar)	She loves that son a lot
No lo conocen a Perón en Córdoba, lo confunden con un cantante de tangos (J. Asís, dialogue, Argentina; Spain *no conocen. . .*)	They've never heard of Perón in Córdoba. They think he's a tango singer
Convénzalo a su amigo de que acepte la beca (M. Vargas Llosa, Peru, dialogue; Spain *convenza a su amigo. . .*)	Persuade your friend to accept the grant

11.16.5 Redundant pronouns in relative clauses

Redundant pronouns occur in spoken Spanish in relative clauses, especially in non-restrictive clauses, and may appear in writing, particularly if several words separate the *que* and the verb that depends on it:

Te voy a hacer una confesión que nunca me animé a hacerla a nadie (Lat. Am., from Kany, 150)	I'm going to make you a confession I never had the courage to make to anybody
Los gramáticos aconsejan muchas cosas que nadie las dice (Spain, informant)	Grammarians recommend lots of things that no one says
Sólo por ti dejaría a don Memo a quien tanto le debo (C. Fuentes, Mexico, dialogue)	Only for you would I leave Don Memo, whom I owe so much

This construction may sound uneducated, especially in restrictive clauses (the first two examples), and is best left to native speakers.

12

Le/les and *lo/la/los/las*

This chapter is devoted to the problem of the relationship between the third-person object pronouns *le/les* and *lo/la/los/las*.

For first and second-person pronouns (including *usted* and *ustedes*) and for third-person subject pronouns (*él, ella, ellos, ellos*), see Chapter 11.

12.1 The *le/lo* controversy: summary of arguments in this chapter

The rules governing the correct choice of third-person object pronouns are complex and vary a great deal throughout the Spanish-speaking world. The problem may be summarized thus:

The personal pronoun used for third-person *direct* objects, human and non-human, in more than 90% of cases and in more than 90% of the Spanish-speaking world, is *lo/la* for the singular and *los/las* for the plural. *Le/les* are used for indirect objects as defined at 11.7.2 and 12.3. This scheme is recommended for beginners pending deeper knowledge of the language.

However, *le/les* is also used for *direct* objects in the following cases:

(a) In the standard language of Spain when the direct object is singular, human and male: *Yo le vi* 'I saw him' instead of *Yo lo vi*. See 12.5.1.
(b) In all countries, with certain verbs, listed at 12.6.4.
(c) Sometimes as the object pronoun for *ustedes*, to denote respect. See 12.6.1.
(d) Frequently when the subject of the verb is inanimate and the direct object is human, especially when the human object is reacting to the action described. See 12.6.2.
(e) When the subject is impersonal *se* and the direct object is human. See 12.6.3.

12.2 Third-person object pronouns: basic rules

Beginners can apply the following scheme, which is based on the Academy's current preferences and is valid for all of Latin America and acceptable to most Spaniards. These rules will produce correct sentences in over 90% of cases.

Preferred third-person object pronouns (from the Academy's *Esbozo. . .*, 3.10.5c):

Singular	Direct object	Indirect object
masculine	*lo*	*le*
feminine	*la*	*le*

Plural	Direct object	Indirect object
masculine	*los*	*les*
feminine	*las*	*les*

Examples:

Ángela vio a Antonio	***lo** vio*
Angela saw Antonio	she saw him
Antonio vio a Ángela	***la** vio*
Antonio saw Angela	he saw her
Vio el libro	***lo** vio*
(S)he saw the book	(s)he saw it
Vio la casa	***la** vio*
(S)he saw the house	(s)he saw it
María dijo hola a Juan	***le** dijo hola*
Maria said hello to Juan (and vice-versa)	she said hello to him/her
Vio a los hombres	***los** vio*
(S)he saw the men	(s)he saw them
Vio a las mujeres	***las** vio*
(S)he saw the women	(s)he saw them
Vio los libros	***los** vio*
(S)he saw the books	(s)he saw them
Vio las casas	***las** vio*
(S)he saw the houses	(s)he saw them
Dijo hola a María y a José	***les** dijo hola*
(S)he said hello to María and José	(s)he said hello to them
Dijo hola a María y a Ángela	***les** dijo hola*
(S)he said hello to Maria and Angela	(s)he said hello to them

Notes

(i) Standard European Spanish prefers the form *le* for a **human** male direct object: *le vi* 'I saw him', although *lo vi* is considered by the Academy to be the correct form and is much more common than in the past; see 12.5.1 for details. However, in the plural *los* is more common than *les* for male human direct objects and is generally preferred; see 12.5.2 for details.

(ii) *Usted/ustedes* 'you' (polite) take third-person object pronouns: *Doctora Smith, le aseguro que la llamé ayer* 'Dr Smith (fem.) I assure you I rang you/her yesterday', *Lo vi ayer* 'I saw him/it/you yesterday', *Le vi ayer* (Spain only) 'I saw you (masc.)/him yesterday', *Los vi ayer* 'I saw them/you yesterday', *Las vi ayer* 'I saw them/you (fem.) yesterday'.

12.3 Use of *le/les* as 'indirect object' pronouns: detailed rules

(*Le/les* are sometimes also used as direct object pronouns: see 12.5-12.6.)

Le/les are often described as third-person 'indirect object' pronouns (*pronombres de complemento indirecto*). However, 'indirect object' is a term that covers many different meanings, and the more general principle underlying the use of *le/les* seems to be the following:

Le/les **replace any person or thing gaining from or losing by the action described in the verb phrase.**

The nature of these gains or losses must be inferred from the meaning of the verb phrase or from clues provided by context. Whatever departures from these examples they may hear, foreign students are advised to use *le/les* in the following contexts.

List A: Typical uses of *le/les*

Le can be translated 'him', 'her', 'it', 'you', *les* as 'you' or 'them'. The choice in the translations may be dictated by context, but in some cases it is arbitrary.

(a) Receiving or acquiring any thing, impression or sensation:

Le di la carta	I gave her/him/you the letter
Voy a darle una mano de pintura	I'll give it a coat of paint
No le dije la verdad	I didn't tell you/him/her the truth
Les suministramos acero y petróleo	We supply them steel and crude oil
Ángel le alcanzó un cuchillo	Angel handed him a knife
Le tirábamos bolas de nieve	We were throwing snowballs at her
Le pusieron una inyección	They gave him/her/you an injection
Le echaron una sábana	They threw a sheet over him
Se le agrega queso rallado	Grated cheese is added to it
Se le pegó una brizna de hierba	A blade of grass stuck to her
Le valió una sonrisa	It earned him a smile
Su padre le contagió sus locuras	His father infected him with his mad ways
Les enseñé el camino	I showed them the way
Le tocó el premio gordo	She got first prize
Les corresponde la mitad	They're/You're entitled to half
Les interesa callarlo	It's in their interest to keep it quiet
Le convenía que fuera así	It suited him that way
No les es ventajoso	It's not advantageous to them
Esa chaqueta no le va	That jacket doesn't suit him/her
Las cosas le iban mal	Things were going badly for her
Le hemos lavado tres camisas	We've washed three shirts for him
No le pasó nada	Nothing happened to him
cuando se le sube el whisky	when the whisky goes to her head
Se le ocurrió llamar a la policía	He had the idea of phoning the police
No le parece mucho	It doesn't seem much to him
Le constaba que . . .	It was a fact to him that . . .
Le suena mal	It sounds wrong to her
Le da igual	It's all the same to him
La secretaria le cayó bien	He took a liking to the secretary
Le gusta la miel	She/he/it likes honey
Le agradó la respuesta	The reply pleased her
Les dolía	It hurt/pained them
Cuánto les pesaba	How sorry they were

(b) Loss or removal from:

Les han robado un millón de pesos	They've stolen a million pesos from them/you
Esto le ha quitado un peso de encima	This has taken a weight off her mind
Mario le ha quitado a Ana	Mario's taken Ana away from him (N.B. personal *a*)
Le he comprado un cuadro	I've bought a picture from him
Le están sacando una muela	They're taking one of her teeth out

Le costó un dineral	It cost her a fortune
Se le cae el pelo	His hair's falling out
Se le ha muerto un hijo	A son of his has died
Se le pasa pronto	She gets over it quickly
Le arrancaron la pistola	They seized the pistol from him

(c) Sufficiency, insufficiency, lack, excess:

Les basta decir que sí	All they have to do is say 'yes'
Le faltan mil pesos	She's 1000 pesos short
Le faltaba un dedo meñique	One of his little fingers was missing
Mil pesetas al día le alcanzaban para vivir	She could manage on 1000 ptas a day

(d) Requesting, requiring, ordering:

Le hicieron varias preguntas	They asked her several questions
Le pidieron sus señas	They asked him his name and address
Les rogaron que se sentasen/sentaran	They requested them to sit down
Les ordenaron rendirse	They ordered them to surrender
Les exigía un esfuerzo continuo	It required continuous effort from them

Note
Compare *Le mandó que comprara/comprase pan* 'He ordered her/him to buy bread' and *La mandó a comprar pan* 'He sent her to buy bread'.

(e) Numerous phrases involving *tener* plus an emotion (although the equivalent verbs, *respetar*, *temer*, etc. may take *lo/la/los/las*):

Le tiene miedo	He fears him/her/you
Su madre le tenía poco cariño	His mother felt little fondness for him
Le tiene ojeriza	She has it in for him
Le tenías una envidia tremenda	You were enormously envious of him

(f) Numerous set phrases consisting of *hacer* plus a noun:

El frío les hacía mucho daño	The cold did them a lot of harm
El chico le hizo una mueca	The boy pulled a face at him
Mi nieto nunca les hacía caso	My grandson never heeded them
Tienes que hacerle frente a la realidad	You have to face up to reality
Le hacía falta reflexionar	He/she needed to reflect

(g) To indicate persons or things affected by something done to a part of their body or to some intimate possession (for further details about this construction and for the omission of the possessive adjective with parts of the body and intimate possessions, see 8.3.4):

¡Le estás pisando los pies!	You're treading on his feet
Los fríos le hielan los dedos	The cold weather freezes her fingers
A esa edad se les ablanda el cerebro	Their brains go soft at that age
Don Juan le acariciaba las mejillas	Don Juan was stroking her cheeks
Los nervios le jugaban malas partidas	His nerves were playing tricks on him
Se le ha hundido la moral	Her morale has collapsed
No le veo la gracia	I don't see what's funny in it
Le he roto la camisa	I've torn his shirt
Le dejaron las gafas hechas añicos (las gafas = Lat. Am. los anteojos)	They shattered her glasses

(h) In a number of less easily classified cases which may all be perceived to convey ideas of 'giving', 'removing', 'benefiting', 'involving', 'affecting intimately':

¿Qué le vamos a hacer?	What can be done about it?
No le hace (Southern Cone; Spain *no tiene que ver*)	That's irrelevant
¡Dale!	Hit him! Go on! Get moving!
Le agradezco	I thank you
El cura les (also *los*) *aconsejaba que no lo hicieran/hiciesen*	The priest advised them not to do it
Le encontraron mil pesos	They found 1000 pesos on her
La respuesta de su hija le afectó mucho (*lo* or *le* possible in Lat. Am.)	His daughter's reply affected him a lot

Note

This multiplicity of meanings can give rise to ambiguities: *Le compré un vestido* 'I bought a dress from her/for her', *Cómprame algo* 'Buy something for/from me', *Ángel me robó una manzana* 'Angel stole an apple from me/for me/on my behalf'. Context nearly always makes the sense plain, or the sentence can be recast: *Compró una calculadora para mí* 'He/she bought a calculator for me', etc.

12.4 Uses of *lo/la/los/las*

Lo/la/los/las are the third-person 'direct object' pronouns, 'direct' object understood here as the person or thing directly affected by a verb phrase but not 'losing' or 'gaining' in the ways described in List A above.

In the following list of examples it will be seen that even when dramatically affected by the verb phrase (as in 'they killed her'), the person or thing denoted by the pronoun is not actively involved as a participant in the action or as an interested party. In fact the condition of the pronoun is very often literally that of an object which merely has the action of the verb done to it.

List B: Contexts normally requiring *lo/la/los/las* (direct object)

The use of *lo* for human males in this list reflects standard Latin-American usage and the Academy's current recommendation. The second of the alternative forms reflects widespread but not obligatory usage in Spain. See 12.2 and 12.5.1 for discussion.

(a) Direct physical actions (although there are exceptions, like *Le pega* 'He beats him/her; see 12.6.4):

Lo/le interrogaron	They interrogated him
La operaron	They operated on her
El perro lo/le mordió	The dog bit him
Coge estos papeles y quémalos	Take these papers and burn them
A usted lo durmieron con algún mejunje en la sidra (J.L. Borges, Argentina, dialogue; Spain *le*)	They put you to sleep with some potion in the cider
Perdone, no quería molestarla	Sorry, I didn't mean to bother you (to a female)
Saca el carburador y límpialo	Take out the carburettor and clean it
—¿Y tu cámara? —La he perdido	'What about your camera?' 'I've lost it'

(b) Verbs of perception – 'seeing', 'hearing', 'knowing', etc.:

Al director no lo/le conozco personalmente	I don't know the director personally
La vi ayer en el mercado	I saw her/you yesterday in the market
Sabía que el ladrón estaba en la habitación porque lo/le oí	I knew the thief was in the room because I heard him
El agente lo/le miraba	The policeman was looking at him

(c) Praise, blame, admiration, love, hatred and other actions denoting attitudes towards a person or thing:

Sus profesores lo/le alaban	His teachers praise him/you
A las monjas las envidio mucho	I envy nuns a lot
Lo/le admiro profundamente	I admire him deeply
Su marido la adora	Her/Your husband adores her
La considero una amiga	I consider her/you a friend

(For some Latin Americans *Lo quieren* = 'They want him', *Le quieren* = 'They love him'.)

(d) 'Naming', 'nominating', 'describing' (but see 12.6.4 for the verb *llamar*):

Los denominaron "los decadentes"	They named them 'the decadents'
Lo/le nombraron alcalde	They nominated him mayor
Las describió en términos despectivos	He described them (fem.) in pejorative terms
Lo calificó de tragedia	He described it as a tragedy

(e) Many other actions done to things or persons but not 'involving' them in the ways described in List A, 12.3:

La crisis energética no la podrá solucionar ningún gobierno elegido	The energy crisis won't be solved by any elected government
El Canciller los recibirá a las siete y cuarto	The Chancellor will receive you/them at 7.15
Este país no hay quien sepa gobernarlo	There's no one who knows how to govern this country
Habrá que defenderlos	We'll have to defend them
No pude convencerla	I couldn't convince her
Yo intentaba evitarlos	I was trying to avoid them
etc.	

Notes
(i) *Lo/la/los/las* agree in gender with the noun they replace. If they do not replace a specific noun, *lo* is used: *Dijo que llegaría a las siete, pero no lo creo* 'He said he'd arrive at seven, but I don't believe it', *Esto no lo aguanta nadie* 'No one can stand this'. This neuter use of *lo* is discussed at 7.4.
(ii) The first and second-person pronouns *me/te/nos/os* could be used in any of the above sentences in place of the third-person pronoun, provided the result makes sense.

12.5   The *le/lo* controversy: general remarks

Interminable controversy surrounds the use of *le* as a *direct object* pronoun for humans.

Beginners may follow the scheme given in 12.2, but they will soon come across at least some of the variants described hereafter. Some of these variants are local and dialectal and need not concern foreign students. But some of them are basic features of Spanish, particularly the European use (described at 12.5.1) of *le* as a direct object pronoun for human males, and the use of *le* for *lo/la* everywhere in certain types of sentence (12.6).

Section 12.5 describes regional variations. Section 12.6 describes certain subtleties in the use of *le* and *lo* that are found in the best written and spoken styles throughout the Spanish-speaking world.

12.5.1 *Le* for *lo* in Spain (*leísmo*): further details

The standard language of Spain, i.e. the variety used in the media and by most educated speakers in Madrid and central regions, favours *le vi* for *lo vi* when the sentence means 'I saw him' as opposed to 'I saw it':

—¿*Has visto a Miguel?*	'Have you seen Miguel?'
—*No, no **le** he visto*	'No, I haven't seen him'
—¿*Has visto mi boli?*	'Have you seen my ball-point pen?'
—*No, no **lo** he visto*	'No, I haven't seen it'

There is much disagreement about this phenomenon, and the Academy has itself changed its mind on the subject several times in the last 150 years and has now come round to advocating the Latin-American preference for *lo* for both human males and masculine non-human direct objects. But in the face of massive resistance in Spain the Academy officially 'tolerates' forms like *Le vi* for 'I saw **him**'.[1]

Students may still encounter a certain amount of anti-*loísta* prejudice in Spain: *leísmo* is very deeply entrenched in central regions and many Spaniards still claim that *lo vi* applied to a male human being sounds vaguely sub-standard or regional. Students will also note much inconsistency in the use of *le* or *lo* with reference to human males in Spain, *lo* being more frequent in the South and increasingly common, it seems, in all circles.

The Academy's current dislike of *le* as a 'direct object' pronoun, based as it is on an over-rigorous distinction between 'direct' and 'indirect' objects, does not in fact do justice to the subtlety of the Spanish language on either continent. The following pages attempt to provide a succinct account of the complexities of the problem. For a full discussion see E. García (1975).

12.5.2 *Les* for *los* in Spain

Use of *les* for *los*, e.g. *Les vi* 'I saw them' (masc.) is also frequently heard in colloquial language in Spain, especially in Castile, when the pronoun refers to human males, but this construction is less common than *Los vi* and is in fact not 'tolerated' by the Academy or favoured in writing. Seco (1992), 164, says of *No les he visto* applied to human males that 'literary language does not generally admit it'. Use of *les* for *los* sounds old-fashioned to some Spaniards, but it is nevertheless quite often seen in writing:

Les *llevaron a una casa donde estuvieron mucho rato esperando* (Juan Benet, Spain, for *los llevaron . . .*)	They took them to a house where they waited for a long time

12.5.3 *Le* for *la* in Spain: regional usage

Speakers from North-Western Spain, especially Navarre and the Basque provinces, habitually use *le* for female human direct objects as well as for males: *Le vi* = both 'I saw him' and 'I saw her', *Lo vi* (masc.) and *La vi* (fem.) 'I saw it'. This usage sometimes appears in literature and is generally accepted as a regional variant. The same phenomenon is sporadically heard elsewhere, e.g. in Valencia and in Paraguay.

---

[1] The Academy now prefers *lo* on historical grounds. The argument in the *Esbozo* is that since *lo* comes from the Classical Latin accusative *illum* and *le* from the dative *illi*, 'I saw **him**' should be *lo vi* in Modern Spanish and 'I said **to him**' *le dije*.

12.5.4 *La* for *le* (*a ella*) in Spain (*laísmo*)

Older speakers in Madrid and speakers in the countryside of central Spain often use *la* for the **indirect** object pronoun to refer to a female or feminine noun:

?*Yo **la** dije la verdad* (for *Yo le dije la verdad*)	I told her the truth
?*Yo **la** alabo el gusto* (M. Delibes, Spain, dialogue; for *Yo le alabo el gusto*)	I praise her taste

School-teachers have waged a long war against this type of *laísmo* and it is now apparently disappearing in the speech of Madrid. It is common in pre-twentieth century literature. Foreign students should avoid it.

12.5.5 *Lo* for *le* in Latin America

Extreme *loísmo*, i.e. use of *lo* for the indirect object, is reported in popular speech in many parts of Latin America: Kany, p. 137, cites from Guatemala *Ya no tarda en llegar. ¿Quiere hablar**lo**?* 'He won't be long now. Do you want to speak to him?' (for *hablar**le***). The same phenomenon is occasionally heard in dialects in Spain. It should not be imitated.

12.5.6 *Le* for *lo/la* applied to inanimate objects in Spain

In familiar speech in Madrid and in pre-twentieth century texts, one finds *le* used as the direct object pronoun even for inanimate nouns: ?*No **le** he leído todavia* 'I haven't read it [*el libro*] yet', ?*Unos niegan el hecho, otros **le** afirman* 'Some deny the fact, others assert it' (B. Feijoo, mid-eighteenth century).

This extreme *leísmo*, endorsed by the Academy until the 1850s, is nowadays considered sub-standard or dialect unless it is a rare instance of genuine personification. However, it occasionally appears in written language, cf. *. . . hacen que San Prudencio y otros obispos maldigan al pueblo y **le** destruyan* (J. Caro Baroja, Spain) '. . . they make Saint Prudentius and other bishops curse the village and destroy it'.

12.6 *Le* used for human direct objects throughout the Spanish-speaking world

Even when all the regional and dialectal factors are excluded, *le* is still found as a direct object pronoun in the best styles in Spain where *la/las* would be expected, and in Latin America where *lo/los* or *la/las* would be the predicted forms.

This problem arises because a simple distinction between 'direct' and 'indirect' objects does not hold in Spanish. This is demonstrated in the translation of the following sentences, in both of which 'her' is the *direct* object of 'flattered':

(a) 'He flattered her'
(b) 'The joke flattered her'

We expect the Spanish translation to be

*Él **la** halagó*
*La broma **la** halagó*

and this indeed is what many native speakers accept. However, many speakers, Spanish and Latin-American, translate (b) as *La broma* **le** *halagó*, this being the more common form in educated speech (in a questionnaire given to 28 Spaniards from the Madrid region, 90% preferred *le* in the second example and 87% preferred *la* in the first; García, 1975, reports similar results for Buenos Aires).

As a result, although the rules for the use of *le/les* already given at 12.3 and the rules for *lo/la/los/las* given at 12.4 will enable foreign learners to form sentences that are acceptable to the majority of native speakers, they do not always explain the actual use of these pronouns.

12.6.1 Le to denote respect

In certain areas some speakers use *le* for human direct objects as a mark of respect. Spaniards who say *lo vi* for 'I saw him' may prefer *le vi* for the polite *usted* form, 'I saw you'.

Argentine informants were convinced that they would say *No quería molestarle* 'I didn't mean to bother you', speaking to their boss, but *molestarlo* when speaking about him. Colombian informants said *molestarlo* in both cases.

Examples of *le* used with *usted* are:

¡Buenas tardes, hijitos! Les encuentro muy alegres (A. Buero Vallejo, Spain, dialogue)	Good afternoon, my dears! I find you very cheerful
Si le molesta el humo, señora, lo apago	If the smoke troubles you, Señora, I'll put it out

but

Lo apagué porque la molestaba el humo	I put it out because the smoke was bothering her

Note
'Respect' may imply that the object is active. García (1975) reports that Buenos Aires speakers differentiate *Le llevaron al hospital* and *Lo llevaron al hospital*, 'They took him to the hospital', the former implying that the patient is walking or cooperative. For Colombian informants only *lo llevaron* was possible.

12.6.2 Le/les preferred when subject is inanimate

Le/les are often the preferred direct object pronouns when they denote a human being and the subject of the verb is inanimate[2]. This statement applies both to Spain and to Latin America. Compare the following sentences: *La espera su marido* 'Her husband's waiting for her' and *Le espera una catástrofe* 'A catastrophe awaits her/him'.

Le is especially preferred when the human direct object is *reacting* emotionally, as in sentences like 'It surprised him', 'It shocked her', 'He doesn't

---

[2] García notes of Buenos Aires speakers that whereas only 14% of a sample would translate 'he convinced him' as *él le convenció* (the rest say *él lo convenció*), 54% say *este color no le convence* 'this colour doesn't convince him'. We found that of 23 educated Spaniards, mostly from Madrid, only 20% used *le* in *yo la convencí* 'I convinced her', but 70% preferred *le* in *Si a tu suegra este color no le convence, que elija otro* 'If this colour doesn't convince your mother-in-law, let her choose another'.

know what's in store for him'. The phenomenon is vividly illustrated in this Peruvian sentence where *le* reflects an inanimate subject (a tooth) and a human direct object, but the *lo* reflects both a human subject (the dentist) and a human direct object:

Si [la muela] le molesta mucho, lo puedo atender hoy mismo (Peruvian dentist to male patient, from *Variedades*, 238)	If it [the tooth] is troubling you a lot, I can attend to you today

Further examples (all Latin American):

Él se miraba la sangre que le había salpicado (M. Vargas Llosa, Peru)	He looked at the blood that had spattered him
Sin embargo, le molestaba encararse con Parodi (J.L. Borges, Argentina)	Yet it troubled him to come face to face with Parodi
Durante mucho tiempo le angustió esa novedad (E. Sábato, Argentina)	For a long while that new turn of events (lit. 'novelty') filled him with anguish
. . . lo que más le preocupaba de la muerte al doctor Urbino . . . (G. García Márquez, Colombia)	What worried doctor Urbino most about the death . . .

A number of verbs often (but not invariably) take *le/les* when their subject is inanimate. The following examples illustrate this tendency:

Le acometió una duda	A doubt assailed him/her
La angustia le acompañaba siempre	Anguish went with her always
Yo la acompañaba siempre	I always went with her
A Consuelo le admiró que no contestase	It surprised Consuelo that he did not reply
A Consuelo la admiro mucho	I admire Consuelo a great deal
El dolor que le afligía . . .	The pain that afflicted him/her . . .
No sabe la suerte que le aguarda	He/she doesn't know the fate that's waiting for him/her
Yo la aguardé (likewise *esperar*)	I awaited her
No le alcanzan mil pesetas para vivir	1000 ptas aren't enough for him/her to live on
No pude alcanzarla	I couldn't catch up with her
El gas les hace reír	The gas makes them laugh
Yo los haré reír	I'll make them laugh

And similarly such verbs as the following: *asustar* 'to frighten', *ayudar* 'to help', *calmar* 'to calm', *coger* 'to catch', *complacer* 'to please', *convencer* 'to convince', *distraer* 'to amuse'/'to distract', *encantar* 'to enchant'/'to charm', *estorbar* 'to impede'/'to get in the way of', *exasperar* 'to exasperate', *fascinar* 'to fascinate', *fatigar* 'to fatigue', *indignar* 'to outrage', *inquietar* 'to worry', *molestar* 'to trouble', *preocupar* 'to worry', *seducir* 'to charm', *tranquilizar* 'to calm', etc.

Note
It must be remembered that many native speakers do not exploit all the potential of these subtleties, so they will often disagree about the correct pronoun to use in any one context. Moreover, strongly *loísta* speakers, e.g. Colombians, may use *lo/la* where others prefer *le*.

12.6.3 Preference for *le/les* after impersonal or reflexive *se*
If impersonal (or, occasionally, reflexive *se*) precedes a third-person pronoun there is a widespread tendency to prefer *le/les* as the direct object pronouns when the object is human.

Se le notaba tímida y cortada (L. Goytisolo, Spain)

Entonces se le leerá como se le debió leer siempre . . . (M. Vargas Llosa, Peru, essay on Camus)

Hola doctor, ¡qué bien se le ve! (Peruvian speaker, *Variedades* 238, *lo* expected)

Licha se le prendió de la solapa (C. Fuentes, Mexico)

Licha se le volvió a abrazar (*ibid.*)

One could see she was timid and embarrassed

Then he will be read as he always should have been read . . .

Hello doctor, you're looking well!

Licha pulled him to her by his lapels

Licha put her arms round him again/Licha drew him to herself again

Notes

(i) Use of *le/les* for the direct object is here a device for removing some of the ambiguities that arise in Spanish from the scarcity of object pronoun forms.

Use of *lo/la* after *se* invites the interpretation of *se* as a substitute for *le* by the rule that two object pronouns beginning with *l* cannot occur side-by-side (see 11.13.1 for discussion). Thus *Le cortó la cabeza* 'He cut his head off' is pronominalized *Se la cortó* 'He cut it off (him)' (for the expected *Le la cortó). For this reason *Se la notaba pálida* suggests 'He noticed that his/her/their hand, face, head, cheek, chin (or some other grammatically feminine noun) was pale'; *Se le notaba . . .* shows that the object is a person. Compare the following examples in which *se* replaces *le* and the object is not human: *Se lo cobró* 'He took **it** off him/her/you', *Se la vendió a ella* 'He sold **it** (fem.) to her', *Se lo leyó a su padre* '(S)he/read **it** to his/her father'.

(ii) In Spain *le* is occasionally seen even for non-human direct objects after impersonal *se*, although in this example *los* would have been more usual: *A los esperpentos de Valle-Inclán siempre se les ha considerado ejemplos de expresionismo español* (A. Buero Vallejo, Spain) 'Valle-Inclán's *esperpentos* have always been considered examples of Spanish expressionism'.

(iii) Use of *la* after impersonal *se* to refer to a female and, in Latin America, of *lo* to refer to a male, is not, however, impossible: *La luz se apagó y apenas se lo veía* (M. Vargas Llosa, Peru) 'The light went out and one could scarcely see him'.

(iv) The verb *llevarse* seems always to prefer *lo* for a direct object pronoun, human or not, even in Spain: *A mi padre me lo voy a llevar a pasar las vacaciones conmigo* 'I'm going to take my father with me on holiday' (*me le* is possible in Spain but less frequent).

12.6.4 Le/les preferred with certain verbs

The following verbs take *le* for their direct object pronoun:

Gustar/agradar/complacer/placer 'to please', and all verbs of similar or opposite meaning: *Le gusta la miel* 'He/she/it likes honey', *Le disgustaba encontrarse sola* 'She disliked finding herself alone'.

Importar 'to matter'/'to concern', *concernir* 'to concern' and verbs of similar meaning: *No les importa que no tengan dinero* 'They don't care that they have no money'; *Eso no le concierne a usted* 'That doesn't concern you'.

Interesar: *Reiteró que sólo un hombre le interesaba en el mundo* 'She repeated that only one man in the world interested her'.

Tirar, when it means 'to pull' rather than 'throw' or 'throw away': *La amiga le tiraba de la mano* (Javier Marías, Spain) 'Her friend was pulling her by the hand'. Compare *Lo/La tiró* 'He threw it/threw it away'.

Tocar, when it means 'to be the turn of' rather than 'to touch': compare *Le toca a usted, señora* 'It's your turn, Señora' and *La tocó a usted, señora* 'He touched you, Señora'.

Creer 'to believe', when its object is human: *Yo no le creo, señora,* 'Señora, I don't believe you', but *Sí que lo creo* 'I *do* believe it'.

Discutir 'argue'/'to discuss' when it means 'answer back': *¿Desde cuándo le discutía?* 'Since when had she been answering him back?' (M. Vargas Llosa, Peruvian dialogue).

Enseñar when its object is human: *Les enseñaba* 'He taught/showed them' but *Lo enseñaba* 'He showed it'.

Entender 'to understand' when its object is human: *No le entiendo* 'I don't understand him/her/you' but *Lo entiendo* 'I understand it'.

Llamar: many speakers prefer *le/les* when the verb means 'to give a name': *Todo el mundo le llama "Chelo"*, 'Everybody calls her "Chelo"', *Se nos informó en un "briefing", que le llaman* (Cuban TV interview) 'We were told in a "briefing", as they call it'. (For christening, educated usage says *Le pusieron María de nombre* 'They called her "Maria"'.) *La/lo/(le)/los/las* are the usual object pronouns used when the verb means 'phone' or 'call to': *Yo la llamaré apenas haya alguna novedad* 'I'll call you/her as soon as there's news'.

Obedecer 'to obey': *¿Le han obedecido a Mademoiselle Durand?* 'Did you obey Mlle Durand?' (E. Poniatowska, Mexico, dialogue), although the verb is also found with *la/lo*.

Pegar 'to beat': [*Lalita*] *te contó que le pegué* (dialogue in M. Vargas Llosa, Peru) 'Lalita told you I hit her', *Dicen que le pega mucho* 'They say he hits him/her/you a lot'. *Pegarlo/pegarla* etc. is assumed to mean 'to stick (i.e. glue) it'.

Preocupar, inquietar 'to worry': *Le preocupa* 'It worries him/her/you'.

Recordar when it means 'to remind'. Cf. *La recuerdo* 'I remember her' but *Recuérdale que viene esta noche* 'Remind her/him that she/he's coming tonight'.

12.6.5 *Le/les* in double accusative constructions

In *Juan la oyó* 'John heard her' *la* is normal since 'she' is not 'actively participant' in any of the ways described at 12.3, List A. In 'John heard her sing an aria' there are two objects, one, 'aria', less active than the other, 'her'. Spanish speakers often use *le* to denote the more active object: *Juan le oyó cantar un aria* (*la* occurs, particularly in Spain, but may be rejected by educated speakers), *Su padre siempre le/la obliga a decir la verdad* 'Her father always obliges her to tell the truth' (*le* preferred but not obligatory).

Notes
(i) *Ver* normally takes *lo* (in Spain *le*)/*la/los/las*: *Yo me quedé con ella porque quería verla firmar el contrato* 'I stayed with her because I wanted to see her sign the contract'.
(ii) *Dejar* 'to let' may elicit *la* (and in Latin America *lo*) – *La dejaron hacerlo* 'They let her do it'. *Permitir* takes *le*: *Le permitieron hacerlo*.

12.7 Pronouns with verbs of motion

For *Acude a ella* 'He goes to her', *Se le acercó* 'She approached him', see 11.8.

12.8 'Resumptive' or 'echoing' *lo* with *ser* and *estar*

The predicate of *ser, estar, parecer* is resumed or 'echoed' by *lo*:

—*Parece alemana*	'She looks German'
—*Lo es*	'She is'

See 7.4 note **(i)** for details.

12.9 *Se* for *le/les* when they are followed by *lo/la/los/las*

For the obligatory replacement of *le* by *se* when it precedes *lo/la/los/las*, as in *Se lo di* 'I gave it to him' (*never *le lo di*), see 11.13.1.

12.10 Latin-American *se los* for *se lo*

For the colloquial Latin American form *?Se los dije* 'I told them/you' (for the standard *Se lo dije a ellos/ellas/ustedes*), see 11.13.2.

12.11 *Le* for *les*

For the universal colloquial tendency to use *le* for *les* when the latter is a 'redundant' pronoun, see 11.16.3.

13

Forms of Verbs

Contents of chapter:

For ease of reference certain constantly required information is set out in separate Tables as follows:

Overview of Spanish verb forms	Table 1	p.197
Conjugation of regular verbs	Table 2	p.199
Regular spelling changes	Table 3	p.200
Conjugation of *ser*	Table 4	p.202
Conjugation of *estar*	Table 5	p.203
Conjugation of *haber*[1]	Table 6	p.204
Compound tenses	Table 7	p.205

Argentine *vos* forms are mentioned in this chapter since they are normally used in educated speech in that country. *Voseo* is discussed in more detail at 11.3.1.

13.1 General remarks about the Spanish verb system

The following remarks may show that the Spanish verb system is less complicated than it seems.

13.1.1 The three conjugations
All Spanish verbs belong to one of three conjugations distinguished by the vowel of the infinitive: (1) *-ar* (2) *-er* (3) *-ir*, or *-ír* in the case of the half dozen verbs listed at 13.1.4f.

The endings of verbs of the *-ir* conjugation are the same as those of the *-er* conjugations except for:

(a) *vosotros* forms of the imperative: *comed* 'eat' but *vivid* 'live';

(b) *nosotros* forms of the present indicative: *comemos* 'we eat' but *vivimos* 'we live';

(c) *vosotros* form of the present indicative: *coméis* 'you eat' but *vivís* 'you live';

(d) *vos* forms of the present indicative in those countries, e.g. Argentina and most of Central America, where this pronoun is used instead of *tú*. *Vos comés* 'you eat' (= *tú comes*) but *vos vivís* 'you live' (= *tú vives*);

---

[1] Auxiliary verb used for creating compound tenses. It also translates 'there is'/'there are'; see Chapter 30.

(e) forms based on the infinitive, i.e. the future and the conditional: *comerá* 'he'll eat', *vivirá* 'he'll live', *comería* 'he'd eat' but *viviría* 'he'd live'.

The full conjugation of three typical regular verbs in *-ar*, *-er* and *-ir* is shown in Table 2, p.199.

13.1.2 Regular spelling changes

There are predictable spelling changes that affect all verbs. They are discussed at 13.2.2 and the most important are shown in Table 3, p.200.

13.1.3 Irregular verbs : general remarks

Only about two dozen Spanish verbs (not counting compound verbs formed from them) are traditionally defined as truly 'irregular'. These are:

andar	to walk	13.3.5
asir	to seize	13.3.6
caber	to fit into	13.3.8
caer	to fall	13.3.9
dar	to give	13.3.15
decir	to say	13.3.16
estar	to be	see Table 5, p.203
haber	auxiliary verb or 'there is'/'there are'	see Table 6, p.204
hacer	to do/to make	13.3.22
ir	to go	13.3.23
oír	to hear	13.3.28
poder	to be able	13.3.33
poner	to put	13.3.34
producir	to produce (and all verbs ending in *-ducir*)	13.3.36
querer	to want	13.3.37
saber	to know	13.3.41
salir	to go out	13.3.42
ser	to be	see Table 4, p.202
tener	to have	13.3.45
traer	to bring	13.3.46
valer	to be worth	13.3.47
venir	to come	13.3.48
ver	to see	13.3.49

13.1.4 Radical changing verbs

'Radical changing verbs' are numerous: several hundred are in everyday use, although many of them are derived from more familiar verbs, e.g. *descontar* 'to discount', conjugated like *contar* 'to count'/'to tell a story'.

These verbs have regular endings, but a vowel in the stem is modified in some forms, cf. *contar* 'to tell a story' > *cuenta* 'he tells', *perder* 'to lose' > *pierdo* 'I lose', *sentir* 'to feel' > *siente* 'he feels' > *sintió* 'he felt', etc.

Grammarians have traditionally been reluctant to call these verbs 'irregular', but they are certainly not regular in the sense that nothing about their infinitive shows that they are of this type. Compare *renovar* 'to renovate', which is a radical changing verb, and *innovar* 'to innovate' which is not, or *atender* 'to attend to', radical changing, and *pretender* 'to claim', regular. Radical changing verbs are listed at 13.4.

A few verbs are uncertain or have become regular. These include: *cimentar* 'to cement', like *cerrar* or, more usually, regular

derrocar 'to overthrow', nowadays regular
mentar 'to mention', educated usage may still conjugate it like *cerrar*
derrengar 'to twist', nowadays regular
plegar 'to fold', like *cerrar* or optionally regular

Note also the following:

regular		**if conjugated like**
apostar	to post a sentry	*contar*; to bet
aterrar	to terrorize	*cerrar*; to level/raze to the ground
asolar	to parch	*contar*; to level/raze to ground[2]

The following list shows the common types of radical changing verbs and a selection of verbs that occur constantly and should be learned first.

A few of these verbs show other irregularities, so they should all be checked against the list at 13.4.

Commonly occurring Radical changing verbs

(a) Conjugated like *contar* 'to tell'/'to count' (13.3.14):

acordarse de	to remember	*encontrar*	to find/meet
acostarse	to go to bed	*esforzarse*	to make an effort
apostar	to bet	*mostrar*	to show
aprobar	to approve/pass an exam	*probar*	to prove/try
avergonzarse	to be ashamed		(i.e. 'sample', 'test')
colarse	to slip through/gatecrash	*recordar*	to remember/remind
colgar	to hang	*renovar*	to renew
comprobar	to check	*rodar*	to roll
consolar	to console	*soltar*	to release/let out
costar	to cost	*sonar*	to sound
demostrar	to demonstrate	*soñar*	to dream
	(a fact, technique)	*tronar*	to thunder
desaprobar	to disapprove	*volar*	to fly

(b) Conjugated like *cerrar* 'to close' (13.3.11):

acertar	to get right/hit the mark	*helar*	to freeze[3]
apretar	to squeeze/tighten	*manifestarse*	to demonstrate
atravesar	to cross		(i.e. protest)
calentar	to heat	*negar*	to deny
comenzar	to begin	*nevar*	to snow
confesar	to confess	*pensar*	to think
despertar(se)	to wake up	*recomendar*	to recommend
empezar	to begin	*sentarse*	to sit down
encerrar	to lock in/shut in	*temblar*	to tremble
enterrar	to bury	*tropezar*	to stumble
gobernar	to govern		

(c) Conjugated like *mover* 'to move' (13.3.27):

desenvolverse	to develop	*disolver*	to dissolve
devolver	to give back	*doler*	to hurt

---

[2] The regular form is becoming standardized for both meanings.
[3] Used of liquids. *Congelar* (regular) means 'to freeze food products'.

envolver	to wrap up	*resolver*	to resolve
llover	to rain	*soler*	to be in the habit of . . .
morder	to bite		(+ infinitive)
oler	to smell (see 13.3.29)	*volver(se)*	to return/become, etc.
remover	to stir up/remove (Lat. Am.)		

(d) Conjugated like *perder* 'to lose' (13.3.31):

atender	to attend (i.e. pay attention)	*extenderse*	to extend/stretch
defender	to defend		(over a distance)
encender	to light/set fire to	*tender a*	to tend to
entender	to understand		

(e) Conjugated like *pedir* 'to ask for' (13.3.30):

competir	to compete	*impedir*	to hinder/impede
concebir	to conceive	*medir*	to measure
conseguir	to achieve/manage to	*perseguir*	to persecute/chase
corregir	to correct	*rendirse*	to surrender
derretirse	to melt	*repetir*	to repeat
despedir	to fire (i.e. dismiss from job); *despedirse de* to say goodbye to	*reñir* *seguir*	to scold (see 13.3.39) to follow
elegir	to elect/choose	*servir*	to serve/be useful
gemir	to groan	*vestir(se)*	to dress

(f) Conjugated like *reír*[4] 'to laugh' (13.3.38):

desleír(se)	to dissolve/melt	*(re)freír*	to fry
engreírse	to grow conceited	*sonreír*	to smile

(g) Conjugated like *sentir* 'to feel' (13.3.43):

advertir	to warn	*herir*	to wound
arrepentirse	to repent	*interferir*	to interfere
consentir	to consent	*invertir*	to invest
convertir	to convert; *convertirse en* to turn into	*mentir* *preferir*	to tell lies to prefer
desmentir	to deny	*referirse a*	to refer to
disentir	to dissent	*sugerir*	to suggest
divertir(se)	to amuse (oneself)		

(h) *dormir* 'to sleep' and *morir* 'to die' (13.3.18).

(i) *jugar* 'to play' (13.3.24).

(j) *adquirir* 'to acquire' (13.3.3).

(k) Conjugated like *discernir* 'to discern' (13.3.17).

cernirse	to hover/loom (*cerner*, conjugated like *perder*, means the same)
concernir	to concern (third-person only)

---

[4] In fact conjugated like *pedir*, although the absence of the consonant obscures this.

13.1.5 Forms of the present indicative
The endings of the present indicative of regular verbs and of all but a few irregular verbs are:

-ar conjugation:	-o	-as	-a	-amos	-áis	-an
-er conjugation:	-o	-es	-e	-emos	-éis	-en
-ir conjugation:	-o	-es	-e	-imos	-ís	-en

However, there are numerous verbs in the *-er* and *-ir* conjugations in which the first-person singular ending is attached to an irregular stem, e.g. *producir* 'to produce' > *produzco* 'I produce', *poner* 'to put' > *pongo* 'I put', etc. These must be learned separately.

A few irregular verbs have a first-person singular ending in *-y*: *dar* > *doy*, *estar* > *estoy*, *ir* > *voy*, *ser* > *soy*.

Argentine *vos* forms are made by dropping any unstressed *i* from the ending of the European Spanish *vosotros* form: *vosotros habláis* > *vos hablás* 'you speak', *vosotros teméis* > *vos temés* 'you fear', *vosotros sois* > *vos sos* 'you are', *vosotros vivís* > *vos vivís* 'you live', *vosotros decís* > *vos decís* 'you say'.

The uses of the present indicative are discussed at 14.3.

13.1.6 Forms of the imperfect indicative
The endings of the imperfect indicative are:

-ar verbs:	-aba	-abas	-aba	-ábamos	-abais	-aban
-er and ir verbs:	-ía	-ías	-ía	-íamos	-íais	-ían

These endings are added to the stem left after removing the infinitive ending. There are three exceptions:

ser to be:	era	eras	era	éramos	erais	eran
ir to go:	iba	ibas	iba	íbamos	ibais	iban
ver to see:	veía	veías	veía	veíamos	veíais	veían
(instead of the expected						
***vía, *vías, etc.)**						

In Argentina the pronoun *vos* takes the standard *tú* endings: *vos ibas* 'you were going', *vos decías* 'you were saying', etc.

The uses of the imperfect indicative are discussed at 14.5.

13.1.7 Forms of the preterite
The preterite of all regular verbs and of most radical-changing verbs is formed by adding the following endings to the stem left after removing the *-ar*, *-er* or *-ir* of the infinitive:

-ar verbs:	-é	-aste	-ó	-amos	-asteis	-aron
-er and -ir verbs:	-í	-iste	-ió	-imos	-isteis	-ieron

However, the third-person plural ending is *-eron* in the case of:

decir:	*dijeron*
ser:	*fueron*
traer:	*trajeron*
all verbs whose infinitive	
ends in *-ducir*:	*condujeron, produjeron*

Verbs whose infinitive ends in *-ñer*, *-ñir* or *-llir* also lose the *i* in the third-person singular and third-person plural endings. See 13.2.2f.

Most of the irregular verbs listed at 13.1.3 have an irregular preterite stem and many of them do not have a stressed final vowel in the endings. *Hacer* 'to do' and *caber* 'to fit into' are typical:

hice	*hicimos*	*cupe*	*cupimos*
hiciste	*hicisteis*	*cupiste*	*cupisteis*
hizo	*hicieron*	*cupo*	*cupieron*

Verbs conjugated like *sentir* 'to feel', *pedir* 'to ask', and *dormir* 'to sleep' have irregularities in the third person of the preterite:

sintió	*sintieron*	*pidió*	*pidieron*	*durmió*	*durmieron*

In Argentina the endings corresponding to the pronoun *vos* are the same as for *tú* in standard Spanish.

The uses of the preterite are discussed at 14.4.

13.1.8 The future and the conditional
The endings of the future and conditional tenses are identical for all verbs, regular and irregular:

Future:	*-é*	*-ás*	*-á*	*-emos*	*-éis*	*-án*
Conditional:	*-ía*	*-ías*	*-ía*	*-íamos*	*-íais*	*-ían*

The endings corresponding to Argentine *vos* are the same as for *tú*. These endings are always added to the infinitive except in the cases of the following twelve verbs:

Infinitive	Future stem	Infinitive	Future stem
caber to fit in	*cabr-*	*querer* to want	*querr-*
decir to say	*dir-*	*saber* to know	*sabr-*
haber	*habr-*	*salir* to go out	*saldr-*
hacer to do/make	*har-*	*tener* to have	*tendr-*
poder to be able	*podr-*	*valer* to be worth	*valdr-*
poner to put	*pondr-*	*venir* to come	*vendr-*

The use of the future and conditional forms is discussed at 14.6 and 14.7.

13.1.9 Forms of the present subjunctive
The endings of the present subjunctive are easily memorized:

-ar verbs take the endings of the present indicative of regular *-er* verbs except that the first-person *-o* is replaced by *-e*.

-er and *-ir* verbs take the endings of the present indicative of regular *-ar*

verbs, except that first-person -*o* is replaced by -*a*:

-*ar* verbs:	-e	-es	-e	-emos	-éis	-en
-*er* and -*ir* verbs:	-a-	-as	-a	-amos	-áis	-an

As far as regular verbs and the great majority of irregular verbs are concerned, the present subjunctive endings are added to the stem left after removing the -*o* of the first-person present indicative: e.g. *vengo* 'I come' > *venga, conduzco* 'I drive' > *conduzca, quepo* 'there's room for me' > *quepa* (from *caber*, 13.3.8), etc.

The six exceptions among the irregular verbs are:

Infinitive	First-person indicative	Present subjunctive
dar to give	*doy*	*dé, des, dé,* etc.[5]
estar to be	*estoy*	*esté, estés, esté, estemos, estéis, estén*
haber	*he*	*haya, hayas, haya,* etc.
ir to go	*voy*	*vaya, vayas, vaya,* etc.
saber to know	*sé*	*sepa, sepas, sepa,* etc.
ser to be	*soy*	*sea, seas, sea,* etc.

In the case of radical-changing verbs, the usual vowel changes occur, e.g. *cuente, cuentes, cuente, contemos, contéis, cuenten* (from *contar*, see 13.3.14).

Verbs that conjugate like *sentir* 'to feel' show the following irregularity in the present subjunctive:

sienta	*sientas*	*sienta*	*sintamos*	*sintáis*	*sientan*

Two other verbs with slight irregularities in the present subjunctive are *morir* 'to die' and *dormir* 'to sleep'. See 13.3.18 for details.

In Argentina the *vos* forms of the present subjunctive used by careful speakers are the same as the standard *tú* forms. See 16.2.8 for further comments on this topic.

The use of the subjunctive is discussed at length in Chapter 16.

13.1.10 Forms of the past (imperfect) and future subjunctives

There are two sets of imperfect subjunctive endings:

Imperfect subjunctive in -*ra*:					
-*ar* verbs:	-ara	-aras	-ara	-áramos	-arais	-aran
-*er* and -*ir* verbs:	-iera	-ieras	-iera	-iéramos	-ierais	-ieran

---

[5] The accent merely distinguishes the forms from the preposition *de*.

Imperfect subjunctive in -se:

-ar verbs:	-ase	-ases	-ase	-ásemos	-aseis	-asen
-er and						
-ir verbs:	-iese	-ieses	-iese	-iésemos	-ieseis	-iesen

The endings of the future subjunctive (nowadays obsolete in ordinary language) are identical to those of the *-ra* past subjunctive, except that the last *a* is replaced by *e*:

-ar verbs:	-are	-ares	-are	-áremos	-areis	-aren
-er and						
-ir verbs:	-iere	-ieres	-iere	-iéremos	-iereis	-ieren

The past (imperfect) and future subjunctive endings are added to the stem of the third-person singular of the preterite indicative.

In the case of regular verbs this stem is found by removing the infinitive ending, e.g. *habl(ar)* > *habl-*: *yo hablara/hablase, tú hablaras/hablases, él hablara/hablase*, etc.

But in the case of irregular verbs the preterite stem is often irregular, e.g.:

Infinitive	Third-person preterite stem	Past and future subjunctives
sentir 'to feel' and verbs like it	*sint(ió)*	*sintiera/sintiese/sintiere*, etc.
pedir 'to request' and verbs like it	*pid(ió)*	*pidiera/pidiese/ pidiere*, etc.
ser 'to be', *ir* 'to go'	*fu(e)*	*fuera/fuese/ fuere*, etc.
producir 'to produce', and all verbs ending in *-ducir*	*produj(o)*	*produjera/produjese/ produjere*, etc.
tener 'to have'	*tuv(o)*	*tuviera/tuviese/ tuviere*, etc.

Morir and *dormir* have the third-person preterite stems *mur(ió)* and *durm(ió)*, so the past subjunctives are *muriera/muriese, durmiera/durmiese*, etc.

The forms *-ese, -era, -ere*, etc. are used with the following verbs:

decir	*dijera/dijese*
ser	*fuera/fuese/fuere*, etc.
traer	*trajera/trajese/trajere*, etc.
all verbs whose infinitive ends in *-ducir*	*condujera, produjese*, etc.
all verbs whose infinitive ends in *-ñer, -ñir* or *-llir*	*bullera, tañese*, etc.

Argentine *vos* forms coincide with the standard *tú* forms.

The future subjunctive is virtually obsolete and foreign learners will not need to use it. Its limited uses in modern Spanish are discussed at 16.17.

13.1.11 The imperative
All matters connected with the imperative are discussed in Chapter 17.

13.1.12 Forms of the past participle
The formation of the past participle (*hablado, sido, muerto,* etc.) is discussed at 19.2.1.

13.1.13 The compound tenses
The compound tenses, e.g. the perfect[6] *he hablado* 'I have spoken', *has visto* 'you've seen' and the pluperfect *habían tenido* 'they'd had', *habrán hecho* 'they'll have made' and the subjunctive counterparts of these two, are always predictable if one can conjugate *haber* (see p.204) and knows the past participle of the verb. For this reason individual compound tenses are not listed in this chapter, but the full compound tense forms of *ver* 'to see' is shown in Table 7, p.205. The use of the compound tenses is discussed at 14.8–14.10.

13.1.14 Forms of the gerund
The formation of the gerund (*hablando, siendo, muriendo,* etc.) is discussed at 20.2.

13.1.15 Forms of the adjectival participle
Some verbs, but by no means all, have an adjectival participle ending in *-ante* in the case of *-ar* verbs and, unpredictably, *-ente* or *-iente* in the case of *-er* and *-ir* verbs, e.g. *preocupante* 'worrying', *hiriente* 'wounding'. The formation and use of this participle is discussed at 19.4.

13.1.16 Continuous forms of verbs
Spanish has a full range of continuous forms, e.g. *estoy hablando* 'I'm talking', *estuve esperando* 'I was waiting'/'I waited for a time', etc. These are all formed from the appropriate tense of *estar* (see p.203) and the invariable gerund. Their use is discussed in Chapter 15.

13.1.17 Forms of the passive
Use of the passive is discussed in Chapter 28, and typical forms are shown on p.198.

13.2 Variants and spelling rules

13.2.1 Colloquial variants
The verb system is remarkably stable throughout the Spanish-speaking world despite the large number of forms and exceptions. Mistakes caused by attempted regularization of irregular forms, e.g. **cabo* for *quepo* (from *caber* 'to fit into'), **produció* for *produjo* (from *producir* 'to produce'), **andé* for *anduve* (from *andar* 'to walk') are stigmatized.

However, regularized preterites of verbs in *-ducir*, e.g. **conducí*, **produció* are common in popular Latin-American speech and are sometimes heard in Spain. Foreign learners should avoid them.

---

[6] For a clarification of the terminology used to describe past tenses, see 14.1.

Three other popular spoken forms are very common, although all but (**a**) are stigmatized as uneducated and should be avoided by foreigners:

(**a**) use of the infinitive for the *vosotros* form of the imperative: *dar* for *dad* 'give', *callaros* for *callaos* 'shut up!'/'be quiet', *iros* for *idos* 'go away', etc. This usage is very widespread in Spain (the *vosotros* forms not being used in Latin America) but it is avoided in writing. For further discussion see 17.2.4;

(**b**) addition of *-s* to the second-person preterite singular, e.g. ?*distes* for *diste* 'you gave', ?*hablastes* for *hablaste* 'you spoke';

(**c**) pluralization of forms of *haber* (other than *hay*) when it means 'there is'/'there are', e.g. ?*habían muchos* for *había muchos* 'there were many'. This tendency, very common in Catalonia and in Latin America, is discussed further at 30.2.1. note (i);

(**d**) a tendency, sporadically heard in local dialects throughout Latin America and in North-American Spanish, to regularize radical changing verbs, e.g. *cuentamos for *contamos* 'we tell', *detiénete for *detente* 'stop'. These forms are occasionally seen in dialogue in novels but foreigners should not imitate them.

13.2.2 General spelling rules
Certain spelling changes are applied systematically throughout the verb system. The most common are shown in Table 3, p.200.

(**a**) The sound of [g] as in *hago* is spelt *gu* before *e* or *i*: *pagar* > *pague* 'pay', *ruego* > *rogué* 'request', etc.

The sounds [gwe] and [gwi] are written *güe, güi*: *averigüe* (from *averiguar* 'to check'/'to ascertain'), *argüí* (from *argüir* 'to argue', i.e. 'argue a point'; *discutir* means 'to have an argument'), etc.

(**b**) The sound [k] is written *qu* before *e* and *i*, but *c* in all other cases: *sacar* > *saque* 'take out', etc.

(**c**) Z, pronounced θ (like *th* in 'think') in standard Peninsular Spanish, like *s* in 'sin' in Southern Spain and in Latin America, is spelt *c* before *e, i*: *rezar* > *rece* 'pray'. The *z* must be restored before any other vowel: *esparcir* > *esparza* 'scatter'/'strew', *vencer* > *venzo* 'defeat', etc.

Speakers who use Latin-American pronunciation will be unable to predict by sound alone the spelling of such words as *caza* 'hunts' and *casa* 'marry'/'house', or *hace* 'does' and *ase* 'grasps' (from *asir*).

(**d**) The sound [χ] (like the *ch* of Scottish 'loch') must be spelt *j* before *a, o*: *regir* > *rijo* 'guide'/'control', *coger* > *cojo/coja* 'catch',[7] etc. The spelling of syllables pronounced [χe] and [χi] must however be learned separately, cf. *ruge* 'roars' (from *rugir*) and *conduje* 'I drove', which rhyme.

(**e**) The diphthong *ie* is written *ye-* at the beginning of a word. Thus *errar* 'to wander' makes its first-person singular present indicative *yerro* for the predicted *ierro. See 13.3.20 for the conjugation of *errar*.

(**f**) When *-ie* or *ió* follow a consonant that already has an intrinsic *y* sound, i.e. *ñ* or *ll*, the *i* is omitted: *tañer* > *tañó* 'chime' (not *tañió), *zambullir* >

[7] *Coger* also has taboo sexual meanings throughout Latin America. In the Southern Cone *agarrar* 'to seize' is preferred for 'to catch'/'to grasp'/'to grab hold of'.

zambulleron 'dive'[8] (not **zambullieron*), *bullir* > *bullera/bullese* 'boil'/'budge' (not **bulliera/*bulliese*). Other verbs affected are *escabullirse* 'to vanish'/'to slip away'/'to skive off', *plañir* 'to mourn' (rare), *reñir* 'to scold', *teñir* 'to tint'/'to stain', *ceñir* 'to fasten'/'to attach',[9] *mullir* 'to make fluffy'/'to fluff up'.

(g) The diphthong *ue* is written *hue* at the beginning of a word. Thus *oler* 'to smell' makes its first-person singular indicative *huelo* for the predicted **uelo*. See 13.3.29 for the conjugation of *oler*.

13.2.3 Spelling and pronunciation of *aislar, reunir, prohibir* and similar verbs whose stem contains a diphthong

When the last syllable but one of an infinitive contains a falling diphthong (one whose second letter is *i* or *u*), this diphthong may or may not be broken into two syllables when it is stressed:

prohibir, [proyβír] (two syllables)	*prohíbe* [proíβe] (three syllables)
reunir, [rrewnír] (two syllables)	*reúnes* [rreúnes] (three syllables)
but	
causar [kawsár] (two syllables)	*causas* [káwsas] (two syllables)

Since 1959 the stressed vowel in such broken diphthongs has been written with an accent. In the Academy's view the fact that *-h-* appears between the two vowels makes no difference. This ruling affects the following forms of the verb:

Present indicative
aislar to isolate: *aíslo, aísla, aísla, aislamos, aisláis, aíslan*
reunir to bring together[10]: *reúne, reúnes, reúne, reunimos, reunís, reúnen*
prohibir to prohibit: *prohíbo, prohíbes, prohíbe, prohibimos, prohibís, prohíben*

Present subjunctive
aísle, aísles, aísle, aislemos, aisléis, aíslen
reúna, reúnas, reúna, reunamos, reunáis, reúnan
prohíba, prohíbas, prohíba, prohibamos, prohibáis, prohíban

Singular imperative

aísla	*reúne*	*prohíbe*

Among verbs affected are:

ahijar	*amohinar*	*desahitarse*	*maullar*
ahilar	*arcaizar*	*desenraizar*	*prohijar*
ahincar	*aullar*	*enraizar*	*rehilar*
ahitar	*aunar*	*europeizar*	*rehusar*
ahumar	*aupar*	*hebraizar*	*sahumar*
airar	*cohibir*	*judaizar*	*sobrehilar*

In other verbs the diphthong is not broken, i.e. when the diphthong is stressed the accent falls on its first vowel and no written accent appears, e.g.

---

[8] Usually *tirarse al agua* 'to dive into the water'.
[9] cf. *Cíñete más a la versión original* 'Stick closer to the original version'.
[10] *Reunirse* 'to meet' (i.e. 'hold a meeting').

arraigo, encausa, etc. Similar are *amainar, causar, desahuciar* (variable, usually the diphthong is retained), *desenvainar, embaucar, embaular* (variable – the verb is hardly ever used), *envainar, reinar, peinar, recauchar*, etc.

The new spelling is in general use in printed texts in Spain, but some thirty years later most people omit the accent in handwriting and many Latin-American publishers use the old forms without the accent.

13.2.4 Verbs whose infinitive ends in *-iar*

These are of two types. The majority conjugate like *cambiar* 'to change': the *-ia* survives as a diphthong throughout and is always pronounced [ya]:

Infinitive *cambiar*　　　　　　　　**Gerund** *cambiando*
Past participle *cambiado*　　　　　**Imperative** *cambia cambiad*

INDICATIVE

Present	Imperfect	Preterite	Future	Conditional
cambio	*cambiaba*	*cambié*	*cambiaré*	*cambiaría*
cambias	*cambiabas*	*cambiaste*	*cambiarás*	*cambiarías*
cambia	*cambiaba*	*cambió*	*cambiará*	*cambiaría*
cambiamos	*cambiábamos*	*cambiamos*	*cambiaremos*	*cambiaríamos*
cambiáis	*cambiabais*	*cambiasteis*	*cambiaréis*	*cambiaríais*
cambian	*cambiaban*	*cambiaron*	*cambiarán*	*cambiarían*

SUBJUNCTIVE

Present	Imperfect	Future
cambie	*cambiara/cambiase*	*cambiare*
cambies	*cambiaras/cambiases*	etc.
cambie	*cambiara/cambiase*	
cambiemos	*cambiáramos/cambiásemos*	
cambiéis	*cambiarais/cambiaseis*	
cambien	*cambiaran/cambiasen*	

But about fifty verbs conjugate like *liar* 'to tie in a bundle', i.e. the *i* of the diphthong may be stressed:

Infinitive *liar*　　　　　　　　　　**Gerund** *liando*
Past participle *liado*　　　　　　　　**Imperative** *lía liad*

INDICATIVE

Present	Imperfect	Preterite	Future	Conditional
lío	*liaba*	*lié*	*liaré*	*liaría*
lías	*liabas*	*liaste*	*liarás*	*liarías*
lía	*liaba*	*lió*	*liará*	*liaría*
liamos	*liábamos*	*liamos*	*liaremos*	*liaríamos*
liáis	*liabais*	*liasteis*	*liaréis*	*liaríais*
lían	*liaban*	*liaron*	*liarán*	*liarían*

SUBJUNCTIVE

Present	Imperfect	Future
líe	*liara/liase*	*liare*
líes	*liaras/liases*	etc.
líe	*liara/liase*	
liemos	*liáramos/liásemos*	
liéis	*liarais/liaseis*	
líen	*liaran/liasen*	

The following list shows common verbs which conjugate like *liar*, and verbs about which the authorities are in disagreement. Verbs ending in *-iar* that do not appear below can be assumed to conjugate like *cambiar* 'to change':

agriar (disputed, usually like *cambiar*)
aliar
amnistiar
ampliar
ansiar
arriar
ataviar
autografiar
auxiliar (disputed, usually like *cambiar*)
averiar
aviar
biografiar
conciliar (disputed, usually like *cambiar*)
contrariar
criar
dactilografiar
desafiar
descarriar
descriarse
desliar
desvariar
desviar
enfriar
enviar
escalofriar
espiar
expatriar (disputed; also like *cambiar*)

expiar
extasiarse (disputed, usually like *liar*)
extraviar
fiar
filiar (but optionally like *cambiar*)
fotografiar
gloriar(se)
guiar
hastiar
historiar (disputed, usually like *cambiar*)
inventariar
litografiar
malcriar
mecanografiar
paliar (but usually like *cambiar*)
piar
porfiar
radiografiar
recriar
resfriar
rociar
telegrafiar
vaciar
vanagloriarse (almost always like *cambiar*)
variar
vidriar (Academy recommends conj. like *cambiar*)

13.2.5 Verbs whose infinitive ends in *-uar*

Nearly all conjugate like *actuar* 'to act', i.e. the *u* may be stressed. But those that end in *-guar* and *-cuar* conjugate like *averiguar* 'to check'/'to ascertain': the *ua* forms an inseparable diphthong (pronounced [wa]).

Infinitive *actuar*   **Gerund** *actuando*
Past participle *actuado*   **Imperative** *actúa actuad*

INDICATIVE

Present	Imperfect	Preterite	Future	Conditional
actúo	*actuaba*	*actué*	*actuaré*	*actuaría*
actúas	*actuabas*	*actuaste*	*actuarás*	*actuarías*
actúa	*actuaba*	*actuó*	*actuará*	*actuaría*
actuamos	*actuábamos*	*actuamos*	*actuaremos*	*actuaríamos*
actuáis	*actuabais*	*actuasteis*	*actuaréis*	*actuaríais*
actúan	*actuaban*	*actuaron*	*actuarán*	*actuarían*

SUBJUNCTIVE

Present	Imperfect	Future
actúe	*actuara/actuase*	*actuare*
actúes	*actuaras/actuases*	etc.
actúe	*actuara/actuase*	
actuemos	*actuáramos/actuásemos*	
actuéis	*actuarais/actuaseis*	
actúen	*actuaran/actuasen*	

Verbs conjugated like *actuar* are:

acentuar	*habituar*
atenuar	*individuar*
conceptuar	*infatuar*
continuar	*insinuar*
desvirtuar	*perpetuar*
efectuar	*preceptuar*
evaluar	*puntuar*
exceptuar	*redituar*
extenuar	*situar*
fluctuar	*usufractuar*
graduar	*valuar*

Infinitive *averiguar* **Gerund** *averiguando*
Past participle *averiguado* **Imperative** *averigua averiguad*

INDICATIVE

Present	Imperfect	Preterite	Future	Conditional
averiguo	*averiguaba*	*averigüé*	*averiguaré*	*averiguaría*
averiguas	*averiguabas*	*averiguaste*	*averiguarás*	*averiguarías*
averigua	*averiguaba*	*averiguó*	*averiguará*	*averiguaría*
averiguamos	*averiguábamos*	*averiguamos*	*averiguaremos*	*averiguaríamos*
averiguáis	*averiguabais*	*averiguasteis*	*averiguaréis*	*averiguaríais*
averiguan	*averiguaban*	*averiguaron*	*averiguarán*	*averiguarían*

SUBJUNCTIVE

Present	Imperfect	Future
averigüe	*averiguara/averiguase*	*averiguare*
averigües	*averiguaras/averiguases*	etc.
averigüe	*averiguara/averiguase*	
averigüemos	*averiguáramos/averiguásemos*	
averigüéis	*averiguarais/averiguaseis*	
averigüen	*averiguaran/averiguasen*	

Note
Few verbs end in -*cuar*, *evacuar* being the most common. It should be conjugated like *averiguar* – but without the dieresis – although conjugation like *actuar* is a common mistake in Spain and is apparently accepted usage in some Latin-American countries.

13.2.6 Verbs whose infinitive ends in -*ear*
These are all regular. The penultimate *e* is never written with an accent, cf. *pasear* 'to go for a walk':

Present indicative

paseo	*paseamos*
paseas	*paseáis*
pasea	*pasean*

Present subjunctive

pasee	*paseemos*
pasees	*paseéis*
pasee	*paseen*

13.2.7 Verbs whose infinitive ends in *-cer*

If the infinitive ends in *-cer* the spelling changes shown on p.200 are applied in the case of a few verbs (*c* > *z* before *a*, *o*). These affect the first-person singular of the present indicative and all of the present subjunctive.

However, the only verbs ending in *-cer* that are conjugated in this way are:
(a) those in which the *c/z* occurs after a consonant.

convencer	to convince
ejercer	to practise[11] (a profession)
(re)torcer	to twist (radical changing; see 13.3.12)
vencer	to defeat

(b) the following three exceptional verbs.

(re)cocer	to cook (radical changing; see 13.3.12)
escocerse	to sting/smart (conj. like *cocer*; *picar* 'to sting' is more usual)
mecer	to rock/swing; *mecerse* 'to sway'

The rest, which are numerous, conjugate like *parecer*, i.e. *-zc-* replaces *-c-* before *-o* or *-a*. See 13.3.10 for examples.

13.2.8 Verbs whose infinitive ends in *-eer*

All are conjugated like *poseer* 'to possess', shown at 13.3.35.

13.2.9 Verbs whose infinitive ends in *-cir*

The spelling changes shown on p.200 must be applied if the infinitive ends in *-cir*: *c* > *z* before *a*, *o*. However the only totally regular verbs ending in *-cir* are *esparcir* 'to scatter/strew', *zurcir* 'to darn/sew together' and *fruncir* 'to pucker/wrinkle' (the eyebrows). All the others should be sought in the list at the end of this Chapter.

13.2.10 Verbs whose infinitive ends in *-uir*

All are conjugated like *construir* 'to build', shown at 13.3.13.

13.3 Irregular verbs

13.3.1 General

Irregular verbs and model radical changing verbs are listed in alphabetical order, though the very frequent verbs *ser*, *estar* and *haber* are shown in Tables 4, 5 and 6, pp.202-204. Connoisseurs will miss such oddities as the archaic *abarse*, attested only in the imperative singular *ábate* 'get thee hence!', or *usucapir* 'to acquire property rights through customary use', used in legal jargon and only in the infinitive. These and similar verbs unknown in everyday language should be sought in the Academy's publications or in other specialized manuals.

---

[11] US spelling 'to practice'.

13.3.2 *Abolir* 'to abolish'

A defective verb. Only those forms are used in which the verb ending begins with *-i*.

Infinitive *abolir*
Past participle *abolido*

Gerund *aboliendo*
Imperative *abolid*. (**abole* not used)

INDICATIVE

Present	Imperfect	Preterite	Future	Conditional
not used	*abolía*	*abolí*	*aboliré*	*aboliría*
not used	etc.	etc.	etc.	etc.
not used				
abolimos				
abolís				
not used				

SUBJUNCTIVE

Present	Imperfect	Future
no forms	*aboliera/aboliese*	*aboliere*
in use	etc.	etc.

Unused forms must be replaced, e.g. **sin que se abola* by *sin que sea abolido* 'without it being abolished'.

There are a few other verbs that share the same peculiarity, but none besides *abolir* and *agredir* is much used in the modern language:

aguerrir 'to inure/harden' (only past participle in use)
agredir see 13.3.4
arrecirse (Lat. Am.) 'to be frozen stiff'
aterirse 'to be numb with cold' (only infinitive and participle used)
blandir 'to brandish'
despavorir 'to be terrified' (only past participle in use)
empedernir 'to harden/petrify' (participle only in use)
garantir 'to guarantee' (replaced by *garantizar* but still used in Peru and the Southern Cone, where it is often conjugated normally)

13.3.3 *Adquirir* 'to acquire'

The infinitive of this verb was once *adquerir*, which explains the appearance of *-ie-* when the stem vowel is stressed:

Infinitive *adquirir*
Past participle *adquirido*

Gerund *adquiriendo*
Imperative *adquiere adquirid*

INDICATIVE

Present	Imperfect	Preterite	Future	Conditional
adquiero	*adquiría*	*adquirí*	*adquiriré*	*adquiriría*
adquieres	etc.	etc.	etc.	etc.
adquiere				
adquirimos				
adquirís				
adquieren				

SUBJUNCTIVE

Present	Imperfect	Future
adquiera	*adquiriera/adquiriese*	*adquiriere*
adquieras	etc.	etc.
adquiera		
adquiramos		
adquiráis		
adquieran		

13.3.4 *Agredir* 'to assault'/'attack'

This verb is classified by some as defective (like *abolir*), by others as a normal *-ir* verb, the former usage being the more conservative.

13.3.5 *Andar* 'to walk'/'go about'

This verb is conjugated like a regular *-ar* verb throughout, except for the preterite indicative and, consequently, the past and future subjunctive:

Preterite indicative	Imperfect subjunctive	Future subjunctive
anduve	*anduviera/anduviese*	*anduviere*
anduviste	etc.	etc.
anduvo		
anduvimos		
anduvisteis		
anduvieron		

13.3.6 *Asir* 'to grasp'/'seize'

Usually replaced in everyday language by *agarrarse*. In practice, forms that contain a *g* are avoided, although other forms are occasionally heard, e.g. *Me así a una rama para no caerme* 'I clutched hold of a branch so as not to fall'.

Infinitive *asir* **Gerund** *asiendo*
Past participle *asido* **Imperative** *ase, asid*

INDICATIVE

Present	Imperfect	Preterite	Future	Conditional
(asgo)	*asía*	*así*	*asiré*	*asiría*
ases	etc.	etc.	etc.	etc.
ase				
asimos				
asís				
asen				

SUBJUNCTIVE

Present	Imperfect	Future
(asga)	*asiera/asiese*	*asiere*
(asgas)	etc.	etc.
(asga)		
(asgamos)		
(asgáis)		
(asgan)		

13.3.7 *Balbucir* 'to stammer'

This verb is often replaced by the regular *balbucear*. *Balbucir* has the peculiarity that, although it is conjugated regularly, no form containing a *z* is used, so **balbuzo* and the present subjunctive are not found.

13.3.8 *Caber* 'to fit in'

Infinitive *caber*   **Gerund** *cabiendo*
Past participle *cabido*   **Imperative** *cabe cabed*

INDICATIVE

Present	Imperfect	Preterite	Future	Conditional
quepo	*cabía*	*cupe*	*cabré*	*cabría*
cabes	etc.	*cupiste*	etc.	etc.
cabe		*cupo*		
cabemos		*cupimos*		
cabéis		*cupisteis*		
caben		*cupieron*		

SUBJUNCTIVE

Present	Imperfect	Future
quepa	*cupiera*/*cupiese*	*cupiere*
quepas	*cupieras*/*cupieses*	etc.
quepa	*cupiera*/*cupiese*	
quepamos	*cupiéramos*/*cupiésemos*	
quepáis	*cupierais*/*cupieseis*	
quepan	*cupieran*/*cupiesen*	

Usage: *¿Quepo yo?* 'Is there room for me?', *No cabe* 'It won't fit', *No cabíamos* 'There wasn't room for us'.

13.3.9 *Caer* 'to fall'

Infinitive *caer*   **Gerund** *cayendo*
Past participle *caído*   **Imperative** *cae caed*

INDICATIVE

Present	Imperfect	Preterite	Future	Conditional
caigo	*caía*	*caí*	*caeré*	*caeriá*
caes	*caías*	*caíste*	etc.	etc.
cae	*caía*	*cayó*		
caemos	*caíamos*	*caímos*		
caéis	*caíais*	*caísteis*		
caen	*caían*	*cayeron*		

SUBJUNCTIVE

Present	Imperfect	Future
caiga	*cayera*/*cayese*	*cayere*
caigas	*cayeras*/*cayeses*	etc.
caiga	*cayera*/*cayese*	
caigamos	*cayéramos*/*cayésemos*	
caigáis	*cayerais*/*cayeseis*	
caigan	*cayeran*/*cayesen*	

13.3.10 Verbs whose infinitive ends in *-cer*

All verbs ending in *-cer* conjugate as shown hereafter, **except** the regular verbs *ejercer*, *(con)vencer* and *mecer*, and the radical changing verbs *escocer*, *(re)cocer* and *(re)torcer* (for which see 13.3.12).

Nacer 'to be born' is typical of this class of verb: *c* > *zc* before *a* or *o*:

Infinitive *nacer*   **Gerund** *naciendo*
Past participle *nacido*   **Imperative** *nace naced*

INDICATIVE

Present	Imperfect	Preterite	Future	Conditional
nazco	*nacía*	*nací*	*naceré*	*nacería*
naces	*nacías*	*naciste*	etc.	etc.
nace	*nacía*	*nació*		
nacemos	*nacíamos*	*nacimos*		
nacéis	*nacíais*	*nacisteis*		
nacen	*nacían*	*nacieron*		

SUBJUNCTIVE

Present	Imperfect	Future
nazca	*naciera/naciese*	*naciere*
nazcas	*nacieras/nacieses*	etc.
nazca	*naciera/naciese*	
nazcamos	*naciéramos/naciésemos*	
nazcáis	*nacierais/nacieseis*	
nazcan	*nacieran/naciesen*	

13.3.11   *Cerrar* 'to shut/close'

A common type of radical changing verb. The endings are those of regular *-ar* verbs, but the *e* of the stem changes to *ie* when stressed.

Infinitive *cerrar*   **Gerund** *cerrando*
Past participle *cerrado*   **Imperative** *cierra cerrad*

INDICATIVE

Present	Imperfect	Preterite	Future	Conditional
cierro	*cerraba*	*cerré*	*cerraré*	*cerraría*
cierras	etc.	etc.	etc.	etc.
cierra				
cerramos				
cerráis				
cierran				

SUBJUNCTIVE

Present	Imperfect	Future
cierre	*cerrara/cerrase*	*cerrare*
cierres	etc.	etc.
cierre		
cerremos		
cerréis		
cierren		

13.3.12   *Cocer* 'to boil'

This, and *escocer* 'to sting', *torcer* 'to twist' and *retorcer* 'to wring/twist', conjugate exactly like *mover* except for the predictable spelling change *c > z* before *a, o*:

Infinitive *cocer*   **Gerund** *cociendo*
Past participle *cocido*   **Imperative** *cuece coced*

INDICATIVE

Present	Imperfect	Preterite	Future	Conditional
cuezo	*cocía*	*cocí*	*coceré*	*cocería*
cueces	etc.	etc.	etc.	etc.
cuece				
cocemos				
cocéis				
cuecen				

SUBJUNCTIVE

Present	Imperfect	Future
cueza	*cociera/cociese*	*cociere*
cuezas	etc.	etc.
cueza		
cozamos		
cozáis		
cuezan		

13.3.13 *Construir* 'to build'

Verbs ending in *-uir* are quite common. An unstressed *i* between vowels is spelt *y*, e.g. *construyó* for the expected **construió*, and an unexpected *y* is inserted in a number of forms, e.g. *construyes* for the predicted **construes*.

Infinitive *construir* **Gerund** *construyendo*
Past Participle *construido*[12] **Imperative** *construye construid*

INDICATIVE

Present	Imperfect	Preterite	Future	Conditional
construyo	*construía*	*construí*	*construiré*	*construiría*
construyes	etc.	*construiste*	etc.	etc.
construye		*construyó*		
construimos		*construimos*		
construís		*construisteis*		
construyen		*construyeron*		

SUBJUNCTIVE

Present	Imperfect	Future
construya	*construyera/construyese*	*construyere*
construyas	etc.	etc.
construya		
construyamos		
construyáis		
construyan		

Note

Argüir 'to argue (a point)' is spelt with a dieresis whenever the *u* is followed by *i*. This preserves the pronunciation [gwi]: *arguyo, argüimos, argüí, arguya*, etc.

13.3.14 *Contar* 'to count'/'tell a story'

A common type of radical changing verb. The endings are regular but the *o* of the stem changes to *ue* when stressed:

Infinitive *contar* **Gerund** *contando*
Past Participle *contado* **Imperative** *cuenta contad*

INDICATIVE

Present	Imperfect	Preterite	Future	Conditional
cuento	*contaba*	*conté*	*contaré*	*contaría*
cuentas	etc.	etc.	etc.	etc.
cuenta				
contamos				
contáis				
cuentan				

---

[12] No written accent because *u* and *i* are both 'weak' vowels. Contrast *leído, creído,* etc. See 39.2.3b for explanation.

SUBJUNCTIVE

Present	Imperfect	Future
cuente	*contara/contase*	*contare*
cuentes	etc.	etc.
cuente		
contemos		
contéis		
cuenten		

13.3.15 *Dar* 'to give'

Infinitive *dar*   **Gerund** *dando*
Past Participle *dado*   **Imperative** *da dad*

INDICATIVE

Present	Imperfect	Preterite	Future	Conditional
doy	*daba*	*di*	*daré*	*daría*
das	*dabas*	*diste*	etc.	etc.
da	*daba*	*dio* (no accent!)		
damos	*dábamos*	*dimos*		
dais	*dabais*	*disteis*		
dan	*daban*	*dieron*		

SUBJUNCTIVE

Present	Imperfect	Future
dé[13]	*diera/diese*	*diere*
des	*dieras/dieses*	etc.
dé[13]	*diera/diese*	
demos	*diéramos/diésemos*	
deis	*dierais/dieseis*	
den	*dieran/diesen*	

13.3.16 *Decir* 'to say'

Infinitive *decir*   **Gerund** *diciendo*
Past Participle *dicho*   **Imperative** *di decid*

INDICATIVE

Present	Imperfect	Preterite	Future	Conditional
digo	*decía*	*dije*	*diré*	*diría*
dices	etc.	*dijiste*	etc.	etc.
dice		*dijo*		
decimos		*dijimos*		
decís		*dijisteis*		
dicen		*dijeron*		

SUBJUNCTIVE

Present	Imperfect	Future
diga	*dijera/dijese*	*dijere*
digas	*dijeras/dijeses*	etc.
diga	*dijera/dijese*	
digamos	*dijéramos/dijésemos*	
digáis	*dijerais/dijeseis*	
digan	*dijeran/ijesen*	

---

[13] The accent distinguishes it from *de* 'of'.

13.3.17 *Discernir* 'to discern'/'to distinguish'

This shows the common radical changing modification *e* > *ie*, but verbs like *discernir* are very unusual in the *-ir* conjugation: only *cernir* 'to hover'/'to loom', *concernir* (third person only) 'to concern' and *hendir* (Lat. Am.; Spain *hender*) 'to cleave' conjugate like it:

Infinitive *discernir* **Gerund** *discerniendo*
Past Participle *discernido* **Imperative** *discierne discernid*

INDICATIVE

Present	Imperfect	Preterite	Future	Conditional
discierno	*discernía*	*discerní*	*discerniré*	*discerniría*
disciernes	etc.	*discerniste*	etc.	etc.
discierne		*discernió*[14]		
discernimos		*discernimos*		
discernís		*discernisteis*		
disciernen		*discernieron*[14]		

SUBJUNCTIVE

Present	Imperfect	Future
discierna	*discerniera/discerniese*	*discerniere*
disciernas	etc.	etc.
discierna		
discernamos		
discernáis		
disciernan		

13.3.18 *Dormir* 'to sleep', *morir* 'to die'

Dormir and *morir* are the only verbs of this kind.

Apart from the common change *o* > *ue*, the third-person preterite stem vowel is *u*. The *u* also appears in the first and second plural of the present subjunctive and in the gerund.

Infinitive *dormir* **Gerund** *durmiendo*
Past Participle *dormido* (*muerto*) **Imperative** *duerme dormid*

INDICATIVE

Present	Imperfect	Preterite	Future	Conditional
duermo	*dormía*	*dormí*	*dormiré*	*dormiría*
duermes	etc.	*dormiste*	etc.	etc.
duerme		*durmió*		
dormimos		*dormimos*		
dormís		*dormisteis*		
duermen		*durmieron*		

SUBJUNCTIVE

Present	Imperfect	Future
duerma	*durmiera/durmiese*	*durmiere*
duermas	*durmieras/durmieses*	etc.
duerma	*durmiera/durmiese*	
durmamos	*durmiéramos/durmiésemos*	
durmáis	*durmierais/durmieseis*	
duerman	*durmieran/durmiesen*	

---

[14] Not the expected *discirnió, *discirnieron.

13.3.19 *Erguir(se)* 'to rear up'/'to sit up straight'
This verb has alternative forms in some of its tenses, the forms with *y-* being more common.

Infinitive *erguir*   **Gerund** *irguiendo*
Past Participle *erguido*   **Imperative** *yergue/irgue erguid*

INDICATIVE

Present	Imperfect	Preterite	Future	Conditional
yergo/irgo	*erguía*	*erguí*	*erguiré*	*erguiría*
yergues/irgues	etc.	*erguiste*	etc.	etc.
yergue/irgue		*irguió*		
erguimos		*erguimos*		
erguís		*erguisteis*		
yerguen/irguen		*irguieron*		

SUBJUNCTIVE

Present	Imperfect	Future
yerga/irga	*irguiera/irguiese*	*irguiere*
yergas/irgas	etc.	etc.
yerga/irga		
yergamos/irgamos		
yergáis/irgáis		
yergan/irgan		

Usage: *No te agaches – ponte erguido* 'Stop slouching – sit up straight', *Se irguió como una serpiente* 'It rose up like a snake', *El perro irguió las orejas* 'The dog pricked up its ears', etc.

13.3.20 *Errar* 'to wander'/'to err'
This verb conjugates like *cerrar*, i.e. *e* > *ie* when stressed, but the *ie* is written *ye*. In the Southern Cone and Colombia and in some other parts of Latin America it is often regular, i.e. *erro, erras, erra*, etc.

Infinitive *errar*   **Gerund** *errando*
Past Participle *errado*   **Imperative** *yerra errad*

INDICATIVE

Present	Imperfect	Preterite	Future	Conditional
yerro	*erraba*	*erré*	*erraré*	*erraría*
yerras	etc.	etc.	etc.	etc.
yerra				
erramos				
erráis				
yerran				

SUBJUNCTIVE

Present	Imperfect	Future
yerre	*errara/errase*	*errare*
yerres	etc.	etc.
yerre		
erremos		
erréis		
yerren		

13.3.21 *Estar* 'to be' *haber* 'to have' (auxiliary verb)
See Table 5, p.203 and Table 6, p.204.

13.3.22 *Hacer* 'to do'/'to make'

There are several compounds, e.g. *deshacer* 'to undo', *contrahacer* 'to counterfeit'

Infinitive *hacer*   **Gerund** *haciendo*

Past Participle *hecho*   **Imperative** *haz haced*

INDICATIVE

Present	Imperfect	Preterite	Future	Conditional
hago	hacía	hice	haré	haría
haces	etc.	hiciste	etc.	etc.
hace		hizo		
hacemos		hicimos		
hacéis		hicisteis		
hacen		hicieron		

SUBJUNCTIVE

Present	Imperfect	Future
haga	hiciera/hiciese	hiciere
hagas	hicieras/hicieses	etc.
haga	hiciera/hiciese	
hagamos	hiciéramos/hiciésemos	
hagáis	hicierais/hicieseis	
hagan	hicieran/hiciesen	

13.3.23 *Ir* 'to go'

Infinitive *ir*   **Gerund** *yendo*
Past Participle *ido*   **Imperative** *ve id* (see note)

INDICATIVE

Present	Imperfect	Preterite	Future	Conditional
voy	iba	fui (no accent!)	iré	iría
vas	ibas	fuiste	etc.	etc.
va	iba	fue (no accent!)		
vamos	íbamos	fuimos		
vais	ibais	fuisteis		
van	iban	fueron		

SUBJUNCTIVE

Present	Imperfect	Future
vaya	fuera/fuese	fuere
vayas	fueras/fueses	etc.
vaya	fuera/fuese	
vayamos	fuéramos/fuésemos	
vayáis	fuerais/fueseis	
vayan	fueran/fuesen	

Note

The *vosotros* imperative of *irse* is irregularly *idos* (for the predicted **íos*). See 17.2.4 for further discussion of this form.

13.3.24 *Jugar* 'to play'[15]

This verb is unique in that *u* > *ue* when stressed. Note also *g* > *gu* before *e*.

Infinitive *jugar*
Past Participle *jugado*

Gerund *jugando*
Imperative *juega jugad*

INDICATIVE

Present	Imperfect	Preterite	Future	Conditional
juego	*jugaba*	*jugué*	*jugaré*	*jugaría*
juegas	etc.	etc.	etc.	etc.
juega				
jugamos				
jugáis				
juegan				

SUBJUNCTIVE

Present	Imperfect	Future
juegue	*jugara/jugase*	*jugare*
juegues	etc.	etc.
juegue		
juguemos		
juguéis		
jueguen		

13.3.25 *Lucir* 'to show off' (transitive)

Infinitive *lucir*
Past Participle *lucido*

Gerund *luciendo*
Imperative *luce lucid*

INDICATIVE

Present	Imperfect	Preterite	Future	Conditional
luzco	*lucía*	*lucí*	*luciré*	*luciría*
luces	etc.	etc.	etc.	etc.
luce				
lucimos				
lucís				
lucen				

SUBJUNCTIVE

Present	Imperfect	Future
luzca	*luciera/luciese*	*luciere*
luzcas	etc.	etc.
luzca		
luzcamos		
luzcáis		
luzcan		

Note
Verbs ending in *-ducir* are conjugated like *producir* shown at 13.3.36.

13.3.26 *Maldecir* 'to curse', *bendecir* 'to bless'

Conjugated like *decir* in some tenses, and regularly in others. Forms that differ from *decir* are shown in bold type:

Infinitive *maldecir*
Past Participle *maldecido*

Gerund *maldiciendo*
Imperative **maldice** *maldecid*

---

[15] i.e. 'play a game'. *Tocar* = 'to play an instrument'

INDICATIVE

Present	Imperfect	Preterite	Future	Conditional
maldigo	*maldecía*	*maldije*	*maldeciré*	*maldeciría*
maldices	etc.	*maldijiste*	*maldecirás*	*maldecirías*
maldice		*maldijo*	*maldecirá*	*maldeciría*
maldecimos		*maldijimos*	*maldeciremos*	*maldeciríamos*
maldecís		*maldijisteis*	*maldeciréis*	*maldeciríais*
maldicen		*maldijeron*	*maldecirán*	*maldecirían*

SUBJUNCTIVE

Present	Imperfect	Future
maldiga	*maldijera/maldijese*	*maldijere*
maldigas	*maldijeras/maldijeses*	etc.
maldiga	*maldijera/maldijese*	
maldigamos	*maldijéramos/maldijésemos*	
maldigáis	*maldijerais/maldijeseis*	
maldigan	*maldijeran/maldijesen*	

13.3.27 *Mover* 'to move'

A common type of radical changing verb. The endings are regular but the *o* of the stem changes to *ue* when stressed.

Infinitive *mover* **Gerund** *moviendo*
Past Participle *movido* **Imperative** *mueve, moved*

INDICATIVE

Present	Imperfect	Preterite	Future	Conditional
muevo	*movía*	*moví*	*moveré*	*movería*
mueves	etc.	etc.	etc.	etc.
mueve				
movemos				
movéis				
mueven				

SUBJUNCTIVE

Present	Imperfect	Future
mueva	*moviera/moviese*	*moviere*
muevas	etc.	etc.
mueva		
movamos		
mováis		
muevan		

13.3.28 *Oír* 'to hear' (also the rare *desoír* 'to disregard')

Infinitive *oír* **Gerund** *oyendo*
Past Participle *oído* **Imperative** *oye oíd*

INDICATIVE

Present	Imperfect	Preterite	Future	Conditional
oigo	*oía*	*oí*	*oiré*	*oiría*
oyes	*oías*	*oíste*	etc.	etc.
oye	*oía*	*oyó*		
oímos	*oíamos*	*oímos*		
oís	*oíais*	*oísteis*		
oyen	*oían*	*oyeron*		

SUBJUNCTIVE

Present	Imperfect	Future
oiga	*oyera/oyese*	*oyere*
oigas	*oyeras/oyeses*	etc.
oiga	*oyera/oyese*	
oigamos	*oyéramos/oyésemos*	
oigáis	*oyerais/oyeseis*	
oigan	*oyeran/oyesen*	

13.3.29 *Oler* 'to smell'

Oler is conjugated like *mover* but shows the predictable spelling *hue* for *ue* when this diphthong is at the beginning of a word:

Infinitive *oler*   **Gerund** *oliendo*
Past Participle *olido*   **Imperative** *huele* *oled*

INDICATIVE

Present	Imperfect	Preterite	Future	Conditional
huelo	*olía*	*olí*	*oleré*	*olería*
hueles	etc.	etc.	etc.	etc.
huele				
olemos				
oléis				
huelen				

SUBJUNCTIVE

Present	Imperfect	Future
huela	*oliera/oliese*	*oliere*
huelas	etc.	etc.
huela		
olamos		
oláis		
huelan		

13.3.30 *Pedir* 'to ask for'

The endings are regular, but the *e* of the stem changes to *i* when stressed, and also in the gerund, third-person preterite and past and future subjunctive:

Infinitive *pedir*   **Gerund** *pidiendo*
Past Participle *pedido*   **Imperative** *pide* *pedid*

INDICATIVE

Present	Imperfect	Preterite	Future	Conditional
pido	*pedía*	*pedí*	*pediré*	*pediría*
pides	etc.	*pediste*	etc.	etc.
pide		*pidió*		
pedimos		*pedimos*		
pedís		*pedisteis*		
piden		*pidieron*		

SUBJUNCTIVE

Present	Imperfect	Future
pida	*pidiera/pidiese*	*pidiere*
pidas	*pidieras/pidieses*	etc.
pida	*pidiera/pidiese*	
pidamos	*pidiéramos/pidiésemos*	
pidáis	*pidierais/pidieseis*	
pidan	*pidieran/pidiesen*	

13.3.31 *Perder* 'to lose'

A radical changing verb. The endings are regular, but the *e* of the stem changes to *ie* when stressed. This is a common type of verb:

Infinitive *perder*　　　　　**Gerund** *perdiendo*
Past Participle *perdido*　　　**Imperative** *pierde perded*

INDICATIVE

Present	Imperfect	Preterite	Future	Conditional
pierdo	perdía	perdí	perderé	perdería
pierdes	etc.	etc.	etc.	etc.
pierde				
perdemos				
perdéis				
pierden				

SUBJUNCTIVE

Present	Imperfect	Future
pierda	perdiera/perdiese	perdiere
pierdas	etc.	etc.
pierda		
perdamos		
perdáis		
pierdan		

13.3.32 *Placer* 'to please'

This verb is found only in the third person and even then it is nowadays very rare: *gustar* (regular) is the usual word for 'to please'.

It is conjugated like *nacer* (see 13.3.10) except that alternative irregular forms (none of them nowadays in use) exist in the third person of three tenses:

Preterite	Present subjunctive	Imperfect subjunctive
sing. plugo	plega	pluguiera/pluguiese
plur. pluguieron		

13.3.33 *Poder* 'to be able'

Infinitive *poder*　　　　　**Gerund** *pudiendo*
Past Participle *podido*　　　**Imperative not used**

INDICATIVE

Present	Imperfect	Preterite	Future	Conditional
puedo	podía	pude	podré	podría
puedes	etc.	pudiste	etc.	etc.
puede		pudo		
podemos		pudimos		
podéis		pudisteis		
pueden		pudieron		

SUBJUNCTIVE

Present	Imperfect	Future
pueda	pudiera/pudiese	pudiere
puedas	pudieras/pudieses	etc.
pueda	pudiera/pudiese	
podamos	pudiéramos/pudiésemos	
podáis	pudierais/pudieseis	
puedan	pudieran/pudiesen	

13.3.34   *Poner* 'to put'

And also compounds like *componer* 'to compose', *imponer* 'to impose', *proponer* 'to propose', *descomponer* 'to split something up', *suponer* 'to suppose', etc.

Infinitive *poner*   **Gerund** *poniendo*
Past Participle *puesto*   **Imperative** *pon*[16] *poned*

INDICATIVE

Present	Imperfect	Preterite	Future	Conditional
pongo	ponía	puse	pondré	pondría
pones	ponías	pusiste	etc.	etc.
pone	ponía	puso		
ponemos	poníamos	pusimos		
ponéis	poníais	pusisteis		
ponen	ponían	pusieron		

SUBJUNCTIVE

Present	Imperfect	Future
ponga	pusiera/**pusiese**	pusiere
pongas	pusieras/**pusieses**	etc.
ponga	pusiera/**pusiese**	
pongamos	pusiéramos/**pusiésemos**	
pongáis	pusierais/**pusieseis**	
pongan	pusieran/**pusiesen**	

13.3.35   *Poseer* 'to possess'

This verb and others like it, e.g. *leer* 'to read', *creer* 'to believe', requires that a *y* sound between vowels should be written *y* and not *i*:

Infinitive *poseer*   Gerund *poseyendo*
Past Participle *poseído*   Imperative *posee poseed*

INDICATIVE

Present	Imperfect	Preterite	Future	Conditional
poseo	poseía	poseí	poseeré	poseería
posees	etc.	poseíste	etc.	etc.
posee		poseyó		
poseemos		poseímos		
poseéis		poseísteis		
poseen		poseyeron		

SUBJUNCTIVE

Present	Imperfect	Future
posea	poseyera/poseyese	poseyere
poseas	poseyeras/poseyeses	etc.
posea	poseyera/poseyese	
poseamos	poseyéramos/poseyésemos	
poseáis	poseyerais/poseyeseis	
posean	poseyeran/poseyesen	

13.3.36   *Producir* 'to produce'

Conjugated like *lucir* except for the preterite and for forms (past and future subjunctive) based on the preterite stem.

---

[16] Accent on imperative of compounds, e.g. *componer* – *compón* 'compose', *posponer* – *pospón* 'postpone'.

The preterite ending is *-eron* and the past and future subjunctive endings are *-era*, *-ese*, not *-ieron*, *-iera*, *-iese*, etc.

Infinitive *producir*   **Gerund** *produciendo*
Past Participle *producido*   **Imperative** *produce producid*

INDICATIVE

Present	Imperfect	Preterite	Future	Conditional
produzco	*producía*	*produje*	*produciré*	*produciría*
produces	etc.	*produjiste*	etc.	etc.
produce		*produjo*		
producimos		*produjimos*		
producís		*produjisteis*		
producen		*produjeron*		

SUBJUNCTIVE

Present	Imperfect	Future
produzca	*produjera/produjese*	*produjere*
produzcas	*produjeras/produjeses*	
produzca	*produjera/produjese*	
produzcamos	*produjéramos/produjésemos*	
produzcáis	*produjerais/produjeseis*	
produzcan	*produjeran/produjesen*	

Note
Regularized forms of the preterite like *produció, *conducí are common mistakes of foreigners and even of some natives, but they are stigmatized.

13.3.37 Querer 'to want'/'to love'

Infinitive *querer*   **Gerund** *queriendo*
Past Participle *querido*   **Imperative** *quiere quered*

INDICATIVE

Present	Imperfect	Preterite	Future	Conditional
quiero	*quería*	*quise*	*querré*	*querría*
quieres	etc.	*quisiste*	*querrás*	*querrías*
quiere		*quiso*	*querrá*	*querría*
queremos		*quisimos*	*querremos*	*querríamos*
queréis		*quisisteis*	*querréis*	*querríais*
quieren		*quisieron*	*querrán*	*querrían*

SUBJUNCTIVE

Present	Imperfect	Future
quiera	*quisiera/quisiese*	*quisiere*
quieras	*quisieras/quisieses*	etc.
quiera	*quisiera/quisiese*	
queramos	*quisiéramos/quisiésemos*	
queráis	*quisierais/quisieseis*	
quieran	*quisieran/quisiesen*	

13.3.38 Reír 'to laugh'

This verb is in fact conjugated in the same way as *pedir*, although the absence of a consonant between the vowels obscures the similarity:

Infinitive *reír*   **Gerund** *riendo*
Past Participle *reído*   **Imperative** *ríe reíd*

INDICATIVE

Present	Imperfect	Preterite	Future	Conditional
río	reía	reí	reiré	reiría
ríes	reías	reíste	etc.	etc.
ríe	reía	rió[17]		
reímos	reíamos	reímos		
reís	reíais	reísteis		
ríen	reían	rieron		

SUBJUNCTIVE

Present	Imperfect	Future
ría	riera/riese	riere
rías	rieras/rieses	etc.
ría	riera/riese	
riamos	riéramos/riésemos	
riáis	rierais/rieseis	
rían	rieran/riesen	

13.3.39   *Reñir* 'to scold'

This and other verbs in *-eñir* are conjugated like *pedir*, except that, as usual, *ie* > *e* and *ió* > *ó* after *ñ*; see Table 3 item 6, p.200:

Infinitive *reñir*   **Gerund** *riñendo*
Past Participle *reñido*   **Imperative** *riñe reñid*

INDICATIVE

Present	Imperfect	Preterite	Future	Conditional
riño	reñía	reñí	reñiré	reñiría
riñes	etc.	reñiste	etc.	etc.
riñe		riñó		
reñimos		reñimos		
reñís		reñisteis		
riñen		riñeron		

SUBJUNCTIVE

Present	Imperfect	Future
riña	riñera/riñese	riñere
riñas	riñeras/riñeses	etc.
riña	riñera/riñese	
riñamos	riñéramos/riñésemos	
riñáis	riñerais/riñeseis	
riñan	riñeran/riñesen	

13.3.40   *Roer* 'to gnaw'

The bracketed forms are less common alternatives.

Infinitive *roer*   **Gerund** *royendo*
Past Participle *roído*   **Imperative** *roe roed*

---

[17] Note written accent. The only third-person singular preterites in *-io* which have no written accent are *dio* (from *dar*) and *vio* (from *ver*); see 39.2.3 note (i) for further remarks.

INDICATIVE

Present	Imperfect	Preterite	Future	Conditional
roo (roigo, royo)	*roía*	*roí*	*roeré*	*roería*
roes	etc.	*roíste*	etc.	etc.
roe		*royó*		
roemos		*roímos*		
roéis		*roísteis*		
roen		*royeron*		

SUBJUNCTIVE

Present	Imperfect	Future
roa (roiga, roya)	*royera/royese*	*royere*
roas (roigas, royas)	*royeras/royeses*	etc.
roa (roiga, roya)	*royera/royese*	
roamos (roigamos, royamos)	*royéramos/royésemos*	
roáis (roigáis, royáis)	*royerais/royeseis*	
roan (roigan, royan)	*royeran/royesen*	

13.3.41 *Saber* 'to know'

Infinitive *saber*   **Gerund** *sabiendo*
Past Participle *sabido*   **Imperative** *sabe sabed*

INDICATIVE

Present	Imperfect	Preterite	Future	Conditional
sé	*sabía*	*supe*	*sabré*	*sabría*
sabes	*sabías*	*supiste*	etc.	etc.
sabe	*sabía*	*supo*		
sabemos	*sabíamos*	*supimos*		
sabéis	*sabíais*	*supisteis*		
saben	*sabían*	*supieron*		

SUBJUNCTIVE

Present	Imperfect	Future
sepa	*supiera/supiese*	*supiere*
sepas	*supieras/supieses*	etc.
sepa	*supiera/supiese*	
sepamos	*supiéramos/supiésemos*	
sepáis	*supierais/supieseis*	
sepan	*supieran/supiesen*	

13.3.42 *Salir* 'to go out'/'to leave'

Infinitive *salir*   **Gerund** *saliendo*
Past Participle *salido*   **Imperative** *sal salid*

INDICATIVE

Present	Imperfect	Preterite	Future	Conditional
salgo	*salía*	*salí*	*saldré*	*saldría*
sales	etc.	etc.	etc.	etc.
sale				
salimos				
salís				
salen				

SUBJUNCTIVE

Present	**Imperfect**	**Future**
salga	*saliera/saliese*	*saliere*
salgas	etc.	etc.
salga		
salgamos		
salgáis		
salgan		

13.3.43 *Sentir* 'to feel'

A common type of *-ir* verb. The endings are regular, but the stem vowel changes to *ie* or to *i* in certain forms:

Infinitive *sentir*   **Gerund** *sintiendo*
Past Participle *sentido*   **Imperative** *siente sentid*

INDICATIVE

Present	**Imperfect**	**Preterite**	**Future**	**Conditional**
siento	*sentía*	*sentí*	*sentiré*	*sentiría*
sientes	*sentías*	*sentiste*	etc.	etc.
siente	*sentía*	*sintió*		
sentimos	*sentíamos*	*sentimos*		
sentís	*sentíais*	*sentisteis*		
sienten	*sentían*	*sintieron*		

SUBJUNCTIVE

Present	**Imperfect**	**Future**
sienta	*sintiera/sintiese*	*sintiere*
sientas	*sintieras/sintieses*	etc.
sienta	*sintiera/sintiese*	
sintamos	*sintiéramos/sintiésemos*	
sintáis	*sintierais/sintieseis*	
sientan	*sintieran/sintiesen*	

13.3.44 *Ser* 'to be'
See Table 4, p.202.

13.3.45 *Tener* 'to have'/ 'to hold'

Infinitive *tener*   **Gerund** *teniendo*
Past Participle *tenido*   **Imperative** *ten tened*

INDICATIVE

Present	**Imperfect**	**Preterite**	**Future**	**Conditional**
tengo	*tenía*	*tuve*	*tendré*	*tendría*
tienes	etc.	*tuviste*	etc.	etc.
tiene		*tuvo*		
tenemos		*tuvimos*		
tenéis		*tuvisteis*		
tienen		*tuvieron*		

SUBJUNCTIVE

Present	Imperfect	Future
tenga	*tuviera/tuviese*	*tuviere*
tengas	*tuvieras/tuvieses*	*etc.*
tenga	*tuviera/tuviese*	
tengamos	*tuviéramos/tuviésemos*	
tengáis	*tuvierais/tuvieseis*	
tengan	*tuvieran/tuviesen*	

Note
Singular imperative of *detener* 'to detain'/'to stop' = *detén*, *retener* 'to retain' = *retén*.

13.3.46 *Traer* 'to bring'
This verb also shows the change *ie* > *e* after *j*:

Infinitive *traer* **Gerund** *trayendo*
Past Participle *traído* **Imperative** *trae traed*

INDICATIVE

Present	Imperfect	Preterite	Future	Conditional
traigo	*traía*	*traje*	*traeré*	*traería*
traes	*traías*	*trajiste*	*etc.*	*etc.*
trae	*traía*	*trajo*		
traemos	*traíamos*	*trajimos*		
traéis	*traíais*	*trajisteis*		
traen	*traían*	*trajeron*		

SUBJUNCTIVE

Present	Imperfect	Future
traiga	*trajera/trajese*	*trajere*
traigas	*trajeras/trajeses*	*etc.*
traiga	*trajera/trajese*	
traigamos	*trajéramos/trajésemos*	
traigáis	*trajerais/trajeseis*	
traigan	*trajeran/trajesen*	

Note
Truje, trujiste etc. is found in Golden-Age texts and survives sporadically in dialects.

13.3.47 *Valer* 'to be worth'

Infinitive *valer* **Gerund** *valiendo*
Past Participle *valido* **Imperative** *vale valed*

INDICATIVE

Present	Imperfect	Preterite	Future	Conditional
valgo	*valía*	*valí*	*valdré*	*valdría*
vales	*etc.*	*etc.*	*etc.*	*etc.*
vale				
valemos				
valéis				
valen				

SUBJUNCTIVE

Present	Imperfect	Future
valga	*valiera/valiese*	*valiere*
valgas	*etc.*	*etc.*
valga		
valgamos		
valgáis		
valgan		

13.3.48   *Venir* 'to come'

Infinitive *venir*   **Gerund** *viniendo*
Past Participle *venido*   **Imperative** *ven venid*

INDICATIVE

Present	Imperfect	Preterite	Future	Conditional
vengo	venía	vine	vendré	vendría
vienes	venías	viniste	etc.	etc.
viene	venía	vino		
venimos	veníamos	vinimos		
venís	veníais	vinisteis		
vienen	venían	vinieron		

SUBJUNCTIVE

Present	Imperfect	Future
venga	viniera/viniese	viniere
vengas	vinieras/vinieses	etc.
vengas	viniera/viniese	
vengamos	viniéramos/viniésemos	
vengáis	vinierais/vinieseis	
vengan	vinieran/viniesen	

13.3.49   *Ver* 'to see'

Infinitive *ver*   **Gerund** *viendo*
Past Participle *visto*   **Imperative** *ve ved*

INDICATIVE

Present	Imperfect	Preterite	Future	Conditional
veo	veía	vi (no accent!)	veré	vería
ves	veías	viste	etc.	etc.
ve	veía	vio (no accent!)		
vemos	veíamos	vimos		
veis	veíais	visteis		
ven	veían	vieron		

SUBJUNCTIVE

Present	Imperfect	Future
vea	viera/viese	viere
veas	vieras/vieses	etc.
veas	viera/viese	
veamos	viéramos/viésemos	
veáis	vierais/vieseis	
vean	vieran/viesen	

13.3.50   *Yacer* 'to lie' (as in 'he lay there')

Almost never used nowadays: *estar tumbado, estar acostado* are the usual translations. It is conjugated like *nacer*, but there are alternative forms (in brackets):

Infinitive *yacer*   **Gerund** *yaciendo*
Past Participle *yacido*   **Imperative** *yace/yaz yaced*

INDICATIVE

Present	Imperfect	Preterite	Future	Conditional
yazco (yazgo, yago)	*yacía*	*yací*	*yaceré*	*yacería*
yaces	etc.	etc.	etc.	etc.
yace				
yacemos				
yacéis				
yacen				

SUBJUNCTIVE

Present	Imperfect	Future
yazca (yazga, yaga)	*yaciera/yaciese*	*yaciere*
yazcas (yazgas, yagas)		
etc.		

13.4 List of irregular verbs

A number of very rare verbs have been omitted, but this is no guarantee that all of the verbs listed are in common use today. Bracketed forms indicate verbs that are found in the infinitive or past participle forms, which are often the only surviving remains of the verbs that are otherwise obsolete (cf. *aterirse*). For verbs beginning with the prefix in *re-* that are not listed here see the root verb.

Infinitive	model
abastecer	*-cer* 13.3.10
abolir	see 13.3.2
aborrecer	*-cer* 13.3.10
abrir	past participle *abierto*
absolver	*mover* 13.3.27
	past participle *absuelto*
abstenerse	*tener* 13.3.45
abstraer	*traer* 13.3.46
acaecer	*-cer* 13.3.10
acontecer	*-cer* 13.3.10
acordar	*contar* 13.3.14
acostar(se)	*contar* 13.3.14
acrecentar	*cerrar* 13.3.11
adherir	*sentir* 13.3.43
adolecer	*-cer* 13.3.10
adormecer	*-cer* 13.3.10
adquirir	see 13.3.3
aducir	*producir* 13.3.36
advertir	*sentir* 13.3.43
aferrar(se)	*cerrar* 13.3.11
	may be conjugated regularly
agradecer	*-cer* 13.3.10
agredir	see 13.3.4
(aguerrir	*abolir* 13.3.2)
alentar	*cerrar* 13.3.11
almorzar	*contar* 13.3.14
	z > c before *e*
amanecer	*-cer* 13.3.10
andar	see 13.3.5
anochecer	*-cer* 13.3.10

Infinitive	model
anteponer	*poner* 13.3.34
apacentar	*cerrar* 13.3.11
aparecer	*-cer* 13.3.10
apetecer	*-cer* 13.3.10
apostar	*contar* 13.3.14
	regular if it means 'to post a sentry'
apretar	*cerrar* 13.3.11
aprobar	*contar* 13.3.14
acertar	*cerrar* 13.3.11
argüir	*construir* 13.3.13
(arrecirse	*abolir* 13.3.2)
arrendar	*cerrar* 13.3.11
arrepentirse	*sentir* 13.3.43
ascender	*perder* 13.3.31
asentar	*cerrar* 13.3.11
asentir	*sentir* 13.3.43
asir	see 13.3.6
asolar	*contar* 13.3.14
	if it means 'to parch'. Usually regular nowadays
atañer	see Table 3, p.200, item 6
	third-person sing. only
atender	*perder* 13.3.31
atenerse	*tener* 13.3.45
(aterirse	*abolir* 13.3.2)
atraer	*traer* 13.3.46
atravesar	*cerrar* 13.3.11
atribuir	*construir* 13.3.13

Infinitive	model	Infinitive	model
avenir	*venir* 13.3.48	*consolar*	*contar* 13.3.14
aventar	*cerrar* 13.3.11	*consonar*	*contar* 13.3.14
avergonzar	*contar* 13.3.14	*constituir*	*construir* 13.3.13
c before *e*, and diphthong spelt *üe*,		*constreñir*	*reñir* 13.3.39
e.g. subjunctive *avergüence*		*construir*	see 13.3.13
balbucir	see 13.3.7	*contar*	see 13.3.14
bendecir	*maldecir* 13.3.26	*contender*	*perder* 13.3.31
(blandir	*abolir* 13.3.2)*	*contener*	*tener* 13.3.45
bruñir	*gruñir*	*contradecir*	*decir* 13.3.16
see Table 3, p.200,		*contraer*	*traer* 13.3.46
item 6		*contrahacer*	*hacer* 13.3.22
bullir	*zambullir*	*contraponer*	*poner* 13.3.34
see Table 3, p.200,		*contravenir*	*venir* 13.3.48
item 6		*contribuir*	*construir* 13.3.13
caber	see 13.3.8	*controvertir*	*sentir* 13.3.43
caer	see 13.3.9	*convalecer*	*-cer* 13.3.10
calentar	*cerrar* 13.3.11	*convenir*	*venir* 13.3.48
carecer	*-cer* 13.3.10	*convertir*	*sentir* 13.3.43
cegar	*cerrar* 13.3.11	*corregir*	*pedir* 13.3.30
g > gu before *e*		*g > j* before *a, o*	
ceñir	*reñir* 13.3.39	*costar*	*contar* 13.3.14
cerner	*perder* 13.3.31	*crecer*	*-cer* 13.3.10
cernir	*discernir* 13.3.17	*creer*	*poseer* 13.3.35
cerrar	see 13.3.11	*cubrir*	past participle
circunscribir	past participle		*cubierto*
	circunscrito	*dar*	see 13.3.15
cocer	see 13.3.12	*decaer*	*caer* 13.3.9
colar	*contar* 13.3.14	*decir*	see 13.3.16
colegir	*pedir* 13.3.30	*decrecer*	*-cer* 13.3.10
g > j before *a, o*		*deducir*	*producir* 13.3.36
colgar	*contar* 13.3.14	*defender*	*perder* 13.3.31
g > gu before *e*		*deferir*	*sentir* 13.3.43
comenzar	*cerrar* 13.3.11	*degollar*	*contar* 13.3.14
z > c before *e*		diphthong spelt *üe*	
compadecer	*-cer* 13.3.10	*demoler*	*mover* 13.3.27
comparecer	*-cer* 13.3.10	*demostrar*	*contar* 13.3.14
competir	*pedir* 13.3.30	*denegar*	*cerrar* 13.3.11
complacer	*-cer* 13.3.10	*g > gu* before *e*	
componer	*poner* 13.3.34	*denostar*	*contar* 13.3.14
comprobar	*contar* 13.3.14	*dentar*	*cerrar* 13.3.11
concebir	*pedir* 13.3.30	usually *dientar* nowadays	
concernir	*discernir* 13.3.17	*deponer*	*poner* 13.3.34
concertar	*cerrar* 13.3.11	*derrengar*	*cerrar* 13.3.11
concluir	*construir* 13.3.13	often regular nowadays; *g > gu* before *e*	
concordar	*contar* 13.3.14	*derretir*	*pedir* 13.3.30
condescender	*perder* 13.3.31	*derrocar*	nowadays regular;
condolerse	*mover* 13.3.27		*c > qu* before *e*
conducir	*producir* 13.3.36	*desacertar*	*cerrar* 13.3.11
conferir	*sentir* 13.3.43	*desacordar*	*contar* 13.3.14
confesar	*cerrar* 13.3.11	*desagradecer*	*-cer* 13.3.10
confluir	*construir* 13.3.13	*desalentar*	*cerrar* 13.3.11
conmover	*mover* 13.3.27	*desandar*	*andar* 13.3.5
conocer	*-cer* 13.3.10	*desaparecer*	*-cer* 13.3.10
conseguir	*pedir* 13.3.30	*desapretar*	*cerrar* 13.3.11
gu > g before *a, o*		*desaprobar*	*contar* 13.3.14
consentir	*sentir* 13.3.43		

Infinitive	model	Infinitive	model
desasosegar	*cerrar* 13.3.11	*desvergonzarse*	*contar* 13.3.14
g > gu before *e*		*z > c* before *e*; diphthong spelt *üe*	
desatender	*perder* 13.3.31	*detener*	*tener* 13.3.45
desavenir	*venir* 13.3.48	*detraer*	*traer* 13.3.46
descender	*perder* 13.3.31	*devolver*	*mover* 13.3.27
desceñir	*reñir* 13.3.39	past participle *devuelto*	
descolgar	*contar* 13.3.14	*diferir*	*sentir* 13.3.43
g > gu before *e*		*digerir*	*sentir* 13.3.43
descollar	*contar* 13.3.14	*diluir*	*construir* 13.3.13
descomedirse	*pedir* 13.3.30	*discernir*	see 13.3.17
descomponer	*poner* 13.3.34	*disentir*	*sentir* 13.3.43
desconcertar	*cerrar* 13.3.11	*disminuir*	*construir* 13.3.13
desconocer	*-cer* 13.3.10	*disolver*	*mover* 13.3.27
desconsolar	*contar* 13.3.14	past participle *disuelto*	
descontar	*contar* 13.3.14	*disponer*	*poner* 13.3.34
desconvenir	*venir* 13.3.48	*distender*	*perder* 13.3.31
describir	past participle *descrito*	*distraer*	*traer* 13.3.46
descubrir	past participle *descubierto*	*distribuir*	*construir* 13.3.13
		divertir	*sentir* 13.3.43
		doler	*mover* 13.3.27
desdecir	*decir* 13.3.16	*dormir*	see 13.3.18
desempedrar	*cerrar* 13.3.11	*elegir*	*pedir* 13.3.30
desengrosar	*contar* 13.3.14	*g > j* before *a, o*	
desentenderse	*perder* 13.3.31	*embebecer*	*-cer* 13.3.10
desenterrar	*cerrar* 13.3.11	*embellecer*	*-cer* 13.3.10
desenvolver	*mover* 13.3.27	*embestir*	*pedir* 13.3.30
past participle *desenvuelto*		*embravecer*	*-cer* 13.3.10
desfallecer	*-cer* 13.3.10	*embrutecer*	*-cer* 13.3.10
desgobernar	*cerrar* 13.3.11	*empedrar*	*cerrar* 13.3.11
deshacer	*hacer* 13.3.22	*empequeñecer*	*-cer* 13.3.10
deshelar	*cerrar* 13.3.11	*empezar*	*cerrar* 13.3.11
desherrar	*cerrar* 13.3.11	*z > c* before *e*	
desleír	*reír* 13.3.38	*empobrecer*	*-cer* 13.3.10
deslucir	*lucir* 13.3.25	*enaltecer*	*-cer* 13.3.10
desmembrar	*cerrar* 13.3.11	*enardecer*	*-cer* 13.3.10
desmentir	*sentir* 13.3.43	*encanecer*	*-cer* 13.3.10
desmerecer	*-cer* 13.3.10	*encarecer*	*-cer* 13.3.10
desobedecer	*-cer* 13.3.10	*encender*	*perder* 13.3.31
desoír	*oír* 13.3.28	*encerrar*	*cerrar* 13.3.11
desollar	*contar* 13.3.14	*encomendar*	*cerrar* 13.3.11
despedir	*pedir* 13.3.30	*encontrar*	*contar* 13.3.14
despedrar	*cerrar* 13.3.11	*encubrir*	past participle *encubierto*
despertar	*cerrar* 13.3.11		
despezar	*cerrar* 13.3.11		
usually *despiezar*, regular; *z >c* before *e*		*endurecer*	*-cer* 13.3.10
desplacer	*-cer* 13.3.10	*enflaquecer*	*-cer* 13.3.10
desplegar	*cerrar* 13.3.11	*enfurecer*	*-cer* 13.3.10
g > gu before *e*; now often regular		*engrandecer*	*-cer* 13.3.10
despoblar	*contar* 13.3.14	*engreírse*	*reír* 13.3.38
desproveer	*poseer* 13.3.35	*engrosar*	*contar* 13.3.14
past participle *desprovisto/desproveído*		now usually regular	
desteñir	*reñir* 13.3.39	*engullir*	*zambullir* see Table 3, p.200, item 6
desterrar	*cerrar* 13.3.11		
destituir	*construir* 13.3.13	*enloquecer*	*-cer* 13.3.10
destruir	*construir* 13.3.13	*enmendar*	*cerrar* 13.3.11
desvanecer	*-cer* 13.3.10	*enmohecer*	*-cer* 13.3.10

Infinitive	model	Infinitive	model
enmudecer	*-cer* 13.3.10	*gemir*	*pedir* 13.3.30
ennegrecer	*-cer* 13.3.10	*gobernar*	*cerrar* 13.3.11
ennoblecer	*-cer* 13.3.10	*gruñir*	see Table 3,
enorgullecer	*-cer* 13.3.10		p.200, item 6
enriquecer	*-cer* 13.3.10	*guarecer*	*-cer* 13.3.10
enronquecer	*-cer* 13.3.10	*guarnecer*	*-cer* 13.3.10
ensangrentar	*cerrar* 13.3.11	*haber*	see Table 6, p.204
ensordecer	*-cer* 13.3.10	*hacer*	see 13.3.22
entender	*perder* 13.3.31	*heder*	*perder* 13.3.31
enternecer	*-cer* 13.3.10	*helar*	*cerrar* 13.3.11
enterrar	*cerrar* 13.3.11	*henchir*	*pedir* 13.3.30
entreabrir	past participle	*hender*	*perder* 13.3.31
	entreabierto	*hendir*	*discernir* 13.3.17
entredecir	*decir* 13.3.16	*herir*	*sentir* 13.3.43
entreoír	*oír* 13.3.28	*herrar*	*cerrar* 13.3.11
entretener	*tener* 13.3.45	*hervir*	*sentir* 13.3.43
entrever	*ver* 13.3.49	*holgar*	*contar* 13.3.14
third-person present *entrevé(n)*		*g > gu* before *e*	
entristecer	*-cer* 13.3.10	*hollar*	*contar* 13.3.14
entumecer(se)	*-cer* 13.3.10	*huir*	*construir* 13.3.13
envanecer	*-cer* 13.3.10	*humedecer*	*-cer* 13.3.10
envejecer	*-cer* 13.3.10	*impedir*	*pedir* 13.3.30
envilecer	*-cer* 13.3.10	*imponer*	*poner* 13.3.34
envolver	*mover* 13.3.27	imperative singular *impón*	
past participle *envuelto*		*incensar*	*cerrar* 13.3.11
equivaler	*valer* 13.3.47	*incluir*	*construir* 13.3.13
erguir	see 13.3.19	*indisponer*	*poner* 13.3.34
errar	see 13.3.20	*inducir*	*producir* 13.3.36
escabullirse	*zambullir*	*inferir*	*sentir* 13.3.43
	see Table 3, p.200,	*influir*	*construir* 13.3.13
	item 6	*ingerir*	*sentir* 13.3.43
escarmentar	*cerrar* 13.3.11	*injerir*	*sentir* 13.3.43
escarnecer	*-cer* 13.3.10	*inquirir*	*adquirir* 13.3.3
escocer	*cocer* 13.3.12	*instituir*	*construir* 13.3.13
escribir	past participle *escrito*	*instruir*	*construir* 13.3.13
esforzar	*contar* 13.3.14	*interferir*	*sentir* 13.3.43
z > c before *e*		*interponer*	*poner* 13.3.34
establecer	*-cer* 13.3.10	*intervenir*	*venir* 13.3.48
estar	see Table 5, p.203	*introducir*	*producir* 13.3.36
estremecer	*-cer* 13.3.10	*intuir*	*construir* 13.3.13
estreñir	*reñir* 13.3.39	*invernar*	*cerrar* 13.3.11
excluir	*construir* 13.3.13	now usually regular	
expedir	*pedir* 13.3.30	*invertir*	*sentir* 13.3.43
exponer	*poner* 13.3.34	*investir*	*pedir* 13.3.30
extender	*perder* 13.3.31	*ir*	see 13.3.23
extraer	*traer* 13.3.46	*jugar*	see 13.3.24
fallecer	*-cer* 13.3.10	*languidecer*	*-cer* 13.3.10
favorecer	*-cer* 13.3.10	*leer*	*poseer* 13.3.35
florecer	*-cer* 13.3.10	*llover*	*mover* 13.3.27
fluir	*construir* 13.3.13	*lucir*	see 13.3.25
fortalecer	*-cer* 13.3.10	*maldecir*	see 13.3.26
forzar	*contar* 13.3.14	*manifestar*	*cerrar* 13.3.11
z > c before *e*		*mantener*	*tener* 13.3.45
fregar	*cerrar* 13.3.11	*medir*	*pedir* 13.3.30
g > gu before *e*		*mentar*	*cerrar* 13.3.11
freír	*reír* 13.3.38	*mentir*	*sentir* 13.3.43
past participle *frito*		*merecer*	*-cer* 13.3.10

Infinitive	model	Infinitive	model
merendar	*cerrar* 13.3.11	*producir*	see 13.3.36
moler	*mover* 13.3.27	*proferir*	*sentir* 13.3.43
morder	*mover* 13.3.27	*promover*	*mover* 13.3.27
morir	see 13.3.18	*proponer*	*poner* 13.3.34
mostrar	*contar* 13.3.14	*proseguir*	*pedir* 13.3.30
mover	see 13.3.27	*gu > g* before *a*	
mullir	*zambullir*	*prostituir*	*construir* 13.3.13
	see Table 3, p.200	*proveer*	*poseer* 13.3.35
nacer	-*cer* 13.3.10	past participle *provisto/proveído*	
negar	*cerrar* 13.3.11	*provenir*	*venir* 13.3.48
g > gu before *e*		*pudrir*	regular;
nevar	*cerrar* 13.3.11		see also *podrir*
obedecer	-*cer* 13.3.10	*quebrar*	*cerrar* 13.3.11
obscurecer	see *oscurecer*	*querer*	see 13.3.37
obstruir	*construir* 13.3.13	*raer*	*caer* 13.3.9
obtener	*tener* 13.3.45	*rayo* is an alternative to *raigo*	
ofrecer	-*cer* 13.3.10	*reaparecer*	-*cer* 13.3.10
oír	see 13.3.28	*reblandecer*	-*cer* 13.3.10
oler	see 13.3.29	*recaer*	*caer* 13.3.9
oponer	*poner* 13.3.34	*recluir*	*construir* 13.3.13
oscurecer	-*cer* 13.3.10	*recocer*	*cocer* 13.3.12
pacer	-*cer* 13.3.10	*recomendar*	*cerrar* 13.3.11
padecer	-*cer* 13.3.10	*reconocer*	-*cer* 13.3.10
palidecer	-*cer* 13.3.10	*reconvenir*	*venir* 13.3.48
parecer	-*cer* 13.3.10	*recordar*	*contar* 13.3.14
pedir	see 13.3.30	*recostar(se)*	*contar* 13.3.14
pensar	*cerrar* 13.3.11	*reducir*	*producir* 13.3.36
perecer	-*cer* 13.3.10	*reelegir*	*pedir* 13.3.30
permanecer	-*cer* 13.3.10	*g > j* before *a, o*	
perseguir	*pedir* 13.3.30	*referir*	*sentir* 13.3.43
gu > g before *a, o*		*reforzar*	*contar* 13.3.14
pertenecer	-*cer* 13.3.10	*z > c* before *e*	
pervertir	*sentir* 13.3.43	*refregar*	*cerrar* 13.3.11
placer	see 13.3.32	*g > gu* before *e*	
plegar	*cerrar* 13.3.11	*regar*	*cerrar* 13.3.11
g > gu before *e*		*g > gu* before *e*	
poblar	*contar* 13.3.14	*regir*	*pedir* 13.3.30
poder	see 13.3.33	*g > j* before *a, o*	
podrir	variant of *pudrir*	*rehacer*	*hacer* 13.3.22
-*u*- used for all forms except		*reír*	see 13.3.38
past participle *podrido*		*rejuvenecer*	-*cer* 13.3.10
poner	see 13.3.34	*remendar*	*cerrar* 13.3.11
poseer	see 13.3.35	*remorder*	*mover* 13.3.27
posponer	*poner* 13.3.34	*remover*	*mover* 13.3.27
tú imperative *pospón*		*rendir*	*pedir* 13.3.30
predecir	*decir* 13.3.16	*renegar*	*cerrar* 13.3.11
predisponer	*poner* 13.3.34	*g > gu* before *e*	
preferir	*sentir* 13.3.43	*renovar*	*contar* 13.3.14
prescribir	past participle *prescrito*	*reñir*	see 13.3.39
presuponer	*poner* 13.3.34	*repetir*	*pedir* 13.3.30
prevalecer	-*cer* 13.3.10	*replegar*	*cerrar* 13.3.11
prevaler	*valer* 13.3.47	*g > gu* before *e*	
prevenir	*venir* 13.3.48	*repoblar*	*contar* 13.3.14
prever	*ver* 13.3.49	*reponer*	*poner* 13.3.34
third-person present *prevé(n)*		*reprobar*	*contar* 13.3.14
probar	*contar* 13.3.14	*reproducir*	*producir* 13.3.36

Infinitive	model	Infinitive	model
requebrar	*cerrar* 13.3.11	*sobreponer*	*poner* 13.3.34
requerir	*sentir* 13.3.43	*sobresalir*	*salir* 13.3.42
resentirse	*sentir* 13.3.43	*sobrevenir*	*venir* 13.3.48
resollar	*contar* 13.3.14	*sofreír*	*reír* 13.3.38
resolver	*mover* 13.3.27	past participle *sofrito*	
past participle *resuelto*		*soldar*	*contar* 13.3.14
resonar	*contar* 13.3.14	*soler*	*mover* 13.3.27
resplandecer	*-cer* 13.3.10	future, conditional and	
restablecer	*-cer* 13.3.10	past and future subjunctives not used	
restituir	*construir* 13.3.13	*soltar*	*contar* 13.3.14
estregar	*cerrar* 13.3.11	past participle *suelto*	
g > gu before *e*		*sonar*	*contar* 13.3.14
retemblar	*cerrar* 13.3.11	*sonreír*	*reír* 13.3.38
retener	*tener* 13.3.45	*soñar*	*contar* 13.3.14
reteñir	*reñir* 13.3.39	*sosegar*	*cerrar* 13.3.11
retorcer	*cocer* 13.3.12	*g > gu* before *e*	
c > z before *a, o*		*sostener*	*tener* 13.3.45
retraer	*traer* 13.3.46	*soterrar*	*cerrar* 13.3.11
retribuir	*construir* 13.3.13	*subarrendar*	*cerrar* 13.3.11
retrotraer	*traer* 13.3.46	*subscribir*	see *suscribir*
reventar	*cerrar* 13.3.11	*subvenir*	*venir* 13.3.48
reverdecer	*-cer* 13.3.10	*subvertir*	*sentir* 13.3.43
revertir	*sentir* 13.3.43	*sugerir*	*sentir* 13.3.43
revestir	*pedir* 13.3.30	*suponer*	*poner* 13.3.34
revolar	*contar* 13.3.14	*suscribir*[18]	past participle
revolcar(se)	*contar* 13.3.14		*suscrito*
c > qu before *e*		*sustituir*[19]	*construir* 13.3.13
revolver	*mover* 13.3.27	*sustraer*[20]	*traer* 13.3.46
past participle *revuelto*		*tañer*	see Table 3,
robustecer	*-cer* 13.3.10		p.200, item 6
rodar	*contar* 13.3.14	*temblar*	*cerrar* 13.3.11
roer	see 13.3.40	*tender*	*perder* 13.3.31
rogar	*contar* 13.3.14	*tener*	see 13.3.45
g > gu before *e*		*tentar*	*cerrar* 13.3.11
romper	past participle *roto*	*teñir*	*reñir* 13.3.39
saber	see 13.3.41	*torcer*	*cocer* 13.3.12
salir	see 13.3.42	*c > z* before *a, o*	
satisfacer	*hacer* 13.3.22	*tostar*	*contar* 13.3.14
seducir	*producir* 13.3.36	*traducir*	*producir* 13.3.36
segar	*cerrar* 13.3.11	*traer*	see 13.3.46
g > gu before *e*		*tra(n)scender*	*perder* 13.3.31
seguir	*pedir* 13.3.30	*transcender*	*perder* 13.3.31
gu > g before *a* or *o*		*transcribir*	past participle
sembrar	*cerrar* 13.3.11		*transcrito*
sentar	*cerrar* 13.3.11	*trasferir*	*sentir* 13.3.43
sentir	see 13.3.43	*transgredir*	*abolir* 13.3.2
ser	see Table 4, p.202	sometimes regular	
serrar	*cerrar* 13.3.11	*transponer*	*poner* 13.3.34
servir	*pedir* 13.3.30	*trasegar*	*cerrar* 13.3.11
sobrentender/	*perder* 13.3.31	*g > gu* before *e*	
sobreentender		*traslucir*	*lucir* 13.3.25

---

[18] less commonly *subscribir*
[19] less commonly *substituir*
[20] less commonly *substraer*

Infinitive	model	Infinitive	model
trasponer	*poner* 13.3.34	*venir*	see 13.3.48
trastrocar	*contar* 13.3.14	*ver*	see 13.3.49
c > qu before *e*		*verter*	*perder* 13.3.31
trocar	*contar* 13.3.14	*vestir*	*pedir* 13.3.30
c > qu before *e*		*volar*	*contar* 13.3.14
tronar	*contar* 13.3.14	*volcar*	*contar* 13.3.14
tropezar	*cerrar* 13.3.11	*c > qu* before *e*	
z > c before *e*		*volver*	*mover* 13.3.27
tullir	*zambullir*	past participle *vuelto*	
	see Table 3, p.200	*yacer*	see 13.3.50
	item 6	*zaherir*	*sentir* 13.3.43
valer	see 13.3.47	*zambullir*	see Table 3, p.200, iter

TABLE I *Overview of the Spanish verb*[21]

Spanish verbs may appear in the following forms:

Infinitive	*hablar*	discussed in Chapter 18
Gerund	*hablando*	discussed in Chapter 20
Past participle	*hablado*	discussed in Chapter 19
Imperative	*habla* (tú) *hablad* (vosotros/vosotras)	
	hable (usted) *hablen* (ustedes)	discussed in Chapter 17

ACTIVE VOICE

INDICATIVE

The uses of the indicative tense forms are discussed in Chapter 14.

Present	*yo hablo*, etc.	I speak
Imperfect	*yo hablaba*, etc.	I was speaking
Preterite	*yo hablé*, etc.	I spoke
Future	*yo hablaré*, etc.	I shall/will speak
Conditional	*yo hablaría*, etc.	I would speak
Perfect	*yo he hablado*, etc.	I have spoken
Pluperfect	*yo había hablado*, etc.	I had spoken
Future	*yo habré hablado*, etc.	I will have spoken
Conditional	*yo habría hablado*,	
etc.	or *yo hubiera hablado*	I would have spoken
Pretérito anterior	*yo hube hablado*	I had spoken, etc. (see 14.10.4)

CONTINUOUS (discussed in Chapter 15)

Present	*yo estoy hablando*, etc.	I'm speaking
Imperfect	*yo estaba hablando*, etc.	I was speaking
Preterite	*yo estuve hablando*, etc.	I spoke/had a talk
Future	*yo estaré hablando*, etc.	I'll be speaking
Conditional	*yo estaría hablando*, etc.	I'd be speaking
Perfect	*yo he estado hablando*, etc.	I have been speaking

[21] The following remarks apply throughout these verb tables:

(i) *Vosotros* forms are replaced by *ustedes* forms throughout Latin America.

(ii) The *-ra* form of *hubiera* is an optional alternative for the conditional *habría* in the conditional tenses of the perfect.

(iii) The *-ra* and *-se* forms of the past subjunctive are interchangeable except in the cases mentioned at 16.2.3.

(iv) The future subjunctive is almost obsolete. See 16.17.

(v) All compound tenses are formed with the auxiliary *haber* (see p.204) and the past participle, which does *not* agree in number or gender in these tenses.

TABLE I *Continued*

Pluperfect	*yo había estado hablando*, etc.	I had been speaking
Future	*yo habré estado hablando*, etc.	I shall/will have been speaking
Conditional	*yo habría estado hablando*, etc.	I would have been speaking

SUBJUNCTIVE

Present	*(que) yo hable*, etc.
Imperfect	*(que) yo hablara/(que) yo hablase*, etc.
Future	*(que) yo hablare*, etc.
Perfect	*(que) yo haya hablado*, etc.
Pluperfect	*(que) yo hubiera/hubiese hablado*, etc.
Future	*(que) yo hubiere hablado*, etc.

CONTINOUS

Present	*(que) yo esté hablando*, etc.
Imperfect	*(que) yo estuviera/estuviese hablando*, etc.
Future	*(que) yo estuviere hablando*, etc.
Perfect	*(que) yo haya estado hablando*, etc.
Pluperfect	*(que) yo hubiera/hubiese estado hablando*, etc.
Future	not used

PASSIVE VOICE

There are a number of ways of translating the English passive, the most common being the passive with *ser*, e.g. *Esta novela fue publicada en México*, or (in the case of the third person) the pronominal form, e.g. *Esta novela se publicó en México*. These forms, not always interchangeable, are discussed in Chapter 28, but a selection of the chief tenses are shown here by way of illustration. The participle in the *ser* form must agree in number and gender with the subject of *ser*:

INDICATIVE (third person only shown)

Present	*es publicado/se publica*	it is published
Imperfect	*era publicado/se publicaba*	it used to be published
Preterite	*fue publicado/se publicó*	it was published
Future	*será publicado/se publicará*	it will be published
Conditional	*sería publicado/se publicaría*	it would be published
Perfect	*ha sido publicado/se ha publicado*	it has been published
Pluperfect	*había sido publicado/se había publicado*	it had been published
Future	*habrá sido publicado/se habrá publicado*	it will have been published
Conditional	*habría sido publicado/se habría publicado*	it would have been published

CONTINUOUS

The passive continuous with *ser* is not very common. It is discussed at 15.4.

Present	*está siendo publicado/está publicándose*	it is being published
Imperfect	*estaba siendo publicado/estaba publicándose*	it was being published
Future	*estará siendo publicado/estará publicándose*	it will be being published
Conditional	*estaría siendo publicado/estaría publicándose*	it would be being published
Perfect	*ha estado siendo publicado/ha estado publicándose* (very rare)	
Pluperfect	*había estado siendo publicado/había estado publicándose* (very rare)	

SUBJUNCTIVE

Present	*(que) sea publicado/(que) se publique*
Imperfect	*(que) fuera publicado/(que) se publicara/(que) fuese publicado/(que) se publicase*
Future	*(que) fuere publicado/(que) se publicare*

TABLE I *Continued*

CONTINUOUS
The subjunctive continuous passive is also extremely rare in practice.

Present	*(que) esté siendo publicado/(que) se esté publicando*
Imperfect	*(que) estuviera/estuviese siendo publicado/(que) se estuviera/estuviese publicando*

TABLE 2 *Conjugation of regular verbs*

The three verbs *hablar* 'to speak', *comer* 'to eat' and *vivir* 'to live' conjugate regularly throughout and are unaffected by spelling changes.

Infinitive	*hablar*		*comer*		*vivir*	
Stem	*habl-*		*com-*		*viv-*	
Gerund	*hablando*		*comiendo*		*viviendo*	
Past participle	*hablado*		*comido*		*vivido*	
Imperative	*habla*		*come*		*vive*	
(***Vosotros/as***)	*hablad*		*comed*		*vivid*	
(***Usted***)	*hable*		*coma*		*viva*	
(***Ustedes***)	*hablen*		*coman*		*vivan*	

INDICATIVE

Present

hablo	*hablamos*	*como*	*comemos*	*vivo*	*vivimos*
hablas	*habláis*	*comes*	*coméis*	*vives*	*vivís*
habla	*hablan*	*come*	*comen*	*vive*	*viven*

Perfect

he hablado, etc. *he comido*, etc. *he vivido*, etc.

Imperfect

hablaba	*hablábamos*	*comía*	*comíamos*	*vivía*	*vivíamos*
hablabas	*hablabais*	*comías*	*comíais*	*vivías*	*vivíais*
hablaba	*hablaban*	*comía*	*comían*	*vivía*	*vivían*

Preterite

hablé	*hablamos*	*comí*	*comimos*	*viví*	*vivimos*
hablaste	*hablasteis*	*comiste*	*comisteis*	*viviste*	*vivisteis*
habló	*hablaron*	*comió*	*comieron*	*vivió*	*vivieron*

Pluperfect

había hablado, etc. *había comido*, etc *había vivido*, etc.

Pretérito anterior

hube hablado, **etc.** *hube comido*, etc. *hube vivido*, etc.

Future

hablaré	*hablaremos*	*comeré*	*comeremos*	*viviré*	*viviremos*
hablarás	*hablaréis*	*comerás*	*comeréis*	*vivirás*	*viviréis*
hablará	*hablarán*	*comerá*	*comerán*	*vivirá*	*vivirán*

Future perfect

habré hablado, etc. *habré comido*, etc. *habré vivido*, etc.

Conditional

hablaría	*hablaríamos*	*comería*	*comeríamos*	*viviría*	*viviríamos*
hablarías	*hablaríais*	*comerías*	*comeríais*	*vivirías*	*viviríais*
hablaría	*hablarían*	*comería*	*comerían*	*viviría*	*vivirían*

TABLE 2 *Continued*

Perfect conditional

habría hablado, etc.	habría comido, etc.	habría vivido, etc.
or		
hubiera hablado, etc.	hubiera comido, etc.	hubiera vivido, etc.

SUBJUNCTIVE

Present

hable	hablemos	coma	comamos	viva	vivamos
hables	habléis	comas	comáis	vivas	viváis
hable	hablen	coma	coman	viva	vivan

Perfect

haya hablado, etc.	haya comido, etc.	haya vivido, etc.

Imperfect

(a)-*ra* form

hablara	habláramos	comiera	comiéramos	viviera	viviéramos
hablaras	hablarais	comieras	comierais	vivieras	vivierais
hablara	hablaran	comiera	comieran	viviera	vivieran

(b)-*se* form

hablase	hablásemos	comiese	comiésemos	viviese	viviésemos
hablases	hablaseis	comieses	comieseis	vivieses	vivieseis
hablase	hablasen	comiese	comiesen	viviese	viviesen

Pluperfect

hubiera hablado, etc.	hubiera comido, etc.	hubiera vivido, etc.
hubiese hablado, etc.	hubiese comido, etc.	hubiese vivido, etc.

Future

hablare	habláremos	comiere	comiéremos	viviere	viviéremos
hablares	hablareis	comieres	comiereis	vivieres	viviereis
hablare	hablaren	comiere	comieren	viviere	vivieren

TABLE 3 *Spelling changes*

The following spelling rules apply to all Spanish verbs, regular and irregular:
(**1**) Infinitives ending in -*zar*, -*cer* and -*cir*:

> *z* is spelt *c* before *i* or *e*.
> *c* is spelt *z* before *a*, *o* (although in the majority of verbs ending in -*cer* *c* > *zc* before *a*, *o*):

rezar 'to pray'		vencer 'to defeat'		esparcir 'to scatter'	

Present indicative

rezo	rezamos	venzo	vencemos	esparzo	esparcimos
rezas	rezáis	vences	vencéis	esparces	esparcís
reza	rezan	vence	vencen	esparce	esparcen

Preterite

recé	rezamos	vencí	vencimos	esparcí	esparcimos
rezaste	rezasteis	venciste	vencisteis	esparciste	esparcisteis
rezó	rezaron	venció	vencieron	esparció	esparcieron

Present subjunctive

rece	recemos	venza	venzamos	esparza	esparzamos
reces	recéis	venzas	venzáis	esparzas	esparzáis
rece	recen	venza	venzan	esparza	esparzan

No other forms affected.

 Most verbs in -*cer* and -*cir* are irregular and should be checked against the list at 13.4.

TABLE 3 *Continued*

(2) Infinitives ending in *-car, -quir:*

    c is spelt *qu* before *e* and *u*.
    qu is spelt *c* before *a, o*.

sacar 'to take out'   *delinquir* 'to commit a crime'

Present indicative

saco	sacamos	delinco	delinquimos
saca	sacáis	delinques	delinquís
saca	sacan	delinque	delinquen

Preterite

saqué	sacamos	delinquí	delinquimos
sacaste	sacasteis	delinquiste	delinquisteis
sacó	sacaron	delinquió	delinquieron

Present subjunctive

saque	saquemos	delinca	delincamos
saques	saquéis	delincas	delincáis
saque	saquen	delinca	delincan

No other forms affected.
Delinquir seems to be the only living example of a verb ending in *-quir* and it is very rarely used.

(3) Infinitives ending in *-gar -guir*.

    g is spelt *gu* before *i* and *e*.
    gu is spelt *g* before *a, o*.

llegar 'to arrive'   *seguir* 'to follow' (radical changing,
                                       like *pedir* 13.3.43)

Present indicative

llego	llegamos	sigo	seguimos
llegas	llegáis	sigues	seguís
llega	llegan	sigue	siguen

Preterite

llegué	llegamos	seguí	seguimos
llegaste	llegasteis	seguiste	seguisteis
llegó	llegaron	siguió	siguieron

Present subjunctive

llegue	lleguemos	siga	sigamos
llegues	lleguéis	sigas	sigáis
llegue	lleguen	siga	sigan

No other forms affected.

(4) Infinitives ending in *-guar:*

    The *u* is written *ü* before *e*. See 13.2.5 for examples.

(5) Infinitives ending in *-ger, -gir:*

    g is spelt *j* before *a, o*.

TABLE 3 *Continued*

proteger 'to protect'		*fingir* 'to pretend'	
Present indicative			
protejo	protegemos	finjo	fingimos
proteges	protegéis	finges	fingís
protege	protegen	finge	fingen
Present subjunctive			
proteja	protejamos	finja	finjamos
protejas	protejáis	finjas	finjáis
proteja	protejan	finja	finjan

No other forms affected.

Verbs ending in -jar, e.g. *amortajar*, and -jer, e.g. *tejer*, retain the *j* throughout.

(**6**) Infinitives ending in -ñer, ñir, -llir:

ie is spelt e.
ió is spelt ó.

tañer 'to chime'		*gruñir* 'to grunt'		*zambullir* 'to dive'	
Gerund					
tañendo		gruñendo		zambullendo	
Preterite					
tañí	tañimos	gruñí	gruñimos	zambullí	zambullimos
tañiste	tañisteis	gruñiste	gruñisteis	zambulliste	zambullisteis
tañó	tañeron	gruñó	gruñeron	zambulló	zambulleron
Imperfect subjunctive					
tañera	tañéramos	gruñera	gruñéramos	zambullera	zambullé-ramos
tañeras	tañerais	gruñeras	gruñerais	zambulleras	zambullerais
tañera	tañeran	gruñera	gruñeran	zambullera	zambulleran
tañese	tañésemos	gruñese	gruñésemos	zambullese	zambullé-semos
tañeses	tañeseis	gruñeses	gruñeseis	zambulleses	zambulleseis
tañese	tañesen	gruñese	gruñesen	zambullese	zambullesen
Future subjunctive					
tañere, etc.		gruñere, etc.		zambullere, etc.	

(**7**) Verbs in -eer: all conjugate like *poseer* at 13.3.35.

(**8**) Verbs in -uir: all conjugate like *construir* at 13.3.13.

TABLE 4 *Conjugation of ser 'to be'*

Infinitive	ser	
Gerund	siendo	
Past participle	sido	
Imperative	sé,[22] sed (vosotros/as),	sea (usted), sean (Ustedes)

INDICATIVE

Present		**Imperfect**		**Preterite**	
soy	somos	era	éramos	fui[23]	fuimos
eres	sois	eras	erais	fuiste	fuisteis
es	son	era	eran	fue[23]	fueron

[22] The accent distinguishes it from the pronoun *se*.
[23] No written accent since 1959.

TABLE 4 *Continued*

Future		Conditional	
seré	seremos	sería	seríamos
serás	seréis	serías	seríais
será	serán	sería	serían

SUBJUNCTIVE

Present		Imperfect(-*ra*)		Imperfect (-*se*)		Future	
sea	seamos	fuera	fuéramos	fuese	fuésemos	fuere	fuéremos
seas	seáis	fueras	fuerais	fueses	fueseis	fueres	fuereis
sea	sean	fuera	fueran	fuese	fuesen	fuere	fueren

COMPOUND TENSES

INDICATIVE

Perfect	*he sido*, etc.	I have been
Pluperfect	*había sido*, etc.	I had been
Future	*habré sido*, etc.	I will have been
Conditional	*habría/hubiera sido*, etc.	I would have been

SUBJUNCTIVE

Perfect	*haya sido*, etc.	
Pluperfect	*hubiera/hubiese sido*, etc.	
Future	*hubiere sido*, etc.	

CONTINUOUS[24]

INDICATIVE

Present	*estoy siendo*, etc.	I'm being
Imperfect	*estaba siendo*, etc.	I was being
Preterite	not used	
Future	*estaré siendo*, etc.	I will be being
Conditional	*estaría siendo*, etc.	I would be being

SUBJUNCTIVE

Present	*(que) esté siendo*, etc.
Imperfect	*(que) estuviera/estuviese siendo*

TABLE 5 *Conjugation of estar* 'to be'

(The difference between *estar* and *ser* is discussed in Chapter 29.)

Infinitive	*estar*
Gerund	*estando*
Past participle	*estado*
Imperative[25]	*estate, estaos* (*vosotros/as*) *estese* (*usted*), *estense* (*ustedes*)

INDICATIVE

Present		Imperfect		Preterite	
estoy	estamos	estaba	estábamos	estuve	estuvimos
estás	estáis	estabas	estabais	estuviste	estuvisteis
está	están	estaba	estaban	estuvo	estuvieron

---

[24] Continuous forms of *ser* are increasingly common in the modern language, but are viewed with suspicion by some purists. See 15.4.

[25] The pronominal forms are used in the imperative. See 17.2.1 and 26.6.4 for further discussion.

TABLE 5 *Continued*

Future		Conditional	
estaré	estaremos	estaría	estaríamos
estarás	estaréis	estarías	estaríais
estará	estarán	estaría	estarían

SUBJUNCTIVE

Present		Imperfect		or	
esté	estemos	estuviera	estuviéramos	estuviese	estuviésemos
estés	estéis	estuvieras	estuvierais	estuvieses	estuvieseis
esté	estén	estuviera	estuvieran	estuviese	estuviesen

Future	
estuviere	estuviéremos
estuvieres	estuviereis
estuviere	estuvieren

COMPOUND TENSES
INDICATIVE

Perfect	he estado
Pluperfect	había estado
Future	habré estado
Conditional	habría/hubiera estado

SUBJUNCTIVE

Perfect	haya estado, etc.
Pluperfect	hubiera/hubiese estado, etc.
Future	hubiere estado, etc.

CONTINUOUS

Estar is not used in the continuous: *está estando is not Spanish.

TABLE 6 *Conjugation of auxiliary verb haber*

This verb is used to form the compound tenses of all regular and irregular verbs. (For discussion of compound tenses see 14.8-10.) Compound forms of *haber* are not used to form compound tenses: there is nothing corresponding to the French *il a eu dit*. *Haber* is also used in the third person only as the main 'existential' verb, cf. *Había muchos* 'There were a lot', *Habrá menos de cinco* 'There will be less than five'; when used thus its present indicative form is *hay*. See Chapter 30 for discussion.

Infinitive	haber
Gerund	habiendo
Past participle	habido
Imperative	(not used)

INDICATIVE

Present		Imperfect		Preterite	
he	hemos[26]	había	habíamos	hube	hubimos
has	habéis	habías	habíais	hubiste	hubisteis
ha	han	había	habían	hubo	hubieron
(hay)					

[26] *Habemos* is used in the phrase *nos las habemos* 'we're dealing with', e.g. *En don Luis nos las habemos nuevamente con el Hombre y la Mujer* (J. Montesinos, quoted by Seco (1992), 214) 'In Don Luis we are dealing once again with Man and Woman'.

TABLE 6 *Continued*

Future		Conditional[27]	
habré	habremos	habría	habríamos
habrás	habréis	habrías	habríais
habrá	habrán	habría	habrían

Perfect	Pluperfect	Pretérito anterior
ha habido	había habido	(not used)
etc.	etc.	

Perfect conditional
habría habido or hubiera habido
etc.

SUBJUNCTIVE

Present		Perfect	
haya	hayamos	haya	habido
hayas	hayáis	etc.	
haya	hayan		

Imperfect

(a) -ra form		(b) -se form	
hubiera	hubiéramos	hubiese	hubiésemos
hubieras	hubierais	hubieses	hubieseis
hubiera	hubieran	hubiese	hubiesen

Pluperfect	Future (obsolete in normal styles)	
hubiera habido or	hubiere	hubiéremos
hubiese habido, etc.	hubieres	hubiereis
	hubiere	hubieren

TABLE 7 *Full conjugation of the compound tenses of ver*

Note the irregular past participle *visto*.

INDICATIVE

Perfect 'I have seen'		Pluperfect 'I had seen', etc.	
he visto	hemos visto	había visto	habíamos visto
has visto	habéis visto	habías visto	habíais visto
ha visto	han visto	había visto	habían visto

Future perfect 'I shall have seen'		Conditional 'I would have seen', etc.	
habré visto	habremos visto	habría visto	habríamos visto
habrás visto	habréis visto	habrías visto	habríais visto
habrá visto	habrán visto	habría visto	habrían visto

Pretérito anterior 'I had seen'	
hube visto	hubimos visto
hubiste visto	hubisteis visto
hubo visto	hubieron visto

[27] The -ra subjunctive form is also commonly used for conditional, i.e. *Te hubiera llamado* for *Te habría llamado* 'I would have phoned you'. See 14.7.5 for discussion.

TABLE 7 *Continued*

SUBJUNCTIVE

Perfect

haya visto	*hayamos visto*
hayas visto	*hayáis visto*
haya visto	*hayan visto*

Imperfect   or

hubiera visto	*hubiéramos visto*	*hubiese visto*	*hubiésemos visto*
hubieras visto	*hubierais visto*	*hubieses visto*	*hubieseis visto*
hubiera visto	*hubieran visto*	*hubiese visto*	*hubiesen visto*

14

Use of indicative (non-continuous) verb forms

This chapter discusses the use of the indicative, non-continuous verb forms. Continuous forms (*estoy hablando, estamos trabajando*, etc.) are discussed in Chapter 15; the subjunctive is discussed in Chapter 16.

The range of possible forms of a typical regular verb is shown in Table 1, p.197.

14.1 Names of the tenses

The traditional names of the tenses are misleading because, like the word 'tense' itself, they too strongly suggest that the main function of the various tense forms is to indicate time. However, the names are so entrenched that to use a more scientific terminology would be unhelpful.

The various names given by grammarians to the Spanish tenses are very confusing, and the problem is worsened by the fact that the Spanish word *pretérito* simply means 'past', whereas the English 'preterite'/(US) 'preterit' is the name of a specific type of past tense:

Imperfect (B & B, R & S, H & N)[1], *pretérito imperfecto* (Academia, Seco), *copretérito* (Bello): *hablaba, decía*
Preterite (B & B, R & S), *pretérito perfecto simple* (Academia) *pretérito indefinido* (Seco), *pretérito perfecto absoluto* (Gili y Gaya), *pretérito* (Bello), past definite (H & N): *hablé, dije*
Perfect (B & B, R & S, H & N), *pretérito perfecto compuesto* (Academia), *pretérito perfecto* (Seco), *pretérito perfecto actual* (Gili y Gaya), *antepresente* (Bello), also sometimes called in English 'present perfect': *he hablado, has dicho*
Pluperfect (B & B, R & S, H & N), *pretérito pluscuamperfecto* (Academia, Seco), *antecopretérito* (Bello): *había hablado, había dicho*
Pretérito anterior (B & B, Academia, Seco), preterite perfect (R & S), *antepretérito* (Gili y Gaya, Bello), past anterior (H & N): *hube hablado, hubo dicho*

The conditional (*hablaría, diría*) is called *el potencial* by Seco and some other grammarians, *el condicional* by most writers and in the Academy's *Esbozo*.

The future tense (*hablaré, diré*) is called the *futuro imperfecto* by Seco to distinguish it from the future perfect/*futuro perfecto* (*habré hablado, habré dicho*).

---

[1] B & B Butt & Benjamin, 2nd edition; R & S Ramsey and Spaulding (1958); H & N Harmer and Norton (1957).

14.2 Tense and aspect in Spanish: general remarks

Any attempt at a brief overview of the role of tense and aspect in the Spanish verb system would be confusing, but the following points deserve emphasis:

(a) There is no 'present' tense in Spanish, if by 'present' is meant a tense form whose sole function is to express present time. The uses of the simple 'present' *hablo, fumas, van*, are several and varied. See 14.3 for further discussion.

(b) There is no 'future' tense in Spanish, in the sense that there is no single verb form whose *exclusive* function is to indicate future time. See 14.6 for further discussion.

(c) The difference between the preterite and imperfect tenses, e.g. *quise – quería*, and to some extent between the pluperfect and *pretérito anterior*, e.g. *había terminado – hube terminado*, involves a distinction between perfective and imperfective *aspect*, i.e. between actions that were or were not completed in the past. English does not systematically indicate the difference between complete and incomplete aspect, so that without further information one cannot tell whether the correct translation of a form like 'I went' should be *yo fui* (completed) or *yo iba* (incomplete).

This difference between completed and incomplete past events may be especially subtle for English-speakers when it comes to differentiating sentences like *Era un problema difícil* and *Fue un problema difícil*, which can really only be translated 'It was a difficult problem'. See 14.5.7 for further discussion.

(d) Unlike French and German, Spanish has a full range of continuous forms which misleadingly resemble the English progressive form: *está lloviendo* 'it's raining', *estabas pensando* 'you were thinking', *he estado comiendo* 'I've been eating'.

The main problem lies in the distinguishing the present continuous from the ordinary present tense: the difference between *lee* and *está leyendo* is neither the same nor as clear-cut as the difference between 'he reads' and 'he's reading'. Nor is the difference between the imperfect continuous *estaba hablando* 'I was speaking' and the preterite continuous *estuve hablando* 'I had a talk'/'I spoke' (for a specific length of time) immediately obvious to English-speakers. See 15.2.3 for a discussion of this problem.

(e) The difference between the preterite *hablé* 'I spoke' and the perfect *he hablado* 'I've spoken' is maintained in spoken as well as written Spanish, whereas it is blurred in French, German and Italian. However, this difference only partly coincides with the distinction between 'I spoke' and 'I've spoken'; see particularly 14.9.3. The difference between the perfect and preterite is also governed by different rules in most of Latin America; see 14.9.7. for more details.

14.3 Uses of the present tense

For the use of the present in conditional sentences, e.g. *Si **sales**, compra pan* 'If you go out, buy some bread', see 25.2.

14.3.1 Present tense to indicate timeless or habitual events that still occur

This is probably the commonest use of this verb form:

Llueve mucho en Irlanda	It rains a lot in Ireland
Fumo más de sesenta al día	I smoke more than sixty a day
María es venezolana	Maria's Venezuelan
Las gaviotas comen peces	Sea-gulls eat fish
No tengo tarjeta de crédito	I don't have a credit card
Me deprime comer sola (C. Martín Gaite, Spain)	Eating on my own depresses me
Los que son creyentes tienen ese consuelo (M. Puig, Argentina)	Those who are believers have that consolation

14.3.2 The present tense for events occurring in the present

The chief problem in this case is how to distinguish it from the present continuous.

In English there is very little overlap between the simple present and the progressive: 'he comes' for 'he is coming' is archaic. The difference between the Spanish simple present and the present continuous is not so clear-cut. The following remarks should be read together with the discussion of the continuous form in Chapter 15.

(a) With some verbs and in some contexts there is often only a slight difference between the simple present and the continuous:

Escribe una novela	He's writing a novel
Está escribiendo una novela	
¿Qué haces?	What are you doing?
¿Qué estás haciendo?	
Cuando lo vi lavaba/estaba lavando su coche	When I saw him he was washing his car

(b) The simple present is used with verbs that denote states rather than actions:

¿Por qué estás tan triste?	Why are you so sad?
Hace frío	It's cold
Parece cansada	She seems tired
¡Cómo brilla la luna!	Isn't the moon bright!
Hoy lleva traje de chaqueta	She's wearing a suit today

Occasionally the continuous may be optionally used to emphasize an unusual or surprising state, as in *Está haciendo mucho calor* 'It's very hot (lately)'. See 15.2.2b for explanation.

(c) The simple present is used for events that happen in the present but are not necessarily actually in progress now. In other words, it is used for events that are just about to happen or have just happened or which are really states or habitual actions rather than events that are actually in progress:

Acusamos recibo de su carta del 3 de enero	We acknowledge receipt of your letter of January 3
A mí me suena poco natural	It sounds unnatural to me
La oposición considera una maniobra el aperturismo anunciado por el régimen	The opposition considers the liberalization policy announced by the regime to be a manoeuvre

¿Por qué te metes en ese asunto?	Why are you getting involved in that business?
¿Qué dices?	What did you say (just then)? (or 'What do you say?' or 'What are you saying?')
¿No oyes los perros?	Can't you hear the dogs?
¡Que me ahogo!	I'm drowning!
¡Ya voy!	I'm coming!
Espérate que meto esto en el horno	Wait while I put this in the oven
Merino pasa la pelota a Andreas (soccer commentary)	Merino passes the ball to Andreas

None of the sentences under (**c**) refers to an event which is strictly speaking in progress *now*, but to events that have either just happened (*¿Qué dices?*, *Pasa la pelota*), are about to happen (*¡Que me ahogo!*), or which are present but not necessarily happening at this moment, e.g. *La oposición considera . . ., ¿Por qué te metes? . . .'.*

Nevertheless, the present and continuous forms sometimes overlap in meaning (see 15.1.2-3 for further discussion).

14.3.3 The *presente histórico* or historic present

Use of the present tense to refer to the past is much favoured as a way of dramatizing descriptive passages in literature. But it also occurs in colloquial language, as in familiar English ('Mrs Brown comes up to me and says . . .').

Translation of literary uses of the present tense by an English present often produces an unfortunate effect.

En los primeros matorrales del bosquecillo, frena a la mula y sus ojos claros, ávidos, buscan en una y otra dirección (M. Vargas Llosa, Peru)	He stopped his mule at the first thickets of the copse and his bright, eager eyes sought in both directions
Fue sensacional: Pedro entra del brazo de la chica sin ojos más que para ella. Yo venga a hacerle señas y él ni caso. Se sientan los dos y al volver la cabeza para atraer la atención del camarero se da cuenta de que Antonio está allí (Colloquial Peninsular Spanish[2])	It was amazing. Pedro comes in arm-in-arm with the girl and he's got eyes only for her. I keep on making signs at them, but he pays no attention. They both sit down and when he turns his head to get the waiter's attention he realizes that Antonio's there

Note
The historic present is normal after *por poco* 'all but' and *casi* 'nearly': *Me caí por unas escaleras y por poco/casi me **rompo** el tobillo* 'I fell down a flight of stairs and nearly broke my ankle'.
This usage is not universal: *Por poco me **hizo** llorar de lo cariñosa que es* (M. Vargas Llosa, Peru, dialogue) 'She's so affectionate she nearly made me cry'.

14.3.4 Present tense used as an imperative
This is frequent in everyday speech to produce a rather abrupt imperative: *Tú te callas* 'You just keep quiet'.

All matters connected with the imperative are discussed in Chapter 17.

14.3.5 Use of the present to ask permission
The present is much used when asking for someone's consent:

---

[2] *Venga a . . .* is a colloquial Peninsular expression that emphasizes repetition. The familiar style of the passage makes translation by the English present possible.

¿Te lo traigo yo?	Shall I bring it for you?
¿Escribo a los abuelos para decírselo?	Shall I write to our grandparents to tell them?
¿Llamo para ver si ha venido?	Shall I ring to see whether he's come?

14.4 The preterite: general

The Spanish preterite is past in time and perfective in aspect, i.e. it refers to actions viewed as completed in the past. Occasionally it is inchoative (inceptive) in aspect, i.e. it describes events as *beginning* in the past (see 14.4.2).

Yo fui differs from the English form 'I was' in being marked for time and aspect, whereas the English form is marked only for time. Compare *Yo fui jefe de departamento* 'I was head of department' (and then stopped) and *Yo era jefe de departamento* 'I was head of department' (at the time and may still be).

Similarly, 'He got cross with his dog' means either *Se enfadó con su perro* or *Se enfadaba con su perro*. Correct translation of the English simple past thus requires a decision about which verbal aspect is implied by the English form.

Some English past verb forms are unambiguously imperfect, e.g. 'he **was getting** angry', 'he **used to get** angry', 'at that time he **would get up** at ten-thirty'. Such forms almost always call for translation by the Spanish imperfect.

14.4.1 Preterite used to indicate an event that is past and complete

The difference between the preterite and imperfect often expresses an idea that is not easily translated into English. Compare *Tuvimos que atravesar dos desiertos para llegar al oasis* 'We had to cross two deserts to get to the oasis (and we did)' and *Teníamos que atravesar dos desiertos para llegar al oasis* 'We had (still) to cross two deserts to get to the oasis'. The first (perfective aspect) looks back on the crossing as accomplished, the second (imperfective aspect) envisages the crossing as still to be made and does not in itself tell us whether it took place or not.

Further examples:

Ayer anduve más de quince kilómetros	Yesterday I walked more than fifteen kilometers
Fue un error no devolverle el dinero	It was a mistake not to return the money to him (we didn't)
La fiesta fue un éxito	The party was a success
Primero fui carpintero, después fui taxista, y después fui domador de leones	First I was a carpenter, then I was a taxi driver and then I was a lion tamer
Tuve el sarampión cuando era pequeño	I had measles when I was a child

The preterite may therefore show that a process or event has reached completion:

*Cuando el café **estuvo** listo le alcanzó una tacita* (E. Sábato, Argentina)	When the coffee was ready she handed him a small cup
*La chica avanzó hacia él, y cuando **estuvo** a su lado le dijo . . .* (E. Sábato, Argentina)	The girl advanced towards him, and when she reached his side, said to him . . .
*La conversación se **fue** espaciando* (ir + gerund suggests a longish process, *fue* shows the process was complete)	The conversation gradually petered out

Notes

(i) The imperfect is used for characteristics as opposed to actions or states, cf. *Mi tía era soltera. Nunca estuvo casada* 'My aunt was a spinster. She was never married'. Compare also *Miguel era poeta* 'Miguel was a poet' and *Miguel fue director gerente* 'Miguel was (i.e. 'worked as') chief executive/(British) managing director'. *?Fue poeta* sounds like ? 'He worked as a poet'.

Use of the preterite for a characteristic is a stylistic idiosyncrasy: *Sir Thomas Browne (1605-82) supo el griego, el latín, el francés, el italiano y el español, y fue uno de los primeros hombres de letras que estudiaron anglosajón* (J.L. Borges, Argentina, more usually . . . *sabía griego*) 'Sir Thomas Browne (1605-82) knew Greek, Latin, French, Italian and Spanish, and was one of the first men of letters to study Anglo-Saxon'.

For a further comparison of preterite and imperfect see 14.5.7.

(ii) In 'cleft' sentences (discussed at 36.2), the tense of *ser* is virtually always dictated by the tense of the other verb(s): *Fue usted quien lo hizo* 'It was you who did it', *Era usted quien lo hacía* 'It was you who used to do it'.

(iii) The preterite is very often used in Latin-American Spanish where the perfect is used in Spain. See 14.9.7 for discussion.

14.4.2 Preterite used to indicate the beginning of a state or action

The preterite may be inchoative in meaning (i.e. indicate the beginning of an action). Compare *Mi hija habló a los once meses* (i.e. *empezó a hablar*) 'My daughter started talking at eleven months' and *Mi hija hablaba a los once meses* 'My daughter was talking **by** eleven months'. Also *Mi nieto anduvo al año* 'My grandson started walking at the age of one'.

14.4.3 Preterite used to indicate certainty in the future

The preterite is occasionally used to indicate an absolute certainty in the future:

Cuando llegue, llegó	She'll be here when she's here (and that's that)!
Cuando se acabe, se acabó	When it's finished, it's finished
Para las dos ya lo acabé (Mexican example from J.M. Lope Blanch (1991); Spain *ya lo tendré acabado*)	I'll have it finished by two o'clock
Nos fuimos (colloquial Latin American; Spain *nos vamos*)	We're going/We're leaving right now (lit. 'we left')

14.4.4 Preterite for events occurring within a finite period

The preterite tense must be used for an event that continued for a finite period of time and then ended. By 'finite' is meant a period of time of a specific length, i.e. whose beginning and end are known:

Estuve destinado en Bilbao dos años	I was posted in Bilbao for two years
Te olvidas del tiempo que estuviste casado	You're forgetting the time you were married
Los dinosaurios reinaron sobre la tierra durante millones de años	The dinosaurs reigned on Earth for millions of years
La ETA tuvo menos actividad durante el régimen de Franco que al instalarse la democracia (M. Vargas Llosa, Peru)	ETA (Basque terrorist group) was less active during the Franco régime than when democracy was introduced
Durante años no pudimos hablar de otra cosa (G. García Márquez, Colombia)	For years we could talk of nothing else
Que yo haya oído, en toda mi vida supe de dos casos (D. Navarro Gómez, Spain)	As far as I've heard, I've known of two cases in the whole of my life

Notes
(i) The period of time is often implied rather than explicit. Use of the preterite may, for example, denote a lifetime envisaged as a finite period: *Siempre dormía como* **durmió** *su padre, con el arma escondida dentro de la funda de la almohada* (G. García Márquez, Colombia) 'He always used to sleep as his father (had) slept, with his gun hidden in his pillowcase', *Siempre procuré pasarlo bien* 'I always tried to have a good time', *Nunca me hizo gracia ese hombre* 'I never really liked that man'.
(ii) In sentences involving phrases like *todos los días, todos los años,* the beginning and end of the period are not specified so the imperfect must be used: *Todos los veranos veraneaban en San Sebastián* 'Every summer they spent their holidays/vacation in San Sebastian', *Todas las mañanas regaba el jardín* 'He watered the garden every morning', *Cuando yo era pequeño yo le/lo veía pasar casi todos los días* 'When I was little I saw him pass nearly every day'.
(iii) If the period is specified but the action consists of a series of repeated discontinuous events, either form is possible, the imperfect apparently being commoner: *Aquella semana se levantaba/levantó a las siete, y desayunaba/desayunó a las ocho* 'That week he rose at seven, and breakfasted at eight', *El verano pasado salía/salió todos los días con él* 'Last summer she went out with him every day', *Aquel año trabajaba/trabajó mucho* 'He worked hard that year'.

14.4.5 Special meanings of the preterite of some verbs

Some verbs require special translations when they appear in the preterite. This is especially true of the auxiliary verbs *deber, querer, poder, saber, soler,* which are discussed in Chapter 21.

Other verbs affected are:

Tener: the preterite often means 'to receive'/'to get', the imperfect means 'had' in the sense of 'was in my possession':

Tuve la impresión de que . . .	I got the impression that . . .
Tenía la impresión de que . . .	I had the impression that . . .
Tuve una carta	I got/received a letter
Cuando tuvo ocasión de estudiar consiguió con la universidad a distancia el título de ingeniero (*Cambio16*, Spain)	When he got the chance to study, he graduated as an engineer from the Open University[3]

Conocer: the preterite means 'to meet for the first time', the imperfect means 'to be acquainted with':

Conocí a Antonia	I met Antonia (for the first time)
Conocía a Antonia	I knew Antonia

14.5 The imperfect: general

The Spanish imperfect form expresses past time and incomplete (imperfective) aspect. The English simple past is marked only for time, so that 'I drank two glasses of wine with my lunch' is strictly speaking untranslatable into Spanish unless the context supplies clues about the aspect of the event: 'When I was young, I drank (i.e. 'used to drink') two glasses every day' (imperfective: *bebía dos vasos*) and 'Last night I drank two glasses' (perfective: *anoche bebí*).

English forms like 'I used to drink', 'I was drinking', 'I would (habitually) drink' are unambiguously imperfective and almost always require translation by the Spanish imperfect.

---

[3] i.e. the public university whose courses are transmitted on radio and TV.

In colloquial language the Spanish imperfect may be a substitute for the conditional. See 14.5.2 and 25.5 for discussion.

14.5.1 Imperfect tense to denote incomplete actions

The imperfect form is used for past events that were incomplete at the time. It often indicates that an event was in progress in the past without reference to its beginning or end. The imperfect is therefore used:

(a) To indicate any state or event already in progress when something else happened. It is thus the correct tense for background descriptions:

Me levanté y descorrí las cortinas. Hacía un día espléndido	I got up and drew the curtains. It was a splendid day
Como el cielo estaba despejado fuimos a la playa	Since the sky was clear we went to the beach
Yo volvía del cine cuando vi a Niso	I was coming back from the cinema when I saw Niso
Los monumentos y estatuas que adornaban los paseos y las plazas fueron triturados . . . (E. Mendoza, Spain)	The monuments and statues that adorned the avenues and squares were pulverized
Volví a la sala, pero él ya no estaba (A. Mastretta, Mexico, dialogue)	I went back to the living room, but he was no longer there

(b) To indicate states or actions that continued in the past for an unspecified period. It is thus much used for characteristics, situations and habitual actions.

Matías era un hombre alto, calvo y un poco cargado de hombros	Matías was a tall, bald, slightly round-shouldered man
Le exasperaban estas comidas mexicanas de cuatro o cinco horas de duración (C. Fuentes, Mexico)	These Mexican meals lasting four or five hours exasperated him
Doña Amalia, por otra parte, era obesa, y se negaba a reconocer que la gula era peor pecado y más insalubre vicio que la dipsomanía (C. Barral, Spain)	Doña Amalia, on the other hand, was overweight, and refused to recognise that greed was a worse sin and more unhealthy vice than dipsomania

If the time period is specified, see 14.4.4.

(c) To express an event that is felt to have already begun at the time of some completed event:

Me marchaba ya cuando has llamado (Lat. Am. *llamaste*)[4]	I was just leaving when you rang

14.5.2 Imperfect for the conditional

The imperfect is commonly used as a colloquial alternative to the conditional to indicate an immediate future. This does not apply when the conditional is used for approximations or suppositions, as at 14.7.2:

Prometió que venía/vendría	He promised he would come/he was coming
Juró que lo hacía/haría	He swore he'd do it
Aunque no me gustara, me casaba/casaría con ella	I'd marry her even if I didn't like her

---

[4] In Spain *llamaste* would indicate that the phone conversation is no longer in progress. See 14.9.7 for further discussion.

Pensé que ya no venías/vendrías	I thought you wouldn't come/weren't coming any more

But this is not possible with *ser* or if the future is not immediate:

Creía que sería posible	I thought it would be possible
Juró que me amaría siempre (not *amaba . . .*)	He swore he would love me always

This usage is especially frequent with *poder* and *deber* to show that someone should or could have acted differently in the past, e.g. *Podías/Podrías haberlo hecho, ¿no?* 'You could have done it, couldn't you?'; see 21.2.3d and 21.3.3.

14.5.3 *Hablaba* or *estaba hablando?*
If the event is not habitual and is truly past (e.g. 'I was leaving the next day' is in fact a future in the past), the difference between the continuous and non-continuous imperfect is usually neutralized:

Yo hablaba/Estaba hablando con los vecinos cuando llegaron los bomberos	I was talking to the neighbours when the firemen came

But the continuous is not used with some verbs of motion. See 15.1.2(b).

14.5.4 Imperfect in children's language
An interesting use of the imperfect is found in children's language:

Vamos a jugar a que yo era un vaquero y tú eras un indio	Let's pretend I'm a cowboy and you're an Indian

14.5.5 Imperfect to make courteous requests
The imperfect can be used to show courtesy in requests and enquiries:

¿Qué deseaba?	What would you like?
Perdone, quería hablar con el director	Excuse me, I'd like a word with the manager

14.5.6 Imperfect used for preterite in journalism
In newspaper styles the imperfect is sometimes used as an alternative to the preterite in order to produce a dramatically drawn-out effect:

La historia de cómo . . . un hombre de cincuenta años mataba en la Noche Vieja de 1977 a su amante, una niña de 14 años, es de nuevo actualidad (*Cambio16*, Spain; or *mató*)	The story of how a man of fifty killed his lover, a girl of 14, on New Year's Eve 1977, is in the news again
Un cuarto de hora después . . . dos grapos asesinaban a un policía armado (*El País*; or *asesinaron*)	A quarter of an hour later two members of GRAPO[5] murdered an armed policeman

14.5.7 Imperfect or preterite? Translation problems
The difference between the preterite and imperfect is often elusive for English-speakers as the following examples show:

Fue un error decírselo	It was a mistake to tell him (we committed it)
Era un error decírselo	It was a mistake to tell him (we may or may not have committed it)

---

[5] A terrorist group active in Spain.

*El problema **fue** difícil*	The problem was difficult (but it doesn't exist any more)
*El problema **era** difícil*	The problem was difficult (at the time, and perhaps still is)
***Tuve** que hablar con ella*	I had to talk to her (and did)
***Tenía** que hablar con ella*	I had to talk to her (and may or may not have done)
***Estuve** enfermo*	I was ill/(US) 'sick' (and got better)
***Estaba** enfermo*	I was ill/sick (at the time and may or may not still be
***Fui** a preguntar*	I went to ask (and did)
***Iba** a preguntar*	I was going to ask
*No le **gustó** la comida*	He didn't enjoy his meal (but he ate it)
*No le **gustaba** la comida*	He didn't like his meal (and may or may not have gone on to eat it)
***Estuve** hablando con ella*	I had a talk with her
***Estaba** hablando con ella*	I was (in the process of) talking to her
*Cuando **estuve** en Cuba . . .*	When I visited Cuba . . .
*Cuando yo **estaba** en Cuba . . .*	When I was in Cuba . . .
***Creí** que hablabas en serio*	I thought you were talking seriously
***Creía** que hablabas en serio* (can also mean more or less the same as *creí que . . .*)	I thought/used to think you talked seriously

14.6 Future tense: general

Spanish has several ways of expressing the future, and the so-called 'future tense' (*hablaré, vendrás*) is not the most common in everyday speech (from which it is said to be disappearing except in its 'suppositional' role described at 14.6.3):

(a) *Esta noche vamos al cine*	Tonight we're going to the cinema
(b) *Esta noche vamos a ir al cine*	Tonight we're going to go to the cinema
(c) *Esta noche iremos al cine*	Tonight we'll go to the cinema
(d) *Esta noche hemos de ir al cine*	Tonight we're to go to the cinema

(a) is typically a description of an event which is pre-arranged or is a scheduled event;

(b) is a foreseen or 'intentional' future and it is often an informal substitute for the future tense proper *iremos, seré*, etc;

(c) is less common in colloquial language and very often excludes the idea of pre-arrangement. Consequently it may sound rather uncertain or, depending on tone and context, may sound like an order or promise;

(d) (discussed at 21.4.1) is sometimes heard in Latin America with a future meaning, but in the Peninsula it implies obligation, and is not very common. It is very common in Mexico as an alternative to *deber de* (the latter is discussed at 21.3.2).[6]

---

[6] *Para terminar, el capitán ha de haberse quejado de su soledad. Serafina ha de haberlo compadecido* (J. Ibargüengoitia, Mexico, dialogue) 'Eventually the Captain must have complained about his solitude. Serafina must have taken pity on him'; Spain *debió de haberse quejado, debió de haberlo/le compadecido*.

As was mentioned earlier, the future tense is disappearing from spoken (but not written) Spanish, this process being more advanced in Latin America than in Spain and more deep-rooted in familiar or popular styles. It is usually replaced by the simple present – *Te llamo mañana* 'I'll call you tomorrow' (see 14.6.4) – or by *ir a* + infinitive: *La voy a ver mañana* 'I'm going to see her tomorrow' (see 14.6.5).

14.6.1 Uses of the future tense form to denote future time
Sometimes, particularly in informal speech, the present and future forms are interchangeable. However, the future is used:

(a) for provisional or less certain statements about the future, or for statements about the future when no other word makes it clear that the future is meant:

Nos veremos mañana en Palacio para el premio al profesor Bernstein, ¿no es cierto? (C. Fuentes, Mexico, dialogue)	We'll see one another tomorrow at the Palace for the prize-giving to Prof. Bernstein, won't we?
Si llueve se aplazará el partido	If it rains the match will be postponed
Me ha dado diez mil pesetas. Con esto tiraré hasta la semana próxima, y luego veremos (*luego vemos* is impossible here)	He gave me 10,000 ptas. I'll manage with that till next week, and then we'll see
En un remoto futuro el sol se apagará	In the remote future the sun will go out
Por la noche nos iremos al cine Juan y yo (A. Buero Vallejo, dialogue, *nos vamos* possible)	This evening Juan and I will go/are going to the cinema
Para entonces todos estaremos calvos	We'll all be bald by then (said of something that will take a long time)

Notes
(i) Nevertheless, the difference between sentences like *Te veo mañana* and *Te veré mañana* 'I'll see you tomorrow' is slight. The former is informal and indicates something so firmly pre-arranged as to be felt to be a present reality. The latter is slightly less certain. Thus *Esta noche vamos al teatro* 'Tonight we're going to the theatre' is usual, but if uttered in the morning, with the prospect of many other chores intervening, one might say *Esta noche, cuando lo tengamos todo hecho, iremos al teatro* 'Tonight, when we've got everything done, we'll go to the theatre'. However, in educated speech there is a great deal of overlap between the present and future, cf. *Te llamo a las seis* and *Te llamaré a las seis* 'I'll call you at six o'clock' (almost indistinguishable).
(ii) After words meaning 'perhaps' the subjunctive is normally used, not the future. See 16.3.2.

(b) The future is used for promises, especially long-term ones, which by nature are not pre-arrangements:

Ten confianza en mí. No te decepcionaré	Have confidence in me. I won't disappoint you
¡No pasarán!	They shall not pass!
Hoy eres la Cenicienta, pero mañana serás una princesa	Today you're Cinderella, but tomorrow you'll be a princess
Una verdadera revolución no admitirá jamás la impunidad (*Vindicación de Cuba*, Cuba)	A true revolution will never allow crimes to go unpunished

However, the present can be used (but not with *ser* 'to be') for short-term promises presented as pre-arrangements, e.g. *No te preocupes, te lo devuelvo mañana* 'Don't worry, I'll give it back to you tomorrow'.

14.6.2 Future tense used for stern commands
The future is occasionally used for very for solemn or very authoritarian commands, as in English:

No matarás	Thou shalt not kill
No saldrás de esta casa hasta que yo no te lo permita	You will not leave this house until I allow you to

14.6.3 Suppositional future

An important function of the future tense in ordinary Spanish, especially in Europe, is to express suppositions or approximations. This is apparently the first use of the future form learnt by Spanish children, who tend to acquire it as a pure future tense when they go to secondary school.[7]

Idiomatic use of the future in approximations often produces much more authentic Spanish than clumsy sentences involving *aproximadamente* or *alrededor de*.

In questions, the future expresses wonder, incredulity or conjecture:

María tendrá unos veinte años	Maria's about 20 years old
Un par de años hará . . . Gannon me escribió de Gualeguaychu (J.L. Borges, Argentina)	It must be a couple of years ago that Gannon wrote to me from Gualeguaychu
Albert Hoffman descubrió el LSD hará 50 años (*El País*, Spain)	Albert Hoffman discovered LSD about 50 years ago
¡Habráse visto semejante tontería!	Did anyone ever see such nonsense?!
¿Qué será esto?	I wonder what this is
¿Qué hora será? (Lat. Am. *¿Qué horas serán?*)	I wonder what the time is
—¿Dónde está tu monedero? —Me lo habré dejado en casa	'Where's your purse?' 'I must have left it at home'
¿Qué estará tramando ella?	I wonder what she's up to

Kany, 190, notes that this use of the future is much more common in Spain than in Latin America, where *deber (de)* often replaces it: *deben de ser las cinco* = *serán las cinco* or *deben (de) ser las cinco*. See 21.3.2 for *deber de*.

In Mexico *haber de* is commonly used for *deber de* in this construction. See the footnote to 14.6 for an example.

14.6.4 Present tense with future meaning

The present is much used in informal language to refer to the immediate future. If the subject is human this conveys an idea of certainty and is therefore especially used for fixtures or appointments, cf. English 'I'm going to Spain next year', 'We attack tomorrow'. If the subject is inanimate, the action is foreseen as a certainty or fixture, e.g. *El tren sale mañana a las 7* 'The train's leaving tomorrow at 7' (scheduled departure).

The fact that the verb refers to the future is normally shown by some time phrase like *mañana, esta noche, el año que viene*:

Vamos a España el año que viene	We're going to Spain next year
¿Quién paga mañana?	Who's paying tomorrow?
En seguida bajo	I'll be down right away
Te llamo esta noche	I'll ring you tonight
Dentro de un cuarto de hora estoy en tu casa (G. García Márquez, Colombia, dialogue)	I'll be at your house in a quarter of an hour

---

[7] Gili y Gaya (1972), 117ff, notes that Spanish children use the suppositional future from as early as their fourth year but often do not use the future form as a true future tense until much later.

Si viene por aquí, ¿qué digo?	If he comes round here, what shall I say?
Esta noche hay tormenta, verás	Tonight there'll be a storm, you'll see
Nos vemos	Goodbye/See you again
Espera, lo hago en un momento	Wait, I'll do it in a moment

Notes

(i) This use of the present tense is particularly common with verbs of motion (*ir, venir, salir, llegar*). With other verbs it is best thought of as an informal alternative for the future tense, although there is often a difference of nuance.

(ii) Events in an unspecified future are by nature less certain, so the present tense should not be used: *Si las cosas continúan así, ya no **habrá** árboles* 'If things go on like this there will be no more trees left'.

(iii) If there is nothing in the context that clearly shows that the statement refers to the future, the present tense is assumed to be a true present and the future must be shown by some unambiguous form, e.g. *ir a* + infinitive or the future tense proper. Compare *Me parece que no hay sitio* 'I think there's no room' and *Me parece que no habrá/va a haber sitio* 'I think there won't be room'.

(iv) The present tense of *ser* is used for the future only for calendar statements: *Mañana es jueves* 'Tomorrow is Thursday', but *Mañana el discurso **será** pronunciado por el presidente* 'Tomorrow the speech will be delivered by the president'.

14.6.5 *Ir a* + infinitive

The future is very often expressed by *ir a* + infinitive. This form may express intention or it may simply be a colloquial substitute for the future tense (but only the future tense form can be used for the suppositional future mentioned at 14.6.3).

It is very commonly heard as a substitute for the future tense, to the extent that it virtually replaces the ordinary future tense form in the speech of many people, especially in Latin America:

Si te casas conmigo te voy a hacer feliz (intention, as opposed to promise, which would be *te haré . . .*)	If you marry me I'm going to make you happy
¡Deprisa, que van a cerrar! (expresses someone's intention; also *que cierran* 'they're closing')	Hurry! They're going to close!
Si las cosas continúan así, no vamos a poder respirar el aire de las ciudades (or, slightly more formally, *podremos . . .*)	If things go on like this we won't be able to breath the air in the cities

Note

The imperfect *iba a*, etc. may also be used to form the future in the past. See 14.7.3.

14.7 The conditional: general

For the forms of the conditional see 13.1.8.

The name 'conditional' is apt only insofar as it describes one common use of the form, viz. the expression of the idea that an event is dependent on some other factor, as in *Podríamos ir mañana* 'We could go tomorrow (if the weather's nice, if we're free, etc.)'. But it has other functions that have nothing to do with the idea of conditionality, especially the expression of suppositions or approximations in the past (14.7.2) and the expression of the future in the past (14.7.3).

For the purpose of agreement, the conditional counts as a past tense, so the subjunctive in a subordinate clause governed by the conditional must also be in the past. Compare *Es absurdo que vengas mañana* 'It's absurd for you to come tomorrow' and *Sería absurdo que **vinieras/vinieses** mañana* 'It would be absurd for you to come tomorrow'.

Colloquial language shows a marked tendency to replace the conditional by the imperfect, especially in conditional sentences (see 14.5.2 and 25.5 for discussion).

Replacement of the imperfect subjunctive by the conditional, e.g. *?si yo tendría dinero* for *si yo tuviera dinero* 'if I had some money' is very common in popular speech in Navarre and neighbouring regions, in Argentina and perhaps locally elsewhere, but foreigners should shun this tendency.

14.7.1 Uses of the conditional to express conditions
For the conditional in conditional sentences, see Chapter 25.

The conditional is also used for implied conditions, i.e. conditional statements in which the if-clause has been deleted:

Sería una locura ponerlo en marcha sin aceite	It would be crazy to start it up with no oil
De nada serviría un nuevo golpe porque sólo perjudicaría al país (headline, Bolivian press)	Another coup d'état would be pointless because it would only damage the country

14.7.2 Conditional for suppositions about the past
The conditional is used for suppositions and approximations about the past in the same way as the future is for the present (see 14.6.3):

Aquel día andaríamos más de cincuenta kilómetros	That day we must have walked more than 50 km
Tendría (or Tenía/Debía de tener) unos treinta años	He must have been about thirty
Llevaba un saco sport que en algún tiempo habría sido azul marino (E. Sábato, Argentina. *Saco = americana* or *chaqueta* in Spain)	He was wearing a sports jacket which must once have been navy blue

In some styles, especially journalism and more so in Latin America, the conditional is used for rumours or unsubstantiated reports. This construction is condemned by grammarians (and by the editors of *El País*) as a Gallicism:

Gregorius habría nacido en Glasgow (J. Cortázar, Argentina)	Gregorius was apparently born in Glasgow
. . . *la desaparición de los etarras estaría motivada por cuestiones de seguridad* (*ABC*, Spain)	. . . security reasons are said to be the motive for the disappearance of the ETA[8] members

14.7.3 Conditional for the future in the past
The conditional is used to express the future in the past (i.e. as a close equivalent of *iba a* + infinitive):

Yo sabía que papá bajaría/bajaba/iba a bajar a las once	I knew father would come down at 11 o'clock
Dijo que lo haría/hacía/iba a hacer luego	He said he'd do/was going to do it later

---

[8] A terrorist organization dedicated to the independence of the Basque region.

Cerró la puerta con cuidado; su mujer dormía profundamente. Dormiría hasta que el sol hiciera su primera presencia en la ventana (I. Aldecoa, Spain)	He shut the door carefully; his wife was fast asleep. She would sleep until the sun first showed at the window
Entonces tuvo una aventura que se desarrollaría en tres etapas diferentes	He then had an adventure that was to develop in three different stages
En un rato todo el mundo se iría a dormir la siesta (A. Mastretta, Mexico, dialogue)	Soon everyone would go and take a siesta

14.7.4 Conditional in rhetorical questions

As in English, the conditional is much used for questions to which the speaker already knows the answer:

¿Alguien se atrevería a decir que la "socialización" ha hecho más libres a los diarios? (M. Vargas Llosa, Peru)	Would anyone dare to say that 'socialization' has made newspapers more free?

14.7.5 Replacement of the conditional by the *-ra* form of the subjunctive

The *-ra* subjunctive form is a stylistic variant for the conditional when this is used as a true conditional (and not, for example, as a suppositional tense or future in the past).

This is normal in all styles with the auxiliary *haber*: *Habría sido mejor/Hubiera sido mejor* 'It would have been better'.

It is also common with *querer* and *deber*: *Yo querría/quisiera hacerlo* 'I'd like to do it'; *Deberías/Debieras haberlo hecho* 'You should have done it'.

With *poder* it is rather literary: *podría haber sido/pudiera haber sido*. See Chapter 21 for discussion of these modal verbs.

With other verbs it is nowadays uncommon and very poetic:

*Abril, sin tu asistencia clara, **fuera** invierno de caídos esplendores* . . . (Juan Ramón Jiménez, i.e. *sería* . . .)	April, without thy bright presence, would be a winter of fallen splendours
. . . *un libro **fuera** poco* . . . *para dar cauce a un país como La Mancha* (C.J. Cela, Spain)	A book would be little (lit. 'were little') to do justice to (lit. 'to give channel to') a land like La Mancha

It is used in formal styles in the Southern Cone in certain formulas, e.g. *pareciera que* . . . for *parecería que* . . . 'it would seem that . . .'

Note
Grammarians do not like the use of the *-se* subjunctive for the conditional: it is explicitly banned by the *Libro de estilo* of *El País*. But it is commonly heard in spontaneous speech: . . . *y hubiese* (for *hubiera/habría*) *sido muy sospechoso que yo me negase* (M. Puig, Argentina dialogue) 'and it would have been very suspicious if I'd refused'.

14.8 Compound tenses: general remarks

The compound tenses, e.g. the perfect, pluperfect, *pretérito anterior* and the perfect and pluperfect subjunctive forms, all use the auxiliary *haber* or, much less commonly and the *pretérito anterior* excepted, *tener*. No Spanish verbs form the perfect with *ser* 'to be' as an auxiliary (*llegar, ir, venir* are very rare archaic or journalistic exceptions, cf. *El verano es ido* 'Summer is gone').

Unlike French and Italian, the past participle is invariable and does not agree in number and gender with the object of the verb (unless *tener* is used instead of *haber*: see 14.8.3).

The participle may be deleted in English, but not in Spanish: '"Have you tried the sausages?" "Yes, I have."' —¿*Has probado las salchichas?* —*Sí* or —*Sí, las he probado.* However, deletion occasionally occurs with the pluperfect tense, to judge by ¿*Se había reído? Sí, se había. Pero esta vez sin sarcasmo* (dialogue in M. Vargas Llosa, Peru) 'Had he laughed? Yes, he had. But without sarcasm this time.' Spanish informants thought that this might be a sporadic feature of informal speech.

14.8.1 Compound tenses: word order

Learners should respect the rule that no words may come between the auxiliary and the participle, cf. French *j'ai toujours dit* = *siempre he dicho.* ?*Yo he siempre dicho* is not heard in normal Spanish.

However this rule is occasionally broken in literary style with such words as *ni siquiera, incluso, todavía, aún, ya, nunca, jamás, más que, quizá(s), tal vez*:

Se habrá tal vez olvidado	You may have forgotten
Se ha más que duplicado la cifra (From *Hoja del lunes*)	The figure has more than doubled
. . . *en buena parte por no habérselo aún propuesto con entera seriedad* (S. Pitol, Mexico)	. . . to a great extent because he hadn't yet suggested it to him in all seriousness

14.8.2 Suppression of *haber* in compound tenses

The auxiliary may optionally be suppressed to avoid repetition:

No sólo había tocado la mano y mirado los ojos de la mujer que más le gustaba tocar y mirar del mundo (C. Fuentes, Mexico)	Not only had he touched the hand and looked at the eyes of the woman he most liked to touch and look at in the world
. . . *yo también he pasado por baches y conocido la duda* (L. Goytisolo, Spain, dialogue)	I've been through rough patches as well and known doubt

14.8.3 *Tengo hecho, tengo comprado,* etc.

Tener is occasionally used as an auxiliary, like the English 'to have **got**', to denote the successful acquisition of some object or the fulfilment of some task: compare 'I've painted the windows' and 'I've got all the windows painted' or 'I've done my homework' and 'I've got all my homework done'.

The participle must agree in number and gender with the object of the verb. The verb must also be transitive and must have a direct object (**tengo sido,* cf. Portuguese *tenho sido* 'I have been' is not Spanish):

Ya tengo compradas las entradas	I've already bought the tickets
Después de las vacaciones tendré hechos todos mis deberes	After the holidays/vacation I'll have all my homework done
Yo tenía concertada hora con el jefe	I had arranged an appointment with the boss
. . .*ese jueves de diciembre tenía pensado cruzar a la orilla derecha* (J. Cortázar, Argentina, dialogue)	. . . That Thursday in December I had planned to cross to the right bank

Note
Llevar is occasionally also used in the same way for accumulative actions: *Llevo tomadas tres aspirinas, pero todavía me duele la cabeza* 'I've taken three aspirins, but my head still aches', *Yo llevo vendidos cuatrocientos* (Mexico City, overheard) 'I've sold four hundred'.

14.9 Perfect tense

Spanish differs from French, German and Italian, and broadly resembles English in that the difference in meaning between the preterite – *hablé* 'I spoke' – and the perfect – *he hablado* 'I've spoken' – is maintained in both written and spoken language.

Students of languages in which the distinction is blurred or lost must avoid translating sentences like *Je l'ai vu hier*, *Ich habe ihn gestern gesehen*, *L'ho visto ieri* 'I saw him yesterday' as **Le/Lo he visto ayer* (correctly *Le/Lo **vi** ayer*). Such misuse of the perfect is sometimes heard in popular Madrid speech.

European Spanish usually uses the perfect wherever English does, but the converse is not true: the perfect is often used in Spain where English requires a simple past tense. Moreover, in the majority of the Spanish-speaking world (Galicia, Asturias and most of Latin America) the preterite is in fact much more common than the perfect, cf. *No vino todavía* (Latin America) 'He didn't come yet' and *No ha venido todavía* (Spain), 'He hasn't come yet'.[9] See 14.9.7 for further remarks on the perfect tense in Latin America.

14.9.1 Perfect to denote events occuring in time that includes the present

The perfect is used for events that have happened in a period of time that includes the present, e.g. today, this afternoon, this week, this month, this year, this century, always, already, never, still, yet. In this respect, English – especially British English – and European Spanish coincide:

No he visto a tu madre esta semana	I haven't seen your mother this week
En sólo dos generaciones se ha desertizado un 43% de la superficie terrestre (advert in *ABC*)	In only two generations 43% of the earth's surface has been reduced to desert
Hemos ido dos veces este mes	We've been twice this month
Ya han llegado	They've already arrived
Siempre he pensado que . . .	I have always thought that . . .
Aún/Todavía no han llegado	They haven't arrived yet

Notes
(i) The preterite may be used with the effect of severing the link between the event and the present moment. Compare *Vi a tu suegra esta mañana* and *He visto a tu suegra esta mañana* 'I saw/have seen your mother-in-law this morning'.
(ii) Words like *siempre* and *nunca* may or may not include the present: compare *Yo siempre he sido un problema para mis padres* 'I've always been a problem for my parents (and still am)' and *Yo siempre fui un problema para mis padres* 'I always was a problem for my parents' (e.g. when I was young). But some speakers do not systematically respect the difference of meaning in either language.
(iii) For the Latin-American (and Canary Islands) use of the preterite in the above contexts see 14.9.7.

14.9.2 Perfect for events whose effects are still relevant in the present

The perfect is used for past events that are relevant to the present or whose effects still bear on the present. In this respect European Spanish and English coincide:

---

[9] North-American English resembles Latin-American Spanish in this respect, so readers from the United States will often prefer an English simple past tense to the compound tenses used in the translations in section 14.9.

Alguien ha fumado un cigarrillo aquí. Huelo el humo	Someone's smoked a cigarette here. I can smell the smoke
¿Quién ha roto esta ventana?	Who's broken this window?
Pero aunque es evidente que Simone de Beauvoir ha leído con detenimiento a estos autores y aprovechado sus técnicas . . . (M. Vargas Llosa, Peru)	But although it is obvious that Simone de Beauvoir has read these authors closely and (has) taken advantage of their techniques . . .

Note

This use of the perfect is also quite common in literary Latin-American styles, but everyday Latin-American speech in most regions favours the preterite for any completed event. See 14.9.7.

14.9.3 Perfect of recency

In Spain, but not in Latin America, the perfect may optionally be used for any very recent event, in practice any event that has happened since midnight. Very recent events (e.g. seconds ago) are almost always expressed by the perfect tenses:

Esta mañana me he levantado/me levanté a las seis	I got up at six this morning
¿Has oído la explosión?	Did you hear the explosion?
—¿Quién ha dicho eso? —No he sido yo. Ha sido él	'Who said that (just now)?' 'It wasn't me. It was him'
La he visto hace un momento	I saw her a moment ago
No he podido hacerlo	I couldn't do it
No he querido venir antes por no querer molestar	I didn't want to come earlier so as not to cause bother
Ha muerto Franco (headline)	Franco is dead

Notes

(i) The perfect of recency is confined to standard European Spanish, although Kany, 200, reports its colloquial use in Bolivia and Perú. Other Latin-American regions favour the preterite in these examples, but for speakers of standard European Spanish ?*La vi hace un momento* sounds wrong because the event is very recent.

(ii) The above examples are chosen to show how European Spanish freely uses the perfect of recency with verbs like *querer*, *ser*, where English allows only the simple past: *No he querido hacerlo* 'I didn't want to do it', *¿Quién ha sido el gracioso que se ha llevado las llaves?* 'Who's the clown who took the keys away with him (just now)?'.

(iii) European Spanish thus differs from English in that the perfect is used of any very recent event, completed or not. English allows 'Have you heard the news?' since the news can still be heard, but not *'Have you heard that explosion?'. Cf. *¿Habéis visto el relámpago?* 'Did you see the flash?'.

(iv) One occasionally finds the perfect used in European Spanish in conjunction with some word or phrase that refers to a past not continuing into the present, e.g. 'yesterday', 'two months ago'. However, unless the event happened in the course of the present day, the preterite is safer. Some native speakers of European Spanish strongly preferred the preterite in the following sentences:

Ayer, a la caída de la tarde, cuando el gran acantilado es de cinabrio, he vuelto a la isla (I. Aldecoa, Spain)	Yesterday, at nightfall, when the big cliff is the colour of cinnabar, I returned to the island
Se trata de un ejercicio que ha perdido la iniciativa hace meses (Cambio16, Spain)	It involves an exercise which lost its initiative months ago
A mí todo lo que me ha sucedido me ha sucedido ayer, anoche a más tardar (J. Cortázar, Argentina, dialogue)	Everything that has happened to me happened yesterday, last night at the latest

Hace pocos días, un pacifista danés ha sido acusado de espionaje a favor de Moscú (*La Vanguardia*, Spain)	A few days ago a Danish pacifist was accused of spying for Moscow

(v) Frequent use of the perfect for the preterite is said to be typical of uneducated Madrid speech: *Bueno, he ido a hacerme el análisis hace quince días y mañana o pasado me dan los resultados* (interview in *Cambio16*, Spain) 'Well, I went and got a test done two weeks ago and tomorrow or the day after they'll give me the results'.

14.9.4 Perfect in time phrases
The perfect is often used, especially in Spain, in negative time phrases of the sort:

Hace años que no te he visto (or *no te veo*; Latin Americans may not accept the perfect)	I haven't seen you for years

Positive sentences of this type usually require the present tense: *Hace años que le/lo veo todos los días* 'I've been seeing him every day for years'.

Choice of tenses in statements of this kind is discussed in greater detail in Chapter 32 (Time expressions).

14.9.5 Use of the perfect for quotations
The perfect is sometimes used for famous quotations, e.g. *Aristóteles ha dicho que . . .* 'Aristotles said . . .', though Carnicer, (1972), 176, questions this usage. The present, preterite or imperfect is safer.

14.9.6 Perfect used for future certainties
The perfect is occasionally used in familiar European Spanish, at least in Central Spain, for future actions that are described as certainties:

Cuando vuelvas ya he acabado/ya lo habré acabado (Lat. Am. *ya acabé*)	I'll have finished by the time you come back

14.9.7 The perfect tense in Latin America
In Latin America all completed actions tend to be expressed by the preterite tense, more so in some regions than others. This solution is so favoured in informal styles in some regions that the perfect tense is rarely heard:

*¿Todavía no **llegó** tu padre?*	Hasn't your father come yet?/(US) 'Didn't your father come yet?'
Aún no salieron del cine	They haven't come out of the cinema yet
¿Qué hubo? (Colombia, Venezuela, etc.; Spain *¿Qué hay?*)	How're things?
Ya nos llegó la moderna solución (advert in *El Tiempo*, Colombia)	Now we've got the modern answer!
—¿Ya organizaste? —le pregunté. *—Sí, ya organicé* (A. Mastretta, Mexico, dialogue; Spain *has organizado, he organizado*)	'Have you organized it?', I asked him. 'Yes, I've organized it'
¿Nunca te fijaste en eso? (ibid., Spain *te has fijado*)	Haven't you ever/Didn't you ever notice that?

This use of the preterite is especially typical of spoken language in much of the Southern Cone: the perfect tense is a rarity in everyday speech in Buenos Aires and is said to sound bookish if used in familiar speech.

However, this colloquial usage varies from one region to another. In the spoken language of Bolivia and Peru the perfect is more frequent and its use seems to correspond quite closely to standard European usage. Kany, 201, notes that in popular Bolivian and Peruvian speech one even hears constructions like *?He tenido un mal sueño anoche* 'I had a bad dream last night' where all other regions, including Spain, require the preterite.[10]

Mexican Spanish (and possibly the Spanish of other parts of Latin America) differs from European in that the perfect is not used to indicate a past action that is still relevant to the present, as in the European sentence *Alguien ha fumado un cigarrillo aquí* 'Someone's smoked a cigarette here (I can still smell the smoke)', but an action that is *continuing* in the present or the future: Mexican *He fumado mucho* = 'I **have been** smoking a lot and still am smoking'.

The perfect of recency, frequent in Spain, is not used in Mexico or in most of Latin America: *Ha llegado hace un momento* for *Llegó hace un momento* is not normal in everyday speech.

Lope Blanch[11] remarks that the perfect may occasionally replace the preterite in exclamations, in which case it is strongly emphatic: compare *Esta mañana llovió mucho* 'It rained a lot this morning' and *¡Esta mañana ha llovido mucho!* 'Did it rain a lot this morning!'.

The tendency to use the perfect with a present meaning is taken to extremes further south in Latin America. Kany, 205ff, notes that in colloquial Ecuadorian and southern Colombian the perfect is used, even in educated speech, as an equivalent to the present tense: *?Ya ha sido tarde* = *Ya es tarde* 'It's late', *?Piernas gordas ha tenido la Laura* (i.e. *tiene*) 'Laura's got fat legs'. Occasionally it may even be used as a future: *?El año que viene ha sido* (i.e. *será*) *bisiesto* 'Next year will be a leap year'. Kany further notes that, south from Ecuador, and especially in Argentina, even the pluperfect of *ser* is locally heard in popular speech with a present meaning: *?había sido tarde* = *es tarde*. However, these forms are very aberrant with respect to normal usage elsewhere.

As was mentioned earlier, the Latin-American preference for the preterite to indicate all past completed actions has its counterpart in North-American English. Compare US 'Did you sell your apartment yet?', 'Did they arrive already?' and British '**Have** you sold your flat yet?', '**Have** they arrived already?'.

14.10 The pluperfect: general

The pluperfect is formed with the imperfect of *haber* plus a past participle: *habías comido* 'you had eaten', *habían llegado* 'they/you had arrived'.

The *-ra* form of the verb can also sometimes have an indicative pluperfect meaning in literary Spanish. See 14.10.2.

---

[10] But note European *Anoche **dormí** mal* 'I slept badly last night' and *Esta noche **he dormido** mal*, same meaning.

[11] '*Sobre el uso del pretérito en el español de México*', in Lope Blanch (1991), 131-43.

14.10.1 Uses of the pluperfect

The use of the Spanish pluperfect corresponds quite closely to the English pluperfect: it is used for events or states that preceded some past event and are felt to be relevant to it:

Yo ya me había dado cuenta de que ustedes no estaban	I had already realized that you weren't there
Sabíamos que ya había vendido el coche	We knew that he had already sold the car

Notes

(i) Colloquially the pluperfect may be avoided, especially in Latin-American Spanish, where it is commonly replaced by the preterite or, when it refers to habitual actions, by the imperfect: *Lo encontré donde lo dejé* (for *donde lo había dejado*) (from J.M. Lope Blanch, 1991, 152) 'I found it where I'd left it/where I left it', *Cuando terminábamos* (for *habíamos terminado*) *volvíamos a casa* (habitual) 'When we had finished, we used to return home', *Le faltaban dos dientes y nunca se puso* (Spain *se había puesto/se ponía*) *a dieta ni fue* (Spain *había ido/iba*) *a la gimnasia* (A. Mastretta, Mexico, dialogue) 'He had two teeth missing and he had never been on a diet or gone to the gymnasium'.

(ii) In some cases the English pluperfect will require translation by the preterite. See 14.10.4 note (i).

English occasionally uses a simple past where a Spanish pluperfect is required: 'I didn't imagine ahead to parties . . . or nights alone in the double bed after a divorce which left me stranded' (Mary Ingram, *Now we are thirty*) *No podía imaginarme el futuro, fiestas . . . noches sola en la cama matrimonial después de un divorcio que me **había dejado** abandonada sin saber qué hacer.*

14.10.2 Pluperfect ending in -ra

The *-ra* form of Spanish verbs descends from the Latin indicative pluperfect: Latin *fueram* 'I had been' > Spanish *fuera*. The Spanish form gradually acquired a subjunctive meaning and for most purposes it is now identical in use to the *-se* imperfect subjunctive (see 16.2.3 for further details).

The old indicative pluperfect use of the *-ra* forms survives in literary Spanish and is found in literature and journalism as a supposedly elegant alternative for the ordinary pluperfect using *había*. This is very common in Latin America, but it is also found in Spain among those who think of themselves as stylists. Lorenzo (1980), 135, echoes a typical European attitude to this construction: *Evidentemente, la sentimos como afectada, pero hay muchas gentes que lo son. . . .*

When used thus, the *-ra* form has no subjunctive meaning at all. However, this construction seems to have been contaminated by a feature of the subjunctive: it only occurs in subordinate, chiefly relative clauses. *El libro que había leído* 'the book he had read' can be re-cast in supposedly 'elegant' style as *el libro que leyera*, but *Había leído el libro* 'He had read the book' cannot be rewritten **Leyera el libro.*

Examples:

*Fue el único rastro que dejó en el que **fuera** su hogar de casada por cinco horas* (G. García Márquez, Colombia; for *había sido*)	It was the only trace she left in what had been her marital home for five hours
*Y en la propia Nicaragua, la dinastía de Somoza, que **fuera** directamente colocada en el poder por Estados Unidos . . .* (M. Benedetti in *El País; había sido . . .*)	And in Nicaragua itself, the Somoza dynasty, which had been directly installed in power by the United States . . .

Note
One even finds examples of the imperfect subjunctive in -*se* used as an indicative pluperfect in the same contexts as the -*ra* form described above: *Así había dado con el hombre capaz, muy versado en asuntos económicos, que **conociese** en la Logia* (A. Carpentier, Cuba; for *había conocido* or *conociera*) 'He had thus come across the able man, well versed in economic matters, whom he had met in the (Masonic) Lodge'. But this is very rare on both continents and rather forced.

14.10.3 -*ra* and -*se* pluperfect after *después de que* and *desde que*

The rule for the choice of verb form after *después de que* 'after' and *desde que* 'since' should logically be subjunctive for as yet unfulfilled events, indicative for fulfilled events, i.e. *Comeremos después de que lleguen los demás* 'We'll eat after the rest arrive' (unfulfilled), *Decidimos comer después de que llegasen/llegaran los demás* 'We decided we would eat after the rest arrived' (unfulfilled: they hadn't arrived yet), *Comimos después de que lle**garon** los demás* 'We ate after the rest (had) arrived' (fulfilled):

. . . *después de que las hijas mayores la* ***ayudaron*** *a poner un poco de orden en los estragos de la boda* (G. García Márquez, Colombia)	after the elder daughters (had) helped her to put a bit of order in the devastation left by the wedding
. . . *después de que Victoriano Huerta* ***mató*** *a Madero* (A. Mastretta, Mexico, dialogue)	after Victoriano Huerta killed Madero

However, written and formal spoken language, especially in Spain, and for no very obvious reason, frequently uses the -*ra* or -*se* forms even for fulfilled events in the past:

. . . *después de que Nigeria* ***hiciese*** *pública su decisión de firmar el acta* (El País)	after Nigeria made public its decision to sign the communiqué/minutes
. . . *dos años después de que Batista* ***tomara*** *el poder* (Cambio16, Spain)	two years after Batista took power
. . . *desde que* ***entrara*** *en prisión, el 23 de agosto* (Cambio16, Spain)	since he entered prison on August 23
Vargas Llosa, que conserva muchos amigos en Barcelona desde que ***residiera*** *en España* (ABC, Spain)	Vargas Llosa, who has kept many friends in Barcelona from when he lived in Spain

If the subject of both verbs is the same, *después de que* is replaced by *después de* + infinitive: *Nos fuimos después de haber hecho todo* 'We left after we had done everything'. Even if the subjects are different, colloquial language may still use the infinitive construction, e.g. *?después de llegar Pepe* for *después de que llegó Pepe* 'after Pepe arrived', but learners should probably avoid this. See 18.3 and 16.2.6 for discussion of the infinitive after subordinators.

14.10.4 *Pretérito anterior: hube hablado, hube acabado*

This tense, called the *pretérito anterior*, is a perfective pluperfect and expresses an event completed just before a following past event. It is normally confined to literature and it is now extremely rare in speech:

Cuando hubieron terminado de reírse, examinaron mi situación personal (A. Cancela, quoted Esbozo, 3.14.7)	When they'd finished laughing they examined my personal situation
Se marchó apenas hubo comido	He left as soon as he had eaten
Le escribió el mismo día, no bien se hubo marchado (L. Goytisolo, Spain)	He wrote to her the same day, when she had only just left

. . . *así que, una vez que me hube quitado la blusa* . . . (E. Sábato, Argentina, dialogue)	So as soon as I had taken my blouse off . . .

Notes

(i) This tense is only used after *después (de) que* 'after', *luego que, así que, no bien, enseguida que, en cuanto, tan pronto como* and *apenas*, all translatable as 'as soon as', and after *cuando* and other phrases, to emphasize that the event was completed just before the main event in the sentence. In ordinary language it is replaced by the preterite: *cuando terminaron de reírse* 'when they'd stopped laughing', *Tan pronto como llegamos, pasamos al comedor* 'As soon as we arrived, we went through to the dining room', *Pero apenas entró cambió de opinión* (J. Ibargüengoitia, Mexico, dialogue) 'But he'd hardly entered when he changed his mind' – or, less commonly, by the pluperfect[12]: *Apenas **había ordenado** el señor juez el levantamiento del cadáver para llevarlo al depósito judicial, rompieron el silencio unos gritos de mujer* (F. García Pavón, Spain) 'The judge had scarcely ordered the removal of the body to the official morgue when the silence was broken by women shouting'.

(ii) The *pretérito anterior* refers to a single completed event. After the same time phrases, repeated or habitual events are expressed by the ordinary pluperfect: *En cuanto habíamos terminado el trabajo, volvíamos a casa* 'As soon as we had finished work, we used to return home' – or, colloquially, by the imperfect: *En cuanto terminábamos el trabajo, volvíamos a casa*.

---

[12] Replacement by the pluperfect is uncommon. Busquets & Bonzi (1983), 69, 267, give numerous examples of the pluperfect as alternatives to the preterite.

15

Continuous forms of the verb

15.1 General

15.1.1 Forms and equivalents of the continuous

Spanish has a full range of continuous verb forms constructed with the appropriate tense of *estar* 'to be' and the gerund: *estoy hablando* 'I'm talking', *estuve cenando* 'I had dinner/supper', *estaremos escribiendo* 'we'll be writing', etc. The formation of the gerund is discussed at 20.2.

French has a close equivalent of the Spanish continuous: *Je suis **en train de** parler* 'I'm (in the middle of) speaking' stresses an ongoing action in much the same way as *estoy hablando*. Students of Spanish who know French well should recall that if *en train de . . .* is impossible in French, the continuous will usually be impossible in Spanish. *Je pars demain = salgo mañana. *Je suis en train de partir demain/*Estoy saliendo mañana* are both impossible for 'I'm leaving tomorrow'.

The Italian continuous, *sto lavorando = estoy trabajando* 'I'm working' appears only in the present and imperfect tenses, whereas its Spanish counterpart can appear in any tense.[1]

The Spanish continuous form is apparently more common than fifty years ago and some of its current uses seem to reflect the influence of English, cf. this extract from a commercial circular from Spain: *Su dirección nos ha sido facilitada por nuestra Embajada en su país y nos **estamos permitiendo** distraer un instante su atención para poner nuestros servicios a su disposición . . .* where *nos permitimos distraer . . .* seems more plausible. The Academy's *Esbozo*, 3.12.5, complains bitterly about this abuse of the continuous.

English-speaking learners constantly over-use the continuous and produce sentences like **En este capítulo el autor **está diciendo** que . . .* 'In this chapter the author is saying that . . .' instead of the correct *dice que . . . .* These errors usually arise from a failure to apply the rule that the continuous refers only to actions that are really in progress. In this case the author is obviously not actually saying the words *now*.

Continuous forms seem to be more frequent in Latin-American Spanish than in European. See 15.5 for discussion.

15.1.2 The Spanish continuous and the English progressive compared

Spanish continuous forms, e.g. *Estoy leyendo, Estaban hablando* etc., misleadingly resemble the much-used English progressive verb form, e.g. 'I'm

---

[1] A. & G. Lepschy (1988), 148.

reading', 'they were talking'. Although the two sometimes correspond closely when the English forms are used as present tenses, the Spanish continuous differs from its English analogue in several important respects:

(a) It can only refer to an action that is actually in progress, whereas the English progressive doubles as a future tense and also, sometimes, as a habitual form:

Estoy comiendo	I'm (actually) eating
Estaré durmiendo	I'll be sleeping/asleep (at that time)
Estabas hablando	You were (in the process of) talking

but

Llegamos mañana	**We're arriving** tomorrow (future)
Si te pones así, me voy	If you get like that, **I'm going** (future)
Mi hijo va a un colegio mixto	My son is going to a mixed (i.e. co-educational) school (habitual)
Te envío ésta para decirte que . . .	**I'm sending** you this to tell you that . . . (either really means 'I have sent' or 'I shall send')
Yo salía a la mañana siguiente para París	**I was leaving** the following morning for Paris (future in the past)
Hoy el Barça juega en casa	Today Barcelona is/are playing at home (*está jugando* possible only if the game is in progress)

(b) The Spanish continuous is very rarely used with verbs of motion (see 15.3):

¿Adónde vas?	Where **are you going**?
Ya voy	I'm coming[2]

(c) The Spanish continuous adds a nuance to, but does not substantially alter the meaning of the non-continuous verb form, so that the two forms are are sometimes virtually interchangeable. This should be clear in the following pairs of examples:

¿No hueles que se queman/se están quemando las salchichas?	Can't you smell that the sausages are burning?
Yo hablaba/estaba hablando con Mario	I was talking to Mario/I used to talk to Mario
Ana lee/está leyendo	Ana is reading

(d) A number of common Spanish verbs do not appear in the continuous form, whereas their English counterparts do. See 15.3 for discussion.

15.1.3 Further remarks on the relationship between the simple present tense and the present continuous

The Spanish present tense, e.g. *escribo*, *hago*, etc., is imprecise in terms of time: it may indicate present, future or habitual events, eternal truths or even past events (see 14.3 and 14.6.4). Continuous forms are much more

---

[2] In Spanish 'to go' must be used when referring to the departure point and 'to come' when referring to the arrival point; English is vague in this respect. Thus *No voy a tu fiesta esta noche* = 'I'm not **coming/going** to your party tonight', but not **No vengo a tu fiesta* . . .'. —*¿Vienes conmigo?* —*No, no voy contigo* ' "Are you coming with me?" "No, I'm not coming/going with you" '.

specifically present: compare *Fuma* 'He smokes' or 'He's smoking' and *Está fumando* 'he's (actually) smoking (now)'.

An action must be perceived to be actually in progress for the continuous to be possible. Peninsular informants[3] said *está lloviendo* on seeing rain through a window, and thought that *llueve*, in this case, sounded vaguely poetic or archaic. But most avoided the continuous in the sentences *Asómate a ver si llueve* 'Look out and see if it's raining' and *¿Llueve o no llueve?* 'Is it raining or not?', the reason being that someone who asks whether it is raining has obviously not actually heard or seen rain falling. If the questioner had heard the patter of rain, *¿Está lloviendo?* would be more appropriate since the phenomenon is known to be occurring.

Similarly, when someone up a tree shouts 'I'm falling!', (s)he literally means 'I'm going to fall!', not 'I'm already in mid-air!': a Spanish speaker shouts *¡Que me caigo!*

With some verbs (e.g. *leer* 'to read', *charlar* 'to chat'), or where the duration of an action is emphasized, the continuous is more appropriate than the simple form: *Estuve leyendo toda la mañana* is better Spanish than *Leí toda la mañana* 'I was reading all morning'/'I read all morning' (example and argument from Moliner, II, 1393).

15.2 Uses of the continuous forms

15.2.1 Continuous used to emphasize events in progress
The continuous is frequently used to show that an event is, was or will actually be in progress at the time. In cases in which the action is emphatically in progress at the time, the continuous is obligatory:

Ahora no se puede poner – está haciendo sus cuentas (not . . .*hace sus cuentas*)	He can't come to the phone now, he's doing his accounts
¿Me estarán viendo/Me ven desde esa ventana?	Are they watching me from that window?
Arriba golpearon dos veces, sin mucha fuerza. —*Está matando las cucarachas* —*propuso Gregorius* (J. Cortázar, Argentina, dialogue)	There were two knocks from upstairs, not very loud. 'He's killing the cockroaches', Gregorius suggested
Pero ¡si te estaba escuchando!/¡si te escuchaba!	But I *was* listening to you!

Notes
(i) In the case of the imperfect tense, the continuous and non-continuous are sometimes interchangeable if they really refer to the past, i.e. *pensaba* and *estaba pensando* both mean 'I/he was thinking'. See 14.5.3 for discussion.
(ii) The preterite continuous is different in meaning from the non-continuous preterite. *Hablé con él* means 'I spoke to him', *Estuve hablando con él* means 'I talked to him for a time', i.e. 'I had a talk with him'. See 15.2.3.

15.2.2 Continuous used to denote temporary or surprising events
(a) The continuous may be used to show that an action is temporary or in some way unusual:

---

[3] In this and several other cases, Latin-American informants tended to use the continuous more readily than Peninsular informants.

Vive en París, pero últimamente está viviendo en Madrid	He lives in Paris, but at the moment he's living in Madrid
¿Dónde estás trabajando estos días?	Where are you working these days?
Me estoy sintiendo mal/me siento mal	I'm (suddenly) feeling ill

(b) The continuous may express surprise, indignation or lively interest:

Pero ¿qué estás haciendo?	But what *are* you doing?
¿Qué me estás contando?	What *are* you telling me!?
—¿En qué estábamos pensando tú y yo cuando engendramos a estos seres, me quieres explicar? —le pregunta la madre al padre (Carmen Rico-Godoy, Spain, dialogue)	'Do you mind explaining to me what you and I were thinking of when we conceived these creatures?', the mother asks the father

15.2.3 Continuous used to denote prolonged events

The continuous may show that an action is prolonged over a period of time:

He estado pensando que tú no siempre dices la verdad	I've been thinking that you don't always tell the truth
Pero, ¿vas a estar esperándola todo el día?	But are you going to keep on waiting for her all day?!
El rostro de María sonreía. Es decir, ya no sonreía, pero había estado sonriendo un décimo de segundo antes (E. Sábato, Argentina)	Maria's face was smiling. I mean, it wasn't smiling now, but it had been smiling a tenth of a second before
Acuérdense, el señor ese con el que estuvimos tomando nieves en el zócalo de Atlixco (A. Mastretta, Mexico, dialogue; *nieves* = *helados* in Spain)	Remember, that gentleman we had an ice-cream with in the main square in Atlixco

Note

The preterite continuous, *estuve hablando/comiendo* 'I was speaking/eating for a time' indicates an action that was prolonged in the past but finished, unlike the imperfect forms *hablaba/estaba hablando* which merely indicate that an action was going on at the time.

The preterite continuous is really only possible with verbs that refer to drawn-out actions, e.g. 'think', 'talk', 'read', 'wait', 'eat', etc.. Verbs that refer to instantaneous actions cannot be extended: **Estuvo rompiendo una ventana* 'He was breaking a window (for a certain time)' is not possible, and *Estaba rompiendo una ventana* is only possible if we mean 'He was (in the process of) breaking a window'.

Instantaneous actions can, however, be repeated over a period of time: *Estuvo disparando al aire durante tres minutos* 'He spent three minutes firing into the air'.

15.2.4 Continuous to express repeated events

The continuous may express the idea that an event is or has been constantly recurring.

Está yendo mucho al cine estos días	He's going to the cinema a lot these days
La estás viendo demasiado, hijo	You're seeing too much of her, son
Está viniendo a casa mucho estos días	He comes to the house a lot these days
Lleva años que se está yendo pero nunca acaba de irse	He's been leaving for years but never gets round to going
Está haciendo frío	It's been cold lately/The weather's cold at the moment
Pero está usted tomando muy seguido esas hierbas y seguido hacen daño (A. Mastretta, Mexico, dialogue)	But you're taking those herbs over long periods, and they cause harm when taken over long periods

Venir and *ir* may appear in the continuous form in this sense, but not usually in other contexts.

15.2.5 Future continuous

The future continuous is used either **(a)** to describe events felt already to be happening in the present, or **(b)** to conjecture about what may actually be happening now:

Mañana a estas horas estaremos volando sobre el Pacífico	Tomorrow at this time we'll be flying over the Pacific
Estarán comiendo a estas horas	They'll probably be eating at this time of day

15.3 Restrictions on the use of the continuous

(a) Continuous forms are not normally used with certain verbs that refer to inner mental activities, e.g. *aborrecer* 'to loathe', *amar* 'to love', *odiar* 'to hate', *saber* 'to know'. In this respect Spanish and English coincide, but some verbs which denote inner states or 'invisible' actions may appear in the continuous in Spanish but not in English:

Me estoy creyendo todo lo que dices	?I'm believing everything you say
Estoy viendo que vamos a acabar mal	I can see we're going to end badly
Te estás mereciendo una bofetada	You deserve (i.e. 'are asking for') a slap
Estoy temiendo que va a llegar tarde	I'm afraid he's going to arrive late

Note
Doler 'to hurt' may appear in either form, much as in English: *Me duele/Me está doliendo la barriga* 'My stomach (i.e. intestines) aches/is aching'.

(b) The continuous is not used to describe states rather than actions (English often allows the progressive form for states):

Tres arañas de luces colgaban del techo	Three chandeliers were hanging from the roof
Lo que falta es . . .	What's lacking is . . .
La luna brillaba sobre las olas	The moon was shining on the waves
Parece cansada	She's looking tired
¡Qué bien huele la madreselva hoy!	Isn't the honeysuckle smelling good today!

(c) The continuous is not used with *estar* (*estar estando is not Spanish), *poder*, *haber* or, usually, with *ir, venir, regresar, volver, andar*, except in the frequentative sense (discussed at 15.2.4):

¿Adónde vas?	Where are you going?
Viene ahora	He's coming now
Cuando volvíamos del cine (me) subí un momento a ver a la abuela	When we were coming back from the cinema I went up to see grandmother for a moment
Estás estúpido hoy	You're being stupid today

Notes
(i) Finite forms of verbs that describe physical posture or position can refer only to an action, not to a state. English speakers are often misled by forms like 'He was sitting down' which almost always means *Estaba sentado* 'He was seated'. *Estaba sentándose* = 'He was in the process of sitting down'. Further examples: *Estaban tumbados* 'They were lying down', *Estaba agachado* 'He was bending down' (compare *Estaba agachándose* 'He was in the process of bending down').
(ii) *Tener* 'to have' is not used in the continuous, except in the frequentative sense

described earlier: *Me dijo que estaba teniendo problemas con su vecino* 'He told me he was having problems with his neighbour'.

(iii) *Llevar* is used in the continuous only with the sense of 'to carry': *Lleva camisa* 'He's wearing a shirt', *Está llevando una camisa a su madre* 'He's taking a shirt to his mother'.

(iv) *Parecer* 'to seem' occasionally appears in the continuous: *La situación me está pareciendo cada vez más fea* 'The situation's looking uglier and uglier to me'.

(v) The continuous of *ir, venir* and, regionally, of some other of these verbs is found in colloquial speech in parts of Latin America. See 15.5 for Latin-American usage.

15.4 Continuous forms of *ser*

Some grammarians frown on continuous forms of *ser*, e.g. *está siendo*, as Anglicisms, but they are not uncommon, especially in Latin America, and they occur in speech as well as in writing to judge by the dialogue of some novels. It seems unreasonable to deny the language the nuance supplied by a continuous form of *ser*, e.g.:

Por un instante pensó que de algún modo él, Martín, estaba de verdad siendo necesario a aquel ser atormentado (E. Sábato, Argentina)
For an instant he thought that he, Martin, was really necessary to that tormented creature (lit. 'being necessary')

La convocatoria a las distintas manifestaciones está siendo variada (La Vanguardia, Spain)
(lit.) The calling to the various demonstrations is varied (i.e. the people attending come from various sources)

Yo no estoy siendo juzgado (C. Fuentes, Mexico, dialogue)
I'm not being judged

Estás siendo muy bueno hoy
You're being very good today

15.5 Latin-American uses of the continuous

Written – or at least printed – Latin-American Spanish seems to obey the same rules as European Spanish as far as the use of the continuous is concerned. However, there are numerous regional variants in colloquial usage and it seems, in general, that the continuous is used more extensively in Latin-American speech than in Spain.

In many places, the continuous of *ir, venir* and other verbs of motion are regularly heard:

—*Estamos yendo a Pato Huachana* —*dijo Lalita* (M. Vargas Llosa, Peru, dialogue)
'We're going to Pato Huachana', Lalita said

¿Cómo le va yendo? (Chile, quoted Kany, 282; Spain *¿Cómo le va?*)
How are things with you?

¿Sabes de cuánto tiempo estoy viniendo a Obrajes? (Bolivia, idem; Spain *desde hace cuanto tiempo* and *vengo . . .*)
D'you know how long I've been coming to Obrajes?

Kany, 282ff, reports that in the Andean region (including Chile) verbs like *poder, tener, haber* also appear in the continuous form, especially in popular styles: *Estás pudiendo* = *Puedes* 'You can', *¿Está habiendo?* 'Is there any?' (Spain *¿Hay?*). This is not heard in standard Spanish.

Chilean informants confirm Kany's remark that the continuous is sometimes used in this area to refer to an immediate future, as in English: *estoy yendo* = 'I'm going'/'I'm leaving'.

In colloquial, but not written Mexican, *andar* is much used instead of *estar* to form the continuous: *Ando trabajando* 'I'm working', *¿Qué andas haciendo?* 'What are you doing?'.

Similar forms with *andar* are sometimes heard in popular speech in Spain, e.g. *¿Qué andas haciendo?* for *¿Qué estás haciendo?*, but *andar* + gerund normally means 'to go around doing something'. See 20.8.1 for discussion and examples.

16

The subjunctive

16.1 Index to chapter

The following general topics are discussed in the sections shown:

The importance of the Spanish subjunctive	16.2.1
Forms of the subjunctive	16.2.2
The -*ra* and -*se* forms compared	16.2.3
Tense agreement and the subjunctive	16.2.4, 16.16
When the subjunctive is **not** used in clauses beginning with *que*	16.2.5
Subjunctive or infinitive?	16.2.6
The subjunctive does **not** always indicate doubt or uncertainty	16.2.7
Regional variations in the use of the subjunctive	16.2.8
The future subjunctive	16.17

The following charts indicate the main uses of the Spanish subjunctive and the section where the topic is discussed further (these charts do not include every point raised in the chapter):

Chart 1: Subjunctive in subordinate clauses introduced by *que*

Meaning of main clause	Subjunctive used	Section
Possibility, probability	always	16.3.1
Perhaps	variable	16.3.2
Depending on	always	16.4
Wanting	always	16.5
Needing	always	16.5
Ordering	variable	16.5
Requesting	variable	16.5
Allowing, forbidding	variable	16.5
Causing	always	16.5
Avoiding	always	16.5
Emotional reactions	almost always	16.6
Value judgements	almost always	16.6
Denial	usually	16.7
Doubt	usually	16.8
Fear	usually	16.9
'The fact that . . .'	usually	16.10
Other nouns + *de que*	variable	16.10

Chart 1: continued

Meaning of main clause	Subjunctive used	Section
Believing and suspecting	yes if negated and sometimes if affirmative	16.11.1, 16.7
Stating, declaring	yes if negated	16.7
Knowing	yes if negated	16.7
Understanding	depends on meaning	16.11.2
Hoping	variable	16.11.3

Chart 2: Subjunctive after subordinators

Meaning of subordinator	Subjunctive used	Section
In order that . . .	always	16.12.2
In order that not . . ./lest	always	16.12.2
Because . . ., since (cause)	depends on meaning	16.12.3
in such a way that . . . (manner)	depends on meaning	16.12.4a
Como (= 'as')	depends on meaning	16.12.4b
Without . . .	always	16.12.4c
In case . . .	variable	16.12.5
Before . . .	always	16.12.6
When . . .	depends on meaning	16.12.6
After	depends on meaning	16.12.6
While . . ., as . . . (time)	depends on meaning	16.12.6
Since . . . (time)	depends on meaning	16.12.6
As soon as . . .	depends on meaning	16.12.6
While . . .	depends on meaning	16.12.6
Until . . .	depends on meaning	16.12.6
Provided that/on condition that	always	16.12.7a
Except . . .	depends on meaning	16.12.7b
Unless . . .	depends on meaning	16.12.7b
Although . . .	variable	16.12.8
In spite of . . .	depends on meaning	16.12.8

Chart 3: Other uses of the subjunctive

	Subjunctive used	Section
To translate: whoever, whatever, whenever however, wherever, the more . . . the more . . .	depends on meaning	16.13
In relative clauses	depends on meaning	16.14
After *donde* and *cuanto* introducing clauses	depends on meaning	16.14.3
After superlatives	depends on meaning	16.14.4
For affirmative imperatives	with *usted/ustedes*	16.15.1
To make negative imperative	always	16.15.1
After words expressing wishes	always	16.15.2
In conditional sentences	depends on meaning	Ch. 25
In a few set phrases	always	16.15.3
Tense agreement rules		16.16

16.2 General remarks on the subjunctive

16.2.1 The importance of the Spanish subjunctive

The subjunctive is a very important feature of Spanish and there is no conclusive evidence that it is dying out. But it is true that spontaneous speech, especially Latin-American, occasionally uses the indicative in constructions that require the subjunctive in formal styles. These colloquial uses of the indicative are mentioned throughout the chapter.

16.2.2 Forms of the subjunctive

There are three non-compound tenses of the Spanish subjunctive: present, imperfect and future. Only two of these are in common use: the present, formed as explained at 13.1.9, and the imperfect.

There are two forms of the latter, one in -*ra* and one in -*se*. These forms are explained at 13.1.10 and in Table 2, p. 199. The relationship between the two forms is discussed in the next section.

Compound tenses of the subjunctive, e.g. *haya hablado, hubiera/hubiese hablado*, and continuous forms of the subjunctive, e.g. *esté hablando, estuviera/estuviese hablando*, are also common.

The future subjunctive, discussed at 16.17 is virtually obsolete and has been replaced by the present subjunctive.

16.2.3 The -*ra* and -*se* forms compared

When the -*ra* and -*se* forms are used as subjunctives they seem to be completely interchangeable and the two forms are shown side by side in most of the following examples.[1] The -*ra* form is more frequent and in some parts of Latin America has all but replaced the -*se* form, but not in Argentina to judge by the popular dialogue in Manuel Puig's novels.

The -*ra* form has a few other functions as an indicative form that it does not share with the -*se* form in normal styles:

(a) It may be a supposedly elegant literary alternative for the indicative pluperfect, especially in Latin-American texts: *el hombre que ella **conociera** años antes* 'the man she had met years ago', for *que había conocido* . . . See 14.10.2 for discussion.

(b) It can replace the conditional of *haber* - *habría sido mejor/**hubiera** sido mejor* 'it would have been better' - and less commonly of a few other verbs. See 14.7.5 for discussion.

(c) It is used in a few set phrases: e.g. *Acabáramos* 'Now I see what you're getting at', *Otro gallo nos cantara* 'That would be another story'.

---

[1] It has been claimed that there is a slight difference of meaning between sentences like *Yo quisiera que lo **hiciera*** and *Yo quisiera que lo **hiciese*** 'I wanted him to do it', but most authorities are convinced that they are interchangeable.

For a contrary view, see Bolinger (1991), 274-82. Bolinger suggests that in conditional sentences the -*se* form is remoter in meaning: *si yo pudiese* more strongly implies 'if I could but I can't' than *si yo pudiera*, which implies 'if I can – we'll have to see'. Likewise, he suggests, the difference in meaning between '*No creo que lo fuera/fuese* is the difference between an ordinary opinion, and an uncertain opinion.

Bolinger's argument is based on a relatively small sample, and most educated informants deny the existence of these nuances.

16.2.4 Tense agreement and the subjunctive

This is discussed in detail at 16.16. The idea that there is a 'Rule of Agreement' that governs which tense of the subjunctive must be used in Spanish is one of the myths of traditional grammar, but in the vast majority of cases the following scheme applies:

Tense of verb in main clause	Subjunctive tense
Present, perfect (*he querido*, etc.), future	Present
Conditional, imperfect, preterite, pluperfect	Imperfect

Examples: *Le digo/he dicho/diré que se **vaya*** 'I tell/have told/will tell him to go away'; *Le diría/decía/dije/había dicho que se **fuera/fuese*** 'I would tell/was telling/told/had told him to go away'.

16.2.5 When the subjunctive is *not* used in clauses introduced by *que*

It is much easier to state categorically when the subjunctive is **not** used in clauses introduced by *que* than to list all the cases in which it is used.

The subjunctive is **not** used:

(a) After affirmative statements that simply declare that an event happened, is happening or will happen:

*Es cierto que **hay/hubo** una conspiración*	It's true that there is/was a conspiracy
*Era obvio que lo **había** hecho*	It was obvious that he'd done it
*Se prevé que **habrá** déficit*	A deficit is forecasted

(b) After affirmative statements that declare the subject's belief or opinion:[2]

*Creo que **habla** inglés*	I think she speaks English
*Yo pensaba que él **era** más honrado*	I thought he was more honest
*Dice que **viene***	She says she's coming
*Parece que su mujer **está** enferma*	It seems that his wife is ill

There are occasional exceptions to **(b)** discussed at 16.11.1.

The negative of sentences under **(a)** and **(b)** usually amount to denials of a fact and therefore require the subjunctive, e.g. *No es cierto que **hubiera/hubiese** una conspiración* 'It isn't true that there was a conspiracy', *No parece que su mujer **esté** enferma* 'It doesn't seem that his wife is ill'. See 16.7 for discussion.

(c) After subordinators (words like *cuando, después de que, mientras que*, etc.), when the verb refers to an action that either habitually happens or had already happened at the time of the main verb. Compare *Le pagaré cuando **llegue*** 'I'll pay him when he arrives' and *Le pago cuando **llega*** 'I pay him when he arrives' (habitual). See 16.12 for further discussion.

(d) When the subject of the main verb and the subordinate verb are the same, in which case the infinitive is normally used. See next section.

---

[2] In this respect Spanish differs from Italian and resembles French. Compare *Creo que es verdad*/*Je crois que c'est vrai* (both subordinate verbs indicative) and Italian *Credo che sia certo* (second verb subjunctive).

(e) In relative clauses, when the thing or person pointed to by the relative pronoun is known to exist: *Se casó con una mujer que sabe japonés* 'He married a woman who knows Japanese'. See 16.14.4 for details.

16.2.6 Subjunctive or infinitive?

A subjunctive can often be avoided by using an infinitive.

As a general rule, the subjunctive is only required when the subject in the main clause and the subject in the subordinate clause are different. When they are the same the infinitive is used. Thus *yo quiero* 'I want' + *yo voy* 'I go' = *Yo quiero ir* 'I want to go' (same subject). But *yo quiero* + *él va* 'he goes' = *Yo quiero que él vaya*, 'I want him to go' (different subjects).

Verbs of prohibiting, permitting, requesting and advising may allow either construction (see 16.5.2). The infinitive is also sometimes used in spontaneous language in cases where the subjunctive is required in formal styles.

The use of the infinitive is discussed further in Chapter 18, especially at 18.3, where there are several remarks that are relevant to the use of the subjunctive.

16.2.7 The subjunctive does *not* always indicate doubt or uncertainty

One common misconception about the Spanish subjunctive is that it expresses doubt or uncertainty. This is sometimes true, but the subjunctive is not in fact always obligatory after some common words that express uncertainty (e.g. 'perhaps', 'probably' – see 16.3.2 – and 'to doubt' – see 16.8), and the sentence *Me acostaré cuando se ponga el sol* 'I'll go to bed when the sun sets' does not doubt that the sun will set: the subjunctive is required after *cuando* simply because the sunset is still in the future.

In this respect students of French or Italian must remember that Spanish uses the present subjunctive to indicate future reference in subordinate clauses where the other two languages use the future indicative. Compare *On y ira quand il fera beau temps, Ci andremo quando farà bel tempo* (both verbs future indicative) with *Iremos allí cuando haga buen tiempo* (second verb subjunctive). Portuguese differs from all three in using a future subjunctive in this context: *Iremos lá quando fizer bom tempo.*

The subjunctive also expresses certainties in other types of sentence. In *El hecho de que España no tenga petróleo explica en parte las dificultades económicas del país* 'The fact that Spain has no oil explains in part the country's economic difficulties' there is no doubt about Spain's having no oil. It is simply a rule of Spanish grammar that phrases meaning 'the fact that' usually require the subjunctive, possibly because an idea of cause is involved. See 16.10.1 for further discussion.

16.2.8 Regional variations in the use of the subjunctive

There is very little variation in the use of the subjunctive in educated speech throughout the Spanish-speaking world.

In some regions, especially Navarre, the Basque Provinces and Argentina, there is a strong tendency in familiar speech to replace the imperfect subjunctive by the conditional, e.g. ?*Si tendría dinero, lo compraría* for *Si tuviera/tuviese dinero, lo compraría* 'If I had money, I'd buy it'. This should not be imitated by foreign learners, although it is acknowledged (at least in Spain and not in writing) as a well-known regionalism.

Also to be avoided is the tendency, heard in sub-standard speech in Argentina and elsewhere in Latin America, to replace the subjunctive by the future indicative after subordinators of time, e.g. *?Se lo diré cuando vendrá* for *Se lo diré cuando venga* 'I'll tell him when he comes'. This construction is also sometimes heard in the speech of small children, which is a significant indication of the unconscious link between the subjunctive and the idea of future time in Spanish.

There is also a tendency in Argentina and probably elsewhere in Latin America to use the indicative in familiar language after subordinators even when the action is or was still in the future: *?Te lo diré cuando llega* 'I'll tell you when he gets here' for *Te lo diré cuando llegue*.

In Argentina, where *voseo* is normal and accepted in conversation among all social groups, careful speakers may nevertheless use standard Spanish subjunctive forms with *vos*. The expected *vos* forms with a stressed final vowel are considered a shade too plebeian for some tastes:

Yo no tengo inconveniente en hablar de perros todo lo que querás (Mafalda cartoon, popular style, Argentina; 'correct' style *todo lo que quieras*)	I don't mind talking about dogs as much as you like

Compare this extract from dialogue between educated adults who address one another as *vos*:

Tengo miedo que no vengas . . . que aflojes (J. Asís, Argentina; Spain *miedo de que*)	I'm scared you won't come . . .that you'll go off the idea

See 11.3.1 for more remarks about Argentine *voseo*.

16.3 Subjunctive after statements of possibility and probability

16.3.1 *Es posible/probable que . . .* and similar statements
In sentences of the pattern statement of possibility/probability/plausibility + *que* + subordinate verb, the latter is in the subjunctive. 'Possibility' also includes meanings like 'the risk that', 'the danger that', 'it is inevitable that', etc.

Es posible que haya tormenta	There may be a storm
Era probable que sucediera así	It was probable that it would happen that way
Es previsible que para el año 2500 tengamos ordenadores superinteligentes que les darán ciento y raya a sus inventores humanos	It's foreseeable that by the year 2500 we will have superintelligent computers that leave their human inventors standing
Puede ser que este auge se prolongue y enriquezca con escritores más originales y propios (M. Vargas Llosa, Peru)	This boom may last and be enriched by more original and more native authors
Corrías el riesgo de que te vieran/viesen	You were running the risk of them seeing you

Note
Pueda que is a frequent Latin-American alternative for *puede que/puede ser que* 'maybe'/'it may be that': *Pueda que algo te den y te mejores* (M. Puig, Argentina, dialogue) 'Maybe they'll give you something and you'll get better'.

16.3.2 Subjunctive after words meaning 'perhaps', 'possibly', 'probably'

There are several commonly used words meaning 'perhaps': *acaso, tal vez, quizá(s)*[3], *a lo mejor, igual, lo mismo, posiblemente*.

(a) *Tal vez* (written *talvez* in Latin America) and *quizá(s)* mean the same. When the event referred to is happening in the present or happened in the past, use of the subjunctive is optional[4]:

*Tal vez **fuese** una discusión auténtica. Tal vez **representaban** una comedia en mi honor* (interview, Madrid press; both moods used)	Maybe it was a real argument. Maybe they were putting on an act for my benefit
Tal vez debió irse (*El País*, Spain)	Perhaps he should have gone (i.e. 'resigned')
Quizá ni siquiera entabláramos conversación (J. Marías, Spain; *entablamos* possible)	Perhaps we didn't even start up a conversation
Quizá era pena lo que se traslucía en la sonrisa de mi padre (idem., *fuera/fuese* possible)	Perhaps it was sorrow that came through in my father's smile

If the event is still in the future, only the future indicative or (much more commonly) the present subjunctive may be used, **not** the present indicative:

*Quizá/Tal vez **venga** mañana* (not **viene mañana*)	Perhaps she'll come tomorrow
Quizá éste sea el destino auténtico de la humanidad (E. Mendoza, Spain)	Perhaps this is humanity's true fate
Quizá España podrá desempeñar un papel particularmente activo en el restablecimiento de la paz en Europa Central (*El País*, Spain; *pueda* is possible, but expresses more uncertainty)	Perhaps Spain will be able to play a particularly active part in reestablishing peace in Central Europe

If the event *was* still in the future, only the imperfect subjunctive or the conditional can be used:

*Quizá/Tal vez **vinieran/viniesen/vendrían** al día siguiente* (not **venían*)	Perhaps they would come the following day

The subjunctive can only be used if *quizá(s)* or *tal vez* precede the verb they modify: one can only say *Era, tal vez, un efecto de esta política* . . . 'It was, perhaps, an effect of this policy . . .'.

(b) *Acaso*. When it means 'perhaps' without ironic overtones, *acaso* takes the subjunctive: *Acaso **sea** verdad que* . . . 'Perhaps it is true that . . .', *una generación que acaso no **volviera** a ser feliz fuera de sus retratos* (G. García Márquez, Colombia) 'a generation that would perhaps never again be happy outside its portraits'. This use of *acaso* to mean 'perhaps' is rather literary.

Acaso is, however, frequently followed by the indicative in all styles as a way adding a sarcastic note to questions or to make a rhetorical question. It then loses the element of doubt associated with the meaning 'perhaps' and suggests that the answer to the question is obvious:

---

[3] *Quizá* is more frequent than *quizás* and is preferred in written Spanish in memory of the original spoken Latin form *quis sapit*, which did not end in *s*.

[4] Use of the indicative is ever more frequent, but it may still sound incorrect to some older speakers.

¿Acaso has visto alguna vez que no llueva en verano? (implying 'of course you haven't')	Have *you* ever seen that it didn't rain in Summer?
¿Acaso todos los paganos no odian a los huambisas? (M. Vargas Llosa, Peru, dialogue)	Don't all the Indians (lit. 'pagans') hate the Huambisa tribe?

(c) *A lo mejor* does not take the subjunctive.[5] It is heard everywhere on both continents, but it is confined to spoken language or informal styles:

Ni siquiera la nombró. A lo mejor se ha olvidado de ella (M. Vargas Llosa, Peru, dialogue)	He didn't even mention her. Maybe he's forgotten her
A lo mejor encontramos con gente conocida (G. Cabrera Infante, Cuba, dialogue, Spain *nos encontramos con . . .*)	Maybe we'll meet some people we know

(d) In Spain *igual* and *lo mismo* are also used with the indicative in familiar speech with the meaning 'perhaps': *Si te viera todos los días, igual acabaría despreciándote* (J. A. Zunzunegui, dialogue, quoted B. Steel (1976), 134) 'If I saw you every day I might end up despising you', *Llama a la puerta. Lo mismo te da una propina* 'Knock on the door. Maybe he'll give you a tip'. These two constructions are considered sub-standard by some speakers and they are not heard in Latin America.

(e) *Posiblemente* 'possibly' and *probablemente* 'probably' obey the same rules as *tal vez* and *quizá(s)*: they can be followed by a subjunctive or by an indicative form when they refer to events in the present or past. If they refer to the future or to the future in the past they can be followed by the subjunctive or by a future or conditional tense, but not by any other indicative tense:

Posiblemente **quedara** *algo de alcohol etílico en nuestras venas humorísticas* (G. García Márquez, Colombia; *quedaba* or *quedase* possible)	Perhaps there was still some ethyl alcohol left in the veins of our humour
Posiblemente lo más criollo de nuestra cocina **radica** *en las sopas, los potajes y los guisos* (*Cuba Internacional*, Cuba; *radique* possible. *Guiso* more or less interchangeable with *guisado* in Spain)	Possibly the most authentic (lit. 'creole') aspect of our cuisine lies in the soups, vegetable potages and stews
Posiblemente lleguen/llegarán mañana (not *llegan*)	Possibly they'll arrive tomorrow
. . . alguna oscura sensación de incertidumbre, que probablemente será tan incierta como el resto (J. Cortázar, Argentina)	some obscure sensation of uncertainty which will probably be as uncertain as the rest
Probablemente el mérito sea de Ada (C. Rico-Godoy, Spain, dialogue)	You can probably thank Ada for that

As a direct verbal modifier *posiblemente* is not particularly colloquial: *ser posible que . . .* (always followed by subjunctive), *quizá* or *tal vez* are more common.

---

[5] R. Navas Ruiz (1986), 36, says that the subjunctive is 'infrequent' with *a lo mejor*, but he gives no examples. We have seen it with the subjunctive in the Colombian press but we doubt whether this is accepted usage.

16.4 'Depending'

Statements + *que* that mean 'to depend on . . .' require the subjunctive:

*De las mujeres depende que se **coma** en el mundo* (A. Mastretta, Mexico, dialogue)	It's women who ensure that people eat in this world (lit. 'that one eats in this world depends on women')
*Miguel contaba con que lo **llamaran/ llamasen** aquella noche*	Miguel was counting on them ringing him that night

16.5 Statements of 'influence' + *que*

16.5.1 General

This includes sentences in which the subject of the main clause influences or attempts to influence the outcome of the action in the subordinate clause. Such verbs typically include those that mean wanting, ordering, needing, causing, allowing, prohibiting, advising, persuading, encouraging, avoiding, and excluding.

When these verbs are used with *que* they always require the subjunctive. However, when the subjects of the main verb and the subordinate verbs refer to the same person, the infinitive is used: see 16.5.2a.

Some of these verbs can also optionally be used with an infinitive even when the subjects are different. This possibility is discussed in 16.5.2b.

The following are some common verbs that come under this category (the list is not exhaustive):

aconsejar que	to advise that
animar a que	to encourage to
causar que	to cause
conseguir/lograr que	to succeed in
contribuir a que	to contribute to
cuidar de que	to take care that
decir que	to tell someone to[6]
dificultar que	to hinder
esforzarse porque	to make an effort to
evitar/impedir que	to avoid
exigir que	to require that
hacer falta que	to be necessary that
hacer que[7]	to make
insistir/empeñarse en que	to insist on
mandar/ordenar que	to order that
necesitar que	to need to
obligar a que	to oblige to
oponerse a que	to be against
pedir que	to ask/request that
permitir que	to allow to
preferir que	to prefer that
prohibir/impedir que	to prohibit/prevent from
querer/desear que	to want

---

[6] Not **decir de*, which is not Spanish: cf. French *dire à quelqu'un **de** faire quelquechose* = *deci**r**le a alquien que **haga** algo* 'to tell someone to do something'.

[7] But *hacer que* 'to pretend' takes the indicative: *Hace que **está** enfermo* 'He pretends that he's ill'.

rogar que	to request (literary)
salvar de que	to rescue/save from
ser necesario que	to be necessary that
suplicar que	to implore to
vigilar que/asegurarse de que	to make sure that

But there are many alternative ways of expressing the ideas associated with these verbs and these also require the subjunctive when they are followed by *que*.

Examples:

Quiero que estudies más	I want you to study more
Se esforzaba porque los demás vivieran/viviesen en mejores condiciones (*esforzarse por* 'to make an effort to . . .')	He strove to ensure that the others lived in better conditions
Organicé que todas nos vistiéramos como ellas (A. Mastretta, Mexico, dialogue)	I arranged it so that all of us women should dress like them
Soy partidario de que lo publiquen	I'm in favour of them publishing it
Esto dio como resultado que no le hicieran/hiciesen caso	The upshot of this was that they ignored him/her
Cierta impaciencia generosa no ha consentido que yo aprendiera a leer (J.L. Borges, Argentina)	A certain generous impatience did not allow me to learn to read
El primer paso, le dijo, era lograr que ella se diera cuenta de su interés (G. García Márquez, Colombia)	The first thing to do, she said to him, was to get her to notice his interest
Nadie impidió que Hemingway escribiera y publicase sus libros (G. Cabrera Infante, Cuba)	Nobody prevented Hemingway from writing and publishing his books
Hay que evitar que ellos se enteren	We have to avoid them finding out

Notes

(i) A noun phrase like *la decisión de que* 'the decision that', *la orden de que* 'the order that', *el deseo de que* 'the wish that', etc. can replace the main verb: *La orden de que se apagaran/apagasen las luces fue el coronel quien la dio* 'It was the colonel who ordered the lights to be turned off', *el anhelo de que Dios exista* 'the longing for God to exist', *La idea era que las chicas ayudasen/ayudaran a los chicos* 'The idea was that the girls should help the boys', *La petición de que se la indultara/indultase no llegó a tiempo*, 'The petition for her reprieve didn't arrive in time'.

(ii) Some verbs may or may not imply 'influence', according to their meaning. They take the subjunctive only when an order or wish is implied: *Decidió que lo firmaran/firmasen* 'He decided that they should sign it', *Decidió que lo habían firmado* 'He decided (i.e. 'came to the conclusion') that they had signed it', *Dijo que se terminara/terminase* 'He said (i.e. 'ordered') that it should be finished', *Dijo que se había terminado* 'He said (i.e. 'announced') that it was finished'. Likewise *establecer que* 'to stipulate that' (subjunctive)/'to establish the truth that' (indicative), *pretender que* 'to try to'/'to aim at'/'to wish that' (subjunctive)/'to claim that' (indicative), *escribir* 'to write that' (indicative) 'to write instructing that' (subjunctive).

(iii) Statements of 'hope' are discussed at 16.11.3.

16.5.2 Use of the infinitive with verbs of 'influence'

Some of the verbs listed under 16.5.1 may appear with an infinitive construction in the following circumstances:

(a) If the subject of the main clause and the subject of the subordinate clause are co-referential, i.e. they refer to the same person or thing. (This rule is discussed in more detail at 18.2.):

Quiero hacerlo but *Quiero que **tú** lo hagas*	I want to do it/I want you to do it
No se deja pensar en ella	He doesn't let himself think of her
Determinaron mandarle/lo a un internado	They decided to send him to a boarding-school
Ya has logrado enfadarme	Now you've managed to make me angry

(b) With certain verbs, even when they are not co-referential. These are verbs that can be constructed with an indirect object, as in *Te ayudaré a **conseguir**/a que **consigas** lo que quieres* 'I'll help you to get what you want'.

The most common of these verbs are:

aconsejar a	to advise to (see note (iv))	*mandar/ordenar*	to order
		obligar a	to oblige
animar a	to encourage	*permitir*	to permit (but not *consentir*,
ayudar a	to help		which always takes *que*)
dejar	to allow		
impedir	to prevent	*persuadir a*	to persuade
incitar a	to spur on/incite	*prohibir*	to prohibit
inducir a	to induce/persuade	*proponer*	to propose
invitar a	to invite	*recomendar*	to recommend (see note (iv))

Examples:

*Incitó/Indujo/Animó/Persuadió a los rebeldes a **protestar**/a que **protestaran/protestasen***	He incited/persuaded/encouraged the rebels to protest
Te dejo que me invites/Te dejo invitarme	I'll let you pay for me
Te prohíbo que cantes/Te prohíbo cantar	I forbid you to sing
Le obligan a que llegue pronto/Le obligan a llegar pronto	They make him come early
Me mandan a que recoja el correo/Me mandan a recoger el correo	They send me to collect the post
Había ordenado retirarse a todas sus sirvientas (A. Gala, Spain; or *a todas sus sirvientas que se retirasen/retiraran*)	She had ordered all her ladies-in-waiting to withdraw
Permitió a su hija que bailara/bailase/ Permitió a su hija bailar	He allowed his daughter to dance
Nos propuso trabajar/que trabajásemos/ trabajáramos con él	He proposed that we should work with him

Notes
(i) Some of these verbs can appear without an object in their main clause; English requires an object like 'one': *un delgado vestido que impedía llevar nada bajo él/ . . . que se llevara/llevase nada debajo de él* 'a thin dress that prevented **one** from wearing anything underneath it', *Esto permite pensar que . . .* 'This allows **one** *to think that . . .*'.
(ii) When more than two object pronouns are involved, the subjunctive is, however, preferred: *Te dejo que me lo compres* 'I'll let you buy it for me' is better than ?*Te dejo comprármelo*.
(iii) When the object is inanimate, the subjunctive is obligatory: *El embalse permite que las aguas del río alcancen unos niveles adecuados* (not **permite a las aguas alcanzar . . .*) 'The dam allows the water of the river to reach suitable (or 'adequate') levels'.
(iv) Some verbs seem to be in a transitional state. Two of these are *aconsejar* 'to advise' (especially in the construction *aconsejar que no* 'to advise not to') and *recomendar* 'to recommend'. The conservative construction is with the subjunctive and this is safer for foreigners, but an infinitive construction is frequently heard colloquially: *Te recomiendo que lo hagas/Te recomiendo hacerlo* 'I recommend you to do it', *Te aconsejo que no lo hagas/Te aconsejo no hacerlo* 'I advise you not to do it', but, rather abitrarily, *El médico le aconsejó que no hiciera caso* (not *no hacer caso) 'The doctor advised him not to pay any attention'.

(v) *Pedir* appears with the infinitive when the subjects are identical: *Pidió hablar con el director* 'He asked to speak to the director', *Pidió verme a las seis* 'He asked to see me at six o'clock'. But it requires the subjunctive when the subjects are different, as do other verbs of requesting: *Pidió/Suplicó/Rogó que contestaran/contestasen cuanto antes* 'He asked/implored/requested them to answer as soon as possible'.

16.6 Emotional reactions and value judgements

16.6.1 Emotional reaction or value judgment + *que* + subjunctive

The subjunctive is used in sentences of the pattern 'Emotional reaction' + *que* + subordinate verb. 'Emotional reaction' covers a vast range of possibilities including regret, pleasure, blame, displeasure, surprise, statements of sufficiency and insufficiency, importance, etc. It also includes value judgements like 'it's logical that . . .', 'it's natural that . . .', 'it's enough that . . .'.

The non-pronominal (i.e. 'non-reflexive') verbs and non-verbal expressions in List A are followed only by *que*: *Le enfada que el perro no deje de ladrar* 'It annoys him that the dog won't stop barking'. These verbs do not appear – at least in educated usage – in the pronominal form with *de que*: one says *le irrita que* + subjunctive, not ?*se irrita de que* . . .. If used pronominally *porque* follows: *se irritaba porque* . . . + indicative 'he got irritated because . . .'. The list is not exhaustive.

The verbs in List B (also not exhaustive) have pronominal counterparts followed by *de que*. In these cases one can either say *le aburre que* + subjunctive 'it bores him that . . .' or *se aburre de que* + subjunctive 'he is bored by the fact that . . .'. The expressions in the list not based on verbs are also followed by *de que* + subjunctive.

It is important in Spanish to differentiate between emotional reactions and value judgements on the one hand and statements of fact like *es verdad que* 'it's true that', *es obvio/evidente que* 'it's obvious that', *es indiscutible que* 'it is beyond dispute that'. The latter require the indicative, even though the distinction may sometimes appear arbitrary to an English speaker. For statements like 'it is **not** true that', see 16.7.1.

List A: Emotional reactions and value judgements followed by *que* (and not by *de que*)

enfadarle/enojarle a alguien que	to anger someone that
fastidiarle a alguien que	to bother someone that
irritarle a alguien que	to irritate someone that
deprimirle a alguien que	to depress someone that
apenarle a alguien que	to pain someone that
importarle a alguien que	to matter to someone that
darle lástima a alguien que	to fill someone with pity that
extrañarle a alguien que	to puzzle someone that
satisfacerle a alguien que	to satisfy someone that
parecerle bien/mal a alguien que	to seem good/bad to someone that
gustarle a alguien que	to like: *me gusta que* 'I like the fact that'
encantarle a alguien que	to enchant someone that
aguantar que/tolerar que	to put up with
perdonar que	to excuse the fact that
preferir que	to prefer that
aceptar que	to accept that

merecer que	to deserve that
basta que/falta que	it's enough that/lacking that
es mejor que/peor/igual que	it's better/worse/the same that
es significativo que	it's significant that
es terrible/lógico/natural/curioso que	it's terrible/logical/natural/curious that
es una pena/tragedia/ventaja que	it's a shame/tragedy/an advantage that
está bien/mal que	it's good/bad that
¡qué pena/lástima que!	what a pity that!
ser una suerte que	to be a stroke of luck that
vale más que	it would be better that

List B: Emotional reactions followed by *de que*

The verbs in this list may appear either with *que* and a direct object (as in List A) or as pronominal verbs followed by *de que* (see also 16.6.2 for further remarks on these verbs):

aburrirle a alguien que/aburrirse de que	to bore someone that/to be bored by the fact that
emocionarle a alguien que/emocionarse de que	to excite someone that/to get excited by the fact that
alegrarle a alguien que/alegrarse de que	to cheer someone that/to be happy that
entusiasmarle a alguien que/entusiasmarse de que	to make someone enthusiastic that/to be enthusiastic that
asustarle a alguien que/asustarse de que	to frighten someone that/to be frightened that
horrorizarle a alguien que/horrorizarse de que	to horrify someone that/to be horrified that
sorprenderle a alguien que/sorprenderse de que	to surprise someone that/to be surprised that
avergonzarle a alguien que/avergonzarse de que	to shame someone that/to be ashamed that
indignarle a alguien que/indignarse de que	to make someone indignant that/to be indignant that
entristecerle a alguien que/entristecerse de que	to sadden someone that/to be saddened that
dolerle a alguien que/dolerse de que	to hurt someone that/to be hurt that
es el culpable de que	he is guilty of the fact that
es hora de que/ha llegado el momento de que	it's time that/the time has arrived that

Further examples of both types of construction:

Me molesta que te quejes tanto	It annoys me that you complain so much
Solo/Sólo faltaba que tú dijeras/dijeses eso	All it needed was for you to say that
Es lógico que lo niegue	It's logical for him to deny it
Es una vergüenza que dejen que pasen estas cosas	It's a disgrace that they allow these things to happen
Basta que les des la mitad ahora	It's enough for you to give them half now
Es curioso que todos los asamblearios se fíen más de lo que escuchan por los auriculares (J. Marías, Spain)	It's curious that all conference members have more confidence in what they hear over their headphones
Fue una casualidad que yo me encontrara/encontrase allí	It was pure chance that I was there
¡Qué rabia que no nos suban el sueldo!	What a nuisance that they won't raise our salary!
Se aburre de que Gene Kelly baile siempre con Cyd Charisse (G. Cabrera Infante, Cuba, dialogue)	He gets bored with the fact that Gene Kelly always dances with Cyd Charisse

El catedrático de portugués se sorprendió mucho de que yo me sorprendiera cuando me contó que este año sólo tenía un estudiante (M. Vargas Llosa, Peru)

The professor of Portuguese was very surprised that I was surprised when he told me that he only had one student this year

Estoy hasta el moño de que tengamos que ser siempre nosotras las que debamos recoger la mesa (C. Rico-Godoy, Spain)

I'm sick to death with the fact that it's always us women who have to clear the table

Andrés era el culpable de que me pasaran todas esas cosas (A. Mastretta, Mexico, dialogue)

It was Andrés's fault that all these things were happening to me

Notes

(i) *Menos mal que* 'thank heavens that' takes the indicative: *Menos mal que no se ha roto* 'Thank heavens it's not broken'. The form *mejor . . .* 'it would be best that' is also followed by the indicative. This abbreviation of *sería mejor que* is very common in Latin America, but it is also heard in colloquial language in Spain: *Mejor lo dejamos para más tarde* 'Better that we leave it for later'. Compare *Sería mejor que lo dejáramos/dejásemos para más tarde* 'It would be better to leave it until later'.

(ii) In spontaneous language in Latin America a value judgement about a past or habitual event may be expressed by the indicative. This construction is sometimes seen in writing in Latin America, especially in Argentina: *El innegable genio de Joyce era puramente verbal; lástima que lo gastó en la novela* (J.L. Borges, Argentina) 'Joyce's undeniable genius was purely verbal; a pity that he used it on the novel', *Era curioso que Morelli abrazaba con entusiasmo las últimas hipótesis de trabajo de la ciencia física* (J. Cortázar, Argentina) 'It was curious that Morelli enthusiastically embraced the latest working hypotheses of physical science', *Es curioso que uno no puede estar sin encariñarse con algo* (M. Puig, Argentina, dialogue) It's strange that one can't manage (lit. 'can't be') without getting fond of something', *Me da lástima que terminó* (idem, dialogue) 'I'm sorry it's ended'.

(iii) English speakers should beware of over-using *si* 'if' in sentences involving a value judgement: *Sería maravilloso que/si no hubiera/hubiese hambre en el mundo* 'It would be marvellous if there were no hunger in the world'.

(iv) The subjunctive is still required when the main clause is deleted: *. . . pero que él diga eso . . .* (some phrase like *es increíble que . . .* having been deleted from the sentence) '. . .that he should say that . . .'/'. . .that he should have the nerve to say that . . .'.

16.6.2 Further remarks on emotional reactions followed by *de que*

As was stated in 16.6.1, the subjunctive is used with these expressions and foreigners should respect this rule. But the indicative mood is sometimes heard in popular speech when the verb is in the present or past. This tendency should not be imitated by foreign students:

Me alegré de que (pensaban)/pensaran/ pensasen hacerlo

I was glad that they intended to do it

Se indignaba de que sus suegros (creían)/creyeran/creyesen en la pena de muerte

He/she was outraged that his/her in-laws believed in the death penalty

Se horrorizaba de que la (trataban)/trataran/ tratasen así

He was shocked at their treating her this way

Note

Quejarse de que 'to complain that . . .' seems to foreign speakers to be an emotional reaction, but it is in fact treated as a verb of statement and is always followed by the indicative. *Lamentar* 'to regret the fact that' . . . takes the subjunctive. *Lamentarse de que* 'to lament the fact that . . .' takes the subjunctive when it expresses an emotional reaction and the indicative when it merely makes a statement. *Protestar de que* 'to protest that . . .' takes the indicative: *Se queja de que Berta la **hace** quedarse a dormir la siesta* (M. Puig, Argentina, dialogue) 'She complains about Berta making her stay in to sleep in the afternoon', *Protestaba de que/Se lamentaba de que el gobierno **había** subido los impuestos* 'He was protesting at/lamenting the fact that the Government had raised taxes', *Lamento que ustedes no me **hayan** comprendido* 'I regret that you did not understand me'.

16.6.3 *Lo* + emotional reactions

If an emotional reaction is expressed by a phrase involving the 'neuter article' *lo* + *que* + verb + *ser*, or *lo* + adjective + *ser que* . . ., e.g. *lo que me irrita es que* . . . 'what irritates me is that . . .', *lo trágico fue que* . . . 'the tragic thing was that . . .', the grammar of the subjunctive is slightly different. The subjunctive is obligatory if the verb in the main clause points to an event still in the future:

*Lo peor será que no **venga** nadie*	The worst thing will be if no one comes
*Lo malo sería que no **terminaran**/ **terminasen** el trabajo a tiempo*	The problem would be if they didn't finish the work on time
*Lo más provocante de la ley es que **provoque** una reacción violenta del gobierno cubano* (La Jornada, Mexico)	The most provocative thing about the law is that it may produce a violent reaction from the Cuban government

However, if the main verb is timeless, habitual or in the past, the verb is usually in the indicative, although the subjunctive is also possible:

*Lo que me indigna es que la sociedad todavía **condena** los amores o amoríos entre una señora madura y un jovencito* (C. Rico-Godoy, Spain)	What makes me mad is that society still condemns romances or love affairs between a mature woman and a young man
*Lo que más me sorprendió . . . fue que . . . se **habían** detenido y vuelto* (J. Marías, Spain)	What surprised me most was that they had stopped and turned round

Note
In some cases use of the subjunctive depends on the meaning: *Lo increíble era que Pedro no lo **sabía*** 'The incredible thing was that Pedro didn't know about it', *Lo increíble era que Pedro no lo **supiera**/**supiese***, same translation. In this case there is a slight difference between moods. The indicative assumes that Pedro did not know whereas the subjunctive leaves open the question whether he knew or not. The choice depends on whether the action denoted by the subordinate verb is a reality to the speaker. Compare: *Lo peor es que mi padre nunca **dice** nada* 'The worst thing is that my father never says anything' and a possible reply to this: *Sí, lo peor es que no **diga** nada* 'Yes, the worst thing is that he doesn't say anything' (i.e. *if* that is the case).

In the second example the speaker does not claim knowledge of the facts described by the first speaker. This subtle distinction, based on the nature of the speaker's background knowledge, will be found to operate in many examples of subjunctive use.

16.7 Subjunctive after denials

16.7.1 Subjunctive after firm denials

In sentences of the pattern 'denial' + *que* + subordinate verb, the subordinate verb is usually in the subjunctive. However, statements like 'I don't think that

. . .', 'I don't believe that . . .' may or may not be denials, according to how certain the speaker's knowledge is; see the next section for discussion.

*Niego que **sea** así*	I deny that it's like that
Mayta negó que hubiera intervenido en el rapto (M. Vargas Llosa, Peru, dialogue; or *hubiese*)	Mayta denied he was involved in the kidnapping
Esto no significa que haya que esperar un cambio radical de actitud (J. Cortázar, Argentina)	This doesn't mean that one must expect a radical change of attitude
Yo no he dicho que seas una histérica (C. Rico-Godoy, Spain, dialogue)	I never said you were a hysteric
No ocurre/sucede que haya eclipse todos los días	It doesn't happen that there's an eclipse every day
No se trata de que tengas que quedarte todos los días hasta las nueve de la noche	It's not a question of your having to stay till nine p.m. every day

Notes

(i) The indicative is occasionally found after *negar que* and verbs of similar meaning, although this construction is unusual, especially in Spain: *Niego que hubo bronca* (*Proceso*, Mexico) 'I deny there was a row', *¿También va Vd a negar que los ingleses se lavan?* (J. Camba, Spain; the indicative is appropriate here because a denial would not be reasonable) 'Are you also going to deny that the English wash?', . . . *pero negaban tozudamente que transportaban marihuana en esta ocasión* (*Granma*, Cuba) 'but they stubbornly denied that they were carrying marihuana on this occasion', *Rechaza que Dios existe*[8] (usually *exista*) 'He denies that God exists'.

(ii) Note that a negative question does not amount to a denial, so the indicative is used: *¿No es verdad que **ha** dicho eso?* 'Isn't it true that he said that?', *¿No sientes que el corazón se te ensancha al ver esto?* (J. Ibargüengoitia, Mexico, dialogue) 'Don't you feel your heart getting bigger when you see this?'.

(iii) *No ser que* is a denial and is normally followed by the subjunctive, except in questions: *No es que yo **diga** que es mentira* 'It's not that I'm saying that it's a lie', *No es que se dijeran grandes cosas* (J. Marías, Spain) 'It isn't that important (lit. 'great') things were said', *No es que fueran por lo tanto mejores escultores que los egipcios de aquel período* (E. Sábato, Argentina, interview) 'It isn't that they were, as a result, better sculptors than the Egyptians of that period', *¿No será que no quiere hacerlo?* 'Isn't it the case that he doesn't want to do it?', *¿No sería que no quedaban más?* 'Wouldn't it be that there were none left?'.

Exceptionally *no ser que* is followed by the indicative, in which case the denial is more confident and assertive: *No era que tomaba posesión del mundo* (M. de Unamuno, Spain) 'It wasn't that he was taking possession of the world'.

16.7.2 Subjunctive after negated verbs of knowing, perceiving, stating and communicating

After an affirmative statement of knowledge, perception, belief or communication, e.g. *sé que . . ., veo que . . ., creo que . . ., digo que . . ., afirmo que . . .* 'I claim that . . .', *significa que . . .* 'it means that . . .', *reconozco que . . .* 'I recognise that . . .', the subordinate verb is in the indicative (for occasional exceptions with verbs like *creer, sospechar*, see 16.11.1). This generalization also applies to statements of fact such as *es verdad/cierto/evidente/indudable/seguro que . . .*.

If these expressions appear in the negative, they may amount to a firm denial, in which case the verb in the subordinate clause will be in the subjunctive, as specified at 16.7.1:

---

[8] Example from Navas Ruiz (1986), 69.

*Digo que **es** así/No digo que **sea** así*	I say that it is so/I don't say that it is so
Creo que él lo conoce/No creo que él lo conozca	I think he knows him/I don't think he knows him
Recuerdo que tu madre era esbelta/No recuerdo que tu madre fuera/fuese esbelta	I remember your mother was slim/I don't remember your mother being slim
Claro que aparte de fumar y beber no veía que se pudiera hacer otra cosa (M. Vargas Llosa, Peru, or *pudiese*)	Obviously, apart from smoking and drinking he didn't see that there was anything else to do

However the subjunctive is sometimes optional after such negations, depending on the degree of uncertainty involved. In some cases the subjunctive causes a slight change of meaning:

Yo sabía que él estaba ahí/Yo no sabía que él estaba ahí (concedes that he was there)	I knew he was there/I didn't know he was there
Yo no sabía que él estuviera/estuviese ahí (suggests that the speaker is still not convinced the person was there)	I didn't know he was there

Notes

(i) Choice of the subjunctive in these sentences depends essentially on the speaker's background knowledge. If one knows for a fact that X is a thief, one says *No confesaba que **había** robado el dinero* 'He didn't confess to stealing the money'. If X may be innocent one says *No confesaba que **hubiese/hubiera** robado el dinero*.

For this reason, statements of ascertainable fact, e.g. *Yo no sabía que la puerta **estaba** abierta* 'I didn't know the door was open' are more likely to take the indicative, and matters of opinion, e.g. *No creo que **sea** muy útil* 'I don't think it's very useful', are almost certain to take the subjunctive.

(ii) Compare the different translations of *decir* in the following examples: *Ha dicho que **venía*** 'She said he/she was coming', *No he dicho que **venía*** 'I didn't say I/she/he was coming', *No he dicho que **viniera/viniese*** 'I didn't tell him/her/you to come', *El chofer dijo que él se ganaba la vida como podía, y al que no le gustara que bajase y tomase un taxi para él solito* (C. Fuentes, Mexico, *chofer* = *chófer* in Spain) 'The taxi driver said he earned his living as well as he could and anybody who didn't like it could get out and get a taxi for himself'.

(iii) If the verb in the main clause is in the imperative form, the verb in the subordinate clause remains in the indicative: *No digas que **es** verdad* 'Don't say it's true', *No creas que esto **es** lo único que hacemos* (A. Mastretta, Mexico, dialogue) 'Don't think that this is the only thing we do', *El tal Pepe me tenía a metro y medio, pero no crean ustedes que me **vio*** (C. Rico-Godoy, Spain, dialogue) 'This Pepe was standing a metre and a half from me, but don't get the idea that he saw me'.

16.8 Statements of doubt

Dudar que takes the subjunctive, but used in the negative it is followed by an indicative when it really means 'to be sure that':

Dudo que sea verdad	I doubt whether it's true
No dudo que sea verdad lo que dices	I don't doubt whether what you say is true (tentative remark)

but

*No dudo que **es** verdad lo que dices*	I don't doubt (i.e. 'I'm convinced') that what you say is true
No dudo que vendrá/venga	I don't doubt he'll come
Dudo que yo pueda venir mañana/Dudo poder venir mañana (infinitive possible since the verbs are in the same person)	I doubt I can come tomorrow

No hay duda que ella puede ser discutida (M. Vargas Llosa, Peru; Spain *No hay duda de que . . .*)	There is no doubt that it can be debated

16.9 Statements of fear

Temer/tener miedo de que 'to fear' and other statements of similar meaning may take the subjunctive or a future indicative tense (including future time expressed by *ir a* 'to be going to . . .') or, if they refer to the past, a past subjunctive or an indicative future in the past. For *temerse que* see note (ii):

Temo que le moleste/Temo que le va a molestar/molestará/le vaya a molestar	I'm afraid it may upset him
Temíamos que le molestara/molestase/ Temíamos que le iba a molestar/ molestaría/Temíamos que le fuera a molestar	We were afraid it would upset him
Yo tenía miedo de que te hubieras ido (G. Cabrera Infante, dialogue, Cuba)	I was scared that you'd gone
. . . para no ver el mar por la escotilla porque nos da miedo de que entre (E. Poniatowska, Mexico)	so as not to see the sea through the hatchway, because we're afraid it'll come in

The subjunctive is always used if the main verb is negated:

*No temía que me **fuera** a atacar*	I wasn't afraid he/she/it was going to attack me

Notes
(i) Redundant *no* (see 23.2.4) instead of *que* after *temer(se)* changes the meaning. The subjunctive is obligatory. Compare *Temo que no te va a gustar* 'I'm afraid you're not going to like it' and redundant *no* in *Temo no te vaya a gustar demasiado* 'I'm afraid in case/lest you're going to like it too much', *Temo no te vayas a enfadar* 'I'm afraid in case/lest you get cross'.
(ii) *Temerse que* usually means little more than 'I'm sorry to say that . . .' and it therefore takes the indicative: *Me temo que no he sido muy delicado* 'I fear I haven't been very discreet', *De eso me temo que no **puedo** hablarte* (L. Sepúlveda, Chile, dialogue) 'I'm afraid I can't talk to you about that'.
(iii) *Temer que* may also occasionally be found with the indicative when it refers to timeless or habitual actions: *Temo que la verdadera frontera la trae cada uno dentro* (C. Fuentes, Mexico, dialogue) 'I fear that each one of us carries the real frontier inside ourselves'.

16.10 Subjunctive after 'the fact that . . .' and after other noun phrases

16.10.1 'The fact that . . .'
There are three common ways of translating 'the fact that': *el hecho de que, el que*, and *que*; the latter two items have various other meanings, for which see the Index.
(a) With all of these the subjunctive is used whenever any kind of value judgement or emotional reaction is involved:

*(El) que no **diga** nada no debería afectar tu decisión*	The fact that he says nothing shouldn't affect your decision

*No hay duda de que el hecho de que
me **hayan** dado el Nobel va a dar
mayor resonancia a todo lo que diga y haga
(G. García Márquez, Colombia)*

There is no doubt that the fact that
they've given me the Nobel prize will
give more weight to everything I say and
do

*Lo que me hace insoportable tu vanidad es
el hecho de que **hiera** la mía (Cartoon by
J. Ballesta in Cambio16, Spain)*

What makes your vanity unbearable is
the fact that it wounds mine

*El que en semanas se **haya** conseguido
cabrear[9] a la vez a todos . . . es todo
un síntoma que se debería convertir en
preocupación (Cambio16, Spain)*

The fact that it has been possible to
annoy everybody simultaneously in a
matter of weeks is a symptom which
should become a matter of concern

(b) The indicative is required when the main verb is a verb of knowing,
perceiving, or a statement of a fact. When *el hecho de que* is preceded by a
preposition it almost always states a certain fact and takes the indicative:

*Se ha dado cuenta del hecho de que **tiene** que
trabajar para vivir*

He/she has realized he has to work in
order to live

*No lo hace por el hecho de que no le **gusta***

She doesn't do it because she doesn't
like it

*Le disgustaría que usted no viniera sólo por
el hecho de que **viene** él*

She would be upset if you didn't come
only because he was coming

*Que a las autoridades francesas les **gusta**
tratar amistosamente con terroristas es algo
demostrado (Cambio16, Spain)*

The fact that French authorities like to
have friendly dealings with terrorists is
demonstrably true

*Que el poder **tiende** al abuso . . . no debe
escandalizar a nadie (El País)*

That power tends to abuse is a fact that
should scandalize no one

(c) In some cases the subjunctive and indicative appear to be
interchangeable. We can detect no difference of meaning between the
following alternatives, but foreigners will not go wrong if they apply the
rules set out in (**a**) and (**b**):

*Le molesta el hecho de que no **venga/viene** a
verle*

The fact that she doesn't come to see
him annoys him

*No le daba importancia al hecho de que él no
le **hacía/hiciera/hiciese** caso*

She didn't mind the fact that he paid her
no attention

*No quiero que el hecho de que te
conozco/conozca sea un obstáculo*

I don't want the fact that I know you to
be an obstacle

*El hecho de que no me **veía/viera/viese** me
hacía sentirme seguro*

The fact that she couldn't see me made
me feel safe

Note
El que 'the fact that' must be differentiated from *el que* 'the person that' (sometimes
only context makes the sense clear):

El que haya dicho eso no sabe lo que dice

The person who/Whoever said that
doesn't know what he/she's talking about

El que haya dicho eso no tiene importancia

The fact that he/she said that has no
importance

16.10.2 Subjunctive after other noun phrases used as subordinators

When a noun phrase replaces a verb phrase it is normally connected to a
following subordinate clause by *de que*: compare *Esperamos **que** llueva* 'We

---

[9] *Cabrear* 'to annoy' is considered vulgar by some speakers. *Enfadar* (Lat. Am. *enojar*) is
more respectable.

hope it will rain' and *la esperanza **de que** llueva* 'the hope that it will rain', and see 33.4.2 for more detailed discussion of the use of *de que* after nouns.

In general the mood of the subordinate verb after such noun phrases is governed by the rules that would affect verb phrases of the same meaning, i.e. *la posibilidad de que . . .* 'the possibility that . . .' requires the subjunctive because *es posible que . . .* 'it's possible that . . .' does.

However, there is a series of miscellaneous noun phrases after which choice between the subjunctive and indicative is determined by meaning. Two factors may combine or operate independently to invoke the subjunctive: **(a)** the type of verb in the main clause, **(b)** the reality or non-reality of the event expressed by the subordinate clause.

(a) In the following examples the verb in the main clause is of a type (emotional reaction, possibility, etc.) that would itself require the subjunctive:

*Le contrarió la casualidad de que **encontrase/encontrara** ahí a su primo*	He was annoyed by happening to find his cousin there
*Podría dar la casualidad de que **hubiera/hubiese** huelga*	It could happen that there'll be a strike
*No podía soportar la idea de que no le **dieran/diesen** el puesto*	He couldn't stand the idea of not getting the job

(b) In the following sentences the indicative is used because the subordinate verb indicates an established fact or reality, even though in some cases the person affected may not yet know the truth of the situation:

*Siempre daba la casualidad de que no **llegaban** a tiempo*	It always happened that they never arrived on time (habitual fact)
*Se tenían que enfrentar con el problema de que no **tenían** dinero*	They had to face up to the problem of not having any money (fact)
*Consiguió que aceptara la idea de que no le **darían** el puesto*	She managed to get him to accept the idea that they wouldn't give him/her the job (i.e. accepting a fact)
*Tengo la convicción de que no **hace** nada*	I'm convinced she/he doesn't do anything (knowledge)
*Se encontró con la sorpresa de que **estaba** de mal humor*	He was surprised to find that she was in a bad mood (factual)
*Le atormentaba la obsesión de que su mujer le **engañaba***	He was tormented by the obsession that his wife was being unfaithful to him (factual as far as he knows)

(c) There remains a murky area in which the choice between subjunctive and indicative is either more or less optional or is dictated by some principle so obscure that it defies our ingenuity to explain it. The following examples must speak for themselves:

*Tuve la suerte de que no me **viera/vio***	I was lucky in that he didn't see me (on that occasion; factual, but subjunctive more usual)

but

*Tenía la suerte de que no me **veía***	I was lucky in that he didn't see me (on one or several occasions. Indicative only)

*Tenía siempre la preocupación de que le **iba/fuera** a pasar algo*	He always worried that something might happen to him
*Vivía con la pesadilla de que **perdería** su dinero*	He lived with the nightmare of losing his money (indicative only)
*Le animaba la ilusión de que lo **conseguiría***	He was encouraged by the dream of getting it (same subject for both verbs)
*Le animaba la ilusión de que ella lo **conseguiría/consiguiera/consiguiese***	He was encouraged by the dream that she would get it (different subjects)

16.11 Subjunctive after special verbs

16.11.1 Subjunctive after *creer, parecer, suponer* and *sospechar*

We said at 16.2.5b and 16.7.2 that expressions of belief + *que* take the indicative – *Creo que Dios existe* 'I believe that God exists' – unless they are negated: *No creo que Dios **exista*** 'I don't believe God exists'.

However, the subjunctive occasionally appears after these verbs even when they are not negated. The meaning is then more hypothetical or hesitant, but the difference can barely be translated into English:

*A veces parece que **estás/estés** soñando*	Sometimes it seems you're dreaming
*Sospecho que **es/sea** mentira*	I suspect it's a lie
*como si la Historia fuera una especie de saltamontes; y parece que lo **sea** pero en otro sentido* (A. Sastre, Spain, dialogue)	as if History were a sort of grasshopper; and it seems that it is but in a different sense
*¿Usted cree que esto **ayude**?* (Manuel Puig, Argentina, dialogue; incredulous tone)	Do you really think that this helps?
*¿Usted cree que yo **quiera** lastimar a esta niña preciosa?* (A. Mastretta, Mexico, dialogue)	Do you really think I want to hurt this lovely girl?

The last two examples are Latin American. In Spain the indicative (*ayuda, quiero*) is used in this kind of question.

16.11.2 Subjunctive after *comprender/entender que, explicar que*

All of these verbs take the subjunctive when they are negated, e.g.

*No entiendo que ahora me **pregunten** sobre la ponencia* (interview in *El País*, Spain)	I don't understand why people are asking me now about the written statement/paper

Comprender takes the subjunctive when it means 'to sympathize with':

*Comprendo que no **quieras** pedir dinero prestado*	I understand your not wanting to borrow money
*Yo comprendo que los concejales **defendieran** sus posiciones dentro del partido* (Santiago Carrillo in *Cambio16*, Spain; or *defendiesen*)	I understand the councillors defending their positions inside the party

Explicar usually takes the subjunctive except when it really means 'to state' or 'to say':

*Esto explica que las mutaciones de la literatura **estén** estrechamente ligadas a las innovaciones técnicas*	This explains how changes in literature are intimately linked to technical innovations

but

*Manuel explicó que **había** estado enfermo*	Manuel explained that he had been ill

16.11.3 Subjunctive after *esperar que*

Esperar 'to hope' may be followed by the subjunctive, by the future indicative, by the indicative of *ir a*, or by the conditional. The subjunctive is the commoner form:

*Espero que le **convenzas/convencerás***	I hope you convince him
*la esperanza de que todo **acabe/acabará/va a acabar** bien*	the hope that everything will end well
. . . con la esperanza de que ella haría lo mismo (C. Fuentes, Mexico)	in the hope that she'd do the same
Por un momento la invadió la esperanza de que su marido no habitara ya el reino de los vivos (S. Pitol, Mexico; or *habitase*)	For a moment she was overcome by (lit. 'invaded by') the hope that her husband no longer dwelt in the realm of the living
Espero que me vas a pagar	I hope you're going to pay me

Notes

(i) *Esperar a que/aguardar a que* 'to wait for . . .' take the subjunctive: *Yo estaba esperando/aguardando a que **fuera/fuese** otro el que lo hiciera/hiciese* 'I was waiting for someone else to do it'.

(ii) *No esperar que* always takes the subjunctive: *Yo no esperaba que me **fuera** a escribir* 'I didn't expect she was going to write to me'.

16.12 Subjunctive after subordinators

16.12.1 General

Subordinators are such words as 'before', 'after', 'provided that', 'because', and 'when', which introduce a subordinate clause.

The general rule governing the mood of the verb after subordinators is: if the event referred to has or had occurred, the verb is in the indicative; if the event has or had not yet occurred, the verb is in the subjunctive. Examples:

*Se lo di cuando **llegó*** (the arrival had happened)	I gave it to him when he arrived
*Se lo daré cuando **llegue*** (the arrival hasn't happened yet)	I'll give it to him when he arrives
*Yo iba a dárselo cuando **llegara/llegase*** (the arrival had not yet happened)	I was going to give it to him when he arrived

It follows from this that a few subordinators, e.g. *antes de que* 'before', *para que/a que* 'in order that', always take the subjunctive because they must refer to something that has or had not yet happened. In some cases, e.g. *puesto que* 'since', *debido a que* 'due to the fact that', the event has obviously taken place and the indicative is always required. But in most cases the mood is variable and depends on the rule given.

The subordinate clause may precede or follow the main clause: *Después de que llegaron, empezamos a hablar/Empezamos a hablar después de que llegaron* 'After they arrived we started talking'/'We started talking after they arrived'.

Subordinators that take only the indicative are discussed in Chapter 33.

For replacement of the subjunctive after subordinators by the infinitive see 18.3.

16.12.2 Subjunctive with subordinators of purpose

(a) *A fin de que, para que/porque, con el objeto de que, con el propósito de que, con la intención de que* and *a que* when it means 'in order to', are always followed by a subjunctive because they obviously point to an event that has or had not yet happened:

*Vengo a que/para que me **dejes** un poco de azúcar*	I've come to borrow some sugar
*Me callé porque/para que no me **acusaran/acusasen** de metomentodo*	I kept silent so that they wouldn't accuse me of interfering
*He escrito una circular a fin de que se **enteren** todos*	I've written a circular so that everybody knows about it

Note

For the difference between *por* and *para* when both mean 'in order to', see 34.14.7.

(b) A number of phrases express negative intention or avoidance i.e. 'so that not'. They are not always easily translated into English now that the word 'lest' has fallen into disuse:

*Trabaja más, no sea que te **despidan***	Work harder so that they don't (lit. 'lest they') fire you
*Volvió la cara al pasar no fuera que le **reconocieran/reconociesen***	He turned his face as he passed by to avoid being recognised ('lest he be recognised')
Me subí al coche en tres minutos no se me fuera a arrepentir de la invitación (A. Mastretta, Mexico, dialogue)	I got into the car within three minutes lest he regretted/so that he wouldn't regret the invitation
Llámalo de testigo no vayan a decir que me envenenaste (ibid., dialogue)	Call him as a witness so they don't say that you poisoned me
*Devuélvele el dinero, no ocurra que nos **demande***	Give him back the money. We don't want him to sue us

16.12.3 Subjunctive with subordinators of cause and consequence

(a) The following are always followed by the indicative:

pues	because (see 33.5.3)
puesto que	since
ya que	since/seeing that
en vista de que	seeing that/in view of the fact that
debido a que	due to the fact that

Como, when it means 'since'/'because' is also followed by the indicative. It is discussed in detail at 33.5.2. When followed by the subjunctive, *como* means 'if' and is discussed at 25.8.2.

Cómo means 'how'. This use is discussed at 24.7.

Invítame ya que/puesto que tienes tanto dinero	Since you have so much money you can pay for me
Como tienes tanto dinero me puedes invitar (in this meaning *como* must appear at the head of the phrase; see 33.5.2 for further discussion)	Since you have so much money you can pay for me

(b) *Porque* is usually followed by an indicative, but requires the subjunctive when it means 'just because'/'only because' and the main verb is negated. Sometimes it can be preceded by *sólo/solo*:

*Porque tú lo **digas**, no voy a callarme*	I'm not going to shut up just because *you* say so
*No lo hago porque tú lo **digas***	I'm not doing it just because *you* say so
*Que nadie venga a nosotros porque **piense** que va a obtener enchufes*[10] (*Cambio16*, Spain)	Let no one come to us (just) because they think that they'll get special favours

but

*No lo hago porque tú lo **dices***	I won't do it because you say so/said I should
*No lo hago sólo porque tú lo **dices***	I'm doing it, but not simply because you're telling me to
*No salgo contigo sólo porque **tienes** un Ferrari*	The fact that you have a Ferrari isn't the only reason I go out with you

Compare:

*Sólo porque **tengas** un Ferrari no voy a salir contigo*	The fact that you have a Ferrari isn't a good enough reason for me to go out with you

The subjunctive is used after *bien porque . . . o/ya porque . . . o* meaning 'whether . . . or':

*Bien/Ya porque **tuviera** algo que hacer o porque **estuviera** cansado, el caso es que no estuvo muy amable con nosotros*	Whether he had something to do or whether he was tired, the fact is that he wasn't very kind to us

Note
If *porque* means *para que* (as it does after verbs like *esforzarse porque* 'to make an effort in order that . . .'), the verb is always subjunctive:

*Nos esforzamos porque/para que todos **tengan** agua limpia*	We're making an effort to ensure that everyone has clean water
*Estoy un tanto apurado y como impaciente porque **pase** el trago*	I'm a bit worried and rather impatient for this unpleasantness to pass

(c) *De ahí que* 'hence the fact that' is almost always followed by a subjunctive:

*Su padre murió de una borrachera, de ahí que no **beba***	His father died from a drunken fit, that's why he doesn't drink
*De ahí que visitar nuestra casa se **convirtiese** de vez en cuando en motivo de excursión* (L. Goytisolo, Spain)	This is why visiting our house occasionally became the pretext for an excursion

(d) *Dado que* takes the indicative if it means 'given that', the subjunctive if it means 'if it is the case that':

dado que es así . . .	given that this is the case . . .
dado que él quiera hacerlo . . .	if it's the case that he wants to do it . . .

16.12.4 Subjunctive with subordinators of result, aim and manner
The basic rule is that these take the indicative when they imply result and the subjunctive when they refer to an aim or intention.

---

[10]*El enchufe*, literally 'plug', is also used in Spain to mean 'connections': *Está muy enchufado* 'He's well-connected', *el enchufismo* 'the old boy network', 'the inside favours system'; also *el amiguismo*.

(a) When they indicate the result of an action the following take the indicative:

así que	so (= 'as a result')
conque	" "
de modo que	in such a way that, so
de manera que	" "
de suerte que	" "
de forma que	" "

*Tú sólo tienes la culpa, de modo que/conque/así que no te **puedes** quejar*	You've got only yourself to blame so you can't complain
*Lo hicieron en silencio de modo/forma/manera que no se **enteró** el portero*	They did it in silence so (as a result) the doorman didn't find out

De modo que/de manera que/de forma que may indicate either result or aim, and in the latter case they take the subjunctive. Unfortunately, some varieties of English (e.g. British) in which the subjunctive has virtually disappeared no longer systematically clarify the difference between result and aim in this kind of sentence, so *Lo hizo de modo que nadie se **enteró*** and *Lo hizo de modo que nadie se **enterase/enterara*** may both be translated 'He did it so no one realized', despite the fact that they mean entirely different things in Spanish.

It seems that North Americans systematically differentiate 'He did it so no one realized' (*de modo que nadie se enteró*) and 'He did it so no one **would** realize' (subjunctive only: *de modo que nadie se **enterase/enterara***). But translating from British varieties of English often poses the dilemma that there is no way of knowing whether the original implies result or aim:

*Salió de modo/manera que nadie lo **notara/notase***	He left so no one would notice
*Salió de modo/manera que nadie lo **notó***	She left so/and nobody noticed
*Compórtate de modo/manera que no **sospeche***	Behave so as to avoid him suspecting
*Alguien debería . . .modificar el sistema de enseñanza, de forma que el colegio de los niños **empezara** en junio* (C. Rico-Godoy, Spain)	Someone ought to modify the educational system so that children's school starts in June

(b) *Como* requires the subjunctive when it refers to an action that is or was still in the future[11]:

*Hazlo como **quieras***	Do it however you like
*Lo hizo como **quiso***	He did it the way he wanted
*Te dije que podías venir como **quisieras/quisieses***	I told you you could come any way you liked

For *como* + subjunctive meaning 'if' see 25.8.2; for *como* meaning 'as' (i.e. 'because') see 33.5.2.

(c) *Como si* 'as if' and *sin que* 'without' always take the subjunctive:

*Debes hacerlo sin que **tenga** que decírtelo*	You must do it without my having to tell you

---

[11] In literary styles, *como* is occasionally found with the *-se* or *-ra* forms when it refers to a past action: *como se diese/diera cuenta de que . . .* 'as/when he realized that . . .'.

*Me miró como si no me **viera/viese***	She looked at me as if she couldn't see me
*Éste/Este las trató con gran familiaridad, como si las **viera** todos los días* (C. Fuentes, Mexico)	He treated them very familiarly just as if he saw them every day

Notes

(i) *Comme si* takes the indicative in French: *comme si elle avait quinze ans* = *como si **tuviera** quince años* 'as if she was fifteen years old'.

(ii) *Es como si* 'it's as if . . .' takes the indicative when it means the same as *es como cuando* 'it's the same as when . . .': *Es como si/cuando no **puedes** respirar y te asustas* 'It's the same as when you can't breath and you get scared'.

   Como si . . . is also occasionally found colloquially in Spain with the indicative to mean 'even if': —*No iré hasta las ocho.* —*Como si no **vienes**, a mí me da igual* (Spain, colloquial) '"I won't come until eight o'clock." "Even if you don't come, it's the same to me".'

(iii) *Tan . . . como que . . .* 'such . . . as that . . .' takes the subjunctive: *Dos héroes como nosotros no pueden retroceder por cosas tan sin importancia como que le **coma** a uno un gigante* (children's story book, Spain) 'Two heroes like us can't turn back because of such unimportant things as being eaten by a giant, (lit. 'as that a giant eats one').

16.12.5 Subjunctive with subordinators of possibility

En caso de que calls for the subjunctive:

*Las pondré en la maleta en caso de que las **necesites***	I'll put them in the suitcase in case you need them
*Las puse en la maleta en caso de que las **necesitaras/necesitases***	I put them in the suitcase in case you needed them

But *por si* usually (but not invariably) takes the indicative, although *por si acaso* may take either mood:

*Llévate el paraguas por si (acaso) **llueve/lloviera/lloviese***	Take the umbrella in case it rains
*Está apuntando hacia la otra acera, por si **hay** un ataque por retaguardia* (J. Ibargüengoitia, Mexico, dialogue)	He's aiming at the other pavement/ sidewalk in case there's an attack from the rear
Por si fuera poco . . . (set phrase)	As if this wasn't enough . . .
*Conviene que vayas enterado por si alguien te **pidiera** una aclaración* (E. Mendoza, Spain, or *pidiese*)	It would be best if you were informed (lit. 'went informed') in case anyone asks you for an explanation

Note

Suponiendo que 'supposing that' requires the subjunctive: *Suponiendo que **venga**, ¿le vas a dejar entrar?* 'Supposing he comes, are you going to let him in?'.

16.12.6 Subjunctive with subordinators of time

After subordinators of time the subordinate verb is in the subjunctive when its action is or was still in the future.

   Students of French and Italian must resist the temptation to use the future tense after these subordinators. Compare *Je lui donnerai son livre quand il **arrivera**, Gli darò il suo livro quando **arriverà** and Le daré su libro cuando **llegue** 'I'll give him his book when he arrives':

*Llegamos antes de que **empezara/empezase** a nevar* (for *antes de que* see note (i))	We arrived before it started snowing
*Me saludará cuando **llegue***	She'll greet me when I arrive/she arrives
*Me saluda cuando **llega***	She greets me when she arrives (habitual)

*Iban a cenar cuando **llegaran/llegasen** los demás*	They were going to have supper when the rest arrived (i.e. they had not yet arrived)
*A medida que/según/conforme **vayan** entrando se lo diré*	I'll tell them as they come in
*. . . las ideas se irán haciendo más y más claras en la medida en que nos **aventuremos** más y más por la senda que iremos construyendo* (C. Almeyda in *El País*)	The ideas will get increasingly clear as we venture further along the path we will be building
*Me doy cuenta, a medida que Rosita **pasa** mis notas a máquina, de que he reunido cerca de doscientas páginas* (C. Fuentes, Mexico)	I realize, as Rosita types out my notes, that I've assembled more than 200 sheets of paper
*Tan pronto como **acabe** la huelga, las cosas marcharán mejor*	Things will get better as soon as the strike is over
*Tan pronto como **acabó** la huelga todo se arregló*	As soon as the strike was over everything was all right
*Nomás que **oscurezca** te vas por la carretera* (J. Ibargüengoitia, Mexico, dialogue; for the Latin-American word *nomás* see 23.2.5)	As soon as it gets dark you go down the road
*Apenas **pueda**, te llamo* (J. Asís, Argentina)	As soon as I can, I'll ring you
*Hasta que no **llegue** a ser ministro no se quedará contento*	He won't be satisfied until be becomes a Minister
*Hasta que no **llegó** a ser ministro no se quedó contento*	He wasn't satisfied until he became a Minister
*En cuanto se **estrene** la obra, se agotarán las entradas*	All the tickets will be sold after the first night
*Siempre que la **vea** se lo diré*	I'll tell her every time I see her

Notes

(i) *Antes de que* is always followed by the subjunctive because it must logically always refer to a future event. Both *antes de que* and *antes que* are correct, the former being more common in Spain.

Antes de is used before an infinitive: *Hazlo tú antes de que salga él* 'You do it before he leaves' but *Hazlo antes de salir* 'Do it before you leave'. *Después (de) que* likewise becomes *después de* before an infinitive.

Antes que may mean 'rather than' and must not then be confused with *antes de que*: *cualquier cosa antes que casarse* 'anything rather than get married'.

(ii) *Después (de) que* 'after' and similar phrases – *a los pocos días de que*, 'a few days after', *desde que* 'since', etc. – always take the subjunctive when they refer to an action still in the future. If they refer to a past action they should logically take the indicative, but in written Spanish the *-ra* and *-se* forms are quite common. (For a more detailed discussion see 14.10.3.)

(iii) *Mientras (que)* 'as long as'/'while'. When it means 'on condition that'/'provided that' the subjunctive is obligatory. When it refers to the future and cannot be translated by 'as long as' either mood is possible; when it refers to completed events in the past the indicative is used: *Mañana puedes hacer la comida mientras (que) yo **arreglo** la casa/mientras (que) yo **arregle** la casa* 'Tomorrow you can do the cooking while I tidy the house', *Pero, mientras lo **necesite**, no puedo dejar de verlo* 'But as long as I need him, I can't stop seeing him', *Mientras (que) **sigas** así, no conseguirás nada* 'You won't get anywhere while/as long as you go on like that', *Mientras (que) **respetaba** nuestro arreglo, todo iba bien* (completed) 'So long as/While he/she respected our arrangement, everything went well', *Le dije que no conseguiría nada mientras no **trabajara/trabajase** más* 'I told her she'd achieve nothing as long as she didn't work harder'.

Mientras que can also be a coordinator: *Yo trabajo todo el día mientras que tú no **haces** nada* 'I work all day while you do nothing'. The *que* is normal here.

(iv) *Apenas* 'hardly' and other words of the same meaning are also discussed at 23.5.7.

16.12.7   Subjunctive with subordinators of condition and exception

They all call for the subjunctive. (For *si* 'if' and *como* when it means 'if' see 25.8.1 and 25.8.2).

(a) Condition

con tal (de) que	provided that
siempre que	" "
siempre y cuando (more emphatic)	" "
a condición de que	on condition that
bajo (la) condición de que	" "
a cambio de que	in return for

El Gobierno está preparado a negociar *siempre que/siempre y cuando/con tal (de) que/a condición de que* **sean** *razonables*	The Government is ready to negotiate provided they are reasonable
sin la condición previa de que se **anule** *el contrato . . . (El País)*	Without the pre-condition that the contract should be cancelled . . .
Te convido a cenar con tal (de) que me **dejes** *escoger el restaurante*	I'll buy you dinner provided you let me choose the restaurant
Cuando yo le informé sobre la conducta de usted añadió cincuenta mil pesetas a la minuta a cambio de que yo **hic'era** *esta llamada telefónica* (M. Vázquez Montalbán)	When I told him about your behaviour he added fifty thousand pesetas to my professional fees in return for my making this telephone call

(b) Exception (occasionally followed by indicative in cases discussed in note (i))

a no ser que	unless
salvo que	unless/save that
excepto que	unless/except that
a menos que	" "
fuera de que (less common)	" "
como no (sea que)	unless (in suggestions)
como no fuera que	unless

Me casaré contigo a no ser que/salvo que **hayas** *cambiado de idea*	I'll marry you unless you've changed your mind
Íbamos de vacaciones en agosto salvo/a no ser que/como no fuera que yo **estuviera** *muy ocupado*	We took our holidays/vacation in August unless I was very busy
No sé qué sugerir. Como no (sea que) **vayamos** *al teatro*	I don't know what to suggest unless we go to the theatre

Note
Excepto/salvo que, con la salvedad de que are followed by the indicative when they mean 'except for the fact that':

Ella hablaba mejor, excepto que/salvo que/con la salvedad de que **pronunciaba** *mal las eñes*	She spoke better/best, except for the fact that she pronounced the *eñes* badly

16.12.8   Subjunctive with subordinators of concession

There are several ways of expressing 'although', of which *aunque* is the most common:

aunque	although
así	"
siquiera	"
aun cuando (emphatic)	"

a pesar de que	despite the fact that
pese a que (literary)	" "
a despecho de que (literary)	" "

These require the subjunctive if they point to an event which is or was still in the future. *Así* requires the subjunctive when it means 'although':

Es un valiente, no lo confesará así/aunque le **maten**	He's a brave man, he won't admit it even if they kill him
No lo confesó aunque le **ofrecieron** *dinero*	He didn't confess even though they offered him money
No lo confesaría aunque le **mataran/matasen**	He wouldn't confess it even if they killed him
Tienen que cumplir, así **caminen** *bajo la lluvia* (*La Jornada*, Mexico)	They have to fulfil/(US) 'fulfill' their mission, even if they walk in the rain
Vendieron la finca, a pesar de que el abuelo se **oponía**	They sold the estate, despite the fact that grandfather opposed it
Venderán la finca, a pesar de que el abuelo se **oponga**	They'll sell the estate, despite the fact that grandfather will/may oppose it
Dijeron que iban a vender la finca, a pesar de que el abuelo se **opusiera/opusiese**	They said they would sell the estate despite the fact that grandfather would/might oppose it

Notes
(i) A subjunctive is normally used after *aunque* when something expected is in fact denied: *Aunque* **sea** *español no me gustan los toros* 'Even though I'm Spanish I don't like bullfights', *Las generalidades de esa magnitud, aunque se* **formulen** *con brillantez, no sirven de gran cosa* (M. Vargas Llosa, Peru) 'Generalizations of that magnitude, even when brilliantly formulated, aren't much use'.
(ii) When *siquiera* is used to mean 'although' (literary style) it requires the subjunctive: *. . . dos fuentes independientes . . . a las que se aludirá, siquiera* **sea** *vagamente* (*Libro de estilo de El País*) 'two independent sources, which will be mentioned, even if in vague terms'.

16.13 Translating 'whether . . . or', 'however', 'whatever', 'whoever', 'whichever' and 'the more . . . the more . . .'

The phrases discussed in this section are often translated by the *forma reduplicativa*, i.e. constructions in which the subjunctive verb is repeated, as in *digan lo que* **digan** 'whatever they say', *pase lo que* **pase** 'whatever happens', *No hay salida para ti,* **hagas** *lo que* **hagas**, **vayas** *a donde* **vayas** (C. Fuentes, Mexico, dialogue) 'There's no way out for you, whatever you do, wherever you go'. After a negative the second verb is sometimes omitted: *quieras o no (quieras)* 'whether you want to or not'.

16.13.1 'Whether . . . or'
The *forma reduplicativa* is used:

Estaré de tu parte, tengas razón o no la tengas	I'll be on your side, whether you're right or wrong
Estuviese o no enfermo, lo cierto es que no vino al trabajo	Whether he was ill/(US) sick or not, the fact is he didn't come to work

16.13.2 'However'
Por mucho que/por más que + verb, *por mucho* + noun + verb, *por (muy)* + adjective + verb.

Use of the subjunctive follows the usual rule: if the event referred to is or was a reality, the indicative is used: *Por mucho que/más que se lo dijo, no lo hizo* 'He didn't do it however much she asked him' but *Por mucho que se lo digas, no lo hará* 'He won't do it however much you ask him'.

Further examples:

Por más que las esperanzas de Eulalia y su padre crecían, no lograban contagiar a Andrés (A. Mastretta, Mexico, dialogue; real event)	However much Eulalia's and her father's hopes grew, they didn't manage to inspire (lit. 'infect') Andrés
Por más que llueva no se le van a resucitar los novillos muertos (M. Puig, Argentina)	However much it rains, his dead steers won't come back to life
Por modesta que fuera su familia, no era el más pobre del colegio (M. Vargas Llosa, Peru)	However humble his family may have been, he wasn't the poorest one in the school
Por buena vista que uno tenga no alcanza a ver más que piedras (J. Ibargüengoitia, Mexico, dialogue)	However good one's eyesight is/may be, one can see nothing but stones

Note

With verbs meaning 'say', 'order', etc., the subjunctive may appear even though the action is a reality: *Por mucho que/más que se lo dijera, no lo hacía* 'However often she told him, he didn't do it'. The imperfect indicative *decía/hacía* and the preterite *dijo/hizo* are also possible here. The difference is one of nuance, the subjunctive being rather more emphatic or insistent.

16.13.3 'The more . . . the more'

Cuanto/a/os/as más . . . más. The general rule is applied: if the event is a reality the indicative is used:

Cuanto más coma más querrá	The more he eats the more he'll want
Cuanto más comía, más quería	The more he ate the more he wanted
Cuanta más leche eches, más espesará	The more milk you add, the thicker it'll get
Yo sabía que cuanto más bebiera/bebiese más me emborracharía	I knew that the more I drank, the drunker I would get

For the use of *mientras* in this construction, and, in Latin America, of *entre* instead of *cuanto*, see 5.11.

16.13.4 'Whatever'

The *forma reduplicativa* is normally used to translate 'whatever':

diga lo que diga	whatever he says
Den lo que den, siempre vamos al Metropolitan (E. Poniatowska, Mexico, dialogue)	Whatever's on (lit. 'whatever they give'), we always go to the Metropolitan cinema
Cómpralo sea como sea	Buy it whatever it looks like (or 'Buy it whatever the cost')
Dijo que lo compraría fuera como fuera/fuese como fuese	He said he'd buy it whatever it was like (or 'whatever the cost')

Como quiera (or *comoquiera*) *que sea* and *comoquiera que fuera* could be used in the last two examples, but they are less usual.

Note

The English 'whatever' may mean 'whichever', in which case it is best translated by an appropriate tense form of *sea cual sea*. This construction is preferred in written and spoken language to the rather stilted *cualquiera que* and *comoquiera que*: *Las camelias cualquiera que/sea cual sea su color son bonitas* 'Camelias are pretty whatever their colour'. (For a general discussion of *cualquiera* see 9.8.)

When 'whatever' means 'everything' it will usually be translated by *todo lo que* or *cuanto*: *Trae todo lo que puedas* 'Bring whatever/everything you can', *Aprenderé todo lo que/cuanto pueda* 'I'll learn whatever/everything I can'.

16.13.5 'Whichever'
When this word means 'which', 'whichever one' or 'the one that' it is usually translated by *que* or *el que* + subjunctive:

Escoge la maceta que más te guste	Choose whichever flower pot you like most
—¿Cuál me llevo?	'Which should I take?'
—El que usted quiera	'Whichever (one) you like'

For more details on the use of the subjunctive in relative clauses, see 16.14.

16.13.6 'Whenever'
Cuando with the subjunctive when the event referred to is or was still in the future, and the indicative in all other cases:

Vienen cuando quieren	They come whenever they want
Vendrán cuando quieran	They'll come whenever they want

Cuando quiera que is old fashioned for *cuando*, but it is used as an occasional literary alternative for *siempre que*:

Cuando quiera que en la vida española se ponen tensos los ánimos . . . (R. Pérez de Ayala, quoted by Seco (1992), 126)	Whenever passions are stirred in Spanish life . . .

16.13.7 'Anyone who . . .', 'whoever . . .'
Cualquiera que 'anyone who . . .' cannot be replaced by the *forma reduplicativa*:

Cualquiera que te vea pensará que vas a una fiesta	Anyone who sees you will think you're going to a party

If 'anyone who . . .' means 'those who . . .', 'people who . . .', a nominalizer plus the subjunctive is used, i.e. *quien* or *el que*:

El que/Quien se crea eso está loco	Anyone who believes that is mad

Quienquiera is also found in the same contexts. According to Seco (1992), 317, it is, in Spain, exclusively literary. But the following example suggests that it survives colloquially in other countries: *Quienquiera se crea eso está loco* (G. Cabrera Infante, Cuban dialogue; Spain *el que crea . . .* or *quien crea . . .*) 'Anyone who thinks that is mad'.

Quienquiera que sea 'whoever it is' seems to be in free variation with the *forma reduplicativa*: *No abras la puerta, sea quien sea/quienquiera que sea* 'Don't open the door, whoever it is'.

16.13.8 'Wherever'
Dondequiera or *forma reduplicativa*:

Dondequiera que voy/Vaya donde vaya me lo/le encuentro	Wherever I go I meet him

Dondequiera que vaya/Vaya donde vaya me lo/le encontraré — Wherever I go I'll meet him

Dondequiera que fuese/Fuese donde fuese, me lo/le encontraba (or fuera . . .) — Wherever I went I met him

16.14 Subjunctive in relative clauses

In this section nominalizers such as *el que* 'the one that', *quien* 'the one who', *aquellos que* 'those who' etc., are treated as relative pronouns. They are also discussed under Nominalizers at 36.1.

See 16.13. for *cualquiera que, quienquiera que, cuandoquiera que, dondequiera*.

16.14.1 Subjunctive in relative clauses when the antecedent is not yet identified

Spanish uses the subjunctive in such cases to express a nuance that English usually ignores. Compare *los que **digan** eso* 'those who say that' (if anyone does) and *los que **dicen** eso* 'those who say that' (some do). The difference in Spanish is striking. Contrast:

*Prefiero un coche que **tenga** cuatro puertas* — I prefer a car with four doors (i.e. any car)

*Prefiero ese coche que **tiene** cuatro puertas* — I prefer that car with four doors
*Busco un médico que **sepa** acupuntura* (N.B. no personal *a*) — I'm looking for a doctor (i.e. 'any doctor') who knows acupuncture
*Conozco **a** un médico que **sabe** acupuntura* — I know a doctor who knows acupuncture

*No leo novelas que **tengan** más de doscientas páginas* — I don't read (any) novels that have more than two hundred pages
*Tengo muchas novelas que **tienen** más de doscientas páginas* — I've got many novels with more than two hundred pages

Further examples:

*Me voy a casar con el primero que me lo **pida*** — I'm going to marry the first man who asks me
*Haz lo que **quieras*** — Do whatever you like
*¿Sabes de alguien que **tenga** apellido en este país?* (E. Sábato, Argentina, dialogue) — Do you know anyone in this country who has a surname (i.e. an illustrious name)?
*. . . cualquier reacción que uno **pueda** tener suena a sobreactuado* (C. Rico-Godoy, Spain) — Any reaction one might have sounds like over-acting/sounds overdone
*Dígame qué tienen que **esté** muy sabroso* (J. Ibargüengoitia, Mexico, dialogue) — Tell me what you've got that tastes really good

Notes
(i) Compare French *J'apprendrai ce que je pourrai* (future indicative) and *Aprenderé lo que pueda* 'I'll learn what I can'.
(ii) In literary styles, the subjunctive is common in relative clauses when the main clause is introduced by *como* 'like' or *como si fuera/fuese* 'as if it were . . .': *. . . como un ángel que perdiera/perdiese las alas* ' . . . like an angel that had lost its wings', *. . . el sol se pone súbitamente – como si fuera un interruptor el que lo apagara* (J. Marías, Spain; or *fuese*) ' . . . the sun sets suddenly – as if it were a switch that had turned it off'.

16.14.2 Subjunctive in relative clauses when the existence of the antecedent is denied

If the antecedent does not exist the verb in the relative cause is in the subjunctive:

*No hay nadie que **sepa** tocar más de un violín a la vez*	There is no one who can play more than one violin at once
*No había mendigo a quien él no **diera/diese** limosna*	There was no beggar to whom he wouldn't give alms
*No hay quien le **entienda***	There's no one who can understand him
*En realidad no existen culturas 'dependientes' y emancipadas ni nada que se les **parezca*** (M. Vargas Llosa, Peru)	In reality there are no 'dependent' and emancipated cultures or anything like them
*¿A quiénes conoces que se **vean** feas esperando un hijo?* (A. Mastretta, Mexico, dialogue; *se vean = estén* in Spain)	What women do you know who look ugly when they're expecting a baby?

16.14.3 Subjunctive after the relatives *donde* and *cuanto*

(For *dondequiera que* see 16.13.8.)

The subjunctive is used if the reference is to a yet unknown or non-existent entity:

*Comeré en el pueblo donde me **pare***	I'll eat in **whichever** village I stop in
*Comí en el pueblo donde me **paré***	I ate in the village I stopped in
*Buscó una zona donde el mar **llegara** debilitado* (M. Vázquez Montalbán)	He looked for an area where the sea was coming in with less force
*Te daré cuanto me **pidas***	I'll give you anything you ask
*Le di (todo) cuanto me **pidió***	I gave her everything she asked

16.14.4 Subjunctive in relative clauses after superlative expressions

The Indicative is used after the superlative when comparison is made with things or persons that the speaker knows personally:

*Eres la chica más inteligente que **he** conocido*	You're the most intelligent girl I've met
*Fue el mayor incendio que **he** visto en mi vida*	It was the biggest fire I've ever seen in my life

But if the idea of 'ever' is stressed or the comparison alludes to every example that *may* ever have existed, the subjunctive is normal:

*Eres la chica más inteligente que **haya** existido nunca/jamás*	You're the most intelligent girl that ever existed
*Es la mayor tontería que se **haya** oído nunca/jamás*	It's the greatest lot of rubbish that was ever heard
*la mayor transacción con divisas fuertes que se **haya** hecho en el Río de la Plata* (E.Sábato, Argentina)	the biggest hard-currency deal made in the River Plate region

16.15 Subjunctive in main clauses

The subjunctive is primarily a feature of subordinate clauses, but it may appear in a main clause in certain circumstances.

16.15.1 Subjunctive with the imperative

The subjunctive is required:

(a) To form all negative imperatives: *No me hables* 'Don't talk to me', *No se vayan ustedes* 'Don't go away'.

(b) To form affirmative (i.e. not negative) imperatives with the pronouns *usted, ustedes: Guarden silencio* 'Keep quiet', *Váyase* 'Go away'.

(c) To form first and third-person imperatives, e.g. *Sentémonos* 'Let's sit down', *Que entre* 'Let him come in'.

The imperative is discussed in detail in Chapter 17.

16.15.2 Subjunctive to express wishes

The verb is usually preceded by *ojalá* or by *quién. Así*, used jokingly, parodies a typical gipsy curse and is frequently heard in colloquial language (at least in Spain):

¡Ojalá nos toquen las quinielas!	Let's only hope we win the pools!
Ojalá no se equivoquen, señora	I hope they're not mistaken, Señora
(A. Mastretta, Mexico, dialogue)	
¡Quién fuera millonario!	If only I were a millionaire!

(*Quién* in this expression should not be confused with the word meaning 'who'.)

¡Dios se lo pague!	May God repay you!
¡Así se te pegue mi catarro!	I hope you get my cold!

There is also a less common expression with the same meaning as *ojalá*:

*(Así) **fueran** como tú todas las mujeres . . .*	If only all women were like you . . .

16.15.3 Subjunctive in some common set phrases
(a) *O sea que* 'in other words':

Ha dicho que tiene que trabajar, o sea que no quiere venir	He said he had to work, in other words he doesn't want to come

(b) In the phrases *que yo sepa/que yo recuerde*:

Que yo recuerde es la primera vez que le he visto	As far as I remember it's the first time I've seen him
—¿Ha llegado Pepe? —No, que yo sepa/por lo que yo sé	'Has Pepe arrived?' 'Not as far as I know'
Que se sepa nadie lo ha hecho antes	As far as anybody knows, it hasn't been done before

(c) In a few set phrases:

¡Acabáramos!	Now I see what you're getting at!
Otro gallo nos cantara si le hubiéramos/ hubiésemos hecho caso	It would have been another story if we had listened to him
¡Cómo tiras el dinero! Ni que fueras millonario . . .	The way you throw money about anyone would think you're a millionaire

16.16 Tense agreement: subjunctive

Despite the claims of many traditional grammars, there are no rigidly fixed rules of tense agreement between main and subordinate clauses, but the following are by far the most usual combinations:

(a) Main clause in present indicative

(1) Present subjunctive:

*Me **gusta** que **hable***	I like her to talk
***Quiero** que **dejes** de fumar*	I want you to stop smoking

(2) Perfect subjunctive:

*Me **encanta** que **hayas** venido*	I'm delighted you've come

(3) Imperfect subjunctive (see note (i)):

*Es imposible que lo **dijera/dijese*** It's impossible that he said it

(b) Main clause in future

Present subjunctive or Perfect subjunctive:

*Nos **contentaremos** con que **terminen**/* We'll be content with them finishing by
hayan terminado para finales del mes the end of the month

(c) Main clause in conditional or conditional perfect

Imperfect subjunctive:

*Nos **contentaríamos** con que* We'd be content with them finishing by
***terminaran/terminasen** para finales del mes* the end of the month
*Yo **habría** preferido que se **pintara/pintase*** I'd have preferred it to be painted black
de negro

(d) Main clause in perfect (see note (ii))

Present, perfect or imperfect subjunctive:

*Te **he dicho** que te **estés** quieto* I told you to be still
*Ha sido un milagro que no te **hayan*** It was a miracle that they didn't
reconocido/reconocieran/reconociesen recognise you

(e) Main clause in imperfect, preterite or pluperfect (see notes (iii) and (iv))

(1) Imperfect subjunctive:

*La idea **era** que **cobrarais/cobraseis** los* The idea was that you'd get paid on
viernes Fridays
*Me **sorprendió** que **fuera/fuese** tan alto* It surprised me that he was so tall
*Yo te **había pedido** que me **prestaras/*** I'd asked you to lend me 100 dollars
***prestases** cien dólares*

(2) Pluperfect subjunctive:

*Me **sorprendía** que **hubiera/hubiese*** I was surprised that he had protested
protestado

(f) Main clause in imperative

Present subjunctive:

***Díganles** que se **den** prisa* Tell them to hurry

Notes
(i) The combination present + imperfect subjunctive or perfect subjunctive occurs when a comment is being made about a past event: *No es cierto que él nos devolviera/devolviese/haya devuelto el dinero* 'It isn't true that he returned the money to us'.
   There seems to be little difference between the perfect and imperfect subjunctive in this case, and occasionally the present subjunctive can also be used: *Algunos **niegan** que Cristóbal Colón **fuera/fuese/haya sido/sea** el primer descubridor de América* 'Some deny that Christopher Columbus was the first discoverer of America'.
(ii) The perfect (*ha dicho, ha ordenado*, etc.) is strictly speaking classified as a present tense for the purposes of agreement, but the imperfect subjunctive is occasionally used with it when the event in the subordinate clause is also in the past. Compare *Ha dado órdenes de que nos **rindamos*** 'He's given orders for us to surrender' and *El clima que se está creando **ha llevado** a que se **hablara** de intervención del Ejército* (*Cambio16*, Spain; also *hable*) 'The climate that is being created has led to talk of Army intervention'.

(iii) The combination past indicative + present subjunctive is optionally possible when the subordinate clause refers to a timeless or perpetual event: *Dios **decretó** que las serpientes no **tengan/tuvieran/tuviesen** patas*[12] 'God decreed that snakes should have no legs'.

(iv) When the subordinate event is in the future and the time of the main verb is the recent past, the present subjunctive is sometimes found in the subordinate clause: *El Gobierno vasco **reclamó** ayer que se le **transfiera** el mando efectivo de las fuerzas de seguridad del Estado en el País Vasco* (*El País*) 'The Basque Government demanded yesterday that effective control over the State security forces in the Basque Country should be transferred to itself'.

Use of the present when both verbs refer to the past is common in popular Latin-American speech but is unacceptable to Peninsular speakers (although examples are increasingly frequent in the media): *El inspector aduanero le **pidió** a la muchacha que le **muestre** su casaca* (*La Prensa*, Peru; Spain *mostrara/mostrase*. In Spain *la casaca* = 'dress coat') 'The Customs inspector asked the girl to show him her coat'.

(v) After *como si* 'as if', *igual que si/lo mismo que si* 'the same as if', the verb is always in the imperfect subjunctive: *Le hablaré como si yo no **supiese/supiera** hablar bien el castellano* 'I'll talk to him as if I didn't know how to speak Spanish well'.

16.17 The future subjunctive

The forms of the future subjunctive are discussed at 13.1.10.

The future subjunctive is nowadays obsolete in standard Spanish except in a few literary variants of set phrases such as *sea lo que fuere* (more usually *sea lo que sea*) 'whatever it may be', *venga lo que viniere* (usually *venga lo que venga*) 'come what may'.

It is much used in legal documents, printed regulations, charters and similar offical documents after formulas of the kind 'a person who . . .':

*APUESTA: Contrato bilateral en el que se acuerda que el que **acertare** un pronóstico o **tuviere** razón en una disputa recibirá del perdedor lo pactado* (from a Spanish legal dictionary)

'BET': A bilateral contract whereby it is agreed that a person who makes an accurate forecast or wins an argument shall receive the amount agreed from the loser

It occasionally appears in flowery language to indicate a very remote possibility:

*. . . lo cual ofrece amplísimas ventajas en la extracción del motor o en reparaciones, caso de que las **hubiere*** (advertisement, Spain; *hubiera/hubiese* more normal).

. . . which offers very wide advantages when removing the engine or in repair work – if such a thing should ever arise

It is quite common in Latin-American newspaper style in some regions:

*. . . sólo la aplicación de un plan de estrictas medidas, aun cuando éstas **resultaren** antipopulares, permitirá salir de la actual situación* (*La Nación*, Buenos Aires)

. . . only the application of a plan of strict measures, even if these were unpopular, would permit us to get out of the present situation

Kany, 225, notes examples in written usage from nine American republics.

---

[12] *Las piernas* is used only of human legs.

17
The imperative

17.1 General remarks

The imperative is used to give orders or to make requests. There are various ways of making an imperative sound less abrupt: in this respect intonation and attitude are as important in Spanish as in any language, and a friendly manner counts for much more than use of formulas like *por favor*, *haga el favor* 'please', which English-speakers constantly use unnecessarily.

Other points to watch are:

(a) All negative imperatives (e.g. 'don't do', 'don't say') are formed with the subjunctive: *Vete* 'Go away', *No te vayas* 'Don't go away'.

(b) For Latin-Americans there is no *vosotros* imperative: *ustedes* is used for both strangers and friends, and even for little children and animals.

17.2 Affirmative forms of the imperative

17.2.1 General

For negative imperatives ('don't do', 'don't say', etc.), see 17.3.

For the affirmative imperative of *estar* 'to be' the pronominal form is always used (at least in Spain): *Estate quieto* 'Sit still'/'Stop running about', *Estense listas para las ocho* 'Be ready by eight'. See 26.6.4 (*estar*) for further discussion.

Addition of a subject pronoun to an imperative, especially in the *tú* and *vosotros* forms, can make an order emphatic and brusque:

*¡**Tú** bájate de ahí!*	You! Get down from there!
*¡**Vosotros** calla(r)os!*	You shut up!

17.2.2 The *tú* imperative

The familiar singular imperative (*tú* form) is, with nine exceptions, formed by removing the *-s* of the second-person singular of the present indicative: *llamas > llama, lees > lee*. The exceptions are:

decir	say	*di*
hacer	do/make	*haz*
ir[1]	go	*ve* (*vete* = 'go away')
poner	put	*pon*

---

[1] For the irregular first-personal plural of *ir, vámonos* (and not the expected *vayámonos*), see 17.5.

salir	leave/go out	*sal*
ser	be	*sé*
tener	have	*ten*[2]
venir	come	*ven*

The *tú* imperative of *haber* is theoretically *he*, but it is not in use[3].

17.2.3 The *vos* imperative

The imperative form corresponding to *vos* (Southern Cone, especially Argentina, and Central America) can usually be found by removing the *-d* from the European *vosotros* form; the final vowel is therefore usually stressed: *tened* > *tené, contad* > *contá, decid* > *decí.* Pronominal verbs take the pronoun *te*, so the imperative of *lavarse* is *lavate* (stressed on the second *a*; the standard form is *lávate*). Further examples (all from Argentina; the *tú* form is included for comparison):

Decile que pase (Dile que pase)	Tell him to come in
Vení cuando puedas (Ven cuando puedas.	Come when you can
See 16.2.8 for the popular Argentine	
form *Vení cuando **podás**)*	
Levantate (Levántate)	Get up

For other remarks on *vos* see the item *voseo* in the Index.

17.2.4 The *vosotros* imperative

The familiar European Spanish plural imperative (*vosotros/vosotras*) is formed by replacing the *-r* of the infinitive by *-d*. There are no exceptions:

ser	be	*sed*
ir	go	*id*
tener	have	*tened*
venir	come	*venid*
cantar	sing	*cantad*

This form is replaced by the *ustedes* form of the imperative in Latin America except in very formal styles (e.g. liturgical language), but it is in everyday use in Spain.

The *-d* is dropped in the pronominal form: *dad + os = daos: Daos la mano* 'Shake hands'; *lavad + os = lavaos: Lavaos el pelo* 'Wash your hair'. There is one exception: *id + os = idos* 'go away!' from *irse*, although in everyday speech *iros* is nowadays much more usual.

Note

In informal spoken language in Spain the *vosotros* imperative is commonly replaced by the infinitive: *venid = venir, id = ir, daos = daros, veníos = veniros, Lavaos las manos* 'Wash your hands' = *Lavaros las manos*, etc. Although it apparently has a long history, this construction is still considered slovenly by some speakers, but it is very widespread, e.g. **Tener** (for *tened*) *cuidado con Socorro que ya se ha cargado*

---

[2] Note idiomatic uses: *Ténmelo preparado* 'Have it ready for me', *Tenedme al corriente* 'Keep me informed'.

[3] As Seco (1992), 219, points out, the nowadays rather old-fashioned literary formula *he aquí*, 'here is . . .'/'what follows is . . .' (French *voici* . . .) is not the imperative of *haber*. Examples: *He aquí una imagen de . . .* 'This is an image of . . .', *Henos aquí ante un aspecto de . . .* 'We are here confronted with an aspect of . . .'.

tres matrimonios (E. Arenas, Spain, popular dialogue) 'Watch out for Socorro, she's already messed up three marriages'. Formal styles require the forms in -*d*.

For further remarks on the use of the infinitive as an imperative, see 17.9.

17.2.5 The *usted/ustedes* imperative

The polite pronouns *usted* and *ustedes* have no independent imperative forms: they use the third-person singular or plural present subjunctive endings respectively: ***Dígame*** 'Tell me', ***Tenga*** 'Take'/'Have', ***Dígan**me (ustedes)*, 'Tell (plural) me', ***Avancen***[4] 'Move on'/'Go on', etc.

The plural forms are used for both polite and informal address in Latin America: a Latin-American mother addresses her children as *ustedes*. *Vosotros* forms of the verb are unfamiliar to most Latin Americans.

17.3 Negative forms of the imperative

When an imperative is in the negative form, the imperative forms are replaced by the present subjunctive:

Affirmative imperative		Negative imperative
Canta	sing	*no cantes*
Vete	go away	*no te **vayas***
(Usted) levántese	stand up	*no se levante*
(Vosotros) sentaos	sit down	*no os sent**éis***
(Ustedes) dénselo	give it to him/ her/them	*no se lo **den***

Notes
(i) The Argentine *vos* forms obey the same rules and foreign students should use the standard subjunctive forms with them for the reasons explained at 16.2.8: *Levantate* > *No te levantes* (not *No te levantés*).
(ii) Affirmative forms of the imperative are occasionally used in the negative in popular Spanish speech, e.g. *?No rechistad* 'Don't answer back!' for *No rechistéis*. This should not be imitated.

17.4 Position of object pronouns with the imperative

When an imperative form is used with an object pronoun, the following rules apply:
(a) If the imperative is **affirmative**, the pronouns are attached to the verb in the normal order (shown at 11.12):

(Tú) dame la mano	Hold my hand
(Tú) ponte la chaqueta (Argentina, *[vos]* ponete el saco*)	Put your jacket on
*(Usted) dé**melo***	Give it to me
*(Vosotros/as) dád**melo***	Give it to me
(Vosotros) despertaos (colloquial *despertaros*; see 17.2.4)	Wake up
*(Ustedes) dén**noslo***	Give it to us

---

[4] Spoken Mexican regularly adds *le* to certain common imperatives, e.g. *Aváncenle* 'Move on', *Pásenle* 'Come in', *Ándale* 'Wow!'/'Heavens!'.

(b) If the imperative is **negative**, the pronouns precede it in the normal way (shown at 11.12):

No *me* des la mano	Don't hold my hand
No *te* pongas la chaqueta	Don't put your jacket on
(Usted) no *me lo* dé	Don't give it to me
Vosotros) no *os* quejéis	Don't complain
(Ustedes) no *se lo* enseñen	Don't show it to him/her/them

Notes
(i) When a pronoun ending in a vowel is attached to an affirmative *ustedes* imperative, there is a widespread tendency in popular Latin-American speech either to repeat the plural *-n* at the end of the word or to shift it to the end of the word: ?*Levántensen* or ?*Levántesen* (for *Levántense)* 'Get up' ?*Díganselon* or ?*Dígaselon* (for *Díganselo*) 'Tell it to him'.

Kany, 143ff, gives examples from seventeen Latin-American republics, and in some places these forms are heard even in spontaneous educated speech. This construction is unknown in standard European Spanish and is banned from Latin-American written styles.
(ii) In some regions popular European Spanish puts the pronouns before an affirmative imperative verb and uses a redundant pronoun even for a direct object (this construction should not be confused with imperatives preceded by *que*, discussed at 17.6): ?¡*Le dé* el juguete al niño! (for ¡*Dele* el juguete al niño!) 'Give the toy to the child!', *Las riegue* las plantas (for *Riegue* las plantas) 'Water the plants'.

This construction is usually stigmatized as uneducated and should not be imitated by foreign students.

17.5 First-person imperatives

The present subjunctive can be used to make a first-person imperative, e.g. 'let's go!', 'let's get up'. If the verb is pronominal, the final *-s* is dropped before adding *-nos*:

Empecemos	Let's get started
Levantémonos	Let's get up
Preparémonos	Let's prepare ourselves
Asegurémonos primero de la verdad de los hechos	Let us first assure ourselves of the truth of the facts
No nos enfademos (Lat. Am. No nos enojemos)	Don't let's get angry

With the exception of *vámonos* 'let's go', informal spoken language tends to avoid this construction. This is usually done by using *ir a* or sometimes simply *a* and an infinitive, e.g. *Vamos a sentarnos* 'Let's sit down', *Bueno, a levantarse* 'OK, let's get up' (note third-person pronoun), *Vamos a verlo/A ver* 'Let's have a look'/'Let's see'. Thus *No nos enfademos* 'Let's not get angry' may be expressed by *No vale la pena enfadarse*, *No nos vamos a enfadar*, *No vamos a enfadarnos*. However, *No nos enfademos* is also acceptable in spoken language.

Note
Ir forms its first-person plural imperative irregularly: *Vamos, Vámonos* 'Let's go'. The expected form *Vayámonos* is nowadays virtually extinct and *Vayamos* is used as an imperative only in set phrases, e.g. *Vayamos al grano* 'Let's get to the point'.

17.6 Third-person imperatives

Third-person imperative forms consisting of *que* + subjunctive are common. They are usually translatable by some formula like 'Let him/her/them . . .', 'Tell him/her/them to . . .':

—*Que llaman preguntando por su marido.*	'There's a phone call for your husband.'
—*Pues que le/lo **llamen** a la oficina*	'Then let them call him at his office'
Que nos cuente qué política económica querría que hiciéramos (Felipe González in *El País*)	Let him tell us what economic policy he'd like us to apply (lit 'make')
Que pasen	Let them come in/tell them to come in
Que ella los bañara, los vistiera, oyera sus preguntas, los enseñara a rezar y a creer en algo (A. Mastretta, Mexico, dialogue)	[As far as I was concerned] let her bathe them, clothe them, listen to their questions, teach them to pray and believe in something

See 33.4 for further remarks on the use of the conjunction *que*.

Note
Third-person imperatives without *que* are found in set phrases: ¡*Dios nos coja confesados!* (archaic or humorous) 'Good God!'/'Heavens above!' (lit. 'May God take us after we've confessed!'), ¡*Sálvese quien pueda!* 'Everyone for himself!' (lit. 'Save him/herself he/she who can').

17.7 First and second-person imperatives preceded by *que*

First and second-person imperatives can also be preceded by *que*. This makes the imperative more insistent or emphatic:

¡*Que tengas un buen fin de semana!*	Have a good week-end!
¡*Que no perdáis el dinero!*	Don't lose the money!
¡*Que se diviertan!*	Have a good time! (*ustedes*)

17.8 Impersonal imperatives

It is possible to form an imperative with impersonal *se*, the resulting construction having no exact equivalent in English. It is much used in formal written Spanish to give instructions without addressing the reader directly:

Rellénese en mayúsculas	Fill out in capital letters (lit. 'let it be filled out . . .')
Cuézanse las patatas durante 15 minutos, córtense en rodajitas, déjense enfriar y cúbranse con mayonesa	Boil the potatoes for 15 minutes, cut into slices, leave to cool and cover with mayonnaise

As the last example shows, the verb agrees in number with the logical object of the verb (in this case with *patatas*).

17.9 The infinitive used as an imperative

The infinitive can sometimes be used as an imperative.
(a) In spoken European Spanish as a familiar replacement for the standard affirmative *vosotros* imperative ending in -*d*. This is discussed in the note to 17.2.4.

(b) The infinitive may be used a brief, impersonal imperative, useful for notices and instructions to the reader.

This use of the infinitive is stylistically controversial. Some grammarians reject the use of the infinitive for affirmative commands and admit only negative forms like *No fumar* 'No smoking', *No tocar* 'Don't touch', *No fijar carteles* 'No bill-sticking', *No asomarse a la ventanilla* 'Do not lean out of the window'. Such negative forms are nowadays seen everywhere in Spain and Mexico (and no doubt elsewhere) although they seem to be a recent development; one used to say ***Prohibido** fumar*, etc.

As far as the affirmative forms are concerned, María Moliner says that an imperative like *Callarse todos* for *Cállense todos* 'Everybody be quiet'/'Be quiet all of you' is not acceptable in careful language. Nevertheless, the form is spreading.

No aparcar delante de las puertas (no aparquen . . .)	No parking in front of doors
Poner en una cacerola la cebolla picada en trozos grandes (Spanish Cookery book: *póngase . . .*)	Put the roughly chopped onion in a saucepan
Descolgar y esperar. Percibirá una señal acústica continua y uniforme. No demorar el marcar (instructions in Spanish phone book)	Lift receiver and wait. You will hear a continuous even tone. Do not delay before dialling
Le gustaba su marido. Adivinar la razón, porque él era espantoso (A. Mastretta, Mexico, dialogue)	She liked her husband, God knows why (lit. 'guess why'), because he was ghastly

Note
Haber plus the past participle is often used to make a sarcastic or withering imperative: *—Me arrepiento de haberla llamado. —Bueno, no haberlo hecho . . .* '"I regret ringing her." '"Well, we shouldn't have done it, should we?"'.

(c) With the preposition *a*, the infinitive may be used to give orders in informal styles:

—Lo he hecho mal.	'I've done it wrong'.
—Bueno, a hacerlo bien la segunda vez (tends to sound uneducated without *a*)	'Well do it right the second time'
¡Todos a callar!	Be quiet everybody!
¡A dormir inmediatamente!	Go to sleep right now!

This type of imperative may sometimes include the speaker: *Bueno, ahora a trabajar* 'Okay, now let's get to work'.

Note
In Spain an infinitive is nowadays often used to introduce the last point in radio or TV news items. This is no doubt not an imperative but an abbreviation of some phrase like *Sólo/Solo nos queda . . .* or *Solo/Sólo falta . . .* 'All that remains is to . . .': *Y finalmente, **añadir** que ésta no es la primera vez que el autor recibe un importante premio literario* 'And finally, let's add/we should add that this isn't the first time that the author has received an important literary prize'.

17.10 The present indicative used as an imperative

The present indicative is sometimes used as an imperative in speech, just as in English, e.g. 'You're getting up right now and going to school'. In both languages this tends to be a no-nonsense imperative and the effect may be brusque to the point of rudeness:

De acuerdo. No te guardo el sitio para mañana, pero pasado me **haces** *dos páginas* (C. Rico-Godoy, Spain, dialogue)	Okay. I won't keep the space for you tomorrow, but the day after tomorrow you're doing two pages for me (editor to journalist)
Nomás que oscurezca te **vas** *por la carretera y* **tiras** *en una barranca el cuerpo de una muchacha que se murió* (J. Ibargüengoitia, Mexico, dialogue; *nomás que = en cuanto* or *nada más . . .* in Spain)	As soon as it gets dark, you go down the road and you throw the body of a girl who died into a ravine
Si quieres, me **llamas** *mañana*	If you want to, call me tomorrow

17.11 Ways of mellowing the imperative

The Spanish imperative can sound more like an order than a polite request, especially if one gets the intonation wrong. There are numerous ways of making a request sound friendly, although in any language a politely worded request can still sound rude if the intonation is abrupt or irritable.

Some of the ways of making a request sound more mellow are:

(a) Use the conditional or imperfect of *poder*.

*¿***Podrían/Podían** *hacer menos ruido (por favor)?*	Would you mind making less noise?/Could you make less noise?

(b) Use *querer*. The conditional makes the imperative even milder:

¿Quieres decirme la verdad?	Would you mind telling me the truth?
*¿***Querrías** *(hacerme el favor de) darle un recado a Pedro?*	Would you mind giving a message to Pedro?

The phrases *Quieres/Querrías/Quiere usted hacerme el favor* are very common in everyday Spanish.

(c) Use the phrase *a ver* 'let's see . . .'.

A ver si vienes a verme más a menudo	Try and come and see me more often
A ver si me devuelves el dinero que te presté	Perhaps you could give me back the money I lent you

(d) Turn the request into a question.

¿Me pone con el 261-84-50 (por favor)?[5]	Can you connect me to 261 8450 please?

(e) In Spain, use *tú* instead of *usted*.

Dame una cerveza	Give me a beer (friendly tone)

This is very widespread in Spain and appropriate between young people (say under thirty) even when they are strangers, but it sounds over-familiar when said to older persons or to people in authority. In Latin America *tú* is used much less frequently between strangers.

---

[5] See 10.17 for how to say telephone numbers in Spanish.

(f) Put a direct object noun in the diminutive.

This is a common way of making a request sound friendly. Compare *Deme una barra de pan* 'Give me a loaf of bread' and *Deme una **barrita** de pan* 'I'll just take a loaf of bread, please'. The diminutive does not necessarily imply smallness in this construction; it simply makes the tone warmer (see 38.2.2).

(g) Add some tag like *¿eh?*, *¡puedes?*

Vamos al cine, ¿quieres?/ ¿vale?[6]	Let's go the cinema, okay?
No chilles, ¿eh?	Stop screaming

17.12 Miscellaneous imperative constructions

Oye/Oiga (usted) (por favor)	Excuse me!, Pardon me! (lit. 'hear!')
No lo vuelvas a hacer/No vuelvas a hacerlo	Don't do it again
Mira lo que he comprado	Look what I have bought
Fíjate lo que me ha pasado	Look what has happened to me
Imagínate qué disgusto[7]	Imagine how upset I was (lit. 'imagine what displeasure')
Trae que te lleve la bolsa (colloquial, Spain only?)	Let me carry your bag
Trae aquí (colloquial, Spain only?)	Give it here/Let me take it
No se te ocurra hacer eso	Don't even think of doing that
No dejes de llamarme/No se te olvide llamarme	Don't forget to call me
Vete a saber	Goodness knows/Heaven knows why
No me digas (incredulous tone)	You don't say!

Note

English allows passive imperatives (normally only in the negative): 'Don't be scared **by** him'. A different solution must be found in Spanish: *No te **dejes** engañar por su apariencia* 'Don't be deceived by his looks', *No **dejes** que te hagan cantar a la fuerza* 'Don't be bullied into singing', *No **dejes** que te mangoneen/No te **dejes** mangonear* 'Don't let yourself be pushed around'.

---

[6] The constant use of *vale* 'okay', 'right', is said by Latin-Americans to be typical of European Spanish.

[7] *El disgusto* 'upset'/'displeasure'; *el asco* 'disgust'.

18

The infinitive

18.1 Summary

Spanish infinitives end in *-ar*, *-er* or *-ir*. In a few infinitives, e.g. *freír*, *reír*, *sonreír*, the vowel bears an accent. These are listed at 13.1.4f.

The Spanish infinitive cannot in itself express number, mood, time or person (this latter fact should be remembered by students of Portuguese). It is also sometimes ambiguous as to voice, i.e. it can be passive in meaning, e.g. *tres cartas sin terminar* 'three unfinished letters' (lit. 'three letters without finishing').

The infinitive may act as a verb or noun, and in the latter case it is masculine singular: *Fumar es malo para la salud* 'Smoking is bad for the health'. This kind of English sentence must not be translated using the Spanish gerund: **Fumando es malo para la salud* is emphatically not Spanish.

Like the gerund, the infinitive often takes suffixed personal pronouns, e.g. *antes de hacerlo* 'before doing it', cf. French *avant de le faire*. When the infinitive is governed by a verb, position of the pronouns may in some cases be optional with variable stylistic effects, as in *quiero verlo* and *lo quiero ver* 'I want to see it'. This topic is discussed at 11.14.4 (Personal pronouns) and below at 18.2.3.

For the use of the infinitive as an imperative see 17.9.

18.2 Infinitive governed by a verb

This section refers to constructions like *Sabe nadar* 'He can swim', *Te desafío a hacerlo* 'I challenge you to do it', etc.

These constructions have many parallels in English, although there are some surprises and Spanish is free of the complication raised by the unpredictable choice between the infinitive and the *-ing* form, cf. 'He claimed **to have** done it' = *Pretendía haberlo hecho* and 'He remembered **having** done it' = *Se acordaba de haberlo hecho*.

18.2.1 Co-referential constructions

If the subject of a main clause and of a subordinate clause are co-referential, i.e. they refer to the same person or thing, the verb in the subordinate clause may be replaced by an infinitive. Compare the following sentences:

Él quiere que lo haga	He wants him/her (someone else) to do it (not co-referential)
Él quiere hacerlo	He wants to do it (co-referential)

| *Prefiero que tú lo abras* | I prefer you to open it |
| *Prefiero abrirlo yo mismo* | I prefer to open it myself |

Constantly recurring verbs that require the infinitive are *poder* 'to be able', *saber* 'to know how to', *deber* 'must', *soler* 'to be accustomed to', *tener que* 'to have to', *hay que* 'it is necessary to'. Modal auxiliary verbs like *poder, deber, saber, haber* are discussed further in Chapter 21.

In some cases both languages optionally allow replacement of the finite verb by a non-finite form, and the infinitive (or the English *-ing* form) is unambiguously co-referential in the third-person:

Desmintieron que hubieran/hubiesen lanzado el misil	They denied that they'd launched the missile (i.e. they themselves or someone else)
*Desmintieron **haber** lanzado el misil*	They denied **having launched** the missile
Reconozco que lo hice	I recognise I did it
Reconozco haberlo hecho	I recognise having done it
Afirmaba que él lo hizo	He claimed he did it (himself or someone else)
Afirmaba haberlo hecho	He claimed to have done it
Recuerdo que lo compré	I remember I bought it
Recuerdo haberlo comprado	I remember having bought it

With some verbs Spanish optionally allows an infinitive construction where English does not allow it or the *-ing* form. See the next section for examples.

18.2.2 Infinitive construction with certain verbs

Spanish allows an infinitive construction with a number of verbs of saying, believing, affirming, etc., a construction which may seem bizarre to English-speakers (one cannot say *'He says to be ill' for 'He says he's ill').

The infinitive construction has the advantage of being co-referential, i.e. it eliminates the ambiguity of *Dice que lo sabe* 'He says (s)he knows it', which may refer to a fourth person. Nevertheless, the ambiguous construction with *que* is much more frequently seen. Compare:

| *Dice estar enfermo* | He says he (i.e. himself) is ill |
| *Dice que está enfermo* | He says he is ill/(US) 'sick' (himself or someone else) |

Further examples:

Dijo llamarse Simón . . . tener 42 años, ser casado, mexicano y estar radicado en el Salto de la Tuxpana (J. Ibargüengoitia, Mexico; the text imitates official language)	He said he was called Simón, was 42, married, Mexican and lived in Salto de la Tuxpana
Creo tener razón	I think I'm right
Creo que tengo razón	I think I'm right
Había creído volverse loco, pensado en matarse (M. Vargas Llosa, Peru)	He had imagined he was going mad, thought about killing himself
Dudo poder hacerlo/Dudo que pueda hacerlo[1]	I doubt I can do it
. . . la información . . . revela ser falsa (C. Fuentes, Mexico, dialogue)	the information turns out to be false

---

[1] The infinitive is particularly common after *dudar* + *poder* 'to doubt one is able to . . .': *Dudo poder hacerlo* 'I doubt I can do it'. However, it is not used elsewhere/after *dudar que* when the latter would require the subjunctive: *Dudo que yo sea tan inteligente como ella dice* 'I doubt I'm as intelligent as she says', but not *'Dudo ser tan inteligente como ella dice.*

Note

In written language an infinitive may appear in relative clauses when the subjects refer to different things and the clause includes a verb of saying or believing. This avoids the use of two *ques*: *las tres muchachas, que él creía* **ser** *hijas de don Mateo* (rather than *que él creía que eran . . .*) 'the three girls, whom he believed to be the daughters of Don Mateo'.

18.2.3 Verbs followed by the infinitive

The following list shows some of the more common verbs that can be followed by an infinitive. Common French equivalents are supplied as a reminder to students of that language to avoid all-too-frequent blunders like **Se acercó de él* for *Se acercó* **a** *él* (French *Il s'est approché de lui*).

Verbs (+ prepositions) followed by infinitive
(verbs marked * allow pronoun shifting. See note (i))

abstenerse de	refrain from
*acabar de: acabo de verla	'I've just seen her'
acercarse a	approach (Fr. *s'approcher de*)
*acertar a	manage to/succeed
*aconsejar	advise (Fr. *conseiller de*)
*acordar	agree to
acordarse de	remember (cf. *recordar*)
*acostumbrar a	be in the habit of
acusar de	accuse of
afirmar	claim/state
*alcanzar a	manage to: *Es todo lo que alcancé a ver* 'It's all I managed to see'
amenazar	threaten to (Fr. *menacer de*): *amenazó matarle* or *con matarle*
*anhelar	long to
animar a	encourage to
*ansiar	long to
*aparentar	seem to
*aprender a	learn to
arrepentirse de	regret/repent
*asegurar	assure
atreverse a	dare to
autorizar a	authorize to
avergonzarse de	be ashamed of
*ayudar a	help to
bajar a	go down to
buscar	seek to (Fr. *chercher à*)
cansarse de	tire of
*cesar de	cease from
*comenzar a	begin to
comprometerse a	undertake to
comunicar	announce/communicate
conceder	concede to
condenar a	condemn to
conducir a	lead to
*confesar	confess
*conseguir	succeed in
consentir en	consent to (Fr. *consentir à*)
consistir en	consist of
contribuir a	contribute to
convenir en	agree to

convidar a	invite to
*creer	believe
cuidar de	take care to
deber	must (see 21.3)
*decidir	decide to (Fr. *décider de*)
decir	say
declarar	declare
*dejar	let/allow: *le dejó hacerlo* or *se lo dejó hacer* 'he let her do it'
*dejar de	leave off
*demostrar	demonstrate
desafiar a	challenge to (Fr. *défier de*)
*desear	desire/wish to
desesperar de	despair of
dignarse	deign to
disponerse a	get ready to
disuadir de	dissuade from
divertirse en	amuse oneself by (usually with gerund; Fr. *s'amuser à*)
dudar en	hesitate over (Fr. *hésiter à*)
echar(se) a	begin to
empeñarse en	insist on
*empezar a	begin to
encargarse de	take charge of
*enseñar a	show how to/teach
esforzarse por	strive to
*esperar	hope/expect/wait
*evitar	avoid (Fr. *éviter de*)
excitar a	excite to
figurarse	imagine
fingir	pretend to
*forzar a	force to
guardarse de	take care not to
gustar de	like to (but usually *Le gusta fumar*, etc.)
habituarse a	get used to
*hacer	make e.g. *La hizo callar*, 'He made her keep quiet'
hartarse de	tire of/have enough of
imaginar	imagine
*impedir	prevent from (Fr. *défendre de*)
impulsar a	urge on to
incitar a	incite to
inclinar a	incline to
inducir a	induce/persuade to
insistir en	insist on (Fr. *insister sur*)
instar a	urge to
*intentar	try to
interesarse en (or *por*)	interest in (Fr. *s'intéresser à*)
invitar a	invite to
jactarse de	boast of
*jurar	swear to
juzgar	judge (but usually with *que . . .*)
limitarse a	limit oneself to
luchar por	struggle to
*llegar a	e.g. *Incluso llegó a robar dinero* 'He even went so far as to steal money'
llevar a	lead to
*lograr	succeed in
*mandar	order to (Fr. *ordonner de*)

mandar a	send to
manifestar	state/declare
maravillarse de	marvel at
merecer	deserve to
meterse a	start to
mover a	move to
*necesitar	need to
negar	deny (*negarse a* 'refuse to')
*obligar a	oblige to (Fr. *obliger de*)
obstinarse en	insist obstinately on
ofrecer	offer
*oír	hear (see 20.7)
olvidar,	forget; infinitive *olvidar* alone is uncommon with the
olvidarse de, olvidársele	infinitive; see 26.6.4
optar (usually *optar por*)	opt to/for
*ordenar	order to (Fr. *ordonner de*)
*parar de	stop
*parecer	seem to
*pasar a	go on to
pasar de	to be uninterested in
pedir	ask to (Fr. *demander à* , *demander de*)
*pensar	*pienso hacerlo* 'I plan to do it'
pensaban en hacerlo	'They were thinking about doing it'
*permitir	allow to (Fr. *permettre de*)
persistir en	persist in
persuadir a	persuade to (Fr. *persuader quelqu'un de faire . . .*)
*poder	be able to
precipitarse a	rush to
*preferir	prefer to
prepararse a	get ready to
presumir de	(approx.) boast about
*pretender	claim to
*procurar	try hard to
*prohibir	prohibit from (Fr. *défendre de*)
*prometer	promise to (Fr. *promettre de*)
quedar en	agree to
*querer	want to (see 21.5)
*recordar	remember to[2]
*rehusar	refuse to (Fr. *refuser de*)
*renunciar a	renounce
resignarse a	resign oneself to
resistirse a	resist
*resolver	resolve to (Fr. *résoudre de*)
*saber	know how to (see 21.2)
sentir	regret/be sorry for
*soler: solía hacerlo	'He habitually did it' (see 21.6)
*solicitar	apply to
soñar con	dream of (Fr. *songer à, rêver de*)
tardar en	be late in/be a long time in (Fr. *tarder à*)
*temer	fear to

[2] The construction is *Me acuerdo de haberla visto* or *Recuerdo haberla visto* 'I remember seeing her'.

Recordarse can only mean 'to remember oneself', as in *Me recuerdo como un niño muy tímido* 'I remember myself as a very timid child'. However *recordarse* for 'to remember' is common in familiar Latin-American speech although it is avoided in careful styles.

*tender a	tend to
*terminar de	finish
*tratar de	try to
vacilar en	hesitate over
venir de	come from
*ver	see (see 20.7)
*volver a (hacer)	(do) again (see 32.6a)

Notes

(i) Verbs preceded by * allow pronoun shifting, i.e. one can say *Acabo de hacerlo* or *Lo acabo de hacer*, *Pienso mudarme mañana* 'I'm thinking of moving tomorrow' or *Me pienso mudar mañana*. Doubtful verbs, e.g. *fingir*, *afirmar*, are not marked. Pronoun shifting is discussed in detail at 11.14.4.

(ii) Verbs of motion, e.g. *salir*, *bajar*, *ir*, *volver*, *entrar*, *acercar(se)*, always take *a* before an infinitive: *Bajó a hablar con ella* 'He went down to talk to her', *Entraron a saludar al profesor* 'They went in to say hello to the teacher', etc.

(iii) For the use of the infinitive as a noun, e.g. *Es bueno jugar al tenis* 'It's good to play tennis'/'Playing tennis is good', see 18.6.

18.2.4 Verbs of permitting and forbidding

These, and certain other verbs, allow either a subjunctive or an infinitive construction. They are discussed under the subjunctive at 16.5.2.

It is worth repeating here that when used with the infinitive they can appear without an object or with only one object in Spanish, but not in English: *Esto prohíbe pensar que* . . . 'This prohibits us/one from thinking that . . .'.

18.2.5 Infinitive after verbs of perception

The infinitive is used after verbs like *ver*, *oír*, to denote a completed action. An incomplete action is indicated by the gerund. English makes the same distinction: compare 'I saw him smoke a cigar' and 'I saw him smoking a cigar'. See 20.7 for more examples:

Te vi entrar	I saw you come in
Se lo oí hacer	I heard her do it
Te lo vi firmar	I saw you sign it
Vimos llegar el avión (note word order)	We saw the plane arrive

Note

A passive may be required in the English translation: *Nunca la oí nombrar* 'I've never heard her mentioned'.

18.3 Infinitive after subordinators

An infinitive construction is possible after many subordinators, e.g. *hasta* 'until', *con tal de* 'provided that', *en caso de* 'in the event that', *a pesar de* 'despite', *para* 'in order to', *con el objeto de* 'with the aim of' and other subordinators of purpose, *nada más* 'as soon as', *por* 'by', *sin* 'without', *antes de* 'before', *después de* 'after', etc.

Foreign students should apply the rule of co-referentiality: the infinitive should be used only if the subject of the subordinate verb is the same as the main verb's, as in *Lo hice antes de salir* 'I did it before I went out/before going out'.

If the subjects are not co-referential, the subjunctive or indicative must be used, the choice being determined by the rules laid at out 16.12.1. Compare

Lo haré nada más acabar esto 'I'll do it as soon as I've finished this' and *Lo haré nada más que acabe esto* 'I'll do it as soon as this finishes'. The latter sentence could also mean 'as soon as I finish this', but a third-person interpretation comes most readily to mind when the subjunctive is used. Further examples:

Lo haré después de comer	I'll do it after I've had lunch
Lo haré después de que hayáis comido	I'll do it after you've had lunch
Entré sin verte	I entered without seeing you
Entré sin que tú me vieras/vieses	I entered without you seeing me
Se fue antes de contestar	He left before he answered
Se fue antes de que yo contestase/contestara	He left before I answered
Enfermó (Lat. Am. *Se enfermó*) *por no comer*	He fell ill/(US) 'sick' from not eating
Se enfadó al enterarse	He got angry when he found out
Se hace camino al andar (Antonio Machado, Spain)	One makes one's path as one goes along

Spontaneous language often uses an infinitive construction with these subordinators, and also in the construction *al* + infinitive 'on . . .-ing', even when the subjects are not co-referential. Thus *me di cuenta al llegar* (co-referential) 'I realized on arriving' is correct, ?*Me di cuenta al llegar Juan* literally ?'I realized on Juan's arriving' (not co-referential) is a frequent but dubious way of saying *me di cuenta cuando llegó Juan* 'I realized when Juan arrived'. *Lo terminé antes de que tú llegases/llegaras* 'I finished before you arrived' is correct, ?*Lo terminé antes de llegar tú* is constantly heard in informal speech but is suspect. Use of the infinitive when the subjects are different is best avoided by foreigners, since native speakers often on reflection reject such utterances as badly formed. Examples:

?*Le miraba sin él darse cuenta* (J. Marsé, dialogue: *sin que él se diese/diera cuenta*)	He watched him without him realizing
?¿*Te voy a ver antes de irte?* (Spanish informant, i.e. *antes de que te vayas*)	Am I going to see you before you go?
?*Llegamos antes de empezar la película* (*antes de que empezara/empezase* . . .)	We arrived before the film started
?*Es decir que había comprado marfil para usted vender* (*Vindicación de Cuba*, Cuba, dialogue, for . . . *para que usted lo vendiera/vendiese*)	In other words he had bought ivory for you to sell
?¿*Me podés comprar postales para mandar yo?* (Argentine informant, i.e. *para que yo las mande*; Spain *puedes* for *podés*)	Could you buy me some post-cards for me to send?

18.4 Replacement of finite forms by the infinitive

The infinitive may be used to give a brief answer a question:

—¿*Qué hacemos?*	'What do we do?'
—*Esperar*	'Wait'
—¿*Qué me aconsejas?*	'What do you advise me?'
—*No decir nada*	'Say nothing'
—¿*Pero se puede saber qué está usted haciendo?*	'But do you mind telling me what you're doing?'
—¡*Sacar a mi mujer!* (E. Arenas, Spain, dialogue)	'Getting my wife out!'

18.5   Infinitive: passive or active?

The Spanish infinitive sometimes acquires a passive meaning especially after *sin, por, a* and *para*:

Esto aún está por ver	This is still to be seen
una cerveza sin abrir	an unopened beer
casas a medio construir	half-built houses
un movimiento sin organizar	an unorganized movement
Los republicanos llegan a la convención	the Republicans are arriving at the
con las tácticas electorales sin decidir	Convention with their electoral tactics
(*El País*, Spain)	undecided
En su recámara había cuatro maletas a medio	In her bedroom there were four half-
hacer (A. Mastretta, Mexico, dialogue;	packed suitcases
recámara = dormitorio in Spain)	
. . . *trabajos para hacer por el estudiante*	work to be done (lit. 'to do') by the student

18.6   Infinitive as a noun

The infinitive may function as a noun, in which case it is always masculine and usually singular:

Mañana me toca lavar el coche	It's my turn to wash the car tomorrow
Votar Comunista es votar contra el paro	To vote Communist is to vote against
(election poster)	unemployment
mejor no hacerlo	best not do it
Odio ordenar	I hate sorting/tidying
un atolondrado ir y venir	a mad coming and going
. . . *el envejecer despacio entre laureles*	. . . ageing slowly among withered
marchitos y ciénagas (G. García Márquez,	laurels and swamps
Colombia)	

18.7   Definite articles before the infinitive

The definite article is nowadays not often used with the infinitive except:
(a) In the common construction *al* + infinitive.

Al entrar, se dio cuenta de que no había nadie	On entering he realized no one was there
Tómese una pastilla al acostarse	Take a pill on going to bed

(b) When the infinitive is qualified by an adjective or by a noun phrase joined to the infinitive by *de*.

Oyó el agitado girar de una cucharilla contra	He heard the agitated grating of a
un vaso (L. Goytisolo, Spain)	teaspoon against a glass
con el andar de los años	as the years passed by

(c) When the infinitive refers to some specific or personal action rather than to a general statement. Compare *Vivir separados cuesta más* 'Living apart costs more' (general statement) and *El vivir separados fue cosa de él* 'Living apart was his idea' (specific, personal). Also:

Ayuda mucho dejar de fumar	It helps to stop smoking
Fue idea del médico **el** *dejar de fumar*	Stopping smoking was the doctor's idea

In other cases, use of the definite article often seems to be optional, although it is much less common in informal styles. The article is, however, quite often retained when the infinitive is the subject of a verb.

In all the following examples the definite article before the infinitive could have been omitted, although in the attributed examples it was in fact used. Omission would make the style slightly less literary:

Paula no pudo evitar (el) reírse (J.J. Plans, Spain)	Paula couldn't help laughing
Odiaban (el) vivir en casa de sus abuelos	They hated living in their grandparents' house
(El) hacer esto le costó mucho trabajo	Doing this cost him a great deal of effort
Esto permite a los robots (el) ser reprogramados para . . .	This allows robots to be re-programmed to . . .

The article is retained in some constructions involving *en*:

La moda en el vestir influye en la moda del maquillaje	Fashion in dressing influences fashion in make-up
Algunos españoles son un poco enfáticos en el hablar	Some Spaniards are rather ponderous in their manner of speaking
Le conocí en el andar	I recognised him from his way of walking

After set verb phrases involving a preposition, the article is omitted:

Hice mal en venir aquí	I did wrong in coming here
Tardaron horas en hacerlo	They took hours to do it
Acabaron por no hablarse con nadie	They ended up not talking to anyone
Tratábamos de contactarla	We were trying to contact her

The indefinite article *un* also occurs before a qualified infinitive:

en un abrir y cerrar de ojos	in the wink of an eye
después de dos años de un agitado avanzar	after two years of agitated progress (lit. 'agitated progressing') along the road to
por el camino de la libertad	liberty

18.8 Infinitive as an imperative

This subject is discussed in 17.9.

18.9 'Rhetorical' infinitive

The infinitive may be used in rhetorical questions or to express disbelief or bewilderment:

¡Pagar yo cien mil por eso!	What! Me pay 100,000 for that!
¡Enamorarme yo a mis años!	Me fall in love at my age!
Pero, ¿cómo abrirlo sin llave?	But how (on earth) does one open it without a key?

18.10 Adjective + *de* + infinitive

Students of French must learn the difference between sentences like

Es difícil aprender español	It's difficult to learn Spanish

and

*El español es difícil **de** aprender*	Spanish is difficult to learn

De is not used when the adjective modifies the infinitive itself:

No es fácil creerlo	It isn't easy to believe it
Es increíble pensar que el hombre ha pisado la luna	It's incredible to think that man has walked on the moon
Es imposible comprobar que . . .	It's impossible to prove that . . .

When the adjective does not modify the infinitive but a noun or pronoun (present or implied), *de* is used:

*(Eso) es difícil **de** averiguar (difícil* modifies *eso)*	That's difficult to check
*Creo que es cierto, pero es imposible **de** comprobar*	I think it's true, but it's impossible to prove

18.11 Infinitive preceded by *que*

The following construction must be noted – particularly by students of French: cf. *J'ai beaucoup à faire, Je n'ai rien à faire,* etc.:

*Tengo mucho **que** hacer*	I've got a lot to do
*Voy a comprar algo **que/para** leer*	I'm going to buy something to read
*Dame algo **que/para** hacer*	Give me something to do
*Eso nos ha dado bastante **que** hacer*	This has given us enough to do
*Te queda mucho **que** sufrir en este mundo*	You've a lot left to suffer in this world

But this construction with *que* cannot be used with verbs of needing, requesting, searching:

*Necesito algo **para** comer*	I need something to eat
*Quiero algo **para** beber*	I want something to drink
*Pidió algo **para** calmar su dolor de muelas*	He asked for something to soothe his toothache
*Busco algo **para** . . .*	I'm looking for something to . . .

Note
The construction with *que* must be distinguished from the following similar construction with *qué* 'what'/'anything': *No tengo **qué** comer* 'I haven't got anything to eat', *No sabemos **qué** pensar* 'We don't know what to think'.

18.12 *El problema a resolver, un argumento a tomar en cuenta,* etc.

This combination of noun + *a* + infinitive is an increasingly fashionable alternative way of saying 'something that is to be/ought to be done', e.g . . . *que va a hacerse/que hay que hacer.*

Seco (1992), 5, says that it is a Gallicism reinforced by the influence of English – 'a problem to (be) solve(d)', *un problème à résoudre* – but he welcomes its brevity and points out that it is not strictly equivalent to *por* + infinitive: *cosas por hacer* = 'things still to be done', *cosas a hacer* = 'things to do'.

The Academy's *Esbozo,* 3.11.5, tolerates certain set constructions used in commerce and finance, e.g. *total a pagar* 'total payable', *cantidades a deducir* 'amounts deductible', *asuntos a tratar* 'business pending'/'agenda', but notes that the Academies of all Spanish-speaking countries condemn such sentences as *Tengo terrenos a vender* 'I've got land to sell' (for *que/para vender*), *personas a convocar* 'people to call/summon' (for *que convocar*), etc.

The construction with *a* is very common in Latin America. For more examples see 35.9.

19

Participles

This chapter discusses past participles, e.g. *hablado* 'spoken', *visto* 'seen', and adjectival or present participles ending in *-ante, -(i)ente*, e.g. *perteneciente* 'belonging', *inquietante* 'worrying'.

19.1 Past participle: general

The past participle has several uses:

(a) It is used with *haber* to form the compound tenses of verbs. In this case the participle is invariably in the masculine singular form: *Ha hablado* 'He has spoken', *Yo la he visto* 'I have seen her'. See 14.8 for discussion.

(b) It is occasionally used with *tener* or *llevar* to express the idea of acquisition or accumulation, as in *Tengo compradas las entradas* 'I've bought the entrance tickets', *Llevo tomados tres somníferos* 'I've taken three sleeping tablets'. See 14.8.3 for discussion.

(c) It is used to form the passive: *Fue impreso/a* 'It was printed', *Fueron observados/observadas* 'They were observed'. The passive is discussed in Chapter 28.

(d) It functions as an adjective, in which case it agrees in number and gender like any adjective: *una exagerada reacción* 'an exaggerated reaction', *un argumento improvisado* 'an improvised argument', *una desesperada tentativa* 'a desperate attempt', etc.

These adjectival participles may, like any other adjective, be converted into nouns by use of an article, demonstrative, numeral or some other word that has the effect of nominalizing adjectives: *un muerto* 'a dead body', *ese herido* 'that wounded person', *¿Qué dirán por su parte los censurados?* 'What will those who have been censured have to say for themselves?', *varios condenados* 'several condemned persons'. Such forms can neatly replace an English relative clause: *Nunca olvidaremos a los desaparecidos* 'We'll never forget those who disappeared', *¿Dónde están los recién llegados?* 'Where are the ones who've just arrived'.

Many words ending in *-ado, -ido* are used only as adjectives, e.g. *adecuado* 'appropriate'/'adequate', *desgraciado* 'unhappy', *desmesurado* 'disproportionate', *indiscriminado* 'indiscriminate', *descarado* 'shameless'.

Some past participles have become true adjectives, i.e. they may in appropriate circumstances appear before a noun: *una arriesgada aventura* 'a risky venture', *la controvertida propuesta* 'the controversial proposal', etc. Other past participles remain verbal and may not precede a noun: *un árbol talado* 'a felled tree', *un periódico quemado* 'a burnt newspaper', *una reunión pospuesta/aplazada* 'a postponed meeting', *un libro impreso* 'a printed book'.

Further examples of participles that may also function as true adjectives are:

alabado	praised	*desconocido*	unknown
alarmado	alarmed	*emocionado*	excited/moved
alejado	remote	*justificado*	justified
elevado	elevated	*marcado*	marked
debido	due	*resignado*	resigned
dedicado	dedicated	*supuesto*	alleged/supposed

and many others.

Such adjectival participles may appear with *ser* without creating a passive sentence: *Su reacción era exagerada* 'His reaction was exaggerated', *Mi llanto era desesperado* 'My weeping was desperate', *Su cara me era desconocida,* 'Her/his face was unknown to me'. Verbal participles form passive sentences when used in the same way: *La ciudad fue destruida* 'The city was destroyed', *Eran perseguidos* 'They were persecuted/pursued'.

In this case it may be possible to make the verbal participle adjectival by using *estar*, e.g. *La ciudad estaba destruida* 'The city was in a state of destruction'. (The difference between *estaba destruido* and the passive with *ser*, *fue destruido*, is discussed at 28.2.5).

19.2 Past participles: forms

19.2.1 Regular and irregular past participles
The past participle is formed in most cases by replacing the *-ar* of an infinitive by *ado*, and *-er* and *-ir* by *-ido*: *hablar/hablado, tener/tenido, construir/construido, ir/ido, ser/sido*, etc.

There are a few common irregular past participles:

Infinitive	Past participle
abrir	*abierto*
absolver (and all verbs in *-solver*)	*absuelto*
cubrir (and compounds)	*cubierto*
decir	*dicho*
escribir (and compounds e.g. *describir*, etc.)	*escrito*
hacer	*hecho*
morir	*muerto*
poner (and compounds)	*puesto*
romper	*roto*
ver (and compounds)	*visto*
volver (and compounds)	*vuelto*

A few have separate adjectival and verbal participles, cf. *Está **despierto** porque lo/le he despert**ado*** 'He's awake because I've woken him'. The following list includes the most important examples.

The bracketed forms in the following list are mentioned by the grammarians but they are virtually never found nowadays:

	Verbal	**Adjectival**	
absorber	*absorbido*	*absorto*	absorbed
bendecir	*bendecido*	*bendito*	blessed
confesar	*confesado*	*confeso*	confessed
confundir	*confundido*	*confuso*	confused
despertar	*despertado*	*despierto*	woken up
elegir	*elegido*	*electo*	elected
freír	*(freído)/frito*	*frito*	fried
imprimir	*imprimido*	*impreso*	printed
maldecir	*maldecido*	*maldito*	cursed
prender	*prendido*	*preso*	pinned on[1]
presumir	*presumido*	*presunto*	presumed
proveer	*proveído*	*provisto*	equipped with
soltar	*soltado*	*suelto*	released
suspender	*suspendido*	*suspenso*	failed (exams)

19.2.2 Irregular past participles in Latin America

A number of irregular adjectival participle forms are more widely used in Latin America than in Spain.

These forms are scholarly participles that are either obsolete in Spain or used only in set phrases, e.g. *el presidente electo* 'the president elect'. They are regularly used in Latin America not only as adjectives but also in the formation of passives, e.g. *Resultó electo candidato a la presidencia* (A. Mastretta, Mexico) 'He was elected as presidential candidate', Spain *salió elegido*:

	Spain	**Lat. Am. adjectival**	
convencer	*convencido*	*convicto*	convinced
corromper	*corrompido*	*corrupto*[2]	corrupt
describir	*descrito*	*descripto*	described
dividir	*dividido*	*diviso*	divided
inscribir	*inscrito*	*inscripto*	entered (a written item)
prescribir	*prescrito*	*prescripto*	prescribed

Examples:

Ocurre en las regiones antárticas descriptas con extraordinaria vividez (J.L. Borges, Argentina, Spain *descritas*)	It happens in the Antarctic regions described with extraordinary vividness
Incluye todos los shampoos prescriptos por médicos (*Gente*, Argentina; Spain *recetados/prescritos*)	It includes all the shampoos prescribed by doctors
su apoyo irrestricto (ibid. Spain *incondicional*)	his unlimited support
. . . *escritores que fueron conservadores convictos* (M. Vargas Llosa, Peru; in Spain *convicto* = 'convicted')	writers who were convinced conservatives

Latin-Americans may reject the use of the regular participles in such sentences, but the irregular forms are not accepted by most Peninsular speakers, and certainly not in the formation of the passive.

---

[1]*Prender* has numerous meanings. In Latin America it is often used for 'to switch on' (lights, etc.); Spain *encender*.
[2] Both *una sociedad corrompida* and *una sociedad corrupta* 'a corrupt society' are said in Spain, the latter being nowadays more frequent.

Note

Muerto is the passive participle of *matar* 'to kill' when applied to human beings: *Su padre fue muerto durante la guerra* 'His father was killed in the war' but *Unos bandidos habían matado a su padre* 'Some bandits had killed his father', *Con el tiempo sería muerto por la Gestapo* (Ernesto Sábato, Argentina, interview) 'He was later to be killed by the Gestapo'.

19.3 Participle clauses

Participle clauses are common in Spanish. These clauses often have exact English counterparts, but slight differences occur between the two languages (see also 31.3.4 for sentences like *Aceptó irritada* 'She accepted irritably'):

Me fui, convencido de que él no sabía nada	I left, convinced he knew nothing
el alcalde de Barcelona, acompañado del alcalde de Madrid (acompañado por = 'escorted by')	the mayor of Barcelona, accompanied by the mayor of Madrid
José González, nacido el 23 de marzo	José González, born on 23 March
—¿Dónde vas? preguntó alarmado	'Where are you going?', he asked in alarm
su padre, muerto en 1956 . . .	His father, who died in 1956 . . .

Absolute participle clauses (i.e. participles that do not depend on another verb in the sentence) are quite common, especially in literary styles. Some absolute participle constructions are stylistically normal, others are rather literary. They can rarely be translated word for word:

Llegados a Madrid, se alojaron en el mejor hotel (see note)	Having arrived in Madrid, they stayed at the best hotel
Concluidas las primeras investigaciones, la policía abandonó el lugar de autos	The initial investigations having been concluded, the police left the scene of the crime
Por fin, trascurridos siete años desde la publicación de su primera novela . . .	At last, seven years having passed since the publication of his first novel . . .
Terminada la guerra, muchos ex-combatientes prefirieron no volver a su patria	Once the war was over, many ex-combatants preferred not to return to their own country
Después de vendida la casa, nos arrepentimos (from Seco, (1992), 284)	Once the house was sold, we regretted it
Arrasado el jardín, profanados los cálices y las aras, entraron a caballo los hunos en la biblioteca monástica (J.L. Borges, Argentina, very literary)	Having demolished the garden and profaned chalices and altars, the Huns rode into the monastery library

Note

Llegar seems to be the only verb of motion that allows this construction. One cannot say **Entrada en el agua se puso a nadar* 'Entering the water she began to swim': *Cuando entró en el agua se puso a nadar*, or **Bajados del tren* for *Cuando bajaron del tren* 'When they got out of the train'.

19.4 Participles in *-ante, -iente* or *-ente*

Adjectival present participles may be formed from many, but by no means all verbs. Such participles function like the English adjectival forms in -ing: 'Sleeping Beauty' = *La Bella Durmiente*. New coinages are appearing constantly, many of them inspired by English adjectives ending in -ing.

Adjectival participles are formed:

-ar conjugation: replace the *-ar* of the infinitive by *-ante*: *alarmar* > *alarmante* 'alarming', *inquietar* > *inquietante* 'worrying'.

-er conjugation: replace the *-er* of the infinitive by *-iente* or, in a few cases, by *-ente*.

-ir conjugation: replace the *-iendo* of the gerund by *-iente* or *-ente*, the choice being unpredictable.

Examples from the *-er* and *-ir* conjugations:

	Gerund	**-nte form**	
crecer	*creciendo*	*creciente*	growing
proceder	*procediendo*	*procedente*	proceeding
sorprender	*sorprendiendo*	*sorprendente*	surprising
tender	*tendiendo*	*tendente*	tending (to)
concernir	*concerniendo*	*concerniente*	concerning
conducir	*conduciendo*	*conducente*	leading (to)
existir	*existiendo*	*existente*	existing/extant
dormir	*durmiendo*	*durmiente*	sleeping
herir	*hiriendo*	*hiriente*	wounding
producir	*produciendo*	*producente*	producing (*contra-producente*, counter-productive)
reír	*riendo*	*riente*	laughing
salir	*saliendo*	*saliente*	outgoing, etc.
seguir	*siguiendo*	*siguiente*	following
sonreír	*sonriendo*	*sonriente*	smiling

There are a few irregular formations:

convencer	*convenciendo*	*convincente*	convincing
convenir	*conviniendo*	*conveniente*	suitable (not really a participle)
fluir	*fluyendo*	*fluente*	flowing/fluent
provenir	*proviniendo*	*proveniente*	coming from

Forms in *-nte* cannot be coined from all verbs and should be learnt separately from the dictionary, especially in view of the remark in note (ii). They are often used in written, mainly journalistic style to replace relative clauses in the same way as English participles in *-ing*:

una situación cambiante/estresante	a changing/stressful situation
el ministro saliente	the outgoing minister
condiciones vinculantes (El País, Spain)	binding conditions
resultados sobresalientes	outstanding results
un éxito fulminante	a fulminating success
En 1984 todavía 157.000 personas, pertenecientes a diferentes clases sociales y procedentes de lugares muy distintos de nacimiento, votaron . . . (El País)	In 1984, 157,000 people belonging to various social classes and originating from widely different places, still voted . . .
el millón y medio restante	the remaining 1.5 million

Notes
(i) The gerund in *-ando* or *-iendo* cannot replace the *-nte* form in any of these examples. See 20.3 for discussion.
(ii) It must be emphasized that these participles are formed unpredictably. English speakers often invent non-existent words like **moviente* for 'moving': *piezas movibles*

= 'moving parts', *espectáculo conmovedor* 'moving spectacle'. Compare also *mesa plegable* 'folding table', *agua potable* 'drinking water', *confiado/crédulo* 'confiding', *planta trepadora* = 'climbing plant', *resultados satisfactorios* 'satisfying results', *hechos reveladores* 'revealing facts' and many others.

(iii) Many forms in *-nte* are not strictly speaking participles but non-verbal adjectives, e.g. *brillante* 'shining', *corriente* 'current'/'ordinary', *aparente* 'apparent', *reciente* 'recent', etc.

(iv) With the exception of a few slang or popular words, e.g. *dominanta* 'bossy' (of a woman), *currante* > *curranta* (familiar Peninsular Spanish for 'hard-working'), *atorrante* > *atorranta* 'slacker'/'lay-about', *golfante* > *golfanta* (popular Peninsular Spanish for 'rascal'/'no-good'), neither participles nor adjectives ending in *-nte* have a separate feminine form. However, a few nouns in *-nte* make their feminine with *-nta*. See 1.2.5.

20

The gerund

For the use of the gerund to form the continuous aspect of verbs, e.g. *estoy hablando* 'I'm talking', *está diciendo* 'he's saying', etc. see Chapter 15.

20.1 General

The gerund is invariable in form, but pronouns may sometimes be attached to it: *Estaba esperándolos* or *Los estaba esperando* 'He was waiting for them'. See 11.14.5 for the difference between the two forms.

The Spanish gerund is quite unlike the English *-ing* form, which serves as gerund, present participle, noun and adjective, and also unlike the French form ending in *-ant* which covers the functions of both the Spanish gerund and the participle form in *-ante, -(i)ente* (discussed at 19.4).

The Spanish gerund is theoretically a kind of adverb and can therefore properly only modify verbs, but not nouns. ?*Una caja conteniendo libros* 'a box containing books' is therefore bad Spanish since there is no verb; this mistake is very common among English-speakers. See 20.3 for detailed discussion.

20.2 Forms of the gerund

(a) All verbs of the *-ar* conjugation, including radical changing verbs: replace the *-ar* of the infinitive by *-ando*: *hablar* 'to speak' > *hablando, contar* 'to tell' > *contando*.

(b) Verbs of the *-er* and *-ir* conjugations: replace the infinitive ending with *-iendo*: *temer* 'to fear' > *temiendo, vivir* 'to live' > *viviendo, producir* 'to produce' > *produciendo*.

Irregular verbs form the gerund in the same way – *ser* > *siendo, tener* > *teniendo* – with the following exceptions:

verbs like *construir*	*construyendo, huyendo*
verbs like *poseer*	*poseyendo, leyendo*
verbs ending in *-ñir* or *-ñer*	*tañendo*
verbs ending in *-llir*	*bullendo*
verbs like *pedir*	*pidiendo*
verbs like *sentir*	*sintiendo, riñendo*
verbs like *reír*	*riendo, sonriendo*
dormir, morir	*durmiendo, muriendo*
traer, caer and their compounds	*trayendo, cayendo*
decir and its compounds	*diciendo*

erguirse	*irguiéndose*
ir	*yendo*
oír and its compounds	*oyendo*
poder	*pudiendo*
venir and its compounds	*viniendo*

20.3 'A box containing books', 'a girl speaking French', etc.

English and French regularly replace relative clauses by a participle construction using the *-ing* form or the *-ant* form of the verb: 'We need a girl who speaks French'/'We need a girl speaking French', 'He had a box that contained several books'/'He had a box containing several books', *C'est là une réponse qui équivaut à un refus*/*C'est là une réponse équivalant à un refus*[1] 'That's a reply that amounts/amounting to a refusal'.

Since the Spanish gerund can theoretically only modify verbs and not nouns, such sentences must usually be translated by a relative clause:

Necesitamos una chica que hable francés (not **hablando francés*)	We need a girl who speaks French
Tenía una caja que contenía varios libros (not **conteniendo libros*)	He had a box containing several books
Esa/Ésa es una respuesta que equivale a una negativa (not **equivaliendo a . . .*)	That's a reply amounting to a refusal

The gerund is possible only when there is a verb in the main clause to which it can refer, e.g. *Me **escribió rogándome** que fuera a verla* 'She wrote a letter asking me to go and see her'. *El cartero trajo una carta pidiendo dinero* 'The postman brought a letter asking for money' is therefore correct only if *pidiendo* refers to *trajo* . . . and not to *carta*, i.e. only if the postman himself is asking for money.

However, this rule is broken:

(a) In captions to pictures.

Dos 747 siendo preparados para el despegue	Two 747s being prepared for take-off
El Avante publicó mi foto quitándome los aretes (A. Mastretta, Mexico, dialogue)	*Avante* published a photo of me taking off my earrings[2]

(b) After verbs meaning 'hear', 'imagine', 'see', 'find', usually to show that the action is actually in progress. See 20.7 for more details.

(c) In the exceptional cases of the adjectives *ardiendo* 'burning' and *hirviendo* 'boiling'. See 4.4 for discussion.

(d) In official and administrative documents.

una ley decretando . . . (= *una ley por la que se decreta . . .*)	a Law decreeing . . .

---

[1] Judge & Healey (1983), 183. Unlike Spanish and English, French also allows the *-ant* form to refer to a subject different to that of the main clause: *La pluie tombant à verse, le voyageur s'arrêta sous un hangar* (ibid.) = *Ya que llovía a cántaros, el viajero se detuvo bajo un granero* 'As it was pouring, the traveller stopped under a barn'.

[2] *Los aretes* = 'hoops', i.e. large earrings. Otherwise *los pendientes*.

This construction, sometimes called the *gerundio curalense*, is deeply entrenched in certain documents, e.g. the *Boletín Oficial del Estado*[3], but Seco, (1992), 208 condemns it, as does the Academy's *Esbozo . . .*, 3.16.8.

(e) Occasionally by writers whose style is presumably above reproach:

El propósito de Probo, el hombre solo afrontando a la multitud, no se pudo realizar (Seco, 1992, xiii)[4]	It was not possible to realize the goal of Probus, the man alone facing the multitude

(f) Constantly in spontaneous speech and informal writing:

Tenía mi edad y un hijo viviendo con su mamá (A. Mastretta, Mexico, dialogue)	She was my age and had a son living with her mother
. . . luego ya en mi habitación, recién limpia y oliendo a ambientador de flores (C. Martín Gaite, Spain)	Then back in my room, (which was) recently cleaned and smelling of flower-scented air-freshener
Hombres trabajando a 400m (Mexican road sign)	Men working at 400 metres

Foreign learners should probably avoid all these uses of the gerund except **(a)**, **(b)** and **(c)**. However, the grammarians' wholesale condemnation of **(d)** to **(f)** seems excessive, since in certain contexts these constructions are clearly acceptable to careful native speakers.

Note
The participle form ending in *-nte* may sometimes be used like the English *-ing* form: *. . . personas pertenecientes a diferentes clases sociales* '. . . people belonging to different social classes'. This construction, possible only with a limited number of verbs, is discussed at 19.4.

20.4 Basic uses of the gerund

In the examples shown in 20.4.1 - 20.4.5, the gerund cannot be negated. One cannot say **No dándome cuenta de que estaba presente, me fui* for 'Not realizing he was present, I left' = *Sin darme cuenta de que estaba presente, me fui*. Also 'I've lost a lot of money by not answering the phone' = *He perdido mucho dinero por no contestar al teléfono*, not **. . . no contestando al teléfono*. An exception is *No queriendo molestar, me fui* 'Not wanting to be a nuisance, I left'.

20.4.1 Gerund used to modify the main verb in the sentence
In this case the gerund functions like an adverb. It may be used to indicate simultaneous actions.

The action denoted by the gerund must be happening at the same time as or almost simultaneously with that of the main verb. Sentences like *?El ladrón huyó volviendo horas más tarde* 'The thief fled, returning hours later' should be expressed *El ladrón huyó y volvió horas más tarde*. *?Abriendo la puerta, entró en la casa* (better *Abrió la puerta y entró en la casa*) is rather less acceptable in Spanish than 'Opening the door, he entered the house'.

Se fue gritando	He went off shouting
Se levantó dando por terminada la entrevista	He got up, judging the interview to be at an end

---

[3] A publication containing the definitive text of new Spanish laws.
[4] Despite his unequivocal condemnation of this very construction (p. 208), in which case only *. . . el hombre solo que afrontaba a la multitud* is possible.

Metió la carta en el sobre, cerrándolo a continuación	He put the letter in the envelope, sealing it afterwards

Note

With the verbs *ser* and *estar* the gerund can translate 'when' or 'while', a construction strange to English-speakers: *Estando en París, me enteré de que su padre había muerto* 'While I was in Paris, I found out that his father had died', *Le conocí siendo yo bombero* 'I met him while I was a fireman', *Te lo diré, pero no estando aquí esta señora* 'I'll tell you, but not while this lady is here'.

20.4.2 Gerund to indicate method

The gerund may indicate the method by which an action is performed. English usually requires the preposition 'by':

Hizo su fortuna comprando acciones a tiempo	He made his fortune (by) buying shares at the right time
Te puedes poner en contacto conmigo llamando a este número	You can contact me by ringing this number
Elijo libros a través de las sugerencias de los periódicos y yendo a numerosas conferencias (Queen Sofía, quoted in *El País*)	I choose books from suggestions in the newspapers and by going to numerous lectures

Note

This construction is often equivalent to a condition: *Apretando/Si lo aprietas de ese modo lo vas a romper* 'You'll break it if you squeeze it'/'by squeezing it like that', *Poniéndose/Si se pone así conmigo usted no conseguirá nada* 'You'll get nowhere if you get like that with me', . . .*es probable que este servicio no se ofrezca en su provincia o que, **aun existiendo**, no se haya anunciado* (Spanish *Yellow Pages*) '. . . It is probable that this service does not exist in your province or, even if it exists (lit. 'even existing'), it has not been advertised'.

20.4.3 To express purpose (= *para* + infinitive)

This construction occurs with verbs of communication:

Me escribió diciéndome/para decirme que fuera/fuese a verle	He wrote telling me to come and see him
Nos llamó pidiendo/para pedir dinero	He rang us asking/to ask for money
Letonia y Estonia han aprobado leyes privando a la población rusa del derecho de ciudadanía (*El País*, Spain; *aprobar* functions like a verb of communication here)	Latvia and Estonia have passed laws depriving their Russian population of citizenship

20.4.4 To indicate cause (= *ya que* . . ., *puesto que* . . . + finite verb)

Siendo estudiante, tendrá usted derecho a una beca	Since you're a student, you'll be entitled to a grant
Miguel, viendo que era inútil intentar persuadirla, se fue	Seeing/Since he could see that it was useless to try to persuade her, Miguel left
Confieso que, a mí, siendo editor, lo único que me procupa es que no lean (*Cambio16*, Spain)	I admit that, since I'm a publisher, the only thing that worries me is that they don't read

20.4.5 To express concession (= *aunque* + finite verb)

The Spanish gerund occasionally signifies 'although', often in combination with *aun* 'even'.

Siendo inteligente como es, parece tonto	Although intelligent, he looks stupid
Aun estando enfermo nos resulta útil	He's useful to us, even though he's ill

. . . pueden pensar que el sol tiene un pie de diámetro, siendo que la "realidad" es gigantescamente diferente (E. Sábato, Argentina, interview)	. . . they may think that the sun is one foot in diameter, although 'reality' is vastly different

20.4.6 Preceded by *como* to replace *como si*

Me miró como riéndose (= *como si se estuviera riendo*)	He looked at me as though he were laughing

20.5 *En* + gerund

In older language and in some dialects this is an equivalent of *al* + infinitive: *en llegando al bosque* = *al llegar al bosque* 'on arriving at the woods' (cf. French *en arrivant à*). This construction seems to be virtually extinct in educated usage. Its modern equivalent, *al* + infinitive, is discussed at 18.3.

20.6 Gerund used to qualify the object of a verb

Like the English *-ing* form, the Spanish gerund can also indicate an action performed by the direct object of certain kinds of verb:

(a) With verbs of 'perception' like 'see', 'hear', 'observe': see 20.7 for details.

(b) With verbs like *coger*, *pillar* ('to catch'), *arrestar* 'to arrest', *dejar* 'to leave', *encontrar* 'to find', *sorprender* 'to surprise':

La cogió/pilló robando	He/She caught her stealing
La dejé llorando	I left her crying
Dejamos a Andrés durmiendo (A. Mastretta, Mexico, dialogue)	We left Andrés sleeping
Encontré a mis hermanos discutiendo	I found my brothers (or brothers and sisters) quarrelling
Me sorprendí repitiendo entre dientes . . . (C. Martín Gaite, Spain)	I caught myself repeating between my teeth . . . (i.e. 'muttering')

(c) With verbs of representation like 'paint', 'draw', 'photograph', 'show', 'describe', 'imagine', 'represent', etc.

La pintó tocando el clavicémbalo	He painted her playing the harpsichord
Esta fotografía muestra al rey bajando del avión	This photo shows the King getting out of the plane
Me los imagino emborrachándose	I can imagine them getting drunk

Note

Captions under photos or other pictures fall into this category. In such captions the gerund very often appears with no accompanying finite verb. See 20.3a above.

20.7 Gerund after verbs of perception ('see', 'hear', etc.)

Commonly after the verb *ver* 'to see', and occasionally after *oír* 'to hear', *recordar* 'to remember', *olvidar* 'to forget', the gerund may be used to qualify the object of the main verb.

Usually the infinitive is also possible in this construction, the difference being one of aspect: the infinitive indicates an action that is completed and the gerund an action that is or was not yet complete. Compare *La vi fumando un cigarrillo* 'I saw her (while she was) smoking a cigarette', *La vi fumar un cigarrillo* 'I saw her smoke a cigarette'.

There is usually a colloquial alternative which uses a finite verb: *La vi que fumaba un cigarrillo* 'I saw that she was smoking a cigarette'. Further examples:

Cuando Félix divisó al doctor leyendo una revista política . . .(C. Fuentes, Mexico)	When Felix caught sight of the doctor reading a political magazine . . .
No se me olvida mi hijo bailando con ella	I can't forget my son dancing with her
La recuerdo siempre cantando	I remember her always singing

With verbs of motion the gerund is usually not possible: 'I saw him coming towards me' is *Le/Lo vi venir hacia mí* or *Le/Lo vi que venía hacia mí* but not **Le/Lo vi viniendo hacia mi.*

Oír 'hear' may take a gerund, but prefers either the infinitive or the construction with *que* and a finite verb. The infinitive is the safest option for foreign learners. A gerund could be taken to refer to the subject of the main verb; e.g. ?*La oí entrando* could mean 'I heard her while (I was) entering':

La oí toser/que tosía	I heard her coughing
Oí entrar a alguien/que alguien entraba	I heard someone come in
. . . oyendo a su padre hablar de que[5]	. . . listening to her father talking about
Emiliano Zapato había tomado Chilpancingo (A. Mastretta, Mexico, dialogue)	Emiliano Zapata having occupied Chilpancingo

But the gerund is possible if its subject is inanimate:

Cuando el sargento oye la corneta tocando la retirada . . . (M. Vargas Llosa, Peru)	When the sergeant hears the trumpet sounding the retreat . . .
Oí el ruido del yelo cayendo sobre un vaso (J. Marías, Spain)	I heard the noise of the ice falling onto a glass

20.8 Other uses of the gerund

20.8.1 Gerund with *andar*
This translates the English 'to go around doing something', with the same faintly pejorative implication of pointless activity. *Ir* can usually replace *andar* in this construction:

Siempre anda/va buscando camorra	He always goes round looking for trouble
Anduve maldiciendo todo el jueves (A. Mastretta, Mexico, dialogue)	All that Thursday I went around swearing

Note
Spoken (not written) Mexican often uses *andar* for *estar* to form the continuous: *¿Andas trabajando?* (for *¿Estás trabajando?*) 'Are you working?'; see 15.5.

20.8.2 Gerund with *ir*
(a) Expresses slow or gradual action:

---
[5] *De que* is correct here. For misuse of *de que* after certain verbs, see 33.4.3.

Nos vamos haciendo viejos	We're (gradually) getting older
Cada vez voy teniendo menos memoria	My memory's getting worse and worse
Poco a poco el consumidor ha ido	Gradually the consumer has discovered
descubriendo que las frutas de Cuba están a	that fruit from Cuba is ripe even if it is
punto aunque sean de color amarillo verdoso	greenish yellow in colour
(interview, *Granma*, Cuba)	
Ella se fue doblando hasta caer al suelo	She gradually doubled up until she fell to
(*Cambio16*, Spain)	the ground

Note

Spoken Mexican-Spanish also uses this construction to express an action that is just finishing (examples from J.M. Lope Blanch (1991), 16): *Espera un momento; voy acabando ya* (Spain *estoy acabando ya/estoy a punto de acabar*) 'Wait a moment, I'm just finishing', *Voy llegando ahorita* (Spain *acabo de llegar*) 'I've only just arrived'.

(b) By extension, to express careful, painstaking or laborious actions:

Ya puedes ir preparando todo para cuando lleguen	You can start getting things ready for when they arrive
Gano lo necesario para ir tirando	I earn enough to get by
Ve escribiendo todo lo que te dicte	Write down everything as I dictate it to you

20.8.3 Gerund with *llevar*

This provides a neat translation of 'for' in time expressions:

Llevo dos meses pintando esta casa	I've been painting this house for two months

This construction is discussed at 32.3.1.

20.8.4 Gerund with *quedarse* (see also 27.3.6)

This translates the idea of 'to continue to do something':

Me quedé ayudándolos un rato	I stayed on for a while to help them
Se quedó mirándome	She remained staring at me

20.8.5 Gerund with *salir*

Usually translates English phrases involving 'come out'/'go out':

Salió ganando	He came out the winner
Era lo único que quería: salir volando por la ventana (C. Martín Gaite, Spain, dialogue)	It was all I wanted to do – fly out of the window

20.8.6 Gerund with *seguir* and *continuar*

Seguir and *continuar* with the gerund translate 'to go on . . . -ing', 'to continue to . . .'. See 32.8 for discussion.

20.8.7 Gerund with *venir*

To express an action that accumulates or increases with time. It sometimes conveys mounting exasperation:

Hace años que viene diciendo lo mismo	He's been saying the same thing for years
La sensación de aislamiento en la Moncloa viene siendo progresiva (*Cambio16*, Spain)	The sensation of isolation at the Moncloa (the Spanish Prime Minister's residence) is steadily growing
Los programas que se vienen ejecutando en el campo de la cardiología infantil . . . (interview, *Granma*, Cuba)	The programmes (US 'programs') that have been carried out in the field of child cardiology . . .

Note
The following construction is typically Mexican: *¿Qué, no lo viste? Ah, claro: tú vienes llegando apenas* 'What? Didn't you see it? Oh, of course, you've only just arrived' (from J.M. Lope Blanch (1991), 17).

20.8.8 Gerund with *acabar*
Means 'end by':

Siempre acaba enfadándose	He always ends by getting mad
Acabarás haciendo lo que ella diga	You'll end by/up doing what she says

Acabar por + infinitive is an equivalent and is the more common construction in negative statements:

Acabarás por no salir nunca de casa	You'll end by/up never going out of the house

20.9 Translating the English *-ing* form

The following examples consist mainly of cases where the English *-ing* form may not be translated by the Spanish gerund.

20.9.1 When the *-ing* form is the subject of a verb
This is normally translated by an infinitive or by a suitable noun:

Learning a language is fun	*Aprender un idioma es divertido*
Eating too much butter is bad for the heart	*Comer demasiada mantequilla es malo para el corazón*
No smoking	*Prohibido fumar*
Skiing is expensive	*Esquiar cuesta mucho*
Salmon fishing is an art	*La pesca del salmón es un arte*

20.9.2 When the *-ing* form is the object of a verb
In this case there are two possibilities:
(a) When the same subject performs both actions, use an infinitive or a noun:

He dreads having to start	*Teme tener que empezar*
I like swimming	*Me gusta nadar/Me gusta la natación*
He gave up gambling	*Dejó de jugar/Dejó el juego*
Try ringing him	*Intenta llamarlo/le*
There's nothing I like better than working in the garden	*No hay nada que me guste más que trabajar en el jardín*

(b) When the actions are performed by different subjects, use a clause or noun. The subjunctive must be used where required by the rules laid out in Chapter 16:

I can't stand Pedro singing	*No puedo ver que Pedro cante*
I didn't mind him/his living here	*No me importaba que viviera/viviese aquí*
I recommended promoting her	*Recomendé su ascenso/que la ascendiesen/ ascendieran*
I approve of you(r) getting up early	*Me parece bien que te levantes temprano*

Note
Some verbs allow the gerund. See 20.7.

20.9.3 The *-ing* form used in a passive sense
Care is needed when the English *-ing* form replaces a passive infinitive, cf. 'Your hair needs cutting' (= 'Your hair needs to be cut'). In the Spanish translation an infinitive or a clause must be used:

Your hair needs cutting	*(Te) hace falta que te corten el pelo* or *que te cortes el pelo*
This needs attending to	*Hace falta cuidarse de esto/Hay que atender a esto*
You're not worth listening to	*No vale la pena escucharte*
It wants/needs polishing	*Hace falta sacarle brillo*

20.9.4 The *-ing* form preceded by prepositions
Unless the preposition is 'by' (see 20.4.2), an infinitive or clause must be used:

I'm looking forward to seeing you	*Tengo ganas de verte*
I prefer swimming to running	*Prefiero nadar a correr*
He was punished for being late	*Lo/Le castigaron por llegar tarde*
He's thinking of starting a business	*Piensa empezar un negocio*
You get nothing in life without working	*No se consigue nada en esta vida sin trabajo/sin trabajar*
He was furious at being mistaken for his brother	*Le enfureció que le confundieran/confundiesen con su hermano*

20.9.5 The *-ing* form before nouns
(a) If the *-ing* form is itself a noun, translation is usually by an infinitive or a noun:

driving permit	*el carnet/el permiso de conducir*
dancing shoes	*los zapatos de baile*
fishing rod	*la caña de pescar*

(b) If the *-ing* form is a participle (adjective) then a relative clause may be used, unless a participle in *-ante*, *-(i)ente* exists (see 19.4):

a walking doll	*un muñeco andante*
the chiming bells	*las campanas que tañen/tañían*
a worrying problem	*un problema inquietante*
a convincing reply	*una respuesta convincente*

But often an idiomatic solution must be sought in either case:

flying planes	*aviones en vuelo*
turning point	*el punto decisivo/la vuelta de la marea*, etc.
steering wheel	*el volante*
dining room	*el comedor*

Note
For the exceptional use of *hirviendo* 'boiling' and *ardiendo* 'burning' as adjectives, see 4.4.

21
Modal auxiliary verbs

21.1 General

This chapter discusses the following commonly occurring auxiliary verbs:

poder	to be able to, to be allowed to, can, could
saber	to know how to
querer	to want
soler	to be in the habit of
deber	must, ought to, should
haber (que, de)	to have to

All of these verbs, except *deber*, are conjugated irregularly. Their forms are shown in Chapter 13.

21.2 *Poder* and *saber* 'to be able to'/'to know how to'

21.2.1 *Poder* and *saber* contrasted
Both verbs are often equivalent to 'can' or 'could' but their meanings are slightly different: *saber*, as well as 'to know', means 'to know how to do something', and *poder* means 'to be able to do something'/'to be allowed to do something':

¿Sabes nadar?	Can you swim? (do you know how to?)
¿Puedes nadar hoy?	Can you swim today? (are you able to/are you allowed to?)
Se sabe ganar las simpatías de todo el mundo	She knows how to win people's affections

Notes
(i) Since 'can' and 'could' have no infinitives or participles in English, *poder* is translated by 'to be able to'/'to be allowed to' in compound and future tenses: *Nunca había podido descifrarlo/Nunca podrá descifrarlo* 'She had never been able to decipher it/She'll never be able to decipher it'.
(ii) *No poder (por) menos de* means the same as *no poder evitar* + infinitive: *No podré (por) menos de decírselo* 'I won't be able to stop myself from telling him/her'.
   The Latin-American equivalent is *no poder menos que*.
(iii) Idioms with *poder*: *No puedo más, estoy harta* 'I cannot go on, I'm fed up', *Al menos en ese terreno la vida no ha podido conmigo* (C. Martín Gaite, Spain) 'In this area at least, life hasn't got the better of me'.

21.2.2 Preterite and imperfect of *poder* and *saber*
The preterite refers to one occasion, the imperfect to a period of time usually made clear by the context. The preterite usually means 'to manage to':

No pudo escaparse	He couldn't escape (he didn't manage to)
No podía escaparse	He couldn't escape (at that time; no information about whether he eventually did)
¿Cómo pudiste hacerlo?	How could you/did you manage to do it?
No me pudo ver porque estaba ocupada	She couldn't/didn't get to see me because she was busy

Note

The preterite of *saber* 'to know' means 'found out'; the imperfect means 'knew': *cuando supe la verdad* 'when I found out/heard the truth'; *sabía la verdad* 'I/she knew the truth'.

21.2.3 *Poder* to express possibility and suggestions

Poder is usually translated by 'could' or 'may'. Except where indicated, either the imperfect or the conditional can be used.

(a) Possibility/suggestions

Podíamos/Podríamos ir al cine esta tarde	We could go to the cinema this afternoon/evening
Podía no haberla visto	He may not have seen her
Puedes/Podías/Podrías venir a comer mañana	You could come to lunch tomorrow
Puede/Podría/Podía haberle ocurrido algo (*pudiera haber . . .* is written style)	Something may/could have happened to him

Note

Puede ser, podría/pudiera ser, podría/pudiera haber sido are equivalent to 'it could be', 'it could have been'. *Pudiera* is less often used in the spoken language: *Aun en el caso de que nuestro viejo profesor se hubiera muerto, que bien pudiera ser . . .* (C. Martín Gaite, Spain) 'Even if our old teacher has died, which could well have happened . . .'.

(b) Polite requests

The conditional is perhaps more usual than the imperfect in polite requests, but both are often heard:

¿Podría/Podía usted abrir la ventana?	Could you open the window?
¿Podrías/Podías decirle al jefe que estoy enfermo?	Could you tell the boss I'm ill?

(c) The preterite indicative expresses something that could have happened but did not:

El día que pudo estallar la Tercera Guerra Mundial (*Cambio16*, Spain)	The day World War III could have broken out
Pensando en lo que pudo haber sido y no fue (J. Marsé, Spain)	Thinking of what might have been and wasn't

(d) The imperfect indicative (not the conditional) can also be used to reproach somebody for something done or left undone in the past:

Me lo podías haber dicho	You could have told me
Podías haber puesto algún adornito de Navidad (C. Rico-Godoy, Spain)	You could have put up some Christmas decorations

In answers, *puede ser* can be abbreviated to *puede*:

—¿Vas a pescar mañana? —Puede	'Are you going fishing tomorrow?' 'Perhaps . . .'

For the use of *puede ser que, pudiera ser que, podría ser que, podría/pudiera haber sido que* with the subjunctive, see 16.3.1.

21.2.4 *Poder* used in speculations

Ha llamado alguien. ¿Quién puede/podrá haber sido/ha podido ser?	Somebody rang. Who could it have been?
¿Dónde se puede haber ido/puede haberse ido?	Where can she have gone?

21.3 *Deber, deber de* and *tener que*

21.3.1 *Deber* to express obligation

Su hijo debe trabajar más si quiere aprobar el examen	Your son must work harder if he is to pass the examination
Debes decirme lo que sepas	You ought to/must tell me what you know

In the last two examples *tener que* could be used instead to strengthen the obligation, i.e. *Tienes que decirme . . .*

Notes
(i) The degree of obligation is reduced by using the conditional or, less often, the *-ra* form of *deber*. Since the imperfect may colloquially replace the conditional, *debería hacerlo, debía hacerlo* and *debiera hacerlo* may therefore all have the same meaning, although *debiera* has a more literary flavour: *Debías/Deberías/Debieras haberle/lo llamado* 'You ought to/should have called him'.
(ii) *No tener más remedio que* is a variation of *tener que* often used in every day language to express strong obligation: *No tengo más remedio que despedirla* 'I have to/I'm obliged to fire her'.

21.3.2 *Deber (de)* to express probability or supposition

Deber de can only express probability or supposition, although *deber* alone is nowadays also used with this meaning:

Debía (de) saber mucho	He must/ought to have known a lot
Debiste (de) llegar tarde	You must have arrived late
Debe (de) haber sido muy guapa	She must have been very beautiful
Deben (de) ser las cinco	It must be five o'clock

The loss in modern Spanish of the distinction between obligation (*deber*) and supposition (*deber de*) creates ambiguities. Use of *deber de* to translate 'must' would clarify the following examples:

Debió hacerlo Juan	John ought to have done it (on that occasion)/John must have done it
Debía hacerlo Juan	John used to have to do it/John ought to do it/John must have done it

21.3.3 Preterite, conditional and imperfect of *deber*

The preterite expresses something that should **have been** done. The conditional and the imperfect express something that should **be** done:

Debió decírtelo antes	She ought to/should have told you before
Debía/debería decírtelo antes	She ought to/should tell you before
En ese momento debí desconfiarme, pero no lo hice (J. Ibargüengoitia, Mexico, dialogue)	At that moment I ought to/should have been suspicious, but I wasn't

Volvió al sitio del que nunca debió salir (E. Arenas, dialogue, Spain)	He went back to the place he ought never to have left/should never have left

21.4 *Haber*

Haber is the modal auxiliary used for forming compound tenses. This use is discussed at 14.8.

Haber, present tense *hay*, is used to translate 'there is', 'there are', 'there were', etc., and is discussed in Chapter 30.

21.4.1 *Haber de*

Haber de has the following values:

(a) It expresses mild obligation or future intention. This usage is nowadays rare and literary: *He de hacerlo cuanto antes* 'I have to do it as soon as possible'.

(b) It expresses probability. This usage is also nowadays rare and literary except in Mexico, where it is very common; see 14.6d: *Ha de haberle dicho todo* 'He must have told him everything'.

(c) In the conditional it translates an indignant or mystified 'should . . .': *¿Por qué habría de ofenderse si yo no dije nada?* (or, more colloquially, *iba a ofenderse*) 'Why should she get offended if I didn't say anything?'.

21.4.2 *Haber que*

Haber que means 'to be necessary to . . .'. In this construction the verb is used only in the third-person singular. The present-tense form is *hay que*.

Hay que darles tiempo	One has to give them time/It's necessary to give them time
No había que hacer autopsia (G. García Márquez, Colombia)	There was no need to do an autopsy
Hubo que llamar a los bomberos	It was necessary to call the firemen

21.5 *Querer* 'to want to'

This verb must not be confused with *querer* 'to love' which cannot precede an infinitive: *Adoro nadar* 'I love swimming'.[1]

There is a difference of meaning between the preterite and the imperfect:

Quise hablar con José	I wanted/tried to talk to José (but failed)
Quería hablar con José	I wanted to talk to José (and may or may not have succeeded)

But sometimes the meanings overlap, especially when the speaker is being very assertive:

Lo hice porque quise/quería hacerlo	I did it because I wanted to

The negative preterite means 'to refuse to'. Compare *No quiso hacerlo* 'He didn't want to do it' (so he didn't) and *No quería hacerlo* 'He didn't want to do it' (no information about whether he did it).

The imperfect subjunctive and the conditional are interchangeable:

---

[1]*Querer* 'to love' can only be used with humans and animals: *Adoro el helado de vainilla* 'I love vanilla ice cream'.

No quisiera/querría volver a nacer   I wouldn't like to be reborn/born again

The imperfect indicative can also be used instead of these two tenses in polite enquiries:

Querría/Quisiera/Quería hablar con el encargado   I would like to speak to the manager

21.6 *Soler*

Soler translates the idea of 'usually', 'to be used to'. It is not used in the future, preterite and conditional tenses:

No me suele doler la cabeza	I don't usually suffer from headaches
Los zapatos de tacón alto suelen ser incómodos	High-heeled shoes are usually uncomfortable
Ha acostumbrado a/solido portarse bien conmigo	She's usually behaved well towards me
No es que suela verla a menudo, pero alguna vez la veo	It's not as if I saw her often, but I see her sometimes

Note

Acostumbrar a may replace *soler* in some cases. It is more literary in style and implies 'to be in the habit of': *No acostumbro a/suelo beber* 'I don't usually drink', *Acostumbra a/suele salir temprano* 'He habitually goes out early'. *Acostumbrar* without *a* is found in classical texts in Spain and is still used in Latin America: Seco (1992), 14, quotes the Argentine A. di Benedetto: *Un periodista que acostumbra contar cosas* 'a journalist who habitually tells things'.

21.7 *Deber, poder* and *tener que*: alternative construction with compound tenses

Deber and *poder* allow a variety of constructions in compound tenses, i.e. tenses based on *haber* and a participle. The option of pronoun shifting (discussed at 11.14.4) doubles the number of possibilities:

Ha debido hacerlo/Lo ha debido hacer	He must have done it
Debe haberlo hecho/Lo debe haber hecho	
Ha podido hacerlo/Lo ha podido hacer	He could have done it
Puede haberlo hecho/Lo puede haber hecho	
Habían debido hacerlo/Lo habían debido hacer	They must have done it (before)
Debían haberlo hecho/lo debían haber hecho	
Habían podido hacerlo/Podían haberlo hecho	They could have done it (before)
Podían haberlo hecho/Lo podían haber hecho	
Había debido hacerlo/Lo habría debido hacer	He ought to have done it
Debería haberlo hecho/Lo debería haber hecho	
(*debiera* can replace *debería* here)	

and also *habría podido hacerlo, Podría haberlo hecho*, etc. 'He might have done it'.

Tener que may also appear in the same alternative constructions: *Ha tenido que hacerlo/Tiene que haberlo hecho* 'He had to do it', etc.

22

Personal a

22.1 Personal *a*: general

The use of the preposition *a* before certain kinds of direct object is so important in Spanish that it deserves a separate chapter.

The basic rule is that identified or particularized human direct objects are marked by a preceding *a*: *Vi a María* 'I saw Mary'. Compare *Vi el coche* 'I saw the car' (non-human).

However, 'personal' *a* is a rather inaccurate label since the same *a* also sometimes appears with inanimate direct objects, particularly, but not only, whenever there might be doubt about which is the subject and which the object, as sometimes happens in Spanish where word order is quite flexible.

22.2 Personal *a* before nouns denoting human beings or animals

Personal *a* is required before a direct object that denotes a known or identified human being, or a 'personified' animal.

Before a direct object that is a personal name or title – *Pedro, el jefe, mamá* – personal *a* is never omitted: *Conozco a tu madre* 'I know your mother', *Vi a Mario y a Elena* 'I saw Mario and Helen', *No aguanto al nuevo jefe* 'I can't stand the new boss'.

With animals, use of personal *a* depends on the extent to which the creature is humanized. Pets virtually always take personal *a*, but in other cases use of *a* depends on factors of emotion or context: the more familiar the language, the more likely the use of *a*. At the zoo one is likely to say *Vamos a ver a los monos* 'Let's go and see the monkeys' but, probably, *Vamos a ver los insectos* 'Let's go and see the insects', monkeys being more lovable than cockroaches. Clinical or scientific language would naturally use personal *a* much more sparingly.

In the following examples personal *a* is obligatory:

No conozco a Feliciano	I don't know Feliciano
Acompañé a mi madre a la clínica	I accompanied my mother to the clinic
Llevó a las niñas al zoo	He took the girls to the zoo
La policía busca a un individuo con una cicatriz en el labio inferior	The police are seeking an individual with a scar on his lower lip
¿Quieres pasear al perro?	Do you want to take the dog for a walk?
Dejad de atormentar al gato	Stop tormenting the cat

Compare the following sentences in which the object of the verb is not individually particularized:

Busco un marido que me ayude en la casa	I'm looking for a husband who will help me in the house
Vi un periodista en el jardín	I saw a journalist in the garden
Veía un chico que jugaba en silencio (E. Sábato, Argentina)	I saw a child playing in silence
Este DC-10 ha traído pasajeros desde Berlín	This DC-10 has brought passengers from Berlin
Utilizaron un perro lobo para el experimento	They used an Alsatian dog for the experiment

Note

A proper name may occasionally denote an inanimate object, in which case personal *a* cannot be used: *Dice conocer todo Shakespeare* 'He says he knows the whole of Shakespeare' (i.e. the works), *Van a subastar un Turner* 'They're going to auction a Turner' (painting), *Procura tomar la reina* 'Try to take the queen' (chess).

22.3 Personal *a* with nouns linked by *como*

A noun linked by *como* to a previous noun which itself has a personal *a*, or to a pronoun standing for such a noun, must also take personal *a* (although it may be omitted colloquially if there is no ambiguity):

*Tuve que recoger **a** mi hermana como **a** un fardo*	I had to pick up my sister as though she were a bundle
*Me trataba como **a** una reina* (A. Mastretta, Mexico, dialogue)	He treated me like a queen

?Tuve que recoger a mi hermana como un fardo sounds like ?'I had to pick up my sister as if I were a bundle'.

22.4 Personal *a* before pronouns

22.4.1 Before pronouns other than relative pronouns

When a pronoun stands for a person it takes personal *a*. These pronouns include *alguien, alguno, uno, ambos, cualquiera, nadie, otro, ninguno, este, ese, aquel, quien, todo, él, ella, usted* and other personal pronouns (excepting *me, te, se, nos, os, le, la, lo*). See next section for discussion of the use of personal *a* in relative clauses.

He visto a alguien en el pasillo	I've seen someone in the corridor
Aunque yo no conozco a nadie de la gente que viene aquí (C. Martín Gaite, Spain)	Although I don't know anyone among the people who come here
Era capaz de insultar a cualquiera	He was capable of insulting anybody
¿A quién has visto?	Who(m) did you see?
A ése/ese es al que quiere, no a ti	He's the one she loves, not you

22.4.2 Personal *a* before relative pronouns

Personal *a* may appear before a direct object relative pronoun that refers to a human being, in which case the form of the relative pronoun will be *quien, el que* or *el cual* (see 35.4.2 for discussion). If personal *a* is not used, *que* is the usual relative pronoun.

Personal *a* is not usual when the clause is clearly restrictive (as defined at 35.1.2). But if it is non-restrictive it must be used, though the difference is occasionally elusive. Peninsular informants generally insisted on *a* in the following examples:

*Tengo un profesor **al** que/a quien han nombrado miembro de la Academia*	I have a teacher whom they've appointed as a member of the Academy
*Es el único **al** que la ley no ha condenado*	He's the only one the law hasn't condemned
*Hace unos días, en el puerto, me dijiste que yo era la primera persona **a** la que habías querido* (E. Sábato, Argentina, dialogue)	A few days ago, at the harbour, you told me I was the first person you had loved
*Plutón, esposo de Proserpina, **a** la que/a quien/a la cual robó*	Pluto, the husband of Proserpine, whom he carried off

Notes

(i) The word *único* generates disagreement. One hears *Tú eres el único que quiero* 'You're the only one I love', some prefer . . . *al que quiero*, others accept both.

(ii) *El que* or *quien* are obligatory in all types of clause if *que* alone creates ambiguities – as it quite often does with human antecedents. Compare *Ése/Ese es el autor que siempre ataca* 'That's the author who (or 'whom he') always attacks'. *Al que* or *a quien* . . . show clearly that 'whom he always attacks' is meant. Another example: *los militares que/a los que/a quienes han ascendido* 'the military men (whom) they have promoted' where use of personal *a* excludes the reading 'who have ascended'.

(iii) Personal *a* is rare with non-human objects, but if it occurs *el que* is the preferred relative pronoun: *Hemos encontrado enormes listas de coches a los que tenían controlados* (*Cambio16*, Spain) 'We have found enormous lists of cars that they had under surveillance'.

22.5 Personal *a* before personified nouns

A personified noun usually requires personal *a*. The decision as to whether a noun is personified or not is, however, dependent on complex factors of context:

*Tú temes **al** éxito tanto como **al** fracaso*	You fear success as much as failure
*Los cazas llevan bengalas de magnesio para confundir **a** un misil dirigido* (*Cambio16*, Spain)	The fighters carry magnesium flares to confuse a guided missile

The last example shows how certain verbs, e.g. *confundir* 'confuse', *criticar* 'criticize', *satirizar* 'satirize', *insultar* 'insult', etc. tend, by their meaning, to personify their object. This explains – though does not justify – the occurrence of sentences like *?Criticaba a las novelas de fulano* 'He criticized so-and-so's novels' for *Criticaba las novelas* . . .

22.6 Personal *a* after *tener, querer*

These verbs acquire different meanings when used with personal *a*:

Tengo un hijo y una hija	I've got a son and a daughter
Tenemos una asistenta griega	We have a Greek maid

but:

*Así tiene **al** marido y **a** los hijos, a base de bocadillos, latas y congelados*	That's how she keeps her husband and children – on sandwiches, tins and frozen food
*Tengo **a** mi tío como fiador*	I've got my uncle to act as guarantor

*La humedad de la noche . . . tiene **a** las veredas resbaladizas y brillosas* (M. Vargas Llosa, Perú; *vereda* for Peninsular *acera* 'pavement'; *brillosas = brillantes*)	The dampness of the night makes the pavements slippery and shiny
Quiere una secretaria	He wants a secretary
*Quiere **a** una secretaria*	He loves a secretary

22.7 Omission of personal *a* before numerals

Nouns preceded by a number tend to be unspecified or unidentified and personal *a* is often omitted before them:

Vieron (a) media docena de soldados enemigos	They saw half a dozen enemy soldiers
Bayardo San Román . . . vio las dos mujeres vestidas de negro (G. García Márquez, Colombia)	Bayardo San Román saw the two women dressed in black
Sólo conozco un hombre capaz de componer esta emboscada maestra (idem; personal *a* omitted before *un* when it is a numeral rather than an article)	I only know one man capable of organizing this masterly ambush

Note
A particularized or identified personal noun will, however, take personal *a*: *Yo conocía personalmente **a** sus tres hijas* 'I knew his three daughters personally'.

22.8 Personal *a* combined with dative *a*

Ambiguity may arise when two *as* occur in the same sentence, e.g. ?*Presenté a mi marido a mi jefe* 'I introduced my husband to my boss' or vice-versa. The common solution is to omit personal *a* and place the direct object after the verb and before the dative.

Presenté Miguel a Antonia	I introduced Miguel to Antonia
Denuncié el ladrón al guardia	I denounced the thief to the policeman
Mande el paciente al especialista	Send the patient to the specialist

Note
The problem of *preferir* is also solved in this way: *Yo prefiero Dickens a Balzac* 'I prefer Dickens to Balzac'.

22.9 Personal *a* before collective nouns

Personal *a* is normally used before collective nouns when these refer to human beings:

Sir Walter Raleigh enriqueció a la enclenque corte inglesa (*Cambio16*, Spain)	Sir Walter Raleigh enriched the feeble English court
*No conocía **al** resto del grupo*	I/(S)he didn't know the rest of the group
*un paso que podría poner **a** Estados Unidos en una posición delicada* (*La Prensa*, Argentina)	a step which could put the US in a delicate position

A is obligatory in all these examples.

Compare the following sentences in which the nouns do not refer to inhabitants or members of a group, but to a place:

Los turistas inundan México	Tourists are inundating Mexico
Hitler invadió la Unión Soviética	Hitler invaded the Soviet Union

Notes

(i) Before words like *país, nación, partido, movimiento*, when these words refer – or may refer – to people, *a* seems to be optional: *Criticó duramente al/el movimiento anarquista* 'He criticized the anarchist movement severely', *Será imposible gobernar a Euskadi* (*Cambio16*, Spain: omission possible) 'It will be impossible to govern the Basque country', *Son los sindicatos los que dirigen (a) esta nación* 'It's the unions that run this country', *Un potente terremoto sacudió el/al país* 'A powerful earthquake shook the country', *Luis García Meza, quien gobernó el país entre julio de 1980 y agosto de 1981* (*El País*, *al* possible) 'Luis García Meza, who governed the country between July 1980 and August 1981'.

(ii) Seeing, visiting, leaving or picturing a place does not call for personal *a*: *Estamos deseando ver Lima* 'We're longing to see Lima', *Se negó a visitar Rumania* 'He refused to visit Romania', *Quería pintar Toledo* 'He wanted to paint Toledo', *Abandonaron Madrid* 'They left Madrid'.

22.10 Personal *a* before inanimate objects

Personal *a* cannot appear before a noun denoting an inanimate direct object in straightforward sentences of the following kind:

He comprado un sacacorchos	I've bought a corkscrew
Escribe poesía	He writes poetry
Sus palabras delataban su derrotismo	His words betrayed his defeatism

But, despite its name, personal *a* is used before inanimate nouns:

(a) When there is likely to be ambiguity as to which is the subject and which the direct object of a verb. Such ambiguity is very common in relative clauses, where the verb often precedes the subject:

*Es difícil saber en qué medida afectó esto **a** la economía cubana* (M. Vargas Llosa, Peru)	It is difficult to know to what extent this affected the Cuban economy
*Este producto es el que mejor impermeabiliza **al** algodón*	This product is the one that best waterproofs cotton
*Una organización que protege **a** su coche* (advertisement, *Cambio16*, Spain)	an organization which protects your car
A tres Autos y un Comercio quemaron (Latin-American headline, strange to Peninsular speakers)	Three Cars and Store Burnt

(b) *A* also sometimes appears before inanimate direct objects when both subject and object are inanimate, even though there is apparently no danger of ambiguity.

It seems that this occurs only in those sentences in which the inanimate subject is also the true agent of the action. In a sentence like *La piedra rompió un cristal*, 'The stone broke a pane of glass' or *La novela causó una sensación* 'The novel caused a sensation' it can be argued that the agents of the action are the person who threw the stone or wrote the novel; *piedra* and *novela* are merely instruments. For this reason personal *a* is impossible.

However, if the inanimate subject is the real agent of the action, personal *a* may **optionally** appear. It is as though the native speaker were not entirely confident that word order alone – loose in Spanish – sufficiently clarifies which is the subject and which the object. The issue is not in doubt if one of the nouns is a human being or is the instrument of a human being. But if both are of equal status, *a* identifies the object clearly:

*Ambos creían que los astros regían **a** las pasiones* (Octavio Paz, Mexico)	Both believed the stars ruled the passions
*Este morfema nominal concretiza **al** semantema* (F. Abad Nebot, Spain)	This nominal morpheme makes the semanteme concrete
*El suicidio de la muchacha . . . excitó **a** la opinión pública* (M. Vargas Llosa, Peru)	The girl's suicide . . . stirred public opinion
*Este clima caracteriza **a** la sierra andina*	This climate characterizes the Andes range

A could in fact be omitted in all these examples.

(c) *A* regularly appears after impersonal *se* so as to show that the *se* is indeed impersonal *se* and not any other kind of *se* such as reflexive *se* or passive *se*, etc.:

*En España se llamaba **a** la plata* (Sp. *dinero*) *de los cohechos y sobornos 'unto de México'* (O. Paz, Mexico; cf. *la plata se llamaba* 'money was called . . .')	In Spain they used to call the money from bribery and graft 'Mexican grease'
*¿Se podía llamar **a** eso caridad?* (M. Vargas Llosa, Peru)	Could one call that charity?
*. . . la plataforma, como se llama **a** los andenes en Inglaterra* (J. Marías, Spain)	. . . the 'platform', as they call the *andén* (of a railway station) in England

22.11 A obligatory or preferred with certain verbs

(a) Some verbs always take the preposition *a*, e.g. *agarrarse a* 'to hold on to', *asociarse a* 'to associate oneself with', *suceder a* 'to follow', *sustituir a* 'to substitute', *renunciar a* 'to renounce', *obedecer a*, 'to obey', *ayudar a* to 'help', *gustar/agradar a* 'to please', etc. However, this *a* may not always be personal *a* but some other manifestation of the preposition *a*:

*Considera que la opción más sabia es renunciar gradualmente **a** la energía nuclear* (*El País*: not personal *a*)	He considers that the wisest option is gradually to give up nuclear energy
*Esto obedece **a** unas normas de comportamiento . . .*	This obeys certain norms of behaviour . . .
***A** los osos les gusta la miel*	Bears like honey
*Este nuevo producto ayuda **al** cabello a recobrar su brillo natural* (*a* normal)	This new product helps the hair recover its natural shine
*Este nuevo tipo de transistor sustituye **a** los anteriores*	This new type of transistor replaces the former ones

It is worth recalling at this point that there is an important difference between personal *a* and the dative *a* meaning 'to' after verbs of giving, saying, pointing, etc. The latter *a* is usually reinforced by a redundant pronoun, whereas the former is not – at least in the Peninsula and in careful speech in much of Latin America. Thus one says *Le dije a tu padre . .* 'I said to your father . . .' (redundant *le*) but only *Vi a tu padre* 'I saw your father' not *?Le/Lo vi a tu padre*. Reinforcement with a redundant pronoun is only required when the object precedes the verb – *A tu padre le/lo vi ayer* 'I saw your father yesterday'. This word order device is explained at 11.16.1 and 37.5.3.

Sentences like ?*Lo vi a tu padre* are, however, common in the Southern Cone and are heard in familiar Latin-American speech everywhere. See 11.16.4 for more details.

(b) *A* preferred after some verbs

Some verbs often take *a* before an inanimate direct object. These include *afectar a* 'to affect', *reemplazar a* 'to replace', *superar a* 'to overcome/exceed', *acompañar a* 'to accompany', *combatir a* 'to combat', *llamar a* 'to name/call'. However, usage is uncertain with some of them and Spanish-speakers sometimes disagree about the appropriateness of the use of *a* before an inanimate object:

Los historiadores británicos llaman "guerra peninsular" (a) lo que nosotros denominamos Guerra de la Independencia	British historians give the name 'Peninsular War' to what we call the War of Independence
Estas ventajas permiten al Volkswagen superar a sus rivales (a normal)	These advantages allow the Volkswagen to beat its rivals
Las nuevas medidas también afectan (a) la deuda pública	The new measures also affect the public debt
El nuevo Ford ha reemplazado a la gama anterior	The new Ford has replaced the previous range

23

Negation

23.1 General

Spanish negative words discussed in this chapter are:

no	no, not	*nunca/jamás*	never/ever
nada	nothing	*apenas*	hardly/scarcely
nadie	nobody	*en mi vida*	never in my life
ni	nor/not even	*en absoluto*	absolutely not
ninguno	none/no	*tampoco*	not even/nor
nomás	(Lat. Am.) just/only/ scarcely		

For the construction *no . . . sino* 'not . . . but' see 33.1.

Matters requiring special attention are the stylistic consequences of use or non-use of the double negative, e.g. *No lo he visto nunca/Nunca lo he visto* 'I've never seen it/him', the use of negative words in certain types of positive sentences, e.g. *¿Quién ha dicho* **nunca** *eso?* 'Who ever said that?', *más que* **nada** 'more than anything', and the use of redundant *no*, e.g. *¡Cuántas veces* **no** *te habré dicho!* 'How many times must I have told you!'.

23.2 *No*

23.2.1 Use and position

No usually precedes the word that it negates, but object pronouns are never separated from a verb: *no dije . . .* 'I didn't say . . .', but *No se lo dije* 'I didn't say it to him/her/you/them':

Mario no estaba	Mario wasn't there
No perdamos tiempo	Let us not waste time
No todos son capaces de aprender idiomas	Not everyone is capable of learning languages
Arguyen – y no sin razón – que . . .	They argue – and not without reason – that . . .
No intentaba verla	I/He/She wasn't trying to see her
Intentaba no verla	I/He/She was trying not to see her

If a verb has been deleted, *no* retains its position: *Bebe cerveza pero no bebe vino > Bebe cerveza, pero no vino* 'He drinks beer but not wine', *Viene mañana, pero no esta tarde* 'He's coming tomorrow but not this afternoon/evening', *—¿Sabéis nadar? —Yo sí, pero él no* '"Can you swim?" "I can, but he can't"'.

In very emphatic denials it may follow the noun: *¡Bases nucleares no!* 'No nuclear bases!', *Aquí puede entrar todo el que quiera, pero borrachos no* (or *pero no borrachos*) 'Anyone who wants to can come in here, but not drunkards', *Ah no, eso no* 'Oh no, not that.'

Notes
(i) Compound tenses do not allow participle deletion in Spanish. In answer to *¿Lo has visto?* 'Have you seen him/it?' one says *sí* or *sí, lo he visto*, or *no* or *no, no lo he visto*, but not **no, no lo he . . .* (compare English 'no, I haven't . . .'): —*¿Has sido tú? —No, no he sido yo* '"Was it you?" "No, it wasn't"', —*¿Se lo has dado? —No, no se lo he dado* '"Did you give it to him/her/them?" "No, I didn't"'. This rule is occasionally broken in the pluperfect: see 14.8 for an example.
(ii) Deletion of a gerund or infinitive is, however, possible: —*¿Estabas comiendo? —No, no estaba* '"Were you having lunch?" "No I wasn't"', —*¿Quieres venir? —No, no quiero* '"Do you want to come?" "No I don't"'.
(iii) If it means 'non-' or 'un-', *no* precedes the noun: *Yo estoy por la no violencia* 'I support non-violence', *la política de la no intervención* 'the non-intervention policy', *Es la única imagen no real en todo el libro* (J. Marsé, Spain) 'It's the only non-real image in the whole book'.

23.2.2 'No' and *no* contrasted
The English word 'no' is versatile and may require translation in various ways:

Look, no hands!	*Mira, ¡sin manos!*
'What's the problem?' 'No money'	—*¿Cuál es el problema? —No tengo/tiene/tenemos/tienen* (etc.) *dinero*
no petrol/(US) gas	*no hay gasolina*
no smoking	*prohibido fumar/no fumar*
no way!	*¡ni hablar!*
no kidding!?	*¿en serio?*
There's no need for arguments	*No hay por qué discutir*

23.2.3 *No* as a question tag
¿No? at the end of a statement implies that the asker already knows the answer, cf. 'isn't it?', 'do you?':

Usted habla inglés, ¿no?	You speak English, don't you?
Mejor tarde que nunca, ¿no?	Better late than never, don't you think?

Note
A negative question is handled as in English: i.e. *no* confirms the negative. There is no Spanish equivalent of the contradicting 'yes' of French (*si!*) or German (*doch*): —*¿No vienes? —No* '"Aren't you coming?" "No (I'm not)"', —*¿No vas a enfadarte otra vez? —Sí* '"You aren't going to get cross again?" "Yes I am"', —*¿No cerraste con llave el armario? —Sí* '"Didn't you lock the cupboard?" "Yes. I did"'.

23.2.4 'Redundant' *no*
An apparently superfluous *no* is inserted in certain types of sentence:
(a) Colloquially and optionally, to avoid two *que*s side by side:

*Más vale que vengas conmigo que (**no**) que te quedes solo aquí* (or *. . . a que te quedes solo . . .*)	Better you come with me than that you stay here alone

(b) In informal language redundant *no* is often unnecessarily used in comparisons, especially before an infinitive:

*La obra de R. vale más para un conocimiento de la derecha que **no** para conocer la República* (M. Tuñón de Lara, Spain)	R.'s work is more useful for gaining knowledge of the Right than of the Republic
Mejor que salgas con ellos que (no) con ella	Better you go out with them than with her
*. . . con los ojos más luminosos, más tristes y más agradecidos que ella **no** le vio nunca . . .* (G. García Márquez, Colombia)	. . . with the most luminous, saddest and most grateful eyes she had ever seen in him . . .

(c) Optionally in interjections involving *cuánto* or *qué de* 'how much', 'how many'. Use of *no* is rather literary nowadays:

*¡Cuántas veces **no** lo había soñado en los últimos tiempos!* (L. Goytisolo, Spain)	How often he had dreamt of it lately!
¡Qué de angustias (no) habrán pasado!	What anguish they must have suffered!

(d) Optionally after *hasta* and *a menos que* in negative sentences:

*Adolfito, hasta que **no** te tomes el bocadillo no te vas a jugar* (E. Arenas, Spain, dialogue)	Adolfo, you're not going out to play until you eat your sandwich
*No era noticia hasta que **no** la publicaba ABC* (*Cambio16*, Spain)	It wasn't news until *ABC* published it

But *no* is not used if the main clause is positive:

Siguieron sin hacer nada hasta que llegó el capataz	They carried on doing nothing until the foreman arrived
Me quedaré aquí hasta que se ponga el sol	I'll stay here until the sun sets

(e) In literary usage, after expressions of fear: the *no* does not alter the sense. Note that *que* is used if the *no* is removed: *Temo no le haya sucedido/Temo que le haya sucedido alguna desgracia* 'I'm worried he may have suffered some misfortune', *Tenía miedo no le/Tenía miedo de que le vieran desde arriba* 'He was afraid that they would see him from above'.

23.2.5 *Nomás* (occasionally written *no más*)

Throughout Latin America this phrase has a variety of meanings in colloquial language that it does not have in Spain. The spelling *nomás* is never used in Spain.

—¿Donde está el hospital? —En la esquina nomás (Spain *justo en la esquina*)	'Where's the hospital?' 'Right on the corner'
Pase nomás (Spain *pase, pase*, etc.)	But *do* come in
El gringo viejo se murió en México. Nomás porque cruzó la frontera (C. Fuentes, Mexico, dialogue)	The old gringo died in Mexico. Just because he crossed the frontier
Una invitación del señor Presidente nomás no se rechaza (idem.)	You don't refuse/turn down an invitation from the President himself
nomás que venga . . .	as soon as she/he arrives . . .

Note
On both continents, *no . . . más que* means 'only' and must be distinguished from *no . . . más de* 'not more than'; see 5.5.

23.3 Double negative

One may say *nadie vino* or *no vino nadie* 'no one came'. As the second example shows, if a negative *follows* a verb, the verb must also be preceded by a negative. A negative sentence in Spanish requires that all the constituents of the sentence be negativized: *Pero una **no** debe esperar **nunca nada** de un hombre sino malas noticias* (Carmen Rico-Godoy, Spain) 'But one should never expect anything from a man except bad news':

No dice nada	He says nothing
Nadie dijo nada	No one said anything
Apenas come nada	He scarcely eats anything
Tampoco vino nadie	Nor did anyone come
No sabe ni latín ni francés	He knows neither Latin nor French
No la he visto nunca con nadie	I've never seen her with anyone

Examples of single negatives:

Tampoco vino	He didn't come either
Apenas habla	He scarcely talks
Nadie cree eso	No one believes that
Ni él ni ella podían decir si esa servidumbre recíproca se fundaba en el amor o la comodidad (G. García Márquez, Colombia)	Neither he nor she could have said whether this reciprocal servitude was based on love or convenience
Ninguna era más guapa que ella	No woman was more beautiful than her
Jamás/Nunca la volvería a ver	(S)he was never to see her again

The difference between a double and a single negative, e.g. between *nunca viene* and *no viene nunca*, is sometimes merely stylistic. References under the individual items give guidance on this subject.

Note
The double negative may occasionally be ambiguous, although intonation or context usually make the meaning clear: *Lo que dice no es nada* 'What he says is nothing' (i.e. worthless) or 'What he says isn't nothing' (i.e. it isn't worthless), *Sonia no llora por nada* 'Sonia doesn't cry over nothing'/'Sonia doesn't cry over anything' (cf. *Sonia llora por nada* 'Sonia cries over nothing').[1]

23.4 *Nada, nadie, nunca, jamás, ninguno* in sentences that are affirmative in form or meaning

These words sometimes have the meaning of 'anything', 'ever', 'anyone', 'anything' in certain types of affirmative sentences:
(a) After comparisons:

Más que nada, es taimado	More than anything, he's cunning
Más que a nadie, se parece a su padre	He's more like his father than anyone (else)
En España son muchos los que se precian de asar el cordero mejor que nadie (Cambio16, Spain)	There are many in Spain who pride themselves on roasting lamb better than anyone else

---

[1] Example from Kauffman (1978). *Sonia no llora sin motivo* expresses the first idea unambiguously.

Algo que [. . .] les pareció más violento, más subversivo que nada que jamás oirían (José Donoso, Chile)

Something which seemed to them more violent, more subversive than anything they would ever hear

Salió más temprano que nunca (A. Mastretta, Mexico, dialogue; *jamás* not possible)

She went out earlier than ever before

Ella es más inteligente que ninguna de las otras

She's more intelligent than any of the other girls/women

(b) In sentences that involve expressions of doubt, denial, abstention, impossibility, etc.

Es dudoso que nadie pueda pasar por nativo en más de tres o cuatro idiomas

It's doubtful whether anyone can pass as a native in more than three or four languages

Se negó siquiera a hablar a nadie de la emisora (G. Cabrera Infante, Cuba)

He even refused to talk to anyone from the radio station

Es imposible ver nada de lo que está sucediendo

It's impossible to see anything of what's going on

Es horrible contar todo esto a nadie

It's horrible to tell all this to anyone

Es poco probable que ninguno haya sobrevivido

It's unlikely that any have survived

Me chocaría que jamás/nunca la encontrasen

I'd be amazed if they ever found her

(c) In questions or exclamations that expect a negative answer:

¿A usted cuándo le han preguntado nada?

When did anyone ask you anything?

¿Quién ha visto a nadie que trabaje más que él?

Who has ever seen anyone who works more than he does?

¿Quién hubiera pensado nunca/jamás que se casaría con Josefa?

Who would ever have thought he'd have married Josefa?

¿Habráse visto nunca/jamás . . . ?

Did you ever see . . . ?

¿Crees que ninguno de ellos te va a ayudar?

Do you think any of them is going to help you? (or 'Do you think none of them is going to help you?')

¿Para qué despedirme de nada ni de nadie? (A. Gala, Spain)

Why say goodbye to anyone or anything?

(d) After *antes de, antes que,* and *sin*:

He venido sin nada

I've come without anything

sin nadie que le cuidara

without anyone to look after him

Al otro día me levanté antes que nadie (J. Cortázar, Argentina, dialogue)

The next day I got up before everybody else (lit. 'before anyone')

Esto hay que hacerlo antes de empezar nada

This must be done before starting anything (else)

Note

(i) Statements of emotion involve a subtlety: *Me sorprendería que nadie me llamara/que no me llamara/nadie* 'I'd be surprised if nobody rang me', *Me sorprendería que me llamara nadie* 'I'd be surprised if anyone rang me', *Sentiría que nadie me viera así/que me viera así nadie* 'I'd be sorry if anyone sees me (looking) like this', *Sentiría que nadie me viera así/Sentiría que no me viera así nadie* 'I'd be sorry if no one sees me (looking) like this'.

(ii) In sentences in which English allows 'something' after 'without' Spanish allows *algo: . . . sin que nadie pudiera hacer algo para impedirlo* (L. Spota, *Mexico; hacer nada* also possible) 'without anyone being able to do anything/something to stop it', *No podía dormir sin que algo la despertara/despertase* 'She couldn't sleep without something waking her up'.

23.5 Further remarks on individual negative words

23.5.1 *Nada, nadie*

(a) When *nada* or *nadie* are the complement of a verb or follow a preposition, they usually appear in the double negative construction in ordinary language:

No sé nada	I know nothing/I don't know anything
No conozco a nadie	I don't know anyone
No es nada/nadie	It's nothing/nobody
No hay nada/nadie	There's nothing/nobody
No lo haría por nada/nadie	I wouldn't do it for anything/anyone
porque la palabra "felicidad" no era apropiada para nada que tuviera alguna vinculación con Alejandra (E. Sábato, Argentina)	because the word 'happiness' was not appropriate for anything which had any link with Alejandra

In literary styles they may precede the verb:

. . . nada prometen que luego traicionen (L. Cernuda, Spain)	they promise nothing that they then betray
A nadie conozco más apto para esta labor literaria	I know no one more suited for this literary task
Por nada del mundo quisiera perderme eso (set phrase in everyday use)	I wouldn't miss that for anything in the world
como esos hombres silenciosos y solitarios que a nadie piden nada y con nadie hablan (E. Sábato, Argentina)	like those silent and solitary men who ask nothing from anyone and speak with no one

(b) When *nada, nadie* are the subject of a verb they usually precede it:

Nada parece cierto en todo esto	Nothing seems sure in all this
Nada en la pieza es histórico (M. Vargas Llosa, Peru)	Nothing in the play is historical
Nadie quiso creerle que era honrado (M. Vargas Llosa, Peru, dialogue)	No one was willing to believe he was honest

But a double negative construction is used in questions:

¿No ha venido nadie?	Has no one come?
¿No ha llegado nada?	Hasn't anything arrived?

Note

With some verbs either construction may be used: *No me gusta nada/Nada me gusta* 'I don't like anything', *Nada de lo que tú hagas me molesta/No me molesta nada de lo que tú hagas* 'Nothing you do bothers me'.

23.5.2 *Nada* as intensifier

Nada may be used adverbially with the meaning 'not at all':

Manuel no trabaja nada	Manuel does absolutely no work
No hemos dormido nada	We haven't slept a wink
No ha sido nada cómoda la cárcel	Prison wasn't comfortable at all

23.5.3 Further remarks on *nadie*

Nadie takes personal *a* if it is the object of a verb:

Apenas conozco a nadie	I hardly know anybody
No se veía a nadie en la playa	There was no one to be seen on the beach

Note
Nadie de should not be followed by a plural noun or pronoun: *nadie de la clase* but *ninguno de los alumnos* 'none of the students', *ninguno de ellos* 'none of them', *ninguno de nosotros* 'none of us'.

23.5.4 *Ni*

'Nor', 'neither'. As with other negative words, if *ni* follows the verb to which it refers the verb must itself be negated: *Ni tú ni yo lo sabemos* 'Neither you nor I know (it)', but *No lo sabemos ni tú ni yo* (same meaning).

Constructions like **Ni tú ni yo no lo sabemos* are considered archaic or incorrect.

Unlike 'nor', *ni* is usually repeated before each member of a list: *No han llegado (ni) Antonio, ni Pilar, ni Ana, ni Mariluz* 'Neither Antonio, Pilar, Ana nor Mariluz has arrived' (the first *ni* is optional).

Examples of the use of *ni*:

. . . ya que entonces no había en la tierra ni sólidos ni líquidos ni gases (J.L. Borges, Argentina)	since at that time there were neither solids nor liquids nor gases on Earth
Ni fumo ni bebo/No fumo ni bebo	I neither smoke nor drink
Ni con ella, ni con nadie, me puedo comunicar (M. Puig, Argentina, dialogue)	I can't communicate with her or with anybody

Notes
(i) *Ni* commonly translates 'not even'. It can often be reinforced by *siquiera*: *Ni (siquiera) en mis peores momentos soñé que esto pudiera suceder* 'Not even in my worst moments did I dream this could happen', *Pero ¡si no ha de tener ni (siquiera) diecisiete años!* 'But she can't even be seventeen!', *Eres un inútil, no puedes ni (siquiera) freírte un huevo* 'You're useless, you can't even fry yourself an egg', *experiencia que no les sirvió ni para enfrentarse con un puñado de bandidos* (M. Vargas Llosa, Peru, dialogue) 'experience that didn't even help you take on a handful of bandits', *No entiendo ni una palabra (siquiera)* 'I don't understand a word', *¡Ni se te ocurra (siquiera) venir a verme!* 'Don't even get the idea of coming to see me!'.
(ii) Before a noun it may be an emphatic denial: *—¿Sabes quién es? —Ni idea* '"Do you know who it is?" "No idea"', *—¿Cuánto ganabas? —Ni (siquiera) un céntimo* '"What were you earning?" "Not a cent"'.
(iii) *Ni* is required after *sin*: *Vivía sin dinero ni ganas de tenerlo* 'He lived without money or the urge to have it', *sin mujer ni hijos* 'without wife or children'.

23.5.5 *Ninguno*

'No', 'none', 'nobody' (cf. French *aucun*, German *kein*). The double negative rule applies: if *ninguno* follows the verb, the verb must itself be negated: *Ninguno de ellos lo sabe/No lo sabe ninguno de ellos* 'None of them know', *Nunca compra ninguno* 'She never buys a single one'. In certain types of sentences, it may be an equivalent of 'any': see 23.4 for examples.

It may be either adjectival or pronominal. As an adjective it loses its final *-o* before a masculine noun or noun phrase.

It also often loses its final *-a* before feminine nouns (but not before adjectives) beginning with stressed *a-* or *ha-*: *ningún arma nuclear* 'no nuclear weapon'. (This, at least, is spoken usage, though the full form is properly written before such nouns). Examples:

En ningún momento pensé que . . .	At no point did I think that . . .
en ningún miserable pueblo costero	in no wretched coastal village

No aceptaremos ninguna solución parcial	We shall accept no partial (or 'biased') solution

The plural *ningunos/ningunas* is rare, presumably because there is scant need to mention more than one of something that does not exist. But it occurs with nouns that are always plural: *Ningunas vacaciones en Cataluña son completas sin una excursión al Pirineo* 'No holiday/vacation in Catalonia is complete without a trip to the Pyrenees', *Total, tenía 18 años y ningunas ganas de volver al pueblo* (A. Mastretta, dialogue, Mexico) 'In short/In a word, he was eighteen and had no desire to come back to the village'.

Examples:
(a) Pronominal forms

Ninguno de los que hablan un idioma está libre de dudas . . . (M. Seco, Spain)	None of those who speak a language is free of doubts . . .
O se lleva todos, o ninguno	Either you take them all, or none
Si he sido insincero con ninguno/alguno de vosotros, decídmelo (*ninguno* is more literary)	If I have been insincere with any of you, tell me so

(b) Adjectival forms

El ministro no hizo ningún comentario/no hizo comentario ninguno/alguno	The minister made no comment
—Si es molestia, puedo esperar. —Molestia ninguna/Ninguna molestia	'If it's a nuisance I can wait.' 'No nuisance at all'
. . . había llegado al climaterio con tres hijas y ningún varón (G. García Márquez, Colombia)	. . . she had reached the menopause with three daughters and no male (offspring)

Notes
(i) As the examples show, *alguno*, placed after the noun, may be used as an emphatic variant of *ninguno*: *en momento alguno* = *en ningún momento* 'at no moment at all'. See the note to 9.4.1a for details.
(ii) When *ninguno* is the subject of a verb, person and number agreement seems to be optional when the pronoun appears: *Ninguna de nosotras **tiene/tenemos** marido* 'None of us women has/have a husband', *Ninguno de vosotros **habéis/ha** traído el libro* 'None of you has/have brought the book'.
If the personal pronoun is omitted, the verb ending must make the meaning clear: *Ninguno **hemos** dicho eso* 'None of us said that', *¿No **salisteis** ninguna anoche?* 'Didn't any of you girls go out last night?' (compare *¿No salió ninguna anoche?* 'Didn't any of the girls go out last night?').
(iii) If *ninguno* is a direct or indirect object and is placed before the verb, the redundant pronoun agrees with the accompanying noun or pronoun: *A ninguno de ellos **los** conozco* 'I don't know any of them', *A ninguno de nosotros **nos** quiere dar el dinero* 'He doesn't want to give the money to any of us'.

23.5.6 *Nunca* and *jamás*
Both mean 'never' or, in certain sentences, 'ever'. *Jamás* is somewhat stronger and less usual than *nunca*. It is usually a synonym of *nunca*, but see note (i). The combination *nunca jamás* is strongly emphatic.
Both require a double negative construction when they follow the verb phrase to which they refer: *Nunca viene* = *No viene nunca* 'He never comes', *Nadie viene jamás* 'No one ever comes'.

No sale nunca/jamás de casa	He never goes out of the house

No tiene dinero y tampoco siente	He has no money, nor does he ever feel
nunca/jamás su carencia	the lack of it
Eso no lo volveré a hacer nunca jamás	I'll never ever do that again
¿Has oído nunca/jamás que un elefante	Have you ever heard of an elephant
volase/volara? (see note (ii))	flying?

Notes

(i) *Jamás* cannot appear after comparisons: *ahora más que nunca* 'now more than ever', *Trabaja menos que nunca* 'He's working less than ever', *Está más guapo que nunca* 'He's more handsome than ever'.

(ii) In rhetorical questions inviting the answer 'no' *jamás/nunca* means 'ever': *¿Se vio jamás/nunca tal cosa?* 'Was such a thing ever seen?', *¿Se ha oído jamás/nunca que un hombre mordiera a un perro?* 'Who ever heard' (lit. 'was it ever heard') that a man bit a dog?' Compare non-rhetorical question: *¿Has estado alguna vez en Madrid?* 'Were you ever in Madrid?'.

23.5.7 *Apenas*

'Hardly', 'scarcely', 'barely', 'as soon as'.

The variant *apenas si* is found in literary style for the meanings 'only' and 'scarcely'. It is not used in time statements or when *apenas* follows the verb.

The *pretérito anterior* (*hubo llegado*, etc.) may appear in conjunction with this adverb, especially in literary styles, though it is uncommon in speech. See 14.10.4 for discussion.

No te conozco apenas	I hardly know you
Apenas (si) te conozco	I hardly know you
En una semana apenas si cambió dos palabras	In the course of a week she barely
con su tío (J. Marsé, Spain)	exchanged two words with her uncle
Apenas llegamos/hubimos llegado cuando	We had scarcely arrived when it started
empezó a llover	raining
hace apenas seis años	barely six years ago

Notes

(i) *No bien* (in Argentina and perhaps elsewhere also *ni bien*) is an alternative: *No bien se hubo marchado/se marchó cuando . . .* 'He'd barely left when . . .'.

Nomás (see 23.2.5) may also be used in Latin America to mean 'scarcely'.

(ii) *Nada más* is a colloquial alternative in time statements: *Nada más llegar, pasé por su despacho* 'As soon as I arrived, I dropped in at his office', *Lo haré nada más llegue* 'I'll do it as soon as I arrive'.

23.5.8 *En mi vida, en toda la noche, en absoluto*

The phrases *en mi vida/en la vida*, 'in my life', *en toda la noche* 'in the whole night', *en absoluto* 'absolutely not' are occasionally used as negatives:

En mi vida le/lo he visto (or *No le/lo he visto*	I've never seen him in my life
en mi vida)	
En toda la noche he podido dormir	I've not been able to sleep the whole night
—¿Te molesta? —En absoluto	'Does it bother you?' 'Absolutely not/not at all'

En toda la noche as a negative phrase is rather old-fashioned: *No he podido dormir en toda la noche* is more normal. *En absoluto* may have a positive meaning in Latin America: *Considero que esos términos enunciados en absoluto han de relativizarse* (H. Guglielmi, Argentina) 'I consider that these terms, (which are) stated in an absolute way, should be relativized'.

23.5.9 *Tampoco*

'Not . . . either', 'nor', 'neither' (cf. French *non plus*). It is the opposite of *también* 'also'.

As with other negative particles, it requires a double negative construction if it follows a verb phrase: *Tampoco creo en los ovnis = No creo en los ovnis tampoco* 'Nor do I believe in UFOs'/'I don't believe in UFOs either':

—¿Tienes la llave? —No. —Yo tampoco . .	'Do you have the key?' 'No.' 'Nor do I . . .'
Tampoco dice nada a nadie	Nor does he say anything to anyone
Ellos tampoco hicieron ningún comentario	They didn't make any comment either

Ni or *y* can precede *tampoco*: *Me dijo que no le gustaba el vino, y/ni tampoco la cerveza* 'He told me he didn't like wine or beer'. As this example shows, *ni* can only be combined with *tampoco* if a negative statement precedes.

24

Interrogation and exclamations

Frequent errors in interrogative or exclamatory sentences are: confusion between *qué* and *cuál*, failure to write accents on interrogative or exclamatory pronouns and adverbs, omission or wrong position of the upside-down question mark and exclamation mark, and mistakes in the choice between *qué* and *lo que* in indirect questions.

24.1 Spelling

The interrogative pronouns and adverbs are:

¿cómo?	how?	24.7
¿cuál?	which?/what?	24.3
¿cuándo?	when?	24.8
¿cuánto?	how many/much?	24.6
¿dónde?	where?	24.9
¿para qué?	what for?	24.10
¿por qué?	why?	24.10
¿qué?	what?	24.4
¿quién?	who?	24.5

The accent marks an important feature of pronunciation, i.e. that the interrogative and exclamatory forms are stressed words. Compare *Yo sé que quiere comprar* and *Yo sé **qué** quiere comprar* 'I know that he wants to buy', 'I know *what* he wants to buy'.

24.2 Word order in interrogative sentences

When a sentence or clause begins with one of the above interrogative words, Verb-Subject word order is used:[1]

¿Qué hizo usted?	What did you do?
¿Cómo se llama tu hermana?	What's your sister called?

Word order in interrogative sentences is discussed more fully at 37.2.2.

---

[1] Although in Cuba constructions like *¿Qué usted hizo?* are commonly heard. See note to 37.2.2.

24.3 *Cuál*

24.3.1 Basic uses of *cuál*
Its basic meaning is 'which?', i.e. 'which one?' of a set:

¿Cuál prefieres?	Which one do you prefer?
¿A cuál prefieres?	Which (person) do you prefer?
¿A cuál de los tres se refiere usted?	To which of the three are you referring?

¿Cuál? is appropriate in cases where choice is involved, but one would say *Han venido algunos de tercero, pero no sé* **quiénes** 'Some of the third year have come, but I don't know which/who'.

24.3.2 Translating 'what is/are/were?', etc.
When translating sentences like 'What's the motive?', 'What's the difference?' one normally uses the phrase *¿Cuál es/era la diferencia?* (or *¿Qué diferencia hay/había?*). This is because such sentences basically mean 'which, of the various possible motives, is the motive?', 'which of the possible differences is the difference?'.

¿Qué es? literally means 'what thing?' or 'what kind of thing?', so it must be must be used when asking the definition of something's nature, as in 'What (kind of thing) is democracy?', 'What (kind of thing) is Vermouth?'. Examples:

¿Cuál es el problema? (*¿Qué es el problema?* is not Spanish)	What's the problem?
¿Cuál es su impresión de los acontecimientos?	What is your impression of the events?
(but *¿Qué hora es?*	What's the time?)
¿Cuál fue el motivo del crimen?	What was the motive of the crime?
Ya hay bastante desolación como para poder ver . . . cuáles son los deberes del hombre (E. Sábato, Argentina)	There is already enough desolation for us to be able to see what man's duties are

Compare

¿Qué es la vida?	What is life?
¿Qué es su hermana?	What is his sister? (i.e. what does she do?)
¿Qué griterío es ése?	What's that shouting?

Note
¿Cuál es su nombre? means 'Which one is your name?' and *¿Cuál es la fecha?* means 'Which one's the date?'. *¿Cómo se llama?* = 'What's your name?', *¿A qué fecha estamos?/¿A cuántos estamos?/¿Qué fecha es hoy?* = 'What's the date?'. But cf. *¿Cuál es la fecha de la Batalla de Waterloo?* 'What's the date of the Battle of Waterloo?'.

24.3.3 *Cuál*: dialect differences
In Spain and in some parts of Latin America *cuál* is rarely used adjectivally (i.e. directly before a noun): *¿**Qué** chicas vienen esta noche?* 'Which girls are coming tonight?', not *¿Cuáles chicas vienen esta noche?* However, sentences like the latter are common in many parts of Latin America:

?*No sé a cuáles asuntos se refiere* (Chile, from Kany, 70; *¿Qué asuntos?*)	I don't know what matters he's referring to
?*—Detenga a ese hombre! —¿Cuál hombre?* (Honduras, ibid., i.e. *¿Qué hombre?*)	'Arrest that man!' 'What man?'

?¿Gatos? ¿Cuáles gatos? (C. Fuentes, Mexico, dialogue; Spain *¿Qué gatos?*)   Cats? What cats?

Sentences like *¿Cuál sombrero prefieres?* may occasionally be heard in Spain, but learners of European Spanish should say *¿Qué sombrero prefieres?* or *¿Cuál de los sombreros prefieres?* or simply *¿Cuál prefieres?*.

24.4 Qué

For the conjunction *que* see 33.4. For the relative pronoun *que*, see Chapter 35.

24.4.1 Basic uses of qué
¿Qué? means 'what?', 'what sort of?', but not in sentences like *¿Cuál es el problema?* 'What's the problem?', for which see 24.3.2.
(a) *Qué* as a pronoun

¿Yo qué gano trabajando para ese negrero?	What do I gain by working for that slave driver?
No sé qué decirte	I don't know what to say to you
Discutían sobre qué iban a decirle a Andrés	They were arguing about what they were going to say to Andrés
Por cierto, ¿qué fue de Antonio?	By the way, what became of Antonio?

(b) *Qué* as an adjective (see 24.3.3 for the Latin-American use of *cuál* in this context)

¿A qué párrafo te refieres?	Which paragraph are you referring to?
¿Con qué medios podemos contar?	What means can we count on?
Me pregunto en qué situación estará ahora	I wonder what situation he's in now

Notes
(i) *¿Qué?* is a familiar alternative for the more refined *¿cómo?* when a repetition is required: —*María es muy respondona.* —*¿Qué?* (polite *¿cómo?*)[2] '"Maria answers back a lot." "What?"' (i.e. what did you say?).
(ii) *El qué* may occasionally be used as an interrogative, presumably to make clear that 'what?' is meant rather than 'I beg your pardon': —*Eso es extraño.* —*¿El qué?* '"That's odd." "What is?"', —*Se le olvidó traer el Malibu.* —*¿El qué?* '"He forgot to bring the Malibu." "The what?"'.

24.4.2 Qué and lo que in indirect questions
Either *qué* or *lo que* are possible except immediately before an infinitive, when *qué* is required and *lo que* may sound uneducated:

Sé de lo que te hablo (C. Fuentes, Mexico dialogue)	I know what I'm talking to you about
Ni sé qué piensa y tampoco sé lo que pienso yo (E. Sábato, Argentina, dialogue)	I don't know what he thinks, and I don't know what I think either
No sé qué hacer (**not** **No sé lo que hacer*)	I don't know what to do
Pregúntale qué/lo que tiene	Ask him what he's got
No sé lo que/qué voy a hacer	I don't know what I'm going to do

24.4.3 Qué: idiomatic uses
The following are noteworthy: *¿Qué tal?* 'How are you?/How are things?',

---
[2] Mexicans say *mande* for *¿Cómo?*

¿Qué tal estás? 'How are you?', *¿Qué te parece?* 'What do you think of it?', *¿A santo de qué haces eso?* 'What on earth are you doing that for?', *¿A mí qué?* 'What do I care?', *¿Y qué?* 'So what?'.

24.4.4 Translating 'What a . . . !'

Qué is used without a following article to translate 'what a . . . !' in exclamations:

¡Qué vida ésta!	What a life!
¡Qué día más/tan hermoso!	What a lovely day!
¡Qué cara!	What a nerve/cheek!

A following adjective is preceded by *más* or *tan*:

¡Qué pareja más/tan moderna!	What a modern couple!
¡Qué libro más/tan aburrido!	What a boring book!
¡Qué nevera más/tan estúpida ésta/esta!	Isn't this a stupid refrigerator!

Qué de . . . is a rather old-fashioned alternative for *cuánto* in exclamations:

¡Qué de cosas/Cuántas cosas tengo que contarte! (familiarly *La de cosas que tengo que contarte*)	What a lot of things I've got to tell you!

Note
Use of *cómo* in this context is an archaism that survives in Latin America: *¡Cómo somos desgraciadas las mujeres!* (Spain *¡Qué desgraciadas somos las mujeres!* 'How unhappy we women are!', *¡Cómo es difícil vivir!* (= *¡Qué difícil es vivir!*) 'How difficult living is!'. (Argentine and Uruguayan examples from Kany, 342-3.) J. M. Lope Blanch, (1991), 13, notes that this construction is used by all social classes in Mexico. It is not used in Spain.
The colloquial *cómo . . . de* is common on both continents: *¡Cómo estás de guapa!* 'Aren't you attractive!', *Pero ¡Cómo está de gordo!* 'My, isn't he fat!'.

24.5 Quién

For *quien* as a relative pronoun see Chapter 35. For *quien* as a nominalizer (e.g. *quien dice eso . . .* 'people who say that . . .') see Chapter 36.
Quién/quiénes translates 'who'/'whom' in direct and indirect questions:

¿Quién ha sido?	Who was it?
¿Sabes en quién estoy pensando ahora?	Do you know who(m) I'm thinking of now?
¿Sabes quiénes van a estar?	Do you know who is going to be there?

Notes
(i) Historically *quien* had no plural, and popular speech often uses the singular for the plural, e.g. *¿Sabes quién (quiénes) son?* 'Do you know who they are?'. This construction, frequent in older literature, should not be imitated.
(ii) *Quién* plus the imperfect subjunctive translates 'if only . . .'. See 16.15.2.

24.6 Cuánto

Cuánto may function as a pronoun/adjective or as an adverb. In the former case it agrees in number and gender with the noun; in the latter case it is invariable.

(a) 'How much', 'how many'

¿Cuánto es?	How much is it?
¿Cuánta mantequilla queda?	How much butter is left?
¿Cuántos vienen?	How many are coming?
No ha dicho cuánta gasolina quería	He didn't say how much petrol/US 'gas' he wanted
¿Cuánto han trabajado?	How much have they worked?

(b) In exclamations, 'how much!', 'what a lot!'

In exclamations *cuánto* is shortened to *cuán* before adverbs or adjectives other than *más, menos, mayor, menor, mejor, peor.* However, although it is not yet quite extinct in educated speech, *cuán* is nowadays usually found only in flowery journalese, and *qué*, or *lo* + adjective or adverb (the latter discussed at 7.2.2) are more usual:

¡Cuántas veces (no) te lo habré dicho!	How many times have I told you!
¡Cuánta falta le hace a este niño alguien que le enderece!	How much this child needs someone to keep him on the straight path!
¡Cuánto más trágico!	How much more tragic!
¡Cuánto mejor estarías así!	How much better you'd be like that!
Ella misma se sorprendió de cuán lejos estaba de su vida (G. García Márquez, Colombia)	She herself was surprised at how far he was from her life

Notes

(i) In the comparative phrases *cuanto más/menos . . . más/menos* 'the more . . . the more' 'the less . . . the less', *cuanto* is not used exclamatorily and does not take an accent. See Chapter 5 for further discussion of this construction.

(ii) *Cuanto* may be used as a relative pronoun equivalent to *todo lo que*: *Dime cuanto sabes = Dime todo lo que sabes* 'Tell me everything you know'.

24.7 *Cómo*

'How' in direct and indirect questions and in exclamations.

¿Cómo te llamas?	What's your name?
¿Cómo quieres que me peine?	How do you want me to do my hair?
No sé cómo hacerlo	I don't know how to do it
¡Cómo está el mundo!	What a state the world is in!
¡Cómo llueve!	Look how it's raining!
¿Cómo le dejas ir solo al cine a ese niño?	How can you let that child go to the cinema on his own?

24.8 *Cuándo* 'when'

Little need be said about this word in direct and indirect questions: *¿Cuándo fue eso?* 'When was that?', *No sé cuándo llegarán* 'I don't know when they'll arrive'.

When it is not a question word, *cuando* (no accent) may introduce relative clauses, see 35.12, or it may be a subordinator often requiring the subjunctive, see 16.12.6. For 'whenever' see 16.13.6. For the use of *cuando* in cleft sentences, e.g. *fue entonces cuando . . .* 'it was then that . . .' see 36.2.

It may also occasionally function as a preposition meaning 'at the time of': *Nos casamos cuando el terremoto* 'We got married at the time of the earthquake'.

24.9 *Dónde* 'where'

This word should be differentiated from *¿Adónde?*, which means 'where to?' and is optionally used with verbs of motion, cf. *¿Adónde van ustedes?* or *¿Dónde van ustedes?*. Only *¿Dónde?* can be used when no motion is involved: *¿Dónde estamos?*, not **¿Adónde estamos?*.

When it is not a question word, *donde* (no accent) may introduce relative clauses, see 16.14.3 and 35.10, where the difference between *donde* and *a donde* is discussed. For 'wherever' see 16.13.8. For *donde* in cleft sentences, e.g. *fue allí donde . . .* 'it was there that . . .' see 36.2.

Donde may mean 'at the house of' in some countries, especially Chile, Peru, Ecuador and Central America: *Voy donde Miguel = Voy a casa de Miguel*; the construction is heard in regional popular speech in Spain. *Lo de* has the same meaning in Argentina: *Voy a lo de Miguel*.

24.10 *Por qué, para qué*

Por qué 'why' must be distinguished in spelling and pronunciation from *porque* 'because'. *Para qué* 'what for?' must be distinguished from *para que* 'in order to'.

In questions *para qué* stresses intention, *por qué* stresses cause, and the difference is the same as between 'what *for*?' and 'why?': *¿Para qué vamos a cambiarlo si todo está bien?* 'What are we changing it for if everything's ok?', *¿Por qué se incendió la casa?* 'Why did the house catch fire?' (not *para qué* or 'what for?'). Statistically *por qué* is much more frequent and can often – but not always – replace *para qué*.

25

Conditional sentences

25.1 General

Conditional sentences may be very varied in structure, but the commonest patterns are:

(a) Open conditions: *Si viene me quedo/quedaré* 'If he comes I'll stay', *Si han llegado, me quedaré* 'If they've arrived I'll stay'.

(b) Remote conditions: *Si viniera/viniese, me quedaría/quedaba* 'If he came/were to come, I would stay'.

(c) Unfulfilled conditions: *Si hubiéramos/hubiésemos tenido más dinero, habríamos/hubiéramos comprado la casa* 'If we had had more money we would have bought the house'.

(d) Fulfilled conditions: *Si llegaba temprano comíamos a las doce* 'If he arrived early we had lunch at twelve', *Si dijo eso, comprendo que su hermana se haya enfadado* 'If he said *that*, I understand his sister getting cross'.

One point can hardly be overstressed: *si*, in the meaning of 'if', is never followed by the present subjunctive except in one rare construction. See 25.8.1 for details.

25.2 Open conditions

Open conditions are so called because fulfilment or non-fulfilment of the condition are equally possible. The subjunctive is not used in open conditions and the tense pattern is the same as in English:

(a) *Si* + present + present:

Si tenemos que pagar tanto no vale la pena	If we have to pay so much it's not worth it
. . .*si (el elitismo) significa que selecciona sus miembros en razón de su aptitud, todas las universidades del mundo son elitistas* (M. Vargas Llosa, Peru)	. . . if elitism means that it selects its members according to their ability, every university in the world is elitist

(b) *Si* + present + future (or present with future meaning):

Si el contrato no está mañana en Londres, no hay trato	If the contract isn't in London by tomorrow, the deal's off
Si llueve me quedo/quedaré en casa	If it rains I'll stay at home

(c) *Si* + past tense + present or future, normally only possible when the subject of the verb in the main clause is not yet sure about the facts described in the if-clause:

Si han contestado ya, no les escribiré	If they've already answered, I won't write to them
Si terminaron la semana pasada nos queda poco por hacer	If they finished last week there isn't much left for us to do
Si llevaba minifalda su madre estará enfadadísima	If she was wearing a miniskirt her mother will be really cross

(d) *Si* + present + imperative

Si queréis ver el desfile, salid al balcón	If you want to see the parade, go out on to the balcony

(e) In reported speech referring to the past, the imperfect or pluperfect indicative appear in the if-clause, and the conditional (or colloquially the imperfect indicative) in the main clause.

This is also very common in 'indirect style', i.e. where the text reports someone's unspoken thoughts, e.g. '(He knew that) if it rained everything would be spoilt' (*Sabía que) si llovía se estropearía todo:*

(Me dijo que) me pagaría si había terminado	(He told me) he'd pay me if I'd finished
Dijo que la operarían si tenía algún hueso roto	She said that they'd operate on her if she had any broken bones
Si la policía la detenía, ya escarmentaría (M. Vázquez Montalbán; Spain, unspoken thoughts)	If the police arrested her, that would teach her a lesson
Si no actuaba pronto, Gianni terminaría por resquebrajarse, por acabar en una clínica psiquiátrica (S. Pitol, Mexico)	If she didn't act promptly Gianni would break down, end up in a psychiatric clinic

The prevalence of this type of construction in passages of indirect speech sometimes encourages students to believe that the pattern *si* + imperfect indicative + conditional is also the usual way of forming remote conditions in Spanish, as in French and English, e.g. 'if I had money'/*si j'avais de l'argent* . . ., Spanish *si **tuviera**/**tuviese** dinero* . . . .The next section should correct any such misconception.

(f) The imperfect indicative therefore sometimes also appears in the if-clause when some phrase like 'I think that . . .', 'What I say is' has been omitted:
(Lo que yo digo es) si sabía que sólo era por mi dinero, claro que no me casaría/casaba '(What I say is that), if I knew that it was only for my money, obviously I wouldn't get married'.

25.3 Remote conditions

In these 'remote' conditions the verb in the if-clause is in the imperfect subjunctive (*-ra* or *-se* form); the verb in the other clause is normally in the conditional.

There are two types, which correspond to the English sentences 'If you paid now it would cost less' and 'If I were rich I'd buy you a house'. The first is fulfillable and is merely a slightly hypothetical variant of an equivalent open condition: there is little difference between *Si pagaras ahora, costaría menos* 'If you **paid** now it would cost less' and *Si pagas ahora, costará menos* 'If you **pay** now it will cost less', except that the probability appears more remote in the first example.

In the second type the condition is contrary to fact and the subjunctive construction is the only possible one in Spanish: *Si yo fuera/fuese rico, te compraría una casa,* 'If I were rich, I'd buy you a house' (but I'm not).

English and French-speaking students must avoid using the imperfect indicative in the if-clause (cf. *si j'étais riche* . . .):

Esto quiere decir que si usted realizase seis viajes con estas 15.000 ptas ahorraría más de 4.000 ptas (RENFE advertisement; or *realizara.* Present indicative possible)	This means that if you made six journeys with these 15,000 ptas, you would save more than 4,000 ptas
Si supieras hacer el nudo como todos los chicos de tu edad, no te tendrías que quejar (I. Aldecoa, Spain, dialogue; *supieses* also possible)	If you knew how to make a knot like all the boys of your age, you wouldn't have to complain
Si por lo menos se pudiera limitar el contrabando de cocaína, se ahorrarían muchas muertes (M. Vargas Llosa, Peru, dialogue; or *pudiese*)	If one could at least limit cocaine smuggling, a lot of deaths would be avoided

Notes
(i) Use of the conditional in the if-clause is regional or substandard, but it is common in Navarre, the Basque Provinces and neighbouring parts of Spain, in popular Argentine speech and no doubt elsewhere, e.g. ?*Si no estaría preso, no lo habrían soltado* 'If he wasn't arrested they wouldn't have let him go' (M. Puig, Argentine dialogue, for *estuviera/estuviese*). This should not be imitated.
(ii) For use of the *-ra* subjunctive form as an alternative for the conditional, see 25.6 and 14.7.5.

25.4 Unfulfilled conditions

These refer to a condition in the past that was not fulfilled. The verb in the if-clause is in the pluperfect subjunctive (*hubiera/hubiese hablado,* etc.) and the verb in the main clause is usually in the perfect conditional of the perfect (*habría/hubiera hecho,* etc.):

Si él hubiera/hubiese tenido dinero, hubiera/habría saldado la cuenta	If he'd had money he'd have settled the bill
. . . si no hubiera sido por las contracciónes del estómago, se habría sentido muy bien (J. Cortázar, Argentina, dialogue)	*. . .* had it not been for the stomach cramps, he'd have felt fine

Notes
(i) There are a number of simplified forms of this type of conditional sentence that are often heard in spontaneous speech but are banned from writing or non-spontaneous language and are rather informal for foreign speakers: *Si lo llego a saber, te habría llamado* 'If I'd found out, I'd have rung you', *Si sé que estás enfermo, no vengo* 'If I'd known you were ill, I wouldn't have come', *Dio un tropezón y si se descuida, se cae* 'He slipped and nearly fell down'.
(ii) *Si* + imperfect + imperfect can be heard in popular speech in Argentina *Si me tocabas, te mataba con mi cuchillo* (E. Sábato, Argentina, dialogue) 'If you'd touched me, I'd have killed you with my knife'. One also hears *si* + imperfect + pluperfect subjunctive *Si hace unos años yo veía* (for *hubiera visto*) *en la playa a alguien con esto, hubiera pensado: ese tipo es loco* (Mafalda cartoon, Argentina; *está loco* in Spain) 'If I'd seen someone a few years ago on the beach with that, I'd have thought that guy's crazy'.

25.5 Imperfect indicative for conditional

The imperfect indicative commonly replaces the conditional tense in the main clause in spontaneous speech on both sides of the Atlantic (the subject is further discussed in 14.5.2). This usage is perfectly acceptable in relaxed European Spanish but it is not allowed in formal styles and it may be less tolerated in some American republics than in others:

Desde luego, si yo fuera hombre, no me casaba . . . (L. Goytisolo, Spain, dialogue)	Obviously, if I were a man I wouldn't marry . . .
Si de pronto tuviese/tuviera la certeza de que no voy a vivir más que dos días, de seguro me iba (for *iría*) *a confesar* (M. de Unamuno, *Diario íntimo*, Spain)	If I suddenly found out for certain that I'd only two days to live, I'd certainly go to confession
Si no fuera por vosotros iba yo a aguantar a vuestro padre . . . (set expression: *iría* not used)	If it weren't for you, would I put up with your father?

25.6 *-ra* forms instead of the conditional

The imperfect subjunctive in *-ra* (but not, at least in careful language, the *-se* form) is a very common alternative for the conditional of the auxiliary verb *haber* and also of some other verbs. See 14.7.5 for detailed discussion:

Con él o sin él, hubiera/habría sido igual	With him or without him, it would have been the same

25.7 Fulfilled conditions

These are not really conditions at all but merely an elegant way of saying 'the reason why'/'just because'/'whenever'. The verb is never in the subjunctive:

Si me estaba contando todos aquellos proyectos era porque inexorablemente pensaba realizarlos (F. Umbral, Spain)	If he was telling me about all those plans, it was because he was inevitably intending to carry them out
Si he tenido suerte, la culpa no es mía	It's not my fault if I've been lucky
Si teníamos dinero, íbamos al teatro	If we had any money, we used to go to the theatre

25.8 *Si* 'if'

25.8.1 *Si*: general

Si is never followed by the present subjunctive except occasionally in formal literary style after *saber*: *No sé si **sea** cierto* 'I do not know whether it be true' for *No sé si es cierto*.

Ser cannot be deleted after *si*: *si **es** urgente* 'if urgent', *Ven antes si **es** posible* 'Come earlier if possible'; cf. also French *si nécessaire* 'if necessary', *si es/fuera/fuese necesario*.

Si sometimes has a merely emphatic function: *Pero, ¡si tiene más de cincuenta años!* 'But he's more than fifty years old!'.

In the phrase *apenas si* it has no function: *Apenas (si) la conocía* 'I/he/she/you barely knew her'.

25.8.2 Replacement of *si* by *como*

In informal language in type 1 (open) conditions, *como* with the present or imperfect subjunctive may replace *si*. This is usually confined to threats and warnings:[1]

Como vuelvas a hablarme de mala manera, me voy	If you talk to me in a nasty way again, I'm going
Como no me lo pagues, me lo llevo	If you don't pay me for it, I'll take it away
Me dijo que como no se lo pagara/pagase, se lo llevaba/llevaría	She told me that if I didn't pay her for it, she would take it away

Como with the indicative = 'since'. See 33.5.2:

Como no me lo has pagado, me lo llevo	Since you've not paid me for it, I'm taking it away

25.8.3 Replacement of *si* by *de*

De + infinitive may replace *si* and a finite verb in an if-clause. This is only possible if the verb in the if-clause and the verb in the subordinate clause are in the same person. One can say *De haberlo sabido, me hubiera quedado en casa* 'Had I known, I'd have stayed at home' (both first-person), but not **De llover, me quedo en casa* 'If it rains I'm staying at home' (*Si llueve me quedo/quedaré en casa*):

De seguir así acabarás haciéndote comunista	If you carry on like that, you'll end by becoming a communist
De no haberse hecho la cirugía estética en ese instante a Márgara, se le arrugaría la nariz (J. Asís, Argentina)	If Márgara hadn't had plastic surgery at that moment, her nose would have become wrinkled

When used thus, *de* must have a hypothetical or future reference. One can say *De llover, lloverá mucho* 'If it rains it'll rain a lot', but not **De ser guapa, es mi novia* 'If she's beautiful, she's my girlfriend' (timeless statement). *De* cannot therefore be used in type 4 (fulfilled) conditional sentences (25.7).

25.9 Other ways of expressing conditions

(a) The gerund may sometimes have a conditional force: *Hablando de esa manera no consigues nada* 'You'll get nowhere by talking like that' = *Si hablas de esa manera . . .* 'If you talk like that . . .'. See note to 20.4.2 for more examples.

(b) A negative if-clause may be introduced by some phrase meaning 'unless', e.g. *a menos que, a no ser que* (see 16.12.7b):

Debe estar en casa, a no ser que haya ido al bar con sus amigos	He must be at home, unless he's gone to the bar with his friends

(c) 'If' may be expressed by some phrase meaning 'on condition that', e.g. *con tal (de) que, a condición de que* (see 16.12.7a):

Compraré los riñones, con tal (de) que estén frescos	I'll buy the kidneys provided they're fresh

---

[1] J.M. Lope Blanch (1991) p.146, says that *como* + subjunctive is unknown in Mexican Spanish.

(d) *Al* + infinitive (see 18.7) properly means 'on . . .-ing', but is sometimes seen with a conditional meaning:

?*Al ser verdad esta afirmación se tendrá que repensar todo*	If this claim is true, everything will have to be re-thought

This is not acceptable in Spain and is probably a Latin-American regionalism. It is stylistically dubious.

(e) *A* + infinitive can have conditional force in a few cases:

A no ser por mí, le hubieran matado	Had it not been for me, they'd have killed him
A juzgar por lo que dicen . . . (= *si se juzga por lo que dicen . . .*)	To judge by what they say . . .
A decir verdad, no me cae bien (= *Si digo la verdad . . .*)	To tell the truth, I don't like it/him/her/you

(f) *Por si . . .* forms conditionals of the sort translated by 'in case . . .' or some similar phrase:

Me asomé a la ventana por si venía	I looked out of the window in case he was coming
Compramos otra botella por si acaso	We'll buy another bottle just in case
Por si esto fuera poco, también me han robado el reloj	As if that weren't enough, they've stolen my watch too

25.10 Miscellaneous examples of conditional sentences

The following are translations of typical English conditionals (some taken from Quirk, Greenbaum *et al.* (1972), 11.32):

Had he known, he wouldn't have protested	*Si lo hubiese/hubiera sabido no habría/hubiera protestado* or *De haberlo sabido . . .*
Were that the only reason, there'd be no problem	*Si ésa fuera/fuese la única razón, no habría problema*
If possible, come earlier	*Si es posible, ven antes* (not *si posible . . .*)
I won't compromise, even if he offers/were to offer me money	*No transijo, incluso/aun si me ofrece/ofreciera/ofreciese dinero*
It'll be impossible unless you change your attitude	*Será imposible, a menos que/salvo que/a no ser que cambies de actitud*
Provided no objection is raised, the meeting will be held here	*Con tal (de) que no haya ninguna objección, la reunión se celebrará aquí*
Should it turn out to be true, things will be different	*Si resulta ser verdad, las cosas serán distintas*

25.11 Translating 'if I were you . . .'

If I were you, I'd keep quiet	*Yo de usted/Yo que usted/Si yo fuera usted, me callaría/callaba*

Yo que usted is the older Peninsular formula; *yo de usted* is a Catalanism which is now widespread, although censured by manuals of good usage[2]: *Yo de ti lo dejaba* 'If I were you I would leave it'.

---

[2] E.g. Santamaría et al. (1989), 309.

26

Pronominal verbs

26.1 General

Pronominal verbs are those that are accompanied by an object pronoun (i.e. *me*, *te*, *se*, *nos*, *os*, *se*) which is of the same person as the subject of the verb, for example *Yo me lavo* 'I'm washing (myself)', *Vais a cansaros* 'You're going to tire yourselves/get tired', *(Él) se ha marchado* 'He's gone/left'. The usual object pronouns are used with such verbs, except in the third person (*usted*, *ustedes* included) which uses the invariable pronoun *se* for both singular and plural.

A very large number of Spanish verbs can be pronominalized, even intransitive verbs like 'to be' and 'to die'. Older grammars sometimes call such forms as *me voy*, *se cayó*, *se lava* 'reflexive verbs', but this name is very misleading. Reflexive verbs are those in which the subject performs an action on him/herself, 'I'm washing myself', 'He praises himself', but only a small percentage of pronominal verbs are actually reflexive. The range of meanings associated with pronominalized verbs is illustrated in the following list, which is not exhaustive:

(a) Reflexive (see 26.2)

Se afeita	He's shaving (himself)
No te conoces (a ti mismo/a)	You don't know yourself

(b) Reciprocal (plural verbs only; see 26.3)

Ustedes se insultan mucho	You insult one another a lot
Se querían tanto	They loved one another so much

(c) To denote accidental or unplanned actions (26.6.2 and 26.6.4)

Me caí en la calle	I fell down in the street
El agua se sale por aquí	The water's leaking here

(d) To emphasize the point of departure of a movement (see 26.6.2)

Se salió de la reunión	He walked out of the meeting
Se han ido de casa	They've left home

(e) To show that an action concerns or interests the subject alone (see 26.2, (note iv))

Yo sé lo que me hago (Spain only)	I know what I'm doing
Tú sabrás lo que te dices (Spain only)	You may know what you're saying

(f) To make a transitive verb intransitive (26.5)

La puerta se abrió	The door opened
No te enfades	Don't get angry

(g) To stress the 'totality' of an action (26.6.3)

Se fumó un paquete entero	He smoked a whole packet
Se leyó el libro en una hora	He read the (whole) book in one hour

Other verbs that have pronominal counterparts, e.g. *reír/reírse* 'to laugh', *morir/morirse* 'to die', *ganar/ganarse* 'to earn'/'to win', *estar/estarse* 'to be', *esperar/esperarse* 'to wait'/'to expect', *volver/volverse* 'to become'/'to return'/'to turn back', *conocer/conocerse* 'to know', *escapar/escaparse* 'to escape', are best studied as separate lexical items. The more common of them are discussed at 26.6.4, and all of them should appear in good dictionaries of Spanish. Some pronominal verbs, e.g. *regresarse* 'to return', *enfermarse* 'to get ill' occur in Latin America but are rejected in Spain; see 26.7.

Verbs that translate the English 'become', e.g. *ponerse, hacerse, volverse, convertirse en*, are often pronominal verbs. They are discussed in Chapter 27.

The pronoun *se* also appears in the following third-person constructions:

Se sirven comidas	Meals (are) served
Se ha dicho que . . .	It has been said that . . .
Se vive mejor en España	One lives better in Spain/Life's better in Spain
Se le considera poco honrado	He's considered to be dishonest
Se detuvo a tres contrabandistas	Three smugglers were detained

These passive or impersonal uses of *se* are discussed separately at 28.4-28.6.

Throughout the following discussion it must be remembered that very often the meaning of a pronominal verb is given by the context. Thus out of context *Se critican* means 'They criticize themselves', 'They criticize one another', or 'They are criticized'. Such ambiguities are almost always resolved by reference to the background of the sentence or by appealing to common sense.

26.2 Reflexive meaning of pronominal verbs

This use, not the most common, shows that an action is done by the subject to/for him/herself: *Se está duchando* '(S)he's having a shower', *Os alabáis mucho* 'You praise yourselves a lot', *Me voy a comprar otro traje* 'I'm going to buy (myself) a new suit'. Four important features of this reflexive meaning are:
(a) The subject is always animate (since a door doesn't usually wash or open itself);
(b) The pronoun may stand for the direct or the indirect object: *Me estoy afeitando* 'I'm shaving', *Me estoy quitando la camisa* 'I'm taking my shirt off';
(c) The action can be voluntary or accidental;
(d) The original verb is always transitive.

Examples:

Se está lavando	He/She's washing
Me corté con una lata	I cut myself with a tin
Se ha roto una pierna	He's broken a leg
¡Qué bien te peinas!	How well you do your hair!
¡Cuidado, que te vas a salpicar!	Careful, you're going to get splashed!

Se daban crema para el sol	They were putting suncream on (or reciprocal 'They were putting suncream on each other')
Se mató en un accidente	He got killed in an accident[1]

Notes

(i) The subject in these constructions may be emphasized by use of the subject pronoun, sometimes reinforced by the appropriate form of *solo* 'alone' or *mismo*: *Primero vistió a la niña y luego se vistió ella* 'First she dressed the child, then she dressed herself', *No eches la culpa a nadie, te has manchado tú solo/mismo* 'Don't blame anyone else, you stained yourself', *La niña se pone los zapatos ella sola* 'The little girl puts on her shoes all by herself'.

If a preposition is used (including personal *a*) emphasis is obtained by using the appropriate prepositional form of the personal pronoun (*mí/ti/sí/nosotros/vosotros/sí*) plus the correct number and gender of *mismo*: *Se decía a sí misma que no servía para nada* 'She told herself he was good for nothing', *Me odio a mí mismo/misma* 'I hate myself', *Nos mentimos a nosotros mismos con frecuencia* 'We lie to ourselves frequently'. *Mismo* is not used if the preposition is *para*: *Se decía para sí que no valía la pena* 'She told herself that it wasn't worthwhile'. When the preposition is *con*, the pronouns *mí*, *ti* and *sí* combine with it to form *conmigo, contigo* and *consigo*; see 11.5.2.

(ii) Verbs expressing hurt take either the prepositional or non-prepositional form: *Se hace daño él mismo/a sí mismo* 'He's hurting himself', *Te perjudicas tú mismo/a ti mismo* 'You're damaging yourself'.

(iii) With a few common verbs the pronominal form may mean 'to get something done' as well as 'to do something for or to oneself': *Se va a hacer un abrigo rojo* 'She's going to make herself a red coat'/'She's going to get a red coat made', *Se ha construido un chalet* 'He built himself a house (either himself or to his specifications)', *Me voy a cortar el pelo* 'I'm going to have my hair cut'/'I'm going to cut my hair'.

Ambiguity can be removed by the appropriate use of the personal pronoun followed by *mismo* or *solo*: *Se construyó la casa él mismo/solo* 'He built the house himself', *Te puedes hacer una permanente tú misma/sola en casa* 'You can give yourself a perm at home'. In some cases it is very unlikely that the action will actually be performed by the subject: *Me voy a operar de cataratas* 'I'm going to have an operation for cataracts', *Si te duele esa muela, debías sacártela* 'If that tooth's aching you ought to have it out' (or, less likely, 'you ought to take it out').

(iv) In colloquial language in Spain, but not in Latin America, a reflexive form may emphasize that the action concerns only the subject: *Tú sabrás lo que te dices* 'I guess *you* know what you're talking about', *Yo me entiendo* 'I know what I'm referring to'/'I know what I'm talking about'.

26.3 Reciprocal meaning of pronominal verbs

A plural pronominal verb may have a reciprocal meaning, i.e. show that an action is done to or for one another. *El uno al otro/los unos a los otros* can be added to make clear that the reciprocal meaning is intended: compare *Se entristecen* 'They grow sad'/'They make themselves sad'/'They make one another sad', and *Se entristecen los unos a los otros* 'They make one another sad':

Nos escribimos periódicamente	We write to one another regularly
Hace años que no se hablan	They haven't been talking to one another for years

---

[1] Not 'He committed suicide', merely that he himself was performing the action that killed him. One could not say **Se mató en una riña* for 'He got killed in a fight': *Le mataron en una riña*.

Pasó mucho tiempo sin que nos viésemos/viéramos	We didn't see one another for a long time
Os conocisteis en Córdoba	You met in Cordoba
Siempre se ponen pegas	They're always finding fault with one another

If one subject is feminine and the other masculine, masculine pronouns are used: *Pedro y María se quieren mucho el uno al otro* 'Pedro and María love one another a lot'.

26.4 Pronominal verbs with inanimate subjects

This construction corresponds to the English intransitive form – *La ventana se rompió* 'The window broke' – or to the colloquial construction with 'got' – *Se ha quemado el pastel* 'The cake got burnt'. For obvious reasons, inanimate subjects are usually third person:

La gripe se cura sola	Flu gets better of its own accord
El barco se hundió	The boat sank
Se ha roto el cable	The cable broke
Las manzanas se están pudriendo	The apples are rotting/going rotten
Las suelas se gastan de tanto andar	Soles wear out from so much walking

Note
Me/te/le/nos/os/les are used after *se* to indicate ownership or to disclaim responsibility for an action: *Se me ha roto la jarra* 'My jug has got broken' (it may or may not be the subject's fault), *Se le ha perdido la sortija* 'Her ring has got lost' (ditto).

26.5 Pronominalization and intransitivity

A large number of transitive verbs have pronominal intransitive counterparts. The pronominal form detransitivizes the transitive verb, or more accurately, blocks off the possibility of understanding a verb as transitive. Compare:

abrir	to open (transitive)	*abrirse*	to open (intransitive)
acabar	to finish (transitive)	*acabarse*	to end (intransitive)
acostar	to put someone to bed	*acostarse*	to go to bed
casar	to marry (transitive)	*casarse*	to get married
cerrar	to close (transitive)	*cerrarse*	to close (intransitive)
despertar	to wake someone up	*despertarse*	to wake up
dormir	to put somebody to sleep (also 'to sleep')	*dormirse*	to go to sleep
enamorar	to make someone fall in love	*enamorarse de*	to fall in love with
meter	to put in	*meterse*	to get in, to interfere
perder	to lose	*perderse*	to get lost
preocupar	to worry somebody	*preocuparse*	to worry
presentar	to introduce people	*presentarse*	to appear unexpectedly
tirar	to throw, to pull	*tirarse*	to jump
vaciar	to empty (transitive)	*vaciarse*	to empty (intransitive)

Sometimes the pronominal form of the verb is radically different in meaning:

| *cambiar* | to change | *cambiarse de* | to change clothes/house |
| *correr* | to run | *correrse* | to be ashamed/to 'come' (taboo, vulgar; Spain) |

desenvolver	to unwrap	*desenvolverse*	to get ahead, to be good at something
despedir	to see someone off, to fire/sack	*despedirse de*	to take one's leave, say goodbye
empeñar	to pawn, pledge	*empeñarse en*	to insist on doing something
gastar	to spend	*gastarse*	to wear out
llevar	to take, to wear	*llevarse*	to take with one, to steal
mudar	to change bedclothes	*mudarse*	to move house, to change one's clothes
negar	to deny	*negarse a*	to refuse to do something
oponer	to contrast two views	*oponerse*	to oppose

Sometimes pronominalization can also change the meaning of intransitive verbs, e.g. *parecer* 'to seem', *parecerse* 'to look like'; *suceder* 'to happen', *sucederse* 'to follow one another'. Further examples appear in the next section.

Many pronominal intransitive verbs have no transitive counterparts (at least in normal language), cf. *acatarrarse/constiparse* 'to catch a cold', *arrepentirse* 'to repent', *abstenerse* 'to abstain', *apropiarse de* 'to take possession of', *atenerse a* 'to limit oneself to', *atragantarse* 'to choke', *atreverse* 'to dare', *comportarse* 'to behave', *dignarse* 'to deign to', *equivocarse* 'to make a mistake', *inmiscuirse* 'to interfere', *quejarse* 'to complain', *suicidarse* 'to commit suicide', which appear only in the pronominal form.

26.6 Pronominalization: miscellaneous verbs

26.6.1 Pronominalization and changes of meaning: general

Pronominalized forms of verbs may also express subtle and usually unpredictable modifications of the sense of the non-pronominal verb. Compare *Bajó del árbol* and *Se bajó del árbol* 'He came down from the tree' (the difference between the two is barely translatable) or *Leyó el libro* and *Se leyó el libro* 'He read the book', where the pronominal form stresses the action of reading the *whole* book.

Several points must be made about this construction:

(a) It is confined to a finite number of common transitive and intransitive verbs. The fact that *comer* 'to eat' has a pronominal form *comerse* 'to eat up'/'to eat every morsel of' does not mean that a verb like *consumir* 'to consume' also has a similar form. For this reason these pronominal verbs must be learnt separately.

(b) Some of the pronominalized forms are more characteristic of spoken language and may be replaced by the simple form in formal styles.

(c) The pronominal form often expresses an optional extra nuance. One tends to say *Se fumó veinte cigarrillos en una hora* 'He smoked twenty cigarettes in an hour', but this does not rule out the slightly less expressive and less usual *Fumó veinte cigarrillos en una hora*. On the other hand, there are many cases in which the pronominal forms cannot replace the simple forms. One cannot say *Se fuman mucho for *Fuman mucho* 'They smoke a lot' (because *fumarse*, in this construction, always requires a specific direct object).

(d) It is not guaranteed that all of the examples given below are used in Latin America. There are also some pronominal verbs that are current in the Americas but are avoided in Spain (see 26.7 for examples).

(e) The nuance added by pronominalization is sometimes very subtle. Ability to distinguish pairs like *bajar/bajarse* 'to get out'/'to descend', *salir/salirse* 'to leave'/'to walk out', *llegar/llegarse* 'to arrive'/'to approach', *morir/morirse* 'to die' is the mark of the true master of idiomatic Spanish.

(f) The existence of a pronominal form does not eliminate the possibility that the verb can be pronominalized for one of the reasons discussed earlier in this chapter. Out of context a form like *Se encontraban* may mean 'They found by chance', 'They found themselves', 'They found one another' or 'They were found'. Context will clarify the issue.

26.6.2 Pronominal verbs of motion

Many common verbs of motion acquire an extra nuance in the pronominal form. The pronominal form may:

(a) draw attention to the point of departure as opposed to the destination, cf. *ir* 'to go somewhere', *irse* 'to go *away from* somewhere';

(b) suggest that an action is untimely, accidental or unplanned, e.g. *caer* 'to fall', *caerse* 'to fall over/down'; *salir* 'to leave'/'to come out', *salirse* 'to leave unexpectedly', 'to leak' (of liquids, gases). Sometimes both nuances are combined.

However, in some cases the effect of pronominalization is not easily classifiable. Examples (verbs presented in alphabetical order):

Bajar/bajarse 'to go down', **subir/subirse** 'to go up'

The difference between the two verbs is sometimes difficult to grasp. As far as 'getting on/into' and 'getting off/out of' some kind of vehicle is concerned, the forms are usually interchangeable, although informal language prefers the pronominal form, especially if unplanned exit/entry is involved:

Iba a bajar(me) en la Plaza de la Revolución, pero me voy a bajar aquí	I was getting out at Revolution Square, but I'm going to get out here
—Bájate de ahí, papacito —le decía. —Es peligrosísimo. No te vayas a caer y te lastimes (A. Mastretta, Mexico, dialogue)	'Come down from there, papa', she was telling him. 'It's dangerous. Don't fall and hurt yourself'

In both the previous examples the non-pronominal form could have also been used but it is less often heard. Ordinary going up and down (e.g. stairs, lifts) requires the non-pronominal form unless reference is made to a whole set of stairs. (See 26.6.3 for a more detailed discussion of the latter construction):

Espérame abajo/arriba que bajo/subo enseguida	Wait for me downstairs/upstairs, I'll be down/up in a minute
Subía siempre las escaleras lentamente	He always used to go upstairs slowly
(Se) subió las escaleras de un tirón (the whole flight of stairs)	She rushed upstairs without stopping

Other meanings require the pronominal form: *El gato se subió al árbol* 'The cat **ran up** the tree', *Se subía por las paredes* 'She was **climbing** up the wall' (with rage, not literally).

Notes
(i) *Bajar(se)/subir(se)* can also be used colloquially as transitive verbs meaning 'to take up', and 'to take down': *Bája(te) estos tiestos al jardín* 'Take these flower pots down to the garden'.

(ii) The non-pronominal form is used for the meanings 'to increase', 'to diminish': *Los precios suben/bajan* 'Prices go up/down'.

Caer/caerse 'to fall'/'drop'

Caer is used to stress point of departure or arrival: *El meteoro cayó del cielo* 'The meteor fell from the sky', *El tigre cayó sobre su presa* 'The tiger fell on its prey', *El avión cayó aquí* 'The plane fell here'. It is also used when the point of departure is taken for granted: *Caía una lluvia fuerte* 'Heavy rain was falling'.

Caerse suggests accidental falling ('falling over', 'falling down'):

Se cayó de la mesa	It fell off the table (accidentally)
Me caí por unas escaleras	I fell down a flight of stairs
¡Que no se te caiga el paquete!	Don't drop the parcel!
No tiene donde caerse muerto (figurative)	He hasn't got a cent (lit. 'He has nowhere to drop dead on')
Se le cayó el alma a los pies (figurative)	He suddenly became intensely depressed (lit. 'His soul dropped to his feet')

Entrar/entrarse 'to enter'

Entrar 'to enter' is by far the more common form. The status of *entrarse* is problematic: many Peninsular speakers reject it altogether, although it is heard in popular speech and is quite common in Latin America to emphasize point of departure:

Salió al balcón pero volvió a entrar(se) porque hacía frío (most Peninsular speakers reject *entrarse*)	She went out on to the balcony but came in again because it was cold

Escapar/escaparse 'to escape'

The pronominal form is the more usual. The non-pronominal form is used only in figurative meanings: *escapar con vida* 'to escape alive', *escapar del peligro* 'to escape danger', *escapar a la justicia* 'to escape justice'. Manuel Seco also mentions *escapar a la calle* 'to take to the street'. But *Los prisioneros se escaparon* 'The prisoners escaped'.

Ir/irse 'to go'/'go away'

The difference between the two generally coincides with the difference between 'to go' and 'to go away', French *aller/s'en aller*, Italian *andare/andarsene*:

Vamos a casa de Pepe (destination stressed)	We're going to Pepe's house
Me voy a casa de Pepe (departure stressed)	I'm off to Pepe's house
Vete (point of departure stressed)	Go away

Llegar/llegarse 'to arrive'/'approach'

Llegar means 'to arrive' and is by far the more common form. *Llegarse* means 'to approach', 'to pop over to':

Llegamos a Madrid	We arrived in Madrid
Llégate/Acércate a la tienda de enfrente	Go over to the shop/(US) 'store' opposite

Marchar/marcharse 'to march'/'leave'

Marchar means 'to march' and *marcharse* means 'to leave a place':

¡Mira cómo marchan los soldados!	Look at the soldiers marching!
Me marcho/Me voy	I'm leaving

Pasar/pasarse 'to pass'

As a verb of motion, both forms mean 'to pass'/'to pass by'/'to pass over'. (For *pasar* as a transitive verb meaning 'to pass time', see 26.7.)

Pasar suggests normal motion. It is also used when playing cards, *Paso* 'I pass':

cuando pasó la frontera	when he crossed the frontier
La carretera pasa por el pueblo	The road goes through the village

Pasarse suggests unwanted passage:

Se pasó de la raya	He went beyond the mark/overdid it
No te pases	Don't go too far/Don't overdo it

Salir/salirse 'to leave'

Salir means 'to go out'/'to leave' without further implications. *Salirse* implies untimely or unexpected departure or, applied to inanimates, accidental motion:

Salimos del cine cuando terminó la película (intentional)	We left the cinema when the film ended
Nos salimos del cine porque la película era muy violenta (unexpected)	We left the cinema (before the end) because the film was very violent
El agua sale por aquí (intended)	The water comes out here (where it should)
El grifo se sale (accidental)	The tap's leaking
El tren se salió de la vía (accidental)	The train ran off the tracks

Saltar/saltarse 'to jump'

Saltar is the normal word for 'to jump'. It can also mean 'jump over', but *saltarse* is replacing it in informal language in this last meaning and it can also be used metaphorically:

Saltaban de alegría	They were jumping for joy
Se saltaban los semáforos	They were jumping the traffic lights
Se saltó/Saltó la hoguera	He jumped over the bonfire

Subir/subirse (see *bajar/bajarse*)

Venir/venirse[2] 'to come'

Venirse suggests 'to come away from somewhere'. Applied to inanimates it implies accidental or unexpected coming. *Venir* simply means 'to come to a place':

---

[2] *Venirse* also has the obvious sexual meaning in vulgar usage in Latin America.

Ha venido de París a pasar unos días (destination stressed)	She's come from Paris to spend a few days
Se ha venido de París porque no puede ver a los franceses (point of departure stressed)	He's come here from Paris because he can't stand the French
Dijiste sus nombres cuando te viniste (J. Cortázar, Argentine, dialogue; probably emphasizes permanent departure from somewhere else)	You mentioned their names when you came here
¿Por qué no vienes conmigo? (destination stressed)	Why don't you come with me?
¿Por qué no te vienes conmigo? (point of departure stressed)	Why don't you (leave him/her/this place and) come with me?[3]
Mira la tormenta que se nos viene (accidental)	Look at the storm that's coming down on us

Volver/volverse 'to return'

Volver means 'to return'. It is also used for intangible things, e.g. happiness, summer, fine weather. *Volver a* + infinitive is the most usual way of saying 'to do something again'. It is discussed at 32.6a.

Nunca volveré a aquella casa	I'll never return to that house
Has vuelto muy moreno	You've come back very sun-tanned
Fue a París, se entrevistó con el presidente, y volvió a Londres	He went to Paris, talked to the President and returned to London

Volverse may mean 'to turn round', 'to turn back halfway', 'to return before time' (unplanned return):

Se volvió hacia ella	He turned to (face) her
Me volví antes de llegar	I turned back before arriving

Note
In Latin America, *regresar/regresarse* is used in the same way: *Helen se había regresado a Puebla* (A. Mastretta, Mexico, dialogue, Spain *se había vuelto* or *había regresado*).
  Some countries, e.g. Colombia, also use *devolverse* for 'to return': *. . . pero se había devuelto del Camino Real* (G. García Márquez, Colombia) ' . . . but he'd turned back on the Highway'. *Devolver* (transitive) means 'to give back' or 'to vomit' in standard Spanish.

26.6.3 Pronominal verbs of consumption, perception, knowledge
A curious optional function of the pronominal form of these transitive verbs is to emphasize the totality of an act of consuming, perceiving or knowing. Thus one says *Como pizza* (but not necessarily whole pizzas), but, optionally (though usually), *Me comí una pizza* 'I ate a (whole) pizza'.
  The verb must have a direct object that must refer to a specific item or quantity:

Bebe mucho vino	He drinks a lot of wine
Se bebió un litro de vino	He drank a litre of wine
Nos comimos un par de bolsas King size de patatas fritas (C. Rico-Godoy, Spain)	We finished off a couple of King-size bags of crisps/(US) 'chips'

---

[3] One could also say *¿Por qué no te vienes conmigo a pasar unos días?* 'Why don't you come and spend a few days with me?', with the implication 'rather than stay there'. Also *¿Te vienes al cine con nosotros?* 'Are you coming to the cinema with us?'.

Tardó mucho en comerse el helado	It took her a long time to eat the ice cream
¡No comas de pie!	Don't eat standing up!
No deberías fumar	You shouldn't smoke
Se fuma tres paquetes al día	He smokes three packets a day
Ando mucho	I walk a lot
(Me) anduve cincuenta kilómetros	I walked 50 kilometres
Aprendo francés	I'm learning French
Me aprendí todo el capítulo en una hora	I learnt the whole chapter in an hour
Sabe mucho	She knows a lot
¿Te sabes los verbos irregulares?	Do you know the irregular verbs?
Conozco Valencia	I know Valencia
Me conozco Valencia de cabo a rabo	I know Valencia inside out
Toma somníferos para dormir	He takes sleeping pills to sleep
Tómate un somnífero	Take a sleeping pill
Pero aquella noche se sintió tan humillado que se tomó el brandy de un golpe (G. García Márquez, Colombia[4])	But that night he felt so humiliated that he drank his brandy down in one go
Trago mal	I can't swallow properly
Se lo ha tragado	He's swallowed it
Vi a tu cuñada	I saw your sister-in-law
Se vio todo el museo en diez minutos	He saw the whole museum in ten minutes
Lee muchas novelas	She reads a lot of novels
Vas a tener que releerte las obras completas [de Shakespeare] para que nos entendamos (C. Fuentes, Mexico, dialogue)	You're going to have to re-read the complete works of Shakespeare so that we can understand one another

Notes
(i) *Conocerse* applied to people acquires a nuance: compare *Conozco a Miguel* and *Me conozco a Miguel* 'I know Miguel'/'I know Miguel (and his little tricks)'.
(ii) *Desayunarse* is old fashioned in Spain but is often used in Latin America: *Me he desayunado un café/con un café* 'I had a coffee for breakfast', cf. Spain *Desayuno fruta y cereales* 'I have fruit and cereals for breakfast'.

26.6.4 Miscellaneous pronominal verbs with special meanings
Pronominalization adds nuances to a number of other verbs, of which the following are frequently encountered:

Aparecer/aparecerse 'to appear'

Aparecer means 'to appear' without further nuances. *Aparecerse* is used of apparitions:

La revista aparece todos los días	The journal appears every day
Se le apareció la Virgen	The Virgin appeared before him

Callar/callarse 'to be quiet'

Callar/callarse are in theory interchangeable except when the subject is inanimate, in which case the pronominal form cannot be used. In practice *callarse* is used more often with animate subjects.

---

[4] In Latin America *tomar* 'to take' is often assumed to mean 'to drink alcohol': *Si ha tomado, no maneje* (Mexican street sign) 'If you've been drinking, don't drive' (*manejar* = *conducir* in Spain).

El niño se calló en cuanto le dieron el biberón	The little boy stopped crying as soon as he was given a bottle
La música calló de repente	The music suddenly stopped

Crecer/crecerse 'to grow'

Crecer means to grow in size. *Crecerse* means to grow in worth or value:

La hierba crece mucho con tanta lluvia	The grass grows quickly with so much rain
Hay personas que se crecen con el peligro	There are people who grow stronger/more confident when they are in danger

In parts of Latin America *crecerse* means 'to be brought up': *Yo me crecí* (Spain *me crié*) *en Bolivia*, 'I was raised in Bolivia'.

Creer/creerse 'to believe'

The pronominal form usually implies unfounded belief:

Creo en ella	I believe in her
Ése se cree que habla francés	He thinks he speaks French
Se cree todo lo que le dicen	He believes everything they tell him
Yo (me) creía que él había llegado	I thought he had arrived

Note
Idiom: *Se lo tiene creído* 'He has a high opinion of himself', (British) 'He fancies himself'.

Dar/darse 'to give'

Dar 'to give'/'to show'; *darse* 'to abandon oneself to something'/'to take up'/'to happen':

Dámelo	Give it to me
¿Qué película dan?	Which film are they showing?
Desde entonces se dio a la bebida	From then on he took up drinking
Este caso se da con mucha frecuencia	This happens very often

Dejar/dejarse 'to leave'

Dejar translates 'to let' and 'to leave' (in the sense of 'abandon'). *Dejarse* emphasizes accidental leaving behind:

Deja tu maleta aquí	Leave your suitcase here
Cuando dejó el ejército . . .	When he left the army . . .
Me he dejado el dinero en casa	I've left my money at home

Note
This use of *dejarse* is apparently confined to Spain. Latin-Americans informants said *Dejé la plata . . .* 'I left my money . . .',[5] which in Spain would imply deliberate leaving.

Encontrar/encontrarse 'to find'

The pronominal form means 'to find something by chance':

---

[5] In Spain *la plata* = 'silver' and *el dinero* = 'money'.

Encontré el libro que buscaba	I found the book I was searching for
Me encontré una moneda de oro	I found a gold coin
Todo el dinero es igual. Yo lo agarro de donde me lo encuentro (A. Mastretta, Mexico, dialogue)	All money's the same. I grab it where I find it

Esperar 'to wait'/'hope'

Esperar translates 'to wait for'. Both *esperar* and *esperarse* are used for 'to expect' and 'to wait':

¿(A) qué estás esperando?	What are you waiting for?
Te estamos esperando	We're waiting for you
Eso no (me) lo esperaba yo	I wasn't expecting this
Hay que esperar(se) a que te atiendan	One has to wait to be served

Espera and *espérate* 'wait' seem to be interchangeable in the imperative.

Estar/estarse 'to be'

Estar means 'to be', and its use is discussed in Chapter 29.

The pronominal form *estarse* is used:

(a) to form the imperative of *estar*:

¡Estate quieto!	Sit still!
¡Estese tranquilo!	Be calm/Don't worry!

This is standard usage in Spain, but it is not universal:

Paso a cambiarme como a las ocho. Por favor, está lista (C. Fuentes, Mexico, dialogue)	I'll be home around eight to get changed. Please be ready

(b) to express obligatory or deliberate being in a place. The translation is usually 'to stay':

Se tuvo que estar en casa porque vinieron sus tíos	He had to stay at home because his aunt and uncle came
Me estuve estudiando toda la noche (from María Moliner)	I stayed up all night studying
. . . y aquí que se esté para lo que se ofrezca (A. Mastretta, Mexico, dialogue)	and let him remain here in case anything turns up

Quedarse would have been possible in all but the last example.

Ganar/ganarse 'to win/earn'

Ganar is used in the phrase *ganar mucho/poco dinero* 'to earn a lot/very little money', *¿Cuánto ganas?* 'How much do you earn?' It also means 'to win'. *Ganarse* can sometimes add more emphasis to the amount earned. It is also used for metaphorical meanings or when the way of earning one's living is mentioned.

Imaginar/imaginarse 'to imagine'

Imaginar is a transitive verb meaning 'to conceive of'/'to invent a new idea'. *Imaginarse* means 'to imagine' in the sense of 'suppose' or 'picture':

Imaginó un nuevo modo de hacerlo	He conceived of/invented a new way of doing it
Te puedes imaginar lo que yo estaba pensando	You can imagine what I was thinking
Me los imagino divirtiéndose	I imagine them amusing themselves

Llevar/llevarse 'to carry'

Llevar means 'to wear', 'to take' or 'to carry'. *Llevarse* means 'to take away':

Voy a llevar el traje al tinte	I'm going to take my suit to the cleaner's
No se te olvide llevarte los libros	Don't forget to take the books with you
Llevaba un abrigo negro	She was wearing a black coat

Mejorar/mejorarse 'to improve'

Mejorar as a transitive verb means 'to make better'. As an intransitive verb it means 'to improve'. *Mejorarse* can only mean 'to get better' from an illness and it is not used everywhere in Spain:

La situación ha mejorado	The situation has improved
(Se) ha mejorado mucho/Está mucho mejor	He's a lot better

Morir/morirse 'to die'

Both translate 'to die', but the pronominal form denotes natural death, especially a gradual death: *Su madre se está muriendo* 'His mother is dying'. *Morir* is used for accidental or deliberate death: *(Se) murió de un ataque al corazón* 'He died from a heart attack', *Murió en un accidente de avión* 'He died in a plane accident'. In formal written Spanish *morir* is more usual for all kinds of death:

Ha muerto el primer ministro	The Primer Minister has died
La propia Tránsito Arias se murió convencida de que . . . (G. García Máquez, Colombia)	Tránsito Arias herself died convinced that . . .

Ocurrir/ocurrirse 'to happen'/'occur'

Ocurrir means 'to happen'. *Occurírsele a alguien algo* means 'to occur to one', 'to have a sudden idea':

Esto lleva ocurriendo desde hace algún tiempo	This has been happening for some time
Se me ha ocurrido una idea genial	I've had a brilliant idea

Olvidar/olvidarse(de)/olvidársele algo a uno 'to forget'

Olvidar usually implies intentional forgetting:

No puedo olvidarla	I can't forget her

Olvidarse de implies accidental forgetting:

Se han olvidado de que en la soledad la tentación es más grande (C. Fuentes, Mexico)	They've forgotten that temptation is greater in solitude
¿Te has olvidado de mí?	Have you forgotten me?/Have you left me out?

Olvidársele algo a uno, also implies accidental forgetting and it can be used before nouns or infinitives. The verb agrees in number with the thing forgotten:

Aquel día se me habían olvidado las llaves (lit. 'The keys had forgotten themselves on me')	That day I had forgotten my keys
Se me habían olvidado otras cosas (J. Ibargüengoitia, Mexico, dialogue)	I'd forgotten other things

Parecer/parecerse 'to seem'

Parecer means 'to seem'; *parecerse a* means 'to look like':

Parece cansada	She seems/looks tired
Se parecen a su madre	They look like their mother

Pasar/pasarse 'to spend time'

For the use of these two as verbs of motion, see 26.6.2.

Pasar means 'to spend time somewhere' or 'to pass' applied to time:

Pasó la noche en casa de su hermano	He spent the night in his brother's house
Pasaron tres horas	Three hours passed

Pasarse means 'to spend time doing something':

Se pasa horas mirando por la ventana	He spends hours gazing out of the window
Podíamos pasarnos la vida sin verlos (A. Mastretta, Mexico, dialogue)	We could spend our lives without seeing them

Quedar quedarse 'to stay'/'remain'

Quedar means 'to remain', *quedar en* 'to agree to do something':

Queda por ver si lo hará	It remains to be seen whether he/she'll do it
No queda sal	There's no salt left
La casa te ha quedado bien	You've done the house up very well

Quedarse means 'to stay':

Me quedaré unos días contigo	I'll stay a few days with you

For other meanings of *quedarse* see 27.3.6 and 28.2.6a.

Reír/reírse 'to laugh'

Both mean 'to laugh'. *Reírse* is the more common form; *reír* is rather literary. However *reírse* implies spontaneous laughter (the more usual kind), so it cannot be used when the cause of merriment comes from outside as in *El gas me hizo reír* 'The gas made me laugh', *Ya los haré reír* 'I'll make them laugh'. 'To laugh at' is *reírse de*:

Se rió de su propia risa (G. García Márquez, Colombia)	She laughed at her own laughter
Todos se reían de él	They all made fun of him

Temer/temerse 'to fear'

Temer usually means 'to be afraid' in the literal sense of 'to fear', especially with a direct object; *temer/temerse* are interchangeable only in the sense of 'to suspect'/'to be worried that':

Teme a su padre	He's afraid of his father
(Me) temo que va a llegar tarde	I'm afraid she's going to be late

See 16.9 for further discussion of *temer/temerse*.

Traer/traerse 'to bring'

Both translate 'to bring', but *traerse* is used to emphasize the agent of the action and to indicate that the things mentioned belong to at least one of the speakers. Some native speakers see a difference between

¿Qué quieres que te traiga?	What do you want me to bring you? (meaning something bought)
Si vas al supermercado no se te olvide traer la leche	Don't forget to bring the milk

and

*¿Qué quieres que **me** traiga?*	What do you want me to bring back? (meaning something belonging to one or both of the speakers)
Cuando vayas al garage tráete las herramientas	When you go to the garage bring back the tools with you

Traer can also mean 'to wear':

Traía un traje precioso	She was wearing a lovely dress

Note
Some pronominal verbs are being replaced by the non-pronominal form, as in the case of *entrenar* for *entrenarse* 'to train', which has become common in recent years in spite of the grammarians' complaints, or *encarar* for *encararse con* 'to face up to (a problem)':

Entreno mañana en el gimnasio	I'll train tomorrow at the gymnasium
Arco 93 trata de encarar la crisis del mercado de arte (El País)	Arco 93 is trying to face up to the crisis in the art market

26.7 Latin-American pronominal verbs

Most pronominal forms used in Spain are also current in Latin America, but some pronominal verbs heard in Latin America sound quaint, rustic or simply wrong to Spaniards. The following selection is not exhaustive, and not all the forms are current in educated speech in all countries (the Peninsular equivalent is given in brackets):

crecerse	to be brought up (*criarse*)
devolverse	to return (*volver, regresar*)
enfermarse	to get ill/(US) 'sick' (*enfermar*)
heredarse	to inherit (*heredar*)

(*heredar* in México means 'to leave to someone in a will'):

Estaba seguro de su alcurnia y pudo heredársela entera a su hija (A. Mastretta, México)	He was sure of his pedigree and managed to leave it in his will to his daughter

prestarse	to borrow[6] (*pedir prestado*)
recordarse	remember (*recordar, acordarse*; see footnote to 18.2.3)
regresarse	to return (*volver, regresar*)
robarse	to steal (*robar*)
soñarse	to dream (*soñar*)
verse	to look: *Te ves muy guapa* (A. Mastretta, Mexico, dialogue; Spain *Qué guapa estás . . .* 'You look very pretty')
vomitarse	to vomit (*vomitar, devolver*)

26.8 Interpretation of pronominal verbs with inanimate subjects

A third-person pronominal verb may also be interpreted as a passive: *Se construyó en España* means the same as *Fue construido en España* 'It was built in Spain' (see 28.4 for more details).

An occasional difficulty with sentences containing pronominal verbs, for example *Se abrió la puerta*, is therefore that of deciding whether they are to be interpreted as intransitive, i.e. 'the door opened', or passive 'the door **was** opened'. This problem only arises with certain verbs which have well-established pronominal intransitive forms and have inanimate subjects, e.g. *abrir/abrirse* 'to open', *cerrar/cerrarse* 'to close', *encontrar/encontrarse* 'to find'/'to be located', *esconder/esconderse* 'to hide' and others which will be found listed in good dictionaries. Most transitive verbs, e.g. *construir* 'to build', *derribar* 'to fell', *operar* 'to operate' do not have intransitive counterparts, so confusion is hardly possible.

The general rule for clarifying which sense is intended is as follows:

If a pronominal verb has an established intransitive meaning, e.g. *abrirse* 'to open', *encenderse* 'to light up'/'to switch on', it will usually precede the subject if the passive meaning is intended, although this position does not preclude a non-passive interpretation. Thus *La puerta se abrió* usually means 'The door opened', but *Se abrió la puerta* may mean either 'The door opened' or 'The door was opened'. Similarly:

Las luces se encienden a las nueve	The lights come on at nine
Se encienden las luces a las nueve	The lights are lit/come on at nine
Tres ventanas se rompieron durante la tormenta	Three windows broke in the storm
Se rompieron tres ventanas durante la manifestación	Three windows were broken in the demonstration

In the second of each of the foregoing examples the passive is the more likely meaning. If the verb has no intransitive possibility, then only a passive meaning is possible:

Se derribaron tres árboles/Tres árboles se derribaron	Three trees were felled

---

[6] In Argentina the verb used in popular speech is *emprestar*. This verb is heard in Spain but is considered substandard.

Los motivos se ignoran/Se ignoran los motivos

The motives are unknown

The foregoing points hardly constitute a hard and fast rule, and it must be remembered that complex word order rules, discussed in Chapter 37, govern the choice between sentences like *Los motivos se ignoran* and *Se ignoran los motivos* 'The motives are unknown'.

26.9 Obligatory use of *uno* as impersonal pronoun with pronominal verbs

Uno/una must be used to give an impersonal meaning to a pronominal verb since two *ses* cannot occur with the same verb:

Se muere de frío en esta casa
He/she/it's dying from cold in this house
*Se muere **uno** de frío en esta casa*
One dies from cold in this house
Cuando está así, se irrita fácilmente por cualquier cosa
When he's like that, he gets easily irritated over anything
*Cuando se está así, se irrita **uno** fácilmente por cualquier cosa*
When one is like that, one gets easily irritated over anything

For more details about the pronoun *uno* see 28.7.1.

27
Verbs of becoming

27.1 General

Spanish has no single word for the English 'to become'. The change from a state or a mood to another can often be expressed by a pronominal verb (for pronominal verbs see Chapter 26). There are also some special verbs, e.g. *ponerse, volverse, hacerse, llegar a ser, convertirse, quedarse*, which can in many cases translate 'to become'.

27.2 Pronominal verbs of change

An important type of pronominal verb denotes a change of mood or state with the meaning of 'to become'/'to get':

aburrir	to bore	*aburrirse*	to get bored
alegrar	to cheer someone up	*alegrarse*	to cheer up/ to be happy about something
asustar	to frighten	*asustarse*	to get frightened
cansar	to tire	*cansarse*	to get tired
divertir	to amuse	*divertirse*	to be amused
endurecer	to make hard	*endurecerse*	to grow hard/to harden
enredar	to entangle	*enredarse*	to get entangled
entristecer	to sadden	*entristecerse*	to grow sad
extrañar	to find something odd/to miss	*extrañarse*	to be puzzled
fastidiar	to annoy	*fastidiarse*	to get annoyed
irritar	to irritate	*irritarse*	to get irritated
marear	to make giddy, to annoy	*marearse*	to feel sick
molestar	to bother	*molestarse*	to be bothered
vaciar etc.	to empty	*vaciarse*	to become empty

Note

Some common exceptional cases of non-pronominal verbs denoting 'to become', 'to get' are: *agonizar* 'to be dying', *adelgazar* (*quedarse delgado*) 'to lose weight', *amanecer* 'to dawn', *anochecer: anochece* 'night is falling', *aumentar* 'to increase', *clarear* 'to grow bright', *crecer* (for *crecerse* see 26.6.4) 'to grow', *disminuir* 'to diminish', *empeorar* (Lat. Am. *empeorarse*) 'to get worse', *enfermar* (Lat. Am. *enfermarse*) 'to get ill', *enflaquecer* 'to lose weight', *engordar* (*ponerse gordo*) 'to get fat', *enloquecer* (*volverse loco*) 'to go mad', *enmudecer* 'to be silent'/'to lose one's voice', *enrojecer* 'to go red', *ensordecer* 'to go deaf', *envejecer* (also *envejecerse*) 'to grow old'/'to age' (but compare: *rejuvenecerse* 'to grow young again'), *mejorar* (*mejorarse* = 'to recover' from an illness) 'to improve', *nacer* 'to be born', *oscurecer* 'to get dark' (but *el cielo se oscurece* 'the sky grows dark'), *palidecer* 'to grow pale', *resucitar* 'to come back to life'.

Amanecer and *anochecer* can also be used with animate subjects and objects: *Amanecí detestando mi color de pelo, mis ojeras, mi estatura* (A. Mastretta, Mexico) 'I woke up (lit. 'I dawned') hating the colour of my hair, the bags under my eyes, my height'. They can also be used impersonally with object pronouns: *Me anocheció en medio de la carretera* 'Night found me on the road'.

27.3 Special verbs meaning 'becoming'

Apart from the use of the pronominal forms discussed in the previous section, the following verbs (most, but not all themselves pronominal) are also used with various shades of meaning.

27.3.1 *Ponerse*

Ponerse is used to indicate change of mood, physical condition and appearance. The changes are usually short-lived, with the exception of *ponerse viejo* 'to get old'. Thus there is a contrast between *Se ha puesto muy pesado* 'He's become boring' (temporarily) and *Se ha vuelto muy pesado* 'He's become a bore'. There is some overlap with *quedarse* meaning 'to lose', 'to be left without' (e.g. *quedarse delgado* 'to become thin', 'to lose weight', see 27.3.6). Often there are equivalent pronominal verbs, i.e. *alegrarse* for *ponerse alegre*, *entristecerse* for *ponerse triste*, or non-pronominal ones, i.e. *engordar* for *ponerse gordo*, *enfermar* for *ponerse enfermo*.

Ponerse can be used of animate and inanimate nouns and of situations:

¡Qué pesado/tonto te estás poniendo!	You're becoming such a bore/a fool!
Se puso/Se quedó ronco de tanto hablar	He got hoarse from talking so much
Con tanto como comes te vas a poner gordo (for *delgado* 'thin' see *quedarse*)	You are going to get fat from eating so much
Al verla se puso pálida/palideció	When he saw her he went pale
En poco tiempo se ha puesto muy viejo/se ha aviejado mucho	He's got very old in a short time
¡Qué sucio se ha puesto este mantel!	This table cloth has got very dirty!
La situación se ha puesto insoportable	The situation has got unbearable
El día se ha puesto gris	It's turned grey/(US) 'gray' (i.e. the weather)
El tiempo se está poniendo frío	The weather is getting cold

Ponerse is often used with children to indicate that they are looking bigger or handsomer than ever: *¡Pero qué guapo/grande se ha puesto este niño!* 'Hasn't this child got handsome/big!'.

27.3.2 *Volverse*

Usually translates 'to become'/'to go' and implies involuntary mental or psychological change when applied to animate subjects. It can also be used of abstract inanimate nouns and circumstances. The change is felt to be more permanent than with *ponerse*:

Se volvió loco de tanto pensar	He went mad from thinking too much
Con la edad se ha vuelto muy de derechas	He's become very right-wing with age
últimamente todo se vuelven complicaciones, dificultades y disgustos (see 2.3.3 for agreement of *vuelven*)	Recently everything has become complications, difficulties and upsets
¿Dónde se volvió asesino ese chico? (M. Puig, Argentina, dialogue)	Where did that boy learn to be a murderer?

See 26.6.2 for other meanings of *volver(se)*.

27.3.3 *Hacerse*

This often implies voluntary effort. It is usual for religious, professional or political changes. It can also occasionally be used of circumstances:

Se hizo católico/Se convirtió al catolicismo	He became a Catholic
Para hacerte arquitecto necesitas saber dibujo	You need to know how to draw to become an architect
Se hace tarde	It's getting late

Notes

(i) There is little difference between sentences like *Se está haciendo cada vez más vago* and *Se está volviendo cada vez más vago* 'He's getting lazier and lazier' except that some wilfulness is implied in the first example.

(ii) 'To become' with the meaning of 'to be appointed' is translated into Spanish as *nombrar* or *hacer*: *Le han nombrado/hecho ministro* 'He's become a Minister'.

27.3.4 *Llegar a ser, pasar a ser*

Llegar a ser is used to indicate the result of a slow and sometimes difficult change, i.e. 'to manage to become'/'to become eventually':

Trabajó mucho y con el tiempo llegó a ser alguien/director general/una persona importante	He worked hard and in due time he became someone/general manager/an important person

   Pasar a (ser) means 'to go on to be' and it does not imply difficulty or lapse of time: *De secretario pasó a (ser) jefe* 'From being a secretary he went on to become the boss', *De millonario pasó a mendigo* 'He went from millionaire to beggar'.

27.3.5 *Convertirse en* 'to turn into'

This verb precedes noun phrases but not adjectives. The change can be due to external circumstances:

Nada más tocarle/lo el hada con la varita el príncipe se convirtió en rana	As soon as the fairy touched him with her wand, the prince turned into a frog
Se ha convertido en un drogadicto/un criminal	He's become a drug addict/a criminal
El transporte se ha convertido en un problema para todos	Transport has become a problem for everybody
La silla se convierte fácilmente en una escalera	The chair turns easily into a step ladder

Note

'To convert to' a new belief is *convertirse a*; see also *hacerse*, 27.3.3: *No todos los que se convierten a una religión se vuelven buenos* 'Not everybody who is converted to a religion becomes good'.

27.3.6 *Quedarse*

   This verb may be a verb of becoming especially when it implies loss:
(a) Implying loss, incapacity

Se quedó ciego/mudo/impedido/viudo	He became blind/dumb/disabled/a widow
Se quedó solo en el mundo	He was left alone in the world
Al morir su padre se quedó sin dinero	When her father died she was left without any money
A pesar del frío se quedó en cueros	In spite of the cold he took all his clothes off

¡Qué delgado te has quedado!	Haven't you got thin!
Me he quedado helado esperándote	I've got frozen waiting for you

But note *quedarse embarazada* 'to get pregnant', which does not imply loss.

(b) Other meanings

Se quitó el abrigo y se quedó con una falda	She took her coat off. She was wearing a
gris y una blusa blanca	grey skirt and a white blouse
Se quedó atrás	He was left behind
Me quedo con este sombrero	I'll take this hat
Quédese con la vuelta	Keep the change
Me quedo en este hotel	I'll stay in this hotel
¿Te has quedado contento?	Are you satisfied now?
Me quedé convencido de que era verdad	I was convinced that it was true
El gerente se quedó fastidiado (C. Fuentes, Mexico)	The manager was irritated

See 26.6.4 and 28.2.6 for more remarks about *quedar(se)*.

Notes

(i) *Quedarse helado* can also apply to shock: *Cuando se lo dijeron se quedó helado* 'He had a terrible shock when they told him'.

(ii) In some Spanish regions *quedar* can be used instead of *quedarse* in the first three examples of **(a)** and also in *quedarse embarazada*.

28

Passive and impersonal sentences

28.1 General

This chapter discusses four constructions. Students who know French may find comparison with this language instructive:

(a) Passive with *ser* (28.2): *Fue construido* 'It was built', *Il a été construit;*

(b) Passive *se* (28.4): *Eso no se dice* 'That isn't said', *Cela ne se dit pas* or *On ne dit pas cela;*

(c) The 'mixed' construction with *se* and personal *a* (28.5): *Se recibió a los embajadores* 'The ambassadors were received', *Les ambassadeurs ont été reçus;*

(d) Impersonal *se* (28.6)[1]: *Se entra* 'one enters', *On entre; Se come bien* 'One eats well', *On mange bien.*

These four constructions are used to form impersonal sentences, i.e. those in which the agent of the action is irrelevant, as in *Fue demolido el año pasado* 'It was demolished last year', *Se dice que las zanahorias son buenas para los ojos* 'They say/It's said that carrots are good for the eyes', *Se vive mejor en España que aquí* 'People live/One lives better in Spain than here'.

Passive with *ser* differs from the constructions with *se* in that the agent of the action can be mentioned: *Fue construido **por** los militares* 'It was built by the military'. In this case it is no longer an impersonal construction.

The example under **(d)** shows that Spanish differs from French in allowing the use of *se* with intransitive verbs to form an impersonal sentence, as in *se es/se está . . . (on est . . .), se vive . . . (on vit . . .), se avanza (on avance)*. In such cases *se* can be thought of as equivalent to the French impersonal pronoun *on*, German *man*.

Less clear-cut are those sentences in which *se* seems to be used as an impersonal subject pronoun even with transitive verbs, as in *Se publicaba poco* which may mean either 'It wasn't published much' (passive) or 'People didn't publish much' (impersonal). These are discussed at 28.4. and 28.6.1.

28.2 Passive with *ser*

28.2.1 General

The passive with *ser* is formed from the appropriate tense and person of *ser*

---

[1] Impersonal *se* was not distinguished from passive *se* in the first edition and it is debatable whether they really are distinct constructions. However, it seems to us that it is in fact better, for explanatory purposes, to treat them separately.

'to be' and the past participle, which agrees in number and gender with the subject of *ser*:

Active	Passive
Manuel escribió la respuesta	*La respuesta fue escrita por Manuel*
Manuel wrote the reply	The reply was written by Manuel
Solucionaron los problemas	*Los problemas fueron solucionados*
They solved the problems	The problems were solved

There are several points to be made about this construction:

(a) English is unusual in allowing indirect objects to form a passive construction: 'He was given two pounds', 'They were told a tall story' – *Se le dieron dos libras, Se les contó un cuento chino.* **Él fue enviado una carta* is unintelligble for *Se le envió una carta/Le fue enviada una carta* 'He was sent a letter'.

(b) Whereas passive *se* and impersonal *se* constructions occur in ordinary speech as an impersonal form or as a substitute for the passive, the passive with *ser* is more characteristic of written or non-spontaneous language. In informal speech the passive is usually replaced by impersonal 'they': *Tres manifestantes fueron arrestados* = *Arrestaron a tres manifestantes* 'They arrested three demonstrators', *Fue entrevistado ayer* = *Le entrevistaron ayer* 'They interviewed him yesterday'. In fact some grammarians assert that the passive with *ser* is not found in spontaneous speech, but this is not completely true – assuming that the following extracts really do reflect spontaneous speech:

*Ese jardín es alemán, y la película se ve que **fue hecha** en Alemania* (M. Puig, Argentina, dialogue)	That garden's German, and you can see the film was made in Germany
*. . . y es que traen un telegrama de Berlín que ella **es invitada** a filmar una gran película* (idem.)	and the thing is they bring a telegram from Berlin (saying) she's being invited to make a big movie
*Se trata de los papeles de mi marido . . . Deben **ser ordenado**s antes de que muera* (C. Fuentes, Mexico, dialogue)	It's about my husband's papers. They have to be sorted before I die

However, such examples are noticeably more common in the dialogue of Latin-American novels. The passive with *ser* is rare in spontaneous Peninsular speech.

(c) The passive with *ser* is, however, extremely common in written Spanish on both continents and probably more so in the Americas. Its increasing use is perhaps one of the most obvious developments in written and formal language in the last half century, especially in newspapers, where it may reflect rushed translations of faxes from English-language press agencies. Sentences like *Estos ejemplos **son vistos** como logros enormes* (C. Fuentes, Mexico) 'These examples are seen as enormous successes' would almost certainly have been written . . . *se ven como logros enormes* in the recent past, and still surprise Peninsular speakers. But the advance of this 'Anglicized' passive seems unstoppable, and it may eventually become a pervasive feature of Spanish. Until that day English-speakers should beware of a tendency to over-use it, especially in speech.

(d) If no agent is mentioned, the passive with *ser* is often identical in meaning with passive *se* (explained at 28.4): *Encontraron dos cargas explosivas que fueron* *desactivadas* and *Encontraron dos cargas explosivas que se desactivaron* both mean 'They found two explosive charges which were de-activated', although the first is unambiguous whereas the second might conceivably be read as ' . . . which de-activated themselves'. But often there is a difference of nuance which may become crucial. The passive with *ser* is less impersonal than the *se* construction in the sense that the latter completely eliminates information about the agent from the message, whereas the former does not. Thus it is probably more usual to say *El reo fue sentenciado* 'The prisoner was sentenced' than *Se sentenció al reo* since the agent (the judge) is obviously implicitly present in the message: *se sentenció* . . . almost implies 'someone sentenced the accused'. But *En el siglo II todavía se hablaba latín* 'Latin was still spoken in the second century' is more normal than . . . *el latín era hablado todavía* because the agent, in this case 'people', is too obvious or vague to be worth mentioning.

Por cannot be used with passive *se*: **El latín se hablaba por los romanos* is bad Spanish for *Los romanos hablaban latín*. This constraint reflects the impersonality of *se* and may partly explain the increasing popularity of the passive with *ser*.

(e) The passive with ser is more common with verbs of perfective (completed) aspect (i.e. the preterite, future, perfect, pluperfect tenses) and with the infinitive than with verbs of imperfective aspect (i.e. in imperfect, present and continuous tenses): *Fue entrevistado ayer* is normal for 'He was interviewed yesterday', *Era entrevistado ayer* is unusual or journalese. However, passive sentences in which the verb is timeless or habitual are nowadays increasingly common in writing and non-spontaneous speech, and more so in Latin America than Spain:

Los mismos ascensores son usados para el transporte de enfermos (*Cambio16*, Spain)	The same lifts are used for carrying patients
. . . *mientras Cabinda era defendida heroicamente por los combatientes del MPLA* (Fidel Castro, speech on Angola)	. . . while Cabinda was being heroically defended by fighters of the MPLA
Basta saber que un hombre es buscado para que todos lo vean de manera distinta (C. Fuentes, Mexico, dialogue)	It's enough to know a man's being sought for everyone to look at him in a different way
Algunos de ellos recuerdan que no hace mucho eran corridos por la Policía (*Cambio16*, Spain)	Some of them remember that not so long ago they were being chased by the police
El parlamento gibraltareño tiene 17 miembros, de los que 2 son puestos por el Gobierno inglés (*El País*, Spain)	The Gibraltarian parliament has 17 members, two of whom are appointed by the British Government

Most Peninsular informants found these sentences unnatural and preferred a *se* construction or, where the agent is mentioned, an active sentence, e.g. *los mismos ascensores se usan* . . ., *basta saber que a un hombre se le busca* . . ., *recuerdan que no hace mucho la Policía les corría* . . ., *dos de los cuales los pone* . . ., although they were prepared to tolerate the second example *era defendida heroicamente*. The fact that the example mentioning Gibraltar sounds natural if one substitutes *impuestos* 'imposed' is an indication of the difficulties surrounding the whole question of when the passive is possible.

Examples of the passive with *ser* with verbs of perfective aspect (active alternatives are shown):

Fue alcanzado por una bala (or *le alcanzó una bala*)	He was hit by a bullet
Las muestras les serán devueltas(or *se le devolverán las muestras*)	The samples will be returned to you
El hijo de Pilar Ternera fue llevado a casa de sus abuelos (G. García Márquez, Colombia; or *llevaron al hijo*. *Llevar* cannot be passivized with *ser* if it means 'wear')	Pilar Ternera's son was taken (i.e. carried) to his grandparent's house

Note
The difference between the true passive *La ciudad **fue** destruida* 'The city was destroyed' (action) and *La ciudad **estaba** destruida* 'The city was in a state of destruction' is discussed at 28.2.5.

28.2.2 Constraints on the passive with *ser*
The passive with *ser* is not used:
(a) With an indirect object: *Le dieron dos regalos* 'He was given two presents', **never** **Fue dado dos regalos*.
(b) Usually when the subject of *ser* is partitive, i.e. has no article: *Se venden naranjas aquí* 'Oranges for sale' but not **Naranjas son vendidas aquí* 'Oranges are sold here'.

However, sentences like *En el mercado antiguo eran vendidas manzanas y otras frutas* 'In the old market apples and other fruits were sold' may be found, especially in literary Latin-American Spanish. *Se vendían manzanas y otras frutas* is more normal.
(c) With a present or imperfect tense to denote a single action. The Academy (*Esbozo*, 3.12.9c) says that *La puerta es/era abierta por el portero* 'The door is/was opened by the doorman' can only refer to a habitual or timeless event.

This rule does not apply to all styles. Journalists sometimes use the imperfect for single events – *Momentos después **era** asesinado por un terrorista* 'Seconds later he was murdered by a terrorist' (see 28.2.1e and 14.5.6 for discussion) – and the historic present may function like a preterite: *El 22 de junio de 1941 la Unión Soviética **es** invadida por ejércitos alemanes* 'On June 22 1941, the Soviet Union was (lit. 'is') invaded by German armies'.
(d) With a large number of verbs, and for no obvious reason.

Many verbs do not allow the passive with *ser*. These are more numerous than in English, which has similar constraints, e.g. 'The window was broken by Jill' but not *'The stairs were descended by Jill'. Only familiarity with the language will eliminate such malformations as **Fueron esperados por sus padres* 'They were expected by their parents', **Fue permitido hacerlo* (but *Le fue permitido hacerlo* is correct) 'He was allowed to do it', both of them sentences which should be expressed in active form or, in the second example, by impersonal *se*: *Se le permitió hacerlo*.

The constraints on the Spanish passive often appear to be quite arbitrary: *Fue abandonada por su marido* 'She was abandoned by her husband' is correct, but 'She was beaten by her husband' can only be *Su marido le pegaba* (see 12.6.4 for this use of *le*) although *Fue golpeada por su marido* is possible. Likewise, one can say *La casa fue destruida por una bomba* 'The house was destroyed by a bomb', but not *La ventana fue rota por una piedra* 'The window was broken by a stone', which, curiously, is difficult to translate into Spanish: *Esta ventana la han roto de una pedrada*.

Sometimes the passive is wrong with a personal pronoun, but acceptable with other types of agent: *Él era admirado por todos* 'He was admired by everybody', but not ?*Él era admirado por mí* 'He was admired by me' (*Yo lo/le admiraba*).

In the following sentences passive with *ser* is not used (at least in normal styles), for no very obvious reason:

Me arañó un gato	A cat scratched me
Me dio un periódico	He/she/you gave me a newspaper
La peina un peluquero muy conocido	A very famous hairdresser does her hair
A la niña la lavó la madre	The mother washed the little girl
Me irritó el humo	The smoke irritated me
La despertaron temprano	She was woken up early

It would be beyond the scope of this grammar to establish a comprehensive list of verbs that do not admit passivization with *ser*. As a general rule it seems that verbs commonly used in everyday conversation are less likely to appear in the passive form than verbs usually associated with formal language.

28.2.3 Avoiding the passive

English speakers may be tempted to over-use the passive. It can be avoided by the following stratagems:

(a) Make the sentence active – the simplest solution, although stylistically tedious if overdone:

Los críticos le alabaron (= *Fue alabado por los críticos*)	The critics praised him
Suspendieron la sesión (= *La sesión fue suspendida*)	The session was suspended

(b) Use passive *se* (discussed at 28.4).

The following typical piece of Anglicized journalese *Su bufete privado es utilizado con frecuencia para asuntos propios del Gobierno* (*El País*, Spain) 'His private office is often used for Government business' could be better expressed by . . . *su bufete privado **se** utiliza con frecuencia para asuntos propios del Gobierno*.

This device can only be used if the agent of the action is not included in the sentence: *El fenómeno fue observado por un astrónomo japonés* 'The phenomenon was observed by a Japanese astronomer' cannot be recast using *se*.

(c) Since one function of the passive is to focus attention on the object of a verb – compare 'He preferred Jane' and 'Jane was preferred by him' – the effect of an English passive can often be produced by putting the object in focus position – i.e. before the verb. A redundant object pronoun then usually becomes necessary: *Las puertas las cierran los porteros a las diez* 'The doors are shut by the doormen at ten o'clock'.

This construction is discussed further at 11.16.1.

28.2.4 Passive meaning of the infinitive

The distinction between an active and passive verb is sometimes blurred in infinitive constructions. The following forms sound unfamiliar to English-speakers:

un partido heterogéneo y sin estructurar	A heterogeneous and unstructured political party (lit. 'without structuring')
El edificio está a medio construir	The building is half built
Eso ya era de prever	That could be foreseen

28.2.5 Comparison between *fue convencido* and *estaba convencido*

This subject is also raised at 19.1.

The passive with *ser* denotes an action; the participle with *estar* usually describes a state arising from an action – i.e. it is not dynamic. Compare *La puerta fue abierta* 'The door was open**ed**' and *La puerta estaba abierta* 'The door was **open**'. The possibility of making this contrast is normally confined to verbs with a dynamic meaning, i.e. ones that describe actions, not states. The participle of a non-dynamic verb will probably only denote a state and therefore may only admit *estar*, cf. *Estoy acostumbrado* 'I'm used to', *Estás deprimido* 'You're depressed' (*ser* impossible).

In some cases a special participle is used with *estar*: cf. *Estaba **despierto** porque había sido **despertado** por una voz de hombre* 'He was awake because he had been woken by a man's voice'. See 19.2.1 for further discussion.

Examples (the translations are designed to emphasize the difference):

La ciudad fue destruida	The city was destroyed
La ciudad estaba destruida	The city was in ruins
Fui detenido	I was arrested
Yo estaba detenido	I was under arrest
La reunión fue aplazada por decisión del presidente (action)	The meeting was postponed by a decision of the president
Cuando llegué me encontré con que la reunión estaba aplazada (state)	When I arrived I found the meeting was postponed
Vino aquí . . . convencido de que iba a ser el mandamás. Y se encontró con que todo estaba hecho y muy bien hecho (M. Vargas Llosa, Peru, dialogue)	He came here convinced he was going to run the show. And he found everything was done and done properly
. . . los hechos históricos no están gobernados por leyes (O. Paz, Mexico[2])	. . . historical facts are not governed by laws
La operación estaba ordenada por el Rey (witness, Spain, expressed as a state)	The operation was ordered by the King

28.2.6 Alternatives to *ser* to express passive meaning

Several other verbs may replace *ser* in the passive. They usually add nuances which can barely be translated into normal English.

(a) *Quedar/quedarse*

Quedar/quedarse emphasizes a condition that has arisen from some event, rather like the popular English 'ended up':

Quedó herido	He was injured (as a result)
La Escuela de Periodismo informa que el plazo de inscripción quedará abierto en el mes de octubre (advertisement in *El País*, Spain)	The School of Journalism announces that the registration period will commence (lit. 'be opened') in October

---

[2] Since literary Latin-American Spanish regularly uses the passive with *ser* to express habitual actions, this sentence might well have been expressed as *son gobernados*. *Están gobernados* would be much more normal in European Spanish.

Queda dicho al principio de este párrafo que . . . (Royal Academy, *Esbozo*)	It was stated at the beginning of this paragraph that . . .

The use of *quedar/quedarse* with adjectives and participles is further discussed at 26.6.4 and 27.3.6.

(b) *Resultar*

Resultar also emphasizes, and more explicitly than *quedar*, the idea of a condition arising from an event:

Una veintena de personas resultaron heridas	About twenty people were injured (as a result)

(c) *Verse*

Verse is often used with a participle in literary styles:

Mis ingresos eran reducidos, ya que se veían afectados por la piratería informática (letter in *El País*)	My earnings were low as they were affected by software piracy
. . . más de 450.000 personas se han visto afectadas por la contaminación del agua potable (*El País*)	More than 450,000 people have been affected by pollution of the drinking water

(d) *Venir*

Use of *venir* suggests that a condition has arisen from some previous event. Again, it is confined to literary styles and it is particularly commonly used when quoting some previous statement:

. . . como viene dicho en el párrafo anterior . . .	. . . as was stated in the previous paragraph . . .
En el caso de producirse omisiones y errores en la guía, la Compañía Telefónica vendrá obligada a corregirlos en la siguiente edición (Spanish phone book)	If omissions or error should appear in the directory, the Telephone Company shall be obliged to correct them in the next edition

28.3 General remarks about passive and impersonal *se*

There are three types of passive and impersonal construction that use *se* (and several more personal ones as well, discussed in Chapter 26):

(a) *Se pasivo* or 'passive *se*' (28.4). This is found only with transitive verbs in the third person. The verb and the logical object agree, e.g. *Se discutieron varios problemas* 'Several problems were discussed', *Se vacunaron las vacas* 'The cows were vaccinated', *Se vendieron tres toneladas* 'Three tons were sold', *La amigdalitis se cura con antibióticos* 'Tonsillitis is cured with antibiotics'.

(b) The 'mixed' construction *se* + transitive verb + *a* (28.5). This construction can be considered impersonal or passive according to one's point of view: it is in fact impersonal in form and passive in meaning. The verb is always in singular: *Se detuvo a tres narcotraficantes* 'Three drug-dealers were arrested', *Se llama a los perros con un silbido* 'Dogs are called by whistling'.

(c) *Se impersonal* or 'Impersonal *se*' (28.6). This is most easily identified when it occurs with intransitive verbs, as in *Se vive mejor aquí* 'One lives better here'.

In the view of many grammarians, 'subjectless' sentences involving transitive verbs, e.g. *Se come bien aquí* 'One eats well here', *Se publica menos ahora* 'There is less publishing now'/'Less is published now', are also examples of impersonal *se*. The difference between this impersonal use of *se* with transitive verbs and Passive *se* is discussed at 28.6.

28.4 Passive *se*

28.4.1 Basic rules

Passive *se* can only be used with transitive verbs and in the third person, normally only with inanimate nouns and pronouns so as to avoid clashes of meaning with other uses of *se* (see 28.5 for discussion). It is usually equivalent in meaning to passive with *ser*, but it is common in ordinary speech, more 'impersonal' than the passive with *ser* (see 28.2.1 for discussion) and it cannot be used when the agent of the action is mentioned; see note (ii):

Los cangrejos se cuecen en vino blanco	(The) crabs are cooked in white wine
. . . nunca se oyeron y leyeron en el Perú tantas definiciones de la libertad de información (M. Vargas Llosa, Peru)	. . . never were there heard and read in Peru so many definitions of freedom of information
No se han traído a la Tierra suelo y muestras de minerales del planeta Marte	Soil and mineral samples from the planet Mars have not been brought to Earth
Se reparan relojes	Watches mended
Se veían los árboles desde la ventana	The trees were visible from the window
Esto podría deberse a…	This could be due to . . . (lit. 'owe itself to')
Se acababan de promulgar varias leyes	Several laws had just been published
que se sepa	as far as is known
Eso no se hace	That sort of thing is not done
Se dice que va a dimitir[3]	They say/It's said that she's going to resign

Notes
(i) For a comparison of this construction with the true passive – *El problema se solucionó/El problema fue solucionado* – see 28.2.1(d).
(ii) Passive *se* may not be followed by *por* and the real agent of the verb: **La decisión se tomó por el presidente* is bad Spanish for *La decisión fue tomada por el presidente* 'The decision was taken by the President'. This rule is constantly broken in speech and occasionally in writing, but this is considered incorrect: **El terrorismo no debe atacarse aisladamente por las naciones que lo padecen* (the Spanish Prime Minister Felipe González, in *El País*) 'Terrorism must not be combated individually by those nations that suffer from it'. This blunder could have been avoided either by use of passive with *ser*, or by a simple active construction.
(iii) Passive *se* may be used to form a passive imperative, useful for footnotes, written instructions and so on: *No se crea que . . .* 'Let it not be believed that . . .', *Téngase presente que . .* 'Let it be borne in mind that . . .', *Desarróllese en castellano el siguiente tema* 'Develop the following topic in Spanish'; see 17.8.
(iv) It must be remembered that as far as form is concerned, there is no difference between this passive *se* construction and reflexive or reciprocal *se*. In other words, only common sense tells us that the first example is not to be translated 'The crabs cook themselves in white wine' or 'The crabs cook one another . . .'

---

[3] The older form *dícese que* is probably the origin of a colloquial form, very widespread in Latin America in various guises, e.g. *isque*, *dizque*. It often implies scepticism, cf. Spain *según dicen*: *A los seis años de andar dizque gobernando se puso enfermo* (A. Mastretta, Mexico) 'After six year of governing (so they say) he fell ill'.

28.4.2 Agreement of the verb with passive *se*

In theory, any verb used with *se* must agree with the logical object. This is true for all constructions with *se*, whether reflexive, reciprocal or passive. In other words, there is no formal distinction between passive *se* and other kinds of *se*:

Las tuercas se quitan con llave, no con martillo	Bolts are removed with a spanner, not with a hammer
Se mezclan en el turmix los tomates sin pepitas y sin piel	The tomatoes, with skins and pips removed, are mixed in the liquidizer
Se enviaron los hombres y las armas necesarios para concluirla (i.e. *la lucha*: Fidel Castro, speech, Cuba)	The men and weapons necessary to finish it [the fight] were sent

When passive *se* is used, the rules of agreement are always respected when a plural noun precedes the verb: *Los libros se vendían a mil pesetas* 'The books were sold at 1000 ptas'.

When the verb precedes a plural noun, popular language sometimes breaks the rules of agreement: *?Se compra objetos usados* 'Used articles bought'. This should not be imitated and it may sound quite illiterate in spite of the fact that some grammarians[4] accept this construction on the grounds that it is really an impersonal construction. Foreigners should make the verb agree.

The following forms may be unacceptable to many speakers:

*?Y nunca más se **ha** tenido noticias de su paradero* (*ABC*; for *se han tenido . . .*)	No further news has been received of his whereabouts
?Se necesita agallas para hacer eso (Spanish informant overheard: *se necesitan agallas*)	You need courage to do that
*?Se les **dio** varios premios* (for *se les dieron . . .*)	Several prizes were given to them
?Se vende máquinas de coser usadas (street sign in Mexico D.F.)	Used sewing machines for sale

Note
When passive *se* is followed by *cuánto, qué, cuál*, the verb is singular: *Se calculó cuántos kilos había* 'It was calculated how many kilos there were', *Se averiguó qué existencias quedaban* 'A check was made of what stocks remained'.

28.4.3 Agreement of passive *se* with modal verbs

Agreement with plural nouns is required with modal verbs when they precede the infinitive of a transitive verb. In this case *se* can be suffixed to the infinitive or precede the modal verb:

Se tienen que resolver varios problemas/ Tienen que resolverse varios problemas	Several problems must be solved
. . . cosas que no se quieren hacer/cosas que no quieren hacerse	. . . things one doesn't want to do
En Londres por la calle se pueden observar los tipos de personas más extrañas (*Cosmopolitan*; = *pueden observarse*)	In London one can observe the strangest sorts of people in the streets
Se deben limpiar bien las verduras antes de cocerlas (= *deben limpiarse*)	Greens should be washed well before boiling

---

[4] J.A. de Molina (1974), 23–25.

See 11.14.4 for further discussion of the position of pronouns with the infinitive.

Notes

(i) Singular agreement with modal auxiliary verbs is considererd incorrect but it is commonly seen and heard, cf. ?*Se puede imprimir textos con más rapidez con un procesador de textos* (*Ordenador Personal*, Spain, for *se pueden*) 'Texts can be printed more rapidly with a word-processor'.

(ii) There is, however, a contrary tendency to give non-modal verbs preceding a transitive verb plural agreement with passive *se*, although many grammarians deplore this tendency, cf *Se necesitan resolver muchos problemas para conseguirlo* 'Many problems have to be resolved in order to achieve it', *Cuando se tratan de estudiar los hallazgos de tiempos pasados . . .* (*ABC*, Spain) 'When an attempt is made to study the discoveries of the past . . .'.

28.5 *Se* + transitive verb + personal *a*

This special type of impersonal or passive construction has evolved to remove some of the ambiguities surrounding the overworked pronoun *se*.

Passive *se* as described at 28.4 is usually unambiguous if there is no noun in the sentence that could be understood to be the subject, as is usually the case when the subject is inanimate: *Los platos se lavan* 'The plates are washed' is unlikely to mean 'The plates wash themselves', which can always be said *Los platos se lavan a sí mismos/Los platos se lavan solos*.

However the burden of ambiguity may be intolerable with animate or personified nouns, particularly those referring to humans, since *Se mataron dos ingleses* may mean 'Two Englishmen killed themselves' as well as 'killed one another'. The language has developed a device for removing the ambiguity by marking the object by the preposition *a*. The verb is always singular:

Se mató a dos ingleses	Two Englishmen were killed
Se criticó duramente al cineasta	The film-maker was severely criticized
Se incitaba a las muchachas a trabajar más que los muchachos	The girls were encouraged to work harder than the boys
Se persiguió y encarceló a millares de creyentes (*El País*)	Thousands of believers were persecuted and jailed

Notes

(i) When a pronoun replaces the logical object, many speakers, including Latin-Americans, prefer *le/les* to *lo/la/los/las* in sentences like . . . *hasta que se les pueda evacuar* (Miguel González, *El País*) '. . . until they can be evacuated', *Al escritor se le halaga o se le desprecia* (A. Monterroso, *El País*) 'The writer is praised or despised'. See 12.6.3 for discussion.

(ii) Sometimes one finds sentences like *Se ha comparado a los ordenadores con el cerebro humano* 'Computers have been compared with the human brain', *Se debe amar más a la verdad que a la fama* 'One must love truth more than fame', in spite of the fact that the logical object is inanimate. This is done to avoid all possibility of a reflexive meaning; see 22.10c for further comments.

(iii) If the logical object is not specific, i.e. does not require personal *a*, ordinary passive *se* is used (see 22.2 for discussion of the omission of personal *a* when the direct object is not specific or particularized): *Se ven muchos turistas en el verano* 'You see a lot of tourists in summer/A lot of tourists are seen in summer'.

(iv) A sentence like *Se mató a dos ingleses* exemplifies the peculiarities of *se*. *Se* is traditionally thought of as an 'object' pronoun, but in the above example *a dos ingleses* is clearly the 'direct object' of *matar*, in which case *se* is functioning as a subject.

372 Passive and impersonal sentences

This theoretical problem has troubled many linguists, but it need not concern the practical user of the language.

(v) The verb must be singular in this construction. **Se les notaban cansados* is not heard in Spain although it is sometimes heard in (but not written) Latin America.

28.6 Impersonal *se*

28.6.1 General

There are two types of construction that can be analysed under the heading of 'Impersonal *se*'.

The first occurs with intransitive verbs: *Se está mejor aquí* 'One's better off here' (French *On est mieux ici*), *Se entra por ahí* 'One goes in that way/through there' (French *On entre par là*). Such sentences can obviously not be translated as passive sentences, and they have no equivalent in French, which restricts the use of *se* to transitive verbs, e.g. *Cela ne se dit pas = No se dice eso* 'That isn't said'.[5]

The second occurs with transitive verbs which are always singular and third-person. The distinction between this use of *se* and Passive *se* is as follows:

If we are talking about a specific book, the sentence *En España se lee poco* must be translated 'It isn't read much in Spain' or 'People don't read **it** much in Spain'; this is a clear instance of Passive *se* as discussed at 28.4. But if the sentence has no identifiable subject, it must be translated 'In Spain people don't read much'; the construction has no equivalent in French, which must use *on*: . . . *on ne lit pas beaucoup*. This construction with *se* can be analysed either as a kind of impersonal passive, or as a use of *se* as an impersonal subject pronoun similar to the French *on*; linguists disagree in their explanations.

That native speakers sometimes confuse the two constructions is shown by the popular tendency to treat passive *se* as impersonal in badly-formed sentences like *?Se vende manzanas* for *Se venden manzanas* 'Apples sold/for sale'; see 28.4.2 for discussion. Occasionally the difference between the two constructions may be visible in the word order, as in *La verdad no puede siempre decirse* 'The truth can't always be told' (passive) and *No se puede decir siempre la verdad* 'One can't always tell the truth' (impersonal).

English-speaking learners should sense the difference instinctively since translation by the English passive is impossible in the case of impersonal sentences like *En Francia se bebe mucho* 'People drink a lot in France', and a passive translation comes easily when there is a discoverable subject, as when someone says the same sentence during a conversation about red wine, in which case it will probably mean 'A lot (of it) is drunk in France' or 'People drink it a lot in France'.

28.6.2 Impersonal *se*: examples

The following examples show the use of impersonal *se* with intransitive verbs:

---

[5] Italian impersonal *si* is constructed differently from its Spanish equivalent, compare *si è contenti* and *se está contento* 'one's content'/'people are content' (adjective always singular in Spanish).

En su círculo, o se es rico o no se entra	In her circle one's either rich or one doesn't get in
A las tres de la madrugada pareció llegarse a un acuerdo tácito para descansar (J. Cortázar, Argentina)	At three in the morning it appeared that a tacit agreement was reached to get some rest
Por la mañana se avanzó muy poco	Very little progress was made in the morning
Se cruza si el semáforo está en verde y se espera si está en rojo (*El País*, Spain)	One crosses if the lights are green and one waits if they are red
. . . si sobra ya se pensará en subvenciones (G. Torrente Ballester, Spain)	. . .if there's any (money) left, subsidies could be considered then
No escuchaba cuando se le hablaba (*El País*, Spain)	He didn't listen when somebody talked to him
No se puede entrar	Entrance forbidden
No se debe ir con prisas	One musn't rush

The following examples illustrate the use of impersonal *se* with transitive verbs. In every case it is assumed that there is no recoverable subject in the sentence – otherwise the construction must be analysed as passive *se* as discussed at 28.4:

No puedo vivir en un mundo donde no se ame (i.e. *donde no haya amor*)	I can't live in a world where people don't love
En este país se critica y se insulta mucho	In this country people criticize and insult a lot
. . .un régimen en el que se mata y se tortura	. . .a régime in which killing and torturing take place
En esas reuniones se habla mucho, pero . . .	A lot of talking goes on in those meetings, but . . .

Notes

(i) Impersonal *se* cannot be used with a verb that already has *se* attached to it for some other reason; see 26.9.

(ii) As with most sentences involving *se*, common sense and context often clarify the meaning. Thus *Se iba al teatro* may mean 'He was going off to the theatre' or 'People used to go to the theatre'.

(iii) Impersonal *se* may even appear in combination with passive with *ser*, although this is rare: *No se debe hablar más que con personas a las que se ha sido ya presentado* 'One must only talk to people one has been introduced to' (C. Rico-Godoy, Spain).

(iv) For agreement of *se* with modal verbs preceding the infinitive of a transitive verb see 28.4.3.

28.7 Other impersonal constructions

28.7.1 *Uno/una* as a pronoun

This is similar to the English 'one' in that it is often an oblique or modest way of saying 'I' or 'we'. A woman uses *una* if the pronoun refers to herself, but *uno* if no self-reference is intended. Its object forms are *lo/la/le*. For many Latin-Americans *uno* is the only form used, even by women, but the example from Vargas Llosa suggests that this may not be universal. This construction is often interchangeable with passive or impersonal *se*:

como los pájaros que comen las migas que uno les tira (J. Cortázar, Argentina dialogue, woman speaking, or *que se les tiran*)	like birds eating the crumbs one throws to them

Bueno, si no le dicen a una como hay que hacerlo . . (woman speaking, or *si no se le dice a una*)

Well, if they don't tell one how to do it . . .

Uno no hace mal a la gente que le es indiferente (E. Sábato, Argentina, dialogue, woman speaking; or *no se hace mal a . . .*)

One doesn't do harm to people one is indifferent to

En ese tiempo una no hablaba de eso con las amigas (M. Vargas Llosa, Peru, dialogue, woman speaking) or *no se hablaba de eso*)

In those days one didn't talk about those things with one's women friends

Notes

(i) *Uno* must be used to make an impersonal expression from a verb which already has *se* (since two *se*s cannot occur with the same verb): *En este pueblo se aburre uno mucho* 'In this village one gets bored a lot', *Se empieza fumando unos cigarrillos y poco a poco se convierte uno en un fumador empedernido* 'One starts by smoking a few cigarettes and gradually one becomes a heavy smoker'. See 26.9 for discussion.

(ii) Colloquially *uno/una* may mean 'someone'. See 9.3 note (iv).

28.7.2 Impersonal *tú*

The second-person singular can be used impersonally, much the same as in English. *Usted* is used instead of *tú* in formal contexts but most people use *uno* or *se* when they are on formal terms with the hearer:

Yo nunca voy allí porque te cobran más que en otra parte (*le cobran a uno más*)

I never go there because they charge you more than elsewhere

Es increíble, si lo piensas (*si uno lo piensa*)

It's incredible if you think of it

In theory the second-person singular cannot coexist in the same sentence with impersonal *se*, but it appears in informal speech, just as pronouns are mixed in familiar English: *Es que no se tiene conciencia de que pasa el tiempo cuando eres joven* (Queen Sofía, interview in *El País*, Spain) 'It's that **one** isn't conscious of time passing when **you**'re young'.

28.7.3 Impersonal third-person plural

As in English, the third-person plural is often used impersonally when the speaker does not include him/herself or the hearer in the reference:

Dicen que el ejercicio es bueno para el corazón

They say exercise is good for the heart

Parece que hablan más despacio en Estados Unidos que en Inglaterra

It seems that they speak more slowly in the USA than in England

29

Ser and estar

29.1 General

Ser and *estar* both translate the English 'to be', but the difference between the two Spanish words is fundamental and sometimes elusive.

Basically *ser* denotes nature or identity while *estar* denotes condition, state or place: *Soy español, pero estoy en Londres* 'I'm Spanish, but I'm in London', *Es callado* 'He's the quiet type', *Está callado* 'He's silent'/'He's keeping silent', *Puede que sea así* 'Perhaps he/she/it is like that', *Puede que esté así* 'Perhaps that's the condition/situation he/she/it's in'.

It is misleading to imagine that *estar* always refers to temporary states while *ser* indicates permanence. This is often true but it is contradicted by sentences like *Está muerto* 'He's dead' or by the fact that one can say either *Soy calvo* or *Estoy calvo* 'I'm bald'. Nor is a characteristic expressed by *ser* necessarily permanent. A brunette can change the colour of her hair and then say *Antes era morena pero ahora soy rubia* 'I was a brunette before, but now I've become a blonde', the point being that both colours are nevertheless considered to be essential attributes of the woman, not 'states'.

Ser is used with a few adjectives that indicate states which are often transitory, e.g. *feliz* 'happy', *desgraciado* 'unhappy', *pobre* 'poor', *rico* 'rich', *consciente* 'conscious'; but these are probably best treated as exceptions, cf. *Está deprimido* 'He's depressed', *Está contento* 'He's happy/content', *Está animado* 'He's full of life' (*estar* obligatory).

Some adjectives, e.g. *gordo* 'fat', *divorciado* 'divorced', may be used with either *ser* or *estar* with hardly any significant change of meaning. *Estar* before a noun phrase can usually only denote situation: Compare *¿Es el jefe?* 'Is he the boss?' with *¿Está el jefe?* 'Is the boss in?'.

Learners constantly forget that *ser* must be used for the location of events as opposed to people or things: *¿Dónde es la fiesta?* 'Where's the party?', but *¿Dónde está el libro?* 'Where's the book?'.

Ser is used to form the passive: *fue criticado*; see Chapter 28. *Estar* is used to form the continuous aspect of verbs: *está hablando* 'he's talking'; see Chapter 15.

29.2 Uses of *ser*

29.2.1 In equational sentences of the sort **A** = **B**

Ser is used to link elements in statements of the type 'A = B', where A and B are nouns or pronouns:

París es la capital de Francia	Paris is the French capital
Es médico/abogado/bibliotecario	He's a doctor/lawyer/librarian
Es un estafador	He's a swindler
Miguel es el jefe	Miguel's the boss
Es la una/Son las doce	It's one o'clock/twelve o'clock
Ha sido un año/verano frío	It's been a cold year/summer

Note
Exceptions to this rule in European colloquial speech are *Está un día hermoso* 'It's a beautiful day' and *estar pez*, e.g. *Estoy pez en historia* 'I'm a complete dunce in History'.

29.2.2 *Ser* with adjectives
Ser is used with adjectives or adjectival phrases referring to identity or nature, i.e. physical, moral and mental characteristics:

¿Quién eres?/¿Cómo eres?	Who are you?/What are you like?
Soy, alto, moreno y delgado	I'm tall, dark and slim
Las mariposas son diferentes de las polillas	Butterflies are different from moths
El marxismo es materialista	Marxism is materialist
El cobre es ideal para los cables	Copper is ideal for cables
Esa chaqueta es bien bonita	That jacket is very nice

Notes
(i) 'It is hot'/'it is cold' applied to weather are translated by *hace calor/frío*, but 'It's a beautiful day' *Hace/Está/Es un día estupendo*. For *estar caliente/frío* see 29.3.1.
(ii) For 'cleft' sentences of the type *Ella es la que lo dijo* 'She's the one who said it' see 36.2.2. For *calvo, gordo, delgado*, marital status and behaviour, see 29.4.1b. For time expressions see Chapter 32.

29.2.3 *Ser* with certain adjectives apparently denoting states
Ser is normally used with *pobre/feliz/desgraciado/inocente/culpable/consciente/fiel* 'poor/happy/unhappy/innocent/guilty/aware/faithful' despite the fact that they may be thought of as conditions:

Ella me dijo soy pobre, pero honrada, Tan sólo bailo para ganarme el pan (Argentine tango)	She told me I'm poor but honest, I only dance to earn my living
El acusado dijo que era inocente	The accused said he was innocent
Hay muchos que no se sienten culpables aunque lo sean	There are many people who don't feel guilty even though they are
Soy consciente de mis limitaciones	I'm conscious of my limitations
La gente así no suele ser feliz en la vida, señora (M. Vargas Llosa, Peru)	People like that are not usually happy in life, Señora
Pocas veces fue tan feliz como en las horas que precedieron a la entrevista con Bordenave (E. Sábato, Argentina)	He was seldom so happy as during the hours before his interview with Bordenave
—Soy tan desgraciada —me dijo (G. Cabrera Infante, Cuba)	'I'm so unhappy', she told me

Notes
(i) *Estar rico/pobre/feliz* is sometimes heard in Spain when describing a transitory state, although many Spaniards (but not Latin-Americans) reject *estar* with these adjectives: *Estoy más pobre que una rata* 'I'm as poor as a church mouse' (lit. 'poorer than a rat'), *Ahora estoy feliz y contento* 'Now I'm happy and satisfied' (*contento* also means 'happy'), *Estaban tan felices que me dieron envidia* (A. Mastretta, Mexico) 'They were so happy that they filled me with envy'.

Estar rico generally means 'to be tasty' in Spain, see 29.4.4, but not necessarily in Latin America: *Andrés acompañó al padre José que **estaba** riquísimo y lo oyó jurar* *por la Virgen de Covadonga que no tenía un centavo* (A. Mastretta, Mexico) 'Andrés accompanied Father José, who was extremely rich and he heard him swear by the Virgin of Covadonga that he didn't have a cent'.

(ii) Peninsular usage normally differentiates *ser consciente* 'to be aware' and *estar consciente* 'to be conscious' (i.e. not asleep or knocked out). Latin-American language generally retains the older usage: *Estamos conscientes de que el debate y la discusión en la libertad son demandas de los jóvenes del país* (*Unomásuno*, Mexico) 'We're aware that debate and argument in (an atmosphere of) freedom are demands of the young people of the country'.

29.2.4 Ser de

Ser can be followed by *de* + noun or by *de* + *un* + adjective to denote identity, nature, origin or the material something is made of:

—*¿De dónde eres?* —*De Londres*	'Where do you come from?' 'London'
La situación era de risa	The situation was extremely funny
Es de día/noche	It's day/night
—*¿De qué es la mesa?* —*Es de madera*	'What's the table made of?' 'Wood'
Soy de carne y hueso como tú	I'm made of flesh and blood like you
Esa chica es de miedo	That girl is tremendous
Oye, que es de verdad	Listen, it's true
Es de un pesado	He/she's such a bore

29.2.5 Ser in impersonal statements

Es verdad/mentira/una tontería/una pena/una lata	It's true/a lie/nonsense/a pity/a bore
Es evidente/obvio/terrible	It's evident/obvious/terrible
Es de suponer que me llamará	One assumes she'll ring me
Es de desear que no sea así	It's to be wished that it won't be like that

Note
Está claro 'it's clear/obvious' is the usual European phrase, but *es claro* is common in Latin America.

29.2.6 Ser to denote possession

Todo esto es mío, el día de mañana será tuyo	All this is mine, tomorrow it'll be yours
El piso es de mi yerno	The flat/apartment belongs to my son-in-law

29.2.7 Ser to denote impressions

Me es/resulta simpática	I find her likeable
Esto me es/resulta molesto	This is uncomfortable for me
Todo le era distinto (A. Carpentier, Cuba)	Everything seemed different to her

29.2.8 Ser of events

If 'to be' means 'to be held' or 'to happen' it must be translated by *ser*:

La fiesta es/se celebra en su casa	The party is at his place
Hay un incendio en el edificio pero no sé en qué piso es	There's a fire in the building but I don't know which floor it's on
¿Dónde es la manifestación?	Where is the demonstration?
El entierro sería a las cinco (G. García Márquez, Colombia)	The funeral was to be at five

Use of *estar* may imply a physical object. Compare: *¿Dónde es la conferencia?* 'Where's the lecture (being held)?', *¿Dónde está la conferencia?* 'Where's the lecture?' (i.e. the lecture notes or typescript).

29.3 Uses of *estar*

29.3.1 *Estar* to describe state as opposed to identity or nature
Estar with adjectives that indicate mood, physical condition or non-characteristic features in general:

Está más bien triste	He's rather sad
Estuvo enfermo una temporada	He was ill/(US) 'sick' for a time
Hoy no estoy muy católico	I don't feel very well today
Estoy segura de lo que te digo	I'm certain of what I'm telling you
El agua que se añada tiene que estar caliente	The water to be added has to be hot
El televisor está estropeado	The television doesn't work
Está parado desde febrero	He's been out of work since February

Note
The pervasive use of the passive with *ser* in written Latin-American Spanish, especially to denote habitual or continuous actions, may produce sentences that require *estar* in Spain. This seems to be particularly frequent in Mexico: *Una de las mesas **era** ocupada por el doctor Bernstein* (C. Fuentes, Mexico, Spain *estaba ocupada*) 'One of the tables was occupied by Doctor Bernstein'.

29.3.2 *Estar de*
Estar de + adjective or noun to indicate mood, temporary employment or situation:

Está de buen/mal humor	He's in a good/bad mood
Está de camarero en Inglaterra	He's working as a waiter in England
Está de veraneo	He's taking his summer holidays/vacation
Estamos de charla	We're having a chat

Colloquially: *Estás de un guapo subido* 'You look especially pretty/handsome', *Estaba de un antipático . . .* 'He was in such a bad mood . . .'

29.3.3 *Estar con*
Estar followed by *con* + noun:

Está con gripe	He's got the flu
Estaba con una cara malísima	He looked terrible
Estaba con un traje de chaqueta muy bonito	She was wearing a suit

29.3.4 *Estar* + adverb
Estar followed by an adverb or an adjective used as an adverb:

—¿Cómo estás? —Estoy bien/mal	'How are you?' 'I'm well/not at all well'
El nombre está mal. Se llamaba Luis José (*Cambio16*, Spain)	The name is wrong. His name was Luis José
Estamos fatal	We're feeling rotten

29.3.5 *Estar que*

Está que muerde	He's in an exceedingly bad mood (lit. 'he's ready to bite')
Hoy estás que no hay quien te aguante	You're unbearable today

29.3.6 *Estar* to indicate location
(For *ser* used for the location of events see 29.2.8.)

Segovia está en España	Segovia is in Spain

El cerezo está en el centro	The cherry tree is in the middle
No está (en casa)	He's not at home
Está encima de todo	It's on top of everything

But with nouns that are permanent fixtures or features there is a colloquial tendency to use *ser*: *¿Dónde **es** la casa de tu amigo?* 'Where's your friend's house?', *Aquí **era** la plaza de las Carretas* (J.L. Borges, Argentina, dialogue) 'This is where Carretas Square used to be', *Turku **es** en Finlandia, ¿no?* 'Turku's in Finland, isn't it?'.

Estar would also be correct in these three sentences.

29.3.7 *Estar* meaning 'to suit', or to indicate 'fit'

Este traje te está muy bien	This dress suits you
El abrigo te está corto	The coat is short for you
El puesto de ministro le está grande	The ministerial job is too big for him

For *estar* with *por* and *para* see 34.14.8.

29.4 *Ser* or *estar*?

29.4.1 *Ser* and *estar* more or less interchangeable

(a) With words indicating marital status:

Sale con una chica que es/está divorciada	He's going out with a girl who's divorced
Tiene que mantener a su madre que es/está viuda	He has to keep his widowed mother
Le pregunté si era/estaba casado	I asked him whether he was married

The tendency is to use *ser* for a stranger, although *estar* is not wrong. One would usually ask *¿Es usted casado?* 'Are you married?', but two friends meeting again would say *¿Estás casado?* or *¿Todavía estás soltero?* 'Are you married?' or 'Are you still single?'.

(b) With *calvo*, *gordo* and *delgado*, *estar* is always used when there has been a change of state. Elsewhere the two verbs are practically interchangeable except in generalizations, when *ser* is required:

¡Mujer, pero qué delgada estás!	Good heavens, haven't you **got** thin!
*Siempre **ha sido** calvo/gordo, pero ahora **está** más calvo/gordo que nunca*	He's always been bald/fat but now he's balder/fatter than ever
Ayer conocí a la novia de mi primo. Parece simpática pero está/es muy delgada	Yesterday I met my cousin's girlfriend. She seems nice but she's very thin
*Las mujeres de esa tribu **son** muy gordas* (generalization)	The women of that tribe are very fat

(c) With adjectives describing social manner when 'to be' = 'to behave':

Estuvo/Fue muy cortés conmigo	He/She behaved very courteously towards me
Siempre está/es cariñosa	She's always affectionate
Tienes que estar/ser más amable con él	You must be kinder to him

But *Hoy has **sido** bueno* 'You've behaved well today', because *estar bueno* means 'tasty', 'appetising' and therefore also 'sexually arousing'. Note, however *¡Hoy has estado bueno!* 'You had a good day today!' (ironical, i.e. 'I

don't think . . .'). *Estar* cannot be used for general statements: *Antiguamente los ingleses **eran** muy corteses* 'Formerly the English were very courteous'.
(d) With adjectives applied to events and with *vida* and *situación*:

La conferencia fue/estuvo muy interesante	The lecture was very interesting
La situación es/está caótica	The situation is chaotic
La fiesta fue/estuvo muy animada	The party was very lively
La vida es/está cara hoy día	Life is expensive nowadays

But *La vida es difícil/maravillosa/amarga* 'Life is difficult, marvellous, bitter' can only be general comments on life. *La vida está difícil* means 'Life is difficult **now**'.
(e) With adjectives referring to weather applied to *día* and *tiempo*:

El día es/está bueno	The weather is nice today
Es/está un tiempo soleado, agradable	The weather is sunny and pleasant

29.4.2 *Ser* and *estar* with prices

*¿Cuánto/A cuánto/A cómo **son** las uvas?*	How much are the grapes?
Son a cincuenta pesetas el kilo	Fifty pesetas a kilo
¿Cuánto (es lo que) le debo?	How much do I owe you?
*¿A cuánto/A cómo **están** las uvas?*	How much are the grapes (at this moment)?
*¿A cuánto/A cómo **están** esas acciones?*	What's the price of those shares?

29.4.3 *Estar* implying impression or change of condition

When *estar* denotes impression, sensation or appearance, it often calls for translation by a special verb in English, e.g. 'to look', 'to taste', 'to feel' or 'to get'. Use of *estar* rather than *ser* often shows there has been a change of condition. Compare:

Es muy guapa	She's very good-looking
Está muy guapa	She's looking very attractive
Este niño es muy alto	This child is very tall
Este niño está muy alto	This child has grown very tall
Es muy joven/viejo	He's very young/old
Está muy joven/viejo	He's looking very young/old
¡Qué fuerte eres!	How strong you are!
¡Qué fuerte estás!	How strong you are! (today/these days)
Este sillón es ya viejo	This armchair is old
Este sillón está ya viejo	This armchair is getting old
*El pollo es riquísimo**	(The) chicken is very good
El pollo está riquísimo	The chicken tastes delicious
*El café es horrible**	(The) coffee is horrible
El café está horrible	The coffee tastes horrible
Tráelo como sea	Bring it any way you can
Tráelo como esté	Bring it as it is
Eres muy española	You're very Spanish
Estás muy española	You're looking very Spanish (or behaving like a typical Spanish woman)

The examples marked with an asterisk are ambiguous: *El pollo es riquísimo* is either a general statement about chicken or it could mean 'The chicken (uncooked) is very good quality'. *Estar* could only mean 'to taste'.

29.4.4 *Ser* and *estar* involving change of meaning

There are some words whose meaning is radically affected by choice of *ser* or *estar*. The following list is not exhaustive:

ser aburrido	to be boring	*estar aburrido*	to be bored
ser atento	courteous	*estar atento*	attentive
ser bueno	good	*estar bueno*	tasty
ser cansado	tiresome	*estar cansado*	tired
ser católico	catholic	*no estar católico*	unwell
ser decidido	resolute	*estar decidido*	decided
ser consciente	aware	*estar consciente*	conscious (not asleep or knocked out)
ser despierto	sharp/alert	*estar despierto*	awake
ser un enfermo	be an invalid	*estar enfermo*	be ill
ser interesado	self-seeking	*estar interesado*	interested
ser listo	clever	*estar listo*	to be ready
ser (un) loco	scatterbrained	*estar loco*	mad
ser malo	bad	*estar malo*	ill
ser negro	black	*estar negro*	very irritated
ser orgulloso	proud (pejorative)	*estar orgulloso*	proud of something/ somebody
ser rico	rich	*estar rico*	delicious
ser torpe	slow-witted	*estar torpe*	clumsy, moving with difficulty
ser verde	green/smutty	*estar verde*	unripe
ser violento	violent/ embarrassing	*estar violento*	embarrassed
ser vivo (*ser un vivo*	sharp/alert be unscrupulous)	*estar vivo*	alive

30

Existential sentences

30.1 General

'Existential sentences' are sentences that refer to the existence of things: 'There's bread', 'There is a planet called Pluto', 'God exists'/'There is a God', etc.

In Spanish such sentences usually involve the special verb *haber* (present indicative *hay*), which means 'there is/are'. However, the picture is complicated for foreign students because of the existence of another verb, *estar*, which means 'to be located'/'to be *there*'.

30.2 *Haber (hay)*

30.2.1 Basic uses

Haber has two uses: (**a**) as an auxiliary used to form perfect tenses (discussed at 14.8); (**b**) as a verb meaning 'there is'/'there are', cf. French *il y a*, German *es gibt*.

In the latter sense the verb occurs only in the third-person singular (see note (ii) for a rare exception in popular speech). It is conjugated exactly as the third-person singular of the auxiliary *haber*, except that its present indicative is *hay*, not *ha*. In this chapter, *haber* in the sense of 'there is/are' is referred to as '*hay*' to avoid confusion with the auxiliary.

Hay can occur in any tense with the meaning 'there is/are/were/will be/have been', etc. However, it does not mean '. . . is/are/were *there*' (= *está/están/estaban ahí/allí*). The relationship between *hay* and *estar* is discussed further at 30.3.

Examples of *hay*:

Hay doscientas personas en el aula	There are two hundred people in the lecture hall
Antes había dos puentes	There used to be two bridges
¿Qué hay?	What's happening?/How're things?
¿Qué hubo?/¿Quiubo? (Colombia and surrounding areas only)	How're things?

Notes

(i) *Hay* is not pluralized: *Había tres chicas* 'There were three girls', never **Habían tres chicas*; *Hubo clases de italiano el año pasado* 'There were Italian classes last year', never **Hubieron clases de italiano . . .*

In Spain the plural construction is stigmatized as uneducated, but it is a very common feature of everyday Castilian as spoken in Catalonia. In Latin America it is universally common in everyday, even educated speech, and it quite frequently appears in informal writing (e.g. newspapers), but it is not accepted in careful styles.

(ii) It is used only in the third person: *Hay cinco* 'There are five', but **Somos** *cinco* 'There are five **of us**', *Ustedes* **son** *cinco* 'There are five **of you**', also *Son cinco* 'There are five **of them**'.

A first-person plural construction ?*Habemos cinco* 'There are five of us' (NB. not the usual form *hemos*) occurs in rustic speech in Spain for the more usual *Somos cinco* and is rather more prevalent in popular speech in Latin America, although it is rejected by educated speakers.

(iii) *Hay* is not followed by the definite article, except when it means 'to exist', in which case *existir* is more commonly used: *Ha venido el médico* (not *Hay el médico) 'There's the doctor!' (i.e. he's arrived). But *También hay/existe la posibilidad de . . .* 'The possiblity also exists of . . .'. Constructions like ?*Hay el cartero* 'The postman's there!' are typical Catalanisms.

(iv) For *hay que* 'it is necessary to' see 21.4.2.

30.2.2 Direct object pronouns and *hay*

Hay functions like an impersonal transitive verb. Since transitive verbs in Spanish must normally have a direct object, an object pronoun may be required to indicate the presence of a deleted noun:

*No hubo presiones, ni **las** hay, ni **las** habrá* (Felipe González in *El País*)	There wasn't any pressure, there isn't any and there won't be
. . . el cochero quiso asegurarse de que no había ningún error. No lo había (G. García Márquez, Colombia)	. . .the coach driver sought reassurance that there was no mistake. There wasn't
Los hay con suerte	Some people are lucky/have all the luck

This pronoun is not always used in informal Latin-American speech, but it is normal in Latin-American writing. See 7.4 for resumptive pronoun with *ser*, *estar*, *parecer*.

30.3 *Hay* and *estar* in existential sentences

Estar has many other uses, discussed in detail in Chapter 29.

As far as its relationship with *hay* is concerned, *está* basically means '. . . is **there**' and *hay* means 'there **is/are** . . .'. In other words, *hay* states that something exists, *estar* indicates that it is **located** somewhere.

In certain cases the meanings overlap, as in *No hay nadie* 'There's no one (there)' and *No está nadie* 'No one's there'/'No one's at home'.

30.3.1 Uses of *estar* and *hay* with defined nouns

Nouns accompanied by the definite article, by a possessive adjective or by a demonstrative (*ese, este, aquel*) normally require *estar*. *Hay* used with such noun phrases is restricted in its meaning to 'exists', as is explained at 30.2.1 note (iii):

*Hay **un** gerente en la compañía*	There's a manager in the company (i.e. 'a manager exists')
*Está **el** gerente*	The manager's there/here/in
No hay dinero	There's no money (anywhere)
*No está **el** dinero/**El** dinero no está*	The money isn't here/there
¿Hay tortilla española?	Have you got Spanish omelette/omelet?
*¿Está **la** tortilla española?*	Is the Spanish omelette on the list?/Is the Spanish omelette ready?

*Por un lado hay **las** grandes fiestas, y por*
*el otro, **las** distracciones institucionales*
(Cambio16, Spain; = existen)
—*¿Qué hay en este pueblo?* —*Hay **la***
iglesia . . .[1] (= *existe*)
—*¿Había alguien?*
Estaban ellos y sus padres (does not mean
existen)
Al ascensor sólo tienen acceso los seres
humanos, es decir no se pueden subir
*ni perros ni cosas . . . para eso **está** el*
montecargas (E. Arenas, Spain, dialogue)

On the one hand there are the
major fiestas, and on the other hand
institutionalized amusements
'What is there in this village?' 'There's
the church . . .'
'Was there anyone there?'
'They and their parents were there'

Only people have access to the
lifts/elevators, in other words dogs and
things can't be taken up in them . . . the
service lift's there for that

Note

In relative clauses, *hay* and *estar* seem to be interchangeable in some sentences, but
only *estar* is possible before definite nouns referring to animates (i.e. ones preceded
by *el* or *ese/este/aquel*): *Reconocí al señor que **estaba** en la puerta* (not *hay*) 'I recognised
the gentleman who was at the door', *Reconocí a un señor que **había/estaba** en la puerta*
'I recognised a gentleman who was at the door', *El sitio estratégico es la mesa que **hay***
al lado de la cristalera que da a la calle (E. Arenas, Spain, dialogue; *está* possible) 'The
strategic spot is the table that's next to the window looking out on the street'.

30.3.2 *Estar* for mobile things

Estar implies that a thing is mobile, *hay* merely that it exists. For this reason,
words like 'problem', 'question', 'atmosphere', 'accident' can only appear
with *hay* since they do not move around:

*Ha **habido** un accidente*
*Ha **habido** aquí tres presidentes*

*Han **estado** aquí tres presidentes*

There's been an accident
There have been three presidents
here/We've had three presidents (in this
country)
Three presidents have been here/have
visited here

30.3.3 *Hay* used before partitive nouns and numbers

Before partitive nouns (quantities, parts of a whole), only *hay* can be used:

Hay leche
Había gente

There's (some) milk
There were (some) people

Since *hay* can be used only in the third person (see 30.2.1, note ii), *ser* must
be used for other persons. This construction occurs with numbers:

Había cuarenta personas en la fiesta
Éramos cuarenta en la fiesta
Vais (Lat. Am. *van*) *a **ser** cuarenta en la*
fiesta

There were forty people at the party
There were forty of us at the party
There will be forty of you at the party

---

[1] *Haber* is possible here with the definite article because it answers the question 'What
things exist?' not 'Where is . . .?'. However, use of *haber* in this sentence may not be
acceptable to Latin Americans.

31

Adverbs

31.1 General

Spanish adverbials (i.e. adverbs and adverb phrases) can be divided into two large classes: invariable words and phrases, and adverbs formed from adjectives by adding the suffix *-mente*. Examples of the first type are *mal* 'badly', *ayer* 'yesterday', *adrede* (familiar *aposta*) 'on purpose', *en serio* 'seriously' (i.e. not jokingly). Examples of the latter are *tranquilamente* 'tranquilly', *violentamente* 'violently', *naturalmente* 'naturally'. Although the suffix *-mente* is very productive there are severe and apparently arbitrary constraints on its use.

A few adjectives also function as adverbs: *Hablaban fuerte* 'They were talking loudly'; see 31.3.3.

More common in Spanish than in English, especially in writing, is the use of an adjective where English uses an adverb: *El rey los recibió agradecido* 'The King received them gratefully', *Vivían felices* 'They lived happily'; see 31.3.4.

31.2 Adverbs in *-mente*

31.2.1 Formation

If the adjective has a separate feminine form, *-mente* is added to it. Otherwise it is added to the invariable singular form:

Masc. singular	Fem. singular	Adverbial form	
absoluto	*absoluta*	*absolutamente*	absolutely
cansado	*cansada*	*cansadamente*	in a tired way
evidente	*evidente*	*evidentemente*	evidently
leal	*leal*	*lealmente*	loyally
tenaz	*tenaz*	*tenazmente*	tenaciously

31.2.2 Accent rules for adverbs in *-mente*

The original stress should be preserved in pronunciation. As a result, adjectives that are irregularly stressed form adverbs in *-mente* that have two stress accents, one on the vowel that carries the written accent, another on the penultimate syllable: *crítico/críticamente* 'critical'/ 'critically', *electrónico/electrónicamente* 'electronic'/'electronically', *hábil/hábilmente* 'skilful'/'skilfully', *sarcástico/sarcásticamente* 'sarcastically'. Pronunciation of such words with a single penultimate stress should be avoided.

31.2.3 Consecutive adverbs in *-mente*

If more than one adverb in *-mente* is joined by a conjunction (e.g. *y, ni, pero,* etc.), *-mente* is dropped from all but the last:

Se lo dije sincera y llanamente	I told him sincerely and plainly
Esto presenta un problema político mayor, y ni intelectual, ni política, ni económicamente se puede mantener tal postura (El País)	This presents a major political problem, and neither intellectually, nor politically nor economically can such a position be sustained
Tuvo la desvergüenza de decirme que era poco serio, que ni social ni literariamente era interesante (S. Pitol, Mexico, dialogue)	She had the nerve to tell me that it wasn't serious, that it was neither socially nor artistically (lit. 'literarily') interesting

This is an important rule of written Spanish, though rarely applied in spontaneous speech. But it is not normal when no conjunction is present: *y así, separados por el muro de vidrio, habíamos vivido ansiosamente, melancólicamente* (E. Sábato, Argentina), 'and thus, separated by the wall of glass, we had lived anxiously, melancholically'.

31.2.4 Limits on the use of the suffix *-mente*

-mente cannot be added to all adjectives, although there is no accounting for experiments, as when Julio Cortázar coins *pelirrojamente* 'red-hairedly' in his novel *Rayuela*.

In general, though with important exceptions (cf. *difícil/difícilmente* 'difficult', *lleno* 'full', but 'fully' = *plenamente*), the set of Spanish adjectives that take *-mente* corresponds to the set of English adjectives that allow the adverbial suffix *-ly*. These are chiefly adverbs of manner.

The following do not take *-mente* (at least in normal styles):

(a) Adjectives denoting physical appearance: *rojo* 'red', *negro* 'black', *calvo* 'bald', *gordo* 'fat', *cojo* 'lame', *viejo* 'old'/'aged', etc.

(b) Adjectives denoting origin, nationality, religion: *cordobés* 'Cordoban', *argentino* 'Argentine', *protestante* 'Protestant', *musulmán* 'Muslim', etc. (Two exceptions are *católicamente* and *cristianamente*: *Tienes que educar a tus hijos católicamente* 'You must bring up your children in the Catholic manner'.)

(c) Ordinal numbers, e.g. *segundo* 'second', *quinto* 'fifth', *vigésimo* 'twentieth'. (Exceptions: *primeramente* 'chiefly'/'firstly' and *últimamente* 'lately'/'lastly'. *En segundo lugar* = 'secondly'.)

(d) Some adjectives, for no obvious reason, e.g. *vacío* 'empty', *lleno* 'full' (*plenamente* = 'fully'), *importante* 'important', and most adjectives in *-ón*, cf. *mandón* 'bossy', *peleón* 'aggressive'/'prone to start fights'.

(e) Many verbal participles which cannot, by meaning, function as adverbs.

However, some Spanish participles take *-mente* whereas their English counterparts do not. The following are some of the many participle forms that may take *-mente*. They usually refer to behaviour, or to frequency, speed or some other idea that could have an adverbial use:

abatido	*abatidamente*	downcast
abierto	*abiertamente*	open(ly)
acentuado	*acentuadamente*	marked(ly)
atrevido	*atrevidamente*	daring(ly)
debido	*debidamente*	due/duly
decidido	*decididamente*	decided(ly)

deliberado	*deliberadamente*	deliberate(ly)
equivocado	*equivocadamente*	mistaken(ly)
exagerado	*exageradamente*	exaggerated(ly)
irritado	*irritadamente*	irritated(ly)
perdido ('lost')	*perdidamente*	hopeless(ly) (e.g. in love)
reiterado	*reiteradamente*	repeated(ly)
resuelto	*resueltamente*	resolute(ly)

31.2.5 Popular forms

Popular forms like *buenamente* and *malamente* are occasionally heard in familiar speech with specialized meanings:

Lo terminamos, pero malamente	We finished it, but it was rushed
Hazlo buenamente cuando puedas	Do it in your own time when you can

The forms *?mayormente* 'a great deal'/'especially' (very common in Latin America), *otramente* 'otherwise' (= *de otra manera*) and *?mismamente*, cf. *?mismamente el cura* 'the priest himself', are considered substandard or popular.

31.2.6 Meaning of adverbs in *-mente*

The existence of a derived adverb in *-mente* does not mean that the adjective cannot itself function adverbially or that there does not exist an adverbial phrase with or without the same meaning. Constant reading and dictionary work are the only solution to this problem, e.g.:

en vano/vanamente	in vain/vainly
de inmediato/inmediatamente	immediately
directo/directamente	directly
Siempre obra locamente/a lo loco	He always acts wildly/in a mad fashion

but only:

Está locamente enamorado	He's madly in love

31.2.7 Too many adverbs in *-mente*

It is bad style to include too many adverbs in *-mente* in a single paragraph: the final syllables set off ugly rhymes. The barbarous sentence *?Evidentemente, todas las lenguas evolucionan constantemente, y sería totalmente absurdo pretender detener arbitrariamente su crecimiento* makes passable English in literal translation – 'Clearly, all languages evolve constantly, and it would be totally absurd to attempt to arrest their growth arbitrarily' – but must be recast in Spanish along the lines of *Es evidente que todas las lenguas están en constante evolución, y sería totalmente absurdo pretender detener de manera arbitraria su crecimiento*.

A form in *-mente* can usually be replaced by *con* + an abstract noun or by some other adverbial phrase, e.g. *alegremente* = *con alegría* or *de un modo* (or *manera*) *alegre*, *rabiosamente* = *con rabia* or *de un modo rabioso*, *ferozmente* = *con ferocidad* or *de un modo feroz*. The sentence *Vivían de un modo tranquilo, feliz y libre* 'They lived quietly, happy and free' is much better Spanish than *Vivían tranquila, feliz y libremente*.

For a selection of adverbial phrases, see 31.3.2.

31.2.8 *-ísimamente*

The suffix *-ísimo* (see 4.9) may be added (judiciously) to adverbs of manner and time. The result is very emphatic:

claramente	*clarísimamente*	extremely clearly
intensamente	*intensísimamente*	extremely intensely
recientemente	*recientísimamente*	extremely recently
tiernamente	*tiernísimamente*	extremely tenderly
urgentemente	*urgentísimamente*	extremely urgently

More common alternatives exist, e.g. *con gran claridad, con enorme intensidad, con gran urgencia*, etc.

Note
Lejos and *cerca* can also have *-ísimo* added to them: *lejísimos* (note the final *s*) and *cerquísima*. Colloquially *lejotes* can be used to denote uncomfortable distance, often preceded by *allá/allí*: *Esa casa está allí lejotes* 'That house is miles off/away'.

31.2.9 Adverbs in *-mente* to mean 'from a . . . point of view'
Adverbs in *-mente* are freely used to indicate point of view. This construction is much favoured in journalistic styles:

Económicamente, este país va a la ruina	Economically, this country is on the road to ruin
Personalmente, lo dudo	Personally, I doubt it
Editorialmente, no lo apruebo	From a publishing point of view, I don't approve of it

31.3 Adverbs of manner

31.3.1 General

These include words like *bien* 'well', *mal* 'badly', *despacio* 'slowly', *pronto* 'quickly', *adrede/aposta* 'on purpose', *igual* 'the same', as well as most of the adverbs formed with *-mente*.

There are often regional differences of usage, e.g *deprisa* 'quickly' in Spain, and *aprisa* in Latin America: *Quiero ir muy aprisa* (A. Mastretta, dialogue, Mexico) 'I want to go very fast'.

There are countless adverbial phrases: *a propósito* 'deliberately', *en balde* 'in vain', *a contrapelo* 'unwillingly', *en serio* 'seriously'. A selection appears at 31.3.2.

Adverbs of manner can modify verbs, participles, adjectives or other adverbs:

Habla despacio	He talks slowly
Esto está mal hecho	This is badly made/This is the wrong thing to do
Está bien	It/He/She's okay
Estoy totalmente agotado	I'm totally exhausted
Me da igual	It's all the same to me
Aquí estamos mejor/peor	We're better/worse (off) here

A few can even modify nouns:

Hace mucho tiempo que una cosa así no ocurría en la ONU (El País)	It has been a long time since something like this happened in the UN
Cenamos algunas cosas que ella traía en su equipaje, latas y así (F. Umbral, Spain)	We had supper on a few things she was carrying in her luggage – tins and that sort of thing

una niña bien	a girl from a 'respectable' family (pejorative)
dos coñacs con hielo, y dos cafés igual	two cognacs with ice, and two coffees the same way

Bien and *así de* can intensify adjectives:

Es bien lista	She's pretty clever
Bien bueno que está, ¿eh?	Great, isn't it? (sarcastic)
¿Adónde vas así de guapa? or *. . . vas tan guapa?*	Where are you off to looking so pretty?

31.3.2 Adverbial phrases of manner

These are numerous. They often provide an elegant alternative to an unwieldy adverb in *-mente*. The following is a small sample:

a buen paso	at a smart pace
a conciencia	conscientiously
El agua sale a chorros	The water is pouring out
a destiempo	inopportunely
a escondidas	secretly/clandestinely
a fuego lento	on a low flame
a hurtadillas	by stealth
a la carrera	at full speed
a la fuerza	by force/under obligation
(llorar) a lágrima viva	to shed floods of tears
a mano	by hand
a matacaballo	at break-neck speed
a medias	by halves
a oscuras	in the dark
a quemarropa	point-blank
a ratos perdidos	at odd moments
a regañadientes	reluctantly/unwillingly
a sabiendas de que . . .	fully aware that . . .
a tiempo	in time (e.g. for the train)
a tientas	by touch/by feel
al raso	in the open/out of doors
bajo cuerda	on the sly
con delirio/locura	madly/passionately
con frecuencia/a menudo	frequently
de balde	free (= without paying)
de continuo	continuously
de corrido	at one go/straight off
de costumbre	usually
de golpe	suddenly
de improviso	unexpectedly
(saberse/aprenderse) de memoria	(learn) by heart
de ordinario	normally/usually
de puntillas	on tiptoe
de rodillas	kneeling
de seguro	for certain/sure
de sobra	in excess/more than enough
(leer algo) de un tirón	to read something in one sitting/ straight through
en cambio	on the other hand
en confianza	confidentially
en cueros (vivos)/en pelota	stark naked
en el acto	on the spot

en lo sucesivo	from now on/hereafter
(hablar) por los codos	to talk too much (lit. 'through the elbows')
sin empacho	coolly/unconcernedly
sin reserva	unreservedly
sin ton ni son	willy-nilly/thoughtlessly

31.3.3 Adjectives as adverbs of manner

The masculine singular of a few adjectives may be used as an adverb, but only in certain phrases, e.g. *hablar claro* 'to speak clearly' but only *expresarse claramente/con claridad* 'to express oneself clearly':

Hablan alto/bajo	They talk loudly/softly
Lo hemos comprado barato/caro	We've bought it cheap/dear
El tren va directo a Tuy	The train goes direct to Tuy
Hay que tirar fuerte	You have to pull hard
Se me apiló firme (J. Cortázar, dialogue, Argentina, Spain: *se me arrimó*)	He pushed himself tight up against me
Anda rápido que vamos a llegar tarde (see 31.3.6 for *rápido*)	walk fast or we'll arrive late
Respiraba hondo como si le costara trabajo	He was breathing deeply, as if with difficulty
Me sienta fatal	It doesn't suit me/agree with me at all
Él no juega limpio	He doesn't play fair

The following are typical of familiar speech and are not to everyone's taste:

Lo hemos pasado estupendo/fantástico/bárbaro	We had a tremendous/fantastic time
La chaqueta le sienta bárbaro a Mariluz	The jacket looks terrific on Mariluz
Eso se hace fácil	That's dead easy/That's a cinch

Note
Colloquial Latin-American provides numerous examples unacceptable in Spain but admitted in informal styles in the Americas: *Qué lindo canta* 'Doesn't he/she sing prettily', *Pero toca muy bonito* 'But he plays really well' (both examples from Kany, 53-55), . . . *un gran número de mexicanos que piensan distinto que el PRI* (*Excelsior*, Mexico) '. . . a large number of Mexicans who think differently from the PRI', *Inicialmente pensé que podíamos haber conseguido unos dólares fácil, sin problemas para la revolución* (*Vindicación de Cuba*, Cuba) 'Initially I thought we could easily have got a few dollars, without any problems for the Revolution'.

31.3.4 Adjectives used to modify both subject and verb

Very common in Spanish is the use of an adjective in combination with a verb to produce an effect more easily created by an adverb in English. This is not a true adverbial use of the adjective, since the adjective agrees with the number and gender of the subject. This construction is restricted in the spoken language to a limited range of verbs and adjectives.

The effect is to make the adjective act both as an adverb and an adjective, i.e. it modifies both the verb and the subject of the verb. Sometimes the construction is obligatory: *Las niñas cansadas dormían* 'The tired girls were sleeping' is not the same as *Las niñas dormían cansadas* which is most nearly translated as 'The girls were tired and asleep' or 'sleeping in their tiredness'. But one could hardly say ?*Las niñas dormían cansadamente* 'The girls were sleeping tiredly' which modifies the verb but not the subject!

Obviously, this construction is confined to those adjectives that can equally well modify a noun or a verb, e.g. *inocente* 'innocent', *confuso* 'confused', *feliz* 'happy', but not adjectives like *harapiento* 'ragged' or *azul* 'blue' which can hardly modify a verb:

Se desvistió mientras se miraba distraído en el espejo del armario (J. Cortázar, Argentina; or *distraídamente*)	He got undressed as he gazed absent-mindedly at himself in the wardrobe mirror
Las mujeres protestaban indignadas (or *indignadamente*)	The women were protesting indignantly
Las máquinas de escribir tecleteaban incansables	The typewriters were clattering tirelessly
Sonrió tranquila . . . (J. Marsé, Spain)	She smiled gently
Viven felices (normal style)	They live happily

31.3.5 Nouns used adverbially

For familiar constructions like *llover cantidad, divertirse horrores* see 31.4.7.

31.3.6 *Rápido*

Rápido is an adjective, and is correctly used in phrases like *tren rápido* 'fast train', *comidas rápidas* 'fast meals', etc.

As an adverb it is, like 'quick', familiar; *con prisa, deprisa, rápidamente, pronto* are correct adverbial forms: *¡Rápido (deprisa/pronto), que se va el tren!* 'Quick, the train's going!', *¡Fuera! ¡Rápido!* 'Get out! Quick!'. Forms like *Lo he hecho rápido* 'I've done it quickly' are familiar.

31.3.7 *A la* and *a lo*

Both may form adverbial phrases of manner, but *a la* followed by a feminine adjective is much more common than *a lo*, which is probably nowadays confined to set phrases:

tortilla a la francesa	plain omelette
despedirse a la francesa	to take French leave (i.e. not say good-bye)
Viven todavía a la antigua	They still live in the old style
a lo loco	crazily/without stopping to think

Note
En plan . . . is rather colloquial, like '-style': *viajar en plan turista* 'to travel tourist-style', *hablar en plan Tarzan* 'to talk Tarzan-style'.

31.3.8 Position of adverbs of manner

For further remarks on the position of adverbs see 37.2.6 and 37.4.

An adverb of manner usually follows an intransitive verb:

Trabaja actualmente en una segunda novela	He is now working on a second novel
Este problema está íntimamente ligado al problema del paro	This problem is intimately linked to the problem of unemployment
esa cara de asco que parece ser habitualmente la suya	that look of disgust which seems habitually to be his

In a transitive sentence, an adverb may follow the object – *Habla griego correctamente* – or the verb – *Habla correctamente el griego* 'He speaks Greek perfectly/without making mistakes'.

The difference is usually almost imperceptible, but strictly speaking an adverb that follows the object modifies the whole verb phrase, whereas an adverb that precedes the object modifies only the verb. Thus *Robaba dinero con frecuencia* 'He frequently stole money', but *Robaba con frecuencia dinero . . .*

'He frequently stole money . . .' is the appropriate order if further items, e.g. jewellery, are to follow.

31.4 Intensifiers and moderators

31.4.1 General

Intensifiers and moderators intensify or weaken the force of a verb, adverb, adjective and, occasionally, noun. Typical intensifiers are *muy* 'very', *mucho/poco* 'much'/'little', *intensamente* 'intensely', *algo/más bien* 'rather', *increíblemente* 'incredibly', *sobremanera* (literary) 'exceedingly'. Many intensifiers have other functions, and are dealt with elsewhere, e.g. *algo* and *más bien* see 9.2, *demasiado* see 9.9, *mucho* and *poco* see 9.12.

New colloquial intensifiers appear and vanish as fashion dictates. *Requete-* used to be a popular prefix in Spain and has created permanent expressions like *requeteguapo/a* 'very good-looking' and *requetebién* 'extremely well done'. *Archi-* can still be found in *archiconocido/archisabido* 'very well-known'. Nowadays, at least in Spain, any adjective can be colloquially reinforced by *super-*: *supertonto/superinteligente* 'extremely silly'/'extremely intelligent'.

31.4.2 Muy

Muy 'very' is originally an abbreviated form of *mucho*, and the full form must be used in isolation:

Es muy inteligente	He's very intelligent
¿Es inteligente? Sí, mucho	Is he intelligent? Yes, very

Note

Bien is sometimes used in Spain in the sense of 'very': *Me voy a dar una ducha bien caliente* 'I'm going to have a very hot shower'. This usage is more common in Latin America: *Es bien simpático* (Chilean informant) 'He's very likeable', *¡Si está bien viejo para ti!* (popular Mexican, quoted Arjona Iglesias, 1991, 78) 'He's really/pretty old for you!'.

31.4.3 Intensifiers in -mente

These cannot modify another adverb in *-mente*, i.e. 'He speaks English incredibly fluently' cannot be translated **Habla inglés increíblemente corrientemente* but must be recast, e.g. *Habla inglés con una soltura/facilidad increíble*:

Ha actuado con admirable honradez	He's acted admirably honestly/with admirable honestly
Lo hicieron con una prisa absurda	They did it absurdly quickly/with absurd haste
Le voy a hablar con una franqueza total	I'm going to talk to you totally frankly

31.4.4 Más and menos

For the use of *más* and *menos* in comparisons, see Chapter 5.

Más is used as an intensifier in familiar speech, without any comparative meaning:

Es que eres más tonto . . .	Heavens, are you stupid!
Está más borracho . . .	Is he drunk!

31.4.5 *Lo* as an intensifier

For *lo* in sentences like *Cuéntale lo bien que canta* 'Tell her how well he sings', *Camina lo más lentamente que puedas* 'Walk as slowly as possible', see 7.2.2.

31.4.6 *Qué* and *cuán* as intensifiers

Exclamatory *¿qué?* is discussed at 24.4, *¿cuán(to)?* at 24.6.

For *No recordaba lo guapa que eres* 'I didn't remember how attractive you are', etc., see 7.2.2.

31.4.7 Nouns used as intensifiers

Familiar speech uses some nouns as intensifiers – not to every taste, as the translation shows:

Lo pasamos bomba (already old-fashioned?)	We had a terrific time (lit. 'we had a bomb of a time')
Canta fenómeno	He's a smashing singer
Nos aburrimos cantidad	We were bored stiff/bored to death
Nos hemos reído cantidad	Did we have a laugh!

31.5 Adverbs of doubt

Words meaning 'perhaps', 'probably', 'possibly' may call for the subjunctive and are discussed under 16.3.

31.6 Adverbs of place

31.6.1 *Aquí, ahí, allí*

It is important to distinguish carefully between *ahí* and *allí*: to the untrained ear they tend to sound similar, at least in some varieties of Spanish. These adverbs are closely linked in meaning to the demonstratives:

este	this, near me	*aquí*	here, near me
ese	that	*ahí*	there
aquel	that, further away	*allí*	there, further away

In other words, *ahí* points to space near the hearer or to both hearer and speaker if they are in the same place. Misuse of *ahí* and *allí* produces a bizarre effect. Carnicer, *Nuevas refexiones*, 24, remarks that to ask people from another country *¿Qué tal se vive ahí?* 'What's it like living just there?', instead of *allí*, prompts them to look under their chairs.

Vente aquí a pasar unos días con nosotros	Come here and spend a few days with us
Aquí construiremos la casa, ahí el garaje, y allí al final del jardín, la piscina	We'll build the house here, the garage there, and the swimming pool there at the bottom of the garden
Deja la linterna ahí a tu lado	Leave the torch there next to you
Sería interesante visitar Groenlandia, pero no quisiera vivir allí	It would be interesting to visit Greenland, but I wouldn't like to live there

If the place referred to is out of sight, *ahí* is generally used if it is nearby or in the same town, *allí* for more remote places:

—*Lo he comprado en esa tienda.*	'I bought it in that shop.'

—*Ah, sí, yo compro siempre ahí*	'Oh yes, I always shop there'
Ya están ahí monsieur Fréjus y monsieur Bebé, y quieren cocktails (J. Cortázar, Argentina. dialogue; note *están ahí* = 'have arrived')	M. Fréjus and M. Bebé are here, and they want cocktails
Si vas a Cáceres, mándame una postal desde allí	If you go to Cáceres send me a card from there
Mi hermana nació en Caracas, y yo también nací allí	My sister was born in Caracas, and I was born there too

However, native speakers may use *ahí* for *allí* (but not vice-versa) if they feel emotionally close to the place they are talking about: *¿Conoces la iglesia a la entrada del pueblo? Pues ahí/allí se casaron mis padres* 'Do you know the church on the way in to the village? Well, that's where my parents got married', —*Y al fin llegué a Manaos. De ahí era fácil pasar a Iquitos. —Y ¿ahí fue donde conociste al señor Julio Reátegui?* (M. Vargas Llosa, Peru, dialogue) ' "And I eventually got to Manaos. From there it was easy to cross to Iquitos." "And that was where you met Sr Julio Reátegui?" '.

Notes
(i) Colloquially *por ahí* is used to mean 'somewhere' when the speaker is indifferent or secretive about the exact location: —*¿Dónde has estado? —Por ahí* ' "Where have you been?" "Somewhere" ' —*¿Dónde está Julia? —Por ahí* ' "Where's Julia?" "She's somewhere around" '.
(ii) *Ahí* may encroach on *allí* in Latin-American speech: *Ahí está, dijo, y ahí estaba porque él lo conocía . . .* (G. García Márquez, Colombia, dialogue, pointing to a comet in the sky) ' "There it is", he said, and there it was because he was familiar with it'.

31.6.2 *Acá, allá*
In the Southern Cone and in many other parts of Latin America, *acá* has more or less replaced *aquí*, even in good writing: *Acá en la Argentina si querés una taza de té, tenés que beber mate* = in Peninsular Spanish *Aquí en Argentina, si quieres una taza de té, tienes que beber mate* 'Here in Argentina if you feel like a cup of tea you have to drink *mate*'.

In Spain, *acá* and *allá* are much less common than *aquí, ahí, allí*, and denote vague or non-specific location or, most commonly, movement (often with the preposition *para*):

Ven acá/aquí, que te voy a contar una cosa	Come here, I'm going to tell you something
Íbamos allá/hacia allí cuando nos le/lo encontramos	We were on the way there when we ran into him
Que se venga para acá en cuanto pueda	He must come here as soon as he can

Notes
(i) *Allá* is often used of large distances in Latin America and occasionally in Spain. It can also in both regions express vague yearnings. In time phrases it emphasizes remoteness and may be obligatory: *Allá/Allí en Argentina tenemos mucha familia* (*allí* in Spain) 'We have a lot of family out there in Argentina', *Nos casamos allá en los años veinte* (not *allí*) 'We got married way back in the twenties', *El sur era y es acentuadamente indio; allá la cultura tradicional está todavía viva* (O. Paz, Mexico) 'The south was and is markedly Amerindian; (down) there traditional culture is still alive', *Al otro lado de las lágrimas, allá arriba en lo alto de su rabia, más allá de las ramas del almendro y de las palmeras . . .* (J. Marsé, Spain) 'On the other side of her tears, up there high in her rage, beyond the branches of the almond tree and the palms . . .'.
(ii) *Acá* and *allá* can take an intensifier, unlike *aquí, ahí, allí*: *más allá del sistema solar*

'beyond the solar system', *más acá de la frontera* 'on this side of the frontier', *Muévelo un poco más acá/hacia aquí* 'Move it this way a bit', *¡Un poquito más acá!* 'This way a bit!' *lo más acá/allá posible* 'as far over here/there as possible'.

El más allá is 'the Beyond' of occult literature.

(iii) *Allá* with a pronoun translates 'Let him/her get on with it', 'It's your look-out', etc. *Allá él si hace tonterías* 'If he wants to fool about, that's his affair', *Bueno, allá tú si no me haces caso* 'Well, if you don't pay any attention to me, it's your problem'.

(iv) *Acá* is sometimes used in time expressions in informal language, though it sounds a little old-fashioned (at least in Spain): *¿De cuándo acá no se dice hola a los amigos?* (*desde cuándo . . .*) 'Since when have people not been saying "hello" to their friends?', *Desde las elecciones acá, este país ya no tiene remedio* 'Since the elections, this country's been beyond hope', *De un tiempo acá se le nota cansada* (*desde un tiempo a esta parte . . .*) 'She's been looking tired for some time now'.

31.6.3 Use of adverbs of place as pronouns

One hears uneducated speakers use *aquí/ahí/allí* for *éste/ése/aquél*: *aquí me dice* = *éste me dice* 'this one here says to me' (itself very familiar). The same phenomenon occurs in Latin America, and also with *acá/allá*.

31.6.4 Adverbs of place with prepositions

All the adverbs of place can be preceded by *de, desde, hacia, hasta, por* and, less commonly, *para* (for which see *acá/allá*).

Los melocotones de aquí son mejores que los de Estados Unidos	The peaches (from) here are better than the ones from America
Mira el sombrero que lleva la señora de allí	Look at the hat that lady over there is wearing
Desde aquí se ve el mar	You can see the sea from here
Se sale por aquí	This is the way out

31.6.5 *Dentro/adentro, fuera/afuera*

'Inside' and 'outside' respectively.

In Spain *dentro* and *fuera* are preferred after prepositions (except perhaps *para*) and also to form prepositional phrases when followed by *de*. *Afuera* and *adentro* strictly speaking denote motion *towards* and should be used only in this sense, although they are occasionally found in isolation with the meaning of *fuera, dentro*.

Peninsular usage:

Por dentro era negro, y por fuera blanco	On the inside it was black, on the outside white
Dentro había flores en macetas	Inside there were flowers in pots
Dentro de la caja había otra	Inside the box was another
Ven (a)dentro y te lo explicaré	Come inside and I'll explain it to you
Vamos a cenar fuera	We're eating out (tonight)/We're having dinner outside
He estado fuera unos días	I've been away for a couple of days
Al acabar el discurso se oyeron gritos de ¡fuera! ¡fuera!	When the speech ended shouts of 'out! out!' were heard
¡Las manos fuera de Cuba!	Hands off Cuba!
Afuera quedaba el domingo de verano, despoblado y soso (F. Umbral, Spain. Poetic: *fuera* is more normal in Spain)	Outside was the summer Sunday, empty (lit. 'depopulated') and lifeless

Latin-American usage:

Afuera and *adentro* are the most common forms. *Adentro de* and *afuera de* are also used as prepositional phrases, this usage being considered normal in Argentina and colloquial in most other Latin-American countries:

Adentro de Aqueronte hay lágrimas, tinieblas, crujir de dientes (J.L. Borges, Argentina; Spain *dentro de*)	Within Acheron there are tears, darkness, gnashing of teeth
Afuera en el parque, y adentro, por la casa entera seguían los disparos (José Donoso, Chile; Spain *fuera, dentro*)	Outside in the park, and inside, throughout the house, the shooting continued
El perro se quedó afuera (Spain *fuera*)	The dog was left outside/stayed outside

31.6.6 *Abajo, debajo de*

For the prepositions *bajo, debajo de* see 34.3.

Abajo means 'down below'/'downstairs': *Te espero abajo* 'I'll wait downstairs'. However, a*bajo **de*** is often used in Latin America for the prepositional phrase *debajo de* 'underneath':

¿Chofi guarda las quincenas abajo del colchón? (A. Mastretta, Mexico; *debajo de* in Spain)	Does Chofi keep her salary under the mattress?
La nevera está abajo del bar (C. Fuentes, Mexico, dialogue; *debajo de* in Spain)	The fridge is under the bar

31.6.7 *Detrás, detrás de* and *atrás*

Atrás 'behind'/'backwards' denotes backwards motion in Spain whereas *detrás* and the prepositional phrase *detrás de* 'behind' denote place:

dar un paso atrás	to move a step backwards
Ponte detrás	Stand behind
detrás de mí/detrás de la mesa	behind me/the table

In Latin America *atrás de* often means *detrás de*:

Las demás me veían desde atrás de la mesa (A. Mastretta, Mexico; *me miraban . . .* in Spain)	The others looked at me from behind the table

31.6.8 *Delante, delante de* and *adelante*

In Spain *delante* means 'in front' and the prepositional phrase *delante de* 'in front of' denotes place and *adelante* 'forward(s)'/'onward(s)' denotes motion forward:

Yo iba delante	I was walking ahead
Delante de ti no hablará	She won't say anything in front of you
Sigue adelante que yo te alcanzaré	Go on ahead. I'll catch up with you

Alante is a popular variant for *adelante*.

In colloquial Latin America *adelante de* is often used for *delante de*, but this is not accepted in Spain.

Notes

(i) Only *adentro, afuera, abajo, atrás, delante* and *adelante* should be intensified: *más adentro/abajo/atrás* 'further inside/down/behind', *más afuera* or *más hacia fuera* 'more to the outside', *más hacia delante* 'further forwards'. *Más adelante* means 'later on', e.g. *Ya hablaremos más adelante* 'We'll talk later on'.

(ii) Omission of *de* in the prepositional phrase, common in Latin America, heard in Spain, is considered incorrect: *dentro **de** mi corazón, fuera **de** la casa*.

(iii) *Fuera de* can mean *aparte de* 'apart from' but is rather colloquial: *Fuera de él no hay nadie en que yo pueda confiar* 'Apart from him, there's no one I can trust' (some grammarians prefer *excepto él*).

(iv) *Atrás* is also used in the time phrases *años/meses/días atrás* 'some years/months/days ago'.

(v) *En adelante* can also be used in time phrases and in quantities: *Para esto necesitas de un millón en adelante* 'For this you'll need a million or more', *De ahora en adelante no lo vuelvo a hacer* 'From now on I won't do it again'.

31.7 Adverbs of time

31.7.1 *Ya*

Ya has a wide variety of uses. In many common constructions its meaning is determined by the tense of the verb that it modifies:

Vienen ya	They're coming right now
Ya llegarán	They'll arrive, for sure
Ya han llegado	They've already arrived
Ya llegaron (Latin America)	They already arrived
Ya no vienen	They're not coming any more
Ya no llegarán	They won't arrive any more
(but only *Aún/Todavía no han llegado*	They haven't arrived yet)

Further examples:

los autores que aportaron nuevos recursos estilísticos al ya idioma castellano (or *al que ya era idioma . . .*)	the authors who contributed new stylistic resources to what was already the Castilian language
Eres hombre ya/Ahora eres un hombre	You're a man now
¿Quién se acuerda ya de lo que era el Charleston?	Who can remember what the Charleston was any more?
Estaba perdido, extraviado en una casa ajena donde ya ni nada ni nadie le suscitaba el menor vestigio de afecto (G. García Márquez, Colombia)	He was lost, adrift in a strange house where nothing and nobody aroused the slightest trace of affection in him any more
Ya desde mucho antes, Amaranta había renunciado a toda tentativa de convertirla en una mujer útil (idem)	Long before this (already), Amaranta had abandoned all attempts to change her into a useful woman

Ya also has idiomatic uses, particularly with the non-past tenses. It can indicate impatience, accumulating frustration, fulfilled expectations, resignation, certainty about the future or, in negative sentences, denial of something expected:

Iros, iros a la playa, que ya me quedo yo aquí a lavar la ropa (Carmen Godoy in *Cambio16*; *iros* is familiar Peninsular usage for *idos*. See 17.2.4 for discussion)	Go on, off you go to the beach while I stay here washing the clothes (martyred tone)
Lleva seis meses en la cama. Si eso no es grave, pues ya me dirás	He's been in bed six months. If that's not serious, then you tell me what is
Sirve ya la cena, que hemos esperado bastante	Serve supper now, we've waited long enough
Por mí, que se vaya ya	He can go right now, as far as I'm concerned
El estudiante de nuestros días – ya no pensaré en el estudiante del año 2000 o 2500 . . . (*Variedades*, 174)	The student of our day – I shan't even consider the student of the year 2000 or 2500 . . .

Ya le pasaré la cuenta cuando gane el gallo (G. García Márquez, Colombia, dialogue: *ya* here makes a promise more certain)	I'll send you the bill when your cockerel/rooster wins
¡Basta ya! ¡Calla ya!	That's enough! Not another word!
¡Ya está bien!	That's enough!
Bueno, eso es el colmo ya	Well, that *is* the limit!
Ya puedes tener buen olfato con la nariz que tú tienes	You can well have a good sense of smell with the nose you've got
Por mí, ya puede llover, que tenemos tienda de campaña	As far as I'm concerned, it can go ahead and rain – we've got a tent
Hitler habría sido todavía peor – y ya es decir – si a su criminal racismo hubiera juntado un fanatismo religioso (*ABC*, Spain)	Hitler would have been even worse – and that's saying something – if he had added religious fanaticism to his criminal racism
Cuando ya acabemos de limpiar la casa . . .	When we finally finish cleaning the house . . .
No, no, ya te digo que él no sabía nada de todo aquello	No, no, I'm *telling* you he knew nothing about all that
¡Ya tuviste que contarme el final!	You *would* have to tell me the ending!
Ya lo sé	I already know/I *know*
Ya empezamos . . .	(Oh dear) here we go again . . .
Ya era hora	It's about time
Ya siéntate y deja de interrumpir (A. Mastretta, Mexico, dialogue, impatient tone[1])	Sit down and stop interrupting
—El jefe quiere hablar conmigo. Está muy enfadado. —Ya será menos	'The boss wants to talk to me. He's very angry'. 'Come on, it won't be that bad'

Notes

(i) *Ya . . . ya* is a literary alternative for *o . . . o* 'either . . . or': *Ya porque la idea del matrimonio acabara por asustarle, ya porque no pudiera olvidar a María, no apareció en la iglesia* 'Either because the idea of marriage eventually frightened him or because he could not forget Maria, he did not appear at the church'.

(ii) *Ya* may be an abbreviation of *Ya lo sé* 'I know', or *Ya entiendo* 'I understand': *—Cuando veas la luz verde pulsa el botón rojo. —Ya* '"When you see the green light, push the red button." "Right/Understood"'.

(iii) *Desde ya* 'straightaway' is an expression from the Southern Cone which is sometimes now heard in Spain.

31.7.2 *Recién*

In Spain *recién* can only appear before participles, e.g. *recién pintado* 'newly painted', *recién casado* 'newly wed', *recién divorciado* 'recently divorced', *un chico recién salido del colegio* 'a boy who has recently left school'. Its use before other parts of speech is very rare.

The use of *recién* as a free-standing adverb of time is one hallmark of Latin-American Spanish everywhere. It is very common in speech and also appears even in quite formal written language.

It has two basic meanings:

(a) 'Right now' or 'just now':

Recién lo vi (Spain *Le acabo de ver*)	I've just seen him
—¿Cuándo lo dijo? —Recién (Spain *ahora mismo*)	'When did he say it?' ' Just now'

---

[1] In Spain the *ya* is placed after the imperative: *¡Siéntate ya!* 'Will you sit down!'.

(b) 'Only', as in 'only now', 'only this year'. This usage is colloquial in some regions:

Recién mañana llegará (Spain *No llegará hasta mañana*)	He won't be here till tomorrow
Y él recién entonces se da cuenta de que está herida porque las manos se le están manchando de la sangre de ella (M. Puig, Argentina, dialogue; Spain: . . . *sólo entonces se da cuenta . . .*)	And only then he realizes that she's injured because his hands are being stained with her blood

Used thus, *recién* precedes the word or phrase it modifies. There is a colloquial diminutive *reciencito*.

31.7.3 *Todavía, aún, ya no*

Todavía and *Aún* both mean 'still'/'yet' and are synonymous. With words like *menos, más, menor* and *mayor* they are translated as 'even'. *Aún* 'still' must be distinguished from *aun* meaning 'even'; the latter discussed at 31.8.

Before or after comparative adjectives and adverbs (including *más* and *menos*), 'even' is translated by *todavía, aún* or ocassionally *incluso* (not by *aun*):

Todavía/aún están aquí	They are still here
No han venido aún/todavía	They haven't come yet
Su cara puede verse menos bonita aún, se lo aseguro (C. Fuentes, Mexico, dialogue; or *todavía menos/menos bonita todavía*)	I can assure you, your face can be even less pretty
Es todavía/aún/incluso/hasta más difícil de lo que yo pensaba	It's even more difficult than I thought

31.7.4 *Luego* and *entonces*

Both words are translatable as 'then' but they usually mean different things.

(a) As time words, *entonces* means 'then'/'at that moment', whereas *luego* means 'afterwards'/'later on'. *Luego* in this sense is stressed: ***Luego** viene/Viene **luego*** 'He's coming later'. If the *luego* is not stressed here, it means 'so'/'in that case':

Abrí la puerta, y entonces me di cuenta de lo que había pasado (*luego* here would mean *después* 'afterwards')	I opened the door, and then realized what had happened
Entonces supe que Mario había mentido (*luego* would mean 'later on')	I realized then that Mario had lied
Desde entonces he sido feliz	From that time on I have been happy
Recuerdo que los cines de entonces siempre apestaban a agua de colonia	I remember that cinemas at that time always stank of Eau de Cologne
el entonces catedrático de griego	the professor of Greek at that time/the then professor of Greek
Gary Hart derrotó al hasta entonces favorito demócrata Walter Mondale	Gary Hart defeated the until then democrat favourite Walter Mondale
¿Quién es? Te lo diré luego	Who is it? I'll tell you later
Lo haré luego	I'll do it later
Hasta luego (cf. *Hasta ahora*, 'See you in a minute')	See you later
Según dice mamá, que luego estuvo seis años liada con Tey . . . (J. Marsé, Spain)	According to mother, who later on was involved with Tey for six years . . .

Note
luego de hacerlo (literary) = *después de hacerlo* 'after doing it'.

(b) Both *entonces* and *luego* may mean 'in that case'. In this meaning *luego* is not stressed:

En Madrid hace 40 grados, en Sevilla 38.
Entonces hace más calor en Madrid que en
Sevilla (or Luego, hace . . .)
—Es . . . mi secreto. —Entonces ya me lo
contarás. Los secretos siempre se cuentan
(Buero Vallejo, Spain, dialogue, *luego* not
possible in conjunction with *ya*)
Pienso luego existo (set phrase)

In Madrid it's 40 degrees, in Seville 38.
In that case it's hotter in Madrid than in
Seville
'It's my secret'. 'Then you'll soon tell me.
Secrets always get told'

I think therefore I am

Notes
(i) Use of *luego* to mean 'straightaway'/'immediately' is a regionalism in Spain, but it is common in certain Latin-American countries.
(ii) The following words also convey the idea of 'then': *después*, 'after', *acto seguido* 'next'/'immediately after', *a continuación* 'next'/'immediately after', *en seguida* 'immediately afterwards'.

31.8 Incluso, hasta, aun, siquiera

All these words may translate the English 'even' in such sentences as 'He even speaks Russian and Greek', 'Even in England the sun shines sometimes'.

Incluso and *aun* are synonyms but nowadays *incluso* is more often used:

Incluso/Aun hoy día algunas personas siguen
creyendo en las hadas
Incluso/aun si le das dinero, no lo hará

Even today some people still believe in
fairies
Even if you give him money he won't do
it

Hasta, literally 'until', may also mean 'even':

Ha llovido tanto que hasta/incluso/aun los
patos están hartos

It's rained so much that even the ducks
have had enough/are sick of it

Siquiera means 'at least':

Dame siquiera mil pesetas

Give me one thousand pesetas at least/if
nothing else

Siquiera el General es generoso. Mira el
coche que me regaló (A. Mastrella, Mexico,
dialogue)

At least the General is generous. Look at
the car he gave me

Ni siquiera translates 'not even':

Bueno, los ingleses . . . los autos por la
izquierda . . . ni siquiera han aceptado el
sistema métrico (C. Catania, Argentina,
interview; *los autos = los coches* in Spain)

Well, the English . . . cars on the left-
hand side of the road . . . they haven't
even accepted the metric system

Note
Inclusive is used in Latin America where Peninsular Spanish uses *incluso*: *Para que una persona con un malestar llegue a un bienestar, debe pasar inclusive por un malestar peor que el que ya tenía* (Interview in *Cuba Internacional*; Spain *malestar* = 'discomfort', 'indisposition') 'For people with troubles to get out of them (lit. 'to arrive at well-being'), they have to pass through even worse troubles than they already had'. Grammarians condemn this because *inclusive* should mean 'inclusive', but the construction is deeply rooted in Latin America, even in educated speech and in writing.

32

Expressions of time

32.1 General

This chapter covers such matters as the expression of duration, e.g. 'for *n* days', 'since . . .', 'during . . .', 'still', 'ago', words like 'again', and dates.

32.2 Duration, i.e. 'for *n* days', etc.

Unlike English, European Spanish often uses – and Latin-American normally uses – the present tense to indicate events that are still in progress or are likely to recur: *Es la tercera vez que **pierdo** la misa del domingo desde que **tengo** uso de razón* (G. García Márquez, Colombia, dialogue; Spain . . . *que me **pierdo**/que me **he perdido** la misa . . .*). English uses past tenses in the same kind of sentence: 'It's the third time **I've missed** Sunday Mass since **I've been** able to reason'.

If the event was continuing in the past, European Spanish often uses – and Latin-American normally uses – the imperfect tense whereas English uses the pluperfect: *Desde que llegó a Europa por primera vez **andaba** en el landó familiar* (G. García Márquez; Spain ***iba** a todas partes/**había ido** a todas partes . . .*) 'Since he'd first arrived from Europe he had been driving around in the family landau'.

English speakers constantly forget this and use the compound tenses (perfect and pluperfect) for both completed and incomplete events: 'How long **have you been** in New York?' (the hearer may or may not be remaining there).[1] But the Spanish perfect tense is a past tense, so *¿Cuánto tiempo **has estado** en Nueva York?* means much the same as *¿Cuánto tiempo **estuviste** en Nueva York?* 'How long **did you** stay in New York?'. The present tense would be used if the hearer is intending to remain there: *¿Cuánto tiempo hace que **estás** en Nueva York?* or *¿Cuánto tiempo **llevas** en Nueva York?* French and Italian have similar rules (*Vous **êtes** ici depuis combien de temps?* 'How long have you been here?', *Da quando **sei** a Roma?* 'How long have you been in Rome?').

32.3 Translating 'for' in time phrases

There are various possibilities, not all of them interchangeable, e.g. *llevar . . ., hace . . ., desde hace . . ., desde, durante, en, por, para*.

---

[1] North-American readers may find that they want to substitute simple pasts for the typically British perfect tenses in some of the translations in this chapter.

32.3.1 *Llevar*

This verb can only be used when the event is or was still in progress: one cannot say *Llevo seis meses en España* 'I've been in Spain for six months' after one has left the country for good: *He estado/Estuve seis meses . . .*

A following verb appears in the gerund form, but the gerund cannot be negated: 'I haven't been smoking for years' = *Hace años que **no fumo**/Llevo años que **no fumo**/Llevo años **sin fumar**/No fumo **desde hace** años*, never **Llevo años no fumando*:

Llevamos cinco años viviendo juntos (Carmen Rico-Godoy, Spain)	We've been living together for five years
Lleva veinte años peleando y está como un gallo nuevo (interview in *Granma*, Cuba)	He's been fighting (i.e. boxing) for twenty years, and he's like a fresh fighting cock
Llevo siete días aquí contigo (C. Fuentes, Mexico, dialogue)	I've been here with you for seven days
Llevo aquí desde las seis	I've been here since six o'clock
El ascensor lleva estropeado dos meses (C. Rico-Godoy, Spain)	The lift/elevator has been broken for two months

If the event or state *was* still in progress at the time, the imperfect of *llevar* is used (**he llevado . . .* is not possible): ***Llevaba** dos años en Madrid cuando me puse enfermo* 'I'd/He'd/She'd been in Madrid for two years when I fell ill', ***Llevabas** años diciéndolo* 'You'd been saying it for years'.

Notes

(i) *Llevar* definitely implies a significant period of time. One would not say **Sólo/Solo llevo unos segundos aquí* for *Sólo/Solo he estado aquí unos segundos* 'I've only been here for a few seconds'.

(ii) This construction with *llevar* is very common in Peninsular speech, but less common in written language than *hace . . ./hacía . . .* (described in the next section).

It is little used in the Southern Cone, particularly in Buenos Aires. In Latin America it is widely replaced by *tener*: ***Tengo** dos años aquí*, 'I've been here for two years', ***Tenía** pocos meses de gobernar cuando logró el cambio* (A. Mastretta, Mexico, dialogue) 'He'd only been acting as Governor for a few months when he managed to bring about the change'. This construction is also found in formal writing.[2]

(iii) The following idioms are noteworthy: *Esto me va a llevar mucho tiempo* 'This is going to take me a long time', *Ana me lleva tres años* 'Ana's three years older than me/I'.

32.3.2 *Hace/hacía/hará . . . que . . .*

*Hace dos años que **estoy** en Madrid* means the same as *Llevo dos años en Madrid* 'I've been in Madrid for two years (and my stay is continuing)'.

The present tense is used for events that continue into the present. If the sentence is negative, the perfect tense is, however, optionally found in Spain, but not usually in Latin America: *Hace años que no la **he visto**/no la veo* 'I haven't seen her for years'. Use of past tenses for the present in conjunction with *hace* is rejected by many Latin-Americans, aversion to the compound tenses being apparently stronger in the Southern Cone than elsewhere.[3]

---

[2] cf. *Aunque **tengan** muchos años de vivir allí . . . nadie los confundiría con los norteamericanos auténticos* (Octavio Paz, Mexico) 'Although they've been living there for years, no one would take them for true North-Americans'.

[3] There is, however, much regional variation in this matter. See 14.9.7.

Hacía + the imperfect + *que* translates 'for' in past time and is followed by the imperfect to denote an action that was still in progress: *Hacía tiempo que nos **veíamos*** 'We had been seeing one another for some time'. In this case the pluperfect changes the meaning: *Hacía tiempo que nos **habíamos visto*** 'It had been some time since we had seen one another'.

Hará . . . que + the present tense is commonly used in suppositions or approximations: ***Hará** dos años que no la veo* (Spain also *. . . no la he visto*) 'It must be two years since I've seen her'. Further examples:

Affirmative sentences:

Hace tiempo que pienso/tengo pensado ir a verla	For some time now I've been thinking of going to see her
¿Hace cuánto tiempo que es usted el amor de Joaquín? (M. Vargas Llosa, Peru, dialogue; Spain *¿Cuánto tiempo hace que es usted la amante de Joaquín?*)	How long have you been Joaquín's lover?

Negative sentences:

Hace dos días que no la veo (L. Spota, Mexico, dialogue; Spain also *. . . no la he visto*)	I haven't seen her for two days
Como no bebo hace tiempo . . . (M. Vargas Llosa, Peru, dialogue)	Since I haven't been drinking for some time

Notes
(i) One cannot use the present tense if no preposition is used: ***He estado** tres horas aquí* 'I've been here three hours' (with the implication 'and I'm just leaving'), not **Estoy tres horas aquí*, also ***Llevo** tres horas aquí/**Hace** tres horas que **estoy** aquí/**Estoy** aquí **desde hace** tres horas*.
(ii) The verb *hacer* does not appear in the plural in this construction: **Hacían años que no hablaban de otra cosa* 'They hadn't talked of anything else for years' is bad Spanish for *hacía años que . . . .* This is a common error of popular speech.
(iii) The imperfect tense may be used in negative sentences with a change of meaning. *Hace años que no **tomábamos** café juntos* 'We haven't had coffee together for years' differs from *Hace años que no **tomamos** café juntos* in that the former would be said while one is actually drinking coffee with the friend, whereas the latter implies that it would be a good idea to have coffee together.
(iv) *En* may be used in the same way as the English 'in' in negative sentences, e.g. 'I hadn't seen her in/for three days'; see 32.5.

32.3.3 Translating 'for' when the event is no longer in progress
Verb in a past tense and no preposition (as in English):

Estuvo una temporada en Guatemala, y luego se volvió a California	He was in Guatemala (for) a while and then he returned to California
Esperamos cinco minutos en la parada	We waited at the stop (for) five minutes
*Cuánto tiempo **ha estado** usted/estuvo en Madrid?* (addressed to someone whose stay is over)	(For) how long were you in Madrid?

Hace . . . que with a preterite tense means 'ago' and is discussed at 32.4.

32.3.4 *Durante*
The basic meaning of *durante* is 'during': *durante el siglo veinte* 'during the twentieth century', *durante los tres meses que estuvo aquí* 'in the three months he was here'. Unlike 'during' it is regularly used before plural nouns to mean 'for

a specific period of time': *durante años* 'in years', *durante muchos siglos* 'for/in many centuries'.

When the event terminates with the period mentioned, the verb is in the preterite tense: *Fue Presidente durante tres años* 'He was President for three years' (and then died or stopped being President). Compare *Era Presidente durante los tres años de la Revolución* 'He was President during the three years of the Revolution' (and may have been before or after):

Durante años nunca **supe** *si me contaban fantasías o verdades* (A. Mastretta, Mexico, dialogue)	For years I never knew whether they were telling me truths or fantasies
Fue incapaz de hablar durante muchas horas (J-M. Merino, Spain)	He was unable to speak for hours (on that occasion)

But *Después de los ataques de asma,* **era** *incapaz de hablar durante muchas horas* (imperfect because the condition is habitual) 'After the asthma attacks he used to be unable to speak for hours'.

Notes
(i) Spanish uses the preterite continuous (*estuve hablando, estuvo leyendo*, etc.) to emphasize that an event continued uninterrupted throughout a period of time: *Durante un cuarto de hora* **estuvo** *mirándote* (L. Spota, Mexico, dialogue) 'He was gazing at you for a quarter of an hour'.
(ii) *Durante* is associated with the verb *durar* 'to last' and is therefore appropriate for long periods of time or periods considered long by the speaker: one does not say **durante un segundo*, but one could say *durante cinco minutos* 'for five minutes' or *Quiero que hables sin parar durante cinco segundos* 'I want you to speak non-stop for five seconds' (seen as a long time). Spanish uses *por* for short periods of time or whenever the speaker wishes to emphasize short duration. See the next section for discussion.
(iii) *En* may be used for *durante* in Latin America: *Olga no habló* **en** *varios minutos* (L. Spota, Mexico) 'Olga didn't speak for several minutes'. Use of *en* may also correspond to English in negative sentences like 'I haven't smoked in/for years'; see 32.5.
En may also be an alternative for *dentro de* in sentences like *Tienes que bajar dentro de/en 5 minutos* 'You've got to be down in five minutes'. See 32.5 for discussion.

32.3.5 *Por* meaning 'for' in time phrases
Por is used instead of *durante* meaning 'for' when referring to brief moments of time (seconds, minutes, etc.) or whenever the speaker emphasizes the shortness of the period.

The preposition may be omitted altogether in such sentences:

Entraré sólo **(por)** *un momento*	I'll come in just for a moment
Por *un momento, Bernardo estuvo a punto de ocultar los motivos de la visita . . .* (J.-M. Merino, Spain; set phrase)	For a moment he was about to conceal the reasons for his visit
Por *un instante, Félix sintió que una pantalla plateada los separaba a él y a Mary* (C. Fuentes, Mexico; set phrase)	For a moment Félix felt that a silver screen was separating him and Mary

Notes
(i) *Por* and *para* are interchangeable in time expressions fixing the duration of some future need (see also 32.3.6 for *para* in time phrases): *Sólo/Solo queremos la habitación* **por/para** *unos días* 'We only want the room for a few days'.
(ii) Latin-Americans may use *por* where Peninsulars use nothing or *durante*: **Por** *cuatro o cinco años nos tuvieron acorralados* (M. Vargas Llosa, Peru, dialogue; Spain *durante . . .*) 'They had us cornered for four or five years', *Ahí permaneció* **por** *casi dos semanas* (L. Sepúlveda, Chile; Spain *durante . . .* or no preposition) 'He stayed there for nearly two months'.

32.3.6 *Para* in expressions of duration

Para is used to translate the idea of 'for' a specified period of time in the future:

*Tenemos agua **para** tres días*	We've enough water for three days
*Vamos a tener lluvia **para** rato*	We are going to have rain for some time

Note
Ir para is a colloquial translation of 'for nearly . . .': ***Va para** cinco años que trabajo aquí* 'I've been working here for nearly five years'/'It's getting on for five years that I've been working here'.

32.3.7 *Desde*

Desde translates 'since' or, sometimes, 'for'. *Desde que* is used before verb phrases, *desde* before singular noun phrases, and *desde hace/hacía* before plural or numbered nouns to translate 'since . . . ago'.

Desde can appear before nouns: ***Desde** niña hablo catalán* 'I've spoken Catalan since I was a little girl'.

***Desde que** se casó con el millonario ese, ya no se habla con sus amigos*	Since she married that millionaire she doesn't talk to her friends any more
*No viene/ha venido **desde marzo***	He hasn't come since March
*Estudio castellano desde hace **un año/tres años***	I've been studying Spanish for one year/three years (lit. 'from since one/three years ago')

Events that are still in progress require the present tense, events that were still in progress require the imperfect. However, European Spanish optionally uses the perfect tense with *desde* even when the action is still in progress.

***He estado/Estoy** aquí desde marzo*	I've been here since March
*¿Desde cuándo se **hace** eso? (se ha hecho eso)*	Since when have people been doing that?
*Desde entonces nada le **ha** durado mucho* (J. Marías, Spain; Lat. Am. . . . *nada le dura*)	Since then nothing has lasted long for him
*Lo **sé** desde que te vi en el hospital* (G. García Marquez, Colombia, dialogue; Spain *lo he sabido*)	I've known it since I saw you in the hospital

Events that are or were no longer in progress require a past tense, normally the compound tense (perfect, pluperfect) in Spain and the preterite in much of Latin America:

***He fumado** tres veces desde octubre/**Había fumado** tres veces desde entonces*	I have smoked three times since October/I had smoked three times since then
*Claro que **he vuelto** a hacerlo/**volví** a hacerlo desde entonces* (the preterite may be preferred in Lat. Am.)	Obviously I've done it again since then

Desde hace/desde hacía are required before plural nouns and before numbers. The compound tenses are possible in Peninsular Spanish:

*Me tranquilizo pensando que todos los adolescentes se **han comportado** exactamente igual desde hace tres mil años* (C. Rico-Godoy, Spain; *se comportan* possible in Spain, normal in Lat. Am.)	I console myself with the thought that all adolescents have been acting the same way for three thousand years

Eso es un campo de batalla desde hace un año (M. Vargas Llosa, Peru, dialogue; Spain also *ha sido*)	That's been a battle-field for a year now

Notes

(i) Literary styles often use a *-ra* or *-se* form of the verb after *desde* to indicate a past event: *Esta/Ésta es la primera vez que menciona el asunto desde que ingresara/ingresase/ingresó en la cárcel* 'This is the first time he has mentioned the matter since he entered prison'. This phenomenon is discussed further at 14.10.3.

(ii) The following Mexican example shows that other tenses may be used for events that are still in progress: *Desde que tenía diez años soñé con ser estrella de cine* (L. Spota, dialogue) 'Since I was ten I've dreamt of being a film-star'.

(iii) 'Since' may sometimes need to be translated by *hace que . . ./hacía que* with a past tense: *Hace ya ocho años que nos casamos* 'It's eight years since we (got) married'/'We got married eight years ago'.

(iv) *Desde* is sometimes used in Mexico and elsewhere in Latin America simply to emphasize the moment at which something happened: *Desde el martes llegó mi hermano* 'My brother arrived on Tuesday (already)'.[4]

32.4 Translating 'ago'

Hace/hacía with a preterite or pluperfect (or, in Spain, a perfect of recency – see 14.9.3) is the usual formula:

Le/Lo vi hace años	I saw him years ago
Lo había visto hacía años	I'd seen him years ago/before then
La he visto (Lat. Am. *La vi*) *hace un momento* (European Spanish perfect of recency)	I saw her a moment ago

Atrás is sometimes used in literary styles:

Lo repararon tiempo atrás	They mended it/fixed it some time ago
Le/Lo conocí días atrás	I met him some days ago

32.5 'In *n* days/weeks', etc.

Foreign students often misuse *dentro de* when translating the English 'in'. *Dentro de* can only refer to the future or the future in the past. One cannot say **Lo hice dentro de un año* 'I did it in one year' (i.e. *Lo hice en un año*).

—¿Cuándo empieza? —Dentro de tres días	'When does it start?' 'In three days' time'
Lo haré dentro de un momento	I'll do it in a moment
Me dijo que dentro de un año estaríamos casados	She/He told me that in a year's time we would be married
de hoy en ocho días	in eight days' time
Me faltan/quedan tres días para irme	I'm going in three days' time

Notes

(i) Use of *en* to mean *dentro de* is common in Latin America, much less common in Spain: *No te preocupes, vuelvo en un rato* (A. Mastretta, Mexico, dialogue) 'Don't worry, I'll be back in a minute'. Seco (1992), 170, says that this use of *en* for *dentro de* is an Anglicism. In the following correct sentence it does not mean *dentro de* but 'in the space of': *Lo haré en un momento* 'It'll only take me a moment to do it'.

(ii) *En* can be like the English 'in' in sentences like 'I've not been there in/for years':

---

[4] Example from J.M. Lope Blanch (1991), 18.

*Sabe usted que no nos hemos visto **en** doce años* (C. Fuentes, Mexico, dialogue) 'You know that we haven't seen one another in/for twelve years'.

32.6 'Again'

There are numerous ways of translating 'again':
(a) *Volver a . . .*
   This is probably the most usual construction before a verb:

Han vuelto a hacerlo	They've done it again
Cuando cerró la puerta volví a llorar (A. Mastretta, Mexico, dialogue)	When he shut the door, I started crying again
Como me vuelvas a hablar de esa manera . . . (this use of *como* is discussed at 25.8.2)	If you talk to me like that again . . .

(b) *Otra vez.*
   This also translates 'again':

Hazlo otra vez/Vuelve a hacerlo/Hazlo de nuevo	Do it again
No te lo digo otra vez/No te lo vuelvo a decir/No vuelvo a decírtelo	I won't tell you again
Otra vez no te lo digo	Another time I won't tell you/The next time I won't tell you

(c) *De nuevo* is more literary than *otra vez.*

De nuevo volvieron las suspicacias y los recelos	Once again suspicion and distrust returned

32.7 *Tardar*

Tardar, as well as meaning 'to be late' (*No tardes* 'Don't be late') may translate 'to take' in expressions of time:

Tardó un año en escribirnos	He took a year to write to us/He didn't write to us for a year
Tardará casi tres horas en acabarlo	He'll take nearly three hours to do it
Se tarda media hora andando	It takes an hour to walk it

Note
Llevar may also be used in certain expressions: *Eso te llevará horas* 'That'll take you hours', *Me llevó días* 'It took me days'; but *El viaje duró varias horas* 'The journey took several hours'.

32.8 'Still'

Todavía and *aún* are discussed at 31.7.3.
   A very frequent construction is *continuar* or *seguir* followed by the gerund (**continuar a hacer algo*, 'to continue to do something', French *continuer à faire quelquechose*, is not Spanish).
   Seguir is used before adjectives and participles, i.e. one says *Sigue enfermo* 'He's still ill' rather than *Continúa enfermo*.

Te has dado cuenta de que sigues llevando puesta la chaqueta del pijama (J-M. Merino, Spain, dialogue)	You've realized that you've still got your pyjama/(US) 'pajama' jacket on

Continuaban/Seguían viéndose	They went on seeing one another
Pero ella sigue soltera (C. Fuentes,	But she's still unmarried
Mexico, dialogue)	

32.9 Dates

Months are not written with a capital letter in Spanish.

The usual format is: *15 de mayo de 1999 = quince de mayo de mil novecientos noventa y nueve, 2 (dos) de mayo de 2002, 1 de abril de 1998,* the latter pronounced *primero de abril* or *uno de abril.* Some purists censure the use of *uno* but it is in general use, at least in Spain; Seco (1992), 196, has nothing against it.

The format of dates in Spain is the same as in Britain: dd-mm-yy. In Latin America there is a tendency to adopt the format mm-dd-yy when writing dates in full: *junio 17 de 1997,* Spain *17 de junio de 1999.*

When dates are written in numbers, the European format is used: Spain *3-IV-1998/3-4-1998,* Britain 3-4-(19)98, US 4-3-(19)98 = '3 April 1998'.

Typists often use a point after the thousands when writing years, *1.999,* but this is condemned by *El País* and by Seco (1992), 197.

32.10 Omission of preposition before certain expressions of time

The preposition is omitted before some words and expressions. These are:
(a) Days of the week

Nos vemos el lunes/el viernes	We're meeting on Monday/Friday

(b) With a demonstrative + *año/día/mañana/tarde/noche/vez*:

Aquel día/año llovió mucho	It rained a lot that day/year
Le/Lo vi esta mañana	I saw him this morning

In familiar Latin-American Spanish the preposition may also be omitted before some other words, as in *la ocasión que te vi* (Spain . . . *en que*) 'the occasion I saw you', . . . *cuando la mañana siguiente me anunció que . . .* (A. Mastretta, Mexico, Spain *a la mañana*) '. . . when the following morning he announced to me that . . .'.

33

Conjunctions

This chapter discusses the following words:

pero, sino, mas	but	33.1
o/u	or	33.2
y/e	and	33.3
que, de que	that	33.4
porque, pues, como	and other words meaning 'because', 'since . . .' 33.5.1	
ya que, puesto que, como	and other words meaning 'since'/'seeing that' 33.5.2	
aunque, y eso que	and other words meaning 'although' 33.6	
con tal de que, a menos que	and other expressions of condition and exception 33.7	
words indicating purpose	33.8	
de modo/manera que	and other words expressing result 33.9	

A large number of Spanish subordinating conjunctions, e.g. *cuando, sin que, después de que,* are associated with the subjunctive and are discussed in Chapter 16. They are merely noted in the appropriate section of this chapter.

33.1 *Pero, sino, mas*

All of these translate 'but'. *Mas* (no accent) is virtually extinct, but it is occasionally found in flowery written language and in the bad Spanish of students influenced by French or Portuguese.

The distinction between *pero* and *sino* is crucial:

(a) *Sino* is used in statements of the sort 'not A but B . . .'. It is almost always preceded by a negative statement and is very common in the construction *no sólo/solo . . . sino (que) . . .* 'not only . . . but . . .'. Before a verb phrase *sino que* must be used. Examples:

No quiero pan, sino vino	I don't want bread, but wine
no tú, sino él	not you, but him
no este/éste, sino ese/ése	not this one, but that
. . . mientras no ponía, sino que arrojaba las tazas sobre la bandeja (C. Rico-Godoy, Spain)	. . . while she was not so much putting as flinging the cups on the tray
Yo no dije que fuera mentira, sino que no lo creía	I didn't say it was a lie, but that I didn't believe it

(b) *Pero* is not possible in any of the above examples. *Pero* translates the English word 'but' in all other cases:

Habla francés, pero mal	He speaks French, but badly
No van a misa todos los días, pero rezan en sus cuartos	They don't go to Mass every day, but they do pray in their rooms
Pero ¿es posible?	But can it (really) be possible?

Notes
(i) *Sino* may sometimes be translated as 'except': *¿Qué puedo decir sino que lo siento?* 'What can I say but/except that I'm sorry?' . . . *ni él pudo entenderlo sino como un milagro del amor* (G. García Márquez, Colombia) 'even he couldn't understand it except as a miracle of love'.
(ii) *Sino* must not be confused (as it sometimes is in old texts) with *si no* 'if not'.
(iii) *No. . . sino* may translate 'only': *Yo no podía sino dar gracias a Dios . . .* 'I could only thank God', *No pensaba sino en ella/No pensaba más que en ella* 'He thought only of her', *El pueblo mexicano . . . no cree ya sino en la Virgen de Guadalupe y en la Lotería Nacional* (O. Paz, Mexico) 'The Mexican people . . . now believe in nothing but the Virgin of Guadalupe and the National Lottery'.

33.2 O

'Or'. It is written and pronounced *u* before a word beginning with *o* or *ho*: *hombres o mujeres* 'men or women', but *mujeres **u** hombres* 'women or men'. Spoken language often neglects to use *u*, and *o* is also sometimes retained if it is the first word in a sentence.

O . . . o translates 'either . . . or': *O lo sabe o no lo sabe* 'Either he knows it or he doesn't', *Os digo que u os apartáis, u os araño* (dialogue in a popular novel, Spain; *o os . . .* is more likely in spontaneous speech) 'I'm telling you, either you get out of my way, or I'll scratch you'.

Note
O should be written with an accent when it appears alongside a number to avoid confusion with zero: *6 ó 5* '6 or 5'. However, *El País* prints *6 o 5* on the grounds that no confusion is likely with *605*.

33.3 Y

'And'; used much like its English equivalent. It is written and pronounced *e* before a word beginning with a pure *i* sound, e.g. *Miguel **e** Ignacio, padre **e** hijos*, but not before words beginning with a *y* sound – *carbón y hierro* 'coal and iron' – and not when it means 'what about . . . ?': *¿Y Ignacio?* 'What about Ignacio?'. Substitution of *e* for *y* is not always made in spontaneous speech.

The use of *y* differs from the English 'and' in a few other respects:
(a) It is occasionally translatable as 'after' in sentences like:

Transcurrieron días y días sin tener más noticias de lo ocurrido[1]	Day after day passed without any further news being heard of what had happened (lit. 'without having news of')

[1] Example from Francisco Marsá (1986), 152. This sentence is a good example of a passive infinitive. See 18.5.

(b) As mentioned earlier, it often means 'what about. . . ?':

¿Y la democracia?	What about democracy?
¿Y qué?	So what?/Who cares?
¿Y el perro?	What about the dog?

33.4 Que

Que is an overworked word: it has at least four separate uses in Spanish:
(a) As a relative pronoun: *la mujer que vi* 'the woman that/whom I saw', *el año en que nací* 'the year I was born in'. This use is discussed in Chapter 35;
(b) *Qué* with an accent means 'what' and is best thought of as an entirely different word; it is discussed at 24.4;
(c) *Que* may mean 'than' in comparisons; see Chapter 5;
(d) As a subordinating conjunction; see the next section.

33.4.1 Que as a subordinating conjunction
Que introduces clauses in the same way as the English conjunction 'that'. It differs from the latter in that it cannot be omitted (see 33.4.6 for rare exceptions):

Dice que viene	He says (that) he's coming
Cree que no ha pagado	He thinks (that) he hasn't paid
Parece que va a llover	It seems (that) it's going to rain

However, the absence of a personal infinitive construction in Spanish makes this use of *que* much more common than the English 'that': *Quiero **que** vengas* 'I want you **to come**', *Te aconsejo **que** no lo hagas* 'I advise you not **to do** it', *Les pidió **que** no firmasen* 'He asked them not **to sign**'. Statements followed by *que* that require the subjunctive, for example *quiero que . . .* 'I want . . .', *es necesario que . . .* 'it's necessary that . . .', are discussed in Chapter 16.

33.4.2 *De before que*
In certain circumstances a subordinate clause must be introduced by *de que*. This is necessary:
(a) After noun phrases
This happens when *que* is a conjunction and not a relative pronoun. English does not clearly differentiate between the relative pronoun 'that' and the subordinating conjunction 'that': the phrase 'the idea **that** he liked . . .' is therefore ambiguous out of context. If 'that' can be replaced by 'which', *que* alone is possible in the Spanish translation. Compare:

the idea that/which he liked	*La idea **que** le gustaba . . .* (relative pronoun; *de que* impossible)
The idea that he likes mustard is absurd ('that' not replaceable by 'which')	*La idea **de que** le gusta la mostaza es absurda* (subordinating conjunction)

Further examples:

*Se dio cuenta **de que** ya no llovía*	He realized that it was no longer raining
*Cuando yo era chico y me desesperaba ante la idea **de que** mi madre debía morirse un día . . .* (E. Sábato, Argentina)	When I was a little boy and I despaired at the idea that my mother would have to die one day . . .
*Tenía miedo **de que** . . .*	He was afraid that . . .

*Soy partidario **de que** . . .*	I'm in favour of . . .
*el argumento **de que** . . .*	the argument that . . .
*la creencia **de que** . . .*	the belief that . . .
*la causa **de que** no llegara a tiempo*	the cause of his not arriving on time

(b) After a number of common verbs that require the preposition *de*

*Me acuerdo **de que** . . .*	I remember that . . .
*Me olvidaba **de que** . . .*	I was forgetting that . . .
*Estoy convencido **de que** . . .*	I'm convinced that . . .

and similarly after a number of verbs denoting mental or emotional states such as *aburrirse de que* . . . 'to be bored that . . .'. For a selection of these verbs see 16.6.1, list B.

(c) After certain adjectives and adverbial phrases that are normally followed by *de*

*Estoy seguro **de que** . . .*	I'm sure that . . .
*Estamos contentos **de que** . . .*	We're pleased that . . .
*Estoy cansado/harto **de que** . . .*	I'm tired/fed up with . . .
*Soy consciente **de que** . . .*	I'm aware that . . .
*Estoy hasta la coronilla **de que** . . .*	I'm sick to death with . . .

(d) After subordinators that include *de*

*antes **de que** llegase*	before he arrived
*después **de que** se fueron*	after they went
*a condición **de que** . . .*	on condition that . . .
*a cambio **de que** . . .*	in exchange for . . .
etc.	

Notes

(i) There is a colloquial tendency, much stronger in Latin America than in Spain, to drop the *de* in the more common of these constructions: *Wenceslao se había dado cuenta que la maniobra de Juvenal era extraviar a sus primos* (J. Donoso, Chile) 'Wenceslao had realized that Juvenal's maneouvre was (designed) to lead his cousins astray', . . . *pero estoy segura que es lo que haces* . . . (L. Goytisolo, Spain, dialogue) 'but I'm sure that that is what you're doing', *para que te convenzas que la dignidad no se come* . . . (G. García Márquez, Colombia, dialogue) 'to convince you (lit. so you convince yourself) that one can't eat dignity . . .'. In general, omission of *de* in such cases may be rejected as substandard by Peninsular speakers.

(ii) *Antes que* 'before' seems to be in more or less free variation with *antes de que* everywhere, cf. *Venda ese gallo antes que sea demasiado tarde* (G. García Márquez, Colombia, dialogue) 'Sell that cockerel before it's too late', *Lo conozco desde antes que tú nacieras* (M. Vargas Llosa, Peru, dialogue) 'I've known him since before you were born', *Antes que te cases, mira lo que haces* (Spanish proverb) 'Before you marry, look at what you're doing'. Peninsular informants found *antes que* acceptable in these sentences but much less common than *antes de que*.

33.4.3 Dequeísmo

There is a growing tendency on both continents to insert a redundant *de* after verbs denoting opinions or states of mind, e.g. *decir* 'say', *afirmar* 'claim', *creer* 'believe', *sostener* 'maintain', *negar* 'deny', *pensar* 'think', *confesar* 'confess', *argüir* 'argue', etc. Examples (a question mark denotes sentences that are considered sub-standard):

*?Dice **de que** no viene* (for *Dice que no viene*)	He says he's not coming
*?Creo **de que** no es verdad* (for *Creo que no es verdad*)	I think it's not true

This use of *de que* for *que* is vehemently rejected by educated speakers everywhere and should be avoided at all costs. It is especially frequent in some regions, notoriously Peru, where it is constantly heard on radio and TV.

Notes

(i) *Hablar de que* is correctly used colloquially for 'to talk about . . .' in such sentences as *Habló **de que** Miguel estaba enfermo* 'He talked about Miguel being ill'.

(ii) *Dudar de que* is a legitimate variant of *dudar que* 'to doubt': *Nadie dudó **(de) que** dijera la verdad*[2] 'No one doubted that he told the truth'.

(iii) The construction with *informar* is *informar a alguien de algo* 'to inform someone of something', so *Les informó **de que** no era cierto* is correct for 'He informed them it was not true'. However, *informar que* is also commonly heard.

33.4.4 *Que* at the head of a phrase

Que may appear at the head of a sentence, especially in speech. Its main functions are:

(a) To reinforce the idea that what follows expresses something expected, something repeated or something that is being insisted on. In this case a verb like *decir* or *preguntar* may have been omitted:

*¿**Que** cómo se llama mi película?*	(Did you ask) what's my film called?
¿Que si me gustó?	(Did you ask me) did I like it?
Que no quiero verla	(I said that) I don't want to see her/it
Oye, que aquí pone que no hay que abrirlo	Listen, it says here that it mustn't be opened
¡Que sí! ¡Que no!	Yes! No! (impatient repetition)

(b) As a colloquial subordinator of cause. It is often inserted to connect one idea to another where English uses a pause represented in writing by a dash:

*¡Deprisa! ¡Deprisa! ¡**Que** se va!*	Hurry! Hurry! It's going! (e.g. the train)
Habla más bajo, que es mi jefe	Talk softer – (s)he's my boss
¡¿Dónde está mi marido que lo degüello?!	Where's my husband – I'm going to slaughter him!
¡Socorro! ¡Que me ahogo!	Help! I'm drowning!
*No me des la lata con lo que dicen los lectores, **que** tengo cosas más importantes de que ocuparme* (C. Rico-Godoy in Cambio16, Spain)	Don't pester me with what the readers are saying – I've more important things to bother about

(c) Colloquially, to show that the truth has dawned after some doubt:

¡Ah! Que usted es el fontanero (Lat. Am. *plomero*)	Ah – so you're the plumber then
Que tú eres entonces el que lo hizo	So you're the one who did it then
¿Que no quieres ir conmigo?	You mean you don't want to go with me?

(d) To translate 'that' in colloquial sentences meaning 'It was so . . . that . . .'. In these sentences some word like *tanto* or *tan* has been deleted:

Tengo un sueño que no veo	I'm so tired I could drop (lit. 'that I can't see')
Estaba la habitación que no cabía un alfiler	The room was so crowded that a pin wouldn't fit/you couldn't get a pin in it

---

[2] Example from Francisco Marsá (1986), 155.

(e) With the subjunctive in commands, exhortations and wishes, e.g. *Que venga en seguida* 'Tell him to come/Have him come immediately'. See 17.6 for details.

(f) To mean 'the fact that', in which case it is likely to take the subjunctive. See 16.10.1 for further discussion.

33.4.5 *Que* in indirect questions

Decir que may mean 'to ask'. *Que* is also used optionally after *preguntar* 'to ask':

—*¿Sabes lo que me dijo este animal de bellota?* —*Te dijo* **que** *si estaba la cena lista* (C. Rico-Godoy, Spain, dialogue complaining about husbands)	'Do you know what this pig (lit. 'acorn animal') said to/asked me?' 'He asked you if dinner/supper was ready'
Yo me pregunto (que) dónde estará ella estudiando	I wonder where she's studying

33.4.6 Omission of conjunction *que*

Que is occasionally omitted, but much less so than the English 'that':

(a) If the following verb is in the subjunctive, and especially with the verb *rogar que* 'to request'. This construction is practically confined to business letters and other official language; it is aso found in substandard language:

Les agradeceríamos (que) comunicasen a su sucursal de Sevilla . . .	We would be obliged if you would inform your Seville branch . . .
Les ruego envíen más información sobre la máquina de escribir ES 3 (advertisement in *Cambio16*, Spain)	Please send more information about the ES 3 typewriter
No importa le tilden de bufón (Popular press, Spain; substandard for *no importa que le tilden . . .*)	It doesn't matter if they dub him a clown

Such omission is best avoided by the foreign student.

(b) In relative clauses introduced by *que* so as to avoid too many *que*s. This is probably confined to written language ('#' marks the point of omission):

Desde este punto de vista, que pienso # comparten muchos españoles . . .	From this point of view, which I think many Spaniards share . . .
Me contestó con una serie de argumentos que supongo # están de moda hoy día	She replied with a series of arguments which I suppose are fashionable nowadays

33.4.7 Replacement of subordinating *que* by an infinitive

For a discussion of sentences like *Dice estar enferma* 'She says she's ill' (for *Dice que está enferma*) see 18.2.2.

33.4.8 Miscellaneous examples of *que*

The bracket indicates that the *que* is optional:

Qué bien (que) lo hemos pasado (the redundant *que* sounds uneducated)	What a nice time we've had
. . . y él habla **que** *habla* (colloquial)	and he kept talking away . . .
Yo venga a pedirle el divorcio y él **que** *no* (*venga a* is a colloquial Peninsular form suggesting constant repetition)	I kept on asking him for a divorce and he wouldn't have it/kept saying no

*Lucho por conseguir comprensión, **(que)** no amor*	I'm struggling to get understanding, not love
Le pregunté (que) qué hacía allí	I asked him what he was doing there
*¡Cuidado **que** sois pesados!*	Heavens, are you a nuisance!

✓ 33.5 Causal conjunctions

The most common are:

porque	because
como	since, as
pues	for (= 'because')
ya que	since
puesto que	since
en vista de que	in view of the fact that

33.5.1 *Porque*

Porque means 'because'; *por qué*, spelt and pronounced differently, means 'why'. The noun *el porqué* means 'the reason why'.

    Porque may occasionally require the subjunctive. See 16.12.3b.

    The difference between *porque* 'because' and *por qué* 'why' is crucial: *No sabe, porque es tan ignorante* 'He doesn't know because he's so ignorant', *No sabe por qué es tan ignorante* 'He doesn't know **why** he's so ignorant'.

Notes
(i) *Porque* may also be found as an optional alternative to *para que* after those words which allow *por*, e.g. *esforzarse por* 'to make an effort to . . .' (see the section on *por* and *para* 34.14). For *por qué* and *para qué* 'why', see 24.10.
(ii) *Por* is intimately associated with the idea of cause, e.g. *Te lo mereces, **por** tonto* 'Serves you right for being stupid', *Se perdieron **por** no haber comprado un mapa* 'They got lost as a result of not having bought a map'. See 34.14.4 for more examples.
(iii) *Porque* and *por qué* can never be used to translate 'that's why' or 'that's the reason why'; see 36.2.4.

33.5.2 *Como, ya que, puesto que, que, en vista de que*

All of these may translate 'since'. *Que* is discussed under 33.4.

Puesto/Ya que quieres que me vaya, me voy	Since you want me to go, I'm leaving
La reunión se aplazó en vista de que no vino casi nadie	The meeting was postponed in view of the fact that hardly anybody turned up

    Care is required with the word *como* when it is used to mean 'since'/'because'. When used thus it can appear only at the head of the phrase it refers to. **Yo no comía como no tenía apetito* is not Spanish, but *Como no tenía apetito, yo no comía* 'As I had no appetite, I didn't eat' is correct:

Como/Ya que quieres que me vaya me voy	Since you want me to go, I'm going

Compare *No lo hice como me dijiste* 'I didn't do it the way you told me to', and *No lo hice, como me lo dijiste* (example from *Libro de estilo de El País*) 'I didn't do it, just as you told me' (i.e. 'because you told me not to'). Further examples:

Es de peor educación todavía insinuar que, como soy una mujer, se supone que no soy nadie (C. Rico-Godoy, Spain, dialogue)	It's even more ill-mannered to hint that, since I'm a woman, it's assumed that I'm nobody
Luego, como veía que no llegaban . . .	Then, since he could see that they weren't coming . . .

Pero, como yo no sabía qué hacer . . .   But since I didn't know what to do . . .

Note
Como with the subjunctive translates 'if' in conditional sentences; see 25.8.2.

33.5.3 *Pues*
Pues has numerous uses, but its basic function is probably to show that what follows is inspired by something said just before, or that the speaker has reflected a moment before continuing.

(a) *Pues* meaning 'because'

Pues should be employed very sparingly as a causal conjunction meaning 'because': Gili y Gaya (1972), 15, caustically observes that 'discovery of causal *pues* as a way of adding a certain literary flourish to one's style is typical of writing between childhood and adolescence . . . This phase does not usually last long'.

Pues may be an elegant written variation on *porque* in the hands of a good stylist, just as 'for' is an occasional flowery variant for 'because' in English ('It cannot be done, **for** there is no money'); but non-natives should probably stick to *porque, ya que* or *puesto que*: *La voz no se sabe si es femenina o de hombre, **pues** es aguda, verdaderamente penetrante* (J.-M. Arguedas, Peru) 'You can't tell whether the voice is a woman's or a man's, for it is high-pitched, truly piercing'.

(b) 'In that case . . .'

*—No queremos comer ahora. —**Pues**, cuando ustedes quieran . . .* (or *entonces/en ese caso*)	'We don't want to eat now.' 'In that case, when you like . . .'
—No quiero estar aquí. —Pues vete	'I don't want to be here.' 'Go away then'

(c) Like the English 'well', it may down-tone an answer to a question, adding a modest or tentative note or perhaps showing that the speaker has reflected a moment before answering:

*—¿En qué situación se encuentran las negociaciones entre los dos gobiernos? —**Pues**, el hecho es que no hay negociaciones . . .* (interview, *Cambio16*, Spain)	'What is the state of the negotiations between the two governments?' 'Well, the fact is there are no negotiations . . .'
*—¿Quiénes estaban? —**Pues** . . . Manuel, Antonio, Mariluz . . .*	'Who was there?' 'Er . . . Manuel, Antonio, Mariluz . . .'

(d) It may add emphasis or a note of contradiction:

*—Yo creía que estaba enfermo. —**Pues** no*	'I thought he was ill.' 'Well he isn't'
*No, si ya me figuro dónde está. ¡**Pues** me va a oír!* (A. Buero Vallejo, Spain, dialogue)	No, I can well imagine where she is. Well, she's going to hear what I've got to say!

Notes
(i) In some parts of Latin America and Northern Spain, conversation is sprinkled with *pues*: *oye pues, vámonos pues*, etc.
(ii) Students of French should not confuse *pues* with *puis* which is translated as *después, entonces* and *luego*.

33.6 Concession

33.6.1 Phrases that introduce concessions ('although', etc.)

The main ways of introducing a concession are as follows (asterisked forms are typical of literary language):

aunque/bien que/y eso que/así/aun cuando	although/even though/even in the event that
a pesar de que/pese a que*/por más que/ a despecho de que*	despite the fact that
por mucho que	however much

All of these, except *y eso que*, may appear with the subjunctive and are discussed at 16.12.8. *Por mucho que* is discussed at 16.13.2.

33.6.2 *Y eso que*

Y eso que is stylistically informal and does not take the subjunctive. It can only refer to events that are realities, i.e. it means 'despite **the fact** that': *No la reconocí, **y eso que** la había visto dos días antes* 'I didn't recognise her although/despite the fact that I'd seen her two days before':

. . . *y eso que lo había visto saltar hasta los zapatos* (J. Cortázar, Argentina, dialogue)	. . . even though I'd seen it bounce down to my shoes
. . . *y eso que devolvió de forma increíble varias bolas* (*El País*)	. . . despite the fact that he made some incredible returns (in tennis)

33.7 Condition and exception

(a) The main conjunctions of condition are (all require the subjunctive and are discussed under 16.12.7a):

con tal (de) que	as long as/provided that
a condición de que	on condition that
bajo (la) condición de que	under the condition that
siempre que	as long as
siempre y cuando	provided always that
mientras (no)	as long as
como	as long as

(b) Conjunctions of exception are (all mean 'unless' and are discussed at 16.12.7b):

a menos que	*excepto que/salvo que*
a no ser que	*como no* . . .
fuera de que	*si no* (if not)

33.8 Subordinating conjunctions of purpose and aim

The most common are:

'in order that'	'so that'
para que	*de manera que**
porque	*de modo que**
a que	*de forma que**
a fin de que	'lest'
con el objeto de que	*no sea/fuera/fuese que*

All conjunctions of purpose require the subjunctive and are discussed under 16.12.2. Those that have asterisks may also indicate result and are then followed by the indicative. See 16.12.4 for discussion.

33.9 Subordinating conjunctions of result

Subordinators that express manner can denote either a result or an aim. In the latter case they take the subjunctive. The most common are:

de modo que/de manera que/de forma que/así que	so that (i.e. 'in such a way that')
conque . . .	so . . .

These are discussed under 16.12.4, but it should be noted that the phrases *de **tal** modo que, de **tal** manera que, de **tal** forma que* can only express result, not purpose:

Gritó de tal modo/manera/forma que todos los vecinos se asomaron a la ventana	He shouted in such a way that all the neighbours leaned out of their windows

33.10 Subordinating conjunctions of time

These include such words and phrases as:

a la vez que	at the same time as
a partir del momento en que	from the moment that
a poco de que	shortly after
al mismo tiempo	at the same time as
al poco rato de que	shortly after
antes de que	before
apenas	scarcely
así que	as soon as
cada vez que	every time that
cuando	when
después de que	after
en cuanto	as soon as
en tanto que	as long as
hasta que	until
mientras	while/as long as
nada más que	as soon as
no bien que	scarcely
siempre que	whenever/as long as
tan pronto como	as soon as
una vez que	once/as soon as

All subordinators of time require the subjunctive in certain circumstances (*antes de que* always take the subjunctive). They are discussed at 16.12.6.

For further remarks on *cuando* see 24.8.

34

Prepositions

The following prepositions are discussed in this chapter:

a	de	hacia	según
ante	desde	hasta	sin
bajo	durante	mediante	sobre
con	en	para	tras
contra	entre	por	

Many of these can be combined with other words to form prepositional phrases such as *debajo de* 'underneath', *frente a* 'opposite', *a razón de* 'at the rate of', etc. A list of these phrases is included at 34.19.

Prepositional usage is more subject than other areas of syntax to the vagaries of linguistic change, and the whole subject is plagued with quibbles and doubts. In this chapter special emphasis is given to aspects of Spanish prepositional usage that are likely to be unfamiliar to English-speakers.

34.1 *A*

This very common preposition has many uses. Apart from the problems they have with Personal *a*, discussed in Chapter 22, English speakers tend to misuse it when translating phrases like 'at the dentist's', 'at Cambridge', 'at the station'. See **(d)** for discussion.

(a) Motion, 'to', 'at', 'up', 'down', etc.

Almost any verb of motion is likely to be followed by *a*. As a result its meanings include 'on', 'into', 'onto', 'down', 'up', as well as 'to' and 'at'.

Por fin llegaron a Managua	They finally got to Managua
Fui a/para que me diera hora	I went to make an appointment
Bajó al sótano	He went down to the basement
Se acercó al buzón	He approached the letter box
Me subí al coche/al tren	I got into the car/on the train
Lanzaban piedras a/contra las ventanas	They were throwing stones at the windows
Arrojó la espada al aire	He hurled the sword into the air
Entró a/para saludarnos	He came in to say hello to us
Ha venido a/para/por hablar con usted	He's come to talk to you
Lo pegó al/en el sobre	She stuck it on the envelope
Cuélgaselo al cuello	Hang it round his neck
(cf. *Cuélgalo **en** la pared*	Hang it on the wall)

Cayó al suelo/al mar	It fell to the ground/into the sea
Se tiró al vacío	He threw himself into the void
una expedición a Marte	an expedition to Mars
salida a la calle	way out to the street
tiro al blanco	target shooting

Notes

(i) *A* is omitted after verbs of motion before *aquí, acá, ahí, allí, allá*: *Ven aquí/acá/(Ven para acá)* 'Come here', *Allá voy/Voy para allá* 'I'm going there'.

(ii) Cf. Spain *entrar* **en** *el cuarto*, Latin America *entrar* **al** *cuarto* 'to enter the room', although *entrar a* is also heard in Spain. The noun takes *a*: *entrada a la galería* 'entrance to the gallery'. Spain also prefers *en* with *penetrar* 'penetrate', *ingresar* 'to join' (club, etc.), *introducir* 'to insert', but the use of *a* is widespread in Latin America, cf. *Ingresa como adepto laico a la orden* (J.L. Borges) 'He entered (historic present) the order as a lay follower'.

(iii) *Para* is also found colloquially after *ir*: *Voy para Lugo* 'I'm heading for Lugo'.

(b) Direction, 'at'

Mira al techo y no te entrará agua en los ojos	Look at the ceiling and you won't get water in your eyes

(c) After verbs of giving, sending, informing, etc.

Dáselo a papá	Give it to father
Le envió cien dólares a su hijo	He sent his son $100
Comunicaremos los datos a los aseguradores	We shall inform the insurers of the details

Note

For the use of the redundant pronoun in the first two of these examples see 11.16.2.

(d) Place (static)

The use of *a* to indicate 'at' or 'in' a place is very limited in Spanish. English-speakers – particularly those who know French, German or Italian – must avoid the use of *a* in sentences like *Estoy haciendo mis estudios* **en** *Cambridge* 'I'm studying at Cambridge', *Te esperaré* **en** *la estación* 'I'll wait for you at the station (à la gare, am Bahnhof,* etc.), *Vive* **en** *Londres = Il habite à Londres,* etc. Apart from set phrases like *al lado de* 'at the side of', *a la luz de* 'in the light of', *a* can only be used with a few nouns like *vuelta*, 'turn', *salida* 'exit', *entrada* 'entrance' which denote actions or moments in time rather than places. *Os esperaré a la salida* is best thought of as 'I'll wait for you on the way out' rather than 'at the exit', which is *en la salida*.

In phrases like *Estaba asomado a la ventana* 'He was leaning in/out of the window' *asomar* is a verb of motion: *Estaba en la ventana* is, however, safer than *Estaba a la ventana* 'He was at the window'. The sentence *Fue a estudiar a París* is only a variant of *Fue a París a estudiar* 'He went to Paris to study'; it does not mean 'He went to study at Paris' – . . . *en París*.

A is used to translate 'at' in a number of situations involving close proximity to an object, e.g. *a la barra* 'at the bar', *a la mesa* 'at table' (i.e. 'at mealtime'); but note *Se sienta* **en** *una mesa de la calle y pide una cerveza* (J. Cortázar, Argentina) 'He sits down at a table in the street and asks for a beer':

Vivo a la vuelta	I live round the corner
a orillas del mar	on the sea shore
Oí pasos a mi espalda	I heard footsteps at my back
a mi lado (cf. *de mi lado*, 'on my side')	at my side

Se pasa horas sentado al ordenador	He spends hours sitting at the computer
Se arrodilló a los pies de la Virgen	He knelt at the feet of the Virgin
Está con el agua al cuello	He's up to his neck (in troubles: *hasta* implies real water)
a la izquierda/derecha de	to the left/right of
a lo lejos/en la distancia	in the distance
Se sentaron al sol/a la luz/al calor del fuego/	They sat in the sun/light/warmth of the
a la sombra/al amparo de un roble	fire/shade/in the shelter of an oak

Compare:

Espérame en la parada del autobús	Wait for me at the bus stop
Estaba parado en un semáforo	He was waiting at a traffic light
Mario está en el banco	Mario is at/in the bank
Los niños están en el colegio	The children are in/at school
(cf. *Mi hijo todavía no va al colegio*)	My son isn't at school yet (i.e. doesn't go yet)
La vi en la puerta de la iglesia	I saw her at the church door

Notes
(i) *A la puerta* is good Spanish, but we found that some American informants preferred *en* – but cf. *Morelli habla del napolitano que se pasó años sentado a la puerta de su casa . . .* (J. Cortázar, Argentina) 'Morelli speaks of the Neapolitan who spent years sitting at the door of his house . . .'.
(ii) Spanish thus has no prepositions that can differentiate 'He's at the hospital' and 'He's in (the) hospital': verbs are used instead – *Ha ido al hospital* and *Está en el hospital.*

(e) Manner (adverbial phrases of manner with *a* are numerous)

a pie/a mano/a lápiz	on foot/by hand/in pencil
a golpes/a tiros/a patadas/a gritos	with blows/by shooting/with kicks/by shouting
un documento escrito a máquina	a typed document
El servicio es a voluntad del cliente	Service charge at the customer's discretion
Las patatas están a punto	The potatoes are done
Le cortaron el pelo al rape	They cropped his hair short
Estoy a dieta	I'm on a diet
a oscuras/a la luz del día	in the dark/by daylight
La carpa se puede asar a la parrilla	Carp may be grilled

Note
The curious construction with *a* found in the phrase *Sois dos a ganar* 'There are two of you earning' may perhaps be included under this heading.

(f) In certain time phrases

A is particularly common in the construction *al* + infinitive where it means 'on . . .-ing', e.g. *al ver* 'on seeing', *al volverse* 'as he turned round/back':

a las diez/a medianoche	at 10 o'clock/at midnight
Se cansa a los cinco minutos	He gets tired after five minutes
bonos del Estado a diez años	ten-year Government bonds
Se casaron a los veinte años (*Se casaron con veinte años*)	They got married at the age of twenty
al día siguiente/al otro día	on the following day
a la mañana siguiente	the following morning
al mismo tiempo	at the same time
a su regreso, a su llegada	on his return, on his arrival
Estamos a miércoles/a quince	It's Wednesday/the fifteenth

tres veces al/por día
Al amanecer ya se habían marchado

three times a day
They were gone by dawn

Note
Ya deben estar al llegar 'They must be about to arrive'.

(g) To translate 'of' or 'like' after verbs meaning 'smell', 'taste', 'sound', and also after the nouns derived from some of these:

Me suena a cuento chino
Esto sabe a pescado
Había un leve olor a fritura y a crema
bronceadora (F. Umbral, Spain)
La ginebra tiene un sabor a agua de colonia

It sounds like a tall story to me
This tastes of fish
There was a faint smell of frying and
suntan cream
Gin has a taste like Eau de Cologne

(h) 'Fitted with', 'propelled by'

Grammarians reject *a* as a Gallicism in the following constructions, but most of them are normal in everyday language:

olla a presión
caldera a/de gas-oil
motor a/de dos tiempos
un suplemento a color (El País; also *en color*)
un avión a/de dos motores
un coche que va a/por metanol

pressure cooker
oil-fired boiler
two-stroke motor
a colour supplement
a twin-engined plane
a methanol-powered car

Note
The use of *a* to denote an ingredient is occasionally seen in advertising language but it should not be imitated: *crema bronceadora a lanolina* 'sun-tan cream with Lanoline' (better *con lanolina*).

(i) Rate, measure, speed, amount, distance

Se vende a mil pesos el metro
¿A cómo están las peras?
Volaba a más de dos mil kilómetros por hora

Compraba tebeos de segunda mano que luego
revendía o cambiaba a razón de dos por uno
(L. Goytisolo, Spain)
Está a cinco manzanas (Lat Am *cuadras*) *de*
aquí
a montones
frutas al por mayor
Trabaja a ratos/a veces

It's on sale at 1000 pesos a metre
How much are the pears?
It was flying at more than 2000 km per
hour
He used to buy second-hand comics
which he then resold or swapped at the
rate of two for one
It's five blocks from here

in heaps
wholesale fruit
He works now and again/sometimes

(j) It translates 'from' after a number of words with such meanings as 'steal', 'confiscate', 'buy', and after *oír* 'to hear':

Le robaron una sortija a mi tía
Le compró un coche a su vecino
La policía se instaló en el piso ocupado al
acusado
Se lo oí decir a Amparo

They stole a ring from my aunt
He bought a car from his neighbour
The police moved into the flat/apartment
confiscated from the accused
I heard Amparo say it

and similarly verbs such as *quitar* 'to take away', *sustraer* 'to steal', *confiscar* 'to confiscate', *llevarse* 'to take away', *sacar* 'to take out/remove', etc. However, *recibir* 'to receive', *adquirir* 'to acquire' and *aceptar* 'to accept' take *de*: *aceptar algo de alguien* 'to accept something from someone'.

Note also: *Le encontraron cien pesos a tu primo* 'They found a hundred pesos on your cousin'.

(k) Before certain types of direct object (the so-called 'personal *a*', e.g. *Vi al gitano* 'I saw the gypsy'). See Chapter 22 for detailed discussion.

(l) After verbs meaning 'begin', 'start', 'get ready to . . .'

Rompió a llorar	He burst into tears
Echó a correr	He broke into a run
El cielo empezaba a despejarse	The sky was beginning to clear

and similarly after *comenzar a* 'to begin', *ponerse a* 'to start to', *prepararse a* 'to get ready to', *disponerse a* 'to prepare oneself to'.

(m) After numerous verbs, adjectives and adverbs which must be learned separately, e.g.

Tendían emboscadas a las Ninfas (J.L. Borges, Argentina)	They laid ambushes for the Nymphs
Aspiraba a hacerse médico	He was aiming to become a doctor
Tienes que hacerte al trabajo	You have to get used to the work
Prefiero una vida mediocre a ser héroe	I prefer a mediocre life to being a hero
Te ayudaré a apretar las tuercas	I'll help you tighten the nuts
el viejo argumento de que la religión sirve de freno a los instintos	the old argument that religion serves as a curb on the instincts
jugar al fútbol/al hockey	to play soccer/hockey
tocar algo al acordeón/a la guitarra	to play something on the accordion/guitar
Pudo salvarse agarrándose a/de un árbol	He managed to save himself by clinging to a tree
No hay otro igual a él	There is no other equal to him
Tenía el jersey liado en torno a la cintura	He had his jersey tied round his waist
Es muy parecido al de ayer	It's very much like the one from yesterday

For a list of verbs used with the infinitive see 18.2.3.

(n) To link two nouns whenever ambiguity might arise from the use of *de*. Compare *el amor de Dios* = 'God's love' and *el amor a Dios* 'love for God'. Often either preposition is possible.

A is also frequently used to link two nouns when a common verbal phrase exists which also requires *a*, e.g. *Les tiene miedo a los toros* 'He's afraid of bulls', *su miedo a los toros* 'his fear of bulls':

el amor a la patria	love for one's home country
La Casa Blanca confirmó el boicot a los Juegos de Moscú (Cambio16, Spain)	The White House confirmed the boycott of the Moscow Games
el respeto a la autoridad	respect for authority
Lo denunciaron como traidor a/de su clase	They denounced him as a traitor to his class
Insinué algo en el prólogo al libro de Lafaye . . . (O. Paz, Mexico; del possible)	I hinted something in the prologue to Lafaye's book . . .
El culto al sol tendría sus ventajas	Sun-worship would have its advantages
El departamento se encargará de la protección a/de la carretera	The department will take over responsibility for protecting roads
El ataque a la ciudad costó muchas vidas	The attack on the city cost many lives

34.2 *Ante*

'Before' (i.e. 'in front of') or 'in the presence of', and like its English equivalent it can in literary usage have a spatial meaning, 'facing'/'in front of'; *frente a* or *delante de* are used in ordinary language. *Delante de* makes clear that position rather than 'presence' is implied, cf. *justificarse ante Dios* 'to justify oneself before God', but *arrodillarse delante de/ante la Virgen* 'to kneel before (a statue of) the Virgin'.

Ante is very common in the figurative meaning of 'faced with', 'in the face of'. It must not be confused with the entirely separate word *antes* 'before' (in time):

El taxi paró ante/frente a/delante de la casa	The taxi stopped in front of the house
ante este dilema . . .	faced with this dilemma . . .
ante tamaño insulto . . .	in the face of such an insult . . .
Ante tantas posibilidades, no sabía cuál escoger	Faced with so many possibilities, he didn't know which to choose
Ante todo, quisiera agradecer al organizador . . .	Above all, I would like to thank the organizer . . .

Notes
(i) *Frente a* for *ante* in phrases like *frente a estos problemas* seems to be spreading, but for some it still sounds like 'in front of these problems'.
(ii) For details about *delante de*, see 31.6.8.

34.3 *Bajo*

'Beneath' or 'under'. It may be a literary variant of *debajo de* 'underneath' (discussed at 31.6.6), but in this sense it is spatially less specific (cf. 'under' and 'underneath'): *Se resguardaron bajo un haya* 'They sheltered under/beneath a beech tree' but *Enterró el botín debajo de un roble* 'He buried the loot underneath (i.e. under the roots of) an oak tree'.

Carnicer notes that for those educated speakers who use *bajo*, the difference is that it implies 'a good distance under' or 'under but not close to or touching' – *bajo una masa de nubes* 'under a mass of clouds', *No me quedo ni un minuto más bajo este techo* 'I'm not staying one more minute under this roof' – whereas *debajo de* implies 'underneath and close to whatever is on top': *Hay mucho polvo debajo de la alfombra* 'There's a lot of dust underneath the carpet'.

Thus ?*El perro está bajo la silla* 'The dog's beneath the chair' sounds affected in both languages: *debajo de la silla* 'under(neath) the chair'.

Bajo must be used in the figurative sense of 'under' in phrases like *bajo el gobierno de* 'under the government of', *bajo ciertas condiciones* 'under certain conditions', etc.

Yo prefiero sentarme bajo el (or al) sol/ bajo las estrellas/la lluvia/un cielo azul	I prefer to sit in the sun beneath the stars/in the rain/beneath a blue sky
bajo tierra (or debajo de la tierra)	underground
bajo la monarquía/la república/el socialismo	under the monarchy/republic/socialism
La temperatura alcanzó treinta bajo cero	The temperature reached thirty below zero
bajo los efectos de la anestesia	under the effects of the anaesthetic
bajo juramento/pena de muerte/órdenes	under oath/sentence of death/orders

Note
Abajo de is often heard for *debajo de* in Latin America, but it is not accepted in Spain.

34.4 *Cabe*

An archaic or rustic equivalent of *junto a*, *cerca de* 'by'/'near' occasionally still found in Latin-American authors.

34.5 *Con*

(a) In many contexts it coincides with the English 'with', but it is used more widely than the latter.

Phrases like 'the boy with the blue Mercedes' require *de*: *el chico del Mercedes azul*. But if 'wearing' or 'carrying' are implied, *con* is usual unless the article is habitually associated with the person: cf. *Nunca te he visto con gafas* 'I've never seen you with glasses', but *¿Te acuerdas del viejo **del** impermeable que venía todos los días?* 'Do you remember the old man with/in the raincoat who used to come every day?'.

Fui a la reunión con Niso	I went to the meeting with Niso
Yo sí te he visto con camisa de seda	I have seen you in a silk shirt
Está escrito con/a lápiz	It's written with a/in pencil
Con lo enferma que está . . .	and with her being so ill . . .
té con miel/café con leche	tea with honey/coffee with milk
Se produjeron varios enfrentamientos con la policía	There were several clashes with the police
Se levantó con el sol	He got up with the sun
con la llegada del otoño	with the arrival of autumn

Notes
(i) *Con* cannot be used in combination with the nominalizer *el*: Contrast *el chico con la americana blanca* – *el **de** la americana blanca* 'the boy with/in the white jacket' – 'the one with/in the white jacket'. Phrases like **el con gafas* are not Spanish.
(ii) *Con* differs from *a* in phrases like *con la llegada de la primavera* 'with the arrival of spring' in that *a la llegada* implies 'at the moment of the arrival of', which is too punctual for the onset of a season. Compare: *Todos se marcharon **a** la llegada de la policía* 'They all left on the arrival of the police ', ***Con** la llegada de Pepe, todo empezó a cambiar* 'With Pepe's arrival, everything began to change'.

(b) After phrases meaning 'to show an attitude towards' *con* alternates with *para con*, much as 'with' alternates with 'towards':

Es muy cariñoso (para) con su mujer	He's very affectionate towards/with his wife
Su amabilidad es igual (para) con todos	His kindness is the same towards all

But if the object of the attitude does not benefit by it, *para* is not used:

Es muy crítico con su hijo	He's very critical with/towards his son
Eres muy cruel con tu novia	You're very cruel to your girlfriend

(c) It may be used with expressions signifying meeting, encounter, collision, 'facing up to', 'struggle with', etc.

Me encontré/tropecé hoy con tu jefe	I ran into/met your boss today
Ha vuelto con su marido (*ha vuelto a* is not used in this sense)	She's gone back to her husband (or 'She's come back with her husband')

Tengo que vérmelas con el vecino	I'll have to have it out with the neighbour (i.e. have a frank talk)
Iba en la moto y se dio un golpe con/contra un poste	He was on his motorbike and crashed into a post
Mi bicicleta rozó con un camión	My bicycle scraped against a lorry
Tendremos que enfrentarnos con el problema/enfrentar el problema	We'll have to face up to the problem
Los ingleses suelen dudar con el subjuntivo	English people usually hesitate over the subjunctive
Estamos luchando con el problema del paro	We're struggling with the problem of unemployment
Está regañado con sus tíos	He's fallen out with his uncle and aunt

(d) It may – strangely to English-speakers – mean 'containing':

un vaso con/de agua, un saco con/de patatas	a glass of water/sack of potatoes
Llevaba una cesta con pan, huevos, uvas y vino (*de* is not possible here)	He was carrying a basket of bread, eggs, grapes and wine
una jeringa con morfina	a syringe full of morphine

Note

This use eliminates any ambiguity caused by *de*, which either means 'full of' – *una cesta de huevos* is 'a basketful of eggs' and it cannot contain anything else – or may denote the container but not the contents, cf. *una botella de coñac* 'a bottle of cognac' or 'a cognac bottle'; but *una botella con coñac* 'a bottle with cognac in it'.

(e) 'Despite' or some other concessive phrase (*a pesar de* is often an equivalent):

Con/A pesar de todos sus esfuerzos, nunca llegó a coronel	Despite/for all his efforts, he never made the rank of colonel
Con todo, la vida no es tan terrible	Despite everything, life isn't so awful
Con lo guapa que estarías con el pelo recogido . . .	To think how attractive you'd look if you had your hair up . . .

(f) *Con* plus an infinitive may, like the gerund, have a conditional sense:

Con hacer (or *haciendo*) *lo que yo os digo, todo irá bien*	Provided you (pl.) do what I say everything will go well
Sólo con pulsar una tecla el ordenador almacena los datos	If you simply press a key the computer stores the data

Note

A subjunctive may also follow *con* in this conditional meaning but it has to be preceded by *que*. This must not be confused with the conjunction *conque* or with *con* plus a relative pronoun: *Con que me pagaran mis gastos me conformaba* 'I would be quite happy if they paid my expenses'.

(g) It may, like the gerund, mean 'as a result of':

Se nos ha ido la tarde con hablar/hablando	The afternoon's gone with all this talking
No conseguirás nada con tratarme/ tratándome de esa manera	You'll achieve nothing by treating me that way

(h) It may indicate the cause or origin of a condition:

Estamos muy entusiasmados/ilusionados con la perspectiva de un nuevo gobierno	We're very excited about the prospect of a new government

Compare *Me preocupo **por** ellos* 'I worry about them', and *Me preocupo **de** hacer todo lo posible* 'I take care to do everything possible'.

Se puso enfermo con malaria (or *Enfermó de malaria*, Lat. Am. *se enfermó*)	He fell ill with/from malaria

Se mareó con el vaivén del tren	He felt nauseated/(British) 'sick' because of the swaying of the train
Se alegró con/de la noticia del nacimiento de su nieto	He cheered up at the news of his grandson's birth

Notes

Miscellaneous examples of *con* used in ways unfamiliar to English speakers: *Hace años que él se escribe con ella* 'He and she have been writing to one another for years', *Murió con más de setenta años* 'He died aged more than seventy', *Usted fue el último que le/lo vio con vida* 'You were the last one to see him alive', *Voy a verme con ella esta noche* 'I'm seeing her tonight'.

34.6 *Contra*

A close equivalent of 'against', but it may mean 'at' after verbs meaning firing, throwing, launching, etc.

En contra de is an equivalent of *contra* when the latter means 'in opposition to'; it becomes *en contra de que* before a verb. Use of a possessive instead of a prepositional pronoun is permitted with *en contra*: *Se están organizando en contra tuya/en contra de ti* 'They're organizing themselves against you'.

El régimen ha organizado una campaña contra/en contra de la corrupción	The regime has organized a campaign against corruption
Contra lo que creen algunos, yo no soy pesimista	Despite/to the contrary of what some believe, I am not a pessimist
Apoya tu pala contra el árbol	Lean your spade against the tree
lanzar un misil contra . . .	to launch a missile at . . .
Lanzó la piedra contra el árbol (cf. *La lanzó al árbol* 'He threw it up at the tree', e.g. a lasso or rope)	He threw the stone at the tree
Conviene inyectarse contra la hepatitis antes de viajar a esas regiones (not **inyectarse para . . .*)	It's a good idea to get immunized against/for hepatitis before travelling to those regions
Navegábamos contra viento y marea	We were sailing against wind and tide
Hay que dejar un depósito contra el valor del coche (or *por el coche . . .*)	You have to leave a deposit against the value of the car
¿Está usted en contra de que lo hagan?	Are you against them doing it?

Notes

(i) For *contra mí*, *en contra tuya*, etc. 'against me'/'against you' see note to 8.7.

(ii) The use of *contra* for *cuanto* in such phrases as *Cuanto más trabajas, más te dan* 'The more you work, the more they give you', heard in popular speech everywhere, should be avoided. See 5.11 for details.

34.7 *De*

34.7.I General uses

Section (a) covers those uses of *de* which correspond to the English 'of' or to the genitive ending 's: these sentences should give English speakers no great problems. French speakers must resist the temptation to replace *de* by *a*: *C'est à vous?* = *¿Es de usted?* 'Is it yours?'.

(a) 'Of', 'belonging to'

el primer ministro de Tailandia	the prime minister of Thailand
los discos de mi primo	my cousin's records

la matrícula del coche	the car number-plate
las bisagras de la puerta	the hinges of/on the door
el primero/uno de mayo	the first of May
¿De quién es esto?	Whose is this?

(b) Origin

See 34.7.5 for the difference between *de* and *desde*.

Soy de México	I'm from Mexico
un ser de otro planeta	a being from another planet
un vino de solera	a vintage wine
Este manuscrito es de la Biblioteca Nacional	This manuscript is from the National Library
una oda del siglo quince	a fifteenth-century ode
un dolor de cabeza	a headache

Notes

(i) English speakers tend to use the preposition *en* to denote belonging to or originating from a place: *los hombres de Grecia* 'the men in Greece' (= Greek men), *las flores de los Andes* 'the flowers in (= of) the Andes' *Las colinas de tierra adentro son más verdes* 'The hills inland are greener'.

The temptation is particularly strong after a superlative: *Éste es el mejor restaurante de Madrid* 'This is the best restaurant in Madrid', *el más antiguo monumento del Perú* 'the most ancient monument in Peru', *el mejor momento de mi vida* 'the best moment in/of my life'. However, spoken and journalistic Mexican Spanish regularly uses *en*: *el plan más ambicioso en el mundo* (Mexican television) 'the most ambitious plan in the world', *el mejor surtido en México* 'the best range in Mexico' (advertisement).

(ii) *Viene de Toledo* normally only means 'He's coming from Toledo'; *Es de Toledo* = 'He's **from** Toledo'.

(c) 'Made of', 'consisting of'

una estatua de oro macizo	a solid gold statue
un manuscrito de pergamino	a parchment manuscript
una novela de ciencia-ficción	a science-fiction novel
Tiene una voluntad de hierro	She has an iron will
Este yogur es de leche de oveja	This is ewe's-milk yoghurt

(d) 'About' in the sense of 'concerning'

It is doubtful whether *de* often means 'concerning', except after certain verbs like *hablar, quejarse de, protestar*: *una carta de amor* 'a love letter' is very different from *una carta sobre el amor* 'a letter about love'.

When it is used to mean 'about', *de* implies something less formal than *sobre*, which is closer to 'on the subject of':

No quiero hablar de mis problemas personales	I don't want to talk about my personal problems
Esta noche va a hablar sobre problemas personales	Tonight he's talking on/about 'personal problems'
Es que yo quería hablar con usted de mi salario[1]	Actually I wanted to talk to you about my wages
No hace más que quejarse de que tiene demasiado trabajo	All he does is moan about having too much work
¿De qué va la cosa?	What's it all about?

---

[1] In Spain *el salario* = 'wages', *el sueldo* = 'salary', e.g. *salario de miseria* 'starvation wages'. *Salario* = 'salary' in Latin America.

(e) 'Costing'

Las naranjas de mil pesos son las mejores	The 1000-peso oranges are the best
Han comprado una casa de un millón de libras	They've bought a million-pound house

(f) Emotions arising from something

Tengo miedo del agua (see note)	I'm afraid of the water
el respeto de/a los derechos humanos	Respect for human rights
Me da pena de él	I'm sorry for him

And similarly *el horror de/a/hacia una cosa* 'horror towards/about a thing'.

However, after *sentir, experimentar* and similar verbs the following words take *por* or *hacia*: *compasión* 'pity', *simpatía* 'affection'/'liking', *admiración* 'admiration', *desprecio* 'contempt', *odio* 'hatred', etc.

Note
Also *Le tengo miedo al agua, Tengo miedo de/Le tengo miedo a todo*. See 34.1n.

(g) In certain adverbial phrases of manner

Me puse a pensar de qué modo podría ayudarlos	I set about thinking how I could help them
Sólo he estado en Sevilla de paso	I've only been in Seville on the way to somewhere else
Intentaron entrar de balde	They tried to get in free/without paying
Estuvimos de bromas hasta las tres de la mañana	We were up until three telling jokes/larking about

(h) Condition (English 'as', 'in')
This construction is closely related to the previous one.

De pequeña yo era muy bajita	As a little girl I was very small
Trabajó dos meses de camarero	He worked as a waiter for two months
—¿De qué vas al baile? —De pastora	'What are you going to the ball as?' 'As a shepherdess'
Tú aquí estás de más	You're not needed here
Yo de ti/de usted no lo haría (or *Yo que tú* . . . see 25.11)	If I were you I wouldn't do it
Vi a una criada de blanco paseando al niño	I saw a maid in white taking the child for a walk

(i) To mean 'if'
For *de* plus the infinitive used for *si* in the if-clause of a conditional sentence, see 25.8.3.

(j) Age, measurements

un hombre de cuarenta años	a man aged forty
un pan de tres días	a three-day old loaf
Esta soga tiene tres metros de largo	This rope is three metres long

(k) *De* is used in certain circumstances with adjectives before an infinitive. Compare: *Su conducta es difícil **de** comprender* 'His behaviour is difficult to understand' and *Es difícil comprender su conducta* 'It's difficult to understand his behaviour'. See 18.10 for further examples and discussion.

(l) *De* is used after *más* and *menos* before numerals and quantities: *Ha comprado más/menos de tres kilos* 'He's bought more/less than three kilos'. See 5.5 for further discussion.

(m) *De* replaces *que* in comparisons involving a clause:

Es más listo de lo que parece	He's cleverer than he seems
No uses más de los que necesites	Don't use more than those you need

See 5.6 for discussion.

(n) *De* alternates with *para* in sentences of the type 'His attitude is not to be copied', 'His stories aren't to be believed':

Sus excusas no son de/para creer	His excuses aren't to be believed
Su habilidad no es de/para subestimar	His cleverness is not be underestimated

(o) After certain verbs meaning 'to take by', 'seize by', 'pull on', etc.

La cogió de la mano	He took her by the hand
Me tiraba de la manga	He was pulling on my sleeve
El profesor le asió de una oreja	The teacher took him by an ear

(p) To denote the agent in some types of passive construction and to indicate the author of a work or the main actor in a film or play:

acompañado de su esposa	accompanied by his wife
un cuadro de Velázquez	a painting by Velázquez
una película de Clark Gable	a Clark Gable film

See 34.14.4 note (ii) for discussion of participle + *de*.

(q) In certain set time phrases

de día/de noche	by day/by night
Se levantó muy de mañana	He got up very early in the morning

(r) In construction of the type 'poor you' (*pobre de ti*), 'that fool John', etc.

Tendrás que habértelas con el gandul de Fulano	You'll have to tackle that lay-about so-and-so
¿Sabes lo que ha hecho la pobre de su mujer?	Do you know what his poor wife has done?

(s) Partitive *de*

De is occasionally used before adjectives – particularly demonstrative adjectives – to mean 'some of', 'one of': *Hay de todo* 'There is a bit of everything':

Puedes comprar de todo	You can buy a little of everything
Tráiganos de ese vino que nos sirvió ayer	Bring us some of that wine you served us yesterday

34.7.2 *Deber* or *deber de?*
See 21.3 for details.

34.7.3 *De* before *que*
Some verbs, all verbal phrases involving a noun or adjective, and some adverbial phrases, must be followed by *de que* when they introduce a clause: *Se dio cuenta de que ya no llovía* 'He realized that it was no longer raining'. See 33.4.2 for discussion.

34.7.4 *Dequeísmo*
For the popular (but stigmatized) tendency to use *de que* instead of *que* after verbs of belief and communication, e.g. ?*Dice de que no viene* for *Dice que no viene* 'She says she isn't coming', see 33.4.3.

34.7.5 *Desde* and *de* meaning 'from'

The existence of two Spanish words which both mean 'from' is a source of confusion. Furthermore, the distinction is not always strictly observed by native speakers.

Desde stresses the idea of movement or distance more than *de*. It is therefore appropriate when motion from a place requires some unusual effort or when the point of origin is mentioned but not the destination, as in *Os veo desde mi ventana* 'I can see you from my window'. It is also freely used in time phrases.

Desde nuestro balcón se divisa la cima de Mulhacén	From our balcony one can make out the summit of Mulhacén
Desde aquí el camino es muy bueno	From here the road is very good
Avanzó desde la puerta con un cuchillo en la mano	He moved forward from the door with a knife in his hand
He venido andando desde el centro	I've walked all the way from the centre
Y entonces una soga lo atrapó desde atrás (J. Cortázar, Argentina)	Then he was caught from behind by a rope
Desde hoy/A partir de hoy tienen que llegar a tiempo	From today you must arrive on time
Los tenemos desde cincuenta centavos hasta cinco pesos	We have them from 50 centavos to 5 pesos

Notes
(i) If *a, hasta* or some other preposition of destination appears, *desde* is often interchangeable with *de*: *De/Desde aquí hasta el centro las calles son muy estrechas* 'From here to the centre the roads are very narrow', *De/Desde aquí a la cima mide ocho mil metros* 'From here to the summit it measures 8,000 metres', *Desde/De 1922 a 1942 estuve en Colombia* 'From 1922 to 1942 I was in Colombia', but *He estado en Colombia desde 1922* 'I've been in Colombia since 1922'.
(ii) If no such prepositional phrase of destination occurs *desde* is usually the safer option, though usage is fickle: *las partículas subatómicas que llegan desde/de otras galaxias* 'subatomic particles that arrive from other galaxies', *¿Desde dónde hablas?* 'Where are you talking from?' (e.g. by radio or phone).
(iii) In the following sentences only *de* is possible: *Yo soy de Madrid* 'I'm from Madrid', *Las hojas caen ya de los abedules* 'The leaves are already falling from the birches', *Sacó tres diamantes de la bolsa* 'He took three diamonds from the bag', *Pasó de secretario a jefe en tres meses* 'He went from secretary to boss in three months', *Hizo un modelo de un trozo de madera* 'He made a model from a piece of wood', *Del techo pendía una enorme araña de luces* 'From the ceiling hung an enormous chandelier', *Se ha venido de España a vivir en Inglaterra* 'He's come from Spain to live in England', *de Pascuas a Ramos* 'once in a blue moon' (lit. 'from Easter to Palm Sunday').
(iv) *Desde ya* is commonly found in the River Plate region with the meaning of 'right away'. *Desde luego* means 'of course' on both continents.

34.8 *Durante*

This word and other ways of saying 'for a period of time' is discussed under 32.2.

34.9 *En*

As a preposition of place *en* is disconcertingly vague since it combines the meanings of 'in' and 'on' (French *sur* and *dans*), as well as 'at', 'into', 'onto': *en la caja* 'in the box', *en la mesa* 'on/at the table', *Está en la comisaría* 'He's in/at the police station'. For the relationship between *en* and 'at' in sentences like 'at the station', 'at Cambridge', see 34.1d.

When it means 'on a horizontal surface', it alternates with *sobre* and, sometimes, with *encima de*. Thus one can say *en/sobre/encima de la mesa* 'on the table', but *Mi hijo duerme en mi cama* 'My son sleeps in my bed', since 'inside' is implied.

En may be replaced by *dentro de* 'inside' if clarity or emphasis are required.

(a) As an equivalent of 'in', 'on' or 'at':

Tus camisas están en el cajón	Your shirts are in the drawer
Cuelga el cuadro en la pared	Hang the picture on the wall
Dio unos golpes discretos en la puerta	He tapped discreetly on the door
Gasta mucho dinero en juegos de azar	He spends a lot of money on gambling (lit. 'games of chance')
Los empleados estaban sentados en sus mesas (see note (i))	The clerks were sitting at their tables
El agua ha penetrado en las vigas	The water has soaked into the joists
Uno de mis pendientes se ha caído en el agua (see note (ii))	One of my earrings has fallen into the water
Propusieron convertirlo en sanatorio	They suggested turning it into a sanatorium
en otoño/primavera/1924	In autumn/spring/1924
Todavía está en proyecto	It's still at the planning stage
Te da ciento y raya en latín	He's miles better than you in Latin

Notes

(i) Compare *Se sentó a la mesa* 'He sat down at table' with *Siempre se comporta mal en la mesa* 'He always misbehaves at table'. See 34.1d for discussion.

(ii) The example suggests the wearer was already in the water, e.g. swimming. If trajectory down to the water is meant, *a* is more usual: *Se tiró al río* 'He jumped into the river', *El avión cayó al mar* 'The plane fell into the sea'.

(iii) *Entrar* and similar verbs take *en* (often *a* in Latin America, and occasionally in Spain): *Entró en el cuarto* 'He entered the room'.

(b) To express the thing by which something else is judged or estimated:

Los daños se han calculado en diez millones de dólares	The damage has been calculated at ten million dollars
El tipo oficial quedó fijado en 151,93 por dólar (*El País*)	The official rate was fixed at 151.93 to the dollar
Lo vendieron en/por un millón de pesetas	They sold it for a million pesetas
Te tenía en más	I thought better of you
Me lo presupuestaron en cien mil	They gave me an estimate of 100,000 for it
Se nota que es inglés en su manera de hablar	One can tell he's English by the way he talks

(c) In a number of adverbial phrases:

Lo tomaron en serio	They took it seriously
en cueros/en broma/en balde	Naked/as a joke/pointlessly
en fila/en seguida (or *enseguida*)	in a row/straight away
Estoy en contra	I'm against

(d) To mean 'as'

Como is much more usual nowadays in the following sentences:

Hablar de esa manera, en/como ser superior, es absurdo	To talk like that, as a superior being, is absurd
Os hablo en/como perito	I'm talking to you as an expert

(e) After a number of common verbs, and in several miscellaneous constructions:

Pensé mucho en usted	I thought of you a lot
Quedamos en vernos a las siete	We agreed to meet at seven
Tardaron cinco semanas en reparar el coche	They took five weeks to mend the car
Vaciló en contestarme	He hesitated before answering me
No dudó en devolvérmelo	He didn't hesitate over giving it back to me
No ayuda en nada	He/She/It's no help at all
La reina abdicó en su hijo	The queen abdicated in favour of her son
Se interesa mucho en/por la filatelia	He's very interested in stamp collecting
El fue el primero/último en hacerlo	He was the first/last to do it

Notes
(i) See 18.2 for further remarks about prepositional usage with verbs. For the obsolete construction *en* + gerund see 20.5.
(ii) *En la mañana* may be be used in Latin America for *por la mañana*: *En las mañanas salíamos a montar a caballo* (A. Mastretta, Mexico) 'In the mornings we used to go riding'.

34.10 *Entre*

Both 'between' and 'among'. *Entre* also has a number of uses unfamiliar to English speakers.
   Prepositional pronoun forms are not nowadays used after *entre*: *Entre Juan y tú recogeréis los papeles* 'You and John will pick up the pieces of paper between you' (not **entre Juan y ti*).
(a) 'Between'

Estábamos entre la espada y la pared	We were between the sword and the wall (i.e. 'we had our backs to the wall')
Entre tú/usted y yo . . .	Between you and me . . .
Lo terminaron entre María y su hermana	Maria and her sister finished it between them

Note
The last example is typical of a construction unfamiliar to English speakers: *Llenan el pantano entre cuatro ríos* (from Moliner, I, 1146) 'Four rivers combine to fill the reservoir', *Lo escribieron entre cuatro de ellos* 'Four of them wrote it between them'.

(b) 'Among'
   It is used with a wider range of nouns than its English equivalent, e.g. *entre la niebla* 'in the mist', *Encontraron la sortija entre la arena* 'They found the ring in the sand'.

No pude encontrar el libro entre tantos tomos	I couldn't find the book among so many volumes
Vivió diez años entre los beduinos de Arabia	He lived for ten years among the Bedouins of Arabia
No podía decidir entre tantas posibilidades	I couldn't choose among so many possibilities

> *. . .y entre el ruido de la lluvia se escuchaba*
> *el ladrido de los perros* (L. Sepúlveda,
> Chile)

> . . . and through/above the noise of the
> rain the barking of the dogs was heard

(c) 'Among themselves', 'one from the other'

In the second of these two meanings *entre* is used in a way unfamiliar to English speakers. It is especially liable to appear with the pronoun *sí* (discussed in detail at 11.5.3):

> *En casa hablan castellano entre sí* (or *entre ellos*)

> At home they speak Spanish among themselves

> *Es más fácil que dos personas vivan en armonía cuando se respetan entre sí*

> It's easier for two people to live in harmony when they respect one another

> *Los idiomas que se hablan en la India son muy diferentes entre sí*

> The languages spoken in India differ widely one from another

(d) It can translate the English phrase 'what with'

> *Entre los niños y el ruido que hacen los albañiles, me estoy volviendo loca*

> What with the children and the noise the builders make, I'm going mad

> *entre pitos y flautas . . .*

> what with one thing and another (lit. 'what with whistles and flutes')

(e) In certain phrases, in a way strange to English speakers

> *Van como ovejas al matadero, decía entre sí*

> They're going like lambs to the slaughter, he said to himself

> *Decía entre mí . . .*

> I said to myself . . .

> *El museo está abierto entre semana*

> The museum is open on weekdays and Saturdays

34.11 *Hacia*

(a) A close equivalent of 'towards', but rather wider in application since it also translates the English suffix *-ward/-wards*:

> *El satélite viaja hacia Venus*

> The satellite is travelling towards Venus

> *La muchedumbre se dirigía hacia el palacio presidencial*

> The crowd was making for the presidential palace

> *Hacia el oeste no había más que dunas*

> Towards the west there was nothing but dunes

> *La actitud de la CE hacia tales problemas parece ambigua*

> The attitude of the EC towards such problems seems ambiguous

> *El incidente ocurrió hacia las tres de la tarde*

> The incident occurred towards three in the afternoon

> *Se apoyaba hacia delante en un bastón*

> He was leaning forwards on a stick

In time phrases *hacia* can usually be replaced by *sobre,* and with dates by *para*: *sobre las tres de la tarde,* 'around 3 p.m.', *para octubre* 'towards/around October'.

(b) Emotions, attitudes 'towards'

Por, con and *para con* are also possible, but not always interchangeable. Deep emotions such as love or hatred prefer *hacia* or *por*; attitudes (e.g. kindness, severity, irritability) prefer *hacia* or *con*:

> *su profundo amor hacia/por/a todo lo andaluz*

> his deep love for everything Andalusian

> *Mostraba una indiferencia total hacia/por las críticas*

> He displayed total indifference towards criticisms

la simpatía de los insurgentes hacia el modelo cubano	The insurgents' sympathy for the Cuban model

For *para con* see 34.5b.

34.12 *Hasta*

(a) 'As far as', 'until', 'up to'

hasta ahora . . .	until now/up to now
Llegaron hasta el oasis, pero tuvieron que volverse	They got as far as the oasis, but had to turn back
No nos vamos hasta el día trece	We're not leaving until the thirteenth
Bailaron hasta no poder más	They danced until they were exhausted
Estoy de exámenes hasta la coronilla (or *hasta las narices*)	I've had enough of exams (I'm sick to death of exams)
hasta luego	goodbye/au revoir

(b) *Hasta que no*
See 23.2.4d for this construction.
(c) As an equivalent of *incluso* 'even'

Hasta llegó a ofrecerles dinero	He even went as far as offering them money
Hasta en Inglaterra hace calor a veces	Even in England it's hot sometimes

Note
In Mexico, and in neighbouring countries, *hasta* has acquired the meaning of 'not until': *Perdona que te llame hasta ahora* (C. Fuentes, dialogue), 'Sorry for not ringing you before now', *Bajamos hasta la Plaza de la Independencia* 'We're not getting off until Independence Square', *hasta entonces me di cuenta* 'I realized only then' or 'I didn't realize until then'.

34.13 *Mediante*

A close equivalent of 'by means of' some instrument, argument or device:

Es inútil intentar abolir el abuso del alcohol mediante/por/con decreto	It is useless to try to abolish alcohol abuse by decree
Lograron abrir la caja mediante/con una antorcha de butano	They managed to open the safe by means of a butane torch

34.14 *Para* and *por*

34.14.1 The difference between them
The existence of two prepositions that both sometimes seem to mean 'for', French *pour*, is one of the stumbling blocks of the language. The difference is best learnt from examples and can hardly be stated clearly in abstract. One basic distinction is that *para* expresses purpose or destination and *por* cause or motive; the difference is perhaps most clearly visible in the two sentences *Hago esto para ti* 'I'm **making** this for you (to give to you)' and *Hago esto por ti* 'I'm **doing** this because of you/on your behalf'. But such contrasting sentences are rare. English speakers are usually confused by sentences like

'This fence is for the rabbits': since this really means 'because of the rabbits' one must say *Esta valla es **por** los conejos.*

The Spanish Civil Guards' motto *Todo por la Patria* 'Everything for the home country' exemplifies *por* at its most confusing. It means 'everything (we do is done) for our country', i.e. 'All our actions are inspired by our country', whereas *todo para la Patria* would mean 'everything (we have is) **for** our country', i.e. 'We give all our belongings to our country'.

It is useful to recall that if 'for' can be replaced by 'out of' or 'because of' then *por* may be the correct translation, but not *para: Lo hizo por amor* 'He did it for (out of) love', *Lo hago por el dinero* 'I do it for (because of) the money':

Llevo el abrigo por/a causa de mi madre	I'm wearing this coat because of my mother (she'll be cross/worried if I don't)
Llevo este abrigo para/a mi madre	I'm taking this coat for/to my mother
Han venido por ti	They've come to get you/because of you/instead of you
Han venido estos paquetes para ti	These parcels have come for you
Lo has conseguido por mí	You've got it as a result of me (i.e. I helped you)
Los has conseguido para mí	You've got it for me

Particularly troublesome is the fact that *por* and *para* can be almost identical in meaning in some sentences that state an intention: *Ha venido **por/para** estar contigo* 'He's come to be with you', whereas in others only *para* is possible: *El carpintero ha venido **para** reparar la puerta* 'The carpenter's come to mend the door'. This problem is discussed at 34.14.7.

Note
The form *pa* is substandard for *para* and should be avoided. It is accepted in a few humorous familiar expressions used in Spain (and possibly elsewhere), e.g. *Es muy echao p'alante* 'He's very forward', *Estoy p'al arrastre* 'I'm all in/exhausted', *p'al gato* 'worthless'/'junk' (literally 'for the cat').

34.14.2 Uses of *para*
Para is used:

(a) To indicate purpose, object or destination, e.g. *¿Para quién es esto?* 'Who(m) is this for?', *Trabaja para ganar dinero* 'He works to earn money', etc.

Todo mi cariño es para ti	All my affection is for you
Tomo pastillas para/con el fin de adelgazar	I take pills in order to slim
Una mesa para dos, por favor	A table for two, please
Se preparó para saltar	He got ready to jump
Lo hace para/con el fin de llamar la atención	He does it to attract attention
Estudia para médico	He's studying to become a doctor

Notes
(i) For the distinction between *He venido para verle* and *He venido por verle*, which both mean 'I've come to see him', see 34.14.7.
(ii) *Para* can also express ironic purpose, like the English 'only to': *Se abstuvo durante años de fumar y beber, para luego morir en un accidente de coche* 'He refrained for years from smoking and drinking, only to die in a car accident', *Corrió a casa para encontrarse con que ya se habían marchado* 'He hurried home only to find that they'd already left'.
(iii) The following construction may also be thought of as expressing the object or purpose of something: *Sus historias no son para/de creer* 'His stories aren't to be believed' (lit. 'aren't for believing'), *No es para tanto* 'It's not that serious'/'It doesn't call for that much fuss'.

(b) Direction after verbs of motion

Íbamos para casa cuando empezó a llover	We were on the way home when it started raining
Ya va para viejo	He's getting old now
Va para ministro	He's on the way to becoming a minister

(c) To indicate advantage, disadvantage, usefulness, need

Fumar es malo para la salud	Smoking is bad for the health
La paciencia es un requisito indispensable para los profesores	Patience is an indispensable requirement for teachers
Con esto tenemos para todos	With this we've enough for everybody
Es mucho dinero para tres días de vacaciones	It's a lot of money for three days' holiday/vacation
Tú eres para él lo más importante	You're the most important thing to/for him

(d) Reaction, response, mood

Para mí eso no es justo	That doesn't seem fair to me
Esto para mí huele a vinagre/Esto a mí me huele a vinagre	This smells of vinegar to me
Para mí que hablas mejor que él	My impression is that you speak better than him

Notes

(i) For *para con* in sentences like *Es muy atento para con los invitados* 'He's very courteous towards guests', see 34.5b.

(ii) *Para* can also translate 'not in the mood for': *No estoy para bromas* 'I'm not in the mood for jokes'.

(e) To translate 'for' when it means 'considering', 'in view of'

Está muy alto para su edad	He's very tall for his age
Estás muy viejo para esos trotes	You're very old for all that
Es poco dinero para tanto trabajo	It's not much money for so much work

(f) 'To' in certain reflexive expressions

Me lo guardo para mí	I'm keeping it to/for myself
Esto acabará mal, me decía para mí/entre mí	This will end badly, I said to myself
Murmuraba para/entre sí	He was muttering to himself

(g) 'About' in the meaning of 'on the point of'

Ya deben estar para/al llegar	They must be about to arrive
La leche está para cocer	The milk's about to boil
—Pues yo estoy para cumplir treinta y cinco la semana que viene (E. Arenas, dialogue, Spain)	Well, I'm going to be thirty-five next week

Note

In Latin America *estar por* is used: *Está por llover* 'It's about to rain', *En 1942, cuando volvió definitivamente, estaba por cumplir veinte años* (S. Pitol, Mexico) 'In 1942, when he came back for good, he was on the verge of his twentieth birthday'. In Spain *estar por* means 'to be in favour of/to be thinking about doing something'.

34.14.3 *Para* in time phrases

(a) To translate 'by'

Lo tendré preparado para las cinco	I'll have it ready by/for five o'clock

Estaremos de vuelta para la merienda	We'll be back by tea
Para entonces ya estaremos todos muertos	We'll all be dead by then

(b) 'For'

Para sometimes expresses the idea of 'for *n* days/weeks/years'. See 32.3.6 for further discussion.

(c) 'Around', 'towards'

El embalse estará terminado para finales de noviembre	The dam will be finished around the end of November
Volveremos para agosto	We'll return around August

Notes

(i) In the last example *para* is more precise than *hacia* and *por* and less precise than *en*.

(ii) *Ir para* is a colloquial translation of 'for nearly . . .' in time phrases: *Va para cinco años que trabajo aquí* 'I've been working here for nearly five years'.

(d) 'Not enough to', 'considering how much'

No había tomado suficientes pastillas como para matarse (M. Vázquez Montalbán, Spain)	She hadn't taken enough pills to kill herself
un matrimonio rápido, bastante rápido para lo mucho que siempre se dice que hay que pensárselo (J. Marías, Spain)	a quick marriage, pretty quick considering how much they always say one ought to think it over

34.14.4 Main uses of *por*

(a) *Por* often means simply 'because of', as in *¿por qué?* (two words) 'why?' (i.e. 'because of what?') and *porque* 'because':

No pudimos salir por/a causa de la nieve	We couldn't go out because of the snow
el índice de muertes por/a causa de infecciones pulmonares	the death rate from lung infections
Lo hice por dinero	I did it for money
la razón por la que me voy	the reason for my leaving
muchas gracias por el regalo	many thanks for the present
Te ha pasado por tonto	It happened to you because you're a fool
Las críticas de la izquierda vienen por/a causa de tres temas	Criticism from the left arises from three topics
. . . el profesor la calificó con un cero por no saber la lección (M. Puig, Argentina)	. . . the teacher gave her a zero because she didn't know the lesson
Las empresas navieras sufren un descalabro importante por la situación actual del mercado (ABC, Spain)	Shipping firms have suffered significant losses due to the present state of the market

Por may thus indicate the origin or inspiration of an emotion or mental state:

No lo puedo ver por lo engreído que es	I can't stand him for his conceitedness
Me fastidia por lo mal que canta	He annoys me because of his bad singing
Le/Lo odio por su mal genio	I hate him for/because of his bad temper
su amor por/hacia/a sus hijos	his love for his children
Siento mucho cariño por/hacia ella	I feel great fondness for her
El gobierno demuestra poco interés por los derechos de la mujer	The government shows little interest in women's rights
Tuvo un recuerdo nostálgico por el Londres de su juventud	He had a nostalgic recollection of the London of his youth
La delató por despecho	He informed on her out of spite

(b) *Por* = 'by' in passive constructions

Sus novelas fueron elogiadas por los críticos	His novels were praised by the critics
La catedral fue diseñada por Gaudí	The cathedral was designed by Gaudí
El suelo estaba cubierto por/de un lecho de hierba	The ground was covered by a bed of grass
Sociedad y economía aztecas por M. León-Portilla	*Aztec Society and Economy* by M. León-Portilla

Notes

(i) For *de* meaning 'by' to indicate the author of a work or the main actor in a film or play, see 34.7.1p.

(ii) *De* is not nowadays used in passive sentences to mean 'by', except with certain verbs which are best learnt separately. Where there is a possibility of using either *por* or *de*, the former usually implies an active agent, the latter generally implies a state. *De* is therefore common when *estar* is used; see 28.2.5 for *estar convencido* contrasted with *ser convencido*.

Examples: *Me sentía tentado de tomar el atajo* 'I felt tempted to take the short cut', *Jesús fue tentado por el Diablo* 'Jesus was tempted by the Devil', *María dijo algunas palabras en voz muy baja . . . seguidas de un ruido de sillas* (E. Sábato, Argentina) 'Maria said a few words in a very low voice, followed by a sound of chairs', *El formulario debe estar acompañado de dos fotos* 'The form must be accompanied by two photos', *Llegó acompañado por dos agentes* 'He arrived escorted by two policemen', *Yo nunca he estado persuadido de la verdad de su versión de los hechos* (state) 'I've never been persuaded of the truth of his version of the facts', *Fui persuadido por su versión de los hechos* (action) 'I was persuaded by his version of the facts', *Las zonas pantanosas suelen estar plagadas de mosquitos* 'Marshy zones are usually plagued with mosquitoes', *En verano las vacas están atormentadas por las moscas* 'In summer the cows are tormented by flies'.

(c) 'Runs *on*', 'works *by*', 'by means of'

El sistema de alarma funciona por rayos infrarrojos	The alarm system works by infra-red rays
El tratamiento por/con rayos X ha producido resultados animadores	Treatment by X-rays has produced encouraging results
Un coche que marcha por/con/a gas-oil	A car which runs on diesel oil
Se puede pagar por/con talón bancario	Payment by cheque accepted
Abrieron la puerta por la fuerza	They opened the door by force
[el Buda] enseñaba la aniquilación del dolor por la aniquilación del deseo (J.L. Borges, Argentina)	[the Buddha] taught the extinction of suffering by the extinction of desire

(d) 'In support of'

This includes the idea of effort or activity on behalf of anything:

Yo voté por los liberales	I voted for the Liberals
una campaña por/en pro de/a favor de la libertad de la prensa	a campaign for press freedom
¿Estás tú por la violencia?	Do you support violence?
Él es senador por Massachusetts	He's senator for Massachusetts
Aprendió a tocar el piano por sí misma/ella sola	She learnt to play the piano by herself

(e) Exchange *for*, substitute *for*, distribution *per*

Llévelo al departamento de reclamaciones y se lo cambiarán por uno nuevo	Take it to the complaints department and they'll change it for a new one
Te han dado gato por liebre	They've served you cat for hare (i.e. swindled you)

Te quieres hacer pasar por lo que no eres	You're trying to pass for other than what you are
¿Por quién me toma usted?	Who do you take me for?
Lo doy por supuesto/sentado	I take it for granted
Él dará la clase por mí	He'll give the class instead of me
Come por tres	He eats three persons' share
tres raciones por persona	three helpings per person
cien kilómetros por hora	100 km an hour
40 horas a la/por semana (*a* is more usual)	40 hours a week
El dos por ciento es protestante/son protestantes	Two per cent are Protestants

(f) Prices, amounts of money

un cheque por/de cien dólares	a cheque/(US) 'check' for 100 dollars
Compró una casa por un millón de dólares	He bought a house for one million dollars

Note

Por is used with *pagar* only when the verb has a following direct object: *He pagado mil libras por este ordenador* 'I paid £1000 for this computer', *He pagado mucho por él* 'I paid a lot for it'. But *Yo lo pagué la semana pasada* 'I paid for it last week'.

(g) 'To judge *by*'

por las señas que me ha dado . . .	from the description he's given me . . .
por lo que tú dices . . .	from what you say . . .
por lo visto	apparently

(h) 'In search *of*'

Peninsular speech prefers *a por*, a construction grudgingly admitted by grammarians and rejected by Latin Americans.

Ha ido (a) por agua	He's gone for water
Le enviaron (a) por el médico	They sent him for the doctor
Voy al baño a por Kleenex (C. Rico-Godoy, Spain)	I'm going/I go to the bathroom/toilet to fetch a tissue
Fui por mi abrigo (A. Mastretta, Mexico)	I went for/to get my coat

(i) 'Through' (= 'by means of')

Conseguí el empleo por/a través de mi tío	I got the job through my uncle
Me enteré por un amigo	I found out through/from a friend
Le reconocí por la descripción	I recognised him from the description

(j) *Por* in adverbial phrases of manner

por correo/avión/mar (but *en tren, en coche, en bicicleta, a pie*)	by mail/air/sea
Los denuncio por igual	I denounce both/all sides equally
por lo general/generalmente	generally
por lo corriente/corrientemente	usually
Me lo tendrás que decir por las buenas o por las malas	You'll have to tell me one way or another

(k) 'However . . .' in concessions (see 16.13)

Por más inteligente que seas, no lo vas a resolver	However intelligent you may be, you won't solve it
Por mucho que protestes, te quedas aquí	However much you protest, you're staying here
Por fuerte que ustedes griten, el patrón no les sube el salario	However loud you shout, the boss won't raise your wages

(l) Miscellaneous examples

Por mí haz lo que quieras	As far as I'm concerned, do what you like
¿Por quién pregunta?	Who are you asking for?
Es agrimensor, o algo por el estilo	He's a surveyor, or something like that
Siéntese por Dios (**not** brusque, i.e. not 'Sit down for God's sake'!)	Do please sit down
Cinco por tres son quince	5 times 3 equals 15
Mide 7 por 5	It measures 7 by 5

(m) With numerous verbs

apurarse por	to get anxious about
asustarse por/de	to get frightened about
decidirse por	to decide on
desvelarse por	to be very concerned about
disculparse por	to apologize for
interesarse por	to be interested in
jurar por	to swear by/on
molestarse por	to bother about
optar por	to opt for
preocuparse por/de	to worry about
tomar por	to take for

34.14.5 *Por* in time phrases
(a) *Por* = 'in'

Debió ser por mayo	It must have been in May
por aquellos días	in those days/during those days

For 'just for', 'only for' and a more detailed discussion of *por* in time phrases see 32.3.5.

34.14.6 *Por* as a preposition of place
(a) 'All over', 'throughout'

He viajado por Latinoamérica	I've travelled around Latin America
Había muchos libros desparramados por el suelo	There were many books scattered over the floor

(b) 'In': less precise than *en* and often implying motion

La vi por/en la calle	I saw her in the street
Debe estar por el jardín	It must be somewhere in the garden

(c) 'Up to'

El agua le llegaba por la cintura	The water was up to his waist
Me llegas por los hombros	You reach my shoulders (e.g. to a growing child)

(d) 'Through', 'out of', 'down'

Se tiró por la ventana	He threw himself out of the window
Entró por la puerta	He came through the door
Se cayó por la escalera	He fell down the stairs
Salía agua por el/del grifo	Water was coming out of the tap

(e) In conjunction with adverbs of place, to denote direction or whereabouts

por aquí	this way/around here
por allí	that way/around there

por delante	from the front/in front
por detrás	from behind/behind
por entre	in between

34.14.7 He venido por hablarle or para hablarle?

Both prepositions may translate 'to' or 'in order to' in sentences like 'I've come to talk to you'. In some cases they are virtually interchangeable (see also 33.5.1):

¿Para qué has venido?	What have you come for?
¿Por qué has venido?	Why have you come?
Estoy aquí para/por verle	I'm here to see him

A useful rule seems to be: if the English sentence can be rewritten using a phrase like 'out of a desire to' or 'from an urge to', then *por* can be used. If not, *para* is indicated; i.e. *por* refers to the mental state of the subject, *para* to the goal of his action.

Thus, *Me dijeron que estabas en Madrid y he venido **por** verte de nuevo* 'I heard you were in Madrid and I've come to (out of an urge to) see you again' is possible. But **El fontanero ha venido por reparar el grifo* is as absurd as 'The plumber has come out of an urge to mend the tap'.

Another example may clarify the point: —*¿Para qué salgo a cenar contigo?* —*Para cenar* (not *por*) '"What am I going out to dinner with you for?" "(In order) to eat"', —*¿Por qué salgo a cenar contigo?* —*Por/Para estar contigo* '"Why am I going out to dinner with you?" "To be with you"':

Estuve toda la noche sin dormir por/para no perderme el eclipse	I spent the whole night without sleeping so as not to miss the eclipse
Llegó a las cinco de la mañana por/para cogerlos en la cama	He arrived at five in the morning so as to catch them in bed
No lo haces más que por/para fastidiar	You only do it to annoy
Ella le habría vendido el alma al Diablo por casarse con él (G. García Márquez, Colombia)	She'd have sold her soul to the Devil to marry him
Le prometo que haré lo posible por dar con él (A. Mastretta, Mexico, dialogue)	I promise you I'll do everything possible to find him
Dame una aspirina para calmar el dolor	Give me an aspirin to ease the pain
Incluso contrataron a un detective privado para buscarle/lo	They even hired a private detective to look for him

34.14.8 Some vital differences between por and para

Tengo muchas cosas por/sin hacer	I have a lot of things still undone
Tengo muchas cosas para hacer	I have many things to do
Estoy por hacerlo	I feel inclined to do it
Estoy (aquí) para hacerlo	I'm here in order to do it
Estaba para hacerlo (Lat. Am. *por*)	I was about to do it
Está por/sin acabar	It isn't finished yet
Está para acabar	This has to be finished
Está para acabar de un momento a otro	It's about to finish at any moment

34.14.9 'For' not translated by por or para

la razón de mi queja	the reason for my complaining
Bebía porque no tenía otra cosa que hacer	She drank for want of something else to do

Los días eran cortos pues era ahora noviembre	The days were short, for it was now November
el deseo de fama	the desire for fame
Lloró de alegría	She wept for joy
Es una buena esposa a pesar de lo que gruñe	She's a good wife for all her grumbling
No dijo una palabra durante dos horas	He didn't say a word for two hours
No le/lo he visto desde hace meses	I haven't seen him for months
Llevamos tres semanas sin que recojan la basura	They haven't collected our rubbish/(US) 'trash' for three weeks
Estuvimos horas esperando	We waited for hours
Se podía ver muy lejos	You could see for miles
ir a dar un paseo	to go for a walk
irse de vacaciones	to go for a holiday/vacation
Me voy a Madrid unos días	I'm going to Madrid for a few days

34.15 *Según*

'According to', 'depending on'. As with *entre*, a following pronoun appears in the subject form: *según tú* 'according to you', not **según ti*:

según el parte meteorológico	according to the weather report
Iremos modificando el programa de estudios según el tipo de estudiante que se matricule	We'll modify the syllabus according to the type of student that signs on
Los precios varían según a qué dentista vayas (or según el dentista al que vayas)	The prices vary according to which dentist you go to
Me decidiré luego, según cómo salgan las cosas	I'll decide later, depending on how things turn out

Notes

(i) As the examples show, *según* often functions as an adverbial: *–¿Vas tú también? —Según* '"Are you going too?" "It depends"', *La policía detenía a los manifestantes según iban saliendo del edificio* 'The police were arresting the demonstrators as they came out of the building', *Lo haremos según llegue papá* (*en cuanto llegue* is more usual) 'We'll do it as soon as father arrives', *Según llegábamos al aparcamiento . . . un automóvil abandonaba un lugar grande y espacioso* (C. Rico-Godoy, Spain) 'Just as we were arriving at the parking lot a car was leaving a large and roomy parking space', *Según dicen . . .* 'According to what they say . . .'.

(ii) The following are colloquial or dialect: *?Dirías que es un millonario según habla* (*por la manera en que habla*) 'You'd think he was a millionaire from the way he talks', *?A mí, según qué cosas, no me gusta hacerlas* (regional for *ciertas cosas . . .*) 'There are certain kinds of thing I don't like doing'. The last example is typical of eastern Spain.

34.16 *Sin*

'Without'. *Sin* raises few problems for the English speaker, except when it appears before an infinitive, in which case it sometimes cannot be translated by the English verb form in -ing: cf. *dos Coca-Colas sin abrir* 'two Coca-Colas, unopened' (or 'not opened'). See 28.2.4.

No subas al tren sin billete	Don't get on the train without a ticket
Como vuelva a verte por aquí te echo sin contemplaciones	If I see you around here again I'll throw you out on the spot (lit. 'without consideration for you')
Fumaba sin cesar	He was smoking ceaselessly
Estoy sin blanca	I haven't got a penny

¡Cuántos hay sin comer!	How many there are who have nothing to eat!
Está más guapa sin peinar	She's more attractive without her hair done

34.17 *Sobre*

This preposition combines some of the meanings of the English words 'on', 'over', 'on top of' and 'above'.

(a) As a preposition of place

It is an equivalent of *en* in the sense of 'on': *en/sobre la mesa* 'on the table', *en/sobre la pared* 'on the wall'. *Encima de* is also used of horizontal surfaces: *encima de la mesa* 'on (top of) the table'.

However, where 'on top of' is impossible in English *encima de* is impossible in Spanish: *Los hinchas se encuentran todavía en/sobre el terreno* 'The fans are still on the field/(British) 'pitch':

Querían edificar sobre estos terrenos un hotel nuevo	They wanted to build a new hotel on this land
Este neumático tiene poco agarre sobre mojado	This tyre has poor grip on wet surfaces
Los rebeldes marcharon sobre la capital	The rebels marched on the capital
El castillo está edificado sobre un pintoresco valle	The castle is built overlooking a picturesque valley
Una mujer habla con un chico y un árbol agita unas hojas secas sobre sus cabezas (J. Cortázar, Argentina)	A woman is talking to a boy and a tree is waving a few dry leaves over their heads
Un sol de fuego caía sobre los campos	A fiery sun fell on the plains

Note
Compare *sobre*, *encima de* and *por encima de* in the following examples: *El rey está por encima de/sobre todos* (rest, not motion) 'The King is above everyone', *Mi jefe siempre está encima de mí* 'My boss is always breathing down my neck', *La bala pasó por encima de su cabeza, rozándole el pelo* (motion) 'The bullet passed over his head, just touching his hair', *El avión voló por encima de/sobre la ciudad* (motion: *sobre* implies height and is often more literary than *encima de*) 'The plane flew over the city'.

(b) Approximation (more usually with time)

Llegaremos sobre las cinco de la tarde	We'll arrive around 5 p.m.
Tenía sobre cuarenta años (. . .*unos 40 años* is more usual)	He was around forty years old
Costó sobre cien mil (*unos/unas 100.000* is more usual)	It cost around 100,000

(c) 'About'

In this sense, *sobre* implies formal discourse 'about', i.e. 'on the subject of' something. Informal discourse usually requires *de*, cf. *No he venido a hablar de tus problemas* 'I haven't come to talk about your problems' (not *sobre*):

Pronunció una conferencia sobre los problemas del Oriente Próximo	He delivered a lecture on the problems of the Near East
La OMS advierte sobre el peligro del uso de tranquilizantes sin receta médica	WHO (World Health Organization) warns on use of tranquillizers without medical prescription

(d) Centre of rotation

El mundo gira sobre su eje polar	The world spins about its polar axis
Las puertas se mueven sobre bisagras	Doors turn on hinges
Dio media vuelta sobre el pie izquierdo	He did a half-turn on his left foot

(e) Superiority or precedence 'over'

el triunfo de los conservadores sobre la izquierda	the victory of the conservatives over the left
No tiene derecho a reclamar su superioridad sobre los demás	He has no right to claim superiority over others
Sobre todo, quisiera agradecer a mi mujer . . .	Above all, I would like to thank my wife . . .
El crecimiento, en términos reales, de las exportaciones en el primer mes de 1984 supera el 50% sobre enero de 1983 (El País)	In real terms, the growth in exports in the first month of 1984 is 50% higher than January 1983
impuestos sobre la renta	taxes on income

34.18 *Tras*

'Behind', 'after'. It is a close equivalent of *detrás de* 'behind' (location) and *después de* 'after' (time); it is very rare in everyday speech. Its brevity makes it popular with journalists.

Tras de is an equally literary variant.

Dos siluetas deformes se destacaron tras el vidrio esmerilado (L. Goytisolo, Spain)	Two distorted outlines loomed through/behind the frosted glass
¿Quién sabe qué cosas pasan tras las cortinas de aquella casa?	Who knows what things happen behind the curtains of that house?
un generoso proyecto tras el cual se esconden intenciones menos altruistas	a generous project behind which less generous intentions lurk
Una banda de gaviotas venía tras el barco	A flock of gulls was following the boat

Detrás de could be used in all the above examples.

Así, tras de los duros años de 1936 a 1939 . . . (popular press; *después de* possible)	So, after the hard years between 1936-1939 . . .
Los cazadores denuncian "intereses políticos" tras las críticas de un grupo ecologista andaluz (El Mundo, Spain)	Hunters denounce 'political interests' after criticisms by an Andalusian ecologist group
Tras de sus ojos se fue como imantado (M. de Unamuno, Spain)	He went off after her, drawn by her eyes, as though magnetized

Notes
(i) Occasionally *tras* is unavoidable: *Siguieron el mismo ritmo de trabajo, año tras año/día tras día* 'They followed the same work-pace, year after year/day after day', *Han puesto un detective tras sus pasos* 'They've put a detective after him/on his trail'.
(ii) Note also the following construction: *Tras de tener él la culpa, se enfada* (or *Encima de tener él . . .*) 'Not only is it his fault; he has the nerve to get angry'.

34.19 Prepositional phrases

The following is a list of common prepositional phrases. They can appear before nouns and, if their meaning is appropriate, before pronouns and infinitives:

a base de	based on/consisting of
a bordo de	on board
a cambio de	in exchange for
a cargo de	supervised by
a causa de	because of
a costa de	at the cost of
a despecho de	in spite of
a diferencia de	unlike
a disposición de	at the disposal of
à distinción de	unlike
a espaldas de	behind the back of
a excepción de	with the exception of
a expensas de	at the expense of
a falta de	for lack of/for want of
a favor de	in favour of
a fin de	with the aim of
a finales/fines de	towards the end of
a flor de	flush with/at . . . level (only used with *piel* 'skin', *agua* 'water', *tierra* 'ground')
a fuerza de	by dint of
a guisa de (literary)	= *a modo de*
a gusto de	to the taste of
a juicio de	in the opinion of
a la sombra de	in the shadow of
a más de	as well as . . .
a mediados de	towards the middle of
a modo de	in the manner of
al nivel de	at the level of
a partir de	starting from
a pesar de	despite
a por	see 34.14.4h
a principios de	towards the beginning of
a prueba de	-proof, eg. *a prueba de incendios* 'fire-proof'
a punto de	on the verge of
a raíz de	immediately after/as an immediate result of
a razón de	at the rate of
a riesgo de	at the risk of
a sabiendas de	with the knowledge of
a través de	through/across
a vista de	in the sight/presence of
a voluntad de	at the discretion of
a vuelta de	e.g. *a vuelta de correo* 'by return of post'
además de	as well as
al alcance de	within reach of
al amor de	in the warmth of (e.g. a fire)
al cabo de	at the end of
al contrario de	contrary to
al corriente de	*au fait* with/informed about
al estilo de	in the style of
al frente de	at the head/forefront of
al lado de	next to
alrededor de	around
al tanto de	= *al corriente de*
a la hora de	at the moment of/when it comes to . . .
a la vera de (literary)	= *al lado de*
a lo largo de	throughout/along
bajo (la) condición de que	on condition of

bajo pena de	on pain of
cerca de	near
con arreglo a	in accordance with
con miras a	bearing in mind/with a view to
con motivo de	on the occasion of (an anniversary, etc.)
con objeto de	with the object of
con relación a	in respect of/in relation to
con respecto a	with respect/reference to/in comparison to
con rumbo a	in the direction of (i.e. moving towards)
con vistas a	with a view to/bearing in mind
de acuerdo con	in accordance with
de regreso a	on returning to
debajo de	see 34.3, 31.6.6
delante de	see 34.2, 31.6.8
dentro de	see 31.6.5
después de	after (time); see 14.10.3
detrás de	behind; see 34.18, 31.6.7
en atención a	in consideration of
en base a	on the basis of (i.e. *sobre la base de*)
en busca de	in search of
en caso de	in case of
en concepto de	as/by way of e.g. *Este dinero es en concepto de ayuda* 'this money is by way of assistance'
en contra de	against
en cuanto a	as for . . ./concerning
en forma de	in the shape of
en frente de	opposite
en honor de	in honour of (but *en honor **a** la verdad* 'strictly speaking')
en lugar de	instead of (+ noun or pronoun)
en medio de	in the middle of
en pos de (literary)	in search of (also = *tras de*)
en pro de (literary)	= *a favor de*
en torno a	around (the subject of)/concerning
en vez de	instead of
en vías de	on the way to: *país en vías de desarrollo* 'developing country'
en vísperas de	on the eve of
en vista de	in view of
encima de	see 34.9 and 34.17
fuera de	see 31.6.5
lejos de	far from
mas allá de	beyond
no obstante (literary)	notwithstanding
por causa de	= *a causa de*
por cuenta de	= *a expensas de*
por encima de	over the head of/against the will of
por parte de	on the part of
por razón de	= *a causa de*
sin embargo de (literary)	notwithstanding
so pena de (literary)	= *bajo pena de*
so pretexto de (literary)	on the pretext of
tras de	see 34.18

35

Relative clauses and pronouns

35.1 General

35.1.1 Forms of relative pronouns

There are four relative pronouns in Spanish: *que, quien(es), el que, el cual*.

El que and *el cual* agree in number and gender with their antecedent[1] and can therefore take the forms:

	singular	plural
masc.	el que/el cual	los que/los cuales
fem.	la que/la cual	las que/las cuales

The plural of *quien* is *quienes*, but it has no separate feminine form.

El que is used only after prepositions. Foreign students tend to over-use *el cual* and neglect the more frequent *el que* and *quien*. *El cual* tends nowadays to be confined to formal styles; it is discussed separately at 35.5.

Cuando, donde and *como* may also introduce relative clauses, e.g. *la calle donde/en la que la vi* 'the street I saw her in/where I saw her'. See 35.10-12 for discussion.

35.1.2 Restrictive and non-restrictive relative clauses

This chapter occasionally refers to a distinction between restrictive and non-restrictive clauses.

Restrictive clauses limit the scope of their antecedent: *Las chicas que eran suizas se callaron* 'The girls who were Swiss stopped talking'. This refers only to those girls who were Swiss.

Non-restrictive clauses or appositive clauses do not limit the scope of their antecedent: *Las chicas, que/las cuales eran suizas, se callaron* 'The girls, who were Swiss, stopped talking'. This sentence clearly claims that all the girls are Swiss. In writing non-restrictive clauses are typically marked by a comma, and in speech by a pause.

A relative clause that refers to the whole of a unique entity is bound to be non-restrictive (note that English does not allow 'that' for 'which' in the following sentence): *La abadía de Westminster, que/la cual es uno de los monumentos más visitados por los turistas* 'Westminster Abbey, which is one of the monuments most visited by tourists'.

---

[1] The antecedent of a relative pronoun is the noun or pronoun that it refers to: in 'the dog that I bought', 'dog' is the antecedent of 'that'.

35.1.3 English and Spanish relative pronouns contrasted

Spanish relative clauses differ from English in four major respects:

(a) Prepositions must never be separated from a relative pronoun: 'the path (that/which) we were walking **along**' = *el camino **por el que** caminábamos*. Sentences like **el camino que caminábamos por*, occasionally heard in the Spanish of beginners, are almost unintelligible.

(b) A relative pronoun can never be omitted in Spanish: 'the plane I saw' = *el avión que (yo) vi*.

(c) English and French constantly replace relative pronouns by a gerund or participle form: 'a box containing two books' *une boîte contenant deux livres*. This is usually impossible in Spanish: *una caja **que contiene/contenía** dos libros*. The subject is discussed in detail at 20.3.

(d) Spanish does not allow a relative pronoun to be separated from its antecedent by a verb phrase. The type of sentence sporadically heard in English like ?'The man doesn't exist whom I'd want to marry' (for 'The man (whom) I'd want to marry doesn't exist') cannot be translated by **El hombre no existe con el que yo quisiera casarme*. The correct translations are *No existe el hombre con el que yo quisiera casarme* or *El hombre con el que yo quisiera casarme no existe*. The first of these two translations is preferable, and this has important consequences for the word order of Spanish sentences containing relative clauses. See 37.2.1 for discussion.

Further examples: *Acudieron corriendo los vecinos, que/quienes/los cuales no pudieron hacer nada* 'The neighbours came running, but could do nothing' (literally, 'who could . . .') not **Los vecinos acudieron corriendo, que . . .*; *Han vuelto las cigüeñas que hicieron su nido en el campanario el año pasado* 'The storks that made their nest in the belfry last year have returned', not **Las cigüeñas han vuelto que . . ..*

35.2 The relative pronoun *que*

Que is the most frequent relative pronoun and may be used in the vast majority of cases to translate the English relative pronouns 'who', 'whom', 'which' or 'that'.

However, there are certain cases in which *el que*, *quien* or *el cual* must be used. These are:

(a) In most cases after prepositions; see 35.4.

(b) *El cual* only: in contexts discussed at 35.5.

Examples of *que* as a relative pronoun:

los inversionistas que se quemaron los dedos	the investors who burnt their fingers
las hojas que caían de las ramas	the leaves (that were) falling from the branches
el libro que compré ayer	the book (that) I bought yesterday
las enfermeras que despidieron el año pasado (see 22.4.2 for use of personal *a* in this type of sentence)	the nurses (that) they fired/sacked last year

Note
The word *todo* requires the relative pronoun *el que*: *todos **los que** dicen eso . . .* 'all who say that/everyone who says that'.

35.3 Use of *que*, *quien*, *el cual* in non-restrictive relative clauses

When no preposition appears before the relative pronoun and the relative clause is **non-restrictive** (see 35.1.2 for definition), *que*, *quien* or *el cual* may be used. *Quien* is used for human beings, and *el cual* is emphatic and restricted to formal language:

Fueron a hablar con José, que/quien/el cual estaba de mal humor	They went to talk to José, who was in a bad mood
Tres cajas de ropa que/las que/las cuales, no pudiendo olvidar a su difunto marido, se negaba a vender	Three chests of clothes which, being unable to forget her late husband, she refused to sell
el presidente, que/quien/el cual acababa de pronunciar un discurso	the President, who had just delivered a speech

El cual is more likely to be used whenever the relative pronoun is separated from its antecedent or from the verb of which it is the subject or object. *El cual* is discussed further at 35.5.

Notes
(i) Only *que* can be used after personal pronouns: *Yo que me preocupo tanto por ti . . .* 'I who worry so much about you . . .', *. . . y ahora, hablando con ella, que tenía el sol de la tarde en el rostro* (F. Umbral, Spain) '. . . and now, talking to her, who had the evening sun on her face'.
(ii) In 'cleft' sentences (discussed at 36.2) a nominalizer, e.g. *el que*, *quien*, must be used: *Fue María quien/la que dijo la verdad* 'It was Maria who told the truth', *Soy consciente de que tengo que ser yo misma la que/quien resuelva el problema* (female speaking) 'I'm aware that I must be the one to solve the problem myself'.
(iii) *El que* also translates 'the one who/which' and is discussed under nominalizers at 36.1: *Aquella chica es Charo – la que lleva el chándal rojo* 'That girl over there is Charo – the one wearing the red tracksuit'.

El que is rare as a subject relative pronoun, though the preceding construction is sometimes similar to a non-restrictive clause. Compare *Hacia el final de los debates, comenzó a perfilarse una cuarta opción, la que reclamaba un "nuevo concepto de un nacionalismo pluralista"* (*El País*) 'Towards the end of the discussions a fourth option began to take shape, one which demanded a "new concept of a pluralist nationalism"'.

35.4 Relative pronoun after prepositions

35.4.1 After prepositions *el que*, *quien* or *el cual* are used
When the relative pronoun is preceded by a preposition, *que* alone is used only in the circumstances discussed at 35.4.2.

The relative pronouns required are:
(a) Non-human antecedents: *el que* (or *el cual*).
(b) Human antecedents: *el que*, *quien* (or *el cual*). *Quien* is slightly more formal than *el que*.

Use of *el cual* is discussed separately at 35.5.

. . . la misión a la que ha dedicado su vida (J.L. Borges, Argentina)	. . . the mission to which he has dedicated his life
la amenaza de guerra bajo la que vivimos	the threat of war we're living under
la maniobra en virtud de la que consiguió un éxito inmerecido	the manoeuvre whereby he gained an undeserved success
la calle desde la que/donde he venido andando	the street I've walked from
¿. . . y todas . . . ésas con quien has paseado	and what about all those . . . women

y . . . que has besado? (Buero Vallejo, Spain, dialogue; *quien* for *quienes* is popular style)

you've walked out with and . . . kissed?

Yo era para ella . . . el ser supremo con el que se dialoga, el dios callado con quien creemos conversar (F. Umbral, Spain; both relative pronouns used)

I was for her . . . the supreme being one talks with, the silent god we imagine we are conversing with

Y sin llegar al extremo de un Lezama Lima, para quien todo es metáfora de todo . . . (M. Vargas Llosa, Peru)

And without going to the extreme of a Lezama Lima, for whom everything is a metaphor for everything

. . . la habían hecho sentir una seguridad de la que hasta entonces carecía (S. Pitol, Mexico)

. . . they had made her feel a security that she had lacked until then

Notes

(i) If the gender of a human antecedent is not known, *quien* (genderless) must be used: *No hay nadie con quien hablar* 'There's no one to talk to', *Busca a alguien de quien te puedas fiar* 'Look for someone you can trust'.

(ii) After neuter antecedents like *algo, nada* and *mucho, lo que* or *que* are used: *No hay nada con (lo) que puedas sacarle punta* 'There's nothing you can sharpen it with', *Iba a morir allí, no por algo en lo que creía, sino por respeto a su hermano mayor* (M. Vargas Llosa, Peru) 'He was going to die there, not for something he believed in, but out of respect for his elder brother'.

(iii) The use of personal *a* before relative pronouns is discussed at 22.4.2.

35.4.2 Relative pronoun *que* after a preposition

Que alone is preferred as a relative pronoun after prepositions in certain circumstances difficult to define.

(a) After *a* (when it is not personal *a*), after *con* and after *de* – unless the latter means 'from'. Use of *que* alone is especially common after abstract nouns:

la película a que me refiero

the film I'm referring to

La discriminación a que están sometidas nuestras frutas y hortalizas . . . (*El País*)

The discrimination which our fruits and vegetables are subject to . . .

La notoria buena fe con que Collazos expone sus dudas y sus convicciones (M. Vargas Llosa, Peru)

The well-known good faith with which Collazos expounds his doubts and convictions

Ese conjunto de sutiles atributos con que el alma se revela a través de la carne (E. Sábato, Argentina)

That set of subtle attributes by which the soul reveals itself through the flesh

. . . la aspereza con que la trataba (S. Pitol, Mexico)

the harshness with which he treated her

las especies de escarabajo de que estoy hablando

the species of beetle I am talking about

uno de los más serios percances de que se tiene noticia (*El País*)

one of the most serious mishaps known (lit 'of which there is knowledge')

El que would be possible, though less elegant, in the foregoing examples.

(b) Frequently after *en* when precise spatial location is not intended. Compare *la caja en la que encontré la llave* 'the box I found the key in', but *la casa en que vivo* 'the house I live in', not *'the house **inside which** I live'.

En que is also preferred when the preceding noun is a period of time. After *día, semana, mes, año, momento* the *en* is also often omitted:

el desierto humano en que ella estaba perdida (F. Umbral)

the human desert she was lost in

Me gustaría vivir en un sitio en que/donde no hubiera coches

I'd like to live in a place where there were no cars

las formas racionales en que se basa la vida social (M. Vargas Llosa, Peru)	the rational forms on which social life is based
el momento político en que salía (M. Vargas Llosa, Peru)	the political moment at which it appeared

In all the preceding examples *el que* is also possible, but not in the following:

una noche en que iba a buscarla (F. Umbral)	one night I went to fetch her
el día que te vi	the day I saw you
El único día que se produjeron diferencias de importancia fue el jueves (*La Nación*, Argentina, quoted in *Variedades* 124)	The only day on which any important differences were recorded was Thursday
el año que nos casamos	the year we got married
el mes que llovió tanto	the month it rained so much
en los meses que estuvo Edwards en Cuba (M. Vargas Llosa, Peru)	during the months Edwards spent in Cuba
durante el año y medio que he estado en el cargo	in the year and a half I've been in the job

Note

If the antecedent is precise as to the number of units of time, *el que* is used: *aquellos millones de años en los que el hombre aprendió a cazar y a servirse de sus herramientas* 'those millions of years in which man learned to hunt and use his tools', *Un tipo de genocidio que estará consumado dentro de treinta años, en los que las buenas intenciones de ciertas instituciones . . .* (A. Carpentier, Cuba) 'A type of genocide which will be complete within thirty years in which the good intentions of certain institutions . . .'.

35.5 *El cual*

In general *el cual* is more formal than *el que* or *quien*, and is yielding ground to them; foreigners spoil much good Spanish by overusing it. But it may be preferred or obligatory in the following contexts:

(a) After *según* when it means 'according to' rather than 'depending on' – as it does in —*¿Qué precio tienen?* —*Según los que quiera* ' "What's their price?" "It depends on which ones you want" ':

el argumento según el cual . . .	the argument according to which . . .
José Carlos Mariátegui, según el cual "el marxismo leninismo es el sendero luminoso de la revolución" (M. Vargas Llosa, Peru)	J. C. Mariátegui, according to whom 'Marxist Leninism is the shining path to revolution'

(b) It is often preferred after long prepositions, i.e. of more than one syllable, e.g. *para, contra, entre, mediante,* and after prepositional phrases, e.g. *a pesar de* 'despite', *debajo de* 'underneath', *delante de* 'in front of', *frente a* 'opposite', *en virtud de* 'by reason of', etc. However, *el que* is increasingly common even in these contexts.

El cual is also especially favoured when the antecedent is separated from the relative pronoun by intervening words, or when the relative is separated from its verb:

. . . una formación profesional mediante la cual los funcionarios de grado medio estén capacitados para . . . (*Cambio16*, Spain)	professional training whereby middle-grade civil servants will be equipped to . . .
Hay cuerpos, seres, con atmósfera propia, dentro de la cual es bueno vivir (F. Umbral, Spain)	There are bodies, beings, with their own atmosphere, within which it is good to live

Hay chequetrenes con los que usted puede viajar por un valor de 15.000 a 20.000 pesetas, pero por los cuales usted sólo paga 12.750 y 17.000 ptas respectivamente (Advertisement: *el cual* separated from its antecedent)	There are 'Traincheques' with which you can travel to a value of 15-20,000 pesetas, but for which you only pay 12,750 and 17,000 pesetas respectively

But note *El otro fue alcanzado por ocho balazos, a consecuencia de **los que** moriría minutos más tarde . . .* (*El País*) 'The other one received eight bullet wounds, as a consequence of which he was to die a few minutes later', . . . *la localización de la abadía, sobre **la que** Adso evita toda referencia concreta* (Umberto Eco, translated by R. Pochtar) '. . . the location of the abbey, about which Adso avoids all specific reference'.

(c) *El cual* is used after *algunos de . . ., todos . . ., la mayoría de . . ., parte de . . .* and similar phrases:

los jóvenes españoles, la mayoría de los cuales son partidarios del divorcio	young Spaniards, the majority of whom are in favour of divorce
. . . árboles, pocos de los cuales tenían hojas	trees, few of which had leaves
. . . defender la revolución social, parte integrante de la cual era la emancipación de la mujer	to defend the social revolution, of which an integral part was the emancipation of woman
Corren por Madrid muchos rumores, algunos de los cuales vamos a recoger aquí	Many rumours are circulating in Madrid, some of which we shall report here

(d) As the subject of a verb, *el cual* seems to be obligatory after a heavy pause such as a sentence break – a construction not easily imitated in English and not particularly common in Spanish:

*Fueron a hablar con su tío, un setentón de bigote blanco y acento andaluz, que hacía alarde de ideas muy avanzadas. **El cual**, tras un largo silencio, contestó . . .*	They went to talk with his uncle, a seventy-year old with a white moustache and Andalusian accent who boasted very advanced ideas. Who, after a long silence, replied . . .

35.6 *Lo cual* and *lo que*

These are used when the relative pronoun refers not to a noun or pronoun but to a whole sentence or to an idea, which, being neither masculine nor feminine in gender, require a neuter pronoun. Since the clause is always non-restrictive, *lo cual* is common, especially in writing. Compare: *Trajo una lista de cifras que explicaba su inquietud* 'He brought a list of figures which (i.e. the list) explained his anxiety' and *Trajo una lista de cifras, lo cual/lo que explicaba su inquietud* 'He brought a list of figures, which (i.e. the fact he brought it) explained his anxiety'. Further examples:

En un primer momento se anunció que los misiles eran americanos, lo cual fue desmentido en Washington (*El País*)	Initially it was stated that the missiles were American, which was denied in Washington
Llegué tarde, por lo que/lo cual no pude asistir a la reunión	I arrived late, for which reason I couldn't attend the meeting
El año siguiente fue la exaltación de Amadeo de Saboya al trono de España, lo cual le tuvo vagando por Madrid hasta altas horas de la madrugada (J.M. Guelbenzu, *Spain*)	The following year there occurred the elevation of Amadeo of Savoy to the Spanish throne, which had him wandering round Madrid until the small hours

35.7 Cuyo

This translates 'whose', and is often an elegant alternative for an otherwise tortuous relative clause. It agrees in number and gender with the following noun. If there is more than one noun, it agrees only with the first: *una mujer cuyas manos y pies estaban quemados por el sol* 'a woman whose hands and feet had been burnt by the sun', *una señora cuyo sombrero y guantes eran de seda* 'a lady whose hat and gloves were made of silk':

aquellos verbos cuyo subjuntivo es irregular	those verbs whose subjunctive is irregular
un hombre de cuya honradez no dudo	a man whose honesty I don't doubt
una medida cuyos efectos son imprevisibles	a measure whose effects are unforeseeable

Notes
(i) Grammarians condemn such commonly heard sentences as ?*Se alojó en el Imperial, en cuyo hotel había conocido a su primera mujer* 'He stayed in the Imperial, in which hotel he had met his first wife', better . . . *el Imperial, hotel donde había conocido a su primera mujer*. But this construction is allowed with *caso*: *Nos han alertado acerca de la posibilidad de que todos los hoteles estén completos, en cuyo caso la reunión será aplazada* 'They have warned us of the possibility that all the hotels may be full, in which case the meeting will be postponed'.
(ii) *Del que/de quien* occasionally replace *cuyo*: *un torero, de quien alabó el tesón y el valor a toda prueba* 'a bullfighter, whose indefatigable steadfastness and courage he praised'.
(iii) *Cuyo* is rare in spontaneous speech and virtually unheard in popular styles. See 35.8c for a discussion.
(iv) *Cuyo* is not used in questions (except in some local Latin-American dialects): *¿De quién es esa mochila?* 'Whose rucksack is that?', not *¿*Cuya mochila es ésa?*.

35.8 Relative clauses in familiar speech

Students will encounter a number of popular or familiar constructions that should probably be left to native speakers.
(a) There is a colloquial tendency, which may sometimes sound uneducated, to insert a redundant pronoun in relative clauses:

*Los gramáticos aconsejan muchas cosas que nadie **las** dice* (overheard)	Grammarians recommend many things that no one says
*Sólo por ti dejaría para siempre a don Memo, a quien tanto **le** debo* (C. Fuentes, Mexico, dialogue)	Only for you would I leave Don Memo for ever. I owe him so much

(b) Popular and relaxed informal speech often avoids combining prepositions and relative pronouns by using a type of construction banned from writing:

?*en casa de una mujer que yo vivía con ella* . . . (*con la que yo vivía*)	in the house of a woman I was living with
?*Te acuerdas del hotel que estuvimos el año pasado?* (. . . *en el que estuvimos* . . .)	Do you remember the hotel we stayed in last year?
?*Soy un emigrante que siempre me han preocupado los problemas de la emigración* (. . . *al que siempre han preocupado los problemas*) (Reader's letter in *El País*)	I am an emigrant who has always been concerned with the problems of emigration

This construction is not uncommon in Golden-Age texts, but it should not be imitated by foreign learners.

(c) *Cuyo* is avoided in spontaneous speech. There are many correct alternatives, e.g. *las mujeres cuyo marido las ayuda en casa* 'women whose husbands help them in the house' can be re-cast as *las mujeres que tienen un marido que las ayuda en casa*. However, popular speech often uses a construction called *quesuísmo* which is stigmatized as illiterate:

?los alumnos que sus notas no están en la lista (cuyas notas no están . . .)	the students whose marks aren't on the list

35.9 *Cartas a contestar . . .*, etc.

The following construction is nowadays very common in journalism, official documents or business letters:

*un libro y una tesis **a tomar** muy en serio por estudiosos y ciudadanos en general . . . (Cambio16, Spain, for que deben ser tomados en serio . . .)*	a book and a thesis to be taken very seriously by students and citizens in general

For a discussion of this controversial construction see 18.12.

35.10 *Donde, adonde, en donde* as relatives

Donde is commonly used as a relative, especially after *hacia*, *a* (in the meaning of 'towards'), *desde*, *de* meaning 'from', *por* meaning 'along'/'through', *en* meaning 'place in', etc.

As a relative its use is rather wider than the English 'where':

Lo recogí en la calle donde te vi	I picked it up in the street where I saw you
Añoraba las playas donde se había paseado durante aquel verano	He longed for the beaches where he had strolled that summer
Ése/Ese es el baúl de donde sacó los papeles	That's the trunk from which he took the papers
la ciudad hacia donde avanzaban las tropas enemigas . . .	the city towards which enemy troops were advancing . . .
un balcón desde donde se podía ver el desfile	a balcony from which/where one could see the parade

In all the above restrictive clauses, *el que* or *el cual* could be used with the appropriate preposition. However, in the following non-restrictive clause only *donde* is possible:

Volvieron a encontrarse en París, donde se habían conocido veinte años antes	They met again in Paris, where they had met for the first time twenty years before

Notes
(i) *Adonde* is not the same as *a dónde*. The former is a relative, the latter is found in direct or indirect questions and is always written as two words: *el pueblo **adonde** yo iba* (relative) 'the village I was going to', *No quería decirle **a dónde** iba yo* (indirect question) 'I didn't want to tell him where I was going', *¿(A) **dónde** va usted?* 'Where are you going?'.
(ii) *En donde* is spatially more specific than *donde*, and is rather literary: *Hay una tienda pequeña en Westwood en donde venden infinidad de camisetas con letreros increíbles* (C. Rico-Godoy, Spain) 'There's a little shop/store in Westwood where they sell a vast

range of T-shirts with fantastic things written on them'. . . . *Westwood donde venden* would have come to the same thing.

(iii) *Donde* is sometimes used colloquially in Mexico (and possibly elsewhere in northern Latin America) to mean an apprehensive 'what if . . . ?'. In this context Peninsular Spanish uses *anda que si* + indicative or *anda que como* + subjunctive : *No digas, estoy muy espantada, **donde** a la pobre criatura le salga la nariz de este hombre* (A. Mastretta, Mexico, dialogue; Spain *anda que como le salga* . . .) 'Don't even mention it, I'm really terrified. What if this poor little thing gets this man's nose?!', *No sé cómo se van a casar.* ***Donde** estén igual de ignorantes en lo demás* (idem, Spain *Anda que como estén* . . ., *Anda que si están* . . .) 'I don't know how they're going to get married. What if they're just as ignorant about all the other things?!'.

35.11 *Como* as a relative

Como is officially recommended after *la manera* and *el modo*, although *en que* is used after *forma*, and usually after the other two as well:

*La manera **como** un país se fortalece y desarrolla su cultura es abriendo sus puertas y ventanas* (M. Vargas Llosa, Peru)	The way a country strengthens and develops its culture is by opening its doors and windows
Me gusta la manera como/en que lo hace	I like the way he does it
Me gusta la forma en que lo hace	I like the way he does it

Notes
(i) *En que* is more usual in informal language.
(ii) *Mismo* plus a noun requires *que*: *Lo dijo del mismo modo que lo dijo antes* 'He said it the same way as he said it before', *Llevas la misma falda que yo* 'You're wearing the same skirt as me'.

35.12 *Cuando* as a relative

Cuando occurs only in non-restrictive clauses:

En agosto, cuando les den las vacaciones a los niños, nos iremos al campo	In August, when the children have their holidays/vacation, we'll go to the countryside
incluso en nuestros días, cuando nadie cree ya en las hadas	even in our day, when no one believes in fairies any more

But: *Sólo puedo salir los días (en) que no trabajo* (restrictive) 'I can only go out on the days I'm not working'.

Notes
(i) *Cuando* is used with *apenas, aún, entonces, justo, no, no bien*: *Apenas había aparcado el coche cuando se acercó un policía* 'He had hardly parked the car when a policeman came up', *Aún/Todavía no había empezado a estudiar cuando le dieron un empleo* 'He hadn't yet started studying when they gave him a job', *Empezó entonces, cuando los demás todavía no habían llegado* 'He began then, when the others hadn't yet arrived'.
  Compare the following restrictive clauses: *en un momento en que* . . . 'at a moment when . . .', *en una época en que* . . . 'in a period when . . .', *en un año en que* . . . 'in a year when . . .', etc.
  (ii) *Que* is used in the following phrases: *ahora que usted sabe la verdad* 'now (that) you know the truth', *luego que haya terminado* 'as soon as he's finished', *siempre que haya bastante* 'as long as there's enough', *cada vez que me mira* 'whenever he looks at me', *de modo que/de manera que* . . . 'so that . . .'.
  In 'cleft' sentences *donde, como* or *cuando* may be obligatory and *que* disallowed (especially in Peninsular Spanish): *Es así **como** hay que hacerlo* 'This is how it must

be done', *Fue entonces **cuando** lo notó* 'It was then that he noticed it'. See 36.2 for discussion.

35.13 Relative clauses after a nominalizer

A nominalizer (e.g. *el que* meaning 'the one who/which') cannot be followed by the relatives *el que* or *el cual*. The noun must be repeated or, in written language, *aquel* is used:

Se imagina un nuevo don Julián, una versión moderna de aquel al que rinde homenaje el título del libro (M. Vargas Llosa, Peru; not *el al que . . .)	He imagines a new Don Julian, a modern version of the one to whom the book's title pays homage
Traiga otro plato – no me gusta comer en los platos en los que otros han comido (spoken language)	Bring another plate – I don't like eating off those others have eaten off

35.14 Miscellaneous examples of relative clauses

Falta saber las condiciones en que está	We have yet to know what conditions he is in
Falta saber en qué condiciones está	" "
Falta saber en las condiciones que está	" "
según el cine a que vayas según al cine que vayas (All examples from M. Moliner.)	depending on what cinema you go to
Era la habitación más pequeña en (la) que jamás he estado	It was the smallest room I've ever been in
Era la habitación más pequeña de todas las que he estado (familiar spoken language)	It was the smallest room I've ever been in
¿Cómo se explica el fenómeno singular que fue la victoria de los liberales?	How does one explain the singular phenomenon of the liberals' victory?
el espectáculo conmovedor que son las ruinas de Machu Picchu	the moving spectacle of the Machu Picchu ruins

36

Nominalizers and cleft sentences

36.1 Nominalizers

36.1.1 General

A marked feature of Spanish is the use of the article to create noun phrases from words that are not themselves nouns: *rojo* 'red', *el rojo* 'the red one'; *explotado* 'exploited', *las explotadas* 'exploited women', etc. See 4.1d for discussion.

This device may be applied to possessive adjective/pronouns, e.g. *mío* 'mine', *el mío* 'my one'/'the one belonging to me': see 8.4 for discussion.

36.1 discusses an important type of nominalizer, *el de, lo de, el que, lo que* and *quien* used as pronouns with such values as 'the one from', 'the one belonging to . . .', 'the one who/that . . .', 'the person who . . .', etc., cf. French *celui de, celui qui, celle qui, ceux qui, ce qui,* etc. Some grammars treat these under relative pronouns, but they are in fact devices for turning a verbal or prepositional phrase into a noun phrase: *los que interrogan* is close in meaning to *los interrogadores* 'the interrogators', *los de antes* to *los anteriores* 'the previous ones', *el que/quien habla catalán* to *el hablante de catalán* 'the Catalan-speaker', etc.

36.2 Discusses 'cleft' sentences, e.g. *Fue aquí donde la vi* 'It was here that I saw her', a type of sentence that presents a number of difficulties not found in English or French.

For the use of *el que* and *quien* as relative pronouns, (*El hombre con el que/con quien hablaba, La mesa en la que escribo*) see Chapter 35, especially 35.3 and 35.4. For *quién* in questions, see 24.5.

36.1.2 *El de*

'The one(s) belonging to', 'that/those of', 'the one(s) from', etc. Its use in Spanish avoids repetition of the noun – as in the tragedy example below. It agrees in number and gender with the noun it replaces:

Entre los problemas de España y los de Estados Unidos, creo que los de los EE.UU son más graves	Between the problems of Spain and (those of) the USA, I think the USA's are more serious
Los de Buenos Aires son mejores	The ones from Buenos Aires are better
los de siempre	the same ones as always
La de los refugiados es la gran tragedia de nuestro siglo (El País)	The tragedy of the refugees is the great tragedy of our century
Su rostro era el de un marino griego actual (M. Vázquez Montalbán, Spain)	His face was that of a present-day Greek sailor

Translation by a Saxon genitive or compound noun is sometimes appropriate:

Quita los de ayer y pon los de la semana pasada	Take away yesterday's and put last week's
Tenía los ojos saltones como los de una rana	He had bulging eyes like a frog's
la industria del petróleo y la del carbón	the oil and coal industries
Lo he hecho para aumentar la moral, sobre todo la de los escritores (J.M. Lara, *El País*)	I've done it to raise morale, especially writers' morale

Note
La de can mean 'the amount of'/'how many': *No sé la de temas que tengo apuntados* (C. Martín Gaite, Spain) 'I don't know how many topics I've got jotted down'. See also 3.2.30.

36.1.3 *Lo de*
The neuter version of the above phrases. Like all neuter pronouns, its use is obligatory if there is no noun to which it can refer. *Lo de* has limited applications.

It is a common equivalent of 'the . . . business/affair' in such phrases as *lo del dinero perdido* 'the affair of the lost money':

Se puso enferma por lo de su hijo	She fell ill/(US) 'sick' because of the business of her son
Siempre está a vueltas con lo de que cuándo nos vamos a casar	(S)he's always coming back with the issue of when we're going to get married
La primera vez que vi a Andrés furioso . . . fue cuando lo de la plaza de toros (A. Mastretta, México; for the prepositional use of *cuando* see 24.8)	The first time I saw Andrés furious was at the time of the bullring business
De lo de la abuela poco les debe quedar (C. Martín Gaite, Spain)	They must have very little left of grandma's/of what belongs to grandma

Note
It is common in Argentina and other parts of Latin America in the meaning *en casa* de 'at . . .'s house': *en lo de Ángel* 'at Angel's place'.

36.1.4 *El que*
This translates 'the one(s) who/which', 'that/those which', etc., (French *celui/celle/celles/ceux qui*). It agrees in number and gender with the noun it replaces:

La que está fuera	The one (fem.) who/that is outside
El que llegó ayer	The one (masc.) that arrived yesterday
Los que dicen eso	The ones/those (masc.) who say that
Vivo en la que está pintada de blanco	I live in the one (i.e. *la casa*) painted white
Me atraían las que le tuvieron cariño, las que incluso le parieron hijos (A. Mastretta, Mexico)	I felt attracted towards those who were fond of him, even towards those who had given him children
La que fue considerada doctrina alternativa (*El País*)	That which was considered the alternative doctrine

Notes
(i) *El de* and *el que* can be combined: *La libertad de la televisión debería ser siempre la del que la contempla . . . no la del que la programa* (*El País*) 'Freedom in television should always belong to the person watching it . . . not to the person programming it'.
(ii) For *el que* (invariable) + subjunctive meaning 'the fact that' (*el hecho de que*), see 16.10.1.
(iii) *La que* is often used in humorous warnings: *No sabes la que te espera* 'You don't know what's waiting for you', *¡La que te tienen preparada!* 'What they've got in store for you!'

36.1.5 *Lo que*

The neuter version of the above: it refers to no specific noun. It can normally be translated by the phrase 'the thing that . . .' or by the pronoun 'what' (cf. French *ce qui/ce que*):

Lo que más me irrita es . . .	What most irritates me is that . . .
Se asombró de lo que dijo el portavoz	He was amazed at what the spokesman said
La valla se prolonga todo lo que da de sí la vista	The fence stretches as far as the eye can see
Le pasa lo que a ti	The same thing happens to him as to you
Octavia, un hombre es lo que siente (A. Bryce Echenique, Peru, dialogue)	Octavia, a man is what he feels
. . . tuvo bien acordarse de un chiste tras otro en lo que quedó de cena (A. Mastretta, México)	. . . he was obliging enough to remember joke after joke during what was left of dinner

Compare: *Por Rosario fue por **la** que se pelearon* 'Rosario was **the woman** they fought over' and *Por Rosario fue por **lo** que se pelearon* 'Rosario was **what** they fought over'.

36.1.6 *Quien* as an equivalent of 'the one who'

Quien/quienes can optionally replace *el que* in many contexts provided it refers to a human being. Since *quien* is not marked for gender it is not an exact equivalent of *el que* and must be used when reference to a specific gender is to be avoided. Only *quien* is possible in the meaning of 'no one':

El que diga eso es un cobarde	The person who says that is a coward
Quien diga eso es un cobarde	(same, but rather literary)
Quienes/Los que no estén de acuerdo, que se vayan	Anyone not in agreement should go
Que se lo diga al que/a quien quiera	Let him tell whomever he likes
Quien no es mala persona es el sargento	Someone who's not a bad fellow is the sergeant
El coronel no tiene quien le escriba (G. García Márquez, title, *el que* impossible here)	The colonel has no one to write to him
Tú no eres quien para decirme eso (colloquial, *el que* impossible)	You're no one to tell me that
como quien espera heredar una fortuna	like someone hoping to inherit a fortune

Note
Since it is indeterminate, *quien/quienes* cannot be used when the identity or sex of the person referred to is known and stressed: *Le/Lo vimos con la que vive al lado* (**Le/Lo vimos con quien vive al lado* = *'We saw him with whoever lives next door') 'We saw him with the girl who lives next door'.

36.2 'Cleft' sentences

36.2.1 General

A number of the examples given in 36.1 are in fact 'cleft' sentences. These are sentences in which an object, predicate or adverbial phrase is isolated and focused by using 'to be'. This can be done in one of two ways:

Simple sentence	**Cleft sentence**
The fire started here	It was here that the fire started
	Here was where the fire started

John said it	It was John who said it
	John was the one who said it
I cut it with this knife	It was this knife I cut it with
	This knife is the one I cut it with

The structure of such sentences differs in Spanish from its French and English counterparts, and there are important differences between Peninsular and Latin-American usage with regard to cleft sentences containing a preposition.

36.2.2 'She is the one who . . .', etc.

English speakers, especially those who know French, are tempted to join this type of cleft sentence by the particle *que*, but only a nominalizer (*el que* or *quien*) can be used:

Es este coche el que compré	This car's the one I bought
Este coche es el que compré (**not** **Es este coche que compré*)	It's this car I bought
Fue esa chica la que/quien lo hizo	That girl is the one who did it
Esa chica fue la que/quien lo hizo	It's that girl who did it
Fue usted el que/quien lo dijo	It was you (masc.) who said it
Usted fue el que/quien lo dijo	You were the one who said it
Esto es lo que más rabia me da	This is what makes me most furious
Lo que más rabia me da es esto	" "
porque nunca es ella, doña Pilar, la que aporta el dinero (interview in *Cambio16*, Spain)	because it's never Doña Pilar who brings in the money
El pelaje overo es el que prefieren los ángeles (J.L. Borges, Argentina)	Lamb's fleece is the one that angels prefer
Para entonces será la guerra mundial la que haya solucionado todo (*Cambio16*, Spain)	By then it'll be world war that will have solved everything
Fue probablemente su intuición la que le llevó a seguir aquella línea de conducta (S. Pitol, Mexico)	It was probably his intuition that made him follow that line of behaviour

36.2.3 Cleft sentences involving prepositions

If the first half of the cleft sentence contains a preposition, the preposition must normally be repeated in the second half, i.e. Spanish says 'It's with her **with whom** you must speak', *Es con ella **con la que/con quien** tienes que hablar*.

A major difference exists here between European and Latin-American Spanish. American Spanish, especially spoken but also informal written, regularly uses *que* alone in a way similar to French or English 'that'. This 'Gallicism' is vehemently rejected by many native Spaniards (although it is heard increasingly among younger generations of Spaniards):

Sp. *Es desde esta ventana desde **donde** se ve el mar*	It's from this window that you can see the sea
Lat.Am. *Es desde esta ventana que se ve el mar*	This balcony is where you can see the sea from
*Desde esta ventana es desde **donde** se ve el mar* (avoided in Lat. Am.?)	
Sp. *Fue por este motivo **por el que** decidió cambiar de empleo*	It was for this reason that he decided to change jobs
Lat.Am. *Fue por este motivo que decidió . . .*	

. . . *pero es con la Maga que hablo* (J. Cortázar, Argentina, dialogue; Spain . . . *con la que/quien hablo*)	. . . but it's Maga I'm talking to
No fue por Pepita sino por Teresa por la que/quien se pelearon (Spain)	It wasn't Pepita but Teresa they fought over
Es por eso que en el lenguaje deportivo abundan las hipérboles (*El Litoral*, Argentina, Spain *por eso es por lo que* . . .)	That's why hyperboles abound in sporting language
Es también por eso por lo que se traiciona a cualquiera (J. Marías, Spain)	That's also why one betrays anyone
No fue por el champagne que vine aquí día tras día (S. Pitol, Mexico, Spain *por lo que*)	It wasn't because of the champagne that I came here day after day

Clauses of time, place or manner require *cuando*, *donde* and *como* respectively, although Latin Americans may use *que*, especially in informal speech:

Sp. *Fue aquí **donde** ocurrió*	It was here that it happened
Lat.Am. *Fue aquí **que** ocurrió*	
Sp./Lat.Am. *Aquí fue **donde** ocurrió*	
Es en esta última novela donde se enfrentan los más verídicos tipos clericales trazados por Galdós (*Insula*, Spain)	It is in this last novel where the most lifelike clerical figures drawn by Galdós confront one another
Fue en Pueblo Nuevo que supimos que el novio de Petra no había vuelto más al pueblo (G. Cabrera Infante, Cuban dialogue; Spain *donde*)	It was in Pueblo Nuevo that we found out that Petra's boyfriend had never returned to the village
La chica se acuerda de que es ahí que está la guarida del brujo (M. Puig, Argentina, dialogue, Spain *donde*)	The girl remembers that there is where the wizard's lair is
Fue en casa de ella que tuvo lugar aquel encuentro con Vallejos (M. Vargas Llosa, Peru, Spain *donde*)	It was in her house that this meeting with Vallejos took place
Sp. *Es así como hay que hacerlo*	It's this way that you have to do it
Lat.Am. *Es así que hay que hacerlo*	" "
Sp./Lat.Am. *Así es como hay que hacerlo*	" "
Fue entonces cuando, podríamos decir, comenzó la historia del automóvil (*El País*, Spain)	It was then, we might say, that the story of the car began
Naturalmente tenía que ser en ese momento . . . que sonara el timbre (J. Cortázar, Argentina, Spain *cuando*)	Of course it had to be at that moment . . . that the bell rang

Notes
(i) Care is required with cleft sentences involving *lo que*. The neuter pronoun must be retained, cf. *Lo que me sorprende es su timidez/Es su timidez **lo que** me sorprende* 'What surprises me is his/her/your shyness', *Es la inseguridad lo que le/lo hace reaccionar de esa forma* 'It's insecurity that makes him react like that' (i.e. 'what makes him react thus is insecurity'), *Ha hecho cine, teatro, televisión, pero es con la canción con lo que le gustaría triunfar* (*Cambio16*, Spain) 'He has worked in cinema, theatre and TV, but it is in singing that he would like to make a hit', *Era un traje negro lo que llevaba* 'It was a black suit that he was wearing' (answers question 'What was he wearing?'), but *El que llevaba era el traje negro* 'The one he was wearing was the black suit' (answer to 'Which suit was he wearing?').
(ii) English makes the verb 'to be' singular when it is shifted to the head of a cleft sentence: 'The mosquitoes are what annoys him'/'It's the mosquitoes that annoy him'. *Ser* normally remains plural in such cleft sentences: ***Tenían** que ser los partidos*

socialistas quienes/los que implementaran esta política de austeridad 'It had to be the socialist parties which implemented this austerity policy', **Son** *los mosquitos lo que me irrita* 'The mosquitoes are what annoys me', *Lo que me irrita* **son** *los mosquitos* 'What annoys me is the mosquitoes'. See 2.3.3. for discussion.

(iii) Cleft sentences involving lengthy prepositional phrases may be connected by *que* in Latin-American usage but are likely to be avoided by careful Peninsular speakers: ?*Fue bajo esta impresión que continuamos con el programa* (Spain *Fue así, bajo esta impresión,* **como** *continuamos con el programa*) 'It was under this impression that we carried on with the programme', *teniendo en cuenta que es gracias al número de parados* **que** *podemos mantener la inflación a nivel europeo* (Triunfo, Spain, Argentine writer) 'bearing in mind that it is thanks to the number of unemployed that we are able to keep inflation at European levels', *Fue a causa de eso que lo hizo* (Latin American) or *Lo hizo a causa de eso* or *Fue a causa de eso por lo que lo hizo* 'It was because of that that he did it'.

(iv) The complexities of cleft sentences can of course be avoided altogether by not using *ser: Por eso te digo, Desde esta ventana se ve el mar, Se pelearon por Pepita, no por Teresa.*

(v) The use of *quien* for things was once normal in Spanish and still survives although it should not be imitated: *No fueron las máquinas quienes desencadenaron el poder capitalista, sino el capitalismo financiero quien sometió la industria a su poderío* (E. Sábato, Argentina) 'It wasn't machines that unleashed capitalist power, but finance capitalism which subjected industry to their domination'.

36.2.4 Translating 'that's why'

Porque means 'because' and it cannot be used to translate sentences like 'She's got the flu, **that's why** she didn't come to work'. A construction with *por* is called for: *Está con gripe, por eso no ha venido al trabajo:*

Por eso lo hice	That's why I did it
Fue por eso por lo que no te llamé antes	That's why I didn't ring before
Fue por eso que no te llamé antes (Lat.-Am. equivalent)	" "
Ésa/Esa es la razón por la que no lo compré	That's the reason why I didn't buy it

36.2.5 Agreement in cleft sentences

The view of María Moliner, confirmed by native informants, is that in the singular either *Tú fuiste el que le/lo mataste* or *Tú fuiste el que le/lo mató* 'You're the one who killed him' is correct, but strict agreement seems to be the only possible construction in the plural: *Vosotros fuisteis los que le/lo matasteis* 'You were the ones who killed him'. Further examples:

Yo fui la que me lo bebí	I was the woman who drank it
Yo fui la que se lo bebió	
El que lo sé soy yo	I'm the one (masc.) who knows
El que lo sabe soy yo	
Somos los únicos que no tenemos ni un centavo para apostar (G. García Márquez, Colombia, dialogue)	We're the only ones who haven't got a *centavo* to bet
Vosotros sois los que lo sabéis	You're the ones who know
Ellos son los que trabajan más	They're the ones who work hardest

Note this sentence in which both agreements occur: *Vos sos el que no me aguanta. Vos sos el que no aguantás a Rocamadour* (J. Cortázar, Argentina, dialogue; Spain *tú eres* for *vos sos, aguantas* for *aguantás*), 'You're the one who can't stand me. You're the one who can't stand Rocamadour'.

37
Word order

37.1 General

Compared with English and French, word order in Spanish is free. Many adjectives may be placed before or after the noun that they modify: *en el pasado remoto/en el remoto pasado* 'in the remote past'; see 4.11 for discussion. A subject may follow or precede a verb: *Juan lo sabe/Lo sabe Juan* 'Juan knows' (different emphasis). A direct object noun phrase may follow or precede the verb: *No tengo hambre/Hambre no tengo* 'I'm not hungry' (different emphasis). As in English, adverbs and adverb phrases may occupy various positions in relation to the verb that they modify: *Normalmente lo hace/Lo hace normalmente* 'Normally he does it'/'He does it normally', *A veces llueve/Llueve a veces* 'Sometimes it rains'/'It rains sometimes'.

Usually the factors that call for a particular word order depend on considerations of style, context, emphasis and rhythm of the sort that few non-natives are sensitive to. In this respect word order can be as complex a question in Spanish as intonation and sentence stress are in English.

Sections 37.2-37.4 deal with patterns of word order that can be explained in terms of more or less clearly definable rules. Sections 37.5 considers the more difficult questions of word order that depend on matters of context, emphasis, intonation and style.

This chapter presumes that SV (Subject-Verb) order, e.g. *Mario viene* 'Mario's coming', and SVO (Subject-Verb-Object) order, e.g. *Juan come una manzana* 'John is eating an apple' are 'normal' and that other arrangements of Verb, Subject and Object are departures from the norm.

It is worth repeating that we are here discussing only late twentieth-century Spanish. In texts from earlier periods word order is typically much freer than today.

37.2 General rules of word order

37.2.1 VS (Verb-Subject) order in sentences containing relative clauses
The two principles explained here account for one of the most commonly encountered differences between Spanish and English as far as the position of the verb in relation to its Subject is concerned.

(a) When a sentence includes a relative clause, VS order is very often preferred in the main clause to ensure that the relative pronoun is not separated from its antecedent by a verb phrase:

Lo compró un señor que estuvo en Venezuela
A man who visited Venezuela bought it

and not **Un señor lo compró que estuvo en Venezuela*

The latter incorrect sentence breaks the strong rule (also discussed at 35.1.3d) that a verb phrase (*lo compró*) cannot come between a noun phrase (*un señor*) and a relative pronoun that refers to it (*que*). Another example:

No existe todavía el coche que yo quiera comprar
The car that I want to buy doesn't exist yet

not **El coche no existe todavía que yo quiera comprar*
?The car doesn't exist yet that I want to buy

The second sentence is not Spanish and probably not English either.

In both cases, another more recognisably English order is also possible, but it is usually less elegant in Spanish, especially when the verb is separated from its subject by a long string of words:

Un señor que estuvo en Venezuela lo compró
A gentleman who was in Venezuela bought it

El coche que yo quiero comprar no existe todavía
The car that I want to buy doesn't exist yet

Further examples: *Me llamó un amigo con el que fui de vacaciones* (better than *Un amigo con el que fui de vacaciones me llamó*). *Me llama una chica que se llama América* (C. Rico-Godoy, Spain, dialogue; better than *Una chica que se llama América me llama*) 'A girl called América rings me'.

(b) VS order is also strongly favoured in the relative clause to keep the verb close to the relative pronoun. Spanish dislikes sentences structured like 'That's the dog that my friend from Kansas City **bought**', best translated *Ese/Ése es el perro* **que compró** *mi amigo de Kansas City*, not *?Ese/Ése es el perro que mi amigo de Kansas City compró*. Further examples:

Estas acciones han rendido más que las que compró tu madre	These shares have yielded more than the ones your mother bought
. . . el carnaval de invierno que organiza el Departamento de Turismo (*El Mercurio*, Chile, in *Variedades*, 182)	the Winter Carnival that the Department of Tourism is organizing

When these two rules are combined, sentences are produced whose word order differs markedly from their English equivalents: *Gana la que eligen los jueces* 'The girl/woman whom the judges select wins', literally: 'Wins the one whom elect the judges'.

Further examples of inversion in both main and relative clauses:

Así dice la carta que nos envió tu padre	That's what's in the letter your father sent (lit. 'Thus says the letter that sent your father')
Son innumerables las dificultades que plantea la lucha contra el terrorismo (*La Vanguardia*, Spain)	The difficulties posed by the struggle against terrorism are innumerable
Durante toda mi vida, ahí donde hubiese un duro, ahí estaba yo (interview in *Cambio16*, Spain)	Throughout my life, wherever you could find five pesetas you'd find me (lit. '. . . wherever there was a five-peseta coin, there was I')

However, set verb phrases like *tratar de, tener que,* are not divided unnaturally. *Solía detenerse a hablar con ella en la aldea abrasada por la sal del Caribe donde su madre había tratado de enterrarla en vida* (G. García Márquez, Colombia; rather than . . . *donde había tratado su madre de enterrarla en vida*) 'He used to stop to talk to her in the village, parched by the salt from the Caribbean, where her mother had tried to bury her alive', *[Las maestras] no tienen la culpa: si no existiera la maldita instrucción primaria que ellas tienen que aplicar* . . . (J. Cortázar, Argentina; rather than *que tienen ellas que aplicar*) '[The school mistresses] aren't to blame: if the wretched primary education they have to administer didn't exist . . .'.

37.2.2 Word order in questions (direct and indirect)

(a) VS (Verb-Subject) order is required when a question word opens the sentence. VS order is also required in indirect questions in the clause following the question word. Question words are:

¿cómo?/¿qué tal?	how?	*¿dónde?*	where?
¿cuál (de)?	which (of)?	*¿por/para qué?*	why?
¿cuándo?	when?	*¿qué?*	what?/which? (see note i)
¿cuánto?	how much?/how many?	*¿a quién?*	whom?

Examples (subject in bold):

*¿Cómo va **una** a estar esperando y delgada?* (A. Mastretta, Mexico, dialogue)	How is one going to be expecting a baby and (be) thin?
*¿Qué tal va **tu nuevo trabajo**?*	How's your new job going?
*¿Cuál de los collares prefiere **tu novia**?*	Which of the necklaces does your girlfriend prefer?
*¿A quién arrestó **la policía**?*	Whom did the police arrest?
*No sé cuándo llegan **los demás***	I don't know when the rest are arriving
*Todo el mundo se pregunta por qué no se levanta **Ricardo** más temprano* (less likely . . . *Ricardo no se levanta más temprano*)	Everyone's wondering why Richard doesn't get up earlier
*No recuerdo dónde vive **tu hermano***	I don't remember where your brother lives
*No me imagino qué pensaría **tu mujer** de todo esto*	I can't imagine what your wife would think about all this

As the examples show, a direct object precedes the verb as in English:

¿Qué consejos me das?	What advice do you give me?
¿Cuántas naranjas has comido?	How many oranges have you eaten?

Verb-Object (VO) order can occasionally be used colloquially to express shock or incredulity:

*¿Has comido **cuántos**?* (more usually *¿Cuántos dices que has comido?*)	You've eaten *how many*?

When the sentence contains an object and a separate subject there are three possibilities:

(a) When the object is shorter than the subject, VOS order is usual; (b) when the subject noun phrase is shorter, VSO order is preferred; (c) when subject and object are of equal length, either order may be used (object in bold):

*¿Dónde compran **drogas** los adolescentes?* (short object)	Where do young people buy drugs?

*¿Dónde compran los adolescentes **las drogas vendidas por los narcotraficantes**?* (long object)	Where do young people buy the drugs sold by drug-pushers?
*¿Dónde compra **pan** mamá?/¿Dónde compra mamá **pan**?* (equal length)	Where does Mother buy bread?

Further examples (object in bold):

*¿A quién ha escrito **la carta** tu amigo Federico?* (short object)	To whom did your friend Federico write the letter?/Who did your friend Federico write the letter to?
*¿Por qué ha tenido **tan mala prensa** Antena 3 en su primer año de emisiones?* (Cambio16, Spain) (short object)	Why has Antenna Three had such a bad press during its first year of broadcasting?
*¿Cómo ha afectado la guerra a **su empresa**?*[2] (short subject)	How has the war affected your company?
*¿Cuándo va a incluir su revista **programas y artículos dedicados a ordenadores tales como los ya citados**?* (long object; reader's letter in *El Ordenador Personal,* Spain[3])	When is your magazine going to include programs and articles devoted to computers like the ones mentioned above?
*¿Cuándo piensan hacer**lo** ustedes?/¿Cuándo piensan ustedes hacer**lo**?* (equal length)	When are you thinking of doing it?

Notes

(i) A noun phrase introduced by *¿qué?* meaning 'which?' or by *¿cuál de?* 'which?' always appears before the verb:[4] *¿Qué programas han gustado más al público?* 'Which programmes[5] have pleased the public most?', *¿Cuál de los aviones consume menos combustible?* 'Which of the planes uses least fuel?', *¿Qué frutas ha comprado Inés?* 'What fruits did Inés buy?', *¿Cuál de los proyectos ha aceptado el comité?* 'Which of the projects has the committee accepted?'.

(ii) Cuban Spanish is unusual in optionally retaining SV order after question words (subject in bold): *¿Cómo **usted** conoció que Tony tenía negocio de narcotráfico? (Vindicación de Cuba;* standard Spanish . . . *se enteró **usted** de que . . .)* 'How did you find out that Tony had a drug-peddling business?', *¿En qué fecha **usted** ingresó en la Corporación CIMEX?* (ibid., standard Spanish *ingresó **usted***) 'On what date did you join the CIMEX Corporation?'

37.2.3 Word order in questions that do not contain a question word

When no question word appears, SVO order can be used, in which case question marks or, in speech, interrogative (rising) intonation are the only things that show that a question is intended:

¿Mamá ha comprado leche? (or *¿Ha comprado mamá leche?*)	Has mother bought any milk?
¿Tú también notaste lo bonito que se ríe? (A. Mastretta, Mexico, dialogue)	Did you also notice how prettily she laughs?

---

[2] However, spontaneous speech is less careful about sentence balance and might produce a sentence like *¿Cómo ha afectado la guerra ésta tan terrible que tenemos a su empresa?* 'How has this terrible war we're having affected your company?'.

[3] The usual Latin-American word for computer is *la computadora.*

[4] In many Latin-American varieties of Spanish, *cuál* alone before a noun can mean 'which': *¿cuál programa?*, *¿cuáles frutas?*, etc. This usage is not normal in Spain. See 24.3.3 for discussion.

[5] US spelling 'programs'.

¿El XIII [decimotercer] Congreso va a ser el de la desaparición de su partido? (interview with Communist leader in *Tribuna*, Spain)	Is the 13th Congress going to be the one at which your party disappears?

However, in such sentences VS order is usual if there is no object: *¿Ha llamado mamá?* 'Has mother called?'. If the sentence includes an object, VOS order is usual if the object is shorter than the subject (object in bold): *¿Ha traído **flores** el vecino de tu suegra?* 'Has your mother-in-law's neighbour brought flowers?'. But if the object is longer than the subject, VSO order is usual; and if they are of the same length, the order is optional (object in bold): *¿Ha traído Miguel **las flores que encargamos ayer por la noche**?* (short subject, so not **¿Ha traído las flores que encargamos anoche Miguel?*) 'Has Miguel brought the flowers we ordered last night?'; but *¿Ha traído **flores** Miguel?/¿Ha traído Miguel **flores**?* (same length) 'Has Miguel brought (some) flowers?'.

37.2.4 Word order in exclamations
When one of the words listed at 37.2.2 introduces exclamation (O)VS order is required:

¡Qué guapo es tu hermano!	Isn't your brother good-looking/My, your brother's good-looking!
¡Cómo se parece Ana a su madre!	Doesn't Anna look like her mother!/Anna really looks like her mother!
¡Cuántos piropos te echa el jefe!	What a lot of flirtatious comments the boss makes to you!

37.2.5 Inversion in tags
VS order is required in writing in tags of the sort 'Mary said', 'John replied' when they follow the words quoted. Inversion in this case is nowadays optional in English and is disappearing:

—*Está bien, dijo el presidente*	'Fine', the President said/said the President
—*Lo dudo, contestó Armando*	'I doubt it', Armando replied/replied Armando

37.2.6 Verb-Subject order required after adverbs
VS is very common when certain adverbs and adverbial phrases precede the verb.

When the verb is intransitive, inversion is usual. Speakers of either language would probably prefer sentences (a) to (b) (subject in bold):

(a) *Delante de ella se levantaba **un enorme edificio***
   Before her stood an enormous building

   *Delante de ella aparecieron **dos hombres chillando y gesticulando***
   Before her there appeared two men screaming and gesticulating

(b) *Delante de ella **un enorme edificio** se levantaba*
   ?Before her an enormous building stood

   ?*Delante de ella **dos hombres chillando y gesticulando** aparecieron*
   ?Before her two men screaming and gesticulating appeared

When the verb has an object it seems that either word order is possible in Spanish (subject in bold):

*Delante de ella **dos mujeres** voceaban sus mercancías*
*Delante de ella voceaban sus mercancías **dos mujeres***
Before her two women were calling out their wares

In the following examples, SV order is not always impossible, but it is usually awkward (subject in bold).[6]

*Siempre me dijeron **las brujas y echadoras** **de cartas** que mi número mágico era el tres* (C. Rico-Godoy, Spain)	The witches and card-readers always told me that my magic number was three
*Siempre fue altanera **la Sofía**[7]* (A. Mastretta, Mexico, dialogue)	Sofia was always haughty/arrogant
*Nunca me hablaban **los vecinos***	The neighbours never spoke to me
*Apenas salían **sus padres**, ponía música rock*	He used to put on rock music as soon as his parents went out
*También decía **su madre** que . . .*	His mother also said that . . .
*Bien saben **las autoridades** que . . .*	The authorities know very well that . . .
*Así dice **Platón***	This is what Plato says
*Todavía humeaban **algunos incendios***	Some fires were still smoking
*Ya me habían explicado **mis amigos** todos los detalles*[8]	My friends had already explained all the details to me
*Solamente pueden usarse **las iniciales de la víctima** en este tipo de caso*	Only the victim's initials may be used in this type of case
*Para tales personas existen **las cárceles***	Prisons exist for such people

Adverbial phrases of place especially favour VS order (subject in bold):

*Ahí vivo **yo***	That's where I live
*Aquí dejó la sangre **el muerto*** (J. Ibargüengoitia, Mexico, dialogue)	The dead man left his blood here
*En su mirada veía **yo** con claridad que me estaba pasando de la raya* (C. Rico-Godoy, Spain)	I could see clearly by his expression (lit. 'in his gaze') that I was overdoing it
*Junto a la puerta colgaba **una deshilachada toalla*** (L. Sepúlveda, Chile)	Next to the door hung a frayed towel

See 37.4 for further remarks about the position of adverbial phrases.

---

[6] It is difficult to be precise on this matter. Native speakers who have an ear for sentence structure will know when SV order sounds right: *Nunca los intereses publicitarios motivarán la publicación de un artículo o suplemento* (*Libro de estilo de El País*) 'The publication of an article or supplement will never be motivated by publicity interests', rather than *Nunca motivarán los intereses publicitarios . . .*

[7] See 3.2.21 for remarks on the use of the definite article with personal names.

[8] SVO order after *ya* has a particularly Mexican ring to it: *Ya él había cumplido diez años cuando mataron al alemán* (S. Pitol, Mexico) 'He was already ten when they killed the German', *. . . que ya el general se robó a la compañera de Marta* (A. Mastretta, Mexico, dialogue) '. . . because the General has already stolen Marta's partner' (*robarse* = *robar* in Spain). *Ya* frequently introduces ill-tempered imperatives in Mexican: *¡Ya crezcan, idiotas!* 'Grow up, you idiots!'.

37.3 Miscellaneous word order rules

This section includes a number of miscellaneous but important rules that explain various features of Spanish word order.

37.3.1 The link between a preposition and the word it modifies

Spanish does not usually separate prepositions from the noun or pronoun that they modify. This rule is absolute in relative clauses: a typically English sentence like 'That's the hotel we're going **to**' must be expressed *Ese/Ése es el hotel **al que** vamos* 'That's the hotel to which we're going'.

In general, only *no* should separate a preposition from its infinitive:

Su nombramiento se demoró por estar siempre la vacante ocupada (not **por la vacante estar*)	His appointment (to the post) was delayed because the vacant position was always occupied
*La promesa de una vida de ocio fue frustrada **al negarse** el Fisco a devolverle el dinero* (not **al Fisco negarse*)	The promise of a life of leisure was frustrated when the Revenue Department refused to return the money to him
Se equivocó por no haber pensado antes	He went wrong as a result of not thinking beforehand

37.3.2 Set phrases are not broken up

Set phrases, particularly set verbal phrases like *tener que* 'to have to', *llevar a cabo* 'to carry out', *hacer público* 'to make public', *surtir efecto* 'to produce an effect', *tener lugar* 'to take place', *darse cuenta de que* 'to realize', should not be broken up by the insertion of other words:

Probablemente las obras se llevarán a cabo para febrero (not **se llevarán probablemente a cabo . . .*)	The work will probably be carried out by February
Por eso hacemos pública esta información (and not the typical English word order ? *. . . hacemos esta información pública*)	This is why we are making this information public

37.3.3 No insertion of words between *haber* and participles

As a rule, words should not be inserted between *haber* and a participle, e.g. *siempre he dicho* or *he dicho siempre* 'I've always said', but not **he siempre dicho* (students of French take note: *J'ai presque toujours pensé que* is *Casi siempre he pensado que* or *He pensado casi siempre que*).

This rule is occasionally broken with certain words; see 14.8.1 for discussion.

37.3.4 Unstressed object pronouns remain with their verb

Unstressed object pronouns (*me, te, se, la, lo, le, nos, os, los, las, les*) are never separated from their verb: *Te lo diré luego* 'I'll tell you later', *Sólo te quiero a ti* 'I only love you'/'I love only you', etc.

There are often optional positions when a finite verb governs an infinitive: *No debí decírtelo* or *No te lo debí decir*. This is discussed at 11.14.4.

37.3.5 Adjectival phrases are kept close to the noun they modify

Spanish does not like to separate adjectival phrases from the noun they modify:

Regresó como a las seis y media con | He returned around 6.30 with a
un ejemplar arrugado y manchado de | crumpled and egg-stained copy of the
huevo de las Últimas Noticias del mediodía | mid-day *Últimas Noticias*
(C. Fuentes, Mexico)

This sentence would sound awkward (at least in polished styles) if the adjectival phrase were put at the end: ?. . . *con un ejemplar de las Últimas Noticias del mediodía arrugado y manchado de huevo*.

However, compound nouns formed with *de* are not broken up. One says *un reloj de pared suizo* 'a Swiss wall-clock', not **un reloj suizo de pared*. There is no infallible way in this case of determining whether nouns connected by *de* are inseparable compounds or not. The subject is discussed further at 4.11.5.

37.3.6 Keep verbs close to their subject
VS order is commonly used to avoid separating a subject from its verb. Spanish does not like to leave a verb dangling at the end of a clause or sentence far from its subject. Compare the English and Spanish versions of this sentence:

El tratamiento debe repetirse durante toda | The treatment must be repeated
la vida, salvo que ***se realice*** *con éxito* | throughout [the patient's] life, unless
un trasplante de riñón (*Ercilla*, Chile, | a kidney transplant is successfully
in *Variedades*, 220; rather than . . . *un* | performed
trasplante de riñón se realice con éxito)

37.3.7 Numbers are usually avoided at the beginning of sentences
See the note to 10.16 for discussion.

37.4 Position of adverbials

37.4.1 Adverbials are kept close to the words they modify
Generally speaking, adverbials (i.e. adverbs, adverbial phrases and adverbial clauses) are placed either immediately before or, more usually, immediately after the word(s) that they modify.

In this respect, *El País* (*Libro de estilo*, p.134) specifically admonishes its journalists and editors against:
(a) separating adverbs from their verb: *El Rey ha inaugurado hoy* . . . 'The King today inaugurated . . .', not *Hoy, el Rey ha inaugurado* . . .;
(b) breaking up verbal phrases by inserting adverbs in them: *El presidente está dispuesto claramente a dimitir* 'The president is clearly prepared to resign', not *El presidente está claramante dispuesto a dimitir* (which is the usual English order and, despite *El País*, very common in Spanish);
(c) beginning articles with an adverb other than *sólo/solo* or *solamente*, on the grounds that since adverbs modify other phrases the latter should precede them.

37.4.2 Adverbials not left at the end of sentences
English differs from Spanish in that it regularly puts adverbials at the end of the sentence: 'I saw that lady who lives next door to your grandmother **yesterday**'. For the reason given at 37.4.1, Spanish puts 'yesterday' close to

'saw': *Vi ayer/Ayer vi a esa señora que vive al lado de tu abuela*. If the *ayer* ended the sentence it would seem to modify *vive*.

The Spanish requirement that adverbs should stay close to their verb therefore often produces the unEnglish order Verb-Adverbial-Object (adverbial in bold):

Besó **fervorosamente** la mano de su anfitriona	He kissed his hostess's hand fervently
El tribunal fijará **discrecionalmente** la duración de la fianza (Spanish legal dictionary)	The Court will fix the period of the bail bond at its discretion
. . . casi siempre **a la una** seguía en chanclas y bata (A. Mastretta, Mexico, dialogue; in Spain chanclas = zapatillas)	. . . she was nearly always still in her slippers and dressing-gown/(US) 'bathrobe' at one o'clock

Adverbials of time are very often put before adverbials of place: 'We went to grandma's house yesterday' = *Fuimos ayer a casa de la abuela*.

Note particularly the position of the adverbials in bold in the following sentences (other orders are possible but are not shown here):

Fue inútil que los párrocos advirtieran **en los pueblos** a las mujeres que sus maridos las abandonarían si llegaba la ley del divorcio (*Cambio16*, Spain)	It was no use the parish priests in the villages warning women that their husbands would leave them if the divorce law was introduced
Parece que la habilidad más importante es la de memorizar información para **luego** escupirla en un examen (Spanish popular press)	It seems the most important skill is memorizing information in order to churn (lit. 'spit') it out later in an examination
Alguien dijo que uno de esos desventurados había huido a Mysore, donde había pintado **en un palacio** la figura del tigre (J.L. Borges, Argentina)	Someone said that one of those unfortunates had fled to Mysore, where he had painted the figure of the tiger in a palace
Me di cuenta de que había estado **antes en** aquel sitio	I realized I'd been in that place before
Siempre has creído que **en el viejo centro de la ciudad** no vive nadie (C. Fuentes, Mexico)	You've always believed that no one lives in the old city centre

For further remarks about the position of adverbs see 37.2.6 and 31.3.8.

37.5 Word order not explainable by sentence structure

Even when all the foregoing more or less codifiable rules are taken into account, there are cases in which word order is determined not so much by the structure of the sentence as by much less easily definable factors of context, style, emphasis and rhythm.

It is never easy to explain these factors in a grammar book, which necessarily quotes fragments of language out of context. The following remarks by no means exhaust the subject, which cannot be covered in every detail in a book of this nature.

37.5.1 The most important information usually comes first

The information that is foremost or most urgent in the speaker's mind tends to come first in the sentence. This is especially true of emotive colloquial language, and in this respect English word order (especially British) is more rigid than Spanish:

¡De dinero no quiero volver a oír ni una palabra!	About *money* I don't want to hear another word!
Americano vino uno solamente (Cuban TV interview)	As for Americans, only one came
Como en la foto de la boda no creo que yo vuelva a estar	I don't think I'll be like I was in the wedding photo again
—Lléveme adentro de una de esas casas . . .	'Take me inside one of those houses . . .'
—Casas fueron antes, ahora son oficinas (M. Puig, Argentina, dialogue; Peninsular usage requires *dentro de . . .*)	'They used to be houses, now they're offices'
Lo que yo digo es que la culpa quien la tiene es el Gobierno	What I say is that the one to blame is the Government
Muchas cosas he leído, pocas he vivido (J.L. Borges, Argentina)	I've read many things but lived few

Notes

(i) When a direct object is placed before the verb, it is resumed or echoed by a pronoun: *Al verano inglés debían llamarlo estación de las lluvias* 'The English summer ought to be called the rainy season'. This rule is not applied to nouns that are not preceded by an article or demonstrative adjective. See 11.16.1 for more details.

(ii) One of the functions of the passive with *ser* is to focus attention on the direct object by putting it at the head of the sentence: *Miguel fue atropellado por un coche* 'Miguel was run over by a a car' is more likely than *Un coche atropelló a Miguel* 'A car ran over Miguel', Miguel being more important than the car.

Informal Spanish generally avoids the passive with *ser*, so placing the direct object at the head of the sentence is a good way of producing the same effect as a passive: *A Miguel lo/le atropelló un coche*.

(iii) Latin-American headline writers exploit the fact that in emotive language the most significant information comes first: *A tres coches quemaron* (Colombian headline) 'Three cars burnt', *Ingeniero buscamos* (advertisement, Venezuela) 'Engineer sought', *Causa de deslizamiento verán expertos* (*El Comercio*, Lima) 'Experts to investigate cause of landslide', *Capturan la policía y el ejército a 23 miembros de Sendero Luminoso* (*UnomásUno*, Mexico) 'Police and Army capture 23 Members of "Shining Path" '[9]. This word order sounds odd to Spaniards.

37.5.2 *El profesor viene* or *Viene el profesor*?

This section discusses sentences consisting only of a subject and verb.

The principle explained at 37.5.1 – that the most important information tends to come first in a sentence – explains the difference between *Antonio viene* and *Viene Antonio*, 'Antonio's coming', two sentences that can really only be differentiated by emphasis and intonation in English.

In a neutral statement in which neither subject nor verb is emphasized, Subject-Verb order is usual (when none of the factors listed in 37.2-37.4 operates): *El médico llega a las diez* 'The doctor arrives at ten o'clock'. If the verb is the most important or urgent information, for example when the doctor's arrival is feared, unexpected or impatiently awaited, Verb-Subject order is appropriate: *¡Viene el médico!* 'The doctor's coming!'.

But this is an obvious example. In most cases departures from Subject-Verb order – which are not, in fact, nowadays very common in written language except when produced by the factors mentioned earlier in the chapter – are

---

[9] A Peruvian left-wing terrorist organization.

determined by factors of style and rhythm that cannot easily be explained in abstract terms.

When it is not clearly called for, VS order may produce a heavily literary, even 'Academic' tone: *Recordará el lector que los complementos directos . . .* (Royal Academy, *Esbozo . . .* 3.7.3f) 'The reader will recall that direct objects . . .', where the order *El lector recordará que . . .* would have been less formal.

In plain styles, VS order is sometimes dictated by considerations of rhythm and phrase length, Spanish preferring to put the verb before an unusually long subject: *Con la firma del tratado Start en Moscú el 31 de julio termina **la carrera de armamentos de la guerra fría*** (*Tribuna*, Spain, subject in bold) 'With the signing of the Start Treaty in Moscow on 31 July, the Cold War arms race ends'.

Very often, the choice between SV and VS is optional (subject in bold): *Me siento en una mesa porque me revienta **hacer barra**/Me siento en una mesa porque **hacer barra** me revienta* (Spain, colloquial) 'I sit at a table because I hate standing at the bar' (lit 'doing bar irritates me'). Here the difference is very slight, though SV order would have been unnatural had the subject been longer).

In the following examples, SV order is preferred either because the subject is focussed as the most important or urgent element, or because no element in the sentence is particularly focussed (subject in bold):

Miguel *está leyendo* (answers the question 'What's Miguel doing?')	Miguel's reading
Bentley *se volvió*	Bentley turned round
De repente, **Horacio** *aulló*	Suddenly Horace howled

In the following sentences, the verb is focussed as the most important or urgent element (subject in bold):

Ha muerto **Franco** (headline)	Franco is dead
Han vuelto a España ya **muchos**	Many have returned to Spain already
Se abrió **la puerta** *y entró* **Juan**	The door opened and John came in

37.5.3 Word order in sentences that include direct objects

A sentence consisting of a subject, verb and direct object theoretically appear in Spanish in the following forms:

(a) *Inés leyó el libro*	SVO
(b) *El libro lo leyó Inés*	O (redundant pronoun) VS
(c) *El libro Inés lo leyó*	OS (redundant pronoun) V
(d) (*Inés el libro leyó*	SOV)
(e) *Leyó Inés el libro*	VSO
(f) *Leyó el libro Inés*	VOS

Of these possibilities, only the first three are at all common in everyday language. (d) is very unnatural and might occur in songs or comic verse, and (e) and (f) are only found in questions or archaic or very flowery literary styles.

(a) is a neutral word order corresponding to an English sentence spoken with equal stress on 'Inés' and 'book'. Since, in neutral sentences, the subject of the verb tends naturally to be the most important element, SVO order is normal.

(b) focusses the object as the most significant information in the sentence, cf. 'as for the book, Inés read it'. See 11.16.1 for the use of the redundant pronoun here.

(c) is not particularly common. It also focusses the object of the verb and might occur in contrasts such as *La moto mi marido la compró el año pasado y el coche hace una semana* '(As for the) motor cycle, my husband bought it last year, and the car (he bought) last week'.

38

Diminutive, augmentative and pejorative suffixes

38.1 General

There are numerous suffixes that add an emotional tone to a word, e.g. *-ito*, *-illo*, *-ón*, *-ote*, *-azo*, *-aco*, *-ejo*, etc.

The effect of these suffixes is very unpredictable. Sometimes they simply create new words without any emotional colouring at all: compare *ventana* 'window', *ventanilla* 'window of a vehicle', *la caja* 'box', *el cajón* 'drawer' (in furniture). These words are standard lexical items and must be learnt separately.

Very often they add an emotional tone to a word or phrase, e.g. affection, endearment, contempt, irony, repugnance, and they may sound affected, effeminate, childish or too familiar if used inappropriately. Consequently, foreign learners are advised not to experiment with them since inexpert use may produce unfortunate effects: *Estarías mejor con el pelo recogido* means 'You'd look better with your hair up', *Estarías mejor con el pelo recogidito* means the same, but sounds either painfully condescending or like an adult talking to a little girl; ?*Estarías mejor con el pelito recogidito* is ludicrous and would be said by no one.

In view of this and the fact that the forms and frequency of the suffixes differ widely from continent to continent and region to region, the following account is very summary. For a detailed picture of Peninsular usage see Gooch (1974), from which some of the following examples are taken.

38.2 Diminutive suffixes

Diminutive suffixes have various uses, described at 38.2.1-38.2.5.
Although these suffixes do not always imply smallness, a word must be said about their relationship with the adjective *pequeño*.

Pequeño means 'small', but it does not usually have the emotional overtones of the English word 'little'. It is generally only used between an article and a noun when applied to abstract nouns, in which case it means 'of little importance': *el/un pequeño problema* 'a small/slight problem', *la/una pequeña dificultad* 'a slight difficulty'. In other cases the combination of *el/un* + *pequeño* + noun is more idiomatically expressed by diminutive suffixes. One says not ?*el/un pequeño perro* but *el/un perrito* 'a little dog', not ?*la/una pequeña casa* but *la/una casita* 'a little house': c.f. . . . *desde la primera vez que la vio leyendo bajo los árboles del **parquecito*** (G. García Márquez, Colombia) '. . . since the first time he had seen her reading under the trees in the little park'.

Due to the influence of English and French, use of *pequeño* with the nuances of 'little' is spreading in journalese, but literary and spoken usage still prefers to add a diminutive suffix to convey all the overtones of 'little', French *petit/petite*.

Pequeño follows the noun when it refers to size or age without affective overtones e.g. *un árbol pequeño* 'a small tree', *un niño pequeño* 'a young child'. In Spain a little child is often affectionately called *el chiquitín, el nene, el pequeño* or even *el peque*.

Note
Sometimes abbreviations are used instead of suffixes, e.g. *mami* or *papi* for *mamá* or *papá*, which are in turn abbreviations for *madre* and *padre*; *cole* from *colegio* 'school', *tele* from *televisión*.

38.2.1 Formation of the diminutive

The following are found, *-ito* being the most common in Central Spain and *-illo* used especially in the South. *-ico*, *-iño* and *-ín* have a regional flavour:

Usual form		Variants	
-ito	-cito	-ecito	-ececito
-illo	-cillo	-ecillo	-ececillo
-ico	-cico	-ecico	-ececico
-uelo	-zuelo	-zuelo	-ecezuelo
-ete	-cete	-ecete	
-ín			
-iño			

All are marked for gender in the usual way: a final vowel is replaced by *-a*; *-ín* makes its feminine *-ina*.

The following remarks apply to typical educated usage in Central Spain and probably to educated usage in many places, but they should be checked against the speech habits of different Latin-American republics.

Words of more than one syllable ending in *-n*, *-ol* or *-r*, and words ending in accented *-e* or having the diphthong *-ie* in their first syllable, usually take the form in *-c-*. The following formations were generated spontaneously by Peninsular informants, but not all are guaranteed to be in common use. It must be emphasized that diminutive suffixes are theoretically very productive and could conceivably be added to almost any noun:

surtidor	spout/fountain	*surtidorcito*
mujer	woman	*mujercita*
mejor	better	*mejorcito*
mayor	bigger	*mayorcito*
charlatán	talkative	*charlatancito*
cajón	drawer	*cajoncito*
madre	mother	*madrecita*
padre	father	*padrecito*
cofre	case/box	*cofrecito*
puente	bridge	*puentecito*
nieto	grandson	*nietecito*
piedra	stone	*piedrecita*

But note *el café* > *cafetito* 'coffee'; *el cafecito* usually means 'a little café'; also *el alfiler* > *alfilerito* 'pin'.

Words of one syllable commonly take forms in *-ec-*:

flor	flower	*florecita*
pan	bread	*panecillo* (i.e. 'bread roll')
pez	fish	*pececito/pececillo*
tos	cough	*tosecita/tosecilla*
pie	foot	*piececito* (?*piececillo* – if it is ever used)
voz	voice	*vocecita*
sol	sun	*solecito/solito*

Words ending in an unaccented vowel or diphthong lose their final vowel, but if the vowel is accented it may be preserved and its accent transferred to the *i* of *-ito*:

armario	wardrobe	*armarito*
estatua	statue	*estatuilla*
silla	chair	*sillita*
mamá	mummy	*mamaíta* or *mamita*
papá	daddy	*papaíto* or *papito*

38.2.2 Uses of the diminutive suffix *-ito*

The main effects of this suffix are:

(a) To give a friendly tone to a statement:

This very common use of the diminutive may simply give a warm tone to a remark. In a bakery one might say *Deme una barrita de pan* 'Give me a loaf of bread', which is merely a cheery equivalent of *Deme una barra de pan*. This use of the diminutive does not imply smallness but merely signals the speaker's attitude to the hearer:

Dame un paquetito por ahora	Give me just one packet for now
Me tiras el vaso con el codo. A ver si tenemos más cuidadito . . .	You're knocking my glass over with your elbow. Let's see if we can't have a little bit more care . . .
Voy a echar una siestecita	I'm going to have forty winks/a quick nap
Un momentito, por favor	Just a moment, please
Me lo contó un pajarito	A little birdy told me
¿Alguna cosita más? (often used in shops)	Would you like anything else?
(*¿Alguna cosa más?*	Anything else?)

(b) To modify the meaning of adjectives and adverbs by adding a warm tone or, sometimes, by making them more precise, e.g. *ahora* 'now', *ahorita* (Mexican colloquial) 'right now':

cerquita de la catedral	just by the cathedral
Ahora mismito se lo sirvo	Don't worry, I'll bring it at once
Ya eres mayorcito	You're a big boy now
(*mayor* = grown up, older)	
Está gordito	He's put on a bit of weight
(*Está gordo*	he's fat)
¡tontito!	silly!
(*¡tonto!*	stupid!)

'Nice' or 'lovely' can be the English equivalent of some adjectival and adverbial diminutives in *-ito*:

¿Un café calentito?	A nice cup of hot coffee?
Las empanadas están recientitas	The meat pies are lovely and fresh
despacito	nice and easy/take it easy

(c) To denote endearment or affection: *hermanita* (lit. 'little sister') is often a term of endearment and does not necessarily imply that the sister is younger than the speaker; *abuelita* 'grandma' is an affectionate form for *abuela* 'grandmother':

Vamos, m'hijito	Come on son
(Lat. Am; Spain: *vamos hijo mío*)	
Se ha hecho daño en la patita	It's hurt its (little) paw

(d) To denote smallness:

el perro/el perrito	dog/little dog/doggy
la puerta/la puertecita	door/little door
el sillón/silloncito	armchair/little armchair
el coche/cochecito	car/little car/baby carriage

Note

Occasionally the diminutive form is of different gender: *la maleta* 'suitcase', *el maletín* 'small hand case', *la botella* 'bottle', *el botellín* (typically a small bottle of beer).

38.2.3 Diminutive suffix *-illo*

The suffix *-illo* is used:

(a) As a diminutive:

pan/panecillo	bread/bread roll
flor/florecilla	flower/little flower

(b) To downgrade the importance of something:

Falta una pesetilla	You're just one peseta short
(Compare *Falta una peseta*	You're a peseta short)
Tengo unas cosillas que hacer	I've got a few little things to do
Ahora sólo queda el jaleíllo de las entradas	All that's left is the business of the
(*jaleo* = row, fuss)	entrance tickets
Hacía un airecillo agradable	There was a pleasant breeze

(c) To give an affectionate tone:

Pero ¿qué haces, chiquilla?	But what **are** you doing, my dear girl?
mentirosillo	'fibber'
He comprado un cachorrillo	I have bought a little puppy

Diminutives in *-illo* are typical of Seville but they are also often used in central Spain.

(d) To give a specialized meaning to a word, cf. English 'book'/ 'booklet'. In some of these cases the diminutive ending has no diminutive function:

el palo/palillo	stick/toothpick
la caja/cajetilla	box/box for cigarettes, etc.
la vara/varilla	rod/thin stick, spoke, wand
la guerra/guerrilla	war/guerrilla warfare
el cigarro/cigarrillo	cigar/cigarette
la cama/camilla	bed/circular table covered with a cloth
la manzana/la manzanilla	apple/camomile
la masa/la masilla	dough/mass/putty
la ventana/la ventanilla	window/vehicle window/tickets window
la bomba/la bombilla	bomb/light bulb
la parra/la parrilla	vine/grill
el bolso/el bolsillo	bag/pocket

(e) To denote a combination of diminutive and pejorative:

la cultura/culturilla	culture/'smattering of culture'
mujer/mujercilla	woman/unimportant woman

38.2.4 Diminutive suffix *-ín*

-ín is peculiar to Asturias but it is used to express affection in many contexts in the rest of Spain:

¿Donde está el chiquitín?	Where's the little one?
¡Chiquirriquitín!	My tiny little one!
¡Mi niña chiquitina! (not *¡Mi pequeña niña!*)	My little girl!

and also to form new words:

la espada/el espadín	sword/dress sword
la peluca/el peluquín	wig/small wig
la tesis/la tesina	thesis/dissertation

38.2.5 Diminutive suffixes *-uelo*, *-eto*, *-ete*

(a) *-uelo* can denote a combination of diminutive and pejorative:

la calleja/callejuela	alley/narrow little alley
el arroyo/arroyuelo	stream/trickle, rivulet
el rey/reyezuelo	king/petty king, princeling
tonto/tontuelo (affectionate)	stupid/chump/dumbo

It may form new words:

el paño/pañuelo	cloth/handkerchief

(b) *-eto*, *-ete* may add a specialized meaning:

el avión	aircraft	*la avioneta*	light aircraft
el camión	truck	*la camioneta*	van/light truck
el caballo	horse	*el caballete*	easel

(c) *-ete* may add a humorous tone:

amigo/amiguete	friend/pal
gordo/regordete	fat/chubby

38.2.6 Diminutive forms in Latin America

In many areas of Latin America, diminutive forms pervade everyday speech to an extent that amuses Spaniards:

Viene ya merito (Mexico; i.e. *ahora mismo*)	He's coming right now
merito ayer no más (Mexico) (i.e. *ayer mismo*)/*Ahorita*	only yesterday
lo voy a hacer (i.e. *ahora mismo*)	I'll do it straight away (in practice it usually means 'when I can')
Clarito la recuerdo	I remember her vividly
Apártate tantito, que voy a saltar (Guatemalan, from Kany, 385)	Get out of the way a bit, I'm going to jump
Reciencito llegó (see 31.7.2 for *recién*)	He's just this minute arrived
Las caras de los gringos son todititas igualitas (C. Fuentes, dialogue, Mexico)	Gringos' faces are all exactly the same

38.3 'Augmentative' suffixes

Typical, in order of frequency, are *-ón, -azo, -ote, -udo*.
(a) These are mainly used to denote intensity or large size, almost always with some associated pejorative idea of clumsiness, unpleasantness, awkwardness, excess, etc.:

rico/ricachón	rich/stinking rich/'loaded'
pedante/pedantón	pedant/insufferable pedant
el soltero/solterón	bachelor/confirmed bachelor
contestón	tending to answer back/cheeky
preguntón	constantly asking questions
cursi/cursilón	affected/incredibly affected
fácil/facilón	easy/facile
la broma/el bromazo	joke/joke pushed too far
el coche/cochazo	car/'heck of a car'
el libro/librazo	book/tome
la ginebra/un ginebrazo	gin/an enormous shot of gin
el gringo/gringote	gringo/bloody gringo
la palabra/la palabrota	word/swearword
el favor/favorzote	favour/'heck of a favour'
El airón de la mañana había dejado el cielo azul (A. Mastretta, Mexico, dialogue)	The gusts of breeze in the morning had left the sky blue

(b) To form an entirely new word. The suffix may then have no connotations of size or awkwardness and may even imply smallness:

la rata/el ratón	rat/mouse
la caja/el cajón	box/drawer
la cintura/el cinturón	waist/belt
el fuego/el fogón	fire/stove
la tela/el telón	cloth/theatre curtain
la cuerda/el cordón	string/shoe-lace
la leche/el lechazo	milk/sucking lamb

Note
-azo is also much used to form nouns which denote a blow or flourish with some object:

el aldabón/aldabonazo	knocker/thump with a door knocker, blow on door
el codo/codazo	elbow/dig with elbow
la bayoneta/el bayonetazo	bayonet/bayonet thrust

38.4 Pejorative suffixes

These are not particularly frequent, especially now that graphic insults are often expressed by language once thought shocking. The words formed by them should be learnt as separate lexical items. Typical suffixes are *-aco, -arraco, -acho, -ajo, -astro, -uco, -ucho, -ejo* and a few others.

They variously denote ugliness, wretchedness, squalor, meanness, etc.

el pájaro/pajarraco	bird/sinister bird
el poeta/poetastro	poet/rhymer, poetaster
el pueblo/poblacho	village/'dump', squalid village/dead-end town
el latín/latinajo	Latin/Latin jargon, dog Latin

la casa/casucha	house/pathetic little house
la palabra/palabreja	word/horrible word
el hotel/hotelucho	hotel/dingy hotel

Some of these suffixes may be used affectionately:

¿Cómo va a poder estudiar con tres pequeñajas como esas/ésas?	How is she going to be able to study with three little terrors like them?

39

Spelling, accent rules, punctuation and word division

Index to chapter:

Alphabet and spelling	39.1
Use of the written accent	39.2
Upper and lower-case letters	39.3
Punctuation	39.4
Division of words	39.5

In some cases pronunciation is indicated by phonetic transcription. See footnote to 39.1.3 for an explanation of the signs used.

39.1 Spelling

39.1.1 The *Nuevas normas* and the alphabet

The spelling rules of modern Spanish are laid down by the Academy in the *Nuevas normas de prosodia y ortografía* which came into official use in January 1959. But even thirty years later pre-1959 spelling is still commonly used by persons who are not connected with the world of publishing, and the *Nuevas normas* are still inconsistently applied in print. (For further comments on the status of the *Nuevas normas* see 6.3 – demonstrative pronouns, 9.15 – *solo/sólo* and 13.2.3 – spelling of *prohibir, aislar, reunir*).

The spelling – particularly the use of the accent - in works published before 1959 will therefore differ in detail from this account. Among the more striking innovations were the removal of the accent from the words *fui, fue, dio, vio,* and its adoption in words like *búho, rehúso, reúne, ahínca, prohíbe, ahíto.*

39.1.2 The Spanish alphabet

The Spanish alphabet consists of the following letters:

a	*a*	g	*ge*	m	*eme*	s	*ese*	z	*zeta/zeda*[1]
b	*be*	h	*hache*	n	*ene*	t	*te*		
c	*ce*	i	*i*	ñ	*eñe*	u	*u*		
ch	*che*	j	*jota*	o	*o*	v	*uve*		
d	*de*	k	*ka*	p	*pe*	w	*uve doble*		
e	*e*	l	*ele*	q	*cu*	x	*equis*		
f	*efe*	ll	*elle*	r	*erre/ere*	y	*i griega*		

[1] The Academy recommends *zeda* but usage prefers *zeta.*

Double *r* (*erre doble*) is a separate sound but it is not treated as a separate letter of the alphabet.

Ch and *ll* are traditionally treated as separate letters so that in alphabetical lists words beginning with *ch* or *ll* follow words beginning with *c* or *l*: *mancha* follows *mancornas* and *collado* follows *colza*, etc. This is very inconvenient for computerized sorting and out of line with other languages that use Latin letters, and a number of authorities, including Seco (1992), 92, 247, advocate standard alphabetical order.[2]

The Academy rules that accents should always be written on capital letters, a convention that is also problematic for computers and word-processors and is often ignored.

Note
Letters of the alphabet are all feminine – *la cu, la uve* – and one says *la/una a, la/una hache*, despite the rule that singular feminine words beginning with a stressed *a* sound require the masculine article, cf. *el arma* (fem.) 'the weapon' (see 3.1.2 for discussion).

39.1.3 Relationship between sounds and letters

Spanish spelling is not entirely rational, but it is much more logical than French or English. Basically one sound corresponds to one letter, so one merely needs to hear words like *colocar* [kolokár][3] 'to place', *chaleco* [chaléko] 'waistcoat'/(US) 'vest', *calenturiento* [kalenturyénto] 'feverish', to be able to spell them correctly. However, the rule of one sound for one letter is broken in numerous cases:

(a) *H* is always silent, except in some rural dialects, but it is common in writing, where it is merely a burden on the memory: *hacha* [ácha] 'axe'/(US) 'ax', *hombre* [ómbre] 'man', *Huesca* [wéska], *Honduras* [ondúras], *ahíto* [a-íto] 'gorged'/'satiated', etc.

H had one useful function in the past: it showed that two adjacent vowels did not form a diphthong, as in words like *prohibe* [pro-íβe] 'prohibits', *buho* [bú-o] 'owl', *rehila* 'it quivers' [rre-íla], *la retahila* [larreta-íla] 'volley'/'string' (e.g. of insults). In its wisdom the Academy abolished this rule in 1959, so one must now write *prohíbe, búho, rehíla, la retahíla*, etc.

The sound [w] at the beginning of a syllable – i.e. when it is not preceded by a consonant - is spelt *hu*: *huele* [wéle] 'it smells', *ahuecar* [awekár] 'to hollow out', *Náhuatl* [ná-watl] 'the Nahuatl language (of Mexico)', etc.

(b) *Z* is pronounced [θ] (like the *th* of 'think') in standard European Spanish, like the *s* of 'sit' throughout Latin America and in Southern Spain and the Canary Islands. *Z* is written *c* before *i* or *e*: *cebra* [θéβra/séβra] 'zebra', *hacer*

---

[2]As this book was going to print (27 April 1994), the 10th Conference of Academies of the Spanish Language voted by a large majority to abolish *ch* and *ll* as separate letters, so normal alphabetical order should now be used. The position of *ñ* is unchanged.

[3] Transcription conventions: χ = voiceless velar fricative, i.e. *ch* in 'loch' or *ch* in German *lachen*; β = bilabial voiced fricative (*v* pronounced with both lips); γ = voiced velar fricative (not found in English: *g* as in 'got' but without closure of the throat); θ = 'th' in 'think', δ = 'th' in 'this', ʎ = palatalized 'l', rr = rolled *r*. Stressed syllables marked by acute accent. Other signs should be given their usual Spanish pronunciation.

[aθér/asér] 'to do', *nación* [naθyón/nasyón]] 'nation', etc. For this reason, a verb like *realizar* 'to attain'/'to achieve'/'to bring about' undergoes spelling changes: *realizo, realice, realicé, realizó*, etc. See 13.2.2 for the effect of these and other spelling rules on the verb system.

There are a few exceptions, e.g. *el eczema* (or *el eccema*) 'eczema', *la enzima* 'enzyme', *zeta/zeda* 'zed'/(US) 'zee', *Nueva Zelanda* (in Latin America *Nueva Zelandia*) 'New Zealand', *zigzag* (plural *zigzags*), *Zimbabue/Zimbabwe*, *zinc* (also *cinc*) 'zinc', *zipizape* 'rumpus'/'fuss'/'noisy quarrel'.

Spelling in Latin America and Andalusia is much more troublesome than in central Spain since *z, c(e), c(i)* and *s* are all pronounced identically, so that pairs of words like *caza* 'hunt' and *casa* 'house', *ves* 'you see' and *vez* 'time' (as in 'three times'), *Sena* 'the river Seine' and *cena* 'supper' sound the same.

(c) The sound of *c* in *cama* is written *qu* before *e* and *i*: *querer* [kerér] 'to want', *quiso* [kíso] 'wanted', *saque* [sáke] 'take out' (third-person present subjunctive of *sacar*), etc.

The letter *k* is consequently not needed in Spanish and is found only in foreign words, for example measurements preceded by *kilo-*, or in *kantiano* 'Kantian', *krausismo*, 'Krausism', *el kiwi* [elkíβi] 'kiwi'/'kiwi fruit', *Kuwait* [kuβáyt] 'Kuwait', etc.

The sound [kw] is always written *cu*, e.g. *cuestión* [kwestyón] 'question'[4], *cuáquero* [kwákero] 'Quaker' (students of Portuguese and Italian take note!).

(d) The sound [χ] (like *ch* in 'loch') is always written *j* before *a, o* and *u*, and is usually written *g* before *e* and *i*: *general* [χenerál], *Gibraltar* [χiβraltár], *rige* [rríχe] 'he/she/it rules', *rugir* [rruχír] 'to roar', etc.

There are numerous exceptions to the latter rule, e.g. the preterite of all verbs whose infinitive ends in *ducir* – the preterite of *producir* 'to produce' is *produje, produjiste, produjo, produjimos, produjisteis, produjeron* – and many other words, e.g.

la bujía	spark plug	*la jeta*	thick lips/snout
crujir	to rustle/to crackle	*Jiménez*	(a personal name)
dejé	I left behind (from *dejar*)	*la jirafa*	giraffe
el equipaje	luggage	*el paisaje*	landscape
el garaje	garage	*tejer*	to weave
la jeringa	syringe	*el traje*	suit
el jersey	jersey	*el ultraje*	outrage
el jesuita	Jesuit	etc.	
Jesús	Jesus		

(e) The sound of *g* in *hago* [áɣo] is written *gu* before *e* and *i*: *ruegue* [rrwéɣe] present subjunctive of *rogar* 'to request', *la guirnalda* [laɣirnálda] 'wreath'/'garland'. The *u* is silent and simply shows that the *g* is not pronounced like Spanish *j* [χ].

The syllables pronounced [gwe] and [gwi] (neither very common in Spanish) are written *güe* and *güi*, e.g. *lingüístico* [lingwístiko], *el desagüe* [eldesáɣwe] 'drainage'/'water outlet', *averigüe* [aβeríɣwe] present subjunctive of *averiguar* 'to check', *nicaragüense* [nikaraɣwénse] 'Nicaraguan', *el pingüino*

---

[4] It means 'issue'/'problem'. Compare *la pregunta* 'question', i.e. something one asks.

[elpingwíno] 'penguin'. This is the only use of the dieresis in the modern language.

(f) *B* and *v* sound exactly the same and are most frequently pronounced as a voiced bilabial fricative [β], although they both sound like the English *b* after *n* or *m* or after a pause. The English sound [v] as in 'vat' does not exist in Spanish, and English speakers of Spanish often make a false distinction between the pronunciation of the Spanish written signs *b* and *v*. For this reason they usually do not confuse these letters in writing.

Native speakers who are poor spellers make blunders like *la uba* for *la uva* [la-úβa] 'grape', *Premio Novel* for *Premio Nobel* [prémyonoβél] 'Nobel Prize' – mistakes which are at least the sign of a normal pronunciation.

(g) In Spain, *x* is usually pronounced like *s* before a consonant: *extender* = [estendér] 'to extend', *el extracto,* = [elestrákto] 'extract', etc. Seco (1992), 381, rejects the pronunciation of *x* as [ks] in this position as affected, but many Latin Americans insist on it.

For the pronunciation and spelling of the words *México, mexicano, Oaxaca* see 4.8.1.

X is pronounced [s] at the beginning of words: *la xenofobia* [lasenofóβya] 'xenophobia', *el xilófono* [elsilófono] (colloquially *el xilofón* [elsilofón]) 'xylophone'.

The pronunciation [ks] is normal between vowels and at the end of words: *el examen* [eleksámen] 'examination', *el taxi* 'taxi' [eltáksi], *Xerox* [séroks]. Learners should avoid popular pronunciations like [esámen], [tási], occasionally heard in Spain.

(h) *N* is pronounced *m* before *b, v, p*: *en Barcelona* = [embarθelóna /embarselóna] 'in Barcelona', *invitar* = [imbitár] 'to invite', *en París* = [emparís] 'in Paris'.

(i) *R* and *rr* represent a flapped and a rolled *r* ([r] and [rr]) respectively, and in a few words they indicate a difference of meaning, e.g. *pero* [péro] 'but', *perro* [pérro] 'dog'; *caro* [káro] 'dear', *carro* [kárro] 'car'/'cart'; *enteró* [enteró] 'he informed', *enterró* [enterró] 'he buried'.

But *r* is pronounced like *rr* when it is the first letter in a word, e.g. *Roma* [rróma], *la ropa* [larrópa] 'clothes', or when it occurs after *l, n* or *s*: *Israel* [isrraél], *la sonrisa* [lasonrrísa] 'smile', *alrededor* [alrreðeðór] 'around'.

When a prefix ending in a vowel is added to a word beginning with *r*, the *r* is doubled in writing and is therefore rolled in speech: *infra+rojo* = *infrarrojo* 'infra-red' *contra+revolucionario* = *contrarrevolucionario* 'counter-revolutionary', *anti+republicano* = *antirrepublicano* 'anti-Republican'. Such words are not spelt with a hyphen in Spanish.

(j) *Ll* is properly a palatalized *l* [ʎ] but it is nowadays pronounced like the letter *y* by many speakers, to the dismay of many purists. Poor spellers sometimes make mistakes like *cullo* for *cuyo* 'whose', *la *balloneta* for *la bayoneta* 'bayonet'.

It is much better to pronounce it *y* than to pronounce it like the *lli* of 'million', which is written *li* in Spanish. *Polio* [póljo] 'polio' and *pollo* [póʎo] 'chicken' sound quite different in correct Spanish.

(k) *M* is often pronounced *n* at the end of words by many, though not by all speakers: *el álbum* = [elálβun/elálβum] 'album', *el referéndum* = [elrreferéndun] 'referendum', *el ultimátum* = [elultimátun] 'ultimatum'.

(l) The three initial groups of consonants *ps*, *mn* and *gn* are pronounced *s*, *n* and *n* respectively and may now officially be spelt this way. But few people can bring themselves to write *la sicología* for *la psicología* 'psychology' or *la siquiatría* for *la psiquiatría* 'psychiatry', and it is doubtful whether anyone would write *la nosis* or *nóstico* for *la gnosis*, *gnóstico* 'gnosis', 'gnostic'. The old forms are therefore still used – even by the Academy itself. *El seudónimo* 'pseudonym' is, however, universally used.

(m) The *p* in *septiembre* 'September' and *séptimo* 'seventh' is sometimes silent and may be dropped in writing, according to the Academy. But many find the forms *setiembre*, *sétimo* repugnant and the forms with *p* are much more common.

(n) If the prefix *re-* is added to a word beginning with *e*, one of the *e*s may be dropped in writing: *re+emplazo* > *remplazo* or *reemplazo* 'replacement', *re+embolso* > *rembolso* or *reembolso* 'reimbursement', *reelige* > *relige* 're-elects'. The new spelling is frequently (but not universally) seen in Latin America, but the spelling with *ree-* is much more usual in Spain.

(o) The sound [y] (like the *y* in 'yacht') is always spelt *y* at the end of words: *Paraguay*, *convoy*.

39.1.4 *Trans-* or *Tras-*

Some uncertainty surrounds the spelling of words which begin with the prefix *trans-* or *tras-*. Educated usage seems to be:

Normally *trans-*	Usually *tras-*	Always *tras-*
transalpino	trascendencia	trasfondo
transatlántico	trascendental	trashumancia
transbordar	trascendente	trashumante
transbordo	trascender	trasladar
transcribir	trasponer	traslado
transcripción	trasvasar	traslucir
transcurrir		trasluz
transcurso		trasnochar
transferencia		traspapelar
transferir		traspasar
transformar		traspaso
transformación		traspié
transfusión		trasplantar
transgredir		trasplante
transgresión		traspunte
transgresor		trasquilar
transmigración		trastienda
transmisión		trastocar
transmitir		trastornar
transmisión		trastorno
transparencia		trastrocar
transparentar		trastrueque
transparente		
transpirar		
transpiración		
transpirenaico		
transportar		
transporte		
transposición		
transversal		

Source: Seco (1992), 362. Seco notes that in the case of the first two columns the alternative spellings in *tras-* and *trans-* respectively are tolerated by the Academy but are not in general use.

39.2 The written accent

39.2.1 General rules

Native Spanish speakers are rather careless about the use of the written accent in handwriting, but in printing and formal writing the rules must be observed.

The basic rule is: if a word is stressed regularly, no written accent is required. If a word is stressed irregularly, the position of the stress must be shown by an acute accent on the stressed vowel. Stress is regular:

(a) if the word ends in a consonant other than *n* or *s* and the stress falls on the last syllable;

(b) if the word ends in a vowel or *n* or *s* and the stress falls on the penultimate syllable.

The following words therefore have regular stress and require no written accent:

la calle	street
la cama	bed
contestad	answer (*vosotros* imperative)
el coñac	brandy
denle	give him (plural imperative, *ustedes* form)
la imagen	image
el jueves	Thursday
Madrid	
natural	natural
(el) Paraguay	
redondo	round (adjective)
el reloj	(pronounced *reló*) clock/watch
el sacacorchos	cork-screw
la tribu	tribe
la virgen	virgin
volver	return

The following are stressed irregularly and must have a written accent:

el álbum	album
alérgicamente	allergically
contéstenles	answer them (*ustedes* imperative)
decídmelo	tell me it (*vosotros* imperative)
difícil	difficult
dirán	they will say (from *decir*)
fácil	easy
las imágenes	images
la nación	nation
la química	chemistry
el récord	record (in sports, etc.)
el rehén	hostage
la/las síntesis	synthesis/syntheses
las vírgenes	virgins

Note
Words ending in two consonants of which the second is *s* (all of them foreign words) are regularly stressed on the last syllable: *Orleans, los complots* 'plots', *los cabarets* 'cabarets'. *El/los fórceps* 'forceps', *el/los bíceps* 'biceps', *el/los récords* are exceptions.

39.2.2 Diphthongs, triphthongs and the position of the stress accent
Spanish vowels are divided into two classes:

Strong	**Semi-vowels**
a, e, o	*i* when pronounced [y]
i when pronounced as in *ti*	*u* when pronounced [w]
u when pronounced as in *tú*	

Vowels may appear in combinations of two or three, e.g. *eai, au, uai, iai,* etc. An intervening *h* is disregarded, so that *au* and *ahu, eu* and *ehu, ai* and *ahi,* etc. are treated the same way (at least since the publication of the Academy's *Nuevas normas*).

(a) When two or more **strong** vowels appear side by side, they are pronounced as separate syllables[5] and do not form diphthongs or triphthongs:

leo	[lé-o]	I read
créamelo	[kré-amelo]	believe me
pasee	[pasé-e]	subjunctive of *pasear* 'to go for a walk'
moho	[mó-o]	rust/mildew
Seoane	[se-o-á-ne]	(a surname)

An accent is required to show that an *i* or *u* combined with other vowels is pronounced strong (i.e. is not a semi-vowel): *creí* [kre-í] 'I believed', *aún* [a-ún] 'still'/'yet'.

(b) A combination, in either order, of a **strong vowel** plus a **semi-vowel** creates a diphthong and is counted as a single vowel for the purpose of finding the position of the written accent. Therefore the following words are stressed predictably:

arduo	[árðwo]	arduous
continuo	[kontínwo]	continuous
la lengua	[laléngwa]	tongue/language
Francia	[fránθya/fránsya]	France
la historia	[laystórya]	history/story
produjisteis	[proðuχísteys]	you produced
hablabais	[aβláβays]	you were speaking

and the following words have unpredictable stress and require a written accent:

amáis	[amáys]	you love
debéis	[deβéys]	you owe
volvió	[bolβyó]	he/she returned
continúo	[kontinú-o]	I continue
hacías	[aθías/asías]	you were doing
ella respondía	[eʎarrespondía]	she was answering/responding

---

[5] Adjacent strong vowels are in fact often run together in rapid speech and pronounced as one syllable, a phenomenon known as syneresis. This happens when the last of the vowels in the sequence is stressed or when none of them is stressed. Thus *león* is often pronounced [león] (one syllable) rather than [le-ón], but this has no affect on spelling.

(c) If a semi-vowel is added to a diphthong, a triphthong is formed. Triphthongs are also counted as a single vowel for the purpose of determining where a written accent should appear:

continuáis	[kontinwáys]	you continue (three syllables)
vieiras	[byéyras]	scallops (Spain only; two syllables)
cambiáis	[kambyáys]	you change (two syllables)

Note
Students of Portuguese should remember that Portuguese has very different rules and writes *colónia*, *história*, but *temia* (stressed like the Spanish *temía*).

39.2.3 Written accent on stressed diphthongs and combinations of strong vowels

If one of a group of combined vowels is stressed, the written accent may or may not appear on it. There are three possibilities:

(a) If the combination is **strong vowel + semi-vowel** the stress falls predictably on the strong vowel, so the following require no written accent:

vais	[báys]	you go (*vosotros* form)
el aire	[eláyre]	the air
veis	[béys]	you see (*vosotros* form)
el peine	[elpéyne]	comb
la causa	[lakáwsa]	cause
Palau	[paláw]	(personal surname)
Berneu	[bernéw]	(personal surname)
alcaloide	[alkalóyðe]	alkaloid

and the following are exceptions:

el país	[elpa-ís]	country
el baúl	[elβa-úl]	trunk/car-boot/(US) 'car trunk'
aún	[a-ún]	still/yet (pronounced differently from *aun*, 'even')
reír	[rre-ír]	to laugh
reís	[rre-ís]	you (*vosotros*) laugh
reúne	[rre-úne]	he reunites
prohíbe	[pro-íβe]	he prohibits
heroína	[ero-ína]	heroine/heroin
el arcaísmo	[arka-ísmo]	archaism
ahí	[a-í]	there
oís	[o-ís]	you (*vosotros*) hear
etc.		

(b) If the combination is **semi-vowel** plus **strong vowel**, the stress also falls predictably on the strong vowel, so the following require no accent; but see note (i):

fui	[fwí]	I was
huido[6]	[wíðo]	fled (past participle of *huir* 'to flee'
la ruina	[larrwína]	ruin
tiene	[tyéne]	he has (from *tener*)
luego	[lwéɣo]	then/later
cuenta	[kwénta]	she/he counts
la tiara	[latyára]	tiara

---

[6] *Huido*, *construido* and other words ending in *-uido* are stressed regularly, whereas words like *creído* 'believed' (past participle of *creer*) and *reído* 'laughed' (past participle of *reír*) are written with an accent because they fall under the exceptions to (a).

acuoso	[akwóso]	watery
vio	[byó]	she/he saw
dio	[dyó]	he/she gave
el pie	[elpyé]	foot
la viuda	[laβyúða]	widow

and the following are exceptions:

el dúo	[eldúo]	duet/duo
el búho	[elβú-o]	owl
frío	[frí-o]	cold
ríe	[rrí-e]	he/she laughs (from *reír*)
se fía	[sefí-a]	he/she trusts (from *fiarse*)

(c) If the combination is **strong vowel + strong vowel** the two vowels form separate syllables, so the following are stressed predictably:

los jacarandaes	[losχakarandá-es]	jacaranda trees (plural of *el jacarandá*)
los noes	[losnó-es]	noes
el caos	[elká-os]	chaos
ahonda	[a-ónda]	he/she deepens
feo	[fé-o]	ugly
leen	[lé-en]	they read
la boa	[laβó-a]	boa (the snake may be *el boa* in Lat. Am.)
el moho	[elmó-o]	rust/mildew

and the following are exceptions:

aéreo	[a-éreo]	air (adjective)
el león	[el-le-ón]	lion
el deán	[elde-án]	dean (ecclesiastical)
el rehén	[elrre-én]	hostage

Notes
(i) Accented forms like *rió* [rri-ó] 'he laughed', *lió* [li-ó] 'he tied in a bundle', *huís* [u-ís] 'you (*vosotros*) flee', *huí* [u-í] 'I fled', etc. are apparent exceptions to rule (b) that the second vowel is predictably stressed in the combination semi-vowel + strong vowel: compare *fui* 'I was', *fue* 'he/she was', *vio* 'he/she saw', *dio* 'he/she gave'. The former words are given a written accent to show that the two vowels are pronounced separately, whereas *vio*, *dio*, *fui* and *fue* are pronounced as monosyllabic words [byó], [dyó], [fwí], [fwé]. Compare the pronunciation of *pie* 'foot' ([pyé]) with *pié* [pi-é], first-person preterite of *piar* 'to cheep' (like a bird).
(ii) See 39.2.2 for triphthongs.
(iii) When an object pronoun is added to a finite verb form (this is nowadays rare) an original written accent is retained: *acabó + se = acabóse* for *se acabó* 'it ended'. See 11.14.1 note (ii) for a discussion of this construction.
(iv) If a word bearing a written accent is joined to another to form a compound, the original written accent is discarded: *tío + vivo = tiovivo* 'merry-go-round', *balón + cesto = baloncesto* 'basketball', etc.

39.2.4 Written accent: some common doubtful cases
The following forms are recommended (where *el/la* precedes the noun it may refer to a male or a female; when no accent is written the stressed vowel is shown in bold):

la acrobacia	acrobatics
afrodisiaco	aphrodisiac
amoniaco	ammonia

austriaco	Austrian
cardiaco	cardiac
el/la chófer[7]	driver
el cóctel	cocktail
demoniaco	or *demoníaco* 'demonic'; likewise other words ending in *-iaco/íaco*, the unacented form being more common
la dinamo[8]	dynamo
disponte	familiar imperative of *disponerse* 'to get ready'[9]
el electrodo	electrode
etíope	Ethiopean
la exégesis or *la exegesis*	exegesis
el fríjol[10]	bean
el fútbol[11]	soccer
el géiser	geyser (geological)
hipocondriaco	(see *demoniaco* above)
ibero (less commonly *íbero*)	Iberian
el láser	laser
la metempsicosis	metempsychosis
el meteoro	meteor
el misil (less commonly *mísil*)	missile
la olimpiada	Olympiad
la orgía	orgy
la ósmosis or *osmosis*	osmosis
el pabilo	wick (of a candle)
el parásito	parasite
el/la pediatra	paediatrician/(US) pediatrician
el periodo or *período*	period
el/la políglota	polyglot
el/la psiquiatra	psychiatrist
policiaco	(see *demoniaco* above)
la quiromancia[12]	palmistry/hand-reading
el rádar	radar
el reptil	reptile
el reuma	rheumatism (sometimes also *el reúma*)
el sánscrito	Sanskrit
el termostato	thermostat
la tortícolis	stiff neck
la utopía	utopia
el zodiaco	(see *demoniaco* above)

Some 'mispronunciations' are usual in speech: *el soviet* 'Soviet', *el oceano* 'ocean' (written and correctly pronounced *el océano*).

39.2.5 Accent on interrogative forms

In the case of some words, the interrogative form carries an accent. This indicates a fact of pronunciation: the interrogative form is stressed, as can

---

[7] Written and pronounced *chofer* in many countries of Latin America, including Mexico.
[8] *El dínamo* in some Latin-American countries, including Argentina and Cuba.
[9] Similarly *componte* 'compose yourself', *detente* 'stop'.
[10] Stressed *el frijol* in Latin America.
[11] *El futbol* is heard in some Latin-American countries.
[12] Likewise all words ending in *-mancia* that have the meaning 'divination'.

be seen by contrasting the *que*'s in *Dice que* **qué** *pasa* 'He's asking what's happening' or the *cuando*'s in *cuando llega* 'when he arrives . . .' and *¿***Cuándo** *llega?* 'When is he arriving?'.

These words are:

cómo	how	*dónde*	where
cuál	which	*qué*	what/which
cuándo	when	*quién*	who
cuánto	how much		

See Chapter 24 for further details.

39.2.6 Accent used to distinguish homonyms
In the case of some two dozen common words, the written accent merely eliminates ambiguities:

	without accent	**with accent**
de/dé	of	present subjunctive of *dar*
el/él	the (def. article)	he/it
este/éste/ese/ése	see 6.3	
aquel/aquél		
mas/más	but (rare)	more
mi/mí	my	me (after prepositions)
se/sé	reflexive pronoun	(i) I know, (ii) *tú* imperative of *ser*
si/sí	if	(i) yes, (ii) prepositional form of *se*
solo/sólo (see 9.15)	alone	only (*solamente*)
te/té	object form of *tú*	tea
tu/tú	your	you

Notes
(i) *Dé* loses its accent if a pronoun is attached and the stress is regular: *denos*, 'give us', *deme* 'give me', etc.
(ii) The Academy requires that *o* ('or') should take an accent when it appears between two numerals so as to avoid confusion with zero: *9 ó 5* '9 or 5'. However, *El País* (*Libro de estilo* 11.97) orders its journalists to ignore this rule and write *9 o 5*.
(iii) The following words do **not** have a written accent: *da* 'gives', *di* 'I gave', *fe* 'faith', *ti* prepositional form of *tú*, *vi* 'I saw', *ve* 'sees'.
(iv) *Aun* 'even' [áwn] and *aún* 'still/yet' [a-ún] are in fact pronounced differently in good Spanish.

39.3 Upper and lower-case letters

39.3.1 Upper-case letters
These are used much more sparingly than in English. They are used:
(a) At the beginning of sentences, as in English.
(b) With proper nouns, but not with the adjectives derived from them: *Madrid, la vida madrileña* 'Madrid life'; *Colombia, la cocina colombiana* 'Colombian cooking'; *Shakespeare, el lenguaje shakespeariano* 'Shakespearean (or Shakespeare's) language'.

Adjectives that are part of an official name are capitalized, e.g. *Nueva Zeland(i)a* 'New Zealand', *el Reino Unido* 'the United Kingdom', *Los Estados*

Unidos 'the United States', *El Partido Conservador* 'The Conservative Party', *Las Naciones Unidas* 'The United Nations', etc.

When a proper name includes the definite article, the latter is written with a capital letter *El Cairo* 'Cairo', *La Haya*.

In the case of countries that appear with the definite article, the article is not part of the name, so a lower-case letter is used: *la India* 'India', *la Argentina*. See 3.2.17 for discussion of this use of the article.

39.3.2 Lower-case letters
Lower-case letters are used for:

(a) Months, seasons and days of the week: *julio* 'July', *agosto* 'August', *verano* 'summer', *invierno* 'winter', *jueves* 'Thursday', *viernes* 'Friday', *martes* 'Tuesday', etc.

(b) Names of religions and their followers: *el cristianismo* 'Christianity', *el catolicismo* 'Catholicism', *el protestantismo* 'Protestantism', *el islam* 'Islam', *un testigo de Jehová* 'a Jehovah's witness', *los musulmanes* 'the Muslims', etc.

(c) Official titles, e.g. *el presidente de la República*, 'the President of the Republic', *la reina de Gran Bretaña* 'the Queen of Great Britain', *el papa Juan XXIII* 'Pope John XXIII', *los reyes de España* 'the King and Queen of Spain', *el señor García* 'Sr Garcia', *ministro de Obras Públicas* 'the Minister for Public Works', etc.

(d) Book and film titles: only the first letter is in upper case, as well as the first letter of any proper name that appears in the title: *Cien años de soledad* 'One Hundred Years of Solitude', *El otoño del patriarca* 'The Autumn of the Patriarch', *El espía que surgió del frío* ('The Spy who came in from the Cold'), *Vida de Manuel Rosas* 'The Life of Manuel Rosas', *La guerra de las galaxias* ('Star Wars'), etc.

However, the titles of newspapers and magazines are capitalized: *El País*, *La Nación*, *Ordenador Personal* 'Personal Computer', etc.

(e) For points of the compass: *norte* 'North', *sur* 'South', *este* 'East', *oeste* 'West'. They are capitalized if they are part of a name: *América del Norte*, 'North America', etc.

39.4 Punctuation

These remarks refer only to major differences between Spanish and English. Readers who need a detailed account of Spanish punctuation should refer to specialized manuals.

39.4.1 Full stops/periods and commas
The full stops/(US) 'period' (*el punto*) is used as in English, except that abbreviations are usually always written with a full stop:

English	Spanish
3000 ptas	*3000 ptas.*
Sr González	*Sr. González*

and a point is used in numbers where English uses a comma, and vice-versa: *1.567,50* = 1,567.50 and *1,005* (*uno coma cero cero cinco*) = 1.005 ('one point zero zero five'). Mexico, however, follows the conventions used in English.

Commas (*la coma*) are used much as in English, except for writing decimals (see preceding paragraph). A comma is not written before the conjunction *y* in a series: *pumas, coyotes y monos* 'pumas, coyotes and monkeys'. Two clauses with different subjects are separated by a comma whereas in English the comma is nowadays often omitted: *Juan es uruguayo, y Marta es argentina* 'Juan is Uruguayan and Marta is Argentine'.

39.4.2 Colons

Colons (*dos puntos*) are used as in English except that they appear after salutations in letters: *Muy Sr. mío:*[13] 'Dear Sir,' *Querida Ana*: 'Dear Ana'.

39.4.3 Semi colons

Semi colons (*punto y coma*) are used much as in English, except that they may be used after a series of commas instead of a comma to denote a longer pause:

Tenía pan, huevos y vino; pero no tenía carne	He had bread, eggs and wine, but he had no meat
Miguel entró cansado, confuso; María le siguió, radiante y orgullosa	Miguel came in, tired, confused. Maria followed him, radiant and proud

The semi colon is also much used before connectors, e.g. *sin embargo/no obstante* 'nevertheless', *a pesar de esto* 'despite this', that are themselves followed by a comma: *Le escribí más de una vez; sin embargo, no me contestó* 'I wrote to him more than once. However, he did not reply'.

39.4.4 Quotations and the representation of dialogue

There is no clear agreement over the use of *comillas* and inverted commas.

The signs « and» may be used (at least in Spain) like our inverted commas to indicate quotations or slang, dialect or other unusual forms, and occasionally to indicate dialogue within a paragraph:

Un inspector de bigotillo con acento «pied noir» acompañado de un gendarme de uniforme, va recorriendo las mesas pidiendo documentación: «No pasa nada, es sólo una operación de rutina». Sin embargo, todo este impresionante montaje sorprende a todos. (Cambio16, Spain)

A further quotation within « » is indicated by ' '. However, the *Libro de estilo* of *El País* (11.31) explicitly forbids the use of « » and requires use of "" for quoted material and ' ' for quotations within quotations. This convention is used in many publications, including this one.

Single quotation marks are in used in *El País* to enclose unusual or foreign words: *La palabra 'esnob' viene del inglés* 'the word "snob" comes from English'.

Dashes are used to enclose dialogue. There are three types of dash in Spanish:

el guión	hyphen	short -
el signo de menos	minus sign	medium length –
la raya	dash	double length —

In the representation of continuous dialogue inverted commas are not used, the words spoken being introduced by a *raya*.

---

[13] The formula used in the Southern Cone is *De mi consideración:*.

A *raya* marks either a change of speaker or a resumption of dialogue after an interruption. Dialogue is terminated by another *raya* only if unspoken words follow, as in *)—Ahora váyase —dijo— y no vuelva más hasta que yo le avise.*

Punctuation in direct speech is disconcertingly placed after the *raya*: *—Aprovecha ahora que eres joven para sufrir todo lo que puedas —le decía—, que estas cosas no duran toda la vida.* (G. García Márquez, *El amor en los tiempos del cólera*).

Example:

—¿Te parece que hablo de él con cierto rencor, con resentimiento? —Juanita hace un curioso mohín y veo que no pregunta por preguntar; es algo que debe preocuparla hace mucho tiempo.
—No noté nada de eso —le digo—. He notado, sí, que evitas llamar a Mayta por su nombre. Siempre das un rodeo en vez de decir Mayta. ¿Es por lo de Jauja, porque estás segura que fue él quien empujó a Vallejos?
—No estoy segura —niega Juanita—. Es posible que mi hermano tuviera también su parte de responsabilidad. Pero pese a que no quiero, me doy cuenta que le guardo un poco de rencor. No por lo de Jauja. Porque lo hizo dudar. Esa última vez que estuvimos juntos le pregunté: «¿Te vas a volver un ateo como tu amigo Mayta, también te va a dar por eso?» No me respondió lo que yo esperaba. Encogió los hombros y dijo:
—A lo mejor, hermana, porque la revolución es lo primero.

(M. Vargas Llosa, *Historia de Mayta*, Seix Barral. Printed in Spain.)

39.4.5 Question and exclamation marks
Spanish and Galician are the only two languages in which a question or exclamation must be introduced by an upside-down question or exclamation mark and followed by normal question and exclamation marks.

The logic behind this is that it enables readers to start the intonation for a question or exclamation at the right point, so words that are not included in the interrogatory or exclamatory intonation pattern lie outside the signs:

Oye, ¿quieres una cerveza?	Hey, d'you want a beer?
Hace calor, ¿verdad?	It's hot, isn't it?
Si te digo que no he gastado más que dos mil pesetas, ¿me vas a creer?	If I tell you I've only spent 2000 ptas, will you believe me?
Pero, ¡qué estupidez!	But what stupidity!
¡Lo voy a hacer! ¿Me oyes?	I'm going to do it! Do you hear me?

39.4.6 Hyphens
Hyphens (*guiones*) are used very sparingly, since compound words are usually written as a single word: *latinoamericano* (not **latino-americano*), *antisubmarino* 'anti-submarine', *hispanohablante* 'Spanish-speaking', *tercermundista* 'Third-World'.

They appear between compound adjectives in which each part represents separate things or people (not the case, for example, with *hispanoamericano*). Only the second of two adjectives agrees in number and gender:

las guerras árabe-israelíes	the Arab-Israeli wars
negociaciones anglo-francesas	Anglo-French negotiations
el complejo militar-industrial	the military-industrial complex

In other cases the hyphen may be used to join two nouns:

misiles superficie-aire	surface-to-air missiles
la carretera Madrid-Barcelona	the Madrid-Barcelona road

Hyphens are sometimes printed between compound nouns of the sort *mujer policía* 'police-woman', *año luz* 'light year', but this does not conform either to the Academy's recommendation or to the best editorial practice.

39.5 Division of words at end of line

A thorough knowledge of the structure of Spanish syllables is necessary for a good pronunciation, and readers should consult manuals of phonology and phonetics for precise details. As far as word division at the end of a line is concerned, the following rules apply:

(a) The following combinations of written consonants are not divided: *ch, ll, rr,* and combinations of stops and liquids, i.e.

br	*cr*	*fr*	*gr*	*pr*	*dr*	*tr*
bl	*cl*	*fl*	*gl*	*pl*		

(b) Bearing in mind that the combinations listed under (a) count as one consonant, a single consonant is always grouped with the following vowel:

ha-ba	*ro-ca*	*nu-do*	*a-gua*	*Ma-hón*	*pe-lo*	*ra-za*
ha-cha	*ca-lle*	*pe-rro*	*ca-bra*	*co-fre*	*o-tro*	*co-pla*

and no syllable begins with more than one consonant:

cal-do	*cos-ta*	*cuan-do*	*par-te*
can-cha	*as-ma*	*hem-bra*	*em-ble-ma*
com-bi-nar	*in-na-to*	*ex-cla-mar*	*con-lle-var*
cons-truc-ción	*al-co-hol*	*re-hén*	*pa-guen*
se-quí-a	*blan-den-gue*	*re-zon-gar*	*clor-hi-dra-to*

It is considered inelegant to begin a line with a single vowel, so *Ate-neo, aé-reo* are the preferred divisions.

(c) Combinations of *i* or *u* with another vowel can be split if an accent is written on the *i* or *u*. Thus:

viu-do	*cié-na-ga*	*fiel-tro*	*can-táis*	*a-ma-bais*	*bue-no*
ha-cia	*re-cien-te*	**but** *ha-cí-a-mos*	*de-cí-ais*	*con-ti-nú-as*	

(d) When a prefix ending with a vowel is added to a word beginning with *r-*, the latter consonant is doubled in writing: *contrarrevolucionario* 'counter-revolutionary', *prorrogar* 'to adjourn'. If the prefix is divided from the word at the end of a line, the single *r* reappears: *contra-revolucionario, pro-rogar*.

Notes
(i) The above rules reflect the rules of Spanish pronunciation, but the Academy states that when a word is clearly divisible on etymological grounds it may be divided accordingly. An etymological division is preferred when the usual division does not reflect the correct pronunciation: *su-brogar* for *sub-rogar* 'to substitute' looks and sounds wrong:

Further examples: *de-sa-gra-da-ble* or *des-a-gra-da-ble* 'disagreeable', *sub-rep-ti-cio* (better than *su-brep-t-i-cio*) 'subreptitious', *sub-ru-ti-na* (better than *su-bru-ti-na*) 'subroutine', *sub-ra-yar* (better than *su-bra-yar*) 'to underline', *sud-a-me-ri-ca-no* or *su-da-me-ri-ca-no* 'South American', *vos-o-tros* or *vo-so-tros* 'you', etc.
(ii) Any of these rules is overridden to avoid a comic or shocking result. One does not write *sa-cerdote, cal-culo, al ser-vicio del gobierno*.

(iii) There is confusion over the combination *tl*. The rule is that it is optionally separable, except in the words *a-tlas*, *a-tle-ta* and any of their derivatives. It should also not be separated in Mexican place names of Nahuatl origin like Tenochtitlan, etc.

(iv) Foreign words should be divided according to the rules prevailing in the language of origin.

(v) Words containing the sequence *interr-* are divided thus: *in-ter-re-la-cio-na-do*.

Sources: Macpherson (1975), *Nuevas normas* (1959), Martínez de Sousa (1974), Seco (1992).

Bibliography

The following general works are useful for serious students of Spanish:

El País, Libro de estilo (Madrid: Ediciones *El País*, 1977, many reprints). Based on the house rules of this prestigious daily newspaper. A generally uncontroversial and reliable guide to good Peninsular written usage.

Moliner, M., *Diccionario de uso del español*, 2 vols, (Madrid: Gredos, 1966-67; reprinted). Unwieldy but invaluable. Virtually ignores Latin-American usage.

Ramsey, M. and Spaulding, J.K., *A Textbook of Modern Spanish* (New York, 1958; often reprinted). Composed by Ramsey in the 1880s and revised by Spaulding in the 1940s. Very thorough but dated.

Real Academia Española, *Gramática de la lengua española: Nueva edición* (Madrid, 1931, reprinted). A useful but old-fashioned reference-point.

—— *Esbozo de una nueva gramática de la lengua española* (Madrid: Espasa Calpe, 1973). A sketch of a major project that is still (1994) awaited.

Seco, M., *Diccionario de dudas y dificultades de la lengua española*, 9ª edición renovada y puesta al día, (Madrid: Espasa Calpe, 1992; apparently a reprint of the 1987 edition). Increasingly indispensable amidst the flood of sometimes mutually contradictory guides to good usage now appearing in Spain.

Smith, C., editor, *Collins Spanish-English English-Spanish Dictionary*, 3rd revised edition (Glasgow and New York: HarperCollins, 1993). Rich in Latin-American usage and colloquial examples.

Solé, Y. and Solé C.A., *Modern Spanish Syntax: a Study in Contrast* (Lexington and Toronto: Heath, 1977). A valuable study despite its slight attention to regional variations and its uncertain English.

Mention must also be made of the two series *Problemas básicos del español* published by the Sociedad General Española de Librería of Madrid and *Problemas fundamentales del español*, published by the Colegio de España, Salamanca. Although uneven in quality, all of these booklets contain important information for intermediate and advanced learners of Spanish.

The following works are mentioned in the text:

Arjona Iglesias, M., *Estudios sintácticos sobre el español hablado de México* (Mexico: Universidad Autónoma, 1991)

Batchelor, R.E. and Pountain, C.J., *Using Spanish: A Guide to Contemporary Usage* (Cambridge: Cambridge University Press, 1992). A wide-ranging general survey of lexical and syntactic questions.

Beinhauer, W., *El español coloquial* (Madrid: Gredos, 1964, reprinted)

Bello, A., *Gramática de la lengua castellana destinada al uso de los americanos* (a recent edition is Caracas, 1951)

Bolinger, D., 'The Subjunctive *-ra* and *-se*: Free Variation?', *Hispania* 39 (1956), 345-49, reprinted in *Essays on Spanish: Words and Grammar* (Newark, Delaware: Juan de la Cuesta, 1991), 274-82.

Busquets, L. and Bonzi, L., *Ejercicios gramaticales* (Madrid: Sociedad General Española de Librería, 1983)

Carnicer, R. *Sobre el lenguaje de hoy* (Madrid: Prensa Española, 1969)

—— *Nuevas reflexiones sobre el lenguaje* (Madrid: Prensa Española, 1972)

García, E., *The Role of Theory in Linguistic Analysis: The Spanish Pronoun System* (Amsterdam/Oxford: North-Holland, 1975)

Gerboin, P. and Leroy, C., *Grammaire d'usage de l'espagnol contemporain* (Paris: Hachette, 1991). A new reference grammar useful for students who know French.

Gili y Gaya, S., *Curso superior de sintaxis española, 8ª edición*, (Barcelona: Biblograf, 1958; often reprinted)

—— *Estudios de lenguaje infantil* (Barcelona: Biblograf, 1972)

Gooch, A.L., *Diminutive, Pejorative and Augmentative Suffixes in Modern Spanish*, 2nd ed. (Oxford: Pergamon, 1970)

Hammer, A.E., *German Grammar and Usage*, 1st edition (London: Edward Arnold, 1971)

Harmer, L.C. and Norton, F.J., *A Manual of Modern Spanish*, 2nd ed. (London: University Tutorial Press, 1957; many reprints)

Iannucci, J.E., *Lexical Number in Spanish Nouns with Reference to their English Equivalents* (1952)

Ingamells, L. and Standish, P., *Variedades del español actual* (London: Longman, 1975), a useful collection of texts from all over the Hispanic world.

Judge, A. and Healey F.G., *A Reference Grammar of Modern French* (London: Edward Arnold, 1975)

Kauffman, D., 'Negation in English and Spanish', in *Readings in Spanish-English Contrastive Linguistics*, edited by R. Nash (San Juan de Puerto Rico: Inter-American U.P., 1978), 156-73.

Kany, C.E., *Sintaxis hispanomericana* (Madrid: Gredos, 1970, several reprints). English original published by University of Chicago (1945). A valuable guide to the variety of Latin-American syntax. It does not reliably mark register, so many examples may be substandard even on their own territory.

Lepschy, A. and G., *The Italian Language today*, 2nd ed. (London: Hutchinson, 1988)

Lope Blanch, J.M., *Estudios sobre el español de México* (Mexico City: Universidad Nacional Autónoma, 1991)

Lorenzo, E., *El español de hoy: lengua en ebullición, 3ª edición* (Madrid: Gredos, 1980)

Luque Durán, J. de, *Las preposiciones* (Madrid: Sociedad General Española de Librería, 1978), 2 vols

Macpherson, I.R., *Spanish Phonology: Descriptive and Historical* (Manchester and New York: Manchester University Press, n.d.)

Marsá, F., *Diccionario normativo y guía práctica de la lengua española* (Barcelona: Ariel, 1986)

Martínez de Sousa, J., *Dudas y errores del lenguaje* (Barcelona: Bruguera, 1974)

Molina Redondo, J.A. de, *Usos de se* (Madrid: Sociedad General Española de Librería, 1974)

Navas Ruiz, R., *El subjuntivo castellano* (Salamanca: Colegio de España, 1986)

Quirk, R., Greenbaum, S., Leech, G. and Svartvik, J., *A Grammar of Contemporary English* (London: Longman, 1972)

Repiso Repiso, S., *Los posesivos* (Salamanca: Colegio de España, 1989).

Santamaría, A. et al., *Diccionario de incorrecciones, particularidades y curiosidades del lenguaje* , 5th ed. (Madrid: Paraninfo, 1989)

Steel, B., *A Manual of Colloquial Spanish* (Madrid: Sociedad General Española de Librería, 1976)

Sources of Examples

These are too numerous to be listed individually. Many of the examples are modified versions of extracts from printed or spoken sources; these are not attributed. Attributed quotations are often from sources chosen not for their literary qualities but because they exemplify the unadorned everyday Spanish that this grammar describes. Poetry and poetic prose have been excluded. The following sources and publications are often mentioned:

Argentina: Jorge Asís, Jorge Luis Borges, Julio Cortázar, *Gente*, *La Nación*, Manuel Puig, Ernesto Sábato

Chile: José Donoso, Luis Sepúlveda

Peru: Alfredo Bryce Echenique, *El Comercio*, Mario Vargas Llosa

Colombia: Gabriel García Márquez, *El Tiempo*.

Mexico: *Excelsior*, Carlos Fuentes, Jorge Ibargüengoitia, *La Jornada*, Ángela Mastretta, *El Nacional*, Octavio Paz, Sergio Pitol, Elena Poniatowska, Luis Spota, *UnoMásUno*

Cuba: Reinaldo Arenas (in exile), Guillermo Cabrera Infante (in exile), *Cuba Internacional*, *Granma* (official organ of the Communist Party of Cuba), *Vindicación de Cuba* (the published transcript of a show trial)

Spain: *ABC*, Ignacio Aldecoa, Eloy Arenas, Carlos Barral, Antonio Buero Vallejo, *Cambio16*, Camilo José Cela, Miguel Delibes, *Diario16*, Antonio Gala, Federico García Pavón, Juan Goytisolo, Luis Goytisolo, José María Guelbenzu, Javier Marías, Juan Marsé, Carmen Martín Gaite, Eduardo Mendoza, *El Mundo*, *El Pais*, Soledad Puértolas, Carmen Rico-Godoy, Alfonso Sastre, *La Vanguardia*, Manuel Vázquez Montalbán, Federico Umbral.

Index of English Words

References are made to section number.

The sign = should be read 'when it has the meaning of'. A preceding question mark (e.g. ?*se los dije*) indicates a questionable or disputed form.

English words not listed should be sought under their most obvious translation, e.g. 'to beat' under *pegar*.

'a'/'an', see Indefinite Article
'about' = 'roughly' 14.6.3, 14.7.2; = 'concerning', see *sobre*
'absolutely not' 23.5.8
'according to', see *según*
'accustomed to', see *soler*
'after', see *después de*
'again' 32.6
'ago' 32.4
'all', see *todo*, *cuanto*
'all the more . . .' 5.11 note
'allow', see *permitir*
'almost', see *casi*
'alone', see *solo*
'already', see *ya*
'although', see *aunque*
'among', see *entre*
'and', see *y*
'another', see *otro*
'any', see *alguno*, *cualquier(a)*, partitive nouns, *ninguno*
'anyone', see *alguien*, *nadie*; 'anyone who' 16.13.7
'anything', see *algo*, *nada*
'appear', see *aparecer(se)*, *parecer*
'approximately', see 'about'
'as' = subordinator of time 16.12.6
'as . . . as' 5.15.1
'at' 34.1, 3.2.27
'as far as' 16.15.3b
'as if' 16.12.4c and notes
'as long as' see *mientras*, *con tal de que*
'as soon as' 16.12.6
'as well as' 2.3.4

'barely', see 'hardly'
'be', see *ser*, *estar*
'be quiet', see *callar(se)*
'because', see *porque*, *ya que*
'because of', see *por*
'become', see Verbs of Becoming
'before', subordinator of time 16.12.6
'behind', see *detrás de*
'better', see *mejor*, Comparison
'between', see *entre*
'both', see *ambos*
'but' 33.1
'by', see *por*, *mediante*

'can', see *poder*, *saber*
'certain', see *cierto*
'change into', see *convertirse*
'conscious', see *consciente*

'depends on' 16.4
'despite the fact that . . .' 16.12.8
'die', see *morir(se)*
'double' 10.14
'doubt', see *dudar*
'during', see *durante*

'each' 9.6, 'one each' 10.13
'either', see *o*, *tampoco*
'end by . . . -ing' 20.8.8
'equal' 5.15.2–3
'even', see *incluso*, *hasta*
'even if/though', see 16.12.8
'ever', see *nunca*
'every' see *cada*, *todo*, *cuanto*
'everything', see *todo*

'except', see *excepto*, *menos*; 'except that' 16.12.7b

'fear', see *temer*
'few', see *poco*
'find', see *encontrarse*
'for', see *para*, *por*; 'for *n* years, days', see Expressions of Time
'forget', see *olvidar(se)*
'former', 'the former the latter' 6.4.3

'given that' 16.12.3d
'go around . . . -ing' 20.8.1
'greater', see *mayor*
'grow', see *crecer(se)*

'half', see *medio*, *mitad*, Fractions
'happy', see *feliz*
'hardly' see *apenas*
'have' see *tener*, *haber*
'hence the fact that . . . ' 16.12.3c
'her', see *la*, Possessives
'here' 31.6.1
'him', see *le*, Possessives
'hope', see *esperar*
'how', see *como*, *cómo*, Neuter Pronouns (*lo*); as in 'how(ever) you like' 16.12.4b
'however much/little' 16.13.2
'hundred', see Numerals, *cien(to)*

'if', see *si*
'if only' 16.15.2
'improve', see *mejorar(se)*
'in' see *en*, also 3.2.27
'in case', see *por si*
'in front of', see *delante de*, *ante*
'in order to' 16.12.2
'in return for' 16.12.7a
'in spite of' see 'despite the fact that'
'in that case', see *entonces*, *pues*
'ing' form of verbs in English, see Continuous Forms of Verb, Gerund, esp. 20.9; 'I saw her smoking' 18.2.5, 20.6–7; used as noun 18.6; 'talking doll'/ 'convincing argument' 19.4, 'a man talking French 20.3, 'while living in . . . ' 20.4.1a, 'by working hard' 20.4.2
'inside' see *dentro*
'it', see *lo*, Personal Pronouns, Object
'it's me', 'it's him' 11.6

'know', see *saber*, *conocer*

'less'/'least', see *menos*, Comparison, *menor*; 'the less . . . the less' 5.11, 'less and less . . . ' 5.12, translation problems 5.14
'lest' 16.12.2b
'let's go'/'let's do' 17.5

'likewise' 2.3.4
'little', = 'not much', see *poco*; = *pequeño*, see *pequeño*
'look', see 'seem'
'lots' see 'many'

'many', see *mucho*, *la de*
'more'/'most', see *más*, Comparison; 'the more . . . the more' see *cuanto*, 'more and more . . . ' 5.12; translation problems 5.14
'much more/less' 5.10
'must' in suppositions 21.3, 14.6.3, 14.7.2; see also *deber*, *haber que*, *tener que*

'neither', see *ni*, *tampoco*
'never', see *nunca*
'no', 'not', see *no*; = 'none of', see *ninguno*
'no one', see *nadie*
'none', see *ninguno*
'nor', see *ni*
'not even', see *ni*
'nothing', see *nada*

'on', see *en*, *sobre*
'on condition that' 16.12.7a
'on seeing/arriving' 18.3, 20.5
'one' (impersonal pronoun), see *uno*, Impersonal *se*
'one another' 11.15b, 26.3
'only', see *sólo*
'or', see *o*
'order', see *mandar*
'other', see *otro*
'outside', see *fuera*
'own', see *propio*

'per cent' 10.7
'perhaps' 16.3.2
'provided that' 16.12.7a

'quickly', see *rápido*

'rather' 9.2
'rest, the', see *resto*
'same' 9.11; 5.15.2–3
'say', see *decir*
'scarcely', see 'hardly'
'seem', see *parecer*, also 29.4.3
'self', as in 'the Pope himself' 9.11, 9.14
'several', see *varios*
'since' = 'seeing that', see *ya que*; = 'since the time when', see *desde*, *desde que*
'single' 10.14
'so many/much', see *tanto*
'so', as in 'so nice' 9.16 note (i); = 'with the result that' 16.12.4
'so that' = 'in order to' 16.12.2; = 'in

such a way that' 16.12.4
'so that not . . . ' 16.12.2b
'some' 3.2.8, 9.4
'someone', see *alguien*
'something' see *algo*
'stay', see *quedarse, estarse*
'still' 31.7.3, 32.8
'supposing that' 16.12.5n

'take', as in 'it took *n* days' 32.7
'take away', see *llevarse*
'that', = 'I think **that**' 33.4.1; = '**that** book'
    see Demonstrative adjectives and
    pronouns; = 'the book **that** I read',
    see Relative Clauses; '**that** which',
    see 6.5, *eso, aquello, lo que*
'that's why' 36.2.4
'the fact that' 16.10
'the more the more', see *cuanto*
'the one that/who', see Nominalizers
'the reason why' 25.7, 36.2.3
'the way that/in which' 35.11
'them', see *le, los*
'then' 31.7.4
'there' 31.6.1
'there is/are', see Existential Sentences
'this', see Demonstrative adjectives and
    pronouns, *esto*
'too', see *demasiado*
'toward(s)', see *hacia*

'un' (prefix) 4.13, 18.5
'under(neath'), see *debajo de*
'understand' see *comprender*
'unless' see *a menos que*

'until' 16.12.6

'various' 9.18b
'very' 31.4.2; as in 'the very place/the
    place itself' 9.11, 9.14
'wait', see *esperar*
'want' see *querer*
'we', 'we Americans' 3.2.29; see also
    nosotros
'what?', see *cuál, qué*
'what a! . . . ' 24.4.4, 3.3.13
'what for', see 'why'
'what if?' 35.10 note (iii)
'whatever' 16.13.4, 16.14
'when', see *cuando, cuándo*
'whenever' 16.13.6
'where', see *donde, dónde*
'wherever' 16.13.8, 16.14.3
'whether . . . or' 16.13.1
'which' see Relative Pronouns; 'which?',
    see *cuál*
'whichever' 16.13.4–5, 16.4
'who(m)' see Relative Pronouns
'whoever', 16.13.7, 16.14
'whose', see *cuyo*
'why', see *por qué, para qué*
'win', see *ganar(se)*
'with', see *con*
'without', see *sin, sin que*
'worse', see *peor*, Comparison

'yet' 31.7.3
'you', 'you English' 3.2.29; see also *tú,
    vos, vosotros, usted(es)*

Index of Spanish Words and Grammatical Points

For the conjugation of individual verbs see pp. 170–97 (irregular) and 197–200 (regular). Standard alphabetical order is used, i.e. *ch* follows *cg*, *ll* follows *lk*; *ñ* follows *n*.

a 34.1; Personal *a* **Chap. 22**; ?*problemas a resolver* 18.12, *a* used with certain verbs 18.2.3, 22.11; *a* + infinitive = 'if' 25.9e
a cambio de que 16.12.7a
a condición de que 16.12.7a
a despecho de que 16.12.8
a donde 24.9, 35.10 note (i)
a fin de que 16.12.2
a la/a lo (to form adverbs) 31.3.7
a lo mejor 16.3.2c
a manera de 3.3.12
a medida que 16.12.6
a menos que 16.12.7b, 25.9b
a modo de 3.3.12
a no ser que 16.12.7b
a personal, see Personal *a*
a pesar de que 16.12.8
a que 16.12.2
a solas 9.15 note (ii)
abajo 31.6.6
abolir 13.3.2
aburrido 29.4.4
acá 31.6.2
acabar with gerund 20.8.8
acabáramos 16.15.3c
acaso 16.3.2b
Accents 39.2; on diphthongs and triphthongs 39.2.2–3; doubtful cases 39.2.4; acc. on demonstrative

pronouns (*éste, ése, aquél*) 6.3; on *aislar, reunir, prohibir* 13.2.3; on question words 24.1; on adverbs in -*mente* 31.2.2; acc. to distinguish homonyms 39.2.6; see also Dieresis (*ü*)
acercarse, pronouns with 11.8
–*aco* (suffix) 38.4
acostumbrar 21.6 note (i)
actuar 13.2.5
adelante 31.6.8
adentro, see *dentro*
Adjectival Participle (e.g. *andante, saliente*) 19.4
Adjective Agreement 4.7; with collective nouns 2.3.1, 4.7.3; with nouns joined by *o* or *ni* 4.7.2, of pre-posed adjs 4.7.4, 'neuter agreement' 4.7.5
Adjectives **Ch. 4**; compared with nouns 4.1d, 3.3.11; forms of 4.2, adjs ending in -*or* 4.2.1 esp. note (i), ending in -*í* 4.2.2a, invariable adjs 4.2.3, invariable adjs of colour 4.2.4, 'dark green/blue', etc. 4.3, *hirviendo* 4.4, compound adjs 4.5, short forms of adjs 4.6; agreement of adjs, see Adjective Agreement; adjs from countries 4.8.1, towns 4.8.2; -*ísimo* 4.9, nouns used as adjs 4.10, Position of adjectives 4.11, position and change of meaning

4.11.8, adjs found only before nouns 4.11.9; attributive adjs 4.1c, 4.12; translating 'un-' 4.13; Comparison, see Comparison of Adjectives and Adverbs; *lo bueno/lo interesante* 7.2.1a, *lo guapa que es* 7.2.2; *ser* or *estar* with Ch. 29 *passim*; adjs whose meaning is affected by use of *ser* or *estar* 29.4.4; adjs used as adverbs 31.3.3; *viven felices* 31.3.4; word order with 37.2.6, 37.4, 31.3.8

adonde 24.9, 35.10

adquirir 13.3.3

Adverbs **Ch. 31**; comparison **Ch.5**, superlative 5.4, *lo más arriba*, etc. 7.2.1b, *lo bien que canta*, etc. 7.2.2; ending in -*mente* 31.2, consecutive advs in -*mente* 31.2.3, advs that do not take -*mente* 31.2.4; advs of manner 31.3, adv. phrases 31.3.2, adjectives used as advs 31.3.3–4, nouns used as advs 31.3.5, *rápido* 31.3.6, *al/a lo* 31.3.7, position of advs of manner 31.3.8, 37.2.6, 37.4; intensifiers (*muy*, etc.) 31.4; advs meaning 'perhaps', 'possibly' 16.3; advs of place 31.6, prepositions with advs of place 31.6.4, *dentro/fuera* 31.6.5, *abajo/debajo de* 31.6.6, *atrás/detrás* 31.6.7, *(a)delante* 31.6.8, advs of time 31.7 (or see *ya*, *recién*, *todavía*, *aún*, *luego*, *entonces*); *incluso/aun* 31.8, *luego/entonces* 31.7.4

afectar (a) 22.11a

Affective suffixes, see Diminutive Suffixes, Augmentative Suffixes

afuera, see *fuera*

agredir 13.3.4

Agreement, see Number, Gender, Tense or Adjective Agreement; with *todo* 9.17f; of *uno* and *cientos* 10.3; of personal pronouns (e.g. *soy yo* = 'it's me') 11.6

ahí 31.6.1

aislar 13.2.3

ajeno 9.1

–*ajo* (suffix) 38.4

al 3.1.3; + infinitive = 'on . . . –ing' 20.5, 18.3; = 'if' 25.9d

algo 9.2

alguien 9.3, pers. *a* with 22.4

alguno 9.4; omission of in journalism 3.4.2; short form 4.6b and note (ii), 9.4; *algunos* compared with *unos* 9.4.2

allá 31.6.2

allí 31.6.1

alma 3.1.2

Alphabet 39.1.2

alrededor, possessive with 8.7

amanecer 27.2 note

ambos 9.5; position 4.11.9

americano 4.8.1 note (i)

andar conjugation 13.3.5, + gerund 20.8.1, in Mexico 15.5

–*ando* (suffix), see Gerund

Animals, gender of 1.2.1 and 1.3; personal *a* with Ch. 22

anochecer 27.2 note

ante (preposition) 34.2

–*ante* (suffix) 19.4

Anterior Preterite, see *Pretérito anterior*

antes de que 16.12.6, esp. note (i), 33.4.2 note (ii); replaced by *antes de* + infinitive 18.3

antes que, see *antes de que*; *antes que nada*, *nadie* 23.4d; = *antes de que* 33.4.2 note (ii)

antiguo 4.11.8

aparecer(se) 26.6.4

apenas 23.5.7; 16.12.6

Apposition, def. article in 3.2.25, indef. article in 3.3.10

aquel, see Demonstrative Adjectives and Pronouns; compared with *ese* 6.4.2

aquello 7.5

aquí 31.6.1; = *este* 31.6.3

ardiendo 4.4

argüir 13.3.13, 13.2.2a

arte 1.4.16 note (i)

Articles, see Definite Article, Indefinite Article

así = 'although' 16.12.8; = 'I hope that' 16.15.2

así que 16.12.4

asir 13.3.6

Aspect, Verbal **Ch. 14**, esp. 14.2; see also Preterite, Imperfect

–*astro* (suffix) 38.4

atrás 31.6.7

Attributive Adjectives 4.1c, 4.12

Augmentative Suffixes (e.g. -*ajo*, -*ón*, -*azo*, -*ote*) 38.3

aun 31.8

aún 31.7.3

aun cuando 16.12.8

aunque 33.6.1, subjunctive with 16.12.8, replaced by gerund 20.4.5

averiguar 13.2.5, 13.2.2a

–*avo* (suffix added to numerals) 10.10, 10.12.2

–*azo* (suffix) 38.3

azúcar 1.4.13

bajar, bajarse 26.6.2
bajo (preposition) 34.3
bajo la condición de que 16.12.7a
bastante, use of *lo* with 7.2.1 note (iv)
beber, beberse 26.6.3
Become/becoming, see Verbs of
    Becoming
billón 10.1n
bueno short form of 4.6b, position 4.11.6,
    comparison 5.2
bullir, see *-llir*

cabe (preposition) 34.4
caber 13.3.8
cada 9.6, see also *todo*
cada vez más/menos 5.12
caer conjugation 13.3.9; *caerse* 26.6.2
callar(se) 26.6.4
calor 1.4.13
cámara 1.2.9
cambiar 13.2.4
Capital Letters 39.3
carácter 2.1.8
Cardinal Numbers **Ch. 10** *passim,* esp.
    10.1
casi, historic present with 14.3.3n
castellano 4.8.1 note (ii)
centenar 10.8 note (ii)
–cer, verbs ending in 13.2.7
cerca 31.2.8 note
cerrar 13.3.11
cien(to) 10.6
cientos 10.3
cierto 9.7; article with 3.3.13, position
    4.11.8
–cir, verbs ending in 13.2.9
clave 4.2.3
Cleft Sentences[1] 36.2; tense in 14.4.1 note
    (ii)
cocer 13.3.12
coche cama 2.1.7b
Collective Nouns, number agreement
    with 2.3.1, 10.8; *tipo/clase* de 2.3.2,
    noun + *de* + noun 3.2.11, personal
    a with 22.9; see also Collective
    Numerals
Collective Numerals (*decena, quincena*
    etc.) 10.8
colon 39.4.2
color 1.4.13
Colours 4.2.3–4, 4.3; *lo verde,* etc. 7.2.1
    note (v)
comer, comerse 26.6.3

comillas (quotation marks) 39.4.4
Comma 39.4.1; use with decimals 10.1
    note (iii)
como = subordinating 'how(ever)'
    16.12.4b; = 'like', indef. article
    after 3.3.12; = 'since'/'because'
    33.5.2, 16.12.3; before personal *a*
    22.3, + subjunctive = 'if' 25.8.2,
    introducing relative clauses 35.11, in
    cleft sentences 36.2
cómo 24.7; = *qué* in Lat.-Am.
    exclamations 24.4.4 note
como no fuera que 16.12.7b
como no sea que 16.12.7b
como quiera que 16.13.4
como si 16.12.4c and notes; tenses after
    16.16 note (v); replaced by *como* +
    gerund 20.4.6
Comparison of Adjectives and Adverbs
    Ch. 5; comparative 5.1, irreg.
    comparative 5.2; superlative 5.3,
    subjunctive after 16.14.4; *más que*
    or *más de?* 5.5, *más/menos del que* 5.6;
    see also *grande, pequeño, poco, mucho,
    más, menos, mayor, menor,* 'much
    more/less'; 'the more . . . the more'
    5.11, 'more and more' 5.12, 'as . . .
    as' 5.15.1; comp. of equality 5.15
Compound Nouns, plural 2.1.7, gender
    1.4.9, 4.11.5
Compound Tenses (i.e. Perfect,
    Pluperfect) 14.8; see also Perfect,
    Pluperfect Tenses
comprender, subjunctive with 16.11.2
con 34.5; combined with personal
    pronouns 11.5.2–3, indef. article
    after 3.3.12; see also *hacia con*
con el objeto de que 16.12.2
con la intención de que 16.12.2
con tal (de) que 16.12.7a, 25.9c
Conditional Sentences **Ch. 25**; open
    conditions 25.2, remote conds 25.3,
    unfulfilled conds 25.4, fulfilled
    conds 25.7, uses of *si* 25.8, *como*
    = *si* 25.8.2, *de* + infinitive = 'if'
    25.8.3, other ways of forming cond.
    sentences 25.9, translation problems
    25.10, 'if I were you' 25.11
Conditional Tense, forms 13.1.8, uses
    14.7; in conditions 14.7.1, **Ch. 25**
    passim; replacement by imperfect
    14.5.2, 25.5; for suppositions
    14.7.2, = future in the past 14.7.3,
    in rhetorical questions 14.7.4;

---

[1] i.e. sentences like 'It was there that I saw it', 'It's her that you've got to talk to', 'It's then that you have to do it'.

replacement by past subjunctive
14.7.5, 25.6; used regionally for past
subjunctive 16.2.8, 25.3 note (i)

Conjugation, see Verbs. Regular verbs are
shown on pp. 197–200. Irreg. verbs
are listed at pp. 170–97;

Conjunctions **Ch. 33**, or see *pero, sino,
mas, o, y, que, de que, porque, como,
pues, ya que, puesto que, aunque, y eso
que, con tal de que, a menos que, de
modo que.* For use of subjunctive after
conjunctions see Subordinators

conmigo 11.5.2

conocer, preterite and imperfect
compared 14.4.5, compared with
conocerse 26.6.3 note (i)

conque 16.12.4a

consciente 29.2.3 note (i)

consigo 11.5.3

construir 13.3.13

contigo 11.5.2

continuar 13.2.5, 32.8; gerund with 20.8.6

Continuous Form of Verbs **Ch 15**;
compared with French, Italian 15.1,
with English 15.1.2 and 15.3, with
simple present tense 15.1.3; general
uses 15.2, preterite continuous
15.2.3n, *estaba hablando* and *hablaba*
compared 14.5.3, future continuous
15.2.5, restrictions on use of 15.3,
estar siendo 15.4, cont. in Lat.-Am.
usage 15.5

contra 34.6; with possessives 8.7

convertirse 27.3.5

cortés 4.2.1 note (ii)

Countries, gender of 1.4.7, def. article
with 3.2.17, adjectives from 4.8.1

crecer(se) 26.6.3

creer subjunctive with 16.7.2, 16.11.1,
comp. with *creerse* 26.6.4

cuál 24.3; compared with *qué* 24.3.2; (for
el cual see Relative Clauses)

cualquier(a) 9.8; *cualquiera que* 16.13.4n; =
'anyone who' 16.13.7

cuándo 24.8

cuando, subordinator 16.12.6; =
'whenever' 16.13.6; introducing
relative clauses 35.12; in cleft
sentences, see Cleft Sentences

cuando quiera que 16.13.6

cuanto 'the more . . . the more' 5.11,
subjunctive with 16.13.3; = 'every'
9.17 note (iii), subjunctive with
16.14.3

cuánto 24.6

cuarentena 10.8

cuatro = 'a handful' 10.8 note (i)

cuyo 35.7, 35.8c

dado que 16.12.3d

dar conjugation 13.3.15, *darse* 26.6.3

Dates, how to write them 32.9

de 34.7; comp. with *desde* 34.7.5; = 'some'
3.2.8 note (ii), def. article in
3.2.11, *es difícil **de** hacer* 18.10, *de* +
infinitive = 'if' 25.8.3, *yo de ti* 25.11,
in passive constructions 34.14.4
note (ii)

de ahí que 16.12.3c

de forma/suerte que 16.12.4a

de manera que 16.12.4a

de modo que 16.12.4a

de nosotros = nuestro 8.6

de nuevo 32.6c

de que 33.4.2–3; after verbs denoting
emotional reactions 16.6.1–2, noun
+ *de que* + subjunctive 16.10.2

debajo de, comp. with *bajo* 34.3, comp.
with *abajo* 31.6.6

deber 21.3; replaced by future in
suppositions 14.6.3 or by conditional
14.7.2; *deber* and *deber de* 21.3.2,
various tenses of *deber* contrasted
21.3.3, *debe haberlo hecho* or *ha debido
hacerlo?* 21.7

debido a que 16.12.3

decena 10.8

Decimals, how to write them 10.1 note
(iii)

décimo 10.12.1–2

decir conjugation 13.3.16, subjunctive
with 16.7.2

Defective Verbs (like *abolir*) 13.3.2

Definite Article **Ch. 3**; forms 3.1.1, *el*
before some fem. nouns 3.1.2; uses
and omission of def. art. 3.2; def.
art. compared with French 3.2.2,
with English 3.2.3, *el padre y **la**
madre* 3.2.4, omission in proverbs
3.2.5, with generic nouns 3.2.6
and 3.2.10, omission in lists 3.2.7,
with partitive nouns 3.2.8, before
qualified nouns 3.2.9, in book and
film titles 3.2.13, in headlines 3.2.14,
with unique entities 3.2.15, with
languages 3.2.16, with countries
3.2.17, with other place names
3.2.18–19, with days of week 3.2.20,
with personal names 3.2.21, with
family terms 3.2.23, with *señor, Mr,*
etc. 3.2.24; in apposition 3.2.25, with
numerals 3.2.26, 10.11; 'at work',
'in hospital' etc. 3.2.27, *nosotros
los españoles* 3.2.29, def. art. in
superlative constructions 5.3.1–4; to
replace possessives 8.3.4, used with
infinitive 18.7

Deixis, see Demonstrative Adjectives
  and Pronouns
dejar(se) 26.6.4
del 3.1.3
delante 31.6.8, 34.2; with possessives 8.7
demás 9.13 note (iii)
demasiado 9.9
Demonstrative Adjectives and Pronouns
  Ch. 6; forms 6.1, position 6.2, accent
  on dem. pronouns 6.3, *este, ese* and
  aquel compared 6.4.1, *aquel* or *ese*?
  6.4.2, 'the former, the latter' 6.4.3,
  neuter forms (*esto, eso, aquello*) 7.5
dentro 31.6.5
dentro de 31.6.5, = 'in *n* days' 32.5
dequeísmo 33.4.3
desayunar(se) 26.6.3 note (ii)
desde 34.7.5; = prep. of time 32.3.7
desde hace 32.3.7
desde que, tense forms with 14.10.3
desde ya 31.7.1 note (iii)
después de que, tense forms with 14.10.3,
  replaced by *después de* + infinitive
  18.3
detrás (de) 31.6.7; with possessives 8.7
devolverse (Lat.-Am. = *regresar*) 26.6.2
  note
Dieresis (*ü*) 13.2.2a, 13.2.5
diferente 5.15.2 note (ii)
Diminutive **Ch. 38**; diminutive suffixes
  38.2.1–5; diminutives and *pequeño*
  38.2, dims to soften imperative
  17.11f, 38.2.2a; for augmentative
  suffixes see Augmentative Suffixes
Diphthongs, accents on 39.2.2
discernir 13.3.17
distinto 5.15.2 note (ii)
Division of Words 39.5
docena 10.8
don 3.2.24 note (i)
donde = 'wherever' 16.13.8, 16.14.3; as
  relative 35.10, in cleft sentences 36.2
dónde 24.9
dondequiera 16.13.8
doña 3.2.24 note (i)
dormir 13.3.18
Double Negative 23.3
dudar, subjunctive with 16.8, *d. de que*
  33.4.3 note (ii)
durante 32.3.4
Duration, see Expressions of time

e = 'and' 33.3
–ear, verbs ending in 13.2.6
ejercer 13.2.7
–ejo (suffix) 38.4
el cual, see Relative Clauses
el de 36.1.2

el hecho de que 16.10
el que, as relative pronoun, see
  Relative Clauses; = 'the one that'
  36.1.4; translation problems 6.5a,
  replacement by *aquel* 6.5c; = 'the
  fact that' 16.10; = 'whichever'
  16.13.5; = 'anyone who' 16.13.7,
  16.14; *el que* in cleft sentences, see
  cleft sentences
él, see Personal Pronouns Subject, also
  Emphasis at 11.15
el, see definite article; with fem. nouns
  like *alma, hambre*, etc. 3.1.2
ella(s), see *él*
ello 7.3
ellos, see *él*
Emphasis, of subject pronouns 11.2.1, of
  object pronouns 11.15
en 34.9; in time phrases 32.5
en + gerund 20.5, *en n días* 32.5
en absoluto = 'absolutely not' 23.5.8
en contra, see *contra*
en cuanto 16.12.6
en donde 35.10
en mi vida = 'never in my life' 23.5.8
en vista de que 16.12.3
–ena (suffix added to numerals) 10.8
encima 34.17
–endo (suffix), see Gerund
enfermar(se) 26.7
–ente (suffix) 19.4
entonces 31.7.4
entrar, ?entrarse 26.6.2; *entrar en* or *entrar
  a*? 34.1 note (ii)
entre 34.10
entre más 5.11
entre, personal pronouns after 11.5.1;
  entre sí 11.5.3 note (ii)
erguir(se) 13.3.19
errar 13.3.20
escapar(se) 26.6.2
ese, see Demonstrative Adjectives and
  Pronouns; *?ese arma* 6.1. note (iii),
  compared with *aquel* 6.4.2
eso 7.5; *eso son . . .* 2.3.3
esparcir 13.2.9
espécimen 2.1.8
esperar, subjunctive after 16.11.3;
  compared with *esperarse* 26.6.3
estar conjugation p.203, use in
  continuous (*estoy hablando*, etc.),
  see Continuous Form of Verbs;
  compared with *estarse* 26.6.3;
  compared with *hay*, see Existential
  Sentences; for comparison with *ser*
  see '*Ser* and *Estar*'
este, see Demonstrative Adjectives and
  Pronouns; *?este área*, etc. 3.1.2 note

(v), 6.1 note (iii)

esto 7.5; *esto son . . .* 2.3.3

–ete (suffix) 38.2, esp. 38.2.5

evacuar 13.2.5

excepto, personal pronouns after 11.5.1

excepto que 16.12.7b

Exclamation Marks 39.4.5

Exclamations, see Interrogation and Exclamations; indef. article in 3.3.13

Existential Sentences (i.e. 'there is/there are') **Ch. 30**; basic uses of *hay* (*haber*) 30.2; *hay* never pluralized 30.2.1 note (i); pronouns with 30.2.2; *hay* and *estar* compared 30.3

explicar 16.11.2

Expressions of Time **Ch. 32**; 'for *n* days, etc.' 32.2–3, *llevar n días* 32.3.1, *hace n días* 32.3.2, *durante* 32.3.4, *por n días* 32.3.5, *desde* (*hace*) = 'since' 32.3.7, 'ago' 32.4, 'in *n* days' 32.5, 'again' 32.6, 'it took *n* days' 32.7; 'still' 32.8, 31.7.3; writing the date 32.9, omission of preposition in expressions of time 32.10

Families, plural of 2.1.6, def. article with family terms 3.2.23

feliz, ser with 29.2.3

Foreign Words, gender 1.4.10, plural 2.1.5

forma reduplicativa, e.g. *sea como sea, diga lo que diga* 16.13

Fractions 10.10

frente a 34.2 note (i)

fuera 31.6.5

fuera de que 16.12.7b

Full Stop, see Point

Future Subjunctive 16.17, forms 13.1.10

Future Tense forms 13.1.8, uses 14.6; general remarks 14.6.1, for commands 14.6.2, used for suppositions and approximations 14.6.3, present tense for future 14.6.4, *ir a . . .* 14.6.5, future in the past 14.7.3; regionally used for subjunctive 16.2.8, *estaré hablando*, etc., see Continuous Forms of Verbs

ganar(se), 26.6.4

Gender of Nouns **Ch. 1**; referring to humans 1.2, titles of female professionals 1.2.7, gen. of mixed groups 1.2.8, inanimate nouns applied to humans 1.2.9, invariable for either sex 1.2.11; animals 1.3 and 1.2.1; gen. of inanimates 1.4; masc. by meaning 1.4.1, masc. by form 1.4.2, masc. nouns ending in *-a* 1.4.3; fem. by meaning 1.4.4, fem. by

form 1.4.5, fem. nouns ending in *-ma* 1.4.6; gen. of countries, provinces, regions 1.4.7; cities, towns, villages 1.4.8; compound nouns 1.4.9; foreign words 1.4.10, abbreviations 1.4.11, metonymic gender 1.4.12, doubtful or disputed genders 1.4.13, Lat.-Am. gender 1.4.15, words of two genders 1.4.16, gender of numbers 10.2

Generic Nouns 3.2.6

Gerund **Ch. 20**; see also Continuous Form of Verb, Adjectival Participles; forms of gerund 20.2; 'a box containing books' 20.3; basic uses of gerund 20.4; = 'while' 20.4.1a; = method by 20.4.2; = 'if' 20.4.2 note, 25.9a; = 'in order to' 20.4.3; = 'seeing that' 20.4.4, = 'although' 20.4.5; = 'as if' 20.4.6, *en* + gerund 20.5; 'I saw her smoking', 'I caught them kissing' 20.6–7; gerund in captions 20.6 note; gerund with *andar* 20.8.1, with *ir* 20.8.2, with *llevar* 20.8.3, with *quedarse* 20.8.4, with *salir* 20.8.5, with *seguir/continuar* 20.8.6, 32.8; with *venir* 20.8.7, with *acabar* 20.8.8, translating English *-ing* 20.9

grande forms 4.6, position of 4.11.6, comparison 5.2, *mayor* 5.8, 4.2.1 note (ii)

gruñir, see *-ñir*

guión (= 'hyphen') 39.4.4, 39.4.6; for dividing words 39.5

gustar, use of *le/les* with 12.6.4, *a* with 22.11

haber conjugation p.204; uses 21.4; = 'there is/are', see Existential Sentences; *habérselas con* footnote to p. 204, *haber de* footnote to 14.6; *haber* to form Perfect and Pluperfect tenses 14.8, position 14.8.1, *he hecho* and *tengo hecho* compared 14.8.3, *haber de* 21.4.1, *haber que* 21.4.2

hablar de que 33.4.3 note (i)

hacer(se) conjugation 13.3.22, *hacerse* = 'become' 27.3.3; *hace n días que* 32.3.2

hacia 34.11

hacia con 34.11b

hambre 3.1.2

hasta 34.12; personal pronouns after 11.5.1; = 'even' 31.8

hasta que (no) 16.12.6

hay **Ch. 30**

Headlines 3.2.14

hembra 1.3, 4.2.3

hindú 4.8.1 note (iii)
hirviendo 4.4
hombre rana 2.1.7
hyphen, see *guión*

–iar, verbs ending in 13.2.4
–ico (suffix) 38.2
–iendo (suffix), see Gerund
–iente (suffix) 19.4
igual 5.15.2, 5.15.3; = 'perhaps' 16.3.2d
igualmente 5.15.3
–illo (suffix) 38.2, esp. 38.2.3
imagen 2.1.3 note (iii)
imaginar(se) 26.6.3
Imperative **Ch. 17**; future tense used
    for 14.6.2, *tú* form 17.2.2, *vos*
    form 17.2.3, *vosotros* form 17.2.4,
    usted(es) form 17.2.5, negative
    imp. 17.3, object pronouns with
    17.4, First-person forms 17.5,
    Third-person imp. 17.6, imp.
    preceded by *que* 17.7, impersonal
    imp. 17.8, infinitive used for 17.9,
    present tense used for 17.10,
    mellowing the imperative 17.11,
    poder in requests 21.2.3b
Imperfect Indicative Tense, forms 13.1.6,
    uses 14.5; used for conditional
    14.5.2, 25.5; *hablaba* and *estaba*
    hablando compared 14.5.3; in
    children's language 14.5.4; to make
    polite requests 14.5.5, replacement
    for preterite 14.5.6, contrasted with
    imperfect 14.5.7, in conditional
    sentences, see Ch. 25, esp. 25.2e-f,
    also 25.4 note (ii)
Impersonal Pronouns, see Impersonal
    se, uno, tú, Passive and Impersonal
    Sentences
Impersonal *se* 28.6; comp. with other
    types of *se* 28.3, 26.8; *le/les* after
    12.6.3, in imperative 17.8; *se arrestó a*
    28.5
importar, pronouns with 12.6.4
–ín (suffix) 38.2, esp. 38.2.4
in– (prefix) 4.13
Inchoative aspect (i.e. preterite to denote
    the beginning of an event) 14.4.2–3
inclusive 31.8n
incluso 31.8; personal pronouns after
    11.5.1
Indefinite Article 3.3; forms of 3.3.1, *un*
    alma for ?*una alma* 3.1.2; indef. art.
    compared with French 3.3.3, before
    several nouns 3.3.4, omission of
    3.3.5–8, retained before qualified
    nouns 3.3.9, in apposition 3.3.10, to
    distinguish nouns and adjectives

3.3.11, after prepositions 3.3.12, in
    exclamations 3.3.13, *unos/unas* 3.4
Indicative Mood **Ch. 14**; comp. with
    subjunctive 16.2.5
indio 4.8.1 note (iii)
inferior 4.2.1 note (i)
Infinitive **Ch. 18**; position of personal
    pronouns with 11.14.3; with
    finite verbs 18.2, *dice que lo sabe*
    or *dice saberlo*? 18.2.2, list of inf.
    constructions 18.2.3; with verbs of
    permitting and forbidding 16.5.2;
    after verbs of perception 18.2.5, 20.7;
    to replace subjunctive 16.2.6, 16.5.2;
    quiero verlo or *lo quiero ver*? 11.14.4,
    18.2.3; inf. after subordinators 18.3,
    16.12.1; *al llegar* 18.3, 20.5; inf. for
    vosotros imperative 17.2.4n, for *tú*
    and *usted(es)* imperative 17.9; passive
    meaning of inf. 18.5, 28.2.4; inf.
    noun 18.6, def. article with 18.7,
    to express incredulity 18.9, *es difícil*
    hacerlo and *es difícil de hacer* 18.10,
    cosas que hacer 18.11, ?*problemas a*
    resolver 18.12
informar de que 33.4.3 note (iii)
Intensifiers (*muy*, etc.) 31.4
interesar, pronouns with 12.6.4
Interrogation and Exclamations **Ch. 24**;
    word order in 37.2.2–4; see also *cómo,*
    cuál, cuándo, dónde, ¿para qué?, ¿por
    qué?, qué, quién, cuánto, Interrogation
    Marks
Interrogation Marks 39.4.5
–iño (suffix) 38.2
ir conjugation 13.3.23, *ir a*, personal
    pronouns with 11.14.4 note (i),
    used for future tense 14.6.5; *ir* with
    gerund 20.8.2; *ir* and *irse* compared
    26.6.2
Irregular Verbs, general 13.3; for
    conjugation seek infinitives in Index
    or on pp. 170–97
–ísimamente (suffix) 31.2.8
–ísimo (suffix) 4.9
–ito (suffix) 38.2, esp. 38.2.2

jamás 23.5.6; = 'ever' 23.4
jugar conjugation 13.3.24, def. article
    with 3.2.28
la de = 'lots of' 3.2.30
la, see def. article; not elided 3.1.1; see
    also Personal Pronouns Object;
    compared with *le*, see *le*
Languages, def. article with 3.2.16
las, see Definite Article; see also Personal
    Pronouns Object; compared with
    les, see *le*

Latin Words, plural 2.1.4c
Latinoamérica 4.8.1 note (i)
le and *les* Compared with *lo/la/los/la* **Ch. 12**; Academy's rules 12.2, main uses of *le/les* 12.3, main uses of *lo* 12.4, general remarks on *le/lo* controversy 12.5, *leísmo* 12.5.1–3, 12.5.6; *loísmo* 12.5.5; *le* used for human direct objects throughout Hispanic world 12.6, *le* to denote respect 12.6.1, *le* preferred when subject inanimate 12.6.2, *le* preferred after impersonal and reflexive *se* 12.6.3, *le* in double accusatives 12.6.5, replacement by *se* 11.13; see also Personal Pronouns, Object; *le* as redundant pronoun 11.16.2, *le* used for redundant *les* 11.16.3
leísmo 12.5.1–3, 12.5.6
lejos 31.2.8 note
les, see *le*
liar 13.2.4
llamar, pronouns with 12.6.4
llegar forms p.201, pronouns with 11.8; compared with *llegarse* 26.6.2; *llegar a ser* = 'become' 27.3.4
llevar(se), pronouns with 12.6.3 note (iv), + gerund 20.8.3, *llevar* and *llevarse* compared 26.6.4, *llevo tres días aquí* 32.3.1
–llir, verbs ending in 13.2.2 and p. 202
lo, neuter article 7.2; *lo bueno*, etc. 7.2.1; *lo guapa que es, lo bien que canta* 7.2.2; *lo* = neuter pronoun 'it' 7.4, *lo hay/lo es* etc. 7.4; as redundant pronoun 11.16.4, as third-person object pronoun, see Personal Pronouns, Object; compared with *le*, see *le*; *lo* + emotional reactions + subjunctive 16.6.3
lo de 36.1.3
lo mismo que 5.15.2
lo que 35.6; = 'that which' 36.1.15, = 'what' and compared with *qué* 24.4.2
loísmo 12.2, (extreme forms) 12.5.5
los, see Definite Article, Personal Pronouns, Object; compared with *les*, see *le*
lucir 13.3.25
luego 31.7.4

macho 1.3, 4.2.3
malamente 31.2.5
maldecir 13.3.26
malo, short form of 4.6b, position 4.11.6, comparison 5.2
mandar, subjunctive with 16.5
mar 1.4.14

marchar, marcharse 26.6.2
mas = 'but' 33.1
más 5.1; *más de* or *más que*? 5.5, *más del/de lo que* 5.6, *más* as an intensifier 5.7, with adverbs of place 31.6.8 note (i)
Mathematical expressions 10.9
mayor 5.8, forms 5.2.1 note (i); use of *tanto* with 9.16 note (i)
mayoría 2.3.1
mayormente 31.2.5
me, see Personal Pronouns, Object
Measurements 10.15
mediante 34.13
medio 9.10
Méjico, see *México*
mejor 5.2; 4.2.1 note (i); *tanto* with 9.16 note (i)
mejorar(se), 26.6.3
menor 5.9; forms 5.2, 4.2.1 note (i)
menos 5.1, *menos de* or *menos que*? 5.5, *menos del/de lo que* 5.6; = 'except' 11.5.1; with adverbs of place 31.6.8 note (i)
–mente (suffix) 31.2, 31.4.3
mero, position 4.11.9
México, mexicano spelling of, 4.8.1 note (iv)
mi/mío see Possessive adjectives and Pronouns
mí 11.5.1, 11.15.
mientras (que) 16.12.6 note (iii)
mientras más 5.11
mil (= 1000) 10.1; gender of 10.2, *mil y uno* 10.1 note (iv)
millón 10.4, 10.1
ministro/a 1.2.7
minoría 2.3.1
mismo 9.11; *lo mismo que* 5.15.2, *lo mismo* = 'perhaps' 16.3.2d
míster 3.2.24
Modal Auxiliary verbs (e.g. *poder, deber, tener que, saber, haber de*) **Ch. 21** or consult individual verb in Index; word order 21.7; agreement with passive *se* 28.4.3
modelo 2.1.7b, 4.2.3
montés 4.2.1 note (ii)
morir conjugation 13.3.18, comp. with *morirse* 16.6.4
mover 13.3.27
mucho 9.12; comparison 5.2, *mucho(s) más/menos* 5.10; = *muy* 31.4.2
muy 31.4.2

nada 23.5.1; as intensifier 23.5.2; = 'anything' 23.4; *nada más* = 'hardly' 23.5.7 note (ii)
nadie 23.5.1; with personal *a* 22.4; =

'anyone' 23.4

Names, plural of 2.1.6, def. article with 3.2.21

negar, subjunctive with 16.7.1

Negation **Ch. 23**; neg. imperative 17.3, double negative 23.3; translating 'anyone', 'anything', 'ever' in questions, comparisons, exclamations and after *antes que*, 23.4; see also *nada, nadie, ninguno, nunca, jamás, apenas, en mi vida*

Neuter pronouns **Ch. 7**; see also *lo, ello, esto, eso, aquello; lo mío*, etc. 8.4.3; *lo cual, lo que* as relative pronouns 35.6

ni 23.5.4

ninguno 23.5.5; short form of 4.6

no 23.2; used with *temer* 16.9 note (i); redundant *no* 23.2.4

no bien ='scarcely' 23.5.7

no fuera que 16.12.2b

no más que . . . = 'only' 9.15 note (i)

no sea que 16.12.2b

no ser que 16.7.1 note (iii)

no vaya a 16.12.2b

nomás, nomás que (Lat.-Am.) 23.2.5; = 'as soon as' 16.12.6

Nominalizers (i.e. *el que, el de, quien* = 'the one/person that/who' **Ch. 36**; see also *el de, el que, quien*; translating 'the one in/of/for which' 35.13. *See also* Cleft Sentences

norteamericano 4.8.1 note (i)

nos, see Personal Pronouns, Object

nosotros, see Personal Pronouns, Subject, esp. 11.4; see also emphasis 11.15, *nosotros* imperative 17.5

Nouns, compared with adjectives 3.3.11, 4.1; used as adjectives 4.10, used as adverbs 31.3.5, used as intensifiers (e.g. *pasarlo bomba*) 31.4.7

nuestro, see Possessive adjectives and Pronouns

Nuevas normas 39.1.1; rulings on accents: see *este, solo, prohibir*, Diphthongs

nuevísimo 4.9.3c

nuevo, position 4.11.7

Number agreement 2.3; see also collective nouns, collective numerals; *esto son . . .* 2.3.3; agr. after *y, o*, 'as well as' 2.3.4; agr. with passive *se* 28.4.2

Numerals **Ch. 10**; gender of 10.2, agreement of *uno* and *cientos* 10.3, *billón* 10.1, *cien* or *ciento*? 10.6, percentages 10.7, collective numerals 10.8, mathematical expressions 10.9, fractions 10.10, def. article with numbers 10.11,

3.2.26; ordinal numbers 10.12, distribution ('one each', etc.) 10.13; 'single', 'double', etc. 10.14, dimensions and measurements 10.15; rules for writing numerals 10.16, telephone numbers 10.17, omission of personal *a* before numerals 22.7

nunca 23.5.6; = 'ever' in questions 23.4

–ñer, verbs ending in 13.2.2f and p.202

–ñir, verbs ending in 13.2.2f and p.202

o 33.2; number agreement with 2.3.4; accent on 39.2.6 note (ii)

o sea que 16.15.3a

obedecer 12.6.4

oceano/océano 39.2.4

ocurrir 16.6.4

oír 13.3.28, with infinitive 20.7

ojalá 16.15.2

oler 13.3.29

olvidar(se), olvidársele 16.6.4

–ón (suffix) 38.3

Ordinal numbers 10.12

os, see Personal Pronouns, Object

–ote (suffix) 38.3

otra vez 32.6b

otro 9.13; no indef. article with 3.3.13, *algunos/unos y otros* 9.4.2

otro gallo nos cantara 16.15.3c

país 2.1.3 note (iv)

país miembro 2.1.7b

para 34.14; main uses 34.14.2, *ir para* 32.3.6n, 34.14.2 note (ii), *he venido para* or *por hablarle?* 34.14.7, *para* contrasted with *por*, 34.14 *passim*, esp. 34.14.8

para que 16.12.2, *algo para/que leer* 18.11, *para* + infinitive replaced by gerund 20.4.3

para qué 24.10

parecer, subjunctive with 16.7.2, 16.11.1; compared with *parecerse* 16.6.3

Participles, see Past Participle, Adjectival Participle (i.e. forms in *-ante, -(i)ente*)

Partitive nouns 3.2.8

pasar, pasarse = verb of motion 26.6.2; = 'pass time' 26.6.3; *pasar a ser* = 'become' 27.3.4

pasear 13.2.6

Passive and Impersonal Sentences (i.e. *fue construido, se construyó*, etc.) **Ch.28**; pass. with *ser* 28.2, avoiding pass. 28.2.3; pass. meaning of infinitive 28.2.4, 18.5; *fue destruido* and *estaba destruido* compared 28.2.5, 19.1; other alternatives for *ser* in passive 28.2.6; third-person plural used impersonally 28.7.3; pass. *se*, see Passive *se*; impersonal *se*, see Impersonal *se*; see also *uno, tú*

Passive of Verbs, forms p. 198, meaning of infinitive 18.5

Passive *se* 28.4; compared with other types of *se* and pass. with *ser* 28.3; overlap with impersonal *se* 26.8; agreement of verb 28.4.2-3, *se arrestó a*, etc. 28.5

Passive, see Passive and Impersonal Sentences; *por* and *de* with 34.14.4 note (ii)

Past Participle **Ch. 19**; forms 19.2.1, Lat.-Am. usage 19.2.2, participle clauses 19.3, pos. of personal pronouns with 11.14.6

pedir conjugation 13.3.30, subjunctive with 16.5.1, 16.5.2 note (v)

pegar 12.6.4

peor 5.2; 4.2.1 note (i), *tanto* with 9.16 note (i)

pequeño, position 4.11.6, comparison 5.2, 5.9; expressed by diminutive 38.2

Perfect Tense, forms p. 197, uses 14.8, 14.9; perfect of recency 14.9.2, perfect in time phrases Ch. 32, see also *desde*; Lat.-Am. usage 14.9.7; *tengo hecho*, etc. 14.8.3, perfect imperative (*no haberlo hecho*) 17.9.b note

Period, see Point

periodo, período 39.2.4

permitir, subjunctive with 16.5, pronouns with 12.6,16.5.2

pero 33.1

Personal *a* **Ch. 22**; before nouns denoting human beings or animals 22.2, after *como* 22.3, with pronouns 22.4, with relative pronouns 22.4.2, before personified nouns 22.5, after *tener, querer* 22.6, with numerals 22.7, combined with dative *a* 22.8, with collective nouns 22.9, before inanimates 22.10, with impersonal *se* 22.10c, preferred with certain verbs 22.11; used after *se* 28.5

Personal Pronouns (see also Pers. Pronouns Subject, Pers. Pronouns Object) Forms 11.1, prepositional forms 11.5; *conmigo, contigo* 11.5.2

Personal Pronouns, Object (*me, te, lo/la/los/las, le/les, nos, os*) 11.7-16 (but for comparison of *le* with *lo*, see *le*); forms 11.7.1, general uses 11.7.2, forms used for *usted(es)* 11.7.3, with verbs of motion 11.8, with *ser*

and *resultar* 11.9; *lo es, lo está*, see Resumptive Pronoun; *se me fue, cuídamelo* 11.11; Order of pronouns 11.12, replacement of *le* by *se* 11.13, *?se los dije* (Lat. Am.) 11.13.2; position 11.14, with imperative 17.4; *quiero verlo* or *lo quiero ver*? 11.14.4, pos. with gerund 11.14.5, pos. with past participle 11.14.6, emphasis of object pronouns 11.15, 'one another' 11.15b, redundant pronouns 11.16, 22.11; prons with *hay* 30.2.2

Personal Pronouns, Subject (*yo, tú/vos, él, ella, usted(es), nosotros, vosotros*) 11.1-6; general uses 11.2, *voseo* 11.3.1, *usted* or *tú*? 11.3.2, *ustedes* or *vosotros*? 11.3.3-4, *nosotros* 11.4, 'it's me'/'it's you', etc. 11.6

pese a que 16.12.8

placer 13.3.32

Pluperfect Tense 14.10; pluperfect in *-ra*, 14.10.2-3; *Pretérito anterior* (*hube visto*, etc.) 14.10.4

Plural of nouns **Ch. 2**; plural in *-s* 2.1.2, in *-es* 2.1.3; of nouns ending in *-á*, *-í*, *-ú* 2.1.3c; invariable nouns 2.1.4, Latin words 2.1.4, other foreign words 2.1.5, proper names 2.1.6, compound nouns 2.1.7, irregular plurals 2.1.8; syntax and semantics of plural 2.2, *las atenciones, las bondades*, etc. 2.2.1, 'scissors', 'pants', etc. 2.2.2; nouns always plural 2.2.3; *tienen novio, se cortaron la mano*; 2.2.4, singular for plural 2.2.5; agreement, see Number Agreement

pobre 29.4.4

poco 9.12; with adjectives 4.13, comparison 5.2, *pocos más* 5.10

poder conjugation 13.3.33, preterite and imperfect compared 21.2.2, compared with *saber* 21.2.1-2, used to express possibility 21.2.3a, in polite requests 21.2.3b, *ha podido hacerlo* or *puede haberlo hecho*? 21.7

Point 39.4.1; to separate hundreds 10.1 note (iii)

poner conjugation 13.3.24, *ponerse* = 'to become' 27.3.1

por 34.14; main uses 34.14.4; in passive constructions 34.14.4 note (ii); with adverbs of place 31.6.4, *por n días* 32.3.5. See also *hacia con*. For comparisons with *para*, see *para*

por ahí 31.6.4, 31.6.1 note (ii)

por ciento 10.7

por eso es (por lo) que 36.2.4

por, indef. article after 3.3.12

por más/mucho/poco que 16.13.2
por poco 14.3.3n
por qué 24.10, 33.5.1
por si (acaso) 16.12.6, 25.9f
porque 33.5.1; subjunctive after 16.12.3b
poseer 13.3.35
posiblemente 16.3.2e
Possessive adjectives and pronouns **Ch. 8**; forms 8.2.1-2, uses of short forms (*mi, tu, su,* etc.) 8.3, replacement by def. article 8.3.4; uses of long forms ((*el*) *mío,* etc.) 8.4, *es mío* or *es el mío?* 8.4.2; *lo mío,* etc. 8.4.3; replaced by *de* + personal pronoun 8.5; possessives in Lat.-Am. usage 8.6; poss. combined with *otro* 9.13 note (ii), ?*delante mío,* etc. 8.7
preferir, personal *a* with 22.8
Prepositional Phrases, list 34.19
Prepositions **Ch. 34** or see *a, ante, bajo, con, contra, de, desde, durante, en, entre, hacia, hasta, mediante, para, por, según, sin, sobre, tras;* def. article with preps 3.2.10a, ?*delante mío* (for *delante de mí*) 8.7; forms of personal pronouns after 11.5; *conmigo, contigo* 11.5.2; omitted in expressions of time 32.10
Present Indicative Tense forms 13.1.5, uses 14.3; used for past 14.3.3, used for imperative 17.10, used for future 14.6.4; Present Continuous, see Continuous Forms of Verb; pres. tense in conditional sentences, see Ch. 25, esp. 25.2a-d
Presente histórico 14.3.3
Preterite Tense forms 13.1.7, uses 14.4; to denote beginning of events 14.4.3; for events over finite periods 14.4.4; replaced by imperfect 14.5.6, contrasted with imperfect 14.5.7; special uses of preterite of *poder, deber, querer, saber, conocer, tener,* consult these verbs in Index; *estuve hablando* 15.2.3n
pretérito, meaning of Spanish term 14.1
Pretérito anterior (i.e. *hube visto*) 14.10.4
primero 10.12.1; short form of 4.6b
probablemente 16.3.2e
producir 13.3.36
Professions, feminine of 1.2.7; indef. article omitted before 3.3.6
prohibir conjugation 13.2.3, subjunctive with 16.5
Pronominal Verbs (i.e. *lavarse, irse, morirse,* etc.) **Ch. 26**; classification of types 26.1, reflexive meaning of 26.2, reciprocal meaning 26.3;

se with inanimate subject 26.4, to make intransitive verbs 26.5, miscellaneous verbs 26.6 (or see infinitive in index); *me comí una pizza, se leyó el libro entero* 26.6.3; unclassifiable uses of *se* with various verbs 26.6.4, misc. Lat.-Am. forms 26.7, word order used to differentiate types of *se* 26.8, use of *no* with pron. verbs 26.9; pron. verbs denoting 'become' 27.2
Pronouns, see Personal Pronouns, Neuter Pronouns, Demonstratives; personal *a* with 22.4
Pronunciation **Ch. 39** *passim*
Proper names, see Names
propio 9.14
proteger p. 202
Proverbs 3.2.5
puede/pueda que 16.3.1 note
pues 33.5.3
puesto que 33.5.2, 16.12.3, replaced by gerund 20.4.4
Punctuation 39.4

que as conjunction 33.4; in comparisons **Ch. 5,** *passim;* as relative pronoun, see Relative Clauses and also 22.4; *cosas* **que** *hacer* 18.11; *que* as conjuction: used at beginning of sentence 33.4.4, in indirect questions 33.4.5, occasional omission 33.4.6, used after verbs denoting emotional reactions 16.6.1-2; = 'the fact that' 16.10, before imperatives 17.6-7, replaced by infinitive 18.2.2, misc. examples of *que* 33.4.8; *que* = 'because' 33.4.4b; *qué* 24.4; compared with *cuál* 24.3.2, compared with *lo que* 24.4.2, in exclamations 24.4.4, 3.3.13
que yo sepa 16.15.3b
quedar(se) 27.3.6, 26.6.4; to form passive 28.2.6a
quejarse 16.6.2 note
querer conjugation 13.3.37, uses 21.5; *querer que* + subjunctive 16.5, pers. *a* with 22.6
Questions, see Interrogation and Exclamations
quien = 'anyone who' 16.13.7, 16.14; as relative pronoun, see Relative Clauses, also 22.4; = 'the one/person who . . . ' 36.1.6
quién 24.5; = 'if only' 16.15.2
quienquiera 16.13.7
quizá(s) 16.3.2a
Quotation Marks 39.4.4

–*ra* pluperfect 14.10.2-3, -*ra* subjunctive
    used for conditional 14.7.5, 25.5
Radical Changing Verbs, 13.1.4; listed
    pp. 157–9
radio 1.4.16 note (ii)
rápido 31.3.6
raya (i.e. 'dash') 39.4.4
recién 31.7.2
Reciprocal Construction ('one another'),
    see Pronominal Verbs; emphasis of
    pronoun in 11.15b
recordar 12.6.4, ?*recordarse* 18.2.3 footnote
Redundant *no*, see *no*
Redundant Object Pronouns 11.16, 22.11
Reflexive Construction (e.g. *yo me lavo*),
    see Pronominal Verbs
régimen 2.1.8
regresar(se) 26.6.2 note
Regular Verbs. *See* Verbs. For conjugation
    see pp. 199–200
reír conjugation 13.3.38, comp. with
    reírse 26.6.4
Relative Clauses **Ch. 35**; word order in
    37.2.1, forms of relative pronouns
    35.1.1, uses of *el cual* 35.5, English
    and Spanish rel. clauses compared
    35.1.3; *que* as rel. pronoun 35.2–3,
    35.4.2; occasional omission of
    que 33.4.6b; rel. pronouns in
    non-restrictive clauses 35.3, rel.
    prons after prepositions 35.4, *cuyo*
    35.7, 35.8c; colloquial variants 35.8,
    rel.clauses following *donde* 35.10,
    following *como* 35.11, by *cuando*
    35.12; 'the one in which', see
    Nominalizers; rel. clauses involving
    idea of 'every' 9.17f, redundant
    pronouns in rel. clauses 11.16.5,
    personal *a* in rel. clauses 22.4,
    subjunctive in 16.14, ?*problemas
    a resolver* 18.12, 'a box containing
    books' 20.4
Relative pronouns, see Relative Clauses,
    Nominalizers
reñir 13.3.39
resto 2.3.1, 9.13 note (iii)
resultar, object pronouns with 11.9a; to
    form passive sentences 28.2.6b
Resumptive Pronoun (i.e. *lo hay, lo es*) 7.4,
    11.9
reunir 13.2.3
rezar, conjugation p. 200
rico 29.2.3 note (i)
roer 13.3.40
rosa 4.2.4

saber conjugation 13.3.41, preterite and
    imperfect contrasted 21.2.2n, *no sabe*

que + subjunctive 16.7.2, compared
    with *poder* 21.2, *se lo sabe todo* 26.6.3
sacar, conjugation p. 201, indef. art. with
    3.3.8
salir conjugation 13.3.42, with gerund
    20.8.5, comp. with *salirse* 26.6.2
saltar, saltarse 26.6.2
salvo 11.5.1; *salvo que* 16.12.7b note
san(to) 4.6 n (v)
sartén 1.4.13
se, see Pronominal Verbs, Impersonal *se*,
    Passive *se*; *se*, to replace *le/les* 11.13,
    se with impersonal *a* 22.10c
se impersonal, see Impersonal *se*
?*se los dije* (Lat. Am.) 11.13.2
sé(p)timo 10.12.1 note (ii)
sea cual sea 16.13.4n
seguir, conjugation p.201, gerund with
    32.8, meaning 'still' 32.8
según 34.14; pronouns after 11.5.1, *según*
    in relative clauses 35.14
segundo 10.12.1
semi colon 39.4.3
sendos 10.13, position 4.11.9
sentar(se) 15.3c note (i)
sentir 13.3.43
ser, conjugation p. 202, omission of
    indef. article after 3.3.7; object
    pronouns with, see Resumptive
    Pronoun, also 11.9b, *estar siendo*
    15.4, Passive with *ser*, see Passive
    and Impersonal Sentences; see also
    under '*ser* and *estar*'
ser and *estar* **Ch. 29**; *fue destruido* and
    estaba destruido compared 28.2.5;
    uses of *ser* 29.2, *ser* of events
    29.2.8, uses of *estar* 29.3, both verbs
    interchangeable 29.4.1; *estar* =
    impression or change of condition
    29.4.3; meaning of adjectives
    affected by 29.4.4; for *estar* to
    denote location see also Existential
    Sentences
si ('if') Ch. 25 *passim*, esp. 25.8; replaced
    by *como* + subjunctive 25.8.2,
    replaced by *de* + infinitive 25.8.3, 'if
    I were you' 25.11
sí (personal pronoun) 11.5.3
siempre que 16.12.7a
siempre y cuando 16.12.7a
sin 34.16; indef. article after 3.3.12
sin que 16.12.4c, replaced by *sin* +
    infinitive 18.3
sino 33.1
siquiera = 'even if' 16.12.8, *ni siquiera*
    23.5.4 note (i); = 'even', 'at least' 31.8
situar 13.2.5
sobre 34.17; = 'on the subject of', comp.

with *de* 34.7d;
solamente, see solo
soler 21.6
solo/sólo 9.15
soñar(se) 26.7
Spelling **Ch. 39**; see also Accents; the
    Nuevas normas 39.1; the alphabet
    39.1.2, relationship between
    sound and letters 39.1.3, *trans-* or
    tras-? 39.1.4, doubtful spellings
    39.2.4, spelling rules affecting all
    verbs 13.2 and p.165; accents, see
    Accents; capital letters 39.3; see also
    Punctuation, Word Division
su, suyo, see Possessive adjectives and
    Pronouns
subir, subirse 26.6.2
Subject Pronouns (*yo, tú, él, ella, nosotros,*
    etc.) see Personal Pronouns,
    Subject; Object Pronouns (*me, te, le,*
    lo, nos, etc.) see Personal Pronouns,
    Object
Subjunctive **Ch. 16**; forms of present
    13.1.9, of imperfect 13.1.10;
    general remarks on subj. 16.1–2;
    -ra and *-se* forms compared 16.2.3;
    when the subj. is *not* used 16.2.5;
    does not always indicate doubt
    or uncertainty 16.2.7; regional
    variations 16.2.8; past subj. used
    for conditional 14.7.5; past subj. in
    conditional sentences Ch. 25, esp.
    25.3–4; *-ra* form used for pluperfect
    14.10.2; after noun + *de que* 16.10.2;
    used after statements implying:
        possibility 16.3, 'perhaps' 16.3.2
        'depends on' 16.4, 'influence'
        'want', 'order', 'persuade',
        'cause', 'permit', 'prohibit', 'ask',
        etc. 16.5; emotional reactions
        and value judgements 16.6, denial
        16.7, 'doesn't say/think/know
        that' 16.7.2, 'doubt' 16.8 'fear',
        16.9; 'the fact that' 16.10,
        'believe', 'suppose', 'seem'
        16.11.1, 'understand', 'explain'
        16.11.2, 'hope' 16.11.3. *See also*
        Subordinators
Subordinators, subjunctive after, 16.12,
    or consult individual words in index;
    subjunctive after subordinators
    implying:
        purpose 16.12.2a, 'lest' 16.12.2b,
        'because', 'since' 16.12.3, 'hence
        the fact that' 16.10.1, result
        16.12.4, manner 16.12.4, 'in
        case', 'supposing that' 16.12.5,
        subordinators of time ('when',

'before', etc.) 16.12.6, condition
    16.12.7a, exception 16.12.7b,
    concession 16.12.8, 'in spite'
    16.12.8 'however', 'whatever',
    'whenever', 'whoever', 16.13
    Subjunctive in Relative Clauses
    16.14, after superlative 16.14.4; in
    main clauses 16.15, after *ojalá*, etc.
    16.15.2; Tense Agreement with
    subj. 16.16; Future Subjunctive
    16.17, Subjunctive used in negative
    imperatives 17.3, in positive
    imperatives 17.2.5, 17.5–7
sud- (prefix) 4.8.1 note (i)
suficiente, see bastante
superar (a) 22.11b
superior 4.2.1 note (i)
Superlative of adjectives 5.3, of adverbs
    5.4
suponer, subjunctive with 16.11.1
    suponiendo que 16.12.5 note
Suppositions, see deber
sur- (prefix) 4.8.1 note (i)
sustituir (a) 22.11a
suyo, see Possessive adjectives and
    Pronouns
Syllable Division 39.5

tal 3.3.13
tal como 5.15.2
tal vez 16.3.2a
tampoco 23.5.9
tan . . . como 5.15.1, *tan . . . como que*
    16.12.4 note (iii)
tan pronto como 16.12.6
tanto 9.16, singular after (*tanto turista,*
    etc.) 2.2.5
tanto . . . como, 5.15.1; number agreement
    after 2.3.4c
tanto . . . cuanto 5.11n
tanto es así 9.16, esp. note (ii)
tanto . . . que 5.15.1
tañer, see *-ñer*
tardar 32.7
te, see Personal Pronouns, Object
Telephone numbers 10.17
temer and other words meaning 'fear',
    subjunctive with 16.9; compared
    with *temerse* 26.6.4
tener conjugation 13.3.45, omission of
    indef. article after 3.3.8, preterite
    and imperfect compared 14.4.5;
    tengo hecho, tengo compradas, 14.8.3;
    tener que 21.3, pers. *a* with *tener* 22.6;
Tense Agreement 16.16
Tenses of Verbs, uses of **Ch. 14**, or
    consult individual tenses in Index;
    names of 14.1; tenses in conditional

sentences, see Conditional
Sentences

tercero 10.12.1; short form 4.6b,
compared with *tercio* 10.10

Thousands, how to write them 10.1 note
(iii)

ti 11.5.1, 11.15

tierra virgen 2.1.7

Time, see Expressions of Time; preterite
tense for events lasting specific time
14.4.4

tipo de 2.3.2

tirar 12.6.4

Titles, *majestad, excelencia*, etc. 1.2.11,
forms of professional titles 1.2.7;
def. article in book, film titles 3.2.13,
def. article before *señor, míster*, etc.
3.2.24

tocar pronouns with 12.6.4

todavía 31.7.3

todo 9.17; *todo son . . .* 2.3.3

todo el mundo 9.17 note (ii)

traer conjugation 13.3.46, comp. with
traerse 26.6.4

trans- (prefix) 39.1.4

tras 34.18

tras- (prefix) 39.1.4

Triphthongs 39.2, esp. 39.2.2

tu, tuyo see Possessive adjectives and
Pronouns

tú, see Personal Pronouns, Subject;
tú imperative 17.2.2, *tú*
used to soften imperative
17.11e; impersonal use of *tú*
28.7.2

u = 'or' 33.2

ü, see Dieresis

–uar, verbs ending in 13.2.5

–ucho (suffix) 38.4

–uco 38.4

–uelo (suffix) 38.2, esp. 38.2.5

único 9.15 note (iii), with relative
pronouns 22.4.2 note (i)

uno/una, see Indefinite Article;
as numeral Ch. 10, esp.
10.3 and 10.5; as impersonal
pronoun 28.7.1; required
with pronominal verbs
26.9

unos/unas 3.4, omission of in journalism
3.4.2, compared with *algunos*
9.4.2

usted compared with *tú* 11.3.2,
compared with *vosotros*
11.3.3, general uses 11.3.4,
object pronouns 11.7.3,
12.6.1, imperative forms
17.2.5

valer 13.3.47

vámonos 17.5 note (i)

varios 9.18

vencer 13.2.7

venir conjugation 13.3.48; object
pronouns with 11.8 note (iv), with
infinitive 18.2.5, with gerund 20.8.7,
comp. with *venirse* 26.6.2; + past
participle to form passive 28.2.6d

ver conjugation 13.3.49; with infinitive
20.7; *verse* = 'to seem' 26.7; *verse* to
form passive 28.2.6c

Verbs of Becoming **Ch. 27**, see also
*ponerse, hacerse, volverse,
convertirse, llegar, pasar*

Verbs, for conjugation of individual
verbs not listed in Index see pp.
197–199; for tables of regular verbs
see pp. 199–200. General remarks on
forms of verbs 13.1–13.2; irregular
verbs, discussion 13.1.3; radical
changing verbs, discussion 13.1.4;
colloquial variants in conjugation
13.2.1, spelling rules affecting
conjugation 13.2, verbs in *-iar* 13.2.4,
in *-uar* 13.2.5, in *-ear* 13.2.6, in *-cer*
13.2.7, in *-eer* 13.2.8, in *-cir* 13.2.9;
defective verbs (like *abolir*) 13.3.2.
For uses of finite and of non-finite
forms see Present, Imperfect,
Preterite, Future, Conditional,
Pluperfect, Subjunctive, Infinitive,
Gerund, Imperative, Participles,
Continuous Forms of Verb, Passive.
For Pronominal verbs (i.e. dictionary
inf. ends in *-rse*) see Pronominal
Verbs

viejo, position 4.11.7

violeta 4.2.4

volver, volverse 26.6.2; *volverse* = 'become'
27.3.2; *volver a* = 'again' 32.6a

volver en sí 11.5.3 note (iii)

vos = *tú* 11.3.1; *vos* imperative 17.2.3

vosotros, see Personal Pronouns, Subject;
compared with *ustedes* 11.3.3;
emphasis 11.15, imperative forms
17.2.4

vuestro see Possessive adjectives and
Pronouns

Word Division 39.5.

Word Order **Ch 37**; in rel. clauses 37.2.1,
in questions 37.2.2–4; —*Buenos días
—dijo Juan* 37.2.5; order of adverbs
37.2.6, 37.4, 31.3.8; position of
adjectives 4.11, with *otro* 9.13 note
(ii); of object pronouns 11.12,17.4;
quiero verlo or *lo quiero ver?* 11.14.4,

18.2.3; position of *haber*, see haber; order with *deber*, *poder* and *tener* *que* 21.7; in interrogations and exclamations 37.2.2–4; word order used to differentiate types of *se* 26.8, used to simulate passive 28.2.3

y 33.3; number agreement with 2.3.4

y eso que 33.6.2
ya 31.7
ya no 31.7.3
ya que 33.5.2, 16.12.3; replaced by gerund 20.4.4
yacer 13.3.50
yo que tú 25.11
yo, see Personal Pronouns, Subject